J2ME™

GAME PROGRAMMING

THOMSON
COURSE TECHNOLOGY

J2ME™
GAME PROGRAMMING

MARTIN J. WELLS

SVP, Course Professional, Trade, Reference Group:
Andy Shafran

Publisher:
Stacy L. Hiquet

Senior Marketing Manager:
Sarah O'Donnell

Marketing Manager:
Heather Hurley

Manager of Editorial Services:
Heather Talbot

Acquisitions Editor:
Mitzi Koontz

Associate Marketing Manager:
Kristin Eisenzopf

Project Editor:
Jenny Davidson

Technical Reviewer:
Cristiano Garibaldi

Retail Market Coordinator:
Sarah Dubois

Copy Editor:
Cathleen Snyder

Interior Layout Tech:
Marian Hartsough

Cover Designer:
Steve Deschene

CD-ROM Producer:
Brandon Penticuff

Indexer:
Sharon Shock

Proofreader:
Sara Gullion

THOMSON

COURSE TECHNOLOGY
Professional ■ Trade ■ Reference

Course PTR, a division of Course Technology
25 Thomson Place
Boston, MA 02210
http://www.courseptr.com

For G. I.

ACKNOWLEDGMENTS

I f you've never written a book, I have to tell you that it's not easy. Once upon a time I was an armchair critic of books—in hindsight, maybe that's why I decided to write one. The thing that strikes you when you embark on writing something like this is the sheer mountain of (hard) work involved. In fact, it's so much work that it really isn't possible for one person to do it alone. Throughout the writing of this book, I've been helped in so many ways by so many people that I can't hope to get across how grateful I am. All I can do is say a thank you and trust you to know how much I mean it.

I will, however, attempt to recognize some of the people who deserve a little acknowledgment—if I've forgotten you, then obviously you didn't deserve it. . . . :)

First, thanks to André LaMothe for giving me the opportunity to contribute to such an excellent series. To Mitzi Koontz, Jenny Davidson, and Cathleen Snyder for the excellent feedback, continual support, and understanding when things didn't quite go according to plan—we got there in the end. Thanks also to Cristiano Garibaldi for covering all the technical bases (and learning along with me).

To Colin Pyle and J. Alexander von Kotze: Thanks for never giving up on the dream of making games for a living (and an extra thanks to Colin for supplying the excellent sprites used in the examples).

To Blake, for allowing me to use his laptop sometimes, and to Ryan, for showing me how a CD drive opens a thousand times. To Vandana and Pratibha Rai for buying me some time (and thanks for the math books laaa). To Scott, Rhandy, Simon, Rob, Gibbo, Mike, Jules, Kristy, Kat, Lee, and the rest of the team for keeping the day job challenging, interesting, and fun.

To Tarek, Sahar, Radfan, and Suleiman for the encouragement and support only friends can give.

To Rick, my only mentor, for showing me that computing really is a science.

To my mum, for showing me that being creative is a way of life and dad for throwing in regular doses of reality.

And finally, to the one and only G.I.: Thanks for believing from day one we could do it, and then bearing the brunt of following through on that belief.

ABOUT THE AUTHOR

MARTIN J. WELLS began programming his own games on a Tandy micro-computer more than 20 years ago. Throughout an extensive career in the IT industry, he has worked in many diverse fields involving a huge variety of computer languages and systems, including Java from its origins. He has extensive experience in media, communications, and entertainment industry development and has founded successful companies in all of these areas.

Martin lives with his wife and two sons in Sydney, Australia. He loves playing soccer and inline hockey, reading, and playing with anything cool and interesting (including his sons).

About the Series Editor

ANDRÉ LAMOTHE, CEO, Xtreme Games LLC, has been involved in the computing industry for more than 25 years. He wrote his first game for the TRS-80 and has been hooked ever since! His experience includes 2D/3D graphics, AI research at NASA, compiler design, robotics, virtual reality, and telecommunications. His books are top sellers in the game programming genre, and his experience is echoed in the Premier Press *Game Development* books.

Letter from the Series Editor

Writing games for PCs is fun, but it just doesn't have the feel of a console or other hand-held device. However, the thought of creating an embedded game for a phone was completely out of the question a few years ago, unless you wanted to call up Nokia or Motorola and see if you could have the contract to create the on-board games. (I wish someone would have; they are terrible!) Anyway, luckily for us, new phones support a number of technologies that allow programmers to create fantastic applications. One such technology is Java II Micro Edition, or J2ME. And that's what this book is all about—writing games for any phone that supports the J2ME standard.

When I first thought of doing a book on J2ME game programming, I knew that I wanted it to push the envelope to set a new standard on what can be done on a phone. That means I had to find an author who was an expert on the platform, but was also willing to push limits and do the impossible, in a manner of speaking. I have to say that I am very happy with this book. The author, Martin Wells, had the same vision about wanting to create the most amazing book on phone/J2ME game programming. For example, he knew that he had to put a chapter on 3D in the book and talk about optimization and other advanced topics. The bottom line is that this book is the best book on the market about making real games on the J2ME platform; moreover, it's written by someone who has made numerous games on the platform. Marty knows the ins and outs and tricks of the system, which is invaluable in such a complex subject area with so many other choices to confuse you.

The other amazing thing about this book is that it is completely self-contained; if you don't know Java 2, there is a Java 2 primer contained within, so more or less all you need is your phone, the book, and some time and you are going to be creating J2ME games on your own phone! I think that this is an amazing thing to be able to do. It's like having your own little game console in your hand. You can play your own games or give them to your friends, or possibly even sell and market them (which is also covered within the book).

In conclusion, if you have been interested in writing games for phones under the J2ME platform, but don't know where to start, how to integrate all the technology, or make sense of all the different APIs, then this is the book for you. Rarely can a single book empower someone to do so much, but Martin Wells has done an amazing job of it.

André LaMothe
Series Editor, Premier *Game Development* Series

Contents at a Glance

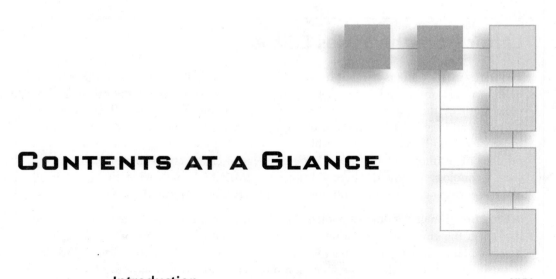

Introduction xxv

Part I   What Is J2ME? 1

Chapter 1   J2ME History 3

Chapter 2   J2ME Overview 13

Chapter 3   J2ME-Enabled Devices 39

Part II   Show Me the Code! 47

Chapter 4   The Development Environment .49

Chapter 5   The J2ME API 77

Chapter 6   Device-Specific Libraries 173

Chapter 7   Game Time 211

Part III   Game On 245

Chapter 8   The Project 247

Chapter 9   The Graphics 269

Chapter 10   The Action 303

Chapter 11   The World 367

Chapter 12   The Game 433

Chapter 13   The Front End 465

Chapter 14   The Device Ports 493

Chapter 15   The Optimizing 519

Chapter 16   The Localization 535

PART IV   SELL, SELL, SELL 541

Chapter 17   Marketing Material 543

Chapter 18   Sales Channels 553

PART V   WHAT NEXT? .569

Chapter 19   CLDC 1.1 and MIDP 2.0 .571

Chapter 20   Isometric Games 621

Chapter 21   Ray Casting 639

Chapter 22   Making the Connection 669

Appendix A   Java 2 Primer 693

Index 738

CONTENTS

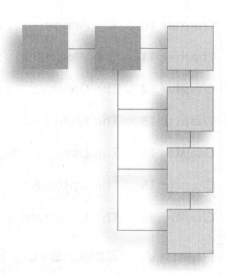

Introduction xxv

PART I   **WHAT IS J2ME?** 1

Chapter 1   **J2ME History** 3
Java's Acorn 3
Java's Growth in the Sun 6
So What Is Java? 6
Multiple Editions 9
Micro Devices Everywhere 9
Micro Software 10
Conclusion 12

Chapter 2   **J2ME Overview** 13
I Shall Call It Mini-ME 13
J2ME Architecture 14
     Configurations and Profiles 15
     Two Sizes Fit All 17
MIDP 28
     Target Devices 28
     MIDP Applications 31
     MIDP 1.0 Libraries 35
MIDP 2.0 37
Conclusion 38

Chapter 3   **J2ME-Enabled Devices** 39

MID Overview 39

    Nokia 40

    Sony Ericsson 44

    Motorola 45

Conclusion 46

PART II   **SHOW ME THE CODE!** **47**

Chapter 4   **The Development Environment** .49

Getting the Tools 49

Installing the Software 50

    Setting Up the JDK 51

    Setting Up the MIDP 51

    Making Path Changes 52

    Setting MIDP_HOME 53

    Updating CLASSPATH 54

    Testing the Setup 54

Baking Some MIDlets! 55

    Compiling Your Application 58

    Preverifying Your Class File 58

    Running Your MIDlet 59

Creating the Full Package 59

    Hello, Again 60

    Building the Class 61

    Creating the JAR 61

    Creating the JAD 62

    Running the Package 63

The J2ME Wireless Toolkit 64

    Installing the Toolkit 64

    Using the KToolbar 65

Working with Other Development Environments 70

    JBuilder 71

    Sun ONE Studio 73

    Other IDEs 75

Conclusion 76

Chapter 5   **The J2ME API** . . . . **.77**

MIDP API Overview 77

The MIDlet Application 78

Using Timers 86

Networking 90

Working with the Connector 90

Working with HttpConnection 92

Persistence (RMS) 95

Record Store 96

Record 98

Locking 103

Enumerating 103

Comparing 104

Filtering 106

Listening In 108

Exceptions 109

User Interface (LCDUI) 110

UI Basics 111

Display 114

Commands 118

Command Listeners 120

High-Level UI 123

Screens 123

Forms and Items 135

Low-Level UI 150

Conclusion 172

Chapter 6   **Device-Specific Libraries** . . . . **.173**

Device-Specific Libraries 173

Nokia 174

Installing the Tools 174

The Nokia UI API 176

Siemens 198

Installing 198

SMS and Phone API 199

Device Control 200

Sounds and Tunes 201

Advanced Graphics and Gaming 202

Motorola 203
    Setup 203
    GameScreen 204
    Sprites and PlayField 207
    ImageUtil 208
    PaletteImage 208
Other Extensions 210
Conclusion 210

Chapter 7   **Game Time** **211**
Game Time 211
Game Design 211
The Application Class 212
The Menu 214
The Game Screen 216
The Game Loop 217
Adding the Graphics 221
    Double Buffering 221
    Drawing the World 223
    Linking to the Application 225
The Actors 226
    Many Roles 226
    The Wombat 230
    Movement 231
    Cars and Trucks 233
    Bringing Them to Life 235
Input Handling 239
Collision Detection 240
Game Over 242
Conclusion 244

PART III   **GAME ON** **245**

Chapter 8   **The Project** **247**
The State of Play 247
    Platform Issues 248
Game Types 250
    Action Games 250
    Puzzle Games 251

Adventure Games 251
Strategy Games 251
Traditional Games 252
Designing Your Game 252
The Platform 253
What Makes a Good Game? 255
The Inspiration 257
Visualize Things 258
The Design Document 258
The Development Process 260
Creating a Prototype 260
Developing the Game 261
Finish What You 262
Your Idea 263
Game Type 263
Game Name 264
Setting 264
Game Play 265
Features 265
Interface 267
Resources 267
Conclusion 268

Chapter 9   The Graphics . . . . **.269**
Sprite Basics 269
Preparing Graphics 270
Loading the Images 273
Getting Some Action 277
Advanced Sprites 282
States Versus Frames 282
More Action 297
And Beyond 301
Conclusion 302

Chapter 10   The Action . . . . **.303**
Getting Some Action 303
Basic Movement 304

Moving at an Angle 304
    Cartesian Space 305
    Directional Movement 305
    Simulating Floating-Point Math 307
    A Moving Example 311
Advanced Motion 317
    Velocity 318
    Acceleration 318
    Free Flight 319
    Adding Bounce 321
Collision Detection 325
    Basic Intersection 325
    Intersection through Exclusion 326
    Reacting to a Collision 328
    Advanced Collision Detection 330
    A Collision Example 332
Actors 342
    The New Actor Class 342
    Revised Ship Class 345
    Revised Game Screen 347
    Adding Weapon Fire 349
The Enemy 355
    Computing Distance 355
    Targeting an Angle 356
    Turning through Spin 358
    Aligning Directions 361
    Creating an Enemy 364
    Creating a Brain 365
Conclusion 366

Chapter 11   **The World** **367**
A New World 367
    Nature of the Universe 367
    World Coordinates 368
    Scrolling the View Port 369
    Panning the View Port 370

Creating a Tile Engine 373
    The Tile Map 374
    Rendering the Tile Layer 376
    Tile Collision Detection 378
    Animated Tiles 379
    Activator Tiles 380
    Non-Collidable Tiles 383
    Background Layers 384
    Putting It All Together 386
Building Worlds 388
    Level Design 388
    Array Maps 390
    Random Level Generator 390
    Using a Map Editor 407
Advanced Object Management 416
    Object Pooling 417
    Linked Lists 418
    Mutually Exclusive Lists 421
    Tracking Object Use 422
    The Actor Pool Class 423
    Adapting the World to Pooling 428
Conclusion 432

Chapter 12   **The Game** . . . . **.433**
The Game Screen 433
Game State 433
    Adding State to GameScreen 434
The Primary Actor 437
    Ship Types 438
    Expanding the Enemy 442
Dealing with Damage 445
    Adding Energy 446
    The Shield Effect 448
    Energy Bar 450
    Dealing with Death 452
Saving and Loading 458
Conclusion 464

Chapter 13   The Front End **465**

Front End Overview 465

The Application Class 467

    Configuration Options 470

    Configuring Keys 472

    Saving and Loading Settings 475

The Menus 479

The Splash Screen 488

Conclusion 492

Chapter 14   The Device Ports **493**

Nokia Customization 493

    FullCanvas 493

    Vibration 495

    Using Reflection and Rotation 496

Build Systems 500

    Setting Up Ant 501

    Creating a Build File 502

    Using Antenna 505

Multi-Device Builds 512

    Device-Specific Code 512

    Managing Resources 514

    The Complete Build 515

Conclusion 518

Chapter 15   The Optimizing **519**

Speed, Glorious Speed 519

    When to Optimize 519

    Don't Optimize Blindly 520

    Method Profiling 521

    Memory Profiling 523

    Garbage Monitoring 525

Optimization 527

    High-Level Optimizations 527

    Low-Level Optimizations 529

Conclusion 534

Chapter 16   The Localization **535**

Localizing 535

    The Locale Class 536

    Adapting Star Assault 539

    The Build Step 539

Conclusion 540

PART IV   SELL, SELL, SELL **541**

Chapter 17   Marketing Material **543**

Game Guide 543

    Section 1: Introduction 544

    Section 2: Playing the Game 545

    Section 3: Reference 545

Taking Screenshots 546

Making Movies 547

    The Camera 547

    Shooting 549

    The Editing 550

    Making an Animated GIF .550

Company Presence 551

Conclusion 552

Chapter 18   Sales Channels **553**

J2ME Business Model 553

    Carrier Downloads 553

    Carrier Revenue Shares 554

    Internet Downloads 554

    Designing for Revenue 555

Ways to Market 556

    Distributors 556

    Using a Distributor 559

    Publishers 559

    Turning Publishers On 561

Approaching the Publisher 563
   In Person 563
   Trade Shows 564
   Over the Internet 564
   The Response 565
Doing the Deal 565
Conclusion 567

PART V   WHAT NEXT? 569

Chapter 19   CLDC 1.1 and MIDP 2.0 .571
The Next Generation 571
   CLDC 1.1 572
   MIDP 2 572
Developing with MIDP 2 574
   MIDP 2 Build System 574
Sound 577
Enhanced LCDUI 578
   CustomItem 578
   Form Control 581
   Spacer Item 584
   ChoiceGroup and List 586
   Item Commands 588
   Graphics 589
   Other Extras 600
Game API 601
   GameCanvas 601
   Layer upon Layer upon 606
   Bringing It All Together 612
Communications 616
   Server Sockets 616
   Secure Connections 617
   Low-Level Communications 618
Push Registry 618
Conclusion 618

Chapter 20   Isometric Games . . . . **.621**

What Is Isometric Projection? 621

    Vertical-Only Perspective 622

The Graphics 623

    The Basic World 624

    Drawing with Perspective 625

    Handling Actors 627

    Using Sectoring 628

    Collision Detection 634

Conclusion 638

Chapter 21   Ray Casting . . . . **.639**

What Is Ray Casting? 639

The Fundamentals 641

    The Map 641

    Field-of-View 643

    Casting Columns 644

    Focal Distance 645

    Faster Math 646

The Engine 647

    Horizontal and Vertical Rays 647

    Projecting a Ray 649

    The First Step 651

    Getting a Hit 652

    Calculating the Distance 652

    Adding Some Limits 653

    The Main Loop 655

    Drawing the Wall 659

    Distortion 660

    Wall Shading 662

    Adding a Background Image 665

    Wrapping Up 665

Advanced Features 666

    Sprites and Actors 666

    Collision Detection 666

    Textures 667

Conclusion 668

Chapter 22   **Making the Connection** **669**

Mobile Communications 669

SMS/MMS 669

Bluetooth 670

HTTP 671

Network Gaming 672

Latency and Dropouts 672

The Cost Factor 672

Practical Uses 673

A Simple Networked MIDlet 674

The Server Side 676

Setting Up Tomcat 677

Creating a Servlet 677

Deploying a Servlet 679

Online Scoring for Star Assault 680

Basic Scoring 680

The Online Scoring Class 682

The Scoring Servlet 686

Advanced Networking 689

Using Sessions 689

Server-Side Persistence 690

Multi-Server 691

Other Considerations 692

Conclusion 692

Appendix A   **Java 2 Primer** **693**

Java 2 693

The Nature of a Program 694

Objects Everywhere 694

So What Is an Object Anyway? 694

Java Objects 696

Instantiation 696

Methods 697

Fields 698

Constructors 698

Objects and Memory 700

Basic Syntax 702
   Comments 702
   Primitive Types 703
   Literals 704
   Declaring Primitive Types 705
   Basic Operators 706
   Statements and Blocks 709
   Conditionals 711
   The do and while Statements 712
   Strings 715
   Arrays 717
Advanced Object-Oriented Programming .717
   Basic Inheritance 718
   Object Base 721
   Method Overriding 722
   Abstract 723
   Interfaces 724
   Visibility 725
   Inner Classes 726
   Finalize 728
   This 729
   Statics 729
   Final 733
Exceptions 734
Packages, Import, and CLASSPATH 736

Index **738**

INTRODUCTION

Whether you're just starting out or you're already a veteran, game programmers are a special breed—part scientist, part storyteller, and all dreamer. Over the years I've found game development to be the most frustrating, painful process I've ever undertaken, and yet I keep coming back for more. There's just nothing like coding a game and seeing a player's eyes light up as he traverses a world of your creation.

In *J2ME Game Programming*, I'm going to teach you how to create games for micro devices. Even more, I'll show you how much fun they can be and just how cool the resulting games can look and play.

I'm not a kid with a hobby; I develop games for fun, but also for profit. In the book, I'll also cover how to earn real revenue from your games by taking them to market.

What's in the Book?

This book will show you how to code games using J2ME, with a clear focus on creating games for mobile phones (the bulk of the J2ME device marketplace). The chapters in this book are intended to be read sequentially, so if you're already familiar with the content covered in a particular section, I recommend you skim over it rather than skipping it entirely—just pick out the funny bits along the way.

Part I will give you an introduction to the world of J2ME, including its origins and current position in the marketplace. You'll also take a look at a range of typical J2ME devices and see the sort of gear for which you'll be developing.

In **Part II** you'll grab all the tools you need and set up your environment for development. Then you'll review the APIs provided as part of Sun's J2ME SDK, along with the added features available with device-specific libraries. At the end of this part, you'll put all these tools into action and create a small action game.

Part III covers what I'd call real project development. You'll look at how to refine game ideas into project plans before you embark on the development of a full-scale action game called *Star Assault*. Then, through nine chapters I'll cover all aspects of developing a commercial-quality game, including graphics, physics, environments, front ends, device-specific customization, and finally localization.

Part IV moves into the world of marketing and publishing your game. You'll look at how to create marketing material to promote your game, as well as how and where you can earn revenue.

Part V takes J2ME game development further by covering the features available in MIDP 2. I'll also show you how to create different types of games by developing both an isometric and 3D ray-casting engine. Finally, you'll explore networking with MIDP and how you can utilize it to create multiplayer games.

Who Are You?

In this book I make the assumption that you're already familiar with Java, or at least another object-oriented programming language. You don't need to be an expert, but you do need to know the basics. The book requires an understanding of rudimentary mathematics; however, the toughest level you get to is simple trigonometry, and even then I explain what I'm doing in a fair bit of detail. I also make the assumption that you're familiar with basic PC operations and can take care of environmental details such as downloading and installing software.

J2ME game development is one of those areas of game programming that (at least at present) offers real opportunities for you to profit from the games you make. I make the assumption that you're also a bit of an entrepreneur and you will want to profit from your development.

Other than that, learning J2ME game programming requires a desire to make fun games. You need to be creative, inventive, and persistent—but most of all, you'll learn to appreciate what you have and make the best of it.

Who Am I?

A very long time ago I remember being dragged through a shopping center by my mother. (I just loved going shopping as a 10-year-old.) As we rounded one corner, a machine loomed in front of me, bearing the words "Space Invaders." On the screen were rows of monochrome aliens inexorably marching downward toward a lone defender. Without comprehending what she was truly doing, my mother gave me 20 cents, and I was instantly and forever hooked to the world of video games.

From that beginning, I bought my first home computer with the sole intent of writing my own games—mostly because I never had enough money to play the arcade machines. I learned BASIC on a Tandy MC10 before moving on to the ZX, Microbee, VIC20, and C64. After studying computing in Sydney, I moved into professional programming on everything from PCs to mainframes.

I've since gone on to work on literally hundreds of projects involving everything from satellite communications systems to massively multiplayer game worlds. I've founded technology companies and watched them both succeed and fail. Through it all, I still love making games.

A few years ago I discovered Java and have since become hooked. (I now prefer it to C++ for most projects.) With the advent of J2ME, I saw an opportunity to build games for a new and emerging environment that goes beyond today's view of electronic entertainment.

Let's Go!

J2ME is a new world. Not because it's Java or because the devices are small by PC standards. We're talking about a completely new aspect to life—the emergence of a ubiquitous device that everybody carries around. Building games around these devices is a completely new field that is waiting for the string of killer games that will define it for years to come. With this book I hope I can teach you the foundations you'll need to build those games. In the words of S.R. Hadden from *Contact*, "Wanna take a ride?"

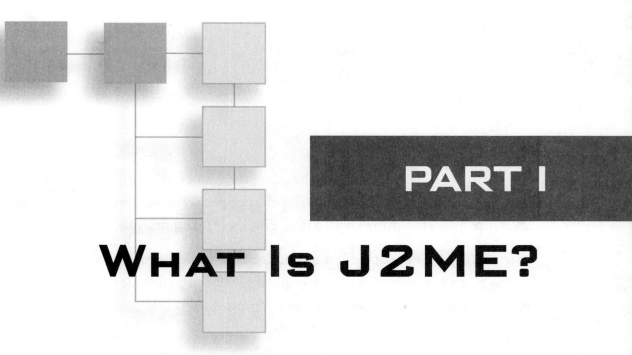

PART I

WHAT IS J2ME?

CHAPTER 1

J2ME History 3

CHAPTER 2

J2ME Overview 13

CHAPTER 3

J2ME-Enabled Devices 39

In Part 1, "What is J2ME", you'll explore the history of micro-device software development (from a game developer's perspective), including how Java, and more importantly the Java 2 Micro Edition (J2ME), fits into the landscape.

Since J2ME game development is all about creating huge games on small devices, I'll also give you a tour of the more popular J2ME compatible devices from manufacturers like Nokia, Motorola, and Sony Ericsson.

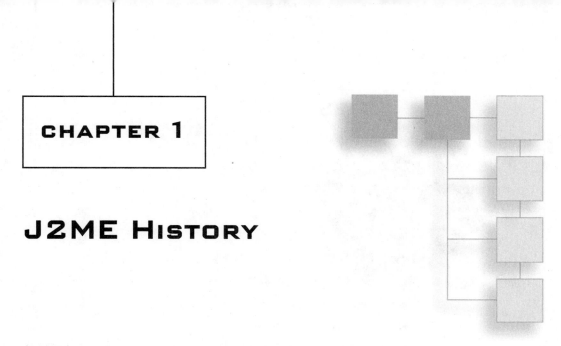

CHAPTER 1

J2ME History

This chapter will cover the history behind the Java language and other related technologies. You'll then look at the capabilities and limitations of devices such as mobile phones before finally looking at the evolution of J2ME.

Java's Acorn

In early 1995, Sun released an alpha version of a new software environment dubbed Java. During the first six months after Java's release, the industry spent most of its time making bad jokes and puns about coffee beans and Indonesian islands. (Is it just irony that there is great surfing around the island of Java?) It didn't take long, however, for the "Write Once, Run Anywhere" call to arms to be taken up. Slowly and inexorably, Java began its march to the top. But before I rush off into Java's glory days, I want to take a brief look at Java's history.

The earliest traces of Java go back to the early 1990s, when Sun formed a special technical team tasked with developing the next wave of computing. After one of those 18-month, secret-location, round-the-clock, caffeine-driven geek-fests—sounds like a game development project, if you ask me—the team emerged with the results: a handheld home-entertainment device controller with an animated touchscreen interface known as the *7 ("star seven"). Figure 1.1 shows *7. And most importantly, the team created a little animated character named Duke to demo their creation. Wow—unheard of!

Figure 1.1 The original *7 device developed by Sun

Now that a decade has passed, I wouldn't really call *7 the next wave of computing, but hey—they didn't even have the Internet or mobile phones, let alone the Internet *on* mobile phones.

The real action, however, wasn't with the device; it was with the back-end technology that powered it. One of the requirements of the project was an embedded software environment that was robust hardware-independent, and that facilitated low-cost development. Enter the hero of our story, James Gosling, a Canadian software engineer working with the team.

Taking some of the best elements of C++, while excluding the troublesome memory management, pointers, and multiple inheritance—along with concepts from the early object-oriented language SIMULA—James created a new language dubbed Oak. (It was named after a tree outside his window. I wonder if an Indonesian island appeared outside his window sometime later, in which case I think he should really lay off the Jolt for a while.)

Oak's power wasn't only in its language design; there were plenty of other object-oriented languages. Oak blossomed because it encompassed *everything*. James didn't create a language and then let other people implement it as they saw fit. The goal of Oak was hardware independence, and with that in mind he created a complete software deployment environment. From virtual computers to functional APIs, Oak provided—and, more importantly, *controlled*—everything.

Unfortunately, *7 floundered around like a legless cow in a butcher shop until 1994, when, during a three-day, non-stop, mountain retreat geek-fest, James (along with Bill Joy, Wayne Rosing, John Gage, Eric Schmidt, and Patrick Naughton) saw a new opportunity for their acorn—the Internet.

Around the same time, that new-fangled Internet thing was emerging as a mainstream technology. The World Wide Web was being used to transfer and display digital content in the form of pictures, text, and even audio almost universally on a variety of hardware.

The goals of the Web were not dissimilar to that of Oak: provide a system to let you write content once, but view it anywhere. Sound familiar? Oak was attempting to do the same thing, but for programming. Imagine if the Internet were used as the framework upon which Oak software could be distributed and universally deployed. James and his pocket-protected buddies were on to something big.

Figure 1.2 The original HotJava browser, showing the first Java home page

Java's Growth in the Sun

After the Oak-meets-Internet epiphany, James and the team at Sun developed a host of technologies around the concept of a universally deployable language and platform. One of their first tasks was to develop the Java-compatible browser known as HotJava (although the early versions had the much cooler name WebRunner, after the movie *Blade Runner*). Figure 1.2 shows the original HotJava browser.

On May 23, 1995, one of the defining moments in the history of computing occurred. The then-young Netscape Corporation agreed to integrate Java into its almost universally popular Navigator Web browser, thus creating an unprecedented audience for the Java software.

Soon programmers from all across the globe flooded the Java Web site to download the new platform. Sun completely underestimated the platform's popularity and struggled to upgrade bandwidth to cope with the rush. Before anyone realized it—even those watching it happen—something changed in the IT world. Kicking and screaming, Java had arrived.

Development of the Java platform continued aggressively over the following years, with the subsequent release of a great deal of supporting technology. New editions, especially one targeting enterprise software development, have arguably become more popular than the original technology.

However, one thing remains the same for me—I still choose Java over any other language. The code is simpler, the development is faster, and the bugs are easier to find. It just works almost everywhere.

So What Is Java?

Java is more than a programming language; it's a way of life. You should immediately terminate all other activities and devote your life entirely to the pursuit of perfection in your Java code. Not! But seriously, coding Java programs is a great way to kill a few hours. (I'm sad, I admit it, but hey—tell me you don't like coding too.)

Java is a little different than your typical programming language. First, most programming languages process code by either compiling or interpreting; Java does both. As you can see in Figure 1.3, the initial compile phase translates your source code (.java files) into an intermediate language called Java bytecode (.class files). The resulting bytecode is then ready to be executed (interpreted) within a special virtual computer known as the JVM (*Java Virtual Machine*).

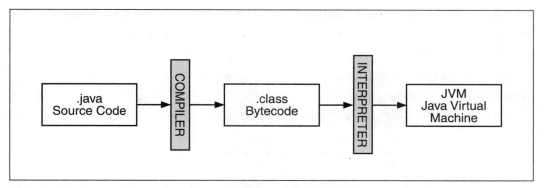

Figure 1.3 Java code goes through two stages: compilation and interpretation.

The Java Virtual Machine is a simulated computer that executes all the bytecode instructions. It's through the JVM that Java gains its portability because it acts as a consistent layer between bytecode and the actual machine instructions—bytecode instructions are translated into machine-specific instructions by the JVM at runtime.

Compiled bytecode is the power behind Java's "Write Once, Run Anywhere" flexibility. As you can see in Figure 1.4, all a target platform needs is a JVM, and it has the power to execute Java applications, regardless of the platform on which they were originally compiled.

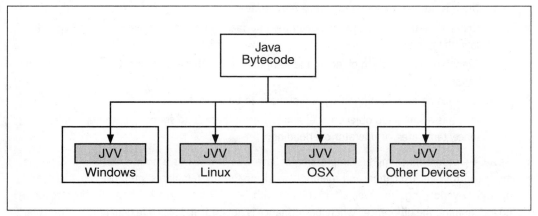

Figure 1.4 Java bytecode becomes a portable program executable on any Java Virtual Machine.

However, to make all this work successfully, you need more than just a programming language—you need a programming platform. The Java platform is made up of three significant components:

- The Java compiler and tools
- The Java Virtual Machine
- The Java API (*Application Programming Interface*)

Java versus C++

Since most of us game programmers are C++ coders first, here's a brief rundown of the significant differences between Java and C++.

Thankfully, Java is based on C++; in fact, James Gosling implemented the initial versions of Java using C++. But James took the opportunity presented by Java's unique language model to modify the structure and make it more programmer-friendly.

The first major difference is memory management. Unlike in C++, in Java you basically aren't trusted enough to peek and poke at your own memory—that's the JVM's job. You can control the construction of objects, but you don't have any sort of fine-tuning control over the destruction of objects. You certainly can't do any of that fancy pointer arithmetic; there's just no concept of addressing an object in memory. However, the good news is that many of those hair-pulling, dangling-pointer, memory-scribbling, blue-screen nightmares just don't happen anymore.

The differences don't end there, though. Java also has the following notable variations from C++.

- There is no preprocessing of source files in Java.
- Unlike C++ there is no split between the interface (.h) and the implementation (.cpp). In Java there is only one source file.
- Everything in Java is an object in the form of a class. (This also means there are no global variables.)
- Java has no auto-casting of types; you have to be explicit.
- Java has a simplified object model and patterns; there is no support for multiple inheritance, templates, or operator overloading.

As a C++ programmer, my first impression of Java was that it was a poor cousin. C++ gave me more control over execution and memory, and I missed my templates, preprocessor tricks, and operator overloading. However, after working with Java for some years, I honestly have to say I no longer mind the differences where performance is not critical. Java code generally performs far better and with fewer bugs. The Java API is a vast pool of free functionality, and the performance seems as good as or better than C++ in most circumstances—if for no other reason than because of the extra time I now spend improving my code.

The JVM's role is to provide an interface to the functionality of the underlying device, whereas the Java API provides a limited view of this functionality to the Java program. In this manner, the JVM is the judge, jury, and executor of program code.

The Java API is a collection of Java classes covering a vast range of functionality including containers, data management, communications, IO, security, and more. There are literally thousands of classes available as part of the Java platform.

Multiple Editions

The Java language has evolved over the years. The first major edition, now known as J2SE (*Java 2 Standard Edition*) was aimed at the development of GUIs, applets, and other typical applications. A few years ago Sun expanded the Java suite with J2EE (*Java 2 Enterprise Edition*), which was built for use in server-side development. This version included expanded tools for database access, messaging, content rendering, inter-process communications, and transaction control.

Sun didn't stop there, though. With a desperate desire to satisfy every programmer on the planet, they set their sights on teeny-weeny devices (yes, that's the true technical term), and thus the rather ingeniously named J2ME (*Java 2 Micro Edition*) squeaked into existence.

Before we get into the nitty-gritty of that edition, take a look at how and why Java found a home in the micro world.

Micro Devices Everywhere

As a child watching reruns of the original *Star Trek* series, I was always wowed when Captain Kirk, usually during some cool away mission, would grandly whip out his little communicator, flip it open, and talk with shipmates over great distances.

Well, a bunch of similar kids were watching those same reruns, but instead of rushing off to write sci-fi video games like I did, they played with their circuit boards and crystal sets and dreamed of building communicators. (I know what I'd rather be doing, but hey— whatever turns you on, right?) Those kids have gone on to create a world of portable phones, pagers, and digital assistants that would blow even Captain Kirk's pastel-colored socks off. (Now all they need is for us to make great games for those devices!)

When I was evaluating the potential of micro-device game development, one of the first things I wanted to know was the size of the market and how large it might grow to be. After a little research, my findings surprised me. The market *is* the exciting thing about micro devices. I mean, let's face it—after about three chapters, you'll know just as well as

I do how technically limited these little things are. There's no pushing the boundaries of graphical interactive entertainment in fewer than 100 pixels and no sound!

But when you're waiting to buy coffee, riding the bus to work, or just waiting for your girl-friend to finish shopping (remember to say it looks great on her), that 10-GHz dual-processor screamer sitting on your desk won't help much. All that stands between you and having to re-read that ad or poster for the thousandth time is those 100 pixels. This is the same all around the world, as millions turn to their mobile phones to kill a few minutes. Now it's up to us to rescue these people from their boredom, to help them break the chains of deskbound PCs, to bring gaming to new worlds, to bring . . . freedom! Now charge! (Oops, got myself a bit worked up there.)

Micro Software

To get a feel for J2ME's place in the landscape, take a look at the world of micro devices. As you can see in Figure 1.5, there are roughly five categories of micro devices.

Over the past decade, micro device manufacturers have generally (sometimes reluctantly) provided programmers and other content creators with various levels of tools to build software applications. There have also been industry attempts to create standard software platforms, which have met with varying degrees of success. Table 1.1 lists some of the development tools used in the recent past.

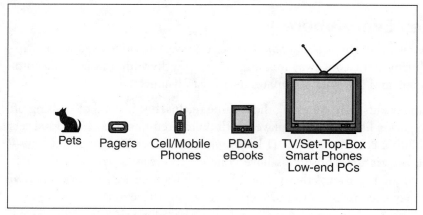

Figure 1.5 The broad categories of micro devices. (Note: One of these categories is rather silly. Can you spot which one? That's right, it's pagers!)

Table 1.1 Non-Java Development Tools

Tool	Description
Manufacturer SDK	The most common development platform was using device manufacturer or operating system (such as Palm, Windows CE, and EPOC/Psion) SDKs (*Software Development Kits*). In most cases, developers would use C/C++.
WAP/WML	WAP (*Wireless Application Protocol),* a standard communications protocol used in mobile devices, is used in a similar way to HTTP and TCP. An early Internet system developed by mobile phone operators used WAP as transport for WML (*Wireless Markup Language)* which serves as a replacement for the more complex HTML (*Hypertext Markup Language)* used by Web browsers. Unfortunately, the end result was nothing like the "mobile internet" promised by promoters.
Web/HTML	Available only to the higher-level devices, the Web was sometimes used as a content delivery tool. Content was usually cosmetically modified to suit the characteristics of micro devices.
Other middleware	Many vendors have also tried to create content-creation middleware and tools such as i-mode and BREW with varying degrees of success.

I-mode

The Japanese market has a hugely popular system known as i-mode. This simple protocol was used to distribute content similarly to WAP. In my opinion, its early success compared to WAP was due to some simple differences, which include the following:

- It was a closed market, so content was targeted and relevant.
- The audience size quickly reached critical mass.
- The carrier (NTT DoCoMo) played a big part in the technology implementation (actually, they invented it), and therefore had significant business motivation to see it succeed.
- It was delivered over a packet-switched network, as opposed to a circuit-switched network, so there was no inconvenient dial-up delay.
- It had color graphics. Mmmm.
- The content was fun.

I-mode has since gone on to greater things (including support for Java), but that's a story for another chapter.

Conclusion

With more than two million programmers, Java is an enormously popular development platform. As a language, it is easy to learn and subsequently master, and it comes prepackaged as a robust, secure, portable, and scalable platform. All of these elements make Java an excellent tool for the micro world.

Things aren't that simple, though. J2SE is too large to fit into the limited capabilities of micro devices, and a lot of the functionality, such as AWT and Swing, isn't applicable or useful anyway.

With J2ME, Sun elected to create a version of Java suited to the weird and wonderful micro world. In the next chapter, you'll take a look at exactly what they came up with.

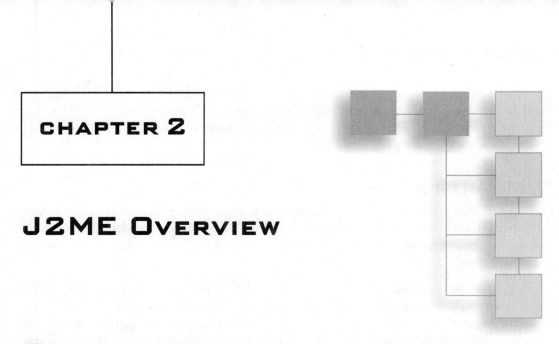

CHAPTER 2

J2ME OVERVIEW

I n this chapter, you'll take a look at J2ME's place in the Java landscape, and you'll get a bird's eye view of the different editions. Then you'll look at the various components that make up J2ME before finally reviewing the tools, configurations, profiles, and virtual machines that make everything tick.

I Shall Call It Mini-ME

Portable devices are an exciting industry. Every time you turn around, there's another sexier model, with a bigger screen, more memory, higher bandwidth, and a faster CPU, usually within an ever-smaller form—and they come in a cool range of colors too.

With all this new hardware horsepower, users are naturally looking for more than just the software that came pre-installed by the manufacturer. I know *Snake II* satisfies all my entertainment needs, but hey, sometimes we have to think about other people.

However, delivering new content is not quite as simple as it sounds. As a developer, you have to cope with the huge variety of hardware, along with the inherently broad range of functionality that comes with such diversity. You then have to wade through the murky swamp of different SDKs to access this functionality. Creating software for multiple versions of one device is hard work; creating it for completely different classes of devices is an exercise in painstaking compromise.

Writing the software isn't the only problem. Delivering it to the device requires a platform capable of installing new software on demand, along with the channels to receive new code. And once installed, users (and device manufacturers acting on their behalf) must consider the security of the software and the device.

So where do you turn for a solution to all these issues? Amidst a blaze of light, a big (but still nerdy) guy in a yellow spandex suit leaps up, hands on hips, chest emblazoned with a big J and a small ME. Never fear, J2ME is here to make you look good in tights—oops, I mean, to bring software to the micro masses! Had you worried, didn't I?

J2ME Architecture

As I mentioned briefly in Chapter 1, Sun elected to create different versions of Java to suit different environments. From the enterprise development tools designed for use in servers to the micro systems for which you're developing, each version has its own place in the Java landscape.

It's important to note that the division between platforms is not simply categorical. The line between different platforms can get blurry. In fact, J2ME development sometimes requires the use of all three platforms (J2ME, J2SE, and J2EE). For example, when you're developing a multiplayer game, you use J2ME for the client-side device software, but you also benefit from the power of J2SE and J2EE when you implement the backend server systems.

In Figure 2.1, you can see the different Java editions, along with the hardware each supports. As you can see, the various editions of Java suit distinctly different device classes. This figure also shows the three virtual machines in use for the different environments. The Hotspot VM is the default virtual machine supplied by Sun for executing the full-scale version of Java—Hotspot is a newer type of virtual machine capable of dynamically

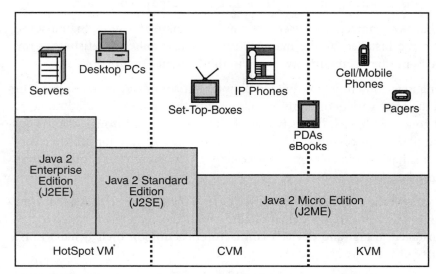

Figure 2.1 The different editions of Java suit different hardware platforms.

optimizing heavily executed code (hotspots) during runtime. The Compact Virtual Machine (CVM) and Kilobyte Virtual Machine (KVM) are smaller virtual machine implementations designed to run within the constraints of the limited resources available on micro devices. We'll look at which virtual machine is used for different devices a little later in the chapter.

In developing J2ME, it was obvious that trying to fit something like J2SE on a mobile phone would be like trying to stuff the Hindenburg down your pants (oh, the humanity).

Since J2SE was obviously way too big to fit on even the larger micro devices, Sun had to shrink it down. But which parts should they remove? With such a large variety of different devices, Sun didn't want to limit all J2ME applications to the lowest compatible hardware set. This would unfairly compromise the functionality of the higher-end devices. Limiting J2ME to the capabilities of low-end pagers just wasn't a practical solution.

The designers of J2ME came up with a solution based on a revised Java architecture that provides for the exclusion of parts of the platform (such as language, tools, JVM, and API) while adding device-category-specific components. This is realized through a combination of J2ME configurations and profiles.

Configurations and Profiles

A *configuration* defines the capabilities of a Java platform designed for use on a series of similar hardware. Essentially, it provides for the minimization of the J2SE platform by removing components such as:

- Java language components
- Minimum hardware requirements, such as the memory, screen size, and processor power for the family of devices
- Included Java libraries

Using this architecture, Sun created two initial configurations to suit the micro world—one for slightly limited devices such as PDAs and Set-Top-Boxes (like digital TV receivers) and one for the "you-wanna-run-Java-on-what?!" class of devices such as pagers, mobile phones, and pets. These two configurations are:

- CDC (*Connected Device Configuration*)
- CLDC (*Connected, Limited Device Configuration*)

You'll review both of these in more detail a little later. The important thing right now is that these configurations let you move forward, confident of the functionality of the underlying target platform. You'll be developing for two platforms at most, not two hundred.

However, configurations don't cover everything; they merely limit Java to a suitable target platform's capabilities—which is essentially a nice way of saying they rip out Java's guts.

Additional functionality is required to handle the new breed of Java devices. Enter J2ME profiles.

A good example of profiles is the UI (*User Interface*) for mobile phones (see Figure 2.2). The J2ME configuration (CLDC) that covers this type of device excludes the typical Java UI libraries, AWT and Swing. The devices aren't capable of displaying anything based on these libraries anyway because the screens are just too small. So there's no point to wasting precious kilobytes on them. The answer was to create a new UI suited to the specific requirements of the humble mobile's LCD screen. The resulting LCD UI is included in the CLDC profile that targets MIDs (*Mobile Information Devices*), hence the name MIDP.

Figure 2.2 A J2ME application is built upon both a profile and a configuration (to a lesser extent).

The LCDUI implementation exemplifies the role that profiles play in adding device-category-specific functionality. This is important because profiles provide a standardization of this functionality, rather than requiring developers to fall back to Java APIs created for each device. Figure 2.3 shows the relationship between all these components.

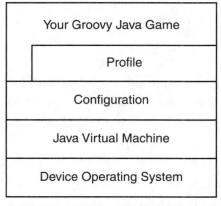

Figure 2.3 J2ME consists of a layer of components. The Java Virtual Machine interfaces with the configuration, which in turn provides functionality to the profile and application layers.

Now that you've reviewed the theory behind the J2ME architecture, take a look at exactly what is available within these configurations and profiles.

Two Sizes Fit All

As I briefly covered in the previous section, the current J2ME architecture provides two distinct configurations, the CDC and CLDC.

The CDC

Built for larger devices such as digital TV set-top-boxes and PDAs (typically with multiple megabytes of memory), the CDC is the bigger brother of the J2ME configurations. It contains a single profile (the Foundation profile) as well as a high-performance virtual machine known as the Compact Virtual Machine (CVM). The Java language implementation and the API pretty much have all the power of J2SE.

Sounds great, doesn't it? Unfortunately, the CDC is not available on the platform where the vast majority of micro-game players are—mobile phones—so it's about as useful as a blind sumo wrestler in a midget-bar brawl.

If you want to develop games for the major audiences out there, then you're interested in those "limited" devices. Enter the CLDC.

The CLDC

The CLDC is all about micro devices, especially mobile phones. It essentially defines a standard used by device manufacturers to implement a Java run-time environment. Third-party developers, following this same standard, are then confident of the platform on which their software can run.

Developed as part of the Java Community Process (JSR-30), the CLDC configuration affects many aspects of Java development and delivery, which include

- Target device characteristics
- The security model
- Application management
- Language differences
- JVM differences
- Included class libraries

Take a look at each of these in more detail.

CLDC's Pedigree

Thankfully, the CLDC wasn't developed in isolation; some of the most influential companies involved in the micro-device industry were involved in the Java Community Process expert group (JSR-30), which was responsible for the development of the specifications. Reading like a who's who of the micro-hardware industry, the list of companies involved includes

- America Online
- Bull
- Ericsson
- Fujitsu
- Matsushita
- Mitsubishi
- Motorola
- Nokia
- NTT DoCoMo

- Oracle
- Palm Computing
- RIM (Research In Motion)
- Samsung
- Sharp
- Siemens
- Sony
- Sun Microsystems
- Symbian

Target Device Characteristics

The first aspect of the CLDC is a definition of the characteristics a supported device should have. Table 2.1 contains a list of these characteristics as defined by the CLDC 1.0a specification.

Table 2.1 CLDC Target Platform Characteristics

Characteristic	Description
Memory	160 KB to 512 KB devoted to the Java platform (minimum 128K available to a Java application)
Processor	16- or 32-bit
Connectivity	Some form of connectivity, likely wireless and intermittent
Other	Low power consumption, typically powered by battery

Note

One thing you might notice right away is that the characteristics of the CLDC don't mention any input methods or screen requirements. That's the job of a particular device class profile, such as the MIDP (*Mobile Information Device Profile*). A configuration just covers the core Java system requirements.

As you can see, the CLDC's target platform isn't exactly awe-inspiring hardware. I mean, what the hell can you do with 128 KB of RAM? And believe it or not, it gets worse.

But that's where the fun is, right? When you get into the real programming in later chapters, you'll learn how to best use the meager space you're given.

The Security Model

J2SE's existing security system was too large to fit within the constraints of the CLDC target platform; it alone would likely have exceeded all available memory. A revised model cuts down many of the features, but requires far less resources. The good news is that this simplification makes it much easier to cover all the details.

There are two main sections to the CLDC security model.

- Virtual machine security
- Application security

I know that security is not the most interesting subject, but I recommend you take the time to review this section. The revised security model for the CLDC lays some important groundwork for application execution models discussed later, and maybe there's a really funny joke hidden in there somewhere—the world's first literary Easter egg, perhaps? Then again, maybe there isn't.

VIRTUAL MACHINE SECURITY   The goal of the virtual machine security layer is to protect the underlying device from any damage executable code might cause. Under normal circumstances, a bytecode verification process carried out prior to any code execution takes care of this. This verification process essentially validates class-file bytecode, thus ensuring it is correct for execution. The most important result of this process is the protection it offers against the execution of invalid instructions—or worse, the creation of scenarios in which memory outside the Java environment is corrupted. Not pretty.

The standard bytecode verification process used with J2SE requires about 50 KB of code space, along with up to 100 KB of heap. While this is negligible on larger systems, it constitutes pretty much all the memory available to Java on many micro devices. Although I have a great desire to spend all my resources doing program verification, some rude people insist on something more, like any form of application. So in an effort to appease this demanding bunch, the CLDC specifications provide an alternative.

The resulting verification implementation within the CLDC's virtual machine requires around 10 KB of binary code space and as little as 100 bytes of run-time memory. From a dynamic memory standpoint, this is a reduction of about 1,000 times. Someone needs to get a little star stamp on the forehead for that one!

The reduction in resources essentially comes from the removal of the iterative dataflow algorithm from the in-memory verification process. The price is that you now have to undertake an additional step known as *pre-verification* to prepare code for execution on the KVM. The result of this process is the insertion of additional attributes into the class file.

Note

Even after undergoing the process of pre-verification, a transformed class file is still valid Java byte-code; the verifier automatically ignores the extra data. The only noticeable difference is that the resulting files are approximately five percent larger.

A tool supplied with the J2ME development environment carries out the process of pre-verifying. It's all rather painless. As you can see in Figure 2.4, the important point is that the resource-intensive part of the verification process is carried out on your (overpowered) development PC (the build server).

Note

To avoid confusion, post-verified class files are commonly called *pclasses*.

APPLICATION SECURITY The class-loader verification process discussed previously is pretty limited. Basically, it just validates that bytecode is the legitimate result of the Java compilation process. Although this is helpful, a further level of security is required to protect a device's resources.

As you might have guessed, the powerful (but rather large) J2SE security model is out the window. The CLDC incorporates a simplified security model based on the concept of a sandbox.

The term *sandbox* really just means that your Java code can play only within the confines of a small, controlled environment. Even if that big blue truck you love is outside and you really wanna play with it, you can't. Anything outside is completely out of bounds. So stop trying, or you're going to your room!

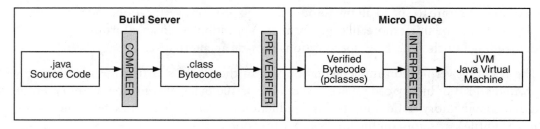

Figure 2.4 A pre-verification process reduces the resources used for the typical class-file verification.

Note

If you've done any development of applets (Java programs executed inside a Web browser), you're already familiar with the concept of sandbox security. The CLCD implementation is very similar.

As you can see in Figure 2.5, your code has restricted what's available in the sandbox environment. The CLDC defines a list of exactly what you can execute, and that's all you get. Protection is also in place so you can't change the base classes that make up the installed API on the device—the so-called *core classes*. The CLDC specifications mandate protection for these classes.

Application Management

Managing applications on micro devices is quite a different experience than doing so on typical PCs. Quite often there is no concept of a file system, let alone a file browser. In some extreme cases, micro devices won't even store class files permanently; they delete them after you finish playing!

Most of the time, especially on typical mobile devices, users have a limited amount of application space in which to store their favorite programs. (This space will be filled with your games, of course.)

To manage these applications, the device should provide a basic ability to review the installed applications, launch an application, and then subsequently delete it if the user so desires. (Hey, don't feel bad—they had to get sick of your game sometime.)

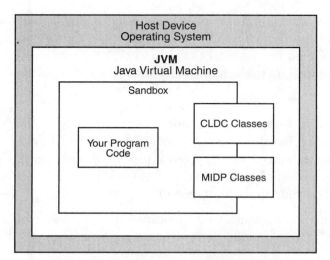

Figure 2.5 The Java sandbox security model provides you access to core classes while protecting the underlying device.

The CLDC doesn't mandate the form the application manager should take; however, typical implementations are simple menu-based tools to browse and launch programs. Nothing fancy, but they certainly do the job.

Language Differences

In the land of the little people, Java isn't quite the same as you know it. They took bits out! Brace yourself; some of them are painful.

FLOATING-POINT MATH   First, there's no floating-point math. That's right—let me say it again. You're programming games, and there's no floating-point math. The reason is that the typical micro device doesn't have dedicated floating-point hardware (which is not surprising, really), and the cost to emulate floating-point math in software was considered too great of a burden on the limited processors.

Never fear, though. In later sections, I'll show you how you can get around this. Actually, it's quite fun.

FINALIZATION   To improve performance and reduce the overall requirements, the CLDC leaves out an automatic object finalization callback. This means there's no `Object.finalize` method.

When using the J2SE under normal circumstances, the garbage collector process will call this method for an object it is about to discard from memory. You can then free any open resources that explicitly require it (such as open files). This doesn't mean the garbage collector doesn't run, it's just that it won't call your finalize method. Some programmers utilize the finalize method in order to free resources when an object is about to be trashed by the garbage collector. Because this method is not available, you need to rely on your own application flow to carry out an appropriate resource cleanup process. This is generally a good practice anyway. You should free resources as soon as they become available; don't leave the timing of this process up to the notoriously strange behavior of the garbage collector.

ERROR HANDLING   Also for resource reasons, the CLDC does not include any of the `java.lang.Error` exception class hierarchy. To refresh your memory, the exceptions shown in Table 2.2 are very much of the fatal heart attack variety. There is pretty much no chance of you recovering from an error such as this; it's really up to the VM to inform the device OS, and the device OS to then panic on your application's behalf.

Because these errors only occur in situations in which your application is about to go bye-bye anyway, there's no need for the CLDC to provide you with access to them.

Table 2.2 java.lang.Error Exceptions

Exception	Description
java.awt.AWTError	Because there is no AWT in the CLDC, this isn't required.
java.lang.LinkageError	An error relating to class compilation inconsistencies. There are many subclasses of this exception, such as java.lang.NoClassDefFoundError.
java.lang.ThreadDeath	One of the only classes in the language with a remotely cool name. You don't need it, though. The application can't really do anything if it encounters this error, except maybe draw a little bomb that has exploded.
java.lang.VirtualMachineError	The virtual machine hierarchy, which includes popular favorites like OutOfMemoryError and StackOverflowError, also are not something your application can really handle.

JVM Differences

The CLDC reference implementation incorporates a revised virtual machine known as the KVM. As you can imagine, the KVM lacks some of the features of its big brother, the J2SE JVM.

The primary features that are not available as part of the KVM and its included libraries are

- Weak references—lets you keep a reference to an object that will still be garbage collected.
- Reflection—the power to "look into" code at runtime.
- Thread groups and daemon threads—advanced thread control (rarely used).
- The JNI (*Java Native Interface*)—lets you write your own native methods, which is not appropriate for sandbox development.
- User-defined class loaders—used to roll your own class loading mechanism (rarely used).

If you have any grand plans involving any of these features, you're out of luck. Thankfully, though, you can live without most of these things, especially in low-resource environments.

Of these limitations, only a couple warrant further mention: reflection and user-defined class loaders.

REFLECTION Reflection is the Java feature that lets your program inspect the code being executed at runtime. This means from your code you can inspect the code in classes, objects, methods, and fields. The KVM does not support reflection in any form, which also means you have no access to features that inherit their functionality from the reflection core, such as the JVMDI (*Java Virtual Machine Debugging Interface*), RMI (Remote Method Invocation), object serialization, and the profiling toolset.

We can live without most of these features in game development. RMI for example, which lets you execute methods across a network, isn't particularly useful since it's a little heavyweight for typical multiplayer game development. We can achieve the same level of functionality by coding a simpler system ourselves. Object serialization is something that would be useful for saving and loading game state; however, again we can code this up ourselves without too much trouble.

While the profiling toolset is also not available, the wireless toolkit from Sun does provide a more limited profiler that suits our needs. Not having the profiling tools just means you can't write your own profiling system. Likewise you won't be able to roll your own debugging system.

USER-DEFINED CLASS LOADERS User-defined class loaders are another feature that is removed from the KVM. These were used primarily to reconfigure or replace the class-loading mechanism with a user-supplied one. Unfortunately, the sandbox security model wouldn't work very well if you could just whack in a new class loader and circumvent the security entirely, so UDCLs got the big shift-delete. This isn't something we really use in general game development anyway.

Included Class Libraries

One of the things I love about Java is the extensive library of classes that comes with the platform. As you can imagine, though, the J2EE and J2SE libraries are too large to use on micro devices.

The designers of the CLDC faced a number of issues regarding the creation of a set of libraries to include with the configuration. The first was, of course, the key driver behind everything—resources. They had less free space than an Aussie backpacker's luggage at the end of a world tour. Some things had to go, and that naturally meant they couldn't please everyone.

This also raised the issue of compatibility, the goal being to retain as much similarity and compatibility as possible with the J2SE libraries. To facilitate this, the designers divided the CLDC libraries into two logical categories—classes that are a subset of J2SE and classes that are specific to the CLDC.

These classes are differentiated by the prefix of the library. J2ME classes that are based on a subset of equivalent J2SE subset classes use the same names as their bigger cousins, so `java.lang.String`, for example, has the same name with J2ME as it does in J2SE, it's just a reduced version. CLDC-specific classes appear under the java extensions hierarchy, `javax.*`. This is reserved only for classes that do not normally appear in J2SE.

Note

CLDC-specific classes sound great, but in reality they don't exist. The CLDC specifies a single group of classes relating to connectivity, but it's not the CLDC's role to implement these; that's the job of a profile, such as the MIDP.

Take a look at exactly what J2SE functionality you have left after the CLDC culling. First, it's important to note that these classes might differ from those found in the J2SE implementation, according to the following rules.

- The package name must be identical to the corresponding J2SE counterpart.
- There cannot be any additional public or protected methods or fields.
- There cannot be changes to the semantics of the classes and methods.

In short this means that a J2SE class implemented in J2ME can only have methods removed, not added, and there can be no change to existing methods (though the actual implementations of those methods could be completely different—not something we really need to care about anyway as long as the methods work the same).

Following is a complete list of the available classes; however, this list can be rather deceiving because many of these J2ME classes have had methods removed.

Note

One thing you might notice when looking through the CLDC class libraries is the distinct lack of a few key elements, such as any form of UI (*User Interface*) or access to device-specific functions. That's the job of a given device category's profile. You'll take a look at these libraries a little later, in the MIDP section.

- System classes
  - `java.lang.Object`
  - `java.lang.Class`
  - `java.lang.Runtime`
  - `java.lang.System`
  - `java.lang.Thread`

- `java.lang.Runnable`
- `java.lang.String`
- `java.lang.StringBuffer`
- `java.lang.Throwable`

■ Input/output classes

- `java.io.InputStream`
- `java.io.OutputStream`
- `java.io.ByteArrayInputStream`
- `java.io.ByteArrayOutputStream`
- `java.io.DataInput` (interface)
- `java.io.DataOutput` (interface)
- `java.io.DataInputStream`
- `java.io.DataOutputStream`
- `java.io.Reader`
- `java.io.Writer`
- `java.io.InputStreamReader`
- `java.io.OutputStreamWriter`
- `java.io.PrintStream`

■ Collection classes

- `java.util.Vector`
- `java.util.Stack`
- `java.util.Hashtable`
- `java.util.Enumeration` (interface)

■ Type classes

- `java.lang.Boolean`
- `java.lang.Byte`
- `java.lang.Short`
- `java.lang.Integer`
- `java.lang.Long`
- `java.lang.Character`

■ Calendar and time classes

- `java.util.Calendar`
- `java.util.Date`
- `java.util.TimeZone`

- Utility classes
  - java.util.Random
  - java.lang.Math
- Exception classes
  - java.lang.Exception
  - java.lang.ClassNotFoundException
  - java.lang.IllegalAccessException
  - java.lang.InstantiationException
  - java.lang.InterruptedException
  - java.lang.RuntimeException
  - java.lang.ArithmeticException
  - java.lang.ArrayStoreException
  - java.lang.ClassCastException
  - java.lang.IllegalArgumentException
  - java.lang.IllegalThreadStateException
  - java.lang.NumberFormatException
  - java.lang.IllegalMonitorStateException
  - java.lang.IndexOutOfBoundsException
  - java.lang.ArrayIndexOutOfBoundsException
  - java.lang.StringIndexOutOfBoundsException
  - java.lang.NegativeArraySizeException
  - java.lang.NullPointerException
  - java.lang.SecurityException
  - java.util.EmptyStackException
  - java.util.NoSuchElementException
  - java.io.EOFException
  - java.io.IOException
  - java.io.InterruptedIOException
  - java.io.UnsupportedEncodingException
  - java.io.UTFDataFormatException
- Error classes
  - java.lang.Error
  - java.lang.VirtualMachineError
  - java.lang.OutOfMemoryError

You might have noticed there are no connectivity classes included in this list, such as those found in the `java.net.*` hierarchy. Because of the interdependencies in the current communications library, connectivity classes could not be included without breaking the migration rules discussed at the beginning of this section. Therefore, the CLDC includes a framework for a new communications class hierarchy known as the *connection framework*. The CLDC's cut-down framework design is exactly that—a design. There are no included classes that actually implement it. For that, you look to the world of profiles.

MIDP

In the previous section, you looked at the functionality of the CLDC, although most of what you reviewed was more about the limitations of the configuration in comparison to J2SE. Also, you might have noticed the omission of some of the things you really need to build an application, such as any form of user interface. These components are device-specific, so it's up to a device category's profile to implement them. This typifies the role of the profile: to add category-specific components on top of a configuration.

The most popular profile—and the only one really useful for your purposes—is MIDP, which targets MIDs (*Micro Information Devices*).

Since MIDP is all about MIDs, take a look at what the profile defines them to be.

Target Devices

MIDs aren't the most capable of computers, and I'm probably using the term *computer* a little loosely here. MIDs are highly portable, uncoupled devices that always compromise functionality for form.

The MIDP specifications reflect this by setting a lowest-common-denominator target platform that can be met by a broad range of handheld devices, especially mobile phones.

The MIDP sets target characteristics that MIDs should (and generally do) meet. There are both hardware and software specifics, both of which I will discuss in more detail in just a moment.

Target Hardware Environment

As you can see in the following list, the characteristics of the target devices are extremely limited. The screens are tiny, the memory is forgettable, and the CPUs move about as fast as I do on a Monday morning.

However, it's important to remember that these characteristics are the minimum target. Many devices dramatically exceed these specifications. Much larger, color screens; more RAM; better input; and next-generation networking are becoming common on an ever-increasing range of devices. Games on the higher-end devices can be downright sexy.

Even on low-end hardware, you can still make some great games; it's just a bit more of a challenge. In later sections, I'll also cover how to develop a game that can adapt itself to take advantage of additional hardware functionality, if available.

The recommended minimum MIDP device characteristics are

- Display
  - 96 × 54 pixels with 1 bit of color with an aspect ratio (pixel shape) of approximately 1 to 1
- Input types
  - One-handed keyboard or keypad (like what you see on a typical phone)
  - Two-handed QWERTY keyboard (resembling a PC keyboard)
  - Touch screen
- Memory
  - 128 KB of non-volatile memory for MIDP components
  - 8 KB of non-volatile memory for application- generated persistent data
  - 32 KB of volatile memory for the Java heap (run-time memory)
- Networking
  - Two-way wireless, possibly intermittent, connectivity
  - Usually quite limited bandwidth

Note

In addition to the listed characteristics, all MIDs are also capable of displaying 2048 × 1536 FSAA 3D graphics and real-time Dolby Digital surround sound. No really—they are! You just have to find the right combination of keys to unlock the secret hardware Easter egg in every phone—and make sure you send me an e-mail if you ever find it.

Target Software Environment

As with the target hardware environment, the software that controls MIDs can vary significantly in both functionality and power. At the higher end of the market, MIDs are not dissimilar to small PCs. At the low end, however, some components you would consider fundamental to the concept of a computer aren't available, such as a file system.

Due to this variety, the MIDP specifications mandate some basic systems software capabilities. The following list shows the most relevant of these capabilities.

- Memory
  - Access to a form of non-volatile memory (for storing things like player name and high scores)

- Networking
  - Sufficient networking operations to facilitate the communications elements of the MIDP API
- Graphics
  - Ability to display some form of bitmapped graphics
- Input
  - A mechanism to capture and provide feedback on user input
- Kernel
  - Basic operational operating system kernel capable of handling interrupts, exceptions, and some form of process scheduling

Note

Volatile memory (also known as dynamic memory, heap memory, or just plain RAM) stores data only as long the device retains power. Non-volatile memory (also known as persistent or static memory, typically using ROM, flash, or battery-backed SDRAM) stores information even after the device has been powered down.

MIDP's Pedigree

Like the CLDC, the MID profile development was part of the Java Community Process expert group (JSR-37). The companies involved were

- America Online
- DDI
- Ericsson
- Espial Group, Inc.
- Fujitsu
- Hitachi
- J-Phone
- Matsushita
- Mitsubishi
- Motorola, Inc.
- NEC
- Nokia
- NTT DoCoMo
- Palm Computing
- RIM (Research In Motion)
- Samsung
- Sharp
- Siemens
- Sony
- Sun Microsystems, Inc.
- Symbian
- Telcordia Technologies, Inc.

MIDP Applications

A Java program written to be executed on a MID is called a MIDlet. (Who comes up with these names? I would prefer to call it something cooler, like a microde or a nanogram—hmm, no, that sounds like a really tiny telegram.)

The MIDlet is subject to some rules regarding its run-time environment and packaging. I'll cover each of these rules in a bit more detail in the next few sections.

Run-Time Environment

It is the role of the device's built-in application manager to start the MIDlet. It's important to know that your application has access to only the following resources:

- All files contained within the application's JAR file
- The contents of the MIDlet descriptor file
- Classes made available as part of the CLDC and MIDP libraries

From this list, you can start to see the structure of a typical MIDlet game package. Most importantly, the JAR file should contain all the classes required to run the application, along with all the resources, such as image files and level data. You can also set application execution options as properties within the plain text MIDlet descriptor file.

Tip

You can bundle multiple MIDlet applications within one JAR file; these applications can then share resources. That's where the term *MIDlet suite* comes from—it's a suite of MIDlets.

Suite Packaging

As I just mentioned, a MIDlet application typically takes the form of a JAR file. This archive should contain all of the class and resource files required for your application. It should also contain a manifest file with the name manifest.mf.

The manifest, stored inside the JAR file, is simply a text file containing attribute value pairs (separated by a colon). Table 2.3 lists all of the types of required and optional attributes included in a manifest file.

In the case where your manifest file contains information on multiple MIDlets (a MIDlet suite), you should use the MIDlet-<N> attributes to specify information on each of the individual MIDlets within the package. Typically, though, your package will only have one application so this isn't too much of a concern.

Of course, you can add your own attributes to the manifest file. The only rule is that they cannot begin with the MIDlet- prefix. Also keep in mind that attribute names must match exactly, including case.

Table 2.3 MIDlet JAR Manifest Attributes

Attribute	Description
Required Attributes	
MIDlet-Name	Descriptive name of the MIDlet suite.
MIDlet-Version	Version number of the MIDlet suite.
MIDlet-Vendor	The owner/developer of the application.

MIDlet-\<n\>	The name, icon filename, and class of each of the MIDlets in the suite. For example:
	
	`MIDlet-1: SuperGame,/supergame.png,com.your.SuperGame`
	`MIDlet-2: PowerGame,/powergame.png,com.your.PowerGame`

MicroEdition-Profile	The name of the profile required to execute the MIDlets in this suite. The value should be exactly the same as the value of the system property microedition.profiles. For MIDP version 1, use MIDP-1.0.
MicroEdition-Configuration	The name of the configuration required to run the MIDlets in this suite. Use the exact name contained in the system property microedition.configuration, such as CLDC-1.0.
Optional Attributes	
MIDlet-Icon	Name of a PNG image file that will serve as a cute little picture identifying this MIDlet suite.
MIDlet-Description	Text describing the suite to a potential user.
MIDlet-Info-URL	URL pointing to further information on the suite.
MIDlet-Jar-URL	The URL from which the JAR can be downloaded.
MIDlet-Jar-Size	Size of the JAR in bytes.
MIDlet-Data-Size	Minimum number of bytes of non-volatile memory required by the MIDlet (persistent storage). The default is zero.

You might also wonder what the point of the MIDlet-Jar-URL attribute is. Given that the manifest file has to be included within a JAR, you might rightly ask, why bother having a URL to go and download a JAR when you obviously must have the JAR to know the URL in the first place? The answer is, you don't need to bother having this attribute in your manifest file—it's intended for use in the application descriptor (JAD) file reviewed later in this section. The attribute is in the list because the manifest file also serves as the default for any attributes not contained within the JAD. The creators of the specifications for MIDP elected to create a single set of attributes for both the manifest and JAD files. A reasonable thing to do, but it still left me confused the first time I read the specifications.

Tip

MIDlet version numbers should follow the standard Java versioning specifications, which essentially specify a format of Major.Minor[.Micro], such as 1.2.34. I generally use the major version to indicate a significant functional variation, the minor version for minor features and major bug fixes, and the micro for relatively minor bug fixes.

The following is an example of a manifest file:

MIDlet-Name: Super Games

MIDlet-Version: 1.0

MIDlet-Vendor: Your Games Co.

MIDlet-1: SuperGame,/supergame.png,com.your.SuperGame

MIDlet-2: PowerGame,/powergame.png,com.your.PowerGame

MicroEdition-Profile: MIDP-1.0

MicroEdition-Configuration: CLDC-1.0

Application Descriptors (JADs)

Transferring large amounts of data around mobile networks is a bit like trying to send an encyclopedia via carrier pigeon (otherwise known as CPIP). For this reason, a descriptor file is available to allow users to view the details of a MIDlet JAR without actually having to download the whole thing.

The application descriptor file, or JAD, serves this purpose. It contains essentially the same attributes as those in the manifest, and it naturally exists independent of the JAR file. Figure 2.6 shows the relationship between all the components of a MIDlet suite and a JAD file.

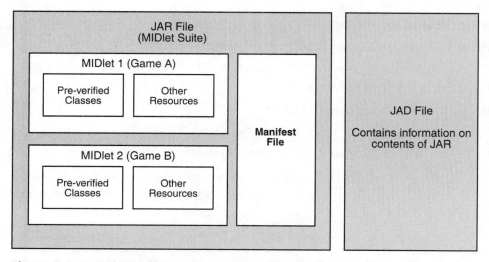

Figure 2.6 A single JAR file contains multiple MIDlet applications, along with their resources. A manifest and JAD are included to describe the details of the contents.

There is a close link between the JAD and the manifest files. You should think of the JAD as a mini-version of the manifest. The following attribute values must be the same in both files, or else the MIDP application manager will reject the MIDlet suite:

- `MIDlet-Name`
- `MIDlet-Version`
- `MIDlet-Vendor`

For all other attributes, the values in the JAD file take precedence.

Caution

At some point in the distant future, a small man wearing a white safari suit and carrying a large briefcase bearing the word "Reviewer" will suddenly appear next to your desk. He will undoubtedly demand—in an upper-class English accent—to know why you have included `MIDlet-<n>` attributes within your JAD files when, upon review of the specification (he will hold it in front of your nose), it clearly says they aren't supposed to be there!

Well, tell him to "nick off"; without the `MIDlet-<n>` attributes, the current Sun MIDP emulator won't display your MIDlets. Assume they're required for now, and argue with the Specinator later.

The following is an example of a JAD file:

> MIDlet-Name: Super Games
>
> MIDlet-Version: 1.0
>
> MIDlet-Vendor: Your Games Co.
>
> MIDlet-1: SuperGame,/supergame.png,com.your.SuperGame
>
> MIDlet-2: PowerGame,/powergame.png,com.your.PowerGame
>
> MicroEdition-Profile: MIDP-1.0
>
> MicroEdition-Configuration: CLDC-1.0
>
> MIDlet-Jar-Size: 2604
>
> MIDlet-Jar-URL: http://your-company.com/MIDlets.jar

As you can see, the primary difference between the JAD and the manifest examples is the inclusion of the two `MIDlet-Jar` attributes. Using these attributes, the application manager can determine the download and device storage requirements for your game.

Tip

The `MIDlet-Jar-Size` attribute is rather cumbersome because it requires updating every time your code or resources change. Constantly updating this value by hand is a pain, so I'll show you a great way to automate the process using a build script in Chapter 14, "The Device Ports."

MIDP 1.0 Libraries

The MIDP specification does a good job of locking down the hardware characteristics of MIDs for you, but there's more to developing applications than just describing the hardware. The MIDP also delivers the real guts of the J2ME mobile software solution—the libraries.

The MIDP libraries provide tools designed specifically for the idiosyncrasies of development on MIDs. This includes access to:

- A user interface catering to small screens and limited input
- Persistent storage (non-volatile memory), also known as record management
- Networking (through an implementation of the CLDC connection framework)
- Timers
- Application management

I'll review the details of all of these API parts in Chapter 5, "J2ME API." For now, you can review the following list of available classes.

- General utility
  - `java.util.Timer`
  - `java.util.TimerTask`
  - `java.lang.IllegalStateException`
- User interface classes
  - `javax.microedition.lcdui.Choice` (interface)
  - `javax.microedition.lcdui.CommandListener` (interface)
  - `javax.microedition.lcdui.ItemStateListener` (interface)
  - `javax.microedition.lcdui.Alert`
  - `javax.microedition.lcdui.AlertType`
  - `javax.microedition.lcdui.Canvas`
  - `javax.microedition.lcdui.ChoiceGroup`
  - `javax.microedition.lcdui.Command`
  - `javax.microedition.lcdui.DateField`
  - `javax.microedition.lcdui.Display`
  - `javax.microedition.lcdui.Displayable`
  - `javax.microedition.lcdui.Font`
  - `javax.microedition.lcdui.Form`
  - `javax.microedition.lcdui.Gauge`
  - `javax.microedition.lcdui.Graphics`

- `javax.microedition.lcdui.Image`
- `javax.microedition.lcdui.ImageItem`
- `javax.microedition.lcdui.Item`
- `javax.microedition.lcdui.List`
- `javax.microedition.lcdui.Screen`
- `javax.microedition.lcdui.StringItem`
- `javax.microedition.lcdui.TextBox`
- `javax.microedition.lcdui.TextField`
- `javax.microedition.lcdui.Ticker`

▪ Application classes
  - `javax.microedition.midlet.MIDlet`
  - `javax.microedition.midlet.MIDletStateChangeException`

▪ Record management classes
  - `javax.microedition.rms.RecordComparator` (interface)
  - `javax.microedition.rms.RecordFilter` (interface)
  - `javax.microedition.rms.RecordListener` (interface)
  - `javax.microedition.rms.RecordStore`
  - `javax.microedition.rms.InvalidRecordIDException`
  - `javax.microedition.rms.RecordStoreException`
  - `javax.microedition.rms.RecordStoreFullException`
  - `javax.microedition.rms.RecordStoreNotFoundException`
  - `javax.microedition.rms.RecordStoreNotOpenException`

▪ Networking classes
  - `javax.microedition.io.Connection` (interface)
  - `javax.microedition.io.ContentConnection` (interface)
  - `javax.microedition.io.Datagram` (interface)
  - `javax.microedition.io.DatagramConnection` (interface)
  - `javax.microedition.io.HttpConnection` (interface)
  - `javax.microedition.io.InputConnection` (interface)
  - `javax.microedition.io.OutputConnection` (interface)
  - `javax.microedition.io.StreamConnection` (interface)
  - `javax.microedition.io.StreamConnectionNotifier` (interface)
  - `javax.microedition.io.Connector`
  - `javax.microedition.io.ConnectionNotFoundException`

MIDP 2.0

With the release of MIDP 2.0, Sun has added significant functionality to the original plat-form. However, because the number of devices supporting these new versions remains limited, we will continue to develop games supporting both platforms, at least for the short term.

My recommended approach to this is to develop for MIDP 1.0 and then take advantage of the new features in the same way you would a MID-device-specific library. In Chapter 14, I'll show you how to achieve this in a relatively painless way using build scripts.

You'll take a much closer look at the new functionality in Chapter 19, "CLDC 1.1 and MIDP 2.0." However, Table 2.4 shows a quick summary of the new features.

There are many great features here—support for quality sound, transparent images (by default), and a new game-oriented API are godsends.

In addition to all this, the hardware requirements for a MIDP 2.0-compatible device are increased; your application can now be as large as 256 KB (up from 128 KB), and the available run-time memory is now 128 KB (up from 32 KB). This is great news because memory capacity, especially the package size, was a severe limitation in MIDP 1.0.

Another related new release is the CLDC 1.1. This version adds some nice features such as floating-point support and a limited form of weak references.

Table 2.4 MIDP 2.0 Features

Category	Features
Networking	Support for HTTPS.
	Incoming data can now "awaken" your MIDlets.
Audio	Play polyphonic tones (MIDI) and WAV samples.
UI	Improved layout tools.
	Better placement control.
	New cool controls including the power to build your own controls.
Games	Support for graphics layers.
	Enhanced canvas tools.
	Integer arrays as images.
	PNG image transparency.
Security	Improved permission-based security system.

Right now, though, the mass market has MIDP 1.0, so you should concentrate on developing for that. Your games will still be more or less the same when developed for the revised platform, just with slightly better everything. Think of developing under the current model as like swinging three bats before you head up to hit.

Conclusion

In this chapter you looked at the motivations, design, and inner workings of J2ME. You saw how the CLDC and MIDP specifications provide you with a solid foundation from which you can confidently develop games for MIDs, and then you reviewed the tools available to you as an application programmer. More importantly, you learned the parts of Java that aren't available.

One of the things that really stands out, though, is the limitations of the CLDC and MIDP platform. The memory, processors, networking, and graphics capabilities don't exactly lead the industry relative to "big box" gaming. But this is where the real difference is: You really can make a top-notch game with limited resources. And the great thing is, you don't need to sell your soul to a publisher to get a two million dollar budget to make a great game—if you even get through the door. Creating a hit J2ME game only takes you and maybe a few of your equally crazy friends. When you're done, you have solid ways of turning your work into real revenue.

You'll get to all this in later chapters. For now, take a look at the popular MIDs on the market and try to get a real feel for the devices for which you're developing.

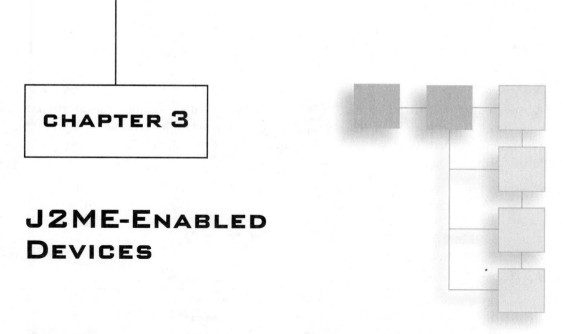

CHAPTER 3

J2ME-Enabled Devices

U p until now you've been dealing with the software behind J2ME. In this chapter, you'll take a quick tour of some of the more popular MIDs on the market and learn about their capabilities as gaming machines.

MID Overview

As I've mentioned in previous chapters, there's a huge range of J2ME-compatible devices already available, and new devices, ranging from mobile phones to PDAs, seem to be released on a daily basis.

The most common form of MID is basically a suped-up mobile phone. Memory is generally limited, with the greatest restriction being that the maximum size of an individual J2ME MIDlet is as low as 30 KB. The input device is typically the traditional phone keypad, although direction pads are becoming popular.

There is, however, a very serious end of the market (in gaming terms), which includes high-end devices such as the Nokia Series 60 (including the N-Gage) and the Sony Ericsson P800/P900. Sporting big screens, tons of memory, and fast processors, these devices provide an excellent experience for gamers.

All right, enough talk—it's time to check out the gear. In the next few sections you'll see what's offered by the likes of Nokia, Sony Ericsson, and Motorola.

Tip

You can always get a reasonably up-to-date list of (some) J2ME devices at http://wireless.java. sun.com/device. This list isn't comprehensive, though.

Nokia

As one of the largest manufacturers of MIDs, Nokia represents a significant proportion of your current (and future) user base, so spending a little time understanding their product range is well worth your while. The best place to find out about Nokia phones is at http://forum.nokia.com.

Although they have a great many different phone models, Nokia standardizes all devices into the five series listed in Table 3.1.

Table 3.1 Nokia Series Devices

Series	Screen	Type	Input Use
Series 30	96 × 65	Monochrome/Color	One-handed
Series 40	128 × 128	Color	One-handed
Series 60	176 × 208	Color	One-handed
Series 80	640 × 200	Color	Two-handed
Series 90	640 × 320	Color	Two-handed

Having all models follow a series is great for us developers. You can develop a game for a particular series and be comfortable that it will work on all phones that conform to the specification. Take a closer look at each of the series and some example phones in the following sections.

Tip

All Nokia J2ME phones support PNG transparency as well as the Nokia UI platform extensions.

Series 30

The Series 30 is mass-market range from Nokia—the sort of thing given away when you buy more than three bananas at the fruit shop. The focus, therefore, is price, and that means the devices don't come loaded with features. However, you can still write games for these devices; you just need to work within their constraint.

The original Series 30 phones were all monochrome (2-bit grayscale), with a maximum MID JAR size of 30 KB and heap memory of around 150 KB. Series 30 phones are always 96 × 65 pixels. There are some newer Series 30 models now available that sport a 4096-color screen, an increased JAR size of 64 KB, and a slightly larger heap. All Series 30 phones use the regular phone keypad layout you see in Figure 3.1. A more advanced version, the 3510i, is shown in Figure 3.2.

Figure 3.1 The low-end Nokia 3410 has a 96 × 65 monochrome screen and a maximum JAR size of 50 KB.

Figure 3.2 The Nokia 3510i, a second-generation Series 30, adds a color display and a 64-KB JAR size.

Tip

Even though the Series 30 devices are limited, don't dismiss them. Although they lack capabilities—especially with regard to JAR size—they make up for it due to the sheer number of these phones in use.

Series 40

The Nokia Series 40 is what you might call the J2ME gaming heartland. They are cheap, extremely popular, and pack enough power to make for some fun gaming. This combination means they are the most widely supported and targeted phone class for J2ME developers.

Tip

The details on different phone models can vary slightly. I recommend you visit Forum Nokia (http://www.forum.nokia.com) to get detailed information on their capabilities.

All Series 40 devices have a 128 × 128-pixel 4096-color screen. They support a minimum MID JAR size of 64 KB and have 200 KB of heap memory (though some devices exceed these capabilities). The input layouts can vary, as you can see in Figures 3.3 and 3.4.

Figure 3.3 The creative Nokia 3300 has a distinct form factor but still follows the Series 40 specification.

Figure 3.4 The Nokia 6820 is a typical Series 40 device.

Series 60

The Nokia Series 60 is where things start to get serious. The standard screen size jumps to the far more respectable 176 × 208, although it's still 12-bit (4096) color. The real news, though, is that the maximum JAR size increases to a whopping 4 MB on average! Heap memory is also up considerably, to 1 MB or more. That's enough space for some serious gaming.

Devices in this series include the 3600, 3650, 6600, 7650, and N-Gage. You can see a picture of a 3650 in Figure 3.5 and an N-Gage in Figure 3.6.

Series 80

The Nokia Series 80 devices are very high-end PDA phones based on the "communicator" range. The form factor is a bi-fold device that opens to present a large screen (640 × 200) and a small QWERTY keyboard. JAR size is a massive 14–16 MB.

Unfortunately the price and bulk of these devices severely limits the total market for your games. If you're developing for the Series 60, consider a port to the Series 80 (or 90). I don't recommend developing a game exclusively for the Series 80, though. You can see a typical Series 60 device in Figure 3.7.

Series 90

The Nokia Series 90 devices are also PDA-come-phones with high-end capabilities. However, they differ from the Series 80 devices in that they do not include the keyboard; they

Figure 3.5 The Nokia 3650 is a classic phone with Series 60 grunt.

Figure 3.6 The Nokia N-Gage is a phone-come-gaming handheld device.

rely instead on pen-based input, so they tend to be of a more manageable size. They're also dead sexy!

A Series 90 device sports a 640×320 16-bit (65536-color) display and a maximum MIDlet size of 64 MB. (Yep, I didn't get that wrong—64 MB!) Now you're talking!

Like the Series 80, however, the 90 has a limited market due to cost. One of the first Series 90 phones is shown in Figure 3.8.

Figure 3.7 The Nokia 9290—a great phone, and when you're done, you can build your house out of about 1,000 used ones.

Figure 3.8 The Nokia 7700—it's not a phone; it's a way of life.

Sony Ericsson

Combining the mobile technology of Ericsson with the style and marketing of Sony seems to have been a successful idea for the partners and consumers. Sony Ericsson has a broad range of capable phones that incorporate strong support for J2ME. To find out more details about developing for Sony Ericsson, visit http://www.sonyericsson.com/developer.

T6xx and Z600 Series

J2ME support starts with the T6xx series of devices, all of which have a 128×160 screen and 16-bit color. Maximum MID size is around 60 KB with 256 KB of RAM. The Z600 also falls into this category because it's a fold-out version of the same platform. You can see an image of the T610 in Figure 3.9.

P800 and P900

At the high end of the market, Sony Ericsson weighs in with the popular P-series (currently the P800 and P900). These are extremely capable devices with screens measuring 208×20; the P800 has 12-bit color and the P900 (shown in Figure 3.10) has 16-bit color. Both units have very fast processors in J2ME terms and 16 MB of base memory. Probably the only drawback is the use of a touchscreen for primary input. This is great for general PDA use, but for gaming it's quite cumbersome and unresponsive.

Figure 3.9 The Sony Ericsson T610, one of the T6xx range

Figure 3.10 The Sony Ericsson P900 . . . mmm

Motorola

Motorola has two distinct ranges of phones, each with its own developer Web site and support system. For the regular GSM and GPRS network-based models, you can use Motocoder for support, which is available at http://www.motocoder.com.

Motorola also supports a range of devices for their iDEN network (mostly sold through Nextel in the United States). The support site for this range is http://idenphones. motorola.com/iden/developer/developer_home.jsp.

In the next couple sections, you can take a look at a few examples of both the device ranges.

General Phones

Motorola has a broad range of Java-enabled phones with varying capabilities. The basic A380 shown in Figure 3.11 has a 96×45 12-bit color display with a max MIDlet size of 100 KB and a heap memory of 1 MB. It's a great gaming phone but a little limited in terms of screen real estate.

Another example of Motorola's J2ME phones is the higher-end A830 is shown in Figure 3.12. With a very respectable 176×220 12-bit color screen, a 100 KB max MIDlet, and 512 KB of RAM, this device is an excellent gaming machine.

Figure 3.11 The Motorola A380 is a solid J2ME phone, although somewhat limited in screen size.

Figure 3.12 The Motorola A830 provides a large screen and fast performance.

iDEN Phones

All Motorola phones that have a model number starting with "i" are within the iDEN range, starting with the i85s, which has a 119 × 64 monochrome screen and a maximum MIDlet size of 50 KB. Like most of the lower-end iDEN phones, memory is limited to 256 KB.

The i730 shown in Figure 3.14 is at the top end of the iDEN offerings. It includes a 130 × 130 16-bit color screen, more than 1 MB of heap, and a maximum MIDlet size of 500 KB—more than enough for some serious gaming.

Figure 3.13 The Motorola iDEN i85s

Figure 3.14 The Motorola iDEN i730 is a more advanced J2ME offering with a larger color screen and more memory.

Conclusion

As you've seen, J2ME has strong support from all the major mobile device manufacturers in the world. There's also a wide variety in terms of both form factor and capability. However, you've only seen a handful of the many models available on the market, and there are more being released all the time. Feel free to also take a look at offerings from companies such as Research In Motion (RIM), Sharp, SAMSUNG, Panasonic, LG Electronics, and Siemens.

PART II

SHOW ME
THE CODE!

CHAPTER 4

The Development Environment 49

CHAPTER 5

The J2ME API 77

CHAPTER 6

Device-Specific Libraries 173

CHAPTER 7

Game Time 211

With the background behind you, it's time to get down to the nitty-gritty of how to develop games. In Part 2, "Show me the code," I'll show you how to set up a complete development environment for creating J2ME games. Once you're ready to go, you'll move on to a complete review of the J2ME MIDP 1 API, as well as the added functionality made available by device manufacturers. Finally, you'll put everything into practice to make a simple action game.

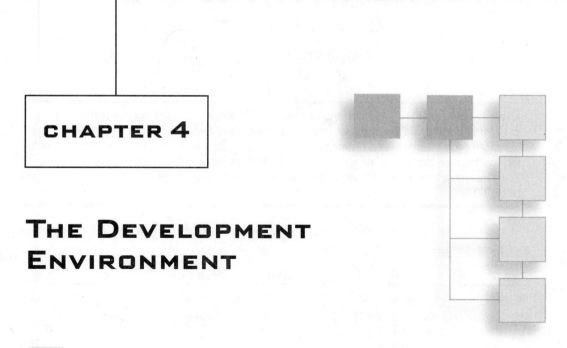

CHAPTER 4

THE DEVELOPMENT ENVIRONMENT

Enough theory; in this chapter, let's see some action!

In the first part of this chapter, you'll download and explore the tools available to compile, pre-verify, and then package your own MIDlet. Then you'll use an emulator to check out your work. Finally, you'll download and look at the Sun's Wireless Toolkit, a set of tools that takes some of the pain out of typical MIDP development tasks.

Getting the Tools

To get started, you need some tools. Table 4.1 lists the packages you need to get started developing a MIDP game. The table also includes a URL that points to a starting location for each of the technologies. Use your Web browser to navigate to the appropriate page, and then follow the links to the appropriate download. For the MIDP download, you want the RI (*Reference Implementation*).

Tip

Whenever Sun develops a new platform they'll often develop an implementation that serves as a demonstration of exactly how the system should perform. The MIDP RI includes all the tools and class files you'll need to develop for the platform.

I recommend you download the latest in the release 1.0.x series of the MIDP. Although later versions are available, for now you need to focus on the first-generation MIDP implementations, which make up the bulk of the current market.

Tip

Knowing how game programmers are, I suspect you've already checked out the features of MIDP 2. I also know you can't wait to get going with those extra features, such as transparent images, advanced sound, and image array manipulation. I'm going to ask you to be patient. Trust me; nothing you learn on the road to developing great MIDP 1 games is going to be redundant in MIDP 2. You'll just have even more with which to work. You'll get to MIDP 2 in Chapter 19, "CLDC 1.1 and MIDP 2.0."

Table 4.1 Basic Development Tools

Tool	Version	Web Site
JDK (*Java Development Kit*—J2SE SDK)	Version 1.4.2	http://java.sun.com/products/j2se
MIDP (*Mobile Information Device Profile*)	Version 1.0.3	http://java.sun.com/products/midp

Using the URLs in Table 4.1, navigate to the Sun Web site and download the latest appropriate versions for each tool.

Installing the Software

Now that you have downloaded the software, you can get started installing things. Along the way, I'll step through the configurations required to get everything working on your development system.

The first thing you should do is create a directory to contain everything you're doing. Use Windows Explorer or another appropriate tool to create a directory named j2me, for example:

```
c:\j2me
```

(You can choose another drive or path if it suits you.) From now on, I'll refer to this as the "j2me home."

Next you need to set up the Java development environment using the JDK before you move on to the MIDP.

Tip

If you already have a working Java development environment of version 1.3 or later, feel free to skip steps as appropriate. Use the tests conducted at the end of the setup to make sure everything is ready to go before you continue.

Setting Up the JDK

When you downloaded the JDK, you likely obtained a file with a name like j2sdk-1_4_1_XX-windows-i586.exe. Execute this program and install the JDK in the directory of your choice. I recommend sticking with the default location suggested by the installation software (see Figure 4.1).

After the installation, the JDK will be pretty much ready to go; the only thing you might need to do is adjust your PATH environment variable to include the JDK binary directories. See the upcoming "Making Path Changes" section for details on doing this.

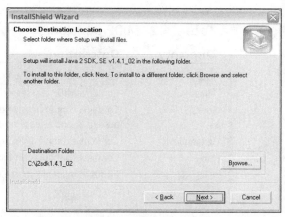

Figure 4.1 Specify the directory where you want to install the JDK.

Setting Up the MIDP

Next you need to install the MIDP. To do this, use your favorite compression tool to unpack the files into a subdirectory of the j2me home. You should end up with a directory something like c:\j2me\midp1.0.3fcs.

After you unpack the files, you will have a number of directories containing all the components of the MIDP package. You should see something like Figure 4.2.

Of these directories, Table 4.2 lists the ones of real interest to you at the moment.

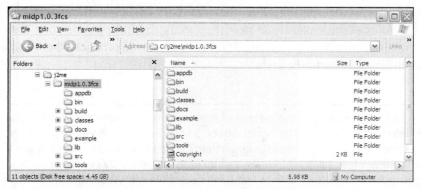

Figure 4.2 After unpacking the MIDP files you should have a directory structure matching this.

Table 4.2 MIDP Directories

Directory	Description
\bin	Contains the command line tools, preverify.exe, and the midp.exe emulator.
\classes	Contains MIDP classes; you'll compile using these as a base.
\docs	Contains comprehensive documentation of the MIDP. Includes guides, reference materials, and release notes.
\example	Contains example JARs and JADs for demonstration purposes.
\lib	Contains configuration files.
\src	Contains example source code.

Feel free to browse around these directories; the MIDP is a comprehensive package, and there's quite a bit to explore.

Making Path Changes

The PATH environment variable is used by operating systems as a list of directories it will search when trying to execute programs or libraries. A common use of the PATH is to specify directories that contain programs you want to execute, without having to navigate to the directory that contains it.

Operating systems define a few default directory locations, including the directory ".", which specifies the current directory. This is why you can change into a directory (CD) and then execute any program within—because the path contains the current directory (note that Windows does this transparently so you won't see a "." entry in the PATH).

Changing the PATH variable to include the MIDP bin directory makes working with the command line much easier—since you don't need to specify the full path of your executable every time you want to run a program. To do so, add the directories where executables reside to your PATH environment variable.

Note

A *command line* (also known as a *shell*) is a method of interacting with an operating system that uses a simple text interface where you enter commands on a line. You can access a command line in Windows by selecting the Command Prompt program from the Accessories menu. For Unix you'll need to open a terminal window. Personally, I make a shortcut to this on my Quick Launch bar, and then adjust settings such as the number of lines and columns and the color scheme.

For example, to run the preverify program with the installation just discussed, you need to enter a command like this:

```
c:\j2me\midp1.0.3fcs\bin\preverify
```

However, if you add this directory to your executable path, you can then simply enter preverify. Because you have two directories (one containing the JDK executables and one containing the MIDP executables), adding them to your PATH will make your life twice as easy.

How you edit your PATH depends on your operating system version. For Windows XP, use the Control Panel to open the System panel, and then select the option to modify your environment variables (see Figure 4.3).

When you have the list of available system variables, select the PATH variable (you might need to scroll down) and hit Edit then type in all of your executable directories on to the end of the existing text. For example, add the following to the end of your path, preceded by a semicolon:

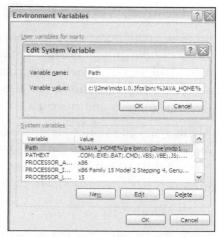

Figure 4.3 Edit the PATH system variable to add the MIDP executable path.

```
;c:\j2me\midp1.0.3fcs\bin;
```

Finally, you should also check and add the JDK binary directory to your path if it isn't already there. For example:

```
c:\j2sdk1.4.1_02\bin;
```

When you've finished editing the PATH and saving the new settings, you should open a new shell. This will cause the new PATH statement to take effect.

Setting MIDP_HOME

The MIDP executable requires you to set an environment variable named MIDP_HOME for the executable to function correctly. This is primarily so the program can access the various configuration files located in the lib directory of the MIDP installation.

Setting the variable is quite similar to adjusting the PATH. However, instead of editing the existing variable, you should create a new one. To do this, open the Environment Variables panel again, and then hit the New button and fill in the fields as shown in Figure 4.4.

Figure 4.4 Add a new environment variable named MIDP_HOME with the value corresponding to where you installed the MIDP RI.

Updating CLASSPATH

Like the operating system, Java has a similar system for locating classes when compiling and executing programs in the virtual machine. The CLASSPATH environment variable is just a list of all the directories which contain your installed class files and libraries. To compile and run your applications, you also need to adjust your Java CLASSPATH—the place where the Java compiler and run time (JVM) will look for classes.

At this stage, all you need to do is add the MIDP classes directory. You can do this by editing the CLASSPATH variable in the same way you edited the PATH variable. If you don't have an existing CLASSPATH_variable just create a new one. Update it by adding the \classes path of your MIDP installation. For example:

```
c:\j2me\midp1.0.3fcs\classes;
```

I also recommend you add the current working directory (specified as a single) to your CLASSPATH. This adds the convenience of allowing you to place class files into the directory with which you're working. The end result is that you can just change into a directory that houses your program class files and run them directly from there—keep in mind that a "." on your path translates to whatever directory you are currently in. This saves you from having to add that directory to your CLASSPATH or having to copy the class files into a directory already contained within your CLASSPATH.

Including the JDK library path, a complete CLASSPATH environment variable generally will look like the following line. (Don't miss that "." at the end!)

```
CLASSPATH=c:\j2sdk1.4.1_02\lib;c:\j2me\midp1.0.3fcs\classes;.
```

Tip

To check the value of your CLASSPATH, you can enter set in the command line. This will show the current values of all environment variables. Don't forget that changes to system variables made through the Control Panel won't take effect until you open a new command line.

Testing the Setup

Now that you've installed the JDK and MIDP, you should test things to make sure you're really ready to go.

Grab a shell and type preverify. The results should match those shown in Figure 4.5.

Next you need to make sure the MIDP emulator is available. Enter midp -version in the shell. The results should look like Figure 4.6.

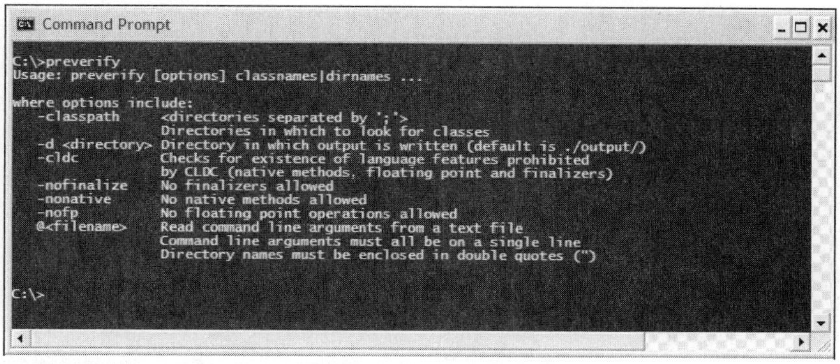

Figure 4.5 Output from the `preverify` command.

Figure 4.6 The results from entering the `midp -version` command in a shell.

Baking Some MIDlets!

Yes, that's right—after that big, long (but incredibly interesting, right?) introduction, you're finally ready to actually code something!

First make a place to store your project by creating a directory called projects within the j2me home. Create a subdirectory within the projects directory called hello. (Feel free to use alternative names if you want; just substitute your choice in any of the examples.)

Okay, you're not going to set the world on fire with your first MIDlet, but at least you'll get to say hello to the micro world. The code for your first MIDlet follows. Create a file named hello.java to contain this code. This code is also available on the CD under the source code for Chapter 4.

```java
import javax.microedition.midlet.MIDletStateChangeException;
import javax.microedition.lcdui.*;
```

```java
/**
 * A simple example that demonstrates the basic structure of a MIDlet
 * by creating a Form object containing the string "Hello, Micro World!"
 *
 * @author Martin J. Wells
 */

public class Hello extends javax.microedition.midlet.MIDlet
        implements CommandListener
{
    protected Form form;
    protected Command quit;

    /**
     * Constructor for the MIDlet which instantiates the Form object and
     * then adds a text message. It then sets up a command listener so it
     * will get called back when the user hits the quit command. Note that this
     * Form is not activated (displayed) until the startApp method is called.
     */
    public Hello()
    {
        // create a form and add our components
        form = new Form("My Midlet");
        form.append("Hello, Micro World!");

        // create a way to quit
        form.setCommandListener(this);
        quit = new Command("Quit", Command.SCREEN, 1);
        form.addCommand(quit);
    }

    /**
     * Called by the Application Manager when the MIDlet is starting or resuming
     * after being paused. In this example it acquires the current Display object
     * and uses it to set the Form object created in the MIDlet constructor as
     * the active Screen to display.
     * @throws MIDletStateChangeException
     */
    protected void startApp() throws MIDletStateChangeException
    {
        // display our form
        Display.getDisplay(this).setCurrent(form);
```

```
}

/**
 * Called by the MID's Application Manager to pause the MIDlet. A good
 * example of this is when the user receives an incoming phone call while
 * playing your game. When they're done the Application Manager will call
 * startApp to resume. For this example we don't need to do anything.
 */
protected void pauseApp()
{
}


/**
 * Called by the MID's Application Manager when the MIDlet is about to
 * be destroyed (removed from memory). You should take this as an opportunity
 * to clear up any resources and save the game. For this example we don't need
 * to do anything.
 * @param unconditional if false you have the option of throwing a
 * MIDletStateChangeException to abort the destruction process.
 * @throws MIDletStateChangeException
 */
protected void destroyApp(boolean unconditional)
        throws MIDletStateChangeException
{
}


/**
 * The CommandListener interface method called when the user executes
 * a Command, in this case it can only be the quit command we created in the
 * constructor and added to the Form.
 * @param command
 * @param displayable
 */
public void commandAction(Command command, Displayable displayable)
{
    // check for our quit command and act accordingly
    try
    {
        if (command == quit)
        {
            destroyApp(true);
```

```
            // tell the Application Manager we're exiting
            notifyDestroyed();
        }
    }

    // we catch this even though there's no chance it will be thrown
    // since we called destroyApp with unconditional set to true.
    catch (MIDletStateChangeException me)
    { }
    }
}
```

Don't worry too much about the details of this example. I should point out, though, that I have not kept things simple. This first MIDlet contains quite a few components, all of which you'll explore soon. For now, I want to just rush blindly on to making something work.

Compiling Your Application

The next step is to compile your application. To prepare for this, open a shell and change to your project's directory by entering `cd \j2me\projects\hello`. To start compiling, enter `javac -target 1.1 -bootclasspath %MIDP_HOME%\classes Hello.java`.

If you've entered everything correctly, the compiler will generate a class file named Hello.class for your program. Feel free to use the `dir` command to check out the results.

Before you move on, take a quick look at the options used to compile because they're a little bit different than what you might typically use.

The `-target 1.1` is there due to a known issue when using JDK 1.4 and the MIDP preverify tool. If you compile normally, you see a Class loading error: Illegal constant pool index error when you attempt to preverify later. To avoid this, you force the Java compiler to output class files in the older 1.1 version format. If you're using a version of the MIDP later than 1.0.3, feel free to give things a go without this option.

The `-bootclasspath %MIDP_HOME%\classes` argument forces the compiler to use only the classes in the MIDP classes directory, which contains the core MIDP and CLDC class files. This ensures that what you're compiling is compatible with the intended run-time target.

Preverifying Your Class File

The next step is to preverify the class file. Enter `preverify -cldc -classpath %MIDP_HOME%\classes;. -d . Hello`. Although this looks complicated, it is a relatively simple command. First, the `-cldc` option checks to see that you're not using any language features not supported by the CLDC, such as floating points or finalizers.

The `classpath` is pretty self explanatory; it should point to both the MIDP class library and the location of your project class files. The `-d` sets the destination directory for the resulting post-verified class files. For now, you'll just overwrite your original class files with the new ones. Later you'll look at better ways of handling this. The final argument is the name of the class you wish to preverify.

Figure 4.7 shows an example of the complete build process.

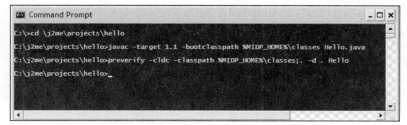

Figure 4.7 The output from building our demo MIDlet.

Running Your MIDlet

Phew, you're almost there! Now that you have a compiled, preverified class file, all you need to do is see the results in action. The simplest way to view a MIDlet is to use the MIDP RI emulator. You can access this straight from the shell using the command `midp -classpath . Hello`.

You should then see the MIDP emulator window with your MIDlet running inside it, as shown in Figure 4.8.

Okay, now stand up, make sure nobody is watching, and give yourself a big high-five—don't ask me how you actually do that. You, my learned friend, have made your first MIDlet!

When you've calmed down enough to continue, move on to the topic of packaging your little wonder.

Creating the Full Package

Now that you've made your first MIDlet, finish things off by creating a full MIDlet suite. The best way to demonstrate this is by including a second MIDlet.

Figure 4.8 Our hello world MIDlet running in the default Sun emulator.

Hello, Again

Using the following code example, create a second MIDlet in a file named Hello2.java.

```java
import javax.microedition.midlet.MIDletStateChangeException;
import javax.microedition.lcdui.*;


/**
 * Another basic MIDlet used primarily to demonstrate how multiple MIDlets make
 * up a MIDlet Suite. This class extends the existing Hello class and overrides
 * the constructor so it displays different content in the Form.
 *
 * @author Martin J. Wells
 */

public class Hello2 extends Hello
{
    /**
     * Constructor for the MIDlet which instantiates the Form object and
     * then adds a text message. It then sets up a command listener so it
     * will get called back when the user hits the quit command. Note that this
     * Form is not activated (displayed) until the startApp method is called.
     */

    public Hello2()
    {
        // create a form and add our text
        form = new Form("My 2nd Midlet");
        form.append("Hello, to another Micro World!");

        // create a way to quit
        form.setCommandListener(this);
        quit = new Command("Quit", Command.SCREEN, 1);
        form.addCommand(quit);
    }
}
```

As you can see, I've taken a little shortcut. Rather than create a new MIDlet, I used the Hello class as a base to derive another class. The only difference is the addition of revised title and text components to the constructor.

Note

Looking at the code for your first MIDlet, you might notice that the three fields—display, form, and quit—are in protected, not private, scope. This way, when you derive Hello2, you have access to these fields inside its constructor.

Building the Class

When you have the `hello2.java` file ready, go ahead and compile, preverify, and test it using the following commands:

```
javac -target 1.1 -bootclasspath %MIDP_HOME%\classes Hello2.java
preverify -cldc -classpath %MIDP_HOME%\classes;. -d . Hello2
midp -classpath . Hello2
```

From these commands, you can see that the only real difference is the class name.

After you correct any errors, you will have not one, but *two* fully operational Battle Stations—oops, I mean MIDlets—within your directory, hello and hello2.

Creating the JAR

Now that you have all your classes ready, the next step is to create the JAR (*Java Archive*) file.

JAR Files

A JAR file is an archiving system used to wrap up the various components of a Java application package, such as class, image, sound, and other data files. The file format is based somewhat on the popular ZIP file, with a few extras such as a manifest, which contains information on the contents of the JAR.

You can create or modify a JAR file using the `jar` command-line tool that comes with the JDK. What's also cool is that you can manipulate JAR files using the `java.util.jar` API.

Table 4.3 provides a short list of some useful JAR commands.

Table 4.3 Useful JAR Commands

Command	Description
`jar -cvf my.jar *`	Creates a new JAR named `my.jar`, which contains all of the files in the current directory.
`jar -cvfm my.jar manifest.txt *`	Creates a new JAR named `my.jar`, which contains all of the files in the current directory. Also creates a manifest file using the contents of the manifest.txt file.
`jar -xvf my.jar *`	Unpacks all of the files in the `my.jar` into the current directory.
`jar -tvf my.jar`	Allows you to view the table of contents for `my.jar`.

As you can see, most commands revolve around the `-f` argument, which specifies the JAR file to work on, and the `-v` argument, which asks for "verbose" output. Combine these with the c, x, and t switches, and you've covered the most common JAR operations.

The next step is to create the corresponding manifest file. Using a text editor, make a new file named manifest.txt in the project directory. This new file should contain the following code:

```
MIDlet-Name: MegaHello
MIDlet-Version: 1.0
MIDlet-Vendor: J2ME Game Programming
MIDlet-1: My First Hello, ,Hello
MIDlet-2: My Second Hello, ,Hello2
MicroEdition-Profile: MIDP-1.0
MicroEdition-Configuration: CLDC-1.0
```

You can then create the JAR file using the command `jar -cvfm hellosuite.jar manifest.txt *.class`. This command will create a new JAR file named `hellosuite.jar` in the directory. If you view the contents of the file now, you should see something like Figure 4.9.

Figure 4.9 The output from a jar command used to create an archive.

You might notice that the manifest file has the name `manifest.mf`, not `manifest.txt`. This is a common point of confusion. The manifest file supplied on the command line is just the input to create a manifest; it isn't the file itself.

Creating the JAD

Now create a corresponding JAD file to represent your suite. Using a text editor, make a new file named `hellosuite.jad` in the project directory. This file should contain the following text. (To save time, you can copy the contents of the `manifest.txt` file and adjust it accordingly.)

```
MIDlet-Name: MegaHello
MIDlet-Version: 1.0
MIDlet-Vendor: J2ME Game Programming
MIDlet-1: My First Hello, ,Hello
MIDlet-2: My Second Hello, ,Hello2
MIDlet-Jar-Size: 2010
MIDlet-Jar-URL: hello.jar
```

There are two differences between this JAD file and the original manifest file. This file no longer has the two version lines, and it has two additional lines referencing the JAR file. The first, MIDlet-Jar-Size is used to specific the size in bytes of the corresponding JAR file, and the second, MIDlet-Jar-URL specifies its location. These variables give a potential user of the JAR the opportunity to see its size (before downloading or installing the JAR) and then to determine where to acquire the JAR file from (such as an internet Web site).

You should check the size of the final hellosuite.jar using the dir command. Make sure it matches the size in the JAD file; it should be around 2000 bytes. Keep in mind that it must be accurate, which also means you'll have to update it every time you change things and recompile. Don't worry, though—Chapter 14, "The Device Ports," will show you how to automate this using build scripts.

Running the Package

Ta da! Your super-kilo-multi-MIDlet-magic-package—try saying that quickly with a mouthful of peanut butter—is ready to go; all you need to do now is run it in the emulator. You can do this using the command midp -classpath . -Xdescriptor hellosuite.jad.

Tip

Take care with the spaces when entering things on the command line. Mistyping them can sometimes result in errors.

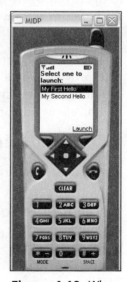

Notice that in this case, you're specifying that a JAD file be executed, not a class file. This is because the emulator will load everything it needs from the JAR file referenced inside the JAD configuration, so you don't need to name a class file to execute.

Once the MIDlet package is running, you should see something like Figure 4.10.

When you run this package, you see the emulator's JAM (*Java Application Manager*) presenting a list of all the MIDlets available in the suite. If you want to play around a little, try expanding the list of MIDlets in the JAD file to four or five. (You can just reference the same class file repeatedly.) Then you'll see each one show up as a unique item in the JAM menu.

If you do this, you might also notice that you don't need to modify the corresponding entries in the manifest file. This is because the entries within the JAD file always take precedence.

This concludes the grand tour of the J2ME command-line development environment. In the next section, you'll look at what Sun's J2ME Wireless Toolkit offers as an alternative.

Figure 4.10 When loading a JAR containing multiple MIDlets the emulator will ask which one to execute.

The J2ME Wireless Toolkit

Command-line development is probably the most basic of programming environments, although personally I'm a big fan of the shell, especially when working on UNIX. However, Sun has another trick up its sleeve to help with development—the J2ME Wireless Toolkit.

The J2ME Wireless Toolkit (or simply the Toolkit, for short) provides some nice features to assist with MIDlet development. These features include

- A host of excellent device emulators on which to test things.
- An application profiler, which provides facilities to analyze method execution time and use frequency.
- A memory monitor tool, which lets you see your application's memory use.
- A network monitor, which shows traffic across a simulated network (including tools to vary the simulated performance).
- Speed emulation tools, which let you adjust the device's operating performance, including slowing bytecode execution.

Before moving on I'd like to clear up a common misconception about the role of the Toolkit. It's not an IDE (*Integrated Development Environment*), so when you load things up, don't go looking for where you can edit source code. When I first downloaded and installed the Toolkit, that was exactly what I expected, so I spent quite some time trying to figure out where the source window was. In fact, I got so frustrated that I finally threw my hands in the air, got up from my desk, shaved my head, flew to Tibet, and became a monk for six years.

All right, so I didn't really shave my head, but this confusion is common. The Toolkit's role is to provide expanded command-line tools, convenience utilities for managing MIDlet creation, and profiling and device emulators. Its role is not the Mobile Jbuilder; you need to look elsewhere for a complete editing suite.

However, the Toolkit does provide some excellent (arguably mandatory) tools for use during J2ME development, so it's certainly worth becoming familiar with it. Even if you later use an IDE to assist with development, you'll still use many of the tools provided with the Toolkit.

Installing the Toolkit

You can download the Toolkit from the Sun Web site at http://java.sun.com/products/j2mewtoolkit.

Tip

Make sure you download version 1.x of the Toolkit. Version 2 is for development using MIDP 2, not MIDP 1.

Once you've downloaded it, follow the instructions for installing the application on your computer.

Tip

When installing the Toolkit, I recommend you set the target directory to one that does not contain spaces, such as `C:\Program Files\Toolkit`. Spaces can interfere with the successful operation of some of the tools.

After you have the Toolkit installed, feel free to browse around the directory to see what's available. In the next few sections, I'll walk you through how to build and run an application, Toolkit-style.

Using the KToolbar

The biggest application in the Toolkit, known as the KToolbar, helps to make the typical process for creating MIDlets faster and easier. It provides a GUI to let you easily create projects, alter manifest and JAD files, and run a host of different MID emulators.

As always, I think the best way to learn about something is to play around with it. Create another MIDlet, this time using the Toolkit to help you.

Creating a New Project

The first step is to create a new project using the KToolbar. To do this, start the KToolbar application using the Start menu item, and then create a new project and `MIDlet` class named HelloToolkit.

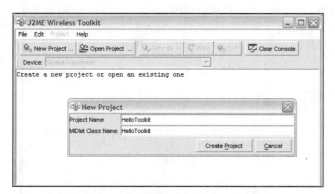

Figure 4.11 Creating a new project using the J2ME Wireless Toolkit

Note

One thing I dislike about the KToolbar is the way it handles project locations and files. I'm not sure why—perhaps to avoid the possibility of the KToolbar conflicting with the role of an IDE—but the KToolbar restricts the locations of your projects, as well as the organization of the files within projects. This means you can't tell the KToolbar to use an existing project directory, such as your `c:\j2me\projects\hello` project, and you can't specify the directories to use within that project space.

Don't worry too much about this for now; later on you'll use the tools directly (from build scripts), rather than from the KToolbar.

Working with Settings

After creating your project, the KToolbar will automatically open the Settings window for your new project. This window lets you quickly and easily edit all the manifest and JAD variables for your project.

Figure 4.12 shows the settings you will use for your project; these are mostly just the default values set by the KToolbar when it created the project.

While you're looking at the KToolbar, I'll also show you how to take advantage of user-defined JAD properties. You can add these attributes to your JAD file and later use them to customize the execution of your MIDlet without having to change code. This use of attributes is a little like command-line arguments, which you don't have in the J2ME environment. The most common use for these properties is to customize your application to suit different environments, such as the variable capabilities of some mobile phone networks. You'll learn more about this in later chapters.

For your sample application, create a custom property by opening the settings window, clicking on User Defined and then creating a new property named "Message" with the value `Hello, World` (see Figure 4.13). Feel free to substitute anything that turns you on here.

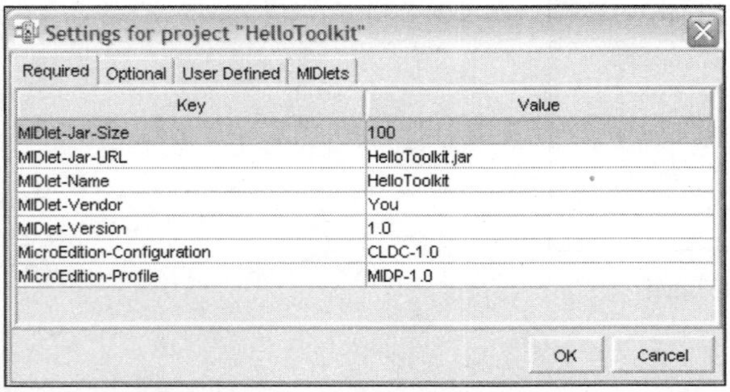

Figure 4.12 The first panel in the KToolbar Settings window lets you easily edit JAD and manifest attributes.

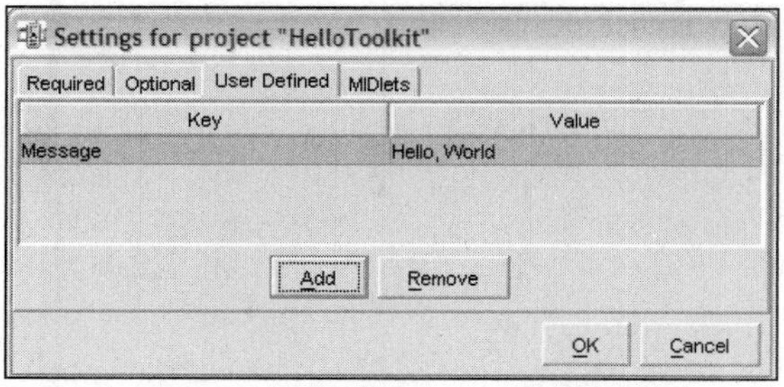

Figure 4.13 Setting a User Defined property.

Your application is going to read this variable and display the message on the screen. Cool, huh?

Hello Toolkit

The next step is to write the code for your new Toolkit-powered MIDlet. Things are pretty much the same as in the previous Hello application, except for some changes to the constructor.

```java
import javax.microedition.midlet.MIDletStateChangeException;
import javax.microedition.lcdui.*;

/**
 * An example used to demonstrate how to access, and then display, a property
 * value set within a JAD file.
 *
 * @author Martin J. Wells
 */

public class HelloToolkit extends javax.microedition.midlet.MIDlet
        implements CommandListener
{
    protected Form form;
    protected Command quit;

    /**
     * Constructor for the MIDlet which instantiates the Form object
     * then uses the getAppProperty method to extract the value associated with
     * the "Message" key in the JAD file. It then adds the value as a text field
     * to the Form and sets up a command listener so the commandAction method
     * is called when the user hits the Quit command. Note that this Form is not
```

```
 * activated (displayed) until the startApp method is called.
 */
public HelloToolkit()
{
   // create a form and add our components
   form = new Form("My Midlet");

   // display our message attribute
   String msg = getAppProperty("Message");
   if (msg != null)
      form.append(msg);

   // create a way to quit
   form.setCommandListener(this);
   quit = new Command("Quit", Command.SCREEN, 1);
   form.addCommand(quit);
}

/**
 * Called by the Application Manager when the MIDlet is starting or resuming
 * after being paused. In this example it acquires the current Display object
 * and uses it to set the Form object created in the MIDlet constructor as
 * the active Screen to display.
 * @throws MIDletStateChangeException
 */
protected void startApp() throws MIDletStateChangeException
{
   // display our form
   Display.getDisplay(this).setCurrent(form);
}

/**
 * Called by the MID's Application Manager to pause the MIDlet. A good
 * example of this is when the user receives an incoming phone call whilst
 * playing your game. When they're done the Application Manager will call
 * startApp to resume. For this example we don't need to do anything.
 */
protected void pauseApp()
{
}

/**
```

```
 * Called by the MID's Application Manager when the MIDlet is about to
 * be destroyed (removed from memory). You should take this as an opportunity
 * to clear up any resources and save the game. For this example we don't need
 * to do anything.
 * @param unconditional if false you have the option of throwing a
 * MIDletStateChangeException to abort the destruction process.
 * @throws MIDletStateChangeException
 */
protected void destroyApp(boolean unconditional)
        throws MIDletStateChangeException
{
}


/**
 * The CommandListener interface method called when the user executes
 * a Command, in this case it can only be the quit command we created in the
 * constructor and added to the Form.
 * @param command
 * @param displayable
 */
public void commandAction(Command command, Displayable displayable)
{
    // check for our quit command and act accordingly
    try
    {
        if (command == quit)
        {
            destroyApp(true);

            // tell the Application Manager we're exiting
            notifyDestroyed();
        }
    }

    // we catch this even though there's no chance it will be thrown
    // since we called destroyApp with unconditional set to true.
    catch (MIDletStateChangeException me)
    {
    }
}

}
```

The main change here is the addition of the getAppProperty call to retrieve the contents of the Message attribute. To integrate this into your project, create a text file containing this source within the src subdirectory of the HelloToolkit project directory (you'll find this under the apps directory of the main Toolkit installation directory), for example C:\WTK104\apps\HelloToolkit\src\HelloToolkit.java.

Building and Running the Program

When your new source file is ready, click on the Build button in the KToolbar. This will automatically compile and preverify your class file. Errors will appear in the console window.

When the build is successful, you can hit the Run button to view the MIDlet running in the default emulator. When you run the MIDlet, you should see the output of the property you set in the JAD file. Feel free to change it and run it with difference values and emulators. After each run, you'll see some pretty useful information about the execution of the MIDlet. Figure 4.14 shows an example of the output.

Figure 4.14 Useful information that appears in the Toolkit console after executing a MIDlet.

Tip

If you're running using version 2 of the Toolkit and you see SecurityException then you may need to remove the MIDP_HOME environment variable to execute this properly.

Working with Other Development Environments

In the preceding sections, you've explored the tools that are available as part of Sun's J2ME platform. However, I'm sure you're wondering how to get all this working in that slick little IDE you use every day. The good news is that most IDEs provide direct integration to make MIDlet development a pretty painless experience.

The following sections include details on integrating J2ME with some of the more popular IDEs. If your particular IDE isn't included below, I recommend reviewing the company's Web site for details on any integration tools they might have available.

JBuilder

JBuilder from Borland/Inprise (I'm not sure even they know who they are) is one of the most popular Java IDEs on the market. If you're already a JBuilder user, you'll be pleased to know that Borland has an OpenTool extension named MobileSet, which provides some good J2ME development integration.

Tip

If you're not already running JBuilder and you want to download a trial version, I recommend steering clear of the Personal edition. It has too many limitations—such as not being able to switch between different JDKs—to make it a practical development solution for J2ME.

You can download the JBuilder MobileSet extension and install it into your JBuilder IDE. Check the Borland Web site for the latest details on compatibility with your version of JBuilder.

After you have installed the extension, you can create a J2ME project using the New Project Wizard. The first step is to specify the setting for the new project. In Figure 4.15, I've created a new project called HelloJBuilder.

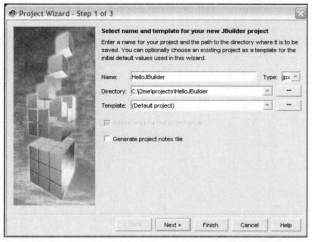

Figure 4.15 The JBuilder project wizard with settings for our HelloJBuilder project.

The next step is where the JBuilder MobileSet kicks in. As you can see in the second Wizard step (shown in Figure 4.16), you need to specify that this project will use the J2ME JDK rather than the default J2SE JDK. If you don't see this option, you should check to make sure you have installed the MobileSet into JBuilder correctly.

Tip

If required, you can set the JDK location to the MobileSet JDK manually using the Configure JDK option in the Tools menu.

After you have completed the New Project Wizard, JBuilder will create a project space for your new masterpiece. That's about as far as it goes, though.

The next step is to create a MIDlet for the project. To do this, use the New command (typically Ctrl+N or File, New from the menu) to bring up the Object Gallery. With the MobileSet installed, you will notice a new panel named Micro at the end. From this panel, you can create both new MIDlets and new Displayable objects (see Figure 4.17). For your project, you need to start with a new MIDlet. This will bring up the New MIDlet Wizard, which contains a host of options relating to the type of MIDlet you want to create. Don't worry too much about the details of the steps at the moment; these options will become relevant in later sections.

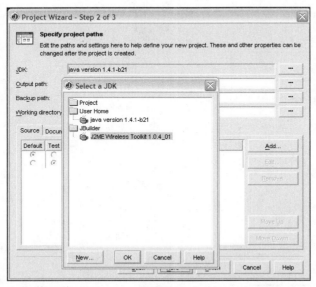

Figure 4.16 Selecting the location of the Mobile Set JDK using JBuilder.

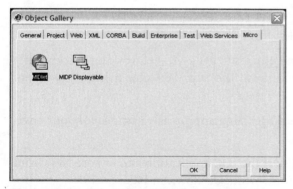

Figure 4.17 Select the MIDlet from the Object Gallery to create a new one.

Upon completion, this Wizard will create two new Java source files, a MIDlet (similar to what you've seen before), and a new MIDP Displayable. If you take a look at the MIDlet source, you'll notice that instead of just instantiating a Form object like the one you used in previous projects, the JBuilder creates a class that extends from the class Form ready for you to customize. You'll learn more about this in later sections.

Now comes the really nice thing about an integrated development environment—just hit the big green Go button. (Okay, it looks more like a Play button.) JBuilder will build, compile, preverify, make the JAD, do your dishes, clean your car, and finally start the emulator running with your MIDlet. How easy is that?

After you've closed the emulator, take a look at the output in the JBuilder Message View. You'll notice that JBuilder is actually just calling the emulator on the command line. This is true for pretty much all J2ME IDE integrations; they automate calling the Sun Toolkit commands. With a good understanding of these tools, you don't really need to use an integration tool such as the MobileSet. For what's its worth, though, it sure makes it easy to get started.

Sun ONE Studio

Sun provides a nice integrated development environment for Java known as Sun ONE Studio, Mobile Edition. The great thing is that this is available free of charge from the Sun Web site, and it's not an evaluation or community edition—it's a full-featured IDE with some excellent extensions for J2ME development (and it doesn't hurt that it's from the makers of J2ME).

Along with all the features you'd expect in a Java IDE, the Mobile Edition adds a good level of integration with J2ME tools. This includes the expected code completion, JAR and JAD management, automated preverification and MIDlet debugging, and an excellent facility for integrating other emulators into the IDE through Sun's Unified Emulator Interface.

As with JBuilder, I want to walk through the process to get a MIDlet working quickly. First you need to download the appropriate files from the Sun Web site, at http://www.sun.com/software/sundev/jde/studio_me/.

After you download the files, install the package using appropriate settings for your environment (see Figure 4.18).

Once you have Sun ONE Studio installed, start the IDE application and choose New from the startup options. You'll see the New Wizard window, shown in Figure 4.19.

The Studio's New Wizard provides many templates for creating new resources. In this case, use the New MIDlet Wizard to whip up a MIDlet framework. Select MIDlet and hit Next.

The next step is to select a location for the new project. I recommend just sticking with the defaults for your first project.

When the Wizard has finished, you'll find it has created a basic MIDlet, including the application lifecycle code. At this point, you just hit the Play button on the application toolbar. The IDE will compile, preverify, and execute the new MIDlet in the emulator. However, if you didn't bother to adjust the MIDlet code created by the Wizard, your MIDlet will be about as exciting as a Romanian puppet maker's, *Secrets of the Master Puppet Stuffers, Volume I*—even if the new edition does have details on PuppetStuffer 6.1!

The IDE output from running your MIDlet is far more interesting; as you can see in Figure 4.20, it includes a good amount of detail on what your MIDlet did.

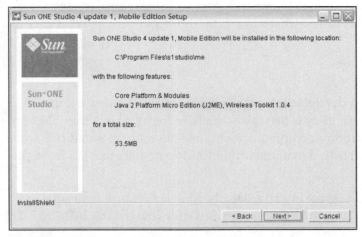

Figure 4.18 The Sun ONE Studio installation program.

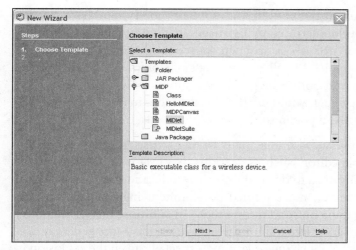

Figure 4.19 The New Wizard lets you specify the type of object you want to create.

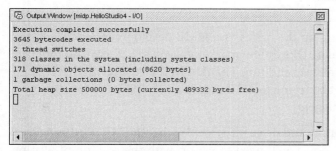

Figure 4.20 The output from executing a MIDlet in Sun ONE Studio.

Feel free to play around with both the code and the other options available in Sun ONE Studio 4. It's a powerful and convenient IDE, especially given the price.

Other IDEs

JBuilder and Sun ONE are certainly not the only IDEs out there. The last time I looked, there were more than 30 popular development environments—all with an excellent range of features—so there's no shortage of Java development tools. However, there are two other IDEs I'd like to mention before you move on: Eclipse (available at http://www.eclipse.org) and IDEA (available at http://www.intellij.com).

Both Eclipse and IDEA are excellent IDEs—IDEA is especially good—and both provide an extensive set of tools for developing in many languages, including Java. Most important, both have excellent support for ANT (an open source tool used to automate the building of Java applications)—which I'll talk about in later chapters—in order to manage a good J2ME build system, and both have good community tools available to assist with J2ME development. Of the two, I would say IDEA is the more mature and powerful, but Eclipse has the advantage of being open source (in other words, free).

On a final note, don't feel too pressured into actually having to use an IDE. Command-line development using a simple editor (such as TextPlus or VIM) is quite practical for J2ME development. All you really need to do is edit files, compile, and run the emulators. (Many developers find this faster on more limited-development machines, given how piggy modern IDEs are getting to be on system resources.) In addition, the vast majority of IDE features—wizards, J2EE server integration, Swing layout tools—are generally useless for J2ME development. This might change over time, especially given the explosion in J2ME popularity, but until then IDEs are mostly a convenience, not a requirement.

Conclusion

In this chapter you looked at setting up the basics of a J2ME development environment, along with some of the more popular IDEs on the market. As you saw, there's no shortage of J2ME tools to make development easy and fun. Thankfully, the pioneering you'll do in micro-software development won't be trying to get things to work, it'll be getting the most game you can out of those little buggers.

Next, you'll bite the head off the bunny and delve into exactly what the MIDP APIs deliver. This will build the foundation of tools you'll need to get on with the real job of writing that gaming masterpiece.

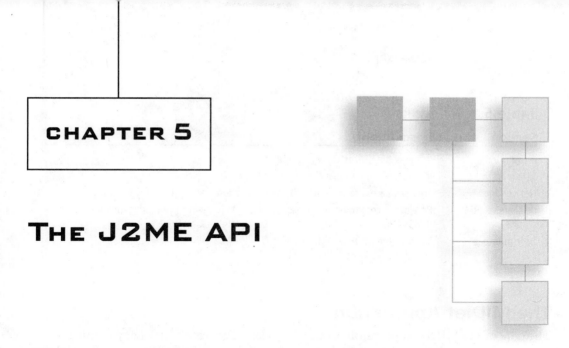

CHAPTER 5

THE J2ME API

In this chapter, you'll get into the details of the functionality available in the MIDP API. This will include examples of typical use, along with general ideas on the practical application of API features in game development. After that, I'll demonstrate how to turn lead into gold using only pencil, some sticky tape, and a 300-foot inflatable penguin—assuming you can actually find a pencil.

MIDP API Overview

All right, you've waded through more introductions than a spinster's ball, so now it's time to get to the meat and potatoes of exactly what you can do with the MIDP API. For an API that covers such little devices, there's a surprising amount of functionality.

Table 5.1 provides an outline of the five significant sections of the MIDP API. As you might have noticed in reviewing the class list included in Chapter 2, the functional grunt of the MIDP API lies in the LCDUI (*Liquid Crystal Display User Interface*), with some extra help from the Persistence (RMS) and Networking APIs.

In the following sections, you'll walk through this functionality and see some examples of the API in action. I'll also try to tell you some practical uses for these tools in developing a real-world game.

Table 5.1 API Sections

Section	Description
Application	Includes the MIDlet class (and friends).
Timers	Includes essentially just the Timer and TimerTask classes.
Networking	Provides access to the (limited) communications capabilities of the device.
Persistence (RMS)	Provides access to device-persistent storage via the Record Management System (RMS) API.
User Interface	Includes the MIDP LCDUI classes.

The MIDlet Application

The core of the MIDlet application is the MIDlet class. To create a MIDlet, you must derive your class from this abstract base class. Table 5.2 provides a list of the methods inherited from the MIDlet class.

Table 5.2 javax.microedition.MIDlet

Method	Description
Access to properties in the JAR and JAD files	
String getAppProperty(String key)	Returns the property value associated with the string key in the JAR or JAD.
Application manager telling your MIDlet something	
abstract void destroyApp(boolean unconditional)	The Application Manager calls this method to give you a chance to do something (such as save state and release resources) before your application is closed.
abstract void pauseApp()	The Application Manager calls this method on your MIDlet when the user has paused the game.
abstract void startApp()	The Application Manager calls this method to tell you that the user wants the game to start again.
Your MIDlet telling the Application Manager something	
abstract void notifyDestroyed()	If your player decides to exit the game, you can call this method to inform the Application Manager.
abstract void notifyPaused()	Call this method to tell the Application Manager that the player has paused the MIDlet.
abstract void resumeRequest()	Call this method to tell the Application Manager that the MIDlet wants to start again (after being paused).

As you can see in Table 5.2, the MIDlet class (apart from the getAppProperty method) is a little weird. That's because you need a little understanding of exactly how the MIDlet fits into the world and, more importantly, the rules it has to live by when under the control of the Application Manager before you can see what the MIDlet class is really doing.

The application manager's role is to control MIDlets. Think of it as something like the Master Control Program from *TRON*; it dictates what's going on, so anytime you want to do anything regarding the state of the application, you need to contact the Application Manager (AM) and let it know what's going on. And likewise, the AM will be kind enough to let you know when these state-change events occur. Happily, though, I don't think it will go power crazy and attempt to take over the world . . . I hope.

Essentially, there are only two states in which your application can practically exist—paused or running. As you can see in Figure 5.1, your MIDlet will be constructed and then placed in the paused state by default. When the AM thinks it's ready—maybe it has to go get a coffee first—it will call the startApp method to notify you that the MIDlet is moving into the running state.

When your MIDlet is running, you can pause it at any time. If the user does this, say by moving to another application, the AM will immediately call your MIDlet's pauseApp method. This gives you a last chance to let go of heavy resources. (Keep in mind that you

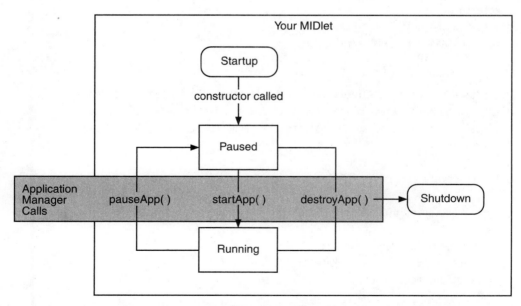

Figure 5.1 The MIDlet class serves as the gateway for communicating application-state changes to the application manager and vice versa.

might be paused indefinitely.) When the user wants to start again, the AM will then call—yep, you guessed it—the startApp method again. This can go on ad infinitum.

Destruction of your MIDlet works the same way; if the user elects to abandon you like a battery-operated toy on the day after Christmas, then the AM is kind enough to call your MIDlet's destroyApp method to let you clean up things.

Of course, not all of these events come from the application manager; quite often the user will choose the Pause or Exit command in your game. You're then obliged to tell the application manager about this event. The two methods you use in this case are—you guessed it—notifyDestroyed and notifyPaused.

To better understand how all this interaction occurs, take a look at some code.

```
import javax.microedition.midlet.*;
import javax.microedition.lcdui.*;

/**
 * A MIDlet which demonstrates the lifecycle of a MIDlet
 * @author Martin J. Wells
 */
public class LifecycleTest extends javax.microedition.midlet.MIDlet
        implements CommandListener
{
    private Form form;
    private Command quit;
    private boolean forceExit = false;

    /**
     * Constructor for the MIDlet which creates a simple Form, adds some text and
     * an exit command. When called this method will also write a message to the
     * console. This is used to demonstrate the sequence of events in a MIDlet's
     * lifecycle.
     */
    public LifecycleTest()
    {
        System.out.println("Constructor called.");

        form = new Form("Life, Jim.");
        form.append("But not as we know it.");
        form.setCommandListener(this);

        // Create and add two commands to change the MIDlet state
```

```java
    quit = new Command("Quit", Command.SCREEN, 1);
    form.addCommand(quit);
}


/**
 * Called by the Application Manager when the MIDlet is starting or resuming
 * after being paused. In this example it acquires the current Display object
 * and uses it to set the Form object created in the MIDlet constructor as
 * the active Screen to display. Also displays a message on the console when
 * called to demonstrate when this method is called in the MIDlet lifecycle.
 * @throws MIDletStateChangeException
 */
protected void startApp() throws MIDletStateChangeException
{
    System.out.println("startApp() called.");
    Display.getDisplay(this).setCurrent(form);
}


/**
 * Called by the MID's Application Manager to pause the MIDlet. A good
 * example of this is when the user receives an incoming phone call whilst
 * playing your game. When they're done the Application Manager will call
 * startApp to resume. For this example we output a message on the console
 * to indicate when this method is called in the MIDlet's lifecycle.
 */
protected void pauseApp()
{
    System.out.println("pauseApp() called.");
}


/**
 * Called by the MID's Application Manager when the MIDlet is about to
 * be destroyed (removed from memory). You should take this as an opportunity
 * to clear up any resources and save the game. For this example we output a
 * message on the console to indicate when this method is called in the
 * MIDlet lifecycle.
 * @param unconditional if false you have the option of throwing a
 * MIDletStateChangeException to abort the destruction process.
 * @throws MIDletStateChangeException
 */
protected void destroyApp(boolean unconditional) throws MIDletStateChangeException
{
```

```java
        System.out.println("destroyApp(" + unconditional + ") called.");

        if (!unconditional)
        {
            // we go through once using unconditional, next time it's forced.
            forceExit = true;
        }
    }


    /**
     * The CommandListener interface method called when the user executes a
     * Command, in this case it can only be the quit command we created in the
     * constructor and added to the Form. We also output a console message when
     * this method is called.
     * @param command the command that was triggered
     * @param displayable the displayable on which the event occurred
     */
    public void commandAction(Command command, Displayable displayable)
    {
        System.out.println("commandAction(" + command + ", " + displayable +
                            ") called.");
        try
        {
            if (command == quit)
            {
                destroyApp(forceExit);
                notifyDestroyed();
            }
        }

        catch (MIDletStateChangeException me)
        {
            System.out.println(me + " caught.");
        }
    }
}
```

This code will display a simple text message and a Quit command. When the user hits the Quit command, a Really? command will take its place (see Figure 5.2). Executing this command will subsequently cause the MIDlet to shut down.

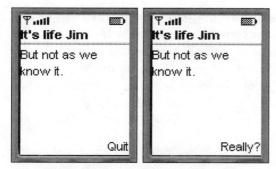

Figure 5.2 The output from our test MIDlet demonstrates the application termination process.

The `System.out.println` lines in this code will also generate the following console output:

```
Constructor called.
startApp() called.
commandAction(Quit) called.
destroyApp(false) called.
javax.microedition.midlet.MIDletStateChangeException caught.
commandAction(Really?) called.
destroyApp(true) called.
```

Take a more detailed look at exactly how this all works. The first two lines are the standard package imports for the MIDP application and user-interface packages—pretty standard stuff. The next line is the class declaration.

```
public class LifecycleTest extends javax.microedition.midlet.MIDlet
        implements CommandListener
```

Here you extend from the base `javax.microedition.midlet.MIDlet` class, which gives you access to the core MIDlet application functionality, and implement the `CommandListener` interface, which lets you "listen" to events generated by commands. (You'll learn more about the ins and outs of this interface later.)

The next section includes the field declarations for the user-interface objects that you need in the MIDlet. There are display and form objects along with two commands (think of them like buttons for now). The constructor then initializes these objects in the correct order and adds them to the display. Again, I don't want to dwell too much on the user-interface aspects of this code; I'll cover that in much more detail later in the chapter.

However, there are a few things to note about how this MIDlet constructs the display objects. First, note that you initialize these in the constructor, not in startApp. This further demonstrates the role of the startApp call. Think of it more as a resume method than as a type of initialization procedure. You will get one call when the application starts, and then after that a subsequent call when a MIDlet is being resumed after it was stopped (say when the user had to answer a call). Because of this you shouldn't use startApp to initialize objects that exist across pauses in execution (in your case, that is all the display objects).

In your case, the startApp method just calls

```
System.out.println("startApp() called.");
display.setCurrent(form);
```

This displays a console message, and then sets the previously initialized display to be the current one. The next section is the pauseApp method.

```
protected void pauseApp()
{
    System.out.println("pauseApp() called.");
}
```

Doesn't do much, I know; however, in later sections you'll see how the pauseApp method can clear out any resources you really don't need before your MIDlet is put on hold. It's good practice to free as many resources as is practical. It is quite acceptable to spend a little time later reinitializing these resources—the user will expect a delay when resuming the game.

From the console output, you also might have noticed that there is no output corresponding to the pauseApp method, which means the Application Manager never called it. This is interesting given that the MIDP specifications state that a MIDlet begins in the paused state, which is why the first post-construction call is the startApp method. You never see an initial call to pauseApp because the Application Manager only calls these methods before you enter a new state. However, since you began in that state when the MIDlet started, the method to notify you of the transition to that state doesn't ever need to be called.

The destroyApp method is a little more interesting.

```
protected void destroyApp(boolean unconditional) throws MIDletStateChangeException
{
    System.out.println("destroyApp(" + unconditional + ") called.");

    if (!unconditional)
        throw new MIDletStateChangeException();
}
```

This code shows you more about exactly what you can do with the destroyApp method. As with pauseApp, keep in mind that this is the Application Manager (or your MIDlet) asking whether it can exit. The keyword here is *ask*—hence you can say no by throwing a hissy fit, also known as a MIDletStateChangeException. However, you won't always have an option, indicated by the Boolean flag passed into the method (the unconditional parameter). If this is true, then Kansas is saying bye-bye, and you don't have a choice in the matter.

If you skip down to the commandAction method, you can see how all of this starts to fit together.

```
public void commandAction(Command command, Displayable displayable)
{
    System.out.println("commandAction(" + command.getLabel() + ") called.");
    try
    {
        if (command == quit)
            destroyApp(false);

        if (command == really)
        {
            destroyApp(true);
            notifyDestroyed();
        }
    }

    catch (MIDletStateChangeException me)
    {
        System.out.println(me + " caught.");
        form.removeCommand(quit);
        form.addCommand(really);
    }
}
```

First, note that you wrap the command processing code in a try block so you can catch the hissy fit when it happens. This wrapped code handles events coming from the Quit and Really? commands. As you can see, when the user hits the Quit command, all you do is call the destroyApp method with the unconditional flag set to false. The destroyApp code then throws the exception via:

```
if (!unconditional)
    throw new MIDletStateChangeException();
```

The catch (MIDletStateChangeException me) block in the commandAction method then catches the exception and makes the change to the user interface by removing the Quit command and adding the Really? command. When you subsequently hit the Really? command, the commandAction method executes the code.

```
if (command == really)
{
    destroyApp(true);
    notifyDestroyed();
}
```

This time the destroyApp method doesn't get a choice—which in your MIDlet's case means it doesn't do anything. The final call to notifyDestroyed then tells the Application Manager to shut down the MIDlet.

Thankfully, the basics of MIDlet application lifecycles (and a bit of user interface) are out of the way. Now I want to leave Kansas for a little while and look at how to get you some rhythm (don't ask how I know that you don't have any) through the use of Timers.

Using Timers

The MIDP API includes two classes related to timing—java.util.Timer and java.util.TimerTask. These are both pretty much the same as what you might be used to with J2SE.

Table 5.3 java.util.Timer

Method	Description
Timer()	Constructs a new Timer object.
void cancel()	Stops a Timer.
void schedule(TimerTask task, Date d)	Schedules a task to run at the specified time d.
void schedule(TimerTask task, Date firstTime, long period)	Schedules a task to run first on the specified date, and then every period milliseconds.
void schedule(TimerTask task, long delay)	Schedules a task to run once after a certain delay in milliseconds has passed.
void schedule(TimerTask task, long delay, long period)	Schedules a task to run after a certain delay in milliseconds has passed, and then every period milliseconds.
void scheduleAtFixedRate(TimerTask task, Date firstTime, long period)	Schedules a task to run continuously from firstTime onward, and then continuously using a fixed interval of period milliseconds.
void scheduleAtFixedRate(TimerTask task, long delay, long period)	Schedules a task to run continuously after delay milliseconds, and then continuously using a fixed interval of period milliseconds.

Table 5.4 java.util.TimerTask

Method	Description
`TimerTask()`	Constructs a new timer task.
`boolean cancel()`	Terminates the task.
`abstract void run()`	This method is overridden with a method containing the code to be executed when the Timer event goes off.
`long scheduledExecutionTime()`	Returns the exact time at which the task was run last.

Timers are useful when you want to execute something at regular intervals, such as when you want to clear unused resources periodically or trigger events within your game. Take a look at a Timer in action.

```
import javax.microedition.midlet.*;
import javax.microedition.lcdui.*;
import java.util.*;

/**
 * A MIDlet which demonstrates a Timer in action.
 * @author Martin J. Wells
 */
public class TimerTest extends javax.microedition.midlet.MIDlet
{
    private Form form;
    private Timer timer;
    private PrintTask task;

    /**
     * MIDlet constructor that creates a form, timer and simple task. See the
     * inner class PrintTask for more information on the task we'll be executing.
     */
    public TimerTest()
    {
        form = new Form("Timer Test");

        // Setup the timer and the print timertask
        timer = new Timer();
        task = new PrintTask();
    }

    /**
```

```
 * Called by the Application Manager when the MIDlet is starting or resuming
 * after being paused. In this example it acquires the current Display object
 * and uses it to set the Form object created in the MIDlet constructor as
 * the active Screen to display.
 * @throws MIDletStateChangeException
 */
protected void startApp() throws MIDletStateChangeException
{
    // display our UI
    Display.getDisplay(this).setCurrent(form);

    // schedule the task for execution every 100 milliseconds
    timer.schedule(task, 1000, 1000);
}


/**
 * Called by the MID's Application Manager to pause the MIDlet. A good
 * example of this is when the user receives an incoming phone call whilst
 * playing your game. When they're done the Application Manager will call
 * startApp to resume. Use this in order to stop the timer from running.
 */
protected void pauseApp()
{
    task.cancel();
}


/**
 * Called by the MID's Application Manager when the MIDlet is about to
 * be destroyed (removed from memory). You should take this as an opportunity
 * to clear up any resources and save the game. For this example we cancel
 * the timer.
 * @param unconditional if false you have the option of throwing a
 * MIDletStateChangeException to abort the destruction process.
 * @throws MIDletStateChangeException
 */
protected void destroyApp(boolean unconditional)
        throws MIDletStateChangeException
{
    timer.cancel();
}
```

```
/**
 * An example of a TimerTask that adds some text to the form.
 */
class PrintTask extends TimerTask
{
    /**
     * To implement a task you need to override the run method.
     */
    public void run()
    {
        // output the time the task ran at
        form.append("" + scheduledExecutionTime());
    }
}
}
```

The TimerTask is the big boss in all of this. Think of it like a manager two days after installing Microsoft Project—it controls execution of all of its associated TimerTasks with mind-numbing precision.

The API to achieve all of this is relatively simple. As you can see in the sample code just shown, a new Timer object and TimerTask are instantiated in the constructor with the following code:

```
timer = new Timer();
task = new PrintTask();
```

Notice from the second line that you're not constructing a TimerTask, but a PrintTask. If you look down in the code, you'll see a declaration for the PrintTask inner class, which extends the TimerTask abstract base class. The PrintTask then implements the required abstract run method; it's this run method that appends the text lines to the display.

The constructor schedules execution of the printTask using:

```
timer.schedule(task, 1000, 1000);
```

You can use a variety of schedule methods to determine when your tasks should run, including running once from a certain time or continuing to run at regular intervals after that time. You can also execute tasks after a certain delay (in milliseconds), optionally continuing at regular intervals.

There are two special scheduleAtFixedRate methods that ensure a task is run an absolute number of times. Use these methods if you always want a task to run the appropriate number of times, even if the application is busy doing something else immediately after the interval time has passed. This is different than regular scheduling, which will execute a task only once even if the allotted interval has passed multiple times; the Timer will run a scheduleAtFixedRate once for every interval that has passed.

Stopping tasks is also pretty easy. You can see an example of this in the pauseApp method.

```
task.cancel();
```

This call will stop all further execution of the task. Note that this is a call to the PrintTask object's cancel method, not to the Timer object. A call to the more general-purpose timer.cancel will result in the timer itself stopping, along with every task scheduled for execution.

Networking

The MIDP includes support for the Generic Connection Framework that is part of the CLDC. However, the MIDP specifications only mandate that an HTTP connection is included in any implementation. This isn't as bad as it sounds; if you had any ideas about writing a high-performance action multiplayer game in the wireless world, I suggest you keep your pants on. Right now you have to design the networking elements of your game around high latency (the time it takes for data to move from one point to another) and high packet loss (the chance that data may not arrive at all). Sub-50ms UDP gaming is out of the question at the moment.

The design of the Generic Connection Framework is reasonably simple. Use the static factory Connector class to build and return a connection. Figure 5.3 shows the full class hierarchy of the available connection types.

Working with the Connector

The Generic Connection Framework design includes the concept of a single super-connector class that serves as a factory for any type of supported connection. Basically, you make a static call to the Connector class's open method, passing in the name of the resource to which you want to connect. This location name should be in the form protocol:address;parameters.

For example, here's how you would get a connection to an HTTP resource:

```
Connector.open("http://java.sun.com");
```

To establish a direct socket connection (if it is supported), you would use something like:

```
Connector.open("socket://127.0.0.1:999");
```

In your case, you'll stick to using the HttpConnection.

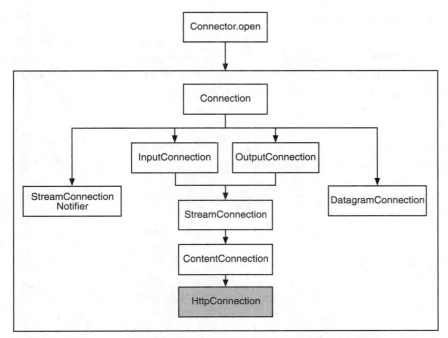

Figure 5.3 The Generic Connection Framework provides a full spread of general-purpose communications classes; however, the MIDP only guarantees support for `HttpConnection`.

Table 5.5 javax.microedition.io.Connector

Method	Description
`static Connection open(String name)`	Constructs, opens, and returns a new connection to the specified URL name.
`static Connection open(String name, int mode)`	Constructs, opens, and returns a new connection to the specified URL name and access mode.
`static Connection open(String name, int mode, boolean timeouts)`	Constructs, opens, and returns a new connection to the specified URL name, access mode, and a Boolean indicating whether you want to see timeout exceptions being thrown.
`static Connection openDataInputStream(String name)`	Opens a connection and then constructs and returns a data input stream.
`static Connection openDataOutputStream(String name)`	Opens a connection and then constructs and returns a data output stream.
`static Connection openInputStream(String name)`	Opens a connection and then constructs and returns an input stream.
`static Connection openOutputStream(String name)`	Opens a connection and then constructs and returns an output stream.

Working with HttpConnection

The `HttpConnection` class is a full-featured HTTP client that serves very well for most (low-latency) network tasks. For games, you can use it to download content on demand (such as a new level), update scores or higher-level meta-game data, or even to implement inter-player communications. You can see all the methods available in the `HttpConnection` class in Table 5.6.

Table 5.6 javax.microedition.io.HttpConnection

Method	Description
Header Methods	
long getDate()	Retrieves the date header value.
long getExpiration()	Retrieves the expiration header value.
String getHeaderFieldKey(int n)	Retrieves the header key by index.
String getHeaderField(int n)	Retrieves the header value by index.
String getHeaderField(String name)	Retrieves the value of the named header field.
long getHeaderFieldDate(String name, long def)	Retrieves the value of the named header field in the format of a date long. If the field doesn't exist, the def value is returned.
int getHeaderFieldInt(String name, int def)	Retrieves the value of the named header field as an integer. If the field doesn't exist, the def value is returned.
long getLastModified()	Returns the last modified header field.
Connection Methods	
String getURL()	Returns the URL.
String getFile()	Get the file portion of the URL.
String getHost()	Returns the host part of the URL.
int getPort()	Returns the port part of the URL.
String getProtocol()	Returns the protocol part of the URL.
String getQuery()	Returns the query part of the URL.
String getRef()	Returns the ref portion of the URL.
int getResponseCode()	Returns the HTTP response status code.
String getResponseMessage()	Returns the HTTP response message (if there was one).
Request Handling Methods	
String getRequestMethod()	Returns the request method of the connection.
void setRequestMethod(String method)	Sets the method of the URL request. Available types are GET, POST, and HEAD.
String getRequestProperty(String key)	Returns the request property value associated with the named key.
void setRequestProperty(String key, String value)	Set the request property value associated with the named key.

In the following sample MIDlet, you'll create a connection to a popular Web site, drag down the first few hundred bytes of content, and then display it. Thankfully, actually doing this is as simple as it sounds.

```java
import java.util.*;
import java.io.*;
import javax.microedition.midlet.*;
import javax.microedition.lcdui.*;
import javax.microedition.io.*;

import java.io.*;
import javax.microedition.midlet.*;
import javax.microedition.lcdui.*;
import javax.microedition.io.*;

/**
 * A demonstration MIDlet which shows the basics of HTTP networking.
 * @author Martin J. Wells
 */
public class NetworkingTest extends javax.microedition.midlet.MIDlet
{
    private Form form;

    /**
     * MIDlet constructor that instantiates a form and then opens up an HTTP
     * connection to java.sun.com. It then reads a few bytes and adds those as
     * a string to the form.
     * @throws IOException if a networking error occurs
     */
    public NetworkingTest() throws IOException
    {
        // Setup the UI
        form = new Form("Http Dump");

        // Create a HTTP connection to the java.sun.com site
        InputStream inStream = Connector.openInputStream("http://java.sun.com/");

        // Open the result and stream the first chunk into a byte buffer
        byte[] buffer = new byte[255];
        int bytesRead = inStream.read(buffer);
        if (bytesRead > 0)
```

```
    {
        inStream.close();

        // Turn the result into a string and display it
        String webString = new String(buffer, 0, bytesRead);
        form.append(webString);
    }
}


/**
 * Called by the Application Manager when the MIDlet is starting or resuming
 * after being paused. In this example it acquires the current Display object
 * and uses it to set the Form object created in the MIDlet constructor as
 * the active Screen to display.
 * @throws MIDletStateChangeException
 */
protected void startApp() throws MIDletStateChangeException
{
    // display our UI
    Display.getDisplay(this).setCurrent(form);
}


/**
 * Called by the MID's Application Manager to pause the MIDlet. A good
 * example of this is when the user receives an incoming phone call whilst
 * playing your game. When they're done the Application Manager will call
 * startApp to resume. For this example we don't need to do anything.
 */
protected void pauseApp()
{
}


/**
 * Called by the MID's Application Manager when the MIDlet is about to
 * be destroyed (removed from memory). You should take this as an opportunity
 * to clear up any resources and save the game. For this example we don't
 * need to do anything.
 * @param unconditional if false you have the option of throwing a
 * MIDletStateChangeException to abort the destruction process.
 * @throws MIDletStateChangeException
```

```
    */
    protected void destroyApp(boolean unconditional) throws MIDletStateChangeException
    {
    }
}
```

Tip

You can see the complete source code in the NetworkingTest.java on the CD (Chapter 5 source code).

All of the action happens in the constructor. The connection is first opened using the following code:

```
    InputStream inStream = Connector.openInputStream("http://java.sun.com/");
```

The static `Connector.openInputStream` is a convenience method to both establish the connection and return an input stream from that connection. If you wanted to play around with the HTTP aspect of things, you could do so in two stages, and thus retain a reference to the `HttpConnection`. For example:

```
HttpConnection http =
(HttpConnection)Connector.openInputStream("http://java.sun.com/");
InputStream inStream = http.openInputStream();
```

The subsequent code within the constructor simply reads the first chunk of data from the input stream into a buffer and displays it. You don't bother reading the whole page because displaying it would be a bit like trying to draw the Mona Lisa with a neon pink highlighter.

Persistence (RMS)

When developing a game, you'll want to save (or "persist") data that you can retrieve later, after the game—or even the phone—is shut off. Like most things in the J2ME world, the functionality is there, it's just in the "It's life, Jim, but not as we know it" category.

Persisting data on a MID is done via the RMS (*Record Management System*), which you'll find in the `javax.microedition.rms` package (Table 5.7 contains a list of all the classes within this package). The RMS stores data as records, which are then referenced using a unique record key. Groups of records are stored in the rather inventively named record store.

Table 5.7 RMS Package (Excluding Exceptions)

Class	Description
Classes	
RecordStore	Allows you access to the record store functionality.
Interfaces	
RecordComparator	Provides an interface you can use to implement a comparator between two records (used by enumeration).
RecordEnumeration	Provides an enumerator for a record store; can be used in conjunction with a comparator and a filter.
RecordFilter	Filters record retrieval.
RecordListener	Provides an interface you can use to "listen" to events that occur in the RMS, such as when records are added, changed, or removed.

Record Store

I had real trouble with that heading; so many lame puns, so little time. . . . Anyway, a record store is exactly what the term implies—a storage mechanism for records. You can see the complete API available in Table 5.8.

As you can see in Figure 5.4, a record store exists in MIDlet suite scope. This means that any MIDlet in the same suite can access that suite's record store. MIDlets from an evil parallel universe (such as another suite) aren't even aware of the existence of your suite's record stores.

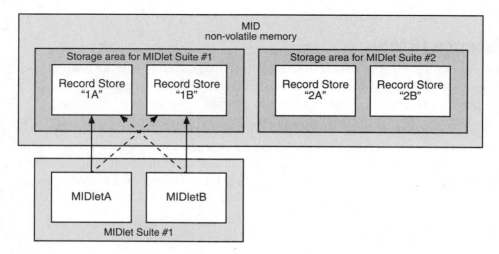

Figure 5.4 A MIDlet only has access to any record stores created in the same MIDlet suite.

Table 5.8 javax.microedition.rms.RecordStore

Method	Description
Store Access Methods	
static RecordStore openRecordStore (String recordStoreName, boolean createIfNecessary)	Opens a record store or creates one if it doesn't exist.
void closeRecordStore ()	Closes a record store.
static void deleteRecordStore (String recordStoreName)	Deletes a record store.
long getLastModified ()	Gets the last time the store was modified.
String getName ()	Gets the name of the store.
int getNumRecords ()	Returns the number of records currently in the store.
int getSize ()	Returns the total bytes used by the store.
int getSizeAvailable ()	Returns the amount of free space. (Keep in mind that records require more storage for housekeeping overhead.)
int getVersion ()	Retrieves the store's version number. (This number increases by one every time a record is updated.)
static String[] listRecordStores ()	Returns a string array of all the record stores on the MID to which you have access.
Record Access Methods	
int addRecord (byte[] data, int offset, int numBytes)	Adds a new record to the store.
byte[] getRecord (int recordId)	Retrieves a record using an ID.
int getRecord (int recordId, byte[] buffer, int offset)	Retrieves a record into a byte buffer. void deleteRecord
(int recordId)	Deletes the record associated with the recordId parameter.
void setRecord (int recordId, byte[] newData, int offset, int numBytes)	Changes the contents of the record associated with recordId using the new byte array.
int getNextRecordID ()	Retrieves the ID of the next record when it is inserted.
int getRecordSize (int recordId)	Returns the current data size of the record store in bytes.
RecordEnumeration enumerate	Records (RecordFilter filter, RecordComparator comparator, boolean keepUpdated) Returns a RecordEnumerator object used to enumerate through a collection of records (order using the comparator parameter).
Event Methods	
void addRecordListener (RecordListener listener)	Adds a listener object that will be called when events occur on this record store.
void removeRecordListener (RecordListener listener)	Removes a listener previously added using the addRecordListener method.

Record

A record is just an array of bytes in which you write data in any format you like (unlike a database table's predetermined table format). You can use `DataInputStream`, `DataOutputStream`, and of course `ByteArrayInputStream` and `ByteArrayOutputStream` to write data to a record.

As you can see in Figure 5.5, records are stored in the record store in a table-like format. An integer primary key uniquely identifies a given record and its associated byte array. The RMS assigns record IDs for you; thus, the first record you write will have the ID of 1, and the record IDs will increase by one each time you write another record.

Figure 5.5 also shows some simple uses for a record store. In this example, the player's name (the string "John") is stored in record 1. Record 2 contains the highest score, and record 3 is a cached image you previously downloaded over the network.

Note

Practically, you likely would store all the details on a player, such as his name, score, and highest level, as a single record with one record per new player. You would then store all these records in a dedicated Player Data record store.

You might also have noticed that there is no `javax.microedition.rms.Record` class. That's because the records are just arrays of bytes; all the functionality you need is in the `RecordStore` class.

Take a look at an example now. In the following code, you'll create a record store, write out some string values, and then read them back again. Doesn't sound too hard, right?

Record Store "A"	
ID	Record data (byte array)
1	"John"
2	"64998"
3	[.png image data]
–	–

Figure 5.5 A record store contains records, each with a unique integer key associated with a generic array of bytes.

Tip

You can see the complete source code for this in the SimpleRMS.java on the CD (Chapter 5 source code).

```java
import java.io.*;
import javax.microedition.midlet.*;
import javax.microedition.rms.*;

/**
 * An example of how to use the MIDP 1.0 Record Management System (RMS).
 * @author Martin J. Wells
 */
public class SimpleRMS extends javax.microedition.midlet.MIDlet
{
    private RecordStore rs;
    private static final String STORE_NAME = "My Record Store";

    /**
     * Constructor for the demonstration MIDlet does all the work for the tests.
     * It firstly opens (or creates if required) a record store and then inserts
     * some records containing data. It then reads those records back and
     * displays the results on the console.
     * @throws Exception
     */
    public SimpleRMS() throws Exception
    {
        // Open (and optionally create a record store for our data
        rs = RecordStore.openRecordStore(STORE_NAME, true);

        // Create some records in the store
        String[] words = {"they", "mostly", "come", "at", "night"};
        for (int i=0; i < words.length; i++)
        {
            // Create a byte stream we can write to
            ByteArrayOutputStream byteOutputStream = new ByteArrayOutputStream();

            // To make life easier use a DataOutputStream to write the bytes
            // to the byteStream (ie. we get the writeXXX methods)
            DataOutputStream dataOutputStream = new DataOutputStream(byteOutputStream);
            dataOutputStream.writeUTF(words[i]);
            // ... add other dataOutputStream.writeXXX statements if you like
```

```
            dataOutputStream.flush();

            // add the record
            byte[] recordOut = byteOutputStream.toByteArray();
            int newRecordId = rs.addRecord(recordOut, 0, recordOut.length);
            System.out.println("Adding new record: " + newRecordId +
                            " Value: " + recordOut.toString());

            dataOutputStream.close();
            byteOutputStream.close();
        }

        // retrieve the state of the store now that it's been populated
        System.out.println("Record store now has " + rs.getNumRecords() +
                        " record(s) using " + rs.getSize() + " byte(s) " +
                        "[" + rs.getSizeAvailable() + " bytes free]");

        // retrieve the records
        for (int i=1; i <= rs.getNumRecords(); i++)
        {
            int recordSize = rs.getRecordSize(i);
            if (recordSize > 0)
            {
                // construct a byte and wrapping data stream to read back the
                // java types from the binary format
                ByteArrayInputStream byteInputStream = new
ByteArrayInputStream(rs.getRecord(i));
                DataInputStream dataInputStream = new DataInputStream(byteInputStream);

                String value = dataInputStream.readUTF();
                // ... add other dataOutputStream.readXXX statements here matching the
                // order they were written above

                System.out.println("Retrieved record: " + i + " Value: " + value);

                dataInputStream.close();
                byteInputStream.close();
            }
        }


    }
```

```
/**
 * Called by the Application Manager when the MIDlet is starting or resuming
 * after being paused. In this case we just exit as soon as we start.
 * @throws MIDletStateChangeException
 */
protected void startApp() throws MIDletStateChangeException
{
    destroyApp(false);
    notifyDestroyed();
}


/**
 * Called by the MID's Application Manager to pause the MIDlet. A good
 * example of this is when the user receives an incoming phone call whilst
 * playing your game. When they're done the Application Manager will call
 * startApp to resume. For this example we don't need to do anything.
 */
protected void pauseApp()
{
}


/**
 * Called by the MID's Application Manager when the MIDlet is about to
 * be destroyed (removed from memory). You should take this as an opportunity
 * to clear up any resources and save the game. For this example we don't
 * need to do anything.
 * @param unconditional if false you have the option of throwing a
 * MIDletStateChangeException to abort the destruction process.
 * @throws MIDletStateChangeException
 */
protected void destroyApp(boolean unconditional) throws MIDletStateChangeException
{
}

}
```

Seems like a lot of work to write a few strings, doesn't it? Fortunately it's not quite as complicated as it looks. The first thing you did was open the record store using the call `rs = RecordStore.openRecordStore(STORE_NAME, true);`.

The Boolean argument on the call to `openRecordStore` indicates that you want to create a new record store if the one you named doesn't already exist.

The next section creates and then writes a series of records to the record store. Because you have to write bytes to the record, I recommend using the combination of a ByteArrayOutputStream and DataOutputStream.

The following code creates our two streams—first the ByteArrayOutputStream, and then a DataOutputStream, which has a target of the ByteArrayOutputStream. As you can see in Figure 5.6, this means that any data you write to using the very convenient writeXXX methods of this class will in turn be written in byte array format through the associated ByteArrayOutputStream.

The code to create this "stream train" is

```
ByteArrayOutputStream byteOutputStream = new ByteArrayOutputStream();
DataOutputStream dataOutputStream = new DataOutputStream(byteOutputStream);
```

You can then use the DataOutputStream convenience methods to write the data before flushing the stream (thus ensuring that everything is committed to the down streams).

```
dataOutputStream.writeUTF(words[i]);
dataOutputStream.flush();
```

Adding the record is simply a matter of grabbing the byte array from the ByteArrayOutputStream and sending it off to the RMS.

```
byte[] recordOut = byteOutputStream.toByteArray();
int newRecordId = rs.addRecord(recordOut, 0, recordOut.length);
```

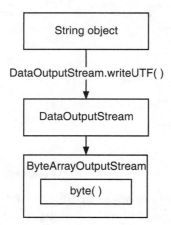

Figure 5.6 DataOutputStreams make byte array formatting easier.

Simple, huh? Here's the output:

```
Adding new record: 1 Value: [B@ea0ef881
Adding new record: 2 Value: [B@84aee8b
Adding new record: 3 Value: [B@c5c7331
Adding new record: 4 Value: [B@e938beb1
Adding new record: 5 Value: [B@11eaa96
Record store now has 5 record(s) using 208 byte(s) [979722 bytes free]
Retrieved record: 1 Value: they
Retrieved record: 2 Value: mostly
Retrieved record: 3 Value: come
Retrieved record: 4 Value: at
Retrieved record: 5 Value: night
```

You can see how easily you can write other data using the various write methods in your `DataOutputStream`. Just be sure you always read things back in the correct order.

Locking

One nice aspect of the RMS implementation is that it takes care of locking for you. The record store implementation guarantees synchronized access, so there is no chance of accidentally accessing storage while another part of your MIDlet, or even another MIDlet in your suite, is hitting it at the same time. Since this type of protection is inherent, you don't need to go to the trouble of coding it yourself.

Enumerating

When you retrieved the records in the previous examples, you used a simple method of reading back the data (an indexing `for` loop). However, you'll encounter cases in which you want to retrieve only a subset of records, possibly in a particular order.

RMS supports the ordering of records using the `javax.microedition.rms.RecordEnumerator` class. Table 5.9 lists all the methods in this class.

You can access an enumerator instance using the record store. For example:

```
RecordEnumeration enum = rs.enumerateRecords(null, null, false);
while (enum.hasNextElement())
{
        byte[] record = enum.nextRecord()  ;
        // do something with the record
            ByteArrayInputStream byteInputStream = new ByteArrayInputStream(record);
            DataInputStream dataInputStream = new DataInputStream(byteInputStream);
```

Table 5.9 javax.microedition.rms.RecordEnumeration

Method	Description
Housekeeping	
void destroy ()	Destroys the enumerator.
boolean isKeptUpdated ()	Indicates whether this enumerator will auto-rebuild if the underlying record store is changed.
keepUpdated (boolean keepUpdated)	Changes the keepUpdated state.
void rebuild ()	Causes the enumerator's underlying index to rebuild, which might result in a change to the order of entries.
void reset ()	Resets the enumeration back to the state after it was created.
Accessing	
boolean hasNextElement ()	Tests whether there are any more to enumerate in the first-to-last ordered direction.
boolean hasPreviousElement ()	Tests whether there are any more to enumerate in the last-to-first ordered direction.
byte[] nextRecord ()	Retrieves the next record in the store.
byte[] previousRecord ()	Gets the previous record.
int previousRecordId ()	Just gets the ID of the previous record.
int nextRecordId ()	Just gets the ID of the next record.
int numRecords ()	Returns the number of records, which is important when you are using filters.

```
        String value = dataInputStream.readUTF();
        // ... add other dataOutputStream.readXXX statements here matching
        // the order they were written above
    System.out.println(">"+value);
}
enum.destroy();
```

You can use the enumerator to go both forward and backward through the results. If you want to go backward, just use the previousRecord method.

Comparing

The previous example retrieves records in ID order, but you can change this order using the ... wait for it ... RecordComparator (the API is shown in Table 5.10).

Table 5.10 javax.microedition.rms.RecordComparator

Method	Description
`int compare (byte[] rec1, byte[] rec2)`	Returns an integer representing whether `rec1` is equivalent to, precedes, or follows `rec2`.

You can use the `javax.microedition.rms.RecordComparator` interface as the basis for a class that will bring order to your enumerated chaos. All you need to do is create a class that compares the two records and returns an integer value representing whether one record is equivalent to, precedes, or follows another record.

Note

The `javax.microedition.rms.RecordComparator` interface includes the following convenience definitions for the `compare` method return values:

- RecordComparator.EQUIVALENT=0   The two records are (more or less) the same for the purposes of your comparison.
- RecordComparator.FOLLOWS=1   The first record should be after the second.
- RecordComparator.PRECEDES=-1   The first record should be before the second.

Here's an example of a record comparator to sort the string values of the previous examples:

```
class StringComparator implements RecordComparator
{
    public int compare(byte[] bytes, byte[] bytes1)
    {
        String value = getStringValue(bytes);
        String value1 = getStringValue(bytes1);

        if (value.compareTo(value1) < 0) return PRECEDES;
        if (value.compareTo(value1) > 0) return FOLLOWS;
        return EQUIVALENT;
    }

    private String getStringValue(byte[] record)
    {
        try
        {
            ByteArrayInputStream byteInputStream = new ByteArrayInputStream(record);
            DataInputStream dataInputStream = new DataInputStream(byteInputStream);
            return dataInputStream.readUTF();
```

```
        }
    catch(Exception e)
    {
        System.out.println(e.toString());
        return "";
    }
  }
}
```

You can then use this comparator in any call to create an enumeration. For example:

```
RecordEnumeration enum = rs.enumerateRecords(null, new StringComparator(),
false);
```

If you were to then enumerate through the records from your previous examples, they would be displayed in a sorted order according to the string value stored in each record.

The output from running this against your previous record store's data follows. (Sounds uncannily like Yoda, doesn't it?)

```
Retrieved record: 4 Value: at
Retrieved record: 3 Value: come
Retrieved record: 2 Value: mostly
Retrieved record: 5 Value: night
Retrieved record: 1 Value: they
```

If you have records containing more complicated data, you need to have your comparator make a logical appraisal of the contents of each record, and then return an appropriate integer to represent the desired order.

You can see a complete working example of this in the SortedRMS.java file on the CD (in the Chapter 5 source code).

Filtering

Sorting enumerations is great! I can't think of anything else I'd like to be doing on a Saturday than sorting enumerators, but sometimes you'll want to limit or filter the records you get back from an enumerator. Enter the javax.microedition.rms.RecordFilter class. . . . . You can see the one and only method in this class defined in Table 5.11.

Table 5.11 javax.microedition.rms.RecordFilter

Method	Description
boolean matches (byte[] candidate)	Returns true if the candidate record validly passes through the filtering rules.

Filtering is just as easy as comparing. (I'm assuming you found that easy.) You just create a class that implements the `javax.microedition.rms.RecordFilter` and then implement the required methods. Here's an example:

```
class StringFilter implements RecordFilter
{
    private String mustContainString;

    public StringFilter(String mustContain)
    {
        // save the match string
        mustContainString = mustContain;
    }

    public boolean matches(byte[] bytes)
    {
        // check if our string is in the record
        if (getStringValue(bytes).indexOf(mustContainString) == -1)
            return false;
        return true;
    }

    private String getStringValue(byte[] record)
    {
        try
        {
            ByteArrayInputStream byteInputStream = new ByteArrayInputStream(record);
            DataInputStream dataInputStream = new DataInputStream(byteInputStream);
            return dataInputStream.readUTF();
        }
        catch (Exception e)
        {
            System.out.println(e.toString());
            return "";
        }
    }
}
```

To use your new filter, just instantiate it in the call to construct the enumerator, like you did with the comparator.

```
RecordEnumeration enum = rs.enumerateRecords(new StringFilter("o"),
new StringComparator(), false);
```

Note that I'm using the comparator and the filter together. It's all happening now!

The output from this is now limited to records with a string value containing an "o" (the result of the indexOf("o") call returning something other than −1). Thus you would only see

```
Retrieved record: 3 Value: come
Retrieved record: 2 Value: mostly
```

Listening In

The RMS also has a convenient interface you can use to create a listener for any RMS events that occur. Using this, you can make your game react automatically to changes to a record store. This is especially important if such a change has come from another MIDlet in your suite because you won't be aware of the change.

To create a listener, you need to make a class that implements the javax.microedition. rms.RecordListener interface (Table 5.12 lists the methods).

Table 5.12 javax.microedition.rms.RecordListener

Method	Description
void recordAdded (RecordStore recordStore, int recordId)	Called when a record is added.
void recordChanged (RecordStore recordStore, int recordId)	Called when a record is changed.
void recordDeleted (RecordStore recordStore, int recordId)	Called when a record is deleted.

For example, the following is an inner class that simply outputs a message whenever an event occurs:

```
class Listener implements javax.microedition.rms.RecordListener
{
    public void recordAdded(RecordStore recordStore, int i)
    {
        try
        {
            System.out.println("Record " + i + " added to " + recordStore.getName());
        }
        catch(Exception e)
        {
            System.out.println(e);
        }
    }
```

```
public void recordChanged(RecordStore recordStore, int i)
{
    try
    {
        System.out.println("Record " + i + " changed in " + recordStore.getName());
    }
    catch (Exception e)
    {
        System.out.println(e);
    }
}

public void recordDeleted(RecordStore recordStore, int i)
{
    try
    {
        System.out.println("Record " + i + " deleted from " + recordStore.getName());
    }
    catch (Exception e)
    {
        System.out.println(e);
    }
}
}
```

Note

The source file ListenerRMS.java on the CD has a complete example of a working RMS Listener.

To activate this listener, use the `RecordStore.addListener` method on a record store you have previously created. This can be used anywhere where you have a record store and want to be notified when it is accessed, for example:

```
RecordStore rs = RecordStore.openRecordStore("Example", true);
rs.addRecordListener(new Listener());
```

Exceptions

I want to make a quick note about exceptions before you leave the world of RMS. In the preceding examples, I've ignored or hacked up pathetic handlers for run-time exceptions that might be thrown. Table 5.13 lists all of these exceptions.

Table 5.13 RMS Exceptions

Exception	Description
InvalidRecordIDException	Indicates that an operation could not be completed because the record ID was invalid.
RecordStoreException	Indicates that a general exception occurred in a record store operation.
RecordStoreFullException	Indicates that an operation could not be completed because the record store system storage was full.
RecordStoreNotFoundException	Indicates that an operation could not be completed because the record store could not be found.
RecordStoreNotOpenException	Indicates that an operation was attempted on a closed record store.

In most cases RMS exceptions occur due to abnormal conditions in which you need to either code around the problem (in the case of the RecordStoreNotFoundException, RecordStoreNotOpenException, and InvalidRecordIDException) or just live with it (in the case of RecordStoreException). The one possible exception to this is RecordStoreFullException, which you might resolve by having your MIDlet clear some space and try again.

Either way, when developing your game, consider the implications of these exceptions and do your best to handle them gracefully, even if all you can do is inform the player that his game save failed.

User Interface (LCDUI)

Okay, on to some more fun stuff—user interfaces. The MIDP allows you to use two distinct interface systems when creating a game—the high-level UI and the low-level UI. The difference between these two UIs comes down to the nature of MIDs themselves; they aren't computers. I know this sounds obvious, but take a minute to review the practical differences; I think it will provide some perspective on the design of the MIDP user interface.

First, device interfaces, form factors, and installed software differ widely across the industry. They all look basically the same (well, most of them do), but there is a never-ending variety of input controls (such as spin dials, mini-joysticks, sliders, flippers, and even fingers), all of which provide distinctly different interface controls.

The basic screen size is much smaller than its desktop computer counterparts. Programming an interface with a 15-inch screen will feel like playing skirmish across the Sahara desert compared to the size of the average mobile phone screen. The screen sizes also vary widely.

Another difference is the amount of interaction you'll get from the user. Typically users play games using one hand, often only for short periods of time. The UI should also take into consideration the fact that the user is not likely to pay continuous attention to what's happening on the device.

Finally, users will be familiar with the controls of the MID's general operating environment, including all the preinstalled software. They will not be terribly interested in learning a new UI every time they download an application. Your game will ask the MID to do something, and it's the MID's job to then do it in a way with which the user is familiar.

Therefore, the high-level UI completely abstracts the device. There is no dependency in your code for how the device will actually implement these things. For example, the high-level UI deals in terms of commands, not in buttons or keys. It's up to the MIDP implementation on that particular device to display a command in a way that the user can see and then execute it. How this occurs is not your problem, it's the MID's.

Which brings you to a problem: Games typically display graphics, and you can't abstract graphics in this manner—it just isn't practical. That's where the low-level UI comes in. You can use it to go wild all over the screen if you want, but you need to handle things like variable screen sizes and key interception all on your own.

When you create a game, however, you won't be using the low-level UI exclusively—you need a mixture of both UIs. For example, your introduction, menus, and most data entry screens will use the high-level UI, but when it comes down to moving the little spaceships around, you use the low-level API. The complete class list for the LCDUI is shown in Table 5.14.

UI Basics

At the heart of the LCDUI is the concept of a screen, which represents a display on the MID. You can only have one screen visible at any point in time. (Reread that sentence a few times—it's a big clue to how all this works.) Think of the user interface as a deck of cards, where only one card is visible at any point in time. Each card is a screen.

There are three types of screens in the LCDUI:

- **Low-level UI**. This is accessible through the `Canvas` class.
- **Form**. This displays groups of simple UI components.
- **Complex components**. These require the whole screen (such as any Screen class object like `TextBox`).

Basically anything displayed on a MID has to either be a screen or exist inside one (in the case of `Form` components).

Table 5.14 javax.microedition.lcdui Class Summary

Class	Description
Interfaces	
Choice	Provides the common interface used to manage a selection of items.
CommandListener	Lets you create a listener for command events from the high-level UI.
ItemStateListener	Lets you create a listener class for changes to an Item object's state.
UI System and Utility Classes	
Display	Represents the manager of the display and input devices of the system.
Font	Obtains font objects, along with their metrics.
Image	Provides a class for holding image data (in PNG format).
AlertType	Provides a helper class that defines the types of Alerts you can create, such as ALARM, CONFIRMATION, ERROR, INFO, WARNING. I sound like the robot from *Lost in Space*.
Displayable	Provides an abstract base class for an object that can be displayed.
High-Level UI	
Command	Abstracts a user action on the interface.
Screen Classes	
Screen	Provides a base class for high-level UI components.
Alert	Provides a screen to alert the user to something.
List	Provides a screen object that contains a list of choices.
TextBox	Provides a screen object used for editing text.
Forms & Items	
Form	Provides a screen that acts as a container for one or more Items.
Item	Provides a base class for something you can stick on a Form (or an Alert).
ChoiceGroup	Provides a UI component for presenting a list of choices.
DateField	Provides a UI component to get the user to enter a date.
Gauge	Displays pretty graph bar to show progress.
ImageItem	Provides an Item that is also an Image. (See the Item entry for more information.)
StringItem	Provides an Item object for displaying a String.
TextField	Provides an Item used to edit text.
Ticker	Provides an Item that scrolls a band of text along the display.
Low-Level UI	
Graphics	Provides 2D graphics tools.
Canvas	Provides the base class used to create low-level UI graphics.

The LCDUI class hierarchy is reasonably complex, so I'll also give you a quick rundown of how it all fits together (you can see the entire class hierarchy laid out in Figure 5.7). First, the classes all fall into one of following functional categories:

- System or utility classes (such as Display, Font, AlertType, and Ticker)
- Low-level API classes (such as Canvas and Graphics)
- High-level API Screen classes (such as Alert, Form, List, and TextBox)
- High-level API Form component classes (classes derived from Item, such as Choice-Group, DateField, Gauge, ImageItem, StringItem, and TextField)

You might be wondering about the difference between the Screen classes, which essentially take over the display, and the Form component classes, which appear functionally similar.

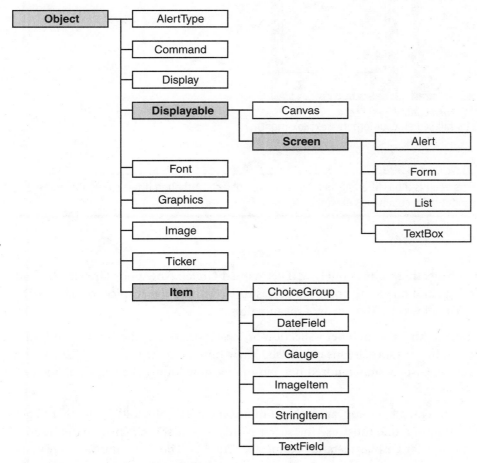

Figure 5.7 The LCDUI class hierarchy.

For example, what's the difference between a `TextBox` and a `TextField`? The answer really comes down to sophistication. A `TextField` is a simple control you can embed inside a form; it's a simple control with limited capabilities. The `TextBox` is the "level boss" of text-entry tools; it uses the entire screen and has additional features, such as clipboard (cut, copy, and paste) tools.

Another important distinction is that `TextBox` is a full-fledged screen in its own right, so you can give it a title, add commands, and listen for command events. In Figure 5.8, you can see the difference between a full-screen `TextBox` and its `TextField` counterpart.

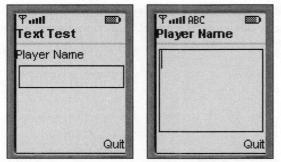

Figure 5.8 A `Form` control `TextField` (`left`) compared to its full-screen counterpart, `TextBox` (right)

Note

The `Alert` screen is a bit different than other `Screen` objects. Although it takes over the entire display, it cannot have commands like other `Screens`.

Display

Once upon a time, there was a lonely MIDlet named Gretel. Now poor Gretel, who had no arms, no legs, and no way to communicate, survived under the auspices of the evil Dr. AM. Life for Gretel was boring; life was meaningless.

One day, while looking through her collection of `TimerTasks`, Gretel the MIDlet noticed a knight riding in the distance. By his colors, she knew him to be the brave Sir Display. She cried out, but Sir Display only ignored her. No matter how loudly she yelled, he seemed deaf to her pleas.

At that very moment, a fairy appeared. (No, I'm not the fairy.) She told Gretel that to get Sir Display's attention, one must use the secret words—`getDisplay`. When Gretel uttered this strange phrase, Sir Display instantly connected with her. They were immediately married and lived happily ever after—at least until about eight seconds later, when the user accidentally dropped the mobile phone into his beer.

Table 5.15 javax.microedition.lcdui.Display

Method	Description
void callSerially(Runnable r)	Serially calls a java.lang.Runnable object later.
Displayable getCurrent()	Gets the current Displayable object.
static Display getDisplay(MIDlet m)	Retrieves the current Display object for the MIDlet.
boolean isColor()	Determines whether the device supports color.
int numColors()	Determines the number of colors (or gray levels, if not color).
void setCurrent(Alert alert, Displayable nextDisplayable)	Displays Alert, and then falls back to display the nextDisplayable object.
void setCurrent(Displayable nextDisplayable)	Shows the nextDisplayable object.

This fairy tale (if you can call it that) gives you a somewhat vague idea of the relationship between the MIDlet and the Display object—the API is shown in Table 5.15. In short, there's only one Display object per MIDlet. It's available by default; you just have to access it using the getDisplay method. For example:

```
Display display = Display.getDisplay(this);
```

Then you can have any Displayable class object (such as a Screen or a Canvas) presented on the screen within a Display. To do this, you don't add the objects to the Display, you set the Displayable object to be current using the setCurrent method. You can see this concept illustrated in Figure 5.9. For example, the following code creates a TextBox object and sets it to be the current Screen on the display. (Remember, TextBox is derived for the Screen class, which in turn is derived from Displayable.)

```java
import javax.microedition.midlet.*;
import javax.microedition.lcdui.*;

/**
 * A demo of the TextBox Screen.
 * @author Martin J. Wells
 */
public class TextBoxTest extends MIDlet implements CommandListener
{
    private TextBox textBox;
    private Alert alert;
    private Command quit;
    private Command go;
```

```
/**
 * MIDlet constructor creates a TextBox Screen and then adds in a go and
 * quit command. We then set this class to be the listener for TextBox
 * commands.
 */
public TextBoxTest()
{
    // Setup the UI
    textBox = new TextBox("Enter Thy Name", "Sir ", 20, TextField.ANY);
    go = new Command("Go", Command.SCREEN, 1);
    quit = new Command("Quit", Command.EXIT, 2);
    textBox.addCommand(go);
    textBox.addCommand(quit);
    textBox.setCommandListener(this);
}


/**
 * Called by the Application Manager when the MIDlet is starting or resuming
 * after being paused. In this example it acquires the current Display object
 * and uses it to set the Form object created in the MIDlet constructor as
 * the active Screen to display.
 * @throws MIDletStateChangeException
 */
protected void startApp() throws MIDletStateChangeException
{
    Display.getDisplay(this).setCurrent(textBox);
}


/**
 * Called by the MID's Application Manager to pause the MIDlet. A good
 * example of this is when the user receives an incoming phone call whilst
 * playing your game. When they're done the Application Manager will call
 * startApp to resume. For this example we don't need to do anything.
 */
protected void pauseApp()
{
}


/**
 * Called by the MID's Application Manager when the MIDlet is about to
 * be destroyed (removed from memory). You should take this as an opportunity
 * to clear up any resources and save the game. For this example we don't
```

```
 * need to do anything.
 * @param unconditional if false you have the option of throwing a
 * MIDletStateChangeException to abort the destruction process.
 * @throws MIDletStateChangeException
 */
protected void destroyApp(boolean unconditional) throws MIDletStateChangeException
{
}


/**
 * The CommandListener interface method called when the user executes a
 * Command, in this case we handle the the quit command we created in the
 * constructor and added to the Form, as well as the go command, which we
 * use to create and display an Alert.
 * @param command the command that was triggered
 * @param displayable the displayable on which the event occurred
 */
public void commandAction(Command command, Displayable displayable)
{
    try
    {
        if (command == quit)
        {
            destroyApp(true);
            notifyDestroyed();
        }

        if (command == go)
        {
            alert = new Alert("", "Greetings " + textBox.getString(), null,
AlertType.CONFIRMATION);
            Display.getDisplay(this).setCurrent(alert);
        }


    }

    catch (MIDletStateChangeException me)
    {
        System.out.println(me + " caught.");
    }
}
}
```

Note

A reference to a `Display` object is only valid between the application manager's calls to `startApp` and `destroyApp`. Don't be tempted to grab the `Display` object in your classes constructor and then cache it for the entire time the application runs. Just use the direct call to `getDisplay` whenever you need to.

Table 5.16 shows the API for the `Displayable` class. Keep in mind this is an abstract base class for the `Screen` and `Canvas` objects.

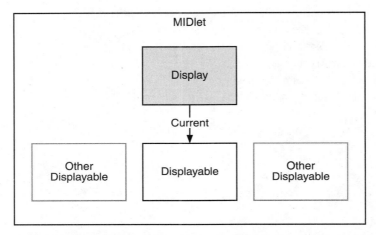

Figure 5.9 A MIDlet can have many displayable objects instantiated, but only one can be current on the screen at any given time.

Table 5.16 javax.microedition.lcdui.Displayable

Method	Description
`boolean isShown ()`	Asks whether you are really on screen.
`void addCommand (Command cmd)`	Adds a new `Command`.
`void removeCommand (Command cmd)`	Removes a `Command`.
`void setCommandListener (CommandListener l)`	Sets a `CommandListener`.

Commands

One thing common to all `Displayables` is the ability to create and display commands to the user and subsequently fire events relating to these commands to a nominated command listener. Remember that a command is an abstract concept; it's up to the MID to turn it into a reality. As you saw in previous examples, commands are objects inserted into a Screen. For example:

```
goCommand = new Command("Cancel", Command.SCREEN, 1);
myForm.addCommand(goCommand);
```

Note

For a full working example of using commands, check out the CommandListenTest.java source file on the CD.

This code creates a new command with the label Cancel and a type of Command.SCREEN.

There's a slightly better way to do this, though. You can use the command type to specify a system-dependant default action. In other words, you can have the UI decide the best way to display a typical command. Cancel is a good example of this; by specifying a command type of Command.CANCEL, you can leave it up to the UI to use its typical label. For example:

```
goCommand = new Command("Cancel", Command.CANCEL, 1);
```

Table 5.17 shows a full list of the command types.

Table 5.17 javax.microedition.lcdui.Command

Type	Description
Command Types	
BACK	Returns to the previous screen.
OK	Provides a standard way to say "yup!"
CANCEL	Provides a standard way to say "nuh!"
EXIT	Provides a standard application quit.
HELP	Asks for help.
ITEM	Hints to the UI that this command relates to an Item.
SCREEN	Indicates that the command is something you just made up.
STOP	Provides a standard way to issue a stop signal.
Methods	
Command(String label, int commandType, int priority)	Constructs a new command.
int getCommandType()	Returns the type of the command.
String getLabel()	Gets the label.
int getPriority()	Gets the priority.

The other parameter used in the construction of a command is the priority. The UI uses the priority as an indication of the order in which you would like commands displayed. Basically, the lower the number, the higher it is in the list.

Command Listeners

Having the user select a command is wonderful, but it's not going to do a lot unless you see that event and then do something about it. You can do this using command listeners.

To create a listener, you need to implement the—you guessed it—CommandListener interface. Thankfully it's an easy one to use. Here's an example of a simple MIDlet that listens for a command:

```java
import javax.microedition.midlet.*;
import javax.microedition.lcdui.*;


/**
 * A MIDlet that demonstrates how to use the CommandListener interface in
 * order to capture command events when triggerd by the user (such as when they
 * hit OK on a command item).
 *
 * @author Martin J. Wells
 */
public class CommandListenTest extends MIDlet implements CommandListener
{
    private Form form;          // form we'll display
    private Command quit;       // quit command added to form


    /**
     * Constructor for the MIDlet which instantiates the Form object then
     * populates it with a string and a "Quit" command.
     */
    public CommandListenTest()
    {
        // Setup the UI
        form = new Form("Listener");
        form.append("Do you wish to quit?");
        form.setCommandListener(this);

        // Create and add two commands to change the MIDlet state
        quit = new Command("Quit", Command.EXIT, 1);
        form.addCommand(quit);
```

```
}

/**
 * Called by the Application Manager when the MIDlet is starting or resuming
 * after being paused. In this example it acquires the current Display object
 * and uses it to set the Form object created in the MIDlet constructor as
 * the active Screen to display.
 * @throws MIDletStateChangeException
 */
protected void startApp() throws MIDletStateChangeException
{
    Display.getDisplay(this).setCurrent(form);
}

/**
 * Called by the MID's Application Manager to pause the MIDlet. A good
 * example of this is when the user receives an incoming phone call whilst
 * playing your game. When they're done the Application Manager will call
 * startApp to resume. For this example we don't need to do anything.
 */
protected void pauseApp()
{
}

/**
 * Called by the MID's Application Manager when the MIDlet is about to
 * be destroyed (removed from memory). You should take this as an opportunity
 * to clear up any resources and save the game.  For this example we don't
 * need to do anything.
 * @param unconditional if false you have the option of throwing a
 * MIDletStateChangeException to abort the destruction process.
 * @throws MIDletStateChangeException
 */
protected void destroyApp(boolean unconditional) throws MIDletStateChangeException
{
}

/**
 * The CommandListener interface method called when the user executes
 * a Command, in this case it can only be the quit command we created in the
 * constructor and added to the Form.
 * @param command
```

```
 * @param displayable
 */
public void commandAction(Command command, Displayable displayable)
{
    // output the command on the console
    System.out.println("commandAction(" + command + ", " + displayable +
                        ") called.");
    try
    {
        // compare the command object passed in to our quit command
        if (command == quit)
        {
            destroyApp(true);
            notifyDestroyed();
        }
    }

    catch (MIDletStateChangeException me)
    {
        System.out.println(me + " caught.");
    }
}
}
```

The first part of setting up a command listener is, of course, creating the listener class. For simplicity, your sample MIDlet class serves as both the application and the listener for commands. To do this, you implement the CommandListener interface using the following code:

```
public class CommandListenTest extends MIDlet implements CommandListener
```

To comply with this interface, you implement the commandAction method.

```
    public void commandAction(Command command, Displayable displayable)
```

Inside this method, you simply check which command object triggered the call and react accordingly.

```
        if (command == quit)
        {
            destroyApp(true);
            notifyDestroyed();
        }
```

Table 5.18 javax.microedition.lcdui.CommandListener

Method	Description
void commandAction (Command c, Displayable d)	The method called with Command c is executed on Displayable d.

High-Level UI

As described previously, the high-level UI provides an abstract interface to the MID. You'll get a lot of functionality by using it, without having to worry about the mechanics of handling the variety of devices on the market.

You use the high-level API by creating components, adding them to the screen, and then reacting to their results. All high-level UI components fall into two broad categories—screens and items.

Why Not AWT?

If you're familiar with Java GUI application development, you may ask why they didn't use the AWT (*Abstract Windowing Toolkit*) or a subset of it as the basis for the MIDP UI.

According to the MIDP specifications, the reason really comes down to the foundation of the AWT. Being designed for large-screen, general-purpose computers resulted in the following unsuitable characteristics.

- Many of the foundation features, such as window management and mouse-operated controls are not appropriate on MIDs.
- AWT is based around having some type of pointer device (mouse or pen); when this is removed, the entire design foundation of AWT is compromised.
- The design of AWT requires the instantiation and subsequent garbage collection of a large number of objects for some pretty basic operations.

Screens

As I covered earlier, screens are full class components that take up the entire interface (input and display). One of those screens, the Form, is special in that it gives you the ability to construct a screen using smaller subcomponents, also known as *items*. Figure 5.10 provides a breakdown of both the Screens and Form items available in the MIDP.

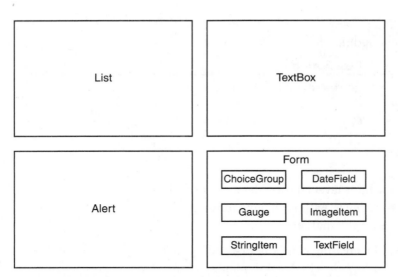

Figure 5.10 The Form screen can contain item components.

In the next section, you'll look at each of these screen objects. We'll leave the Form screen and its little friends until last.

List

A List (you can see the full API in Table 5.20) is a component that presents the user with a list of choices. (Imagine that!) The class implements the javax.microedition.lcdui.Choice interface. (The ChoiceGroup item also implements this interface.) Table 5.19 lists the three pre-defined choice types, and Figure 5.11 shows an example of these types.

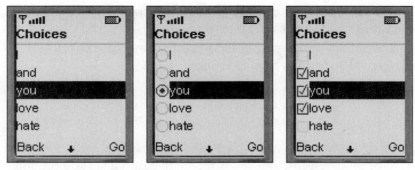

Figure 5.11 The three types of Lists as rendered by the default emulator.

Table 5.19 Choice Types

Type	Description
IMPLICIT	Provides a list of choices where selection generates a single event (a list).
EXCLUSIVE	Provides a list of choices with one selection at a time (radio buttons).
MULTIPLE	Provides a list of choices for multiple selections (check boxes).

Table 5.20 javax.microedition.lcdui.List

Method	Description
List (String title, int listType)	Constructs a list using the given title and list type.
List (String title, int listType, String[] stringElements, Image[] imageElements)	Constructs a list with a predefined set of options and corresponding images.
int append (String stringPart, Image imagePart)	Adds an element (choice) to the list (as well as an optional image).
void delete (int elementNum)	Removes an element.
void insert (int elementNum, String stringPart, Image imagePart)	Inserts an element (string and image) into the list.
void set (int elementNum, String stringPart, Image imagePart)	Directly sets an element's string and image.
Image getImage (int elementNum)	Returns the image associated with an element.
String getString (int elementNum)	Returns the string associated with an element.
boolean isSelected (int elementNum)	Returns a Boolean indicating whether a particular element is currently selected.
int getSelectedIndex ()	Returns the currently selected element index.
void setSelectedIndex (int elementNum, boolean selected)	Sets a selection by element index.
int getSelectedFlags (boolean[] selectedArray_return)	Fills in the current selection choices in a Boolean array.
void setSelectedFlags (boolean[] selectedArray)	Directly sets the selections based on an array of Booleans.
int size ()	Returns the number of elements in the list.

Take a look at the List component in action. In the example code that follows, you'll let the user select new words from a list. Each time the user selects an entry, it will be added to the underlying form. This example also illustrates nicely how a MIDlet switches screens.

```java
import javax.microedition.midlet.*;
import javax.microedition.lcdui.*;

import javax.microedition.midlet.*;
import javax.microedition.lcdui.*;

/**
 * A demonstration of a List screen.
 * @author Martin J. Wells
 */
public class ListTest extends MIDlet implements CommandListener
{
    private Form form;
    private Command quit;
    private Command add;
    private Command back;
    private Command go;
    private List list;

    /**
     * Constructor for the MIDlet which creates a List Screen and appends
     * a bunch of items on the list as well as a Form containing an Add
     * and Quit command.
     */
    public ListTest()
    {
        // Setup the UI
        String[] choices = { "I", "and", "you", "love", "hate",
                             "kiss", "bananas", "monkeys", "that" };

        list = new List("Choices", List.IMPLICIT, choices, null);
        go = new Command("Go", Command.OK, 1);
        back = new Command("Back", Command.BACK, 2);
        list.addCommand(go);
        list.addCommand(back);
        list.setCommandListener(this);
```

```
    // build the form
    form = new Form("Make-a-Story");
    add = new Command("Add", Command.SCREEN, 1);
    quit = new Command("Quit", Command.EXIT, 2);
    form.addCommand(add);
    form.addCommand(quit);
    form.setCommandListener(this);
}


/**
 * Called by the Application Manager when the MIDlet is starting or resuming
 * after being paused. In this example it acquires the current Display object
 * and uses it to set the Form object created in the MIDlet constructor as
 * the active Screen to display.
 * @throws MIDletStateChangeException
 */
protected void startApp() throws MIDletStateChangeException
{
    Display.getDisplay(this).setCurrent(form);
}


/**
 * Called by the MID's Application Manager to pause the MIDlet. A good
 * example of this is when the user receives an incoming phone call whilst
 * playing your game. When they're done the Application Manager will call
 * startApp to resume. For this example we don't need to do anything.
 */
protected void pauseApp()
{
}


/**
 * Called by the MID's Application Manager when the MIDlet is about to
 * be destroyed (removed from memory). You should take this as an opportunity
 * to clear up any resources and save the game. For this example we don't
 * need to do anything.
 * @param unconditional if false you have the option of throwing a
 * MIDletStateChangeException to abort the destruction process.
 * @throws MIDletStateChangeException
 */
```

```java
protected void destroyApp(boolean unconditional) throws MIDletStateChangeException
{
}


/**
 * The CommandListener interface method called when the user executes a
 * Command. This method handles the standard quit command as well as an add
 * command which triggers the display to be switched to the list. It then
 * handles commands from the list screen to either select an item or abort.
 * @param command the command that was triggered
 * @param displayable the displayable on which the event occurred
 */
public void commandAction(Command command, Displayable displayable)
{
    System.out.println("commandAction(" + command + ", " + displayable +
                       ") called.");
    try
    {
        // form handling
        if (displayable == form)
        {
            if (command == quit)
            {
                destroyApp(true);
                notifyDestroyed();
            }

            if (command == add)
            {
                Display.getDisplay(this).setCurrent(list);
            }
        }

        // list handling
        if (displayable == list)
        {
            if (command == go)
            {
                form.append(list.getString(list.getSelectedIndex()) + " ");
                Display.getDisplay(this).setCurrent(form);
            }
```

```
            if (command == back)
                Display.getDisplay(this).setCurrent(form);
        }

    }

    catch (MIDletStateChangeException me)
    {
        System.out.println(me + " caught.");
    }
}
}
```

You create the list using the following code within the MIDlet constructor:

```
String[] choices = { "I", "and", "you", "love", "hate",
                     "kiss", "bananas", "monkeys", "that" };
list = new List("Choices", List.IMPLICIT, choices, null);
```

This creates your List object with a preset list of choices from the array of strings. Since List is a screen, you also add commands to let the user take some action.

```
go = new Command("Go", Command.OK, 1);
back = new Command("Back", Command.BACK, 2);
list.addCommand(go);
list.addCommand(back);
list.setCommandListener(this);
```

Note that the listener is set to the MIDlet. If you look further down, you'll notice the form screen also sets its listener to the MIDlet. This is perfectly fine because your commandAction method can determine the screen (Displayable, actually) from which a command came.

```
public void commandAction(Command command, Displayable displayable)
{
...

    // form handling
    if (displayable == form)
    {
        if (command == quit)
        {
            ...
        }
    }

    // list handling
```

```
if (displayable == list)
{
    if (command == go)
    {
        form.append(list.getString(list.getSelectedIndex()) + " ");
        ...
    }
}
```

Note

This is a simple example dealing with a single-choice list. You can use both implicit and exclusive list types without any code change. However, multiple-type lists are a little bit different. You will need code to deal with multiple selections.

The real action here is the call to `list.getString(list.getSelectedIndex())`. This simply gets the currently selected item from the list. Figure 5.12 shows how it looks when it's running.

Figure 5.12 An example of a `List` in action.

And that's it! Next time you're out at a nightclub, swagger over to that hot chick at the bar and say, "I can present and select a J2ME LCDUI List any way I want, baby." Trust me; she'll be so impressed she won't know what to say.

TextBox

A `TextBox` component is the word processor of the micro world! Well, not really. It just lets you enter more than one line of text, but hey—what do you expect here?

The `TextBox` class has some great features (you can see the API in Table 5.21), however. You can have the player enter multiple lines of text; cut, copy, and paste from a clipboard (even across other components); and filter the data being entered (such as permitting only numbers).

Table 5.21 javax.microedition.lcdui.TextBox

Method	Description
TextBox (String title, String text, int maxSize, int constraints)	Constructs a new text box.
void delete (int offset, int length)	Deletes chars from an offset.
int getCaretPosition ()	Returns the current cursor position.
int getChars (char[] data)	Gets the contents of the TextBox as an array of chars.
int getConstraints ()	Returns the constraints.
int getMaxSize ()	Gets the maximum number of chars that can be stored in this TextBox.
String getString ()	Returns the current contents as a String.
void insert (char[] data, int offset, int length, int position)	Inserts text into the contents.
void insert (String src, int position)	Inserts text into the contents.
void setChars (char[] data, int offset, int length)	Replaces chars with new values.
void setConstraints (int constraints)	Changes the constraints.
int setMaxSize (int maxSize)	Changes the maximum size.
void setString (String text)	Sets the contents to a String.
int size ()	Returns the number of chars used.

Now I want to jump straight into an example of a TextBox in action, and then I'll walk you through the code.

```
import javax.microedition.midlet.*;
import javax.microedition.lcdui.*;

public class TextBoxTest extends MIDlet implements CommandListener
{
    private TextBox textBox;
    private Alert alert;
    private Command quit;
    private Command go;

    public TextBoxTest()
    {
        // Set up the UI
```

```java
        textBox = new TextBox("Enter Thy Name", "Sir ", 20, TextField.ANY);
        go = new Command("Go", Command.SCREEN, 1);
        quit = new Command("Quit", Command.EXIT, 2);
        textBox.addCommand(go);
        textBox.addCommand(quit);
        textBox.setCommandListener(this);
    }

    protected void startApp() throws MIDletStateChangeException
    {
        Display.getDisplay(this).setCurrent(textBox);
    }

    protected void pauseApp()
    {
    }

    protected void destroyApp(boolean unconditional) throws MIDletStateChangeException
    {
    }

    public void commandAction(Command command, Displayable displayable)
    {
        try
        {
            if (command == quit)
            {
                destroyApp(true);
                notifyDestroyed();
            }

            if (command == go)
            {
                alert = new Alert("", "Greetings " + textBox.getString(), null,
AlertType.CONFIRMATION);
                display.setCurrent(alert);
            }

        }

        catch (MIDletStateChangeException me)
        {
```

```
            System.out.println(me + " caught.");
        }
    }
}
```

This MIDlet will display a text box on startup, let you enter your name, and return a cute little greeting, as shown in Figure 5.13.

Figure 5.13 A TextBox in action.

The code should be getting rather familiar to you now. The constructor instantiates a new TextBox screen object and then adds quit and go commands.

```
textBox = new TextBox("Enter Thy Name", "Sir ", 20, TextField.ANY);
go = new Command("Go", Command.SCREEN, 1);
quit = new Command("Quit", Command.EXIT, 2);
textBox.addCommand(go);
textBox.addCommand(quit);
```

I already covered the rest of the example in previous sections, so I'll just skip to the guts of the result—the commandAction method handling of the go command.

```
alert = new Alert("", "Greetings " + textBox.getString(), null, AlertType.CONFIRMATION);
display.setCurrent(alert);
```

Here you're sneaking a look at the next section—the Alert screen. The code just grabs the current contents of the textBox object and displays them as an Alert.

You can also use constraints to restrict the input to the typical data types shown in Table 5.22. These are all pretty self-explanatory, but you should be aware that you can combine the password constraint with other types by using a logical OR. You can then use the CONTRAINT_MASK to strip out any constraint modifiers (such as the password) by using a logical AND.

Table 5.22 Text Entry Constraints

Constraint	Description
ANY	Provides no constraints.
EMAILADDR	Formats an e-mail address.
NUMERIC	Allows only numbers.
PASSWORD	Allows a hidden text entry.
PHONENUMBER	Allows a phone number.
URL	Allows a URL.
CONSTRAINT_MASK	Provides a mask constant used to separate constraints.

Alert

Remember Davros from *Dr. Who*? No evil ever conjured by Hollywood can top the might of the trundling Dalecs—lucky they didn't have stairs in the future. Using an MIDP Alert is sort of the same as when Dalecs stop and electronically excrete their "exterminate," but in a completely different and far more boring way.

You can think of an Alert as a very simple dialog box; you use it to display a message (and because an Alert is a screen, it takes over the entire screen). You can see the full API in Table 5.23 and the different types of Alerts in Table 5.24.

There are really only two categories of Alerts—one that displays for a set period and then kills itself, and one that waits for the user's acknowledgement. (The latter type is also known as a *modal* Alert.)

Creating an Alert is a relatively simple process. For example, in the previous section you created an alert when the user entered his name.

```
alert = new Alert("", "Greetings " + textBox.getString(), null, AlertType.CONFIRMATION);
display.setCurrent(alert);
```

This is a typical use for an Alert—to display a message to the user and then resume operations on another Displayable. Alerts are a little bit different from regular Displayables, however. First, they can't be the only items in your MIDlet. An Alert must be associated with a Displayable from which it was spawned (the default); otherwise, you have to identify specifically a Displayable onto which the Alert should fall back after the user has dismissed it.

Also, Alerts do not have commands, even though they are subclasses of Screen, which in turn is a subclass of Displayable. The methods relating to commands—namely addCommand, removeCommand, and setCommandListener, will trigger exceptions if called.

For an example of an Alert in action, see the previous "TextBox" section.

Table 5.23 javax.microedition.lcdui.Alert

Method	Description
Alert (String title)	Constructs a simple Alert that automatically disappears after a system-defined period of time.
Alert (String title, String alertText, Image alertImage, AlertType alertType)	Constructs an Alert using a title, message, image, and type.
int getDefaultTimeout ()	Gets the default timeout used by the MID.
Image getImage ()	Gets the Alert's image.
String getString ()	Gets the Alert's string.
int getTimeout ()	Gets the current timeout.
AlertType getType ()	Gets the current type.
void setImage (Image img)	Sets the image.
void setString (String str)	Sets the Alert message.
void setTimeout (int time)	Sets the timeout.
void setType (AlertType type)	Sets the type.
void addCommand (Command cmd)	Not available! Calling this will result in an exception.
void setCommandListener (CommandListener l)	Not available! Calling this will result in an exception.

Table 5.24 javax.microedition.lcdui.AlertType

Type	Description
ALARM	Alerts the user to an event for which he has previously requested notification.
CONFIRMATION	Confirms a user's action.
ERROR	Indicates that something bad happened.
INFO	Indicates something informative.
WARNING	Warns the user of something.
boolean playSound (Display display)	Plays the sound associated with an Alert without having to actually construct the Alert.

Forms and Items

A Form is a Screen that can contain one or more of the following components derived from the Item class—StringItem, ImageItem, TextField, ChoiceGroup, DateField, and Gauge.

To use a Form, you simply construct it like any other Screen, and then use the append, delete, insert, and set methods to manipulate the Items, images, and strings. Then it's up to the MID to determine exactly how items are laid out within the Form. (Typically they are laid out in a simple vertical list.)

Note

You can also add simple images and strings to a Form. However, these are just convenience methods that automatically construct the equivalent Item for you. For example:

```
form.append("hello")
Is actually identical to:
form.append(new StringItem("hello"))
```

This reinforces an important point: Only Items can exist in a Form.

Table 5.25 lists the full API for the Form class.

In previous examples, you saw some simple uses for Forms. For example, you might remember this usage:

```
form = new Form("Make-a-Story");
...
form.append(list.getString(list.getSelectedIndex()) + " ");
```

This simply constructs a new form and then appends a string to it.

Nothing too complicated, as far as I know. The fun stuff really starts when you let Items on the dance floor. As I've previously mentioned, there are six Items available (StringItem, ImageItem, TextField, ChoiceGroup, DateField, and Gauge). You can arbitrarily construct these and add them to a form. The trick to using Items lies in how you subsequently interact with them.

Table 5.25 javax.microedition.lcdui.Form

Method	Description
Form (String title)	Constructs a form with a given title.
Form (String title, Item[] items)	Constructs a form with a title, and that is pre-populated with an array of items.
int append (Image img)	Appends an image.
int append (Item item)	Appends an Item class object.
int append (String str)	Appends a string.
void delete (int itemNum)	Removes an item by index number.
Item get (int itemNum)	Returns an item by index number.
void insert (int itemNum, Item item)	Inserts a new item at a certain index.
void set (int itemNum, Item item)	Sets an item at a particular index.
void setItemStateListener (ItemStateListener iListener)	Sets a listener for changes in item states.
int size ()	Returns the number of items in the form.

Table 5.26 javax.microedition.lcdui.ItemStateListener

Method	Description
void itemStateChanged (Item item)	Called when an Item's state changes.

Items have their own event-handling mechanism that is quite different from the command structure used by screens. Each item can register an ItemStateListener (you can see the interface in Table 5.26) that will trigger a method call when—you guessed it—the state of the item changes. Take a look at an example.import javax.microedition.midlet.*;

```
import javax.microedition.lcdui.*;

import javax.microedition.midlet.*;
import javax.microedition.lcdui.*;

/**
 * A demonstration of a TextField.
 * @author Martin J. Wells
 */
public class TextFieldTest extends MIDlet implements CommandListener,
        ItemStateListener
{
    private Form form;
    private TextField textFieldItem;
    private Command quit;

    /**
     * MIDlet constructor that creates a form and then adds in a TextField item
     * and a quit command.
     */
    public TextFieldTest()
    {
        // Construct a form.
        form = new Form("Text Field Test");

        // Construct the textfield item and a quit command
        textFieldItem = new TextField("Enter text:", "", 10, TextField.ANY);
        quit = new Command("Quit", Command.EXIT, 2);

        // Add everything to the form.
        form.addCommand(quit);
```

```
    form.append(textFieldItem);

    // And register us as the listening for both commands and item state
    // changes.
    form.setCommandListener(this);
    form.setItemStateListener(this);
}


/**
 * Called by the Application Manager when the MIDlet is starting or resuming
 * after being paused. In this example it acquires the current Display object
 * and uses it to set the Form object created in the MIDlet constructor as
 * the active Screen to display.
 * @throws MIDletStateChangeException
 */
protected void startApp() throws MIDletStateChangeException
{
    Display.getDisplay(this).setCurrent(form);
}


/**
 * Called by the MID's Application Manager to pause the MIDlet. A good
 * example of this is when the user receives an incoming phone call whilst
 * playing your game. When they're done the Application Manager will call
 * startApp to resume. For this example we don't need to do anything.
 */
protected void pauseApp()
{
}


/**
 * Called by the MID's Application Manager when the MIDlet is about to
 * be destroyed (removed from memory). You should take this as an opportunity
 * to clear up any resources and save the game. For this example we don't
 * need to do anything.
 * @param unconditional if false you have the option of throwing a
 * MIDletStateChangeException to abort the destruction process.
 * @throws MIDletStateChangeException
 */
protected void destroyApp(boolean unconditional) throws MIDletStateChangeException
{
}
```

```
/**
 * This method is called as a result of the item's state be changed by the
 * user (ie. they entered some text). After checking we have the right item
 * we then popup a little alert acknowledging the event.
 * @param item
 */
public void itemStateChanged(Item item)
{
    System.out.println("item state changed for " + item);
    if (item == textFieldItem)
    {
        Display.getDisplay(this).setCurrent(
                new Alert("", "You said  " + textFieldItem.getString(),
                        null, AlertType.INFO));
    }
}


/**
 * The CommandListener interface method called when the user executes a
 * Command, in this case it can only be the quit command we created in the
 * constructor and added to the Form.
 * @param command the command that was triggered
 * @param displayable the displayable on which the event occurred
 */
public void commandAction(Command command, Displayable displayable)
{
    try
    {
        if (command == quit)
        {
            destroyApp(true);
            notifyDestroyed();
        }
    }

    catch (MIDletStateChangeException me)
    {
        System.out.println(me + " caught.");
    }
}
}
```

First you'll notice the addition of the ItemStateListener in the class's implements list. This is required to set your MIDlet to be a receiver of these events. (It's essentially the same as implementing the command listener.)

To comply with this interface, you then implement the method.

```
public void itemStateChanged(Item item)
```

This method is subsequently called when the user changes the state of the Item's value. And unlike what you'd expect from something like a Windows UI, it really *is* that simple.

Note

An Item cannot appear on more than one form. Doing so will result in an InvalidStateException being thrown.

In the next sections, you'll take a quick look at all of the available Items, including any idiosyncrasies they might have.

StringItem

A StringItem lets you add a simple text message to a form. It doesn't do much, really—the user can't edit the text, so you won't see any events. Table 5.27 lists the available methods.

There are two ways to add a StringItem to a form. The first method is the most obvious.

```
StringItem text = new StringItem("Label:", "Value");
form.append(text);
```

Figure 5.14 shows this StringItem in operation.

Figure 5.14 A StringItem in action.

As an alternative, you can also use

```
form.append("string");
```

The `append` method will automatically construct a new `StringItem` object using the string you pass it. If you don't plan to change the string (or its label) after you add it to the form, I'd recommend using this shortcut. However, if you really want, you can gain access to the `StringItem` by using the `Index` integer returned by the method. For example:

```
int stringItemIndex = form.append("string");
StringItem stringItem = form.get(stringItemIndex);
```

ImageItem and Image

`ImageItem` is similar to `StringItem`, except that it obviously lets you display images, rather than strings. However, in addition to simply containing an image, the `ImageItem` class provides tools to lay out where the image will appear on the screen.

Looking at the details of the `ImageItem` API in Table 5.28, you can see things are relatively simple. There are three essential functions—change the image, change the layout, or change the alternative text.

Table 5.27 javax.microedition.lcdui.StringItem

Method	Description
StringItem (String label, String text)	Constructs a new `StringItem` object using the supplied label and text.
String getText ()	Gets the current text.
void setText (java.lang.String text)	Sets the text.

Table 5.28 javax.microedition.lcdui.ImageItem

Method	Description
ImageItem (java.lang.String label, Image img, int layout, String altText)	Constructs a new `ImageItem`.
Image getImage ()	Gets the image associated with this `Item`.
void setImage (Image img)	Changes the image.
int getLayout ()	Gets the current layout for the `Item`.
void setLayout (int layout)	Changes the layout.
String getAltText ()	Gets the text to be displayed if the image could not be rendered on the device.
void setAltText (java.lang.String text)	Changes the alternative text.

You use a mixture of double-byte (int) values to control image layout. (Table 5.29 displays the full list of the preset values.) You should note that the first four values are all on the right side of the double-byte values, so you can't mix them. You can, however, combine the two NEWLINE layout values with the four primary controls. For example, the following lines are not valid:

```
// not a valid construct
ImageItem.LAYOUT_RIGHT | ImageItem.LAYOUT_CENTER
```

Not that you'd ever really want to do that, right? You can, however, do the following:

```
// valid construct
ImageItem.LAYOUT_NEWLINE_BEFORE | ImageItem.LAYOUT_RIGHT |
ImageItem.LAYOUT_NEWLINE_AFTER
```

The other attribute you can set on an ImageItem is the alternative text. This string will be displayed in place of the image if for some reason the MID couldn't render the image—perhaps due to limited display capabilities, insufficient space, or just because you looked at the MID the wrong way during lunch. This also applies to the layout controls. The MID will happily take your advice on how to do things, but in the end it's up to the MID to make it happen (in its own way).

Before you move on to an example of the ImageItem in action, I need to show you how to actually create an image.

The Image class (Table 5.30 shows the available methods) encapsulates an in-memory graphical image that exists independent of the display. Images are subsequently rendered to the display through an ImageItem, ChoiceGroup, List, or Alert.

Table 5.29 ImageItem Layout Modifiers

Method	Description
Mutually Exclusive	
LAYOUT_DEFAULT	Use the device implementation's default alignment.
LAYOUT_CENTER	Centers the image.
LAYOUT_RIGHT	Right-aligns the image.
LAYOUT_LEFT	Left-aligns the image.
Modifiers (Can be mixed with the modifiers above)	
LAYOUT_NEWLINE_AFTER	Adds a line break after displaying the image.
LAYOUT_NEWLINE_BEFORE	Adds a line break before displaying the image.

Table 5.30 javax.microedition.lcdui.Image

Method	Description
static Image createImage (byte[] imageData, int imageOffset, int imageLength)	Creates an immutable image from a byte array in PNG format.
static Image createImage (Image source)	Creates an immutable image from another image.
static Image createImage (int width, int height)	Creates a mutable image buffer of a set width and height.
static Image createImage (java.lang.String name)	Creates an immutable image from a PNG resource file.
Graphics getGraphics ()	Gets a graphics object for drawing on this image.
int getHeight ()	Gets the image's height.
int getWidth ()	Gets the image's width.
boolean isMutable ()	Determines whether the image is mutable.

Images come in two forms—immutable and mutable. An *immutable* image represents the static resource from which it was created (such as from a file stored in your JAR), whereas a *mutable* image can be changed through the low-level graphics system. Just to confuse you a little (because I'm that kind of guy), you can convert a mutable image into an immutable image, but not vice versa. You'll explore mutable images more when you look at the low-level UI. I'll even show you how to create a mutable image from an immutable one.

Looking at the Image API, you'll notice there are no constructors, only factory methods. To create an image, you need to use one of these create methods.

PNG is the only image-file format available. It is a compact, flexible, no-loss format most graphical applications will output happily for you. The following sample MIDlet creates an immutable image from a PNG file, and then adds it to a form through an ImageItem object.

Note

This example references the image file alienhead.png. You can obtain this from the CD in Chapter 5 source directory or alternatively replace the file with a PNG of your choice and then change the filename within the source. To work, the image file must be in the same directory as the MIDlet class file.

Tip

You can create a PNG image file using most popular graphics applications (such as Adobe Photoshop). For more information check out Chapter 9, "The Graphics".

```java
import javax.microedition.midlet.*;
import javax.microedition.lcdui.*;
import java.io.IOException;

/**
 * An example MIDlet that shows how to use an ImageItem
 *
 * @author Martin J. Wells
 */
public class ImageItemTest extends MIDlet implements CommandListener
{
    private Form form;
    private ImageItem imageItem;
    private Command quit;

    /**
     * Constructs the MIDlet by creating a Form object and then populating it
     * with an ImageItem and a quit command.
     */
    public ImageItemTest()
    {
        form = new Form("ImageItem Test");

        Image alienHeadImage = null;
        try
        {
            // Construct the imageitem item and a quit command
            alienHeadImage = Image.createImage("/alienhead.png");
        }
        catch(IOException ioe)
        {
            form.append("unable to load image");
        }


        // construct the image item using our alien head image and append it
        // to the form
        imageItem = new ImageItem(null, alienHeadImage, ImageItem.LAYOUT_RIGHT,
                                  null);
```

```
    form.append(imageItem);

    quit = new Command("Quit", Command.EXIT, 2);
    form.addCommand(quit);

    form.setCommandListener(this);
}


/**
 * Called by the Application Manager when the MIDlet is starting or resuming
 * after being paused. In this example it acquires the current Display object
 * and uses it to set the Form object created in the MIDlet constructor as
 * the active Screen to display.
 * @throws MIDletStateChangeException
 */
protected void startApp() throws MIDletStateChangeException
{
    Display.getDisplay(this).setCurrent(form);
}


/**
 * Called by the MID's Application Manager to pause the MIDlet. A good
 * example of this is when the user receives an incoming phone call whilst
 * playing your game. When they're done the Application Manager will call
 * startApp to resume. For this example we don't need to do anything.
 */
protected void pauseApp()
{
}


/**
 * Called by the MID's Application Manager when the MIDlet is about to
 * be destroyed (removed from memory). You should take this as an opportunity
 * to clear up any resources and save the game. For this example we don't
 * need to do anything.
 * @param unconditional if false you have the option of throwing a
 * MIDletStateChangeException to abort the destruction process.
 * @throws MIDletStateChangeException
 */
protected void destroyApp(boolean unconditional) throws MIDletStateChangeException
{
}
```

```
/**
 * The CommandListener interface method called when the user executes a
 * Command, in this case it can only be the quit command we created in the
 * constructor and added to the Form.
 * @param command
 * @param displayable
 */
public void commandAction(Command command, Displayable displayable)
{
    try
    {
        if (command == quit)
        {
            destroyApp(true);
            notifyDestroyed();
        }
    }

    catch (MIDletStateChangeException me)
    {
        System.out.println(me + " caught.");
    }
}
}
```

TextField

A TextField is a simple item for capturing text from the user. It's quite similar to its bigger screen-based cousin, TextBox. The differences really come down to TextField being a subclass of Item, and therefore being embeddable within a form. For example:

```
form.append(new TextField("Password:", "", 15, TextField.PASSWORD));
```

When used in a MIDlet, this field appears much like Figure 5.15.

For more information on using the features of a TextField, refer to the "TextBox" section. Table 5.31 lists all the methods available.

Figure 5.15 A TextField Item in action.

Table 5.31 javax.microedition.lcdui.TextField

Method	Description
`TextField (String label, String text, int maxSize, int constraints)`	Constructs a new `TextField`.
`int getConstraints ()`	Gets the constraints.
`void setConstraints (int constraints)`	Changes the constraints.
`void insert (char[] data, int offset, int length, int position)`	Inserts characters into the field.
`void insert (String src, int position)`	Inserts a string into the field.
`void delete (int offset, int length)`	Removes characters from the field.
`int getCaretPosition ()`	Retrieves the current cursor position.
`int getChars (char[] data)`	Gets the current contents of the field as a `char` array.
`void setChars (char[] data, int offset, int length)`	Sets the field using the contents of a `char` array.
`void setString (java.lang.String text)`	Sets the field using a string value.
`String getString ()`	Gets the current contents of the field as a string.
`int getMaxSize ()`	Gets the maximum size of the field.
`int setMaxSize (int maxSize)`	Changes the maximum size of the field.
`int size ()`	Gets the current number of characters in the field.

ChoiceGroup

`ChoiceGroup` is the other `Item` that has a big brother `Screen` equivalent (`List`) that you've already covered. Because you've been over most of the territory already, I'll just talk about the differences between `ChoiceGroup` and `List`.

Of course, the foremost difference is that one is a `Screen` class object and the other—`ChoiceGroup`—is a `Form`-embeddable `Item` class. In addition, unlike in a `List`, you cannot use the `IMPLICIT` control type because you don't have any access to the command events.

You might have wondered about the practical differences between the `IMPLICIT` and `EXCLU-SIVE` choice types. Typically, you'll find that `IMPLICIT` is for single-selection command `List`s, and `EXCLUSIVE` is for single-selection `ChoiceGroup`s. Both `ChoiceGroup` and `List` support the `MULTIPLE` choice type.

Table 5.32 lists all the methods available in the `ChoiceGroup` class.

Following is an example of using a `ChoiceGroup` in the form from the previous example:

```
form.append(new ChoiceGroup("Choose: ", Choice.MULTIPLE,
                new String[]{ "one", "two" }, null ));
```

Table 5.32 javax.microedition.lcdui.ChoiceGroup

Method	Description
`ChoiceGroup (String label, int choiceType)`	Constructs a new `ChoiceGroup`.
`ChoiceGroup (String label, int choiceType, String[] stringElements, Image[] imageElements)`	Constructs a `ChoiceGroup` using a preset list of elements and images.
`int append (String stringPart, Image imagePart)`	Appends a choice (and an associated image).
`void delete (int elementNum)`	Removes a choice.
`Image getImage (int elementNum)`	Returns the image associated with a choice.
`int getSelectedFlags (boolean[] selectedArray_return)`	Returns the selected choices. (This is only relevant when you are using `MULTIPLE`.)
`int getSelectedIndex ()`	Returns the currently selected choice.
`String getString (int elementNum)`	Gets the string associated with an element number.
`void insert (int elementNum, String stringElement, Image imageElement)`	Inserts a choice.
`boolean isSelected (int elementNum)`	Determines whether a choice is selected.
`void set (int elementNum, java.lang.String stringPart, Image imagePart)`	Changes a choice.
`void setSelectedFlags (boolean[] selectedArray)`	Changes the selected items.
`void setSelectedIndex (int elementNum, boolean selected)`	Selects a single entry.
`int public int size ()`	Returns the number of choices.

The output from this (see Figure 5.16) also demonstrates just how different forms are from screens. As you can see, the MID (in this case, the Sun WTK 1.04 emulator) has rendered both the password text field and the choice group on one screen.

DateField

A `DateField` (see Table 5.34 for the API) is one of those things you'll completely ignore until the day you need the player to enter a date (although this rarely occurs in games). I'll give you a quick rundown on using the `DateField`, just in case.

As detailed in Table 5.33, you can use three types of Date-Fields—one for entering just a calendar date, one for only the time, and one for both. However, this practically equates to only two entry types—date and time. Figure 5.17 presents an example of both types in action.

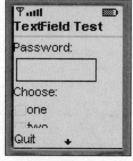

Figure 5.16 An example of a `Form` containing multiple `Items`, including a `ChoiceGroup`.

Table 5.33 DateField Types

Type	Description
DATE	Allows you to enter the calendar date.
DATE_TIME	Allows you to enter both a date and a time.
TIME	Allows you to enter just the time.

In the case of the DATETIME type, the MID generally will provide a way to access both of these types. Figure 5.18 presents an example of this.

You use the DateField item just like you did in the previous examples.

```
form.append(new DateField("Date of Birth?", DateField.DATE_TIME));
```

Figure 5.17 Examples of different DateField types.

Figure 5.18 An example of a DateField of type DATE_TIME.

Table 5.34 javax.microedition.lcdui.DateField

Method	Description
DateField (String label, int mode)	Constructs a new DateField using the specified label and mode.
DateField (String label, int mode, TimeZone timeZone)	Constructs a new DateField using the specified label, mode, and TimeZone.
Date getDate ()	Retrieves the date set in the field.
int getInputMode ()	Returns the field's mode.
void setDate (Date date)	Changes the date value.
void setInputMode (int mode)	Changes the input mode.

Gauge

A Gauge (see Table 5.35 for the list of methods) item lets you display graphically to the user the relative position of something. In other words, it's a cute little bar that shows where you are.

Table 5.35 javax.microedition.lcdui.Gauge

Methods	Description
Gauge (String label, boolean interactive, int maxValue, int initialValue)	Constructs a Gauge.
int getMaxValue ()	Gets the maximum value.
void setMaxValue (int maxValue)	Sets the maximum value.
int getValue ()	Gets the current value.
void setValue (int value)	Sets the current value.
boolean isInteractive ()	Returns a Boolean indicating whether this Gauge is interactive.

A Gauge is optionally interactive, meaning that it will act like an input control. A good example of this is the volume gauge on most mobile phones. In this case, you can slide the gauge value interactively between the minimum and maximum values. Figure 5.19 shows an example form containing both an interactive and a non-interactive Gauge (top and bottom, respectively).

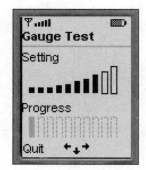

As you can see, the MID can draw interactive Gauges differently than non-interactive ones. The code to create these Gauges is

```
form.append(new Gauge("Setting", true, 10, 1));
form.append(new Gauge("Progress", false, 10, 1));
```

Figure 5.19 Examples of Gauge in action.

You can see that in both examples I've used a maximum value of 10 and a starting (default) value of 1. These values could be pretty much any mix; for example, you could have a maximum of 500 and a starting value of 250. However, keep in mind that every value in this range is represented (not just the number of bars that happen to be displayed), so with numbers that high you'll be hitting the arrow for quite a while before you visually move even one bar.

Low-Level UI

Let me tell you a little about myself. I live in a mansion with endless servants to do my every bidding, 24 hours a day. And I do mean every bidding—I don't have to do anything, ever. No need to clean, dress, or even feed myself. They take care of it all.

If I want to go for a swim in my Olympic-sized, gold-plated, chocolate-milk-filled pool, I have a servant hold my body in place while other servants flap my arms and legs about in a swimming motion. Life's tough. Sure, I have to ask for things to be done, but I'm happy to leave the details to my servants.

All right, this story isn't about me (no . . . really). In fact, it's actually (metaphorically, at least), about your MIDlet. Up until now, it has led a princely life in which things are pretty much all done for it. It just makes requests to create elements on the user interface, and the butler—oops, MID—takes care of getting the job done.

Unfortunately, this is also boring as hell. You have no real power to do things your way, and that just isn't practical for game development. The low-level UI provides a toolkit to move and draw graphics, render fonts, and capture direct key events—just what you need to make that chocolate-milk-swimming-pool racing game.

Canvas

Two classes really make up the low-level UI engine—Canvas (see Table 5.36 for the API) and Graphics (see Table 5.37 for the API). The Canvas is a Displayable object (just like the high-level UI's screen object) that serves as the target for all your graphical activities. The Graphics object (or to be more accurate, the *context*) is your palette of tools with which to draw. You can see this relationship in Figure 5.20.

You'll explore the details of the Graphics object in a little while. First, take a look at how you create and then display a Canvas Displayable.

You don't create a Canvas like you create other Displayable objects. It serves as a base class from which you derive your own custom drawing object. The Canvas base class provides all the tools, and you need to add the content. The only method you need to implement in your derived Canvas class is

```
protected void paint(Graphics graphics)
```

This method is responsible for rendering or drawing the Canvas control on the screen.

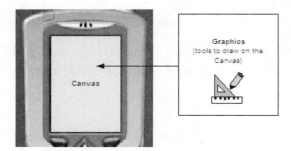

Figure 5.20 Use a Graphics object to draw on a Canvas.

Table 5.36 javax.microedition.lcdui.Canvas

Method	Description
General Methods	
int getGameAction (int keyCode)	Gets the game action associated with a key code.
int getKeyCode (int gameAction)	Gets the key code associated with a game action.
String getKeyName (int keyCode)	Gets the name of a device key (identified by a key code).
int getWidth ()	Returns the display's width.
int getHeight ()	Returns the display's height.
boolean hasPointerEvents ()	Determines whether the device supports pointer press and release events.
boolean hasPointerMotionEvents ()	Determines whether the device supports dragging events.
boolean hasRepeatEvents ()	Checks whether the device will return multiple events if a key is held down.
boolean isDoubleBuffered ()	Gets whether the device graphics are double buffered.
Event Response Methods	
abstract void paint (Graphics g)	Called when the canvas needs repainting.
void hideNotify ()	Called when the canvas has been hidden.
void showNotify ()	Called when you are back in the action.
void keyPressed (int keyCode)	Called when a key has been pressed.
void keyRepeated (int keyCode)	Called when a key begins repeating (when it's held down).
void keyReleased (int keyCode)	Called when a key has stopped repeating (when the key is no longer held down).
void pointerDragged (int x, int y)	Called when the pointer is dragged.
void pointerPressed (int x, int y)	Called when the pointer is pressed.
void pointerReleased (int x, int y)	Called when the pointer is released.
void repaint()	Requests a repaint of the Canvas.
void repaint(int x, int y, int width, int height)	Requests a repaint of only a specified portion of the Canvas.
void serviceRepaints()	Requests that any pending repaint requests be handled as soon as possible.

In the following example, you'll subclass the Canvas object, override the paint method, and then create a work of art involving some rectangles and more shades of gray than a retirement home.

```
import javax.microedition.midlet.*;
import javax.microedition.lcdui.*;
import java.util.Random;
```

```java
/**
 * A MIDlet that demonstrates the basic use of the Canvas class by loading
 * and drawing an image. Note that for this to work you must have the
 * alienhead.png file in the directory where you execute the class.
 *
 * @author Martin J. Wells
 */
public class CanvasTest extends MIDlet implements CommandListener
{
    private MyCanvas myCanvas;
    private Command quit;
    private Command redraw;

    /**
     * An inner class used to customize a Canvas for our needs.
     */
    class MyCanvas extends Canvas
    {
        private Random randomizer = new Random();

        /**
         * @return A simple random range finder (returns a random value between
         * an upper and lower range)
         */
        private int getRand(int min, int max)
        {
            int r = Math.abs(randomizer.nextInt());
            return (r % (max - min)) + min;
        }

        /**
         * Called by the Application Manager when the Canvas needs repainting.
         * This implementation uses the drawImage method to render the previously
         * loaded alienHeadImage.
         * @param graphics The graphics context for this Canvas
         */
        protected void paint(Graphics graphics)
        {
            for (int i=10; i > 0; i--)
            {
                graphics.setGrayScale(getRand(1,254));
                graphics.fillRect(0, 0, i*(getWidth()/10), i*(getHeight()/10));
```

```
            }
        }
    }

    /**
     * Constructor for the MIDlet that firstly loads up a PNG image from a file
     * then constructs the instance of our MyCanvas class and adds a quit and
     * redraw command and sets this MIDlet to be the listener for Command events.
     */
    public CanvasTest()
    {
        // Construct the canvas
        myCanvas = new MyCanvas();

        // we still need a way to quit
        quit = new Command("Quit", Command.EXIT, 2);
        myCanvas.addCommand(quit);

        // and a redraw trigger
        redraw = new Command("Redraw", Command.SCREEN, 1);
        myCanvas.addCommand(redraw);

        myCanvas.setCommandListener(this);
    }

    /**
     * Called by the Application Manager when the MIDlet is starting or resuming
     * after being paused. In this example it acquires the current Display object
     * and uses it to set the Canvas object created in the MIDlet constructor as
     * the active Screen to display.
     * @throws MIDletStateChangeException
     */
    protected void startApp() throws MIDletStateChangeException
    {
        Display.getDisplay(this).setCurrent(myCanvas);
    }

    /**
     * Called by the MID's Application Manager to pause the MIDlet. A good
     * example of this is when the user receives an incoming phone call whilst
     * playing your game. When they're done the Application Manager will call
     * startApp to resume. For this example we don't need to do anything.
```

```
 */
protected void pauseApp()
{
}


/**
 * Called by the MID's Application Manager when the MIDlet is about to
 * be destroyed (removed from memory). You should take this as an opportunity
 * to clear up any resources and save the game. For this example we don't
 * need to do anything.
 * @param unconditional if false you have the option of throwing a
 * MIDletStateChangeException to abort the destruction process.
 * @throws MIDletStateChangeException
 */
protected void destroyApp(boolean unconditional) throws MIDletStateChangeException
{
}


/**
 * The CommandListener interface method called when the user executes
 * a Command, in this case it can be the quit command, in which case we exit
 * or the redraw command, in which case we call MyCanvas repaint method which
 * will in turn cause it to be redrawn through the implement paint method.
 * @param command
 * @param displayable
 */
public void commandAction(Command command, Displayable displayable)
{
    try
    {
        if (command == redraw)
        {
            // ask the canvas to redraw itself
            myCanvas.repaint();
        }

        if (command == quit)
        {
            destroyApp(true);
            notifyDestroyed();
        }
    }
```

```
    catch (MIDletStateChangeException me)
    {
        System.out.println(me + " caught.");
    }
    }
}
```

This MIDlet will look something like Figure 5.21 when it is run.

Take a look at how this MIDlet works. You'll notice the addition of the MyCanvas inner class. As you can see, it extends the javax.microedition.lcdui.Canvas abstract base class.

Figure 5.21 An example using the low-level API to draw shaded rectangles.

```
class MyCanvas extends Canvas
{
    ...

    protected void paint(Graphics graphics)
    {
        for (int i=10; i > 0; i--)
        {
            graphics.setGrayScale(getRand(1,254));
            graphics.fillRect(0, 0, i*(getWidth()/10), i*(getHeight()/10));
        }
    }
}
```

Everything happens in the overridden paint method. Using the passed Graphics object, you set a random drawing color (or shade of gray, to be exact), and then render ever-larger rectangles as you progress through the for loop.

The MIDlet constructor then creates your Canvas using

```
myCanvas = new MyCanvas();
```

As you can see, creating a Canvas is a relatively painless process. But it's a bit like a blank sheet of paper—the real fun is in drawing. That's where the Graphics class rips its pants off and jumps in the Jacuzzi.

Graphics

As you saw in the previous example, you use the Graphics class's tools to carry out basic 2D rendering on a Canvas.

Table 5.37 javax.microedition.lcdui.Graphics

Method	Description
Color	
int getColor ()	Gets the currently set color.
void setColor (int RGB)	Changes the current drawing color.
void setColor (int red, int green, int blue)	Changes the current drawing color.
int getRedComponent ()	Gets the red component (0–255) of the current drawing color.
int getGreenComponent ()	Gets the green component (0–255) of the current drawing color.
int getBlueComponent ()	Gets the blue component (0–255) of the current drawing color.
void setGrayScale (int value)	Sets the current grayscale drawing color.
int getGrayScale ()	Gets the current grayscale drawing color.
Coordinates	
int getTranslateX ()	Returns the current translated X origin.
int getTranslateY ()	Returns the current translated Y origin.
void translate (int x, int y)	Translates the origin in the current graphics context.
Images and Clipping	
void clipRect (int x, int y, int width, int height)	Sets the current clipping rectangle.
int getClipHeight ()	Gets the current clipping-rectangle height.
int getClipWidth ()	Gets the current clipping-rectangle width.
int getClipX ()	Gets the current X offset of the clipping rectangle.
int getClipY ()	Gets the current Y offset of the clipping rectangle.
void setClip (int x, int y, int width, int height)	Intersects the current clipping rectangle with the one passed to the method.
2D Geometry	
void drawArc (int x, int y, int width, int height, int startAngle, int arcAngle)	Draws an arc.
void drawImage (Image img, int x, int y, int anchor)	Renders an image at a certain position.
void drawLine (int x1, int y1, int x2, int y2)	Draws a line.
void drawRect (int x, int y, int width, int height)	Draws a rectangle.
void drawRoundRect (int x, int y, int width, int height, int arcWidth, int arcHeight)	Draws a rounded rectangle.
void fillArc (int x, int y, int width, int height, int startAngle, int arcAngle)	Draws a filled arc.

Table 5.37 javax.microedition.lcdui.Graphics *(continued)*

Method	Description
void fillRect (int x, int y, int width, int height)	Draws a filled rectangle.
void fillRoundRect (int x, int y, int width, int height, int arcWidth, int arcHeight)	Draws a filled, rounded rectangle.
int getStrokeStyle ()	Gets the current stroke style.
void setStrokeStyle (int style)	Sets the current stroke style.
Strings and Fonts	
void drawString (String str, int x, int y, int anchor)	Renders a String.
void drawSubstring (String str, int offset, int len, int x, int y, int anchor)	Renders only part of a String.
void drawChar (char character, int x, int y, int anchor)	Draws a single character.
void drawChars (char[] data, int offset, int length, int x, int y, int anchor)	Draws an array of characters.
Font getFont ()	Gets the current drawing font.
void setFont (Font font)	Sets the current drawing font.

Coordinates

Before you go much further, you really need to understand exactly which way is up in MIDP. The most basic thing is the position of the origin point on the display (also known as 0, 0). As you can see in Figure 5.22, from this point the X and Y mapping of the display should be very much what you're used to.

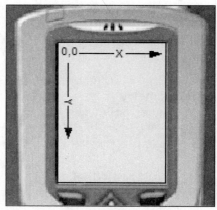

Figure 5.22 Graphics coordinates start at position (0, 0) in the top-left corner of the screen and progress along the X- and Y axes.

All of the draw methods you'll explore later in the chapter take coordinates according to this format. However, there are occasions when you might want to change the origin on the screen. In effect, you can change the world, and thus the position of everything, without changing where things are drawn in real X, Y coordinate terms. For example:

```
graphics.drawRect(25, 25, 10, 10 );
```

This code will result in a rectangle appearing at position (25, 25) and extending for 10 pixels in both directions. Now I'm going to change the nature of the universe itself and add an origin translation of 50 pixels on the Y-axis only.

```
graphics.translate(0, 50);
graphics.drawRect(25, 25, 10, 10 );
```

As you can see in Figure 5.23, the second rectangle is now drawn lower on the screen, at the (translated) coordinates (0+25, 50+25).

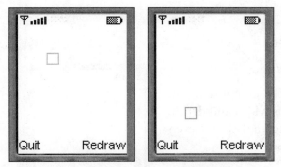

Figure 5.23 Using translate to shift the drawing origin.

You should note that multiple calls to translate are cumulative for the same Canvas. Therefore, the following code will set a translation of (20, 70), not (20, 20):

```
graphics.translate(0, 50);
graphics.translate(20, 20);
```

You can also use negative numbers to adjust the translation. If you want to adjust the absolute position, you need to offset the translation by the current value. For example, if you want to clear any translation, you use:

```
graphics.translate(-graphics.getTranslateX(), -graphics.getTranslateY())
```

2D Drawing Tools

There is a host of simple drawing tools you can use to render onto a Canvas, including: lines, rectangles, and arcs. Let's start on the easy one first and draw a line.

The drawLine method takes four parameters—the X and Y coordinates of the line's starting position and the X and Y coordinates of the end of the line. For example:

```
graphics.drawLine(50, 0, 100, 0);
```

This code will draw a line from position (50, 0) to (100, 0). Unfortunately, I've waited for lunch in more attractive lines than this one, so why don't we spice it up a bit with some color and style?

You can change the current rendering color using the setColor method. Keep in mind this will change the color for everything rendered from that point forward. You can also change the line stroke using the setStroke method to change the style to DOTTED. (The default line stroke is SOLID.) For example, the following code will render a dashed line in bright red:

```
graphics.setStrokeStyle(Graphics.DOTTED);
graphics.setColor(255, 0, 0);
graphics.drawLine(50, 0, 50, 100);
```

Figure 5.24 shows the far more appealing result.

Drawing a rectangle is a very similar process, except that you need to specify things in terms of origin plus width and depth. You can also draw transparent or filled rectangles, and even give them rounded corners (for you Mac users).

The four rectangle methods are drawRect, drawRoundedRect, fill-Rect, and fillRoundedRect. I'll leave you to play around with the results from these. However, I think the arc drawing tools need a little explaining. First, take a look at one in action. The following code will create a red semicircle.

Figure 5.24 An example line drawn using the DOTTED line style.

```
graphics.setColor(255, 0, 0);
graphics.drawArc(25, 25, 50, 50, 90, 180);
```

The output will appear similar to Figure 5.25.

An arc is drawn using six parameters. The first four are the bounding box of the entire circle of the arc.

The other two parameters are startAngle and arcAngle. These relate to the portion of the circle that you want drawn, where an Angle is the number of degrees starting with 0 at right side (at three o'clock) and 180 on the left side (at nine o'clock). Figure 5.27 illustrates these angles.

Figure 5.25 An example of an arc drawn using the drawArc method.

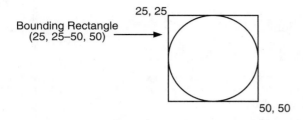

Figure 5.26 The dimensions of an arc are described using six parameters.

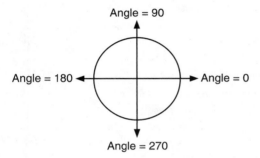

Figure 5.27 The directions represented by angles in the LCDUI.

Drawing Text

You can draw text onto a Canvas using the methods drawChar, drawChars, drawString, and drawSubstring. The major modifier when drawing text is the font used. The font support included with MIDP is vastly simplified compared to typical GUIs. The Font class (you can see the API in Table 5.38) represents both a font and its corresponding metrics.

To save resources, you don't get to create a Font object; it exists in the MID by default. You must acquire a reference to one in order to use it. The getFont method serves this purpose. For example, the following code gets a system font and then sets it to be the current font for all future text-drawing calls:

```
protected void paint(Graphics graphics)
{
    Font f = graphics.getFont(FACE_MONOSPACE, STYLE_BOLD, SIZE_MEDIUM);
    graphics.setFont(f);}
```

Table 5.38 javax.microedition.lcdui.Font

Method	Description
`static Font getFont (int face, int style, int size)`	Gets a system font.
`Font getDefaultFont ()`	Gets the default font.
`int getBaselinePosition ()`	Returns the font's baseline.
`int getFace ()`	Returns the face.
`int getHeight ()`	Gets the font's pixel height.
`int getSize ()`	Returns one of the SIZE constant values representing the font size.
`int getStyle ()`	Returns one of the STYLE constant values representing the style in use.
`boolean isBold ()`	Returns true if the font is bold.
`boolean isItalic ()`	Returns true if the font is italics.
`boolean isPlain ()`	Return true if none of the boys like this font.
`boolean isUnderlined ()`	Returns true if the font is underlined.
`int charsWidth (char[] ch, int offset, int length)`	Gets the pixel width of a `char` array.
`int charWidth (char ch)`	Gets the pixel width of a single `char`.
`int stringWidth (String str)`	Gets the pixel width of a `String`.
`int substringWidth (java.lang.String str, int offset, int len)`	Gets the pixel width of a substring.

Notice the lack of a font name string or font size integer? This really brings home the point that you're just retrieving a standard font from the MID's rather limited library. Table 5.39 shows the full list of font types. (No, really . . . that's all you get.)

To draw using the current font, the most convenient method is drawString. For example, the following code will acquire the default font and then render a string in a rather pleasant shade of blue:

```
protected void paint(Graphics graphics)
{
    graphics.setColor(100, 100, 255);
    graphics.setFont(Font.getDefaultFont());
    graphics.drawString( "Default font", 0, 0, Graphics.TOP | Graphics.LEFT);
}
```

Table 5.39 Font Types

Method	Description
Font Faces (Mutually Exclusive)	
FACE_MONOSPACE	Produces monospaced characters.
FACE_PROPORTIONAL	Produces proportional characters.
FACE_SYSTEM	Produces default system characters.
Font Sizes (Mutually Exclusive)	
SIZE_LARGE	Produces large characters.
SIZE_MEDIUM	Produces medium characters.
SIZE_SMALL	Produces small characters.
Font Styles (Can Be Mixed)	
STYLE_BOLD	Produces bold characters.
STYLE_ITALIC	Produces italicized characters.
STYLE_PLAIN	Produces plain characters.
STYLE_UNDERLINED	Produces underlined characters.

I'm using a shortcut here as well. Font.getDefaultFont() will get you the device's default font for display; typically this is a good one to use. Next you'll take this a little further and draw strings using three different font sizes.

```
protected void paint(Graphics graphics)
{
    graphics.setColor(100, 100, 255);

    int y = 0;
    graphics.setFont(Font.getDefaultFont());

    // draw the first string at position 0, 0
    graphics.drawString("Default font", 0, 0, Graphics.TOP | Graphics.LEFT);

    // move our y axis down by the height of the current font
    y += graphics.getFont().getHeight();

    // change to a SMALL size font
    graphics.setFont(Font.getFont(Font.FACE_SYSTEM, Font.STYLE_PLAIN,  Font.SIZE_SMALL));
    graphics.drawString("System, plain, small", 0, y, Graphics.TOP | Graphics.LEFT);
```

```
    // move our y axis down by the (now different) height of the current font
    y += graphics.getFont().getHeight();

    // change to a MEDIUM size font
    graphics.setFont(Font.getFont(Font.FACE_SYSTEM, Font.STYLE_PLAIN, Font.SIZE_MEDIUM));
    graphics.drawString("System, plain, medium", 0, y, Graphics.TOP | Graphics.LEFT);

    // move our y axis down by the (now different) height of the current font
    y += graphics.getFont().getHeight();

    // and finally change to a LARGE size font
    graphics.setFont(Font.getFont(Font.FACE_SYSTEM, Font.STYLE_PLAIN, Font.SIZE_LARGE));
    graphics.drawString("System, plain, large", 0, y, Graphics.TOP | Graphics.LEFT);
}
```

This code will produce the results shown in Figure 5.28.

If you look carefully, you'll notice I'm maintaining a Y-axis variable to determine where the next line of text is drawn. This illustrates a good practice: Because you can't be sure of the implementation size of a given font, you should always deal in relative terms—in this case by asking the font for its height. You can accomplish a similar task horizontally using the Font.getWidth method.

Figure 5.28 An example of different fonts in use.

Now that you've seen some of the fonts in action, look a little closer at those drawString calls, particularly the last parameter—the anchor point. Table 5.40 lists the various anchor points available. As you can see, there are two distinct types— horizontal and vertical. You must include one from each in any anchor you specify. For example, the following is not valid:

```
// Warning: NOT a valid anchor point
graphics.drawString("Monkeys", 0, y, Graphics.LEFT);
Whereas the following is valid:
// OK, since both the X-axis and Y-axis anchor point modifiers are specified
graphics.drawString("Monkeys", 0, y, Graphics.LEFT | Graphics.TOP);
```

An anchor point's role is to adjust the origin of the text's bounding box. Therefore, when you specify an anchor point horizontally RIGHT, you are in fact moving the X origin all the way to the right of the text.

Table 5.40 Font Anchor-Point Types

Type	Description
Horizontal Modifiers	
HCENTER	Horizontally centers the text
LEFT	Anchors text from the left
RIGHT	Anchors text from the right
Vertical Modifiers	
TOP	Anchors text from the top
BOTTOM	Anchors text from the bottom
BASELINE	Anchors text from the baseline
VCENTER	Vertically centers the text

Images and Clipping

You've seen images used before, when you looked at the ImageItem class. Drawing images in a Canvas is even easier. Simply construct an image and use the drawImage methods to display it. For example:

```
try
{
    // Construct the image
    alienHeadImage = Image.createImage("/alienhead.png");
}
catch (IOException ioe)
{
    System.out.println("unable to load image");
}
...
protected void paint(Graphics graphics)
{
    graphics.drawImage(alienHeadImage, 0, 0, Graphics.LEFT|Graphics.TOP);
}
```

The image created in this example is immutable—in other words, it's designed to stay static. The other type of image (mutable) allows modification at run time. You can use graphics tools to draw on a mutable image. That way, you can construct your own images for later use. Here's an example of a mutable image:

```
// construct a mutable image 50 x 50 pixels
Image i = Image.createImage(50, 50);
```

```
// use the image's graphics object to render a rectangle (note that I am NOT using the
Canvas. The Image object has its own graphics object that we can use to render onto the
actual image)
i.getGraphics().fillRect(0, 0, 49, 49);
// output the results to the canvas's grtaphics object
graphics.drawImage(i, 0, 0, Graphics.LEFT|Graphics.TOP);
```

The first thing you do is create an empty image with a width and height of 50 pixels. Then you do something strange: You ask the image for a graphics object! This illustrates an important concept. As you can see, you can use the image's own graphics object to draw the rectangle. You can then use that graphics object to scribble like a three-year-old.

The important concept here is that you're doing it away from the current display. This means that not only can you prepare things out of the user's sight, but you can also reuse them any time you want, thus saving the time to re-render the image.

Okay, I think you're ready for some serious action, so let's crank it up a gear. See if you can keep up with me.

```
// create a mutable image
Image i = Image.createImage(50, 50);

// get a reference to the image's graphics object
Graphics ig = i.getGraphics();

// set up some positions to make life easier
int centerX = i.getWidth()/2;
int centerY = i.getHeight()/2;

// draw our immutable image onto a mutable one
ig.drawImage(alienHeadImage, centerX, centerY, Graphics.VCENTER | Graphics.HCENTER);

// render two lines
ig.setColor(200, 0, 0);
ig.drawLine(0, 0, i.getWidth()-1, i.getHeight()-1);
ig.drawLine(i.getWidth()-1, 0, 0, i.getHeight()-1);

// get the font
Font f = Font.getFont(Font.FACE_PROPORTIONAL, Font.STYLE_BOLD, Font.SIZE_SMALL);
ig.setFont(f);

// render the text horizontally centered by adjusting the X starting
// draw position by half the string's width in pixels
String text1 = "Say NO to";
```

```
ig.drawString(text1, centerX - (f.stringWidth(text1)/2), 1,
              Graphics.LEFT | Graphics.TOP);
text1 = "Aliens";
ig.drawString(text1, centerX - (f.stringWidth(text1)/2), i.getHeight()-    f.getH-
eight(), Graphics.LEFT | Graphics.TOP);

// ready! Send it to the canvas.
graphics.drawImage(i, 0, 0, Graphics.LEFT|Graphics.TOP);
```

Figure 5.29 illustrates the output from this code. (We're all ready for our anti-aliens demonstration.) In this example, the first thing you do is create your mutable image and set up some convenience variables, such as the location of the center of the image.

Next you do something you're going to find very useful in the future—you turn that resource-loaded immutable image into a mutable one! It's easy to do; you just draw the image onto the mutable one. Once you have this, you go on to render two red lines over the top of the image and then the text.

Figure 5.29 An example of an Image that we've drawn onto using its `Graphics` object.

Also notice the way you rendered the text. I wanted to center it horizontally on the image, so I adjusted the starting position by exactly half its pixel width using the `Font.stringWidth` method.

Before you move on, there's one last thing to cover with regard to drawing images—clipping. Clipping lets you limit graphical output to only a certain area on the display. For example, if I were to set a clipping region starting at 10, 10 and extending to 50, 50, then from that point on, no graphics output would appear in any other part of the display.

To set a clipping region, you use the `setClip` method. For example, add the following clipping rectangle to the previous code:

```
// get a reference to the image's graphics object
Graphics imageGraphics = i.getGraphics();
imageGraphics.setClip(10, 10, 30, 30);
```

As illustrated in Figure 5.30, with this clipping region set, you'll find that much of the output from the previous example no longer appears.

You can also adjust the current clipping rectangle to create multiple clipping regions using the `clipRect` method.

Figure 5.30 An example of an image drawn with clipping bounds set.

Event Handling

As you've seen, you get input from user commands. However, this isn't a practical interface for moving a spaceship around the screen. The low-level UI provides the ability to capture direct key (and pointer) events that are automatically generated by the device.

I want to start with capturing and responding to key events. The setup in your MIDlet for this is surprisingly little. All you need to do is implement one or more of the key event notification methods: keyPressed, keyReleased, or keyRepeated. The MID will then call these methods when the input event occurs (in other words, when the key is pressed, released, or held down).

Note

Some devices don't support repeating keys, so you might not see any calls to keyRepeated. To determine support for repeating keys, check the Boolean returned by the hasRepeatEvents method.

The key event notification methods include an integer representing the input key. Table 5.41 lists the constants that map these integers to keys on the devices. Notice something weird? I don't know about you, but the last time I looked, I couldn't find the Fire key on my mobile phone. The device-mapped keys (also known as *action keys*) are set by the MID on the most appropriate keypad options, as a convenience to us game programmers. (Aren't they nice?)

Table 5.41 Key Event Codes

Key Event	Description	Key Event	Description
Default Keys		**Device Mapped Keys (Actions)**	
KEY_NUM0	Numerical keypad 0	UP	Up arrow
KEY_NUM1	Numerical keypad 1	DOWN	Down arrow
KEY_NUM2	Numerical keypad 2	LEFT	Left arrow
KEY_NUM3	Numerical keypad 3	RIGHT	Right arrow
KEY_NUM4	Numerical keypad 4	FIRE	A fire button
KEY_NUM5	Numerical keypad 5	GAME_A	Game function A
KEY_NUM6	Numerical keypad 6	GAME_B	Game function B
KEY_NUM7	Numerical keypad 7	GAME_C	Game function C
KEY_NUM8	Numerical keypad 8	GAME_D	Game function D
KEY_NUM9	Numerical keypad 9		
KEY_POUND	#		
KEY_STAR	*		

The convenience methods getKeyCode, getKeyName, and getGameAction let you retrieve the name of a key event or action, and vice versa. Take a look at keys in action:

```java
import javax.microedition.midlet.*;
import javax.microedition.lcdui.*;

/**
 * A MIDlet demonstrating how to read and interpret key events from a device.
 * @author Martin J. Wells
 */
public class KeyEventTest extends MIDlet implements CommandListener
{
    private MyCanvas myCanvas;
    private Command quit;

    /**
     * A custom Canvas class we use to draw a string based on a screen
     * position modified by key events.
     */
    class MyCanvas extends Canvas
    {
        private String lastKeyName = "Hit a Key"; // name of the last key they hit
        private int x = 0; // current position
        private int y = 0;

        /**
         * Overriden Canvas.paint method that draws a string at the current
         * position (x, y).
         * @param graphics The graphics context for this Canvas
         */
        protected void paint(Graphics graphics)
        {
            // draw a black rectangle the size of the screen in order to wipe
            // all previous contents
            graphics.setColor(255, 255, 255);
            graphics.fillRect(0, 0, getWidth(), getHeight());

            // draw the string (the name of the last key that was hit)
            graphics.setColor(0, 0, 0);
            graphics.drawString(lastKeyName, x, y, Graphics.LEFT | Graphics.TOP);
        }

        /**
         * Overriden Canvas method called when a key is pressed on the MID. This
         * method sets the key name string and then modifies the position if a
```

```java
     * directional key was hit.
     * @param keyCode the code of the key that was pressed
     */
    protected void keyPressed(int keyCode)
    {
        if (keyCode > 0)
            lastKeyName = getKeyName(keyCode);

        switch (getGameAction(keyCode))
        {
            case UP: y--; break;
            case DOWN: y++; break;
            case RIGHT: x++; break;
            case LEFT: x--; break;
        }

        // request a repaint of the canvas
        repaint();
    }
}

/**
 * MIDlet constructor that creates the custom canvas (MyCanvas) and adds
 * a quit command to it.
 */
public KeyEventTest()
{
    // Construct a the canvas
    myCanvas = new MyCanvas();

    // we still need a way to quit
    quit = new Command("Quit", Command.EXIT, 2);
    myCanvas.addCommand(quit);
    myCanvas.setCommandListener(this);
}

/**
 * Called by the Application Manager when the MIDlet is starting or resuming
 * after being paused. In this example it acquires the current Display object
 * and uses it to set the Form object created in the MIDlet constructor as
 * the active Screen to display.
 * @throws MIDletStateChangeException
 */
protected void startApp() throws MIDletStateChangeException
```

```
{
    // upon starting up we display the canvas
    Display.getDisplay(this).setCurrent(myCanvas);
}


/**
 * Called by the MID's Application Manager to pause the MIDlet. A good
 * example of this is when the user receives an incoming phone call whilst
 * playing your game. When they're done the Application Manager will call
 * startApp to resume. For this example we don't need to do anything.
 */
protected void pauseApp()
{
}


/**
 * Called by the MID's Application Manager when the MIDlet is about to
 * be destroyed (removed from memory). You should take this as an opportunity
 * to clear up any resources and save the game. For this example we don't
 * need to do anything.
 * @param unconditional if false you have the option of throwing a
 * MIDletStateChangeException to abort the destruction process.
 * @throws MIDletStateChangeException
 */
protected void destroyApp(boolean unconditional) throws MIDletStateChangeException
{
}


/**
 * The CommandListener interface method called when the user executes a
 * Command, in this case it can only be the quit command we created in the
 * constructor and added to the Canvas.
 * @param command
 * @param displayable
 */
public void commandAction(Command command, Displayable displayable)
{
    try
    {
        if (command == quit)
        {
            destroyApp(true);
            notifyDestroyed();
        }
```

```
        }

    catch (MIDletStateChangeException me)
    {
        System.out.println(me + " caught.");
    }
  }
}
```

This MIDlet displays a string (which changes when you hit different keys) and moves it around in response to you hitting the arrows keys on the device. The real action happens in the keyPressed method.

```
protected void keyPressed(int keyCode)
{
    if (keyCode > 0)
        lastKeyName = getKeyName(keyCode);

    switch(getGameAction(keyCode))
    {
        case UP: y--; break;
        case DOWN: y++; break;
        case RIGHT: x++; break;
        case LEFT: x--; break;
    }

    repaint();
}
```

Here you take the keyCode passed into the method and set the name of the key. You then check whether the key is one of the default action keys and change the positions of the x and y variables. Not as hard as it looks, is it?

Conclusion

You covered a great deal of ground in this chapter. For an API targeting small devices, the MIDP is certainly big on features.

During your tour, you looked at the networking, timers, and record management system before finally reviewing the power of both the high- and low-level interfaces. As you can imagine, many of the nightmares of trying to code games on MIDs are "alarm-clocked" by J2ME. It really does let you get on with doing what you were born to do—code da gamez!

Next you'll take a look at the popular additional APIs, made available by device manufacturers, which extend this functionality even further.

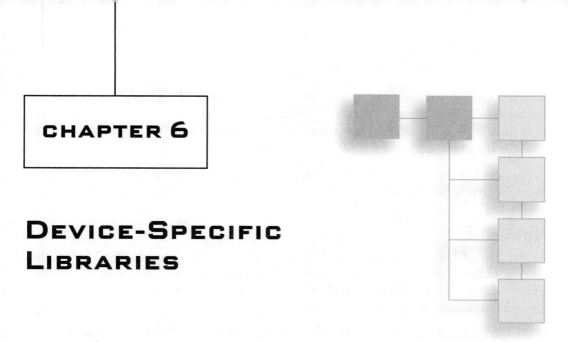

CHAPTER 6

DEVICE-SPECIFIC LIBRARIES

In the previous chapter you saw the functionality offered by the standard MIDP API. Manufacturers, however, provide additional features such as transparent imaging and additional sound capabilities. In this chapter, you'll look at some of the more popular device-specific libraries.

Device-Specific Libraries

You've seen how J2ME does a great job of abstracting the features of an MID. The MIDP API gives you the comfort of working with a (relatively) standard platform to develop your games. MIDP 1.0 represents the features that are common to all MIDs that support that version. There are some exceptions where support is optional, such as repeating keys and pointer device input. Generally, though, what you see in the specifications is what you can expect to get.

As you can imagine, many mobile devices have features beyond those supported by MIDP 1.0—especially features that are unique to particular devices (such as vibration support). This will naturally continue as the hardware improves. The MIDP specifications will continue to be updated. You'll notice that many of the features made available as manufacturer-specific extensions under MIDP 1, such as transparent images and sounds, are now included in MIDP 2. However, it is the nature of a standardized common platform to leave room for manufacturer extensions.

Manufacturers make additional features available to developers through J2ME software development kits (SDKs). For example, Nokia provides an SDK for many of their devices, which provide features such as transparent image blitting, playing sounds, and turning the device into a vibrator (settle down).

You also need to regularly test, if not directly develop, using the various emulators supported for different phones. Trust me; switch phones regularly during development to keep some perspective on the idiosyncrasies of different devices. It'll save you from some monster surprises later.

In the next few sections, you'll take a look at the features made available by some of the more popular MID manufacturers: Nokia, Siemens, and Motorola.

Nokia

As you saw in Chapter 3, Nokia has an impressive range of J2ME-compatible MIDs on the market. In fact, they provide a significant portion of the installed user base you'll target with your games. Fortunately, Nokia has backed their J2ME hardware with solid support for Java developers—especially game developers.

Using the Nokia SDKs, you will be able to add the following features to your games:

- Device control for flashing the lights or making the device vibrate
- Expanded sound support
- Full-screen drawing (beyond `Canvas`)
- Extra graphics, including triangle and polygon drawing, transparent image blitting, rotation, alpha channels, and direct pixel access

Nokia provides two distinct tools to help you develop J2ME games for their range of MIDs—the NDS (*Nokia Developer's Suite*) for J2ME and Java SDKs for individual devices. You'll download and install both of these in the next section.

Installing the Tools

The NDS provides a basic Nokia phone emulator, audio tools, and a simple development environment somewhat similar to Sun's J2ME Wireless Toolkit. (Actually, the NDS is a little better in some ways.) I'm not going to go into detail about using the NDS as an IDE, but feel free to play around with it. Although it's pretty cute, it still doesn't serve as a full-scale IDE.

However, the NDS is a great way to manage and run the various Nokia emulators (in the form of phone SDKs). It also has support for JBuilder and Sun ONE Studio integration, so download it from the Nokia Web site and let's take a tour. To download the NDS, you need to visit Forum Nokia at http://www.forum.nokia.com.

Navigate to the Java section and then to the Tools and SDKs page. (There's a ton of cool stuff around there, so don't get distracted now!) What you're after is the Nokia Developer's Suite for J2ME. You need to become a member of the developer forum (free of charge) to download these tools. As you can see in Figure 6.1, after you download the NDS, install it as you normally would and select the IDE integration you prefer.

Next, set the installation directory to be under your J2ME working directory like that in Figure 6.2 (feel free to use your own directory location).

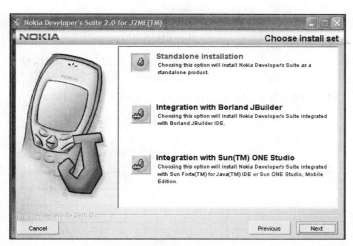

Figure 6.1 The Nokia Developers Suite 2.0 installation options for integration with an existing development environment.

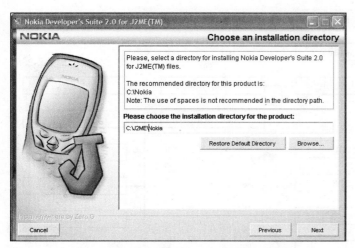

Figure 6.2 Select the directory in which to install the NDS.

The Nokia UI API

Nokia makes additional MIDP features available through the Nokia UI API. You will find a version of the API, in the form of documentation and class files (classes.zip), packaged with most of the device SDKs (such as C:\J2ME\Nokia\Devices\Nokia_7210_MIDP_SDK_v1_0) Each device comes packaged with a complete copy of the Nokia UI, however they are all the same thing.

Life on planet Nokia consists of the classes and interfaces highlighted in Figure 6.3.

To see a Nokia emulator in action you can just run the executable (such as 7210.exe) found in the bin directory for each device (C:\J2ME\Nokia\Devices\Nokia_7210_MIDP_SDK_v1_0\bin) and then use the file menu to open a JAR file containing your classes.

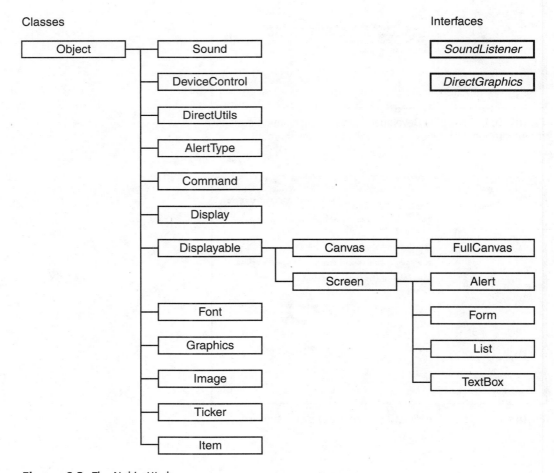

Figure 6.3 The Nokia UI classes

Tip

I would stay away from using the NDS to build your project; use your IDE or the command line to compile the project and then use the NDS device emulators to view it. Also, you only need to include the Nokia UI specific classes (classes.zip) on your classpath if you're using Nokia UI features.

To get things working, you need to add `lib/classes.zip` to your build class path. Then you will be able to use the classes in the `com.nokia.mid.*` package. Take a look at the details of these features.

Device Control

You can control some of the extra physical features of Nokia devices using the `com.nokia.mid.ui.DeviceControl` class. (Table 6.1 shows the methods available.)

Table 6.1 com.nokia.mid.ui.DeviceControl

Method	Description
static void flashLights(long duration)	Flashes the lights.
static void setLights(int num, int level)	Turns the lights on and off.
static void startVibra(int freq, long duration)	Vibrates for a given frequency and time.
static void stopVibra()	Stops vibrating.

The two device elements you can control are the lights and vibration. To temporarily flash the lights on and off, use the `flashLights` method. For example:

```
import com.nokia.mid.ui.DeviceControl;
...
    DeviceControl.flashLights(5000);
```

This code will cause the lights (such as the LEDs) to flash. If there is no support for this feature, then nothing will happen (duh). The integer value specifies the length of time (in milliseconds) to keep the lights on, although the device might override this value if you specify a number that is too large.

The other method relating to lights, `setLights`, allows you to control any of the lights on the device individually, such as the backlight or the LEDs . . . in theory. In reality, Nokia only gives you the ability to control the device's backlight (if it has one). To do this, call the method with the light number (the first integer) set to 0 for the backlight and the level integer set to a number between 0 and 100 (where 0 is off and 100 is the brightest level).

For devices that don't support graded backlighting, all values between 1 and 100 just translate to on. Here's an example of setLights in action:

```
DeviceControl.setLights(0, 100);
```

Tip

A word of warning about playing with the backlight: There is no method to determine the current backlighting level; therefore, you have no way of restoring the lighting to the level the user previously had. Be careful using this function. A user won't be impressed if, while playing in a dark place, you turn the lights out to reward them for completing a level.

If you really want to add this function to your game, consider making it an option the player can enable or disable. This applies to the vibration function as well.

Controlling the vibration of the phone is one of those cool things you really want to do. Crashing into a side railing or taking shield damage feels much cooler if you give the phone a jiggle when it happens. To start the phone vibrating, use

```
DeviceControl.startVibra(10, 1000);
```

The first parameter, the frequency, is an integer in the range of 0 to 100. This number represents how violent the shaking should be. The second integer is the duration of the vibration in milliseconds. You can vary these numbers depending on what's happening in the game. For example, you might make the phone vibrate more violently for bigger shield hits or for a longer duration as the shield weakens.

A call to startVibra will return immediately, regardless of the duration of the call. If the device does not support vibration it will throw an IllegalStateException. This can happen even on a device that supports vibration if, for example, it's docked in a cradle.

To immediately stop any current vibration, use the stopVibra method.

Sound

The Nokia UI also includes the ability to play sounds on compatible MIDs (Table 6.2 lists the available methods). The most basic support you can rely on is playing simple tones as well as Nokia ring-tone format (RTPL) tunes. More advanced MIDs can also play digitized audio using the WAV format.

Playing Tones

The first thing to playing sounds is determining the support for the device. The getSupportedFormats method will return an array of integers containing either FORMAT_WAV or FORMAT_TONE.

Table 6.2 com.nokia.mid.sound.Sound

Method	Description
`Sound(byte[] data, int type)`	Creates a sound object using the byte array data.
`Sound(int freq, long duration)`	Creates a sound object using a frequency and a duration.
`void init(byte[] data, int type)`	Initializes a sound using a byte array.
`void init(int freq, long duration)`	Initializes a sound using a frequency and a duration.
`static int getConcurrentSoundCount(int type)`	Gets the maximum number of simultaneous sounds the device supports.
`static int[] getSupportedFormats()`	Gets the supported formats.
`void release()`	Releases any audio resources owned by the sound.
`int getGain()`	Gets the volume of the sound.
`int getState()`	Gets the state of the sound.
`void setGain(int gain)`	Sets the volume.
`void setSoundListener(SoundListener listener)`	Registers a sound listener for state notifications.
`void stop()`	Stops playing the sound.
`void resume()`	Starts playing the sound again from where you last stopped.
`void play(int loop)`	Starts playing the sound.

You can create a simple tone sound and play it using

```
Sound s = new Sound(440, 1000L);
s.play(1);
```

This code constructs a 440-Hz tone with a duration of 1000 milliseconds. The play method starts the sound playing and immediately returns; your MIDlet continues with the sounds playing in the background. The sound will stop either when the duration expires or when you ask it to stop by calling the stop method.

Tip

All Nokia MIDs at least support frequencies of 400 Hz and 3951 Hz. You should consult the Nokia UI API javadoc for details on the other supported frequencies.

Some MIDs support multiple sounds played simultaneously. You can determine how many sounds are supported using the getConcurrentSoundCount method. If a call to play a sound exceeds the maximum number supported, the last sound playing will stop and the new sound will start.

You can also use the API to play simple tunes, such as the ring tones included with the phone. This functionality is available through Nokia's RTPL (*Ring Tone Programming Language*), which is part of the SMS (*Smart Messaging Specification*). The simplest way to generate RTPL music is to use the Nokia PC suite software.

Tip

Support for more advanced multimedia (including video) on newer MIDs is available through Sun's MMAPI (*Mobile Media API*). For more information, visit http://java.sun.com/products/mmapi.

Listening In

When you're playing sounds, it isn't always easy to determine when a particular sound or RTPL tune has finished playing. For simple sounds (such as weapon fire) you probably don't care, but for background tunes or level-win rewards you need to know when the sound (or song) has finished, by either moving on in the game or starting another song. To determine when a sound or song has ended you use the SoundListener interface.

To set up a listener, create a class (or use your existing MIDlet) that implements the SoundListener interface, and then implement the soundStateChanged method. For example:

```
import com.nokia.mid.sound.Sound;
import com.nokia.mid.sound.SoundListener;
import javax.microedition.midlet.MIDlet;
import javax.microedition.midlet.MIDletStateChangeException;
import javax.microedition.lcdui.*;

/**
 * A demonstration of the Nokia UI Sound API.
 * @author Martin J. Wells
 */

public class NokiaSound extends MIDlet implements CommandListener, SoundListener
{
    private Sound sound;
    private Form form;
    private Command quit;
    private Command play;

    /**
     * MIDlet constructor creates a form and appends two commands. It then
     * instantiates a Nokia Sound class ready to play sounds for us in response
     * to the play command (see the commandAction method).
     */
```

```
public NokiaSound()
{
    form = new Form("Nokia Sound");

    form.setCommandListener(this);
    play = new Command("Play", Command.SCREEN, 1);
    form.addCommand(play);
    quit = new Command("Quit", Command.EXIT, 2);
    form.addCommand(quit);

    // Initialize a sound object we'll use later. We create the object here
    // with meaningless values becuase we'll init it later with proper
    // numbers. A sound listener is then set.
    sound = new Sound(0, 1L);
    sound.setSoundListener(this);
}


/**
 * The Nokia SoundListener interface method which is called when a sound
 * changes state.
 * @param sound The sound that changed state
 * @param state The state it changed to
 */
public void soundStateChanged(Sound sound, int state)
{
    if (state == Sound.SOUND_UNINITIALIZED)
        form.append("Sound uninitialized ");

    if (state == Sound.SOUND_PLAYING)
        form.append("Sound playing ");

    if (state == Sound.SOUND_STOPPED)
        form.append("Sound stopped ");
}



/**
 * Called by the Application Manager when the MIDlet is starting or resuming
 * after being paused. In this example it acquires the current Display object
 * and uses it to set the Form object created in the MIDlet constructor as
 * the active Screen to display.
 * @throws MIDletStateChangeException
 */
```

```java
protected void startApp() throws MIDletStateChangeException
{
    Display.getDisplay(this).setCurrent(form);
}

/**
 * Called by the MID's Application Manager to pause the MIDlet. A good
 * example of this is when the user receives an incoming phone call whilst
 * playing your game. When they're done the Application Manager will call
 * startApp to resume. For this example we don't need to do anything.
 */
protected void pauseApp()
{
}

/**
 * Called by the MID's Application Manager when the MIDlet is about to
 * be destroyed (removed from memory). You should take this as an opportunity
 * to clear up any resources and save the game. For this example we don't
 * need to do anything.
 * @param unconditional if false you have the option of throwing a
 * MIDletStateChangeException to abort the destruction process.
 * @throws javax.microedition.midlet.MIDletStateChangeException
 */
protected void destroyApp(boolean unconditional)
        throws MIDletStateChangeException
{
}

/**
 * The CommandListener interface method called when the user executes a
 * Command, in this case it can only be the quit command we created in the
 * constructor and added to the Form.
 * @param command the command that was triggered
 * @param displayable the displayable on which the event occurred
 */
public void commandAction(Command command, Displayable displayable)
{
    // check for our quit command and act accordingly
    try
    {
        if (command == play)
```

```
        {
            // initliaze the parameters of the sound (440Hz playing for 2
            // seconds - 2000 ms)
            sound.init(440, 2000L);
            sound.play(1);
        }

        if (command == quit)
        {
            destroyApp(true);

            // tell the Application Manager we're exiting
            notifyDestroyed();
        }
    }

    // we catch this even though there's no chance it will be thrown
    // since we called destroyApp with unconditional set to true.
    catch (MIDletStateChangeException me)
    { }
  }

}
```

Tip

The Nokia NDS contains a great sound playing example in the C:\j2me\Nokia\Tools\Nokia_ Developers_Suite_for_J2ME\midp_examples\Tones directory.

Tip

You can control the playback volume using the Sound.setGain method with a number ranging from 0 to 255.

Full-Screen Drawing

Even when you are using the MIDP low-level UI's Canvas class, you still don't get access to the entire screen. This is inconvenient because of the relatively significant space you lose at the top and bottom of the screen that could be put to good use. (For example, you could use the space to display the number of lives the player has left.) As you can see in Figure 6.4, Nokia's FullCanvas is an extension of the MIDP Canvas class that provides full-screen access. You can see the lone method for the class in Table 6.3.

Figure 6.4 Nokia's `FullCanvas` class gives you access to the entire display.

Table 6.3 com.nokia.mid.ui.FullCanvas	
Method	**Description**
`FullCanvas()`	Constructs a new `FullCanvas`.

The price you pay is the loss of the command system. You need to implement this yourself using keystroke responses. (The `addCommand` and `setCommandListener` methods will throw an `IllegalStateException`.) In exchange, you will gain access to the keys previously reserved for commands, as follows:

- `KEY_UP_ARROW`
- `KEY_DOWN_ARROW`
- `KEY_LEFT_ARROW`
- `KEY_RIGHT_ARROW`
- `KEY_SEND`
- `KEY_END`
- `KEY_SOFTKEY1`
- `KEY_SOFTKEY2`
- `KEY_SOFTKEY3`

In the following example, you will draw some random-colored rectangles extending out as far as the canvas will allow. As you can see from the results in Figure 6.1, you can gain a sizeable amount of rendering space when you use `FullCanvas`.

```
import com.nokia.mid.ui.FullCanvas;
import javax.microedition.midlet.*;
import javax.microedition.lcdui.*;
```

```java
import java.util.Random;

/**
 * An example that demonstrates the use of the Nokia UI FullCanvas class.
 * You must have the Nokia UI class files on your classpath and run this example
 * on a Nokia emulator (such as the 7210).
 * @author Martin J. Wells
 */
public class FullCanvasTest extends MIDlet
{
    private MyCanvas myCanvas;

    /**
     * An inner class which extends from the com.nokia.mid.ui.FullCanvas and
     * implements a random rectangle drawer.
     */
    class MyCanvas extends FullCanvas
    {
        private Random randomizer = new Random();

        /**
         * A method to obtain a random number between a miniumum and maximum
         * range.
         * @param min The minimum number of the range
         * @param max The maximum number of the range
         * @return
         */
        private int getRand(int min, int max)
        {
            int r = Math.abs(randomizer.nextInt());
            return (r % (max - min)) + min;
        }

        /**
         * Canvas class paint implementation where we draw the some random
         * rectangles.
         * @param graphics The graphics context to draw to
         */
        protected void paint(Graphics graphics)
        {
            for (int i = 10; i > 0; i--)
            {
                graphics.setColor(getRand(1, 254), getRand(1, 254), getRand(1, 254));
```

```
            graphics.fillRect(0, 0, i * (getWidth() / 10), i * (getHeight() / 10));
        }
    }
}

/**
 * MIDlet class which constructs an instance of our custom FullCanvas.
 */
public FullCanvasTest()
{
    myCanvas = new MyCanvas();
}

/**
 * Called by the Application Manager when the MIDlet is starting or resuming
 * after being paused. In this example it acquires the current Display object
 * and uses it to set the Canvas object created in the MIDlet constructor as
 * the active Screen to display.
 * @throws MIDletStateChangeException
 */
protected void startApp() throws MIDletStateChangeException
{
    Display.getDisplay(this).setCurrent(myCanvas);
}

/**
 * Called by the MID's Application Manager to pause the MIDlet. A good
 * example of this is when the user receives an incoming phone call whilst
 * playing your game. When they're done the Application Manager will call
 * startApp to resume. For this example we don't need to do anything.
 */
protected void pauseApp()
{
}

/**
 * Called by the MID's Application Manager when the MIDlet is about to
 * be destroyed (removed from memory). You should take this as an opportunity
 * to clear up any resources and save the game. For this example we don't
 * need to do anything.
 * @param unconditional if false you have the option of throwing a
 * MIDletStateChangeException to abort the destruction process.
 * @throws MIDletStateChangeException
```

```
    */
    protected void destroyApp(boolean unconditional) throws MIDletStateChangeException
    {
    }
}
```

Direct Graphics

Now you get to the real fun of the Nokia UI—graphics. And let me tell you, what you get is downright cool—transparency, image rotation, triangle and polygon drawing, and monkeys . . . yeah, monkeys . . . little pink, fluffy monkeys will jump out of the device and dance naked for you! Um, all right. There are no monkeys, but seriously, this is where the Nokia UI really comes into its own. Features such as image rotation and transparency are more than just a little bit important for making great games.

These graphics functions are available through the com.nokia.mid.ui.DirectGraphics class (the full API is listed in Table 6.5), which you acquire using the com.nokia.mid.ui. DirectUtils.getDirectGraphics static method (the DirectUtils API is shown in Table 6.6). For example:

```
protected void paint(Graphics graphics)
{
    // Get the Nokia DirectGraphics object
    DirectGraphics dg = DirectUtils.getDirectGraphics(graphics);

    // Call DirectGraphics methods
    ...
}
```

The DirectGraphics object returned in the method call in this example is not the same object as the original Graphics context, nor is DirectGraphics a super of Graphics. However, the two contexts are inherently connected; changes to one will affect the other. This is not only important, it also makes for some great bonus features when you combine the two.

Once you have a DirectGraphics object, any call on the original Graphics object's method to change color (setColor or setGrayScale), clipping (setClip or clipRect), stroke (setStrokeStyle), or translation (translate) will affect the output of any future drawing on the linked DirectGraphics object. Keep in mind that at this point I'm not saying you call these methods on the DirectGraphics object itself. (They aren't there anyway.) You call them on the original Graphics object. The link between the two will result in the change affecting the DirectGraphics object as well. Keep this in mind because I'll get to an example soon.

On the flip side, the DirectGraphics object's setARGBColor method will change the current rendering color on the original Graphics context. What's cool about that? Notice the "A" in the color method call? Yep, that's an alpha channel! You can set a variable level of transparency when drawing graphics. Not only can you do it using the DirectGraphics calls, but you can also do it using the Graphics call. For example, in the following code you'll draw two rectangles using Graphics and DirectGraphics to set an alpha channel color. Both rectangles will have a high level of transparency.

```
protected void paint(Graphics graphics)
{
    // Get the Nokia DirectGraphics object
    DirectGraphics dg = DirectUtils.getDirectGraphics(graphics);

    // Draw a transparent rectangle in the center of the screen
    dg.setARGBColor(0xFFFF0000);
    graphics.fillRect(50, 50, getWidth()-100, getHeight()-100);

    // Draw a rectangle that fills the screen (no transparency)
    dg.setARGBColor(0xFF0000FF);
    graphics.fillRect(0, 0, getWidth(), getHeight());
}
```

The call to setARGBColor uses a four-byte integer value (Quad 8) to represent the alpha-, red-, green-, and blue-channel intensity. For the alpha channel, 00 represents completely transparent and FF (or 255) is fully opaque. Table 6.4 lists a few examples.

The code example you just saw will draw a big blue rectangle. Because the last setARGBColor is fully opaque, none of the underlying smaller red rectangle will show through. If you adjusted the color of the rectangle to have an alpha level of 55 (0x550000FF), you would see a mixture of both colors displayed. If the alpha level were further dampened down to 00 (0x000000FF), only the underlying red rectangle would show. Figure 6.5 shows an example of all three results.

Notice the transitional color of the red rectangle. In the second image, you see a blending of both rectangles on the display at the same time. Remember this trick; it's one of the coolest you've got.

Table 6.4 ARGB Examples

Value	Description
0xFF000000	Black (No transparency)
0xFFFF0000	Red (No transparency)
0x000000FF	Blue (Fully transparent—results in nothing being rendered)
0x80FFFF00	Yellow (Half transparent)
0x2000FF00	Green (Slightly transparent)

Table 6.5 com.nokia.mid.ui.DirectGraphics

Method	Description
void drawImage(Image img, int x, int y, int anchor, int manipulation)	Draws an image.
void drawPixels(byte[] pixels, byte[] transparencyMask, int offset, int scanlength, int x, int y, int width, int height, int manipulation, int format)	Draws pixel data directly with a transparency mask.
void drawPixels(int[] pixels, boolean transparency, int offset, int scanlength, int x, int y, int width, int height, int manipulation, int format)	Draws pixel data directly with optional transparency encoding in the pixel data format.
void drawPixels(short[] pixels, boolean transparency, int offset, int scanlength, int x, int y, int width, int height, int manipulation, int format)	Draws pixel data (short data type version).
void drawPolygon(int[] xPoints, int xOffset, int[] yPoints, int yOffset, int nPoints, int argbColor)	Draws a polygon (a closed, many-sided shape) based on the x and y arrays of points.
void drawTriangle(int x1, int y1, int x2, int y2, int x3, int y3, int argbColor)	Draws a closed triangle.
void fillPolygon(int[] xPoints, int xOffset, int[] yPoints, int yOffset, int nPoints, int argbColor)	Draws a filled polygon based on the x and y arrays of points.
void fillTriangle(int x1, int y1, int x2, int y2, int x3, int y3, int argbColor)	Draws a filled, closed triangle.
int getAlphaComponent()	Gets the alpha component of the current color.
int getNativePixelFormat()	Returns the native pixel format of an implementation.
void getPixels(byte[] pixels, byte[] transparencyMask, int offset, int scanlength, int x, int y, int width, int height, int format)	Copies the pixel values (including any transparency mask) of the graphics context from a specific location to an array of byte values.
void getPixels(int[] pixels, int offset, int scanlength, int x, int y, int width, int height, int format)	Copies the pixel values of the graphics context from a specific location to an array of int values.
void getPixels(short[] pixels, int offset, int scanlength, int x, int y, int width, int height, int format)	Copies the pixel values of the graphics context from a specific location to an array of short values.
void setARGBColor(int argbColor)	Sets the current color (and alpha) to the specified ARGB value (0xAARRGGBB).

Figure 6.5 Three examples of drawing using Nokia alpha channels.

Triangles and Polygons

MIDP limits geometric drawing to just lines and rectangles. Although you can use lines to draw almost any shape, there's no way to fill the compound shape—and it's about as much fun as watching paint dry. The Nokia UI adds the capability to draw outlined or filled shapes with three or more sides (triangles and polygons).

Table 6.6 com.nokia.mid.ui.DirectUtils

Method	Description
`static Image createImage(byte[] imageData, int imageOffset, int imageLength)`	Constructs a mutable image from the given byte array.
`static Image createImage(int width, int height, int ARGBcolor)`	Constructs a mutable image with a specified width, height, and ARGB color.
`static DirectGraphics getDirectGraphics (javax.microedition.lcdui.Graphics g)`	Gets a `DirectGraphics` object using a `javax.microedition.lcdui.Graphics` instance.

The method calls to draw geometry are relatively simple so an example should give you the general idea. The following code draws a triangle and a rectangle.

```
protected void paint(Graphics graphics)
{
    // Get the Nokia DirectGraphics object
    DirectGraphics dg = DirectUtils.getDirectGraphics(graphics);

    // Draw a colored triangle
    dg.fillTriangle(getWidth() / 2, 10, getWidth(), getHeight(), 0, getHeight(),
                    0xFF00FF00);
```

```
    // Poly wants a display
    int[] xPoints = {25, 50, 25, 10};
    int[] yPoints = {10, 25, 50, 25};
    dg.drawPolygon(xPoints, 0, yPoints, 0, xPoints.length, 0x55FF0000);
}
```

Reflecting and Rotating

`DirectGraphics` provides an enhanced `drawImage` method capable of rendering an image using rotation and reflection. Given that graphics are commonly drawn in multiple directions in a game (such as to represent a sprite moving from left and right), you'll find that without reflection or rotation multiple versions (sometimes quite a few) of the same images are required to represent these different directions. A combination of reflection and rotation lets you reuse the same graphics, thus freeing up space in your JAR for yet more graphics.

To render an image using reflection or rotation, use the `DirectGraphics.drawImage` method. Table 6.7 lists the available options. You can combine flipping and rotating.

Table 6.7 Reflection and Rotation Types

Type	Description
FLIP_VERTICAL	Flips the image vertically.
FLIP_HORIZONTAL	Flips the image horizontally.
ROTATE_90	Turns the image 90 degrees counterclockwise.
ROTATE_180	Turns the image 180 degrees counterclockwise.
ROTATE_270	Turns the image 270 degrees counterclockwise.

In the following code, you will use `drawImage` to render an image both rotated and reflected.

```
class MyCanvas extends FullCanvas
{
    private Image alienHeadImage = null;

    /**
     * A custom FullCanvas that loads up a sample image (make sure the
     * image file is in the JAR file!)
     */
```

```
public MyCanvas()
{
    try
    {
        alienHeadImage = Image.createImage("/alienhead.png");
    }
    catch (IOException ioe)
    {
        System.out.println("unable to load image");
    }
}

/**
 * The overriden Canvas paint method draws the previously loaded image
 * onto the canvas using the passed in graphics context.
 */
protected void paint(Graphics graphics)
{
    // Get the Nokia DirectGraphics object
    DirectGraphics dg = DirectUtils.getDirectGraphics(graphics);

    // Draw the alien head rotated by 270 degrees
    dg.drawImage(alienHeadImage, getWidth()/2, getHeight()/2,
                Graphics.HCENTER | Graphics.VCENTER,
                DirectGraphics.ROTATE_270);

    // Draw the alien head upside down
    dg.drawImage(alienHeadImage, getWidth() / 2, (getHeight() / 2) + 20,
                Graphics.HCENTER | Graphics.VCENTER,
                DirectGraphics.FLIP_VERTICAL);
}
}
```

Image Transparency

At the start of this section on DirectGraphics, you saw how you could set transparency, or alpha channels, for graphics rendering. Well here's a news flash: This also extends to the PNG image format! Yep, that's right; you can render images using the full alpha channel in PNG files exported directly from your favorite graphics application.

The most significant use of this feature in a game is when you render a non-rectangular image onto a background. Without transparency support, you cannot draw the image seamlessly over a background image—you'll have ugly bordering. In Figure 6.6, you can see a good example of an image without transparency (top) and with transparency (bottom).

The following code renders these images. As you can see, there is basically no difference when you load or display a transparent image.

Figure 6.6 An example drawing a transparent and non-transparent PNG image.

```
protected void paint(Graphics graphics)
{
    // Get the Nokia DirectGraphics object
    DirectGraphics dg =
DirectUtils.getDirectGraphics(graphics);

    // Fill the screen with pastel green
    graphics.setColor(50, 200, 50);
    graphics.fillRect(0, 0, getWidth(), getHeight());

    // Draw the alien head
    dg.drawImage(alienHeadImage, getWidth()/2, getHeight()/2,
                Graphics.HCENTER | Graphics.VCENTER, 0);

    // Draw the transparent alien head.
    // Note that I'm assuming you've previously loaded a transparent
    // image file into an Image object named transAlienHeadImage.
    dg.drawImage(transAlienHeadImage, getWidth() / 2, (getHeight() / 2) + 20,
                Graphics.HCENTER | Graphics.VCENTER, 0);
}
```

Pixel Data Access

Last but not least, DirectGraphics gives you access to the nuts and bolts of the native pixel data with which a Nokia MID stores images. You can extract pixel data, modify it, and then render your modified version. Uses of direct pixel manipulation are pretty much endless because this function allows your program to modify the image. For example, you can turn one range of colored pixels into another color (or level of transparency). What's good about that? Well imagine the case of a space shooter. At the start of the game you could let the player choose his ship color, and then use pixel manipulation to change one color (such as the go-fast stripes along the wings) into another color of his choice. This could even include different levels of depth that match the original paint job. This wouldn't normally be practical because of the extra space different-colored ships would take up in the JAR file.

Table 6.8 Pixel Data Types

Type	Description
TYPE_BYTE_1_GRAY	One-bit format, two distinct color values (on/off), stored as a byte. Eight pixel values in a single byte, packed as closely as possible.
TYPE_BYTE_1_GRAY_VERTICAL	One-bit format, two distinct color values (on/off), stored as a byte. Eight pixel values are stored in a single byte.
TYPE_BYTE_2_GRAY	Two-bit format, four grayscale colors.
TYPE_BYTE_332_RGB	Three bits for red, three bits for green, and two bits for blue component in a pixel, stored as a byte.
TYPE_BYTE_4_GRAY	Four-bit format, 16 grayscale colors.
TYPE_BYTE_8_GRAY	Eight-bit format, 256 grayscale colors.
TYPE_INT_888_RGB	Eight bits for red, green, and blue component in a pixel (0x00RRGGBB).
TYPE_INT_8888_ARGB	Eight bits for alpha, red, green, and blue component in a pixel (0xAARRGGBB).
TYPE_USHORT_1555_ARGB	One bit for alpha, five bits for red, green, and blue component in a pixel.
TYPE_USHORT_444_RGB	Four bits for red, green, and blue component in a pixel, stored as a short (0x0RGB).
TYPE_USHORT_4444_ARGB	Four bits for alpha, red, green, and blue component in a pixel, stored as a short (0xARGB).
TYPE_USHORT_555_RGB	Five bits for red, green, and blue component in a pixel.
TYPE_USHORT_565_RGB	Five bits for red, six bits for green, and five bits for blue component in a pixel.

This all sounds great, but unfortunately it's not that easy to use. First, different Nokia models store image data internally in different formats. (Table 6.8 lists the various formats.) You need to determine the native storage format using DirectGraphics.getNativePixelFormat. Once you have the format, you can get the image data in the form of an array of integers, shorts, or bytes, depending on the native image format you're requesting. For example, the Nokia 7210 (which you'll use for all the following examples) has a native pixel format of TYPE_USHORT_444_RGB. Quite a mouthful, huh? This format uses the Java short type to store pixel data. With all this in mind, take a look at the code to grab the pixel data.

```
int pixFormat = d g.getNativePixelFormat();

// make sure we have a pixel format we know how to handle properly
if (pixFormat == DirectGraphics.TYPE_USHORT_444_RGB)
{
    // Create an array large enough to hold the pixels we grab (20 x 50)
    short pixels[] = new short[20*50];
```

```
dg.getPixels(pixels, 0, 20, 0, 0, 20, 50, DirectGraphics.TYPE_USHORT_444_RGB);
...
```

The first thing you do in this code is to determine the pixel format of the data you're going to grab. To keep things simple, I've just hard-coded a test to make sure the format is what you expect (TYPE_USHORT_444_RGB). Adding support for other formats is a relatively painless process, but it doesn't make for concise examples at this stage.

Before I move on, I want to talk about exactly what the TYPE_USHORT_444_RGB format means. First, the USHORT indicates that a Java short type (2 bytes, or 16 bits) represents each pixel in the image. To understand all this, you can think of a short as being four sets of 4 bits, commonly written as 4444.

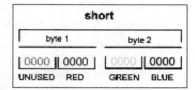

Figure 6.7 The byte layout for a 444_RGB color pixel.

As you can see in Figure 6.7, the 444_RGB—aka 12-bit color—indicates 4 bits for each of the red, green, and blue components of the color. Now because 4 bits can only represent 16 possible combinations, this means there is a maximum of 16 reds, 16 greens, and 16 blues. If you combine all these, you have a maximum of 4096 (16 * 16 * 16) colors on the device. This is the capability of the 7210 display; other MIDs have different capabilities.

One thing you might notice here: Since the Java short type has 2 bytes (16 bits) and the combination of the RGB components is only 12 bits (4 + 4 + 4), what is the purpose of the other 4 bits? The answer is nothing—this format doesn't require them.

All right, now that you have a little background on the 444_RGB format, take a look at things in action. The following code draws an image with a go-fast red stripe down the center. Using the Nokia UI direct pixel access, you're going to change just the red components of the image to green. A free paint job that doesn't waste any precious JAR space!

```
protected void paint(Graphics graphics)
{
    // Get the Nokia DirectGraphics object
    DirectGraphics dg = DirectUtils.getDirectGraphics(graphics);

    // Paint the entire canvas black
    graphics.setColor(0, 0, 0);
    graphics.fillRect(0, 0, getWidth(), getHeight());

    // Draw the original red-striped image
    dg.drawImage(redStripeImage, 0, 0, Graphics.TOP|Graphics.LEFT, 0);
```

```
// Get the native pixel format
int pixFormat = dg.getNativePixelFormat();

// Make sure we have a pixel format we know how to handle properly
if (pixFormat == DirectGraphics.TYPE_USHORT_444_RGB)
{
    int imgWidth = redStripeImage.getWidth();
    int imgHeight = redStripeImage.getHeight();

    // Create an array big enough to hold the pixels
    short pixels[] = new short[imgWidth*imgHeight];

    // Grab them from the graphics context in the array
    dg.getPixels(pixels, 0, imgWidth, 0, 0, imgWidth, imgHeight,
                DirectGraphics.TYPE_USHORT_444_RGB);

    // Loop through the contents of the array looking for the right color
    for (int y=0; y < imgHeight; y++)
    {
        for (int x = 0; x < imgWidth; x++)
        {
            // Pixels are stored in one long array so we need to get an
            // index relative to our x and y
            int a = (y * imgWidth) + x;
            short pixel = pixels[a];

            // Check to see if the pixel has all the RED bits on
            if (pixel == 0x0F00)
                pixels[a] = (short)0x00F0; //
        }
    }

    dg.drawPixels(pixels, false, 0, imgWidth, 60, 0, imgWidth, imgHeight,
                0, DirectGraphics.TYPE_USHORT_444_RGB);

}
}
```

Tip

You can see a complete working example of this on the CD in the Chapter 6 source code directory
under the name NokiaGraphicsTest.

You can recreate this example yourself by creating a PNG image file with some of the pixels set to maximum solid red. The preceding code will loop through the image and replace any pixels matching this color with solid green pixels. You can see the results in Figure 6.8.

This is a simple example of pixel manipulation—directly replacing one pixel with another. Using other techniques, the sky really is the limit to what you can do. For now, here are some ideas of what's possible:

Figure 6.8 The results of turning all the red pixels to green using RGB pixel manipulation.

- **Color shifting.** As you just saw in the example, you can change any set of colors into another. Using a more advanced version of this function, you can also reflect the shade of the original color. This results in much sexier go-fast stripes.

- **Translucent shadows.** You can create a darkened version of a sprite by lowering the pixel intensity. You can then draw this version underneath the sprite to create a translucent shadow effect that saps the light as it passes over the background.

- **Light blasts.** You can create some excellent explosive effects by dramatically increasing the brightness (the opposite of the shadow effect just mentioned) of an expanding area of pixels. This can give the illusion of an impact or an explosion with no images required. (You can use images as maps to create outlines for these effects if you want.) The end results can be spectacular.

- **Pulsing.** You can range through pixels' colors to create blinking and other effects.

- **Weather effects.** You can create daylight, nighttime, and fog effects.

- **Image scaling.** You can change the size of images, which is useful for height or size illusions.

Tip

One thing to keep in mind: Modifying pixels is a relatively slow process, so avoid (as much as possible) doing it on every call to `paint`. If the effect you're using still works, you can just pre-render modified versions (such as the alternative player-colored ships) as new images and then display those during the `paint` method. This has very little cost in terms of rendering speed.

Some effects require that you check pixels on every `paint` pass (such as the dynamic lighting explosions), but doing too much of this will kill the MID's CPU in no time. Give the effect a try (on the real phone) to see how it works. And above all, make these effects optional extras that the player can disable.

Siemens

Like Nokia, Siemens seem to take J2ME development (especially game development) quite seriously. They have expanded beyond MIDP 1.0 with an SDK that provides access to many of the features of their handsets, including:

- Messaging using SMS
- Placing a call
- Play sounds and tunes
- Control-device features such as vibration and lights
- Advanced graphics tools that let you draw and manage sprites, create tiled backgrounds, and directly access pixel data (but don't get too excited)

In the next few sections, you'll take a closer look at these features.

Installing

To get started you should download the SMTK (*Siemens Mobility Toolkit*) for Java from the Siemens Developer Portal at https://communication-market.siemens.de/portal. The SMTK provides the core tools, including the Siemens MIDP extensions API, along with good integration with JBuilder and Sun ONE Studio. However, the SMTK does not include any emulators; you will need to download at least one emulator to get things moving. (The M55 is a good emulator to use.) Once you have downloaded the SMTK and your selected emulator, go ahead and install both.

You can use the SMTK Manager (shown in Figure 6.9) to verify that the emulator is installed and ready to go. If you have multiple emulators installed, you can use the SMTK Manager to switch between them.

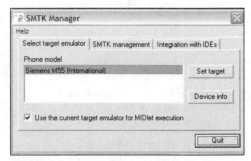

Figure 6.9 You can use the SMTK Manager to review the installed emulators.

Setup Development

To begin using the Siemens API in your MIDlets, you need to locate the library JAR, a file called api.jar (bet it took them a while to come up with *that* name), located in the lib subdirectory of your SMTK installation. Add this to your CLASSPATH—or if you're like me, just copy it into a directory that is already on your CLASSPATH.

You can run any of the emulators you've downloaded by navigating to the associated directory and using Emulator.exe. Once this is loaded, use the Actions panel and choose Start Java Application. Figure 6.10 shows the SL55 emulator running a simple image-draw test. As you can see from the results, the SL55 emulator supports PNG transparency.

Figure 6.10 The Siemens SL55 emulator in action.

Now that you're set up for development, take a look at the Siemens API.

SMS and Phone API

You can use the Siemens GSM (*Global System for Mobile Communications*) tools to send an SMS and even initiate a phone call. These facilities are available through the com.siemens.mp.gsm package in the classes Call, Phonebook, and SMS. You can see a complete list of these classes in Table 6.9.

Table 6.9 com.siemens.mp.gsm Classes

Class	Description
Call	
static void start(String number)	Initiates a call from the handset. (Watch out—your MIDlet will terminate after calling this method.)
PhoneBook	
static String[] getMDN()	Returns a string array of the Missed Dialed Number list.
SMS	
static int send(String number, byte[] data)	Sends a byte array as an SMS to a number.
static int send(String number, String data)	Sends a string as an SMS to a number.

Placing a call is extremely easy. Here's an example:

```
Call.start("555-5555-5555");
```

If you make this call and the phone doesn't support calling from a MIDlet, it will throw a `com.siemens.mp.NotAllowedException`. If the number is not valid, you'll get an `IllegalArgumentException`. One very important thing to keep in mind: If the call is successful (the number is okay and the MID supports this function), your MIDlet will immediately terminate. Doesn't sound so useful after all, eh?

Sending an SMS is just as simple, and you don't get rudely terminated. Here's an example:

```
SMS.send("555-5555-5555", "Hi mom!");
```

Incorrectly formatting the number will cause an `IllegalArgumentException`. If the function is not supported or the network is not available, an `IOException` will result. One thing to keep in mind: The phone might prompt the user to confirm that a message should be sent (given that a message usually has an associated cost).

Device Control

Two primary device control functions are available to a MIDlet—backlight and vibration (Table 6.10 lists the API for these classes). Controlling the backlight is a pretty nice effect. For example, you can make it flash when a player wins a level. Unfortunately, just like with Nokia's UI API, you cannot determine the current state of the backlight before you enable or disable it. Take care when you turn it off because you might leave the player quite literally in the dark.

Here's an example of turning the light on and then off:

```
Light.setLightOn();
Light.setLightOff();
```

You have similar control over vibration on the device. This lets you add a nice sense of realism to those heavy weapon impacts or car smashes. To control vibration, use the `startVibrator` and `stopVibrator` methods, just like you did using the `Light` control. You can also use the `triggerVibrator` method to vibrate for a fixed period. For example:

```
Vibrator.startVibrator();
Thread.sleep(500);     // wait for half a second
Vibrator.stopVibrator();
```

Table 6.10 Device Control Classes

Class	Description
com.siemens.mp.game.Light	
static void setLightOn()	Turns on the backlight.
static void setLightOff()	Turns off the backlight.
com.siemens.mp.game.Vibrator	
static void startVibrator()	Starts vibrating.
static void stopVibrator()	Stops vibrating.
static void triggerVibrator(int duration)	Sets vibration for a certain amount of time.

Sounds and Tunes

The first and easiest way to get some sound out of a Siemens MID is by using the Sound class's playTone method (Table 6.11 has the full API). This simple method plays a sound at a particular frequency (in Hz) for a period of milliseconds. For example:

```
Sound.playTone(550, 1000);
```

Thankfully there are other sound-playing options with a little more sophistication than playTone. Using the MelodyComposer class, you can use common musical constructs to create complex songs and then play them using the Melody class. (Refer to the Siemens API javadoc for a full list of the musical constructs available.) Here's an example that creates and plays a simple tune:

```
try
{
    MelodyComposer composer = new MelodyComposer();
    composer.setBPM(90);
    composer.appendNote(MelodyComposer.TONE_A2, MelodyComposer.TONELENGTH_1_4);
    composer.appendNote(MelodyComposer.TONE_C2, MelodyComposer.TONELENGTH_1_4);

    composer.getMelody().play();
}
catch(Exception e)
{
    // Handle the generic exception being thrown by the MelodyComposer class
}
```

In this code you simply construct a MelodyComposer, add some notes to it, and then extract the resulting melody, which you then play. The try-catch block is there because the MelodyComposer throws the generic exception. (There's no documentation as to why the MelodyComposer would throw a generic exception, and thus I have no idea how to handle it—poorly done.)

Table 6.11 Device Control Classes

Class	Description
com.siemens.mp.game.Sound	
static void playTone(int frequency, int time)	Plays a tone at a certain Hz for a period of time (in milliseconds).
com.siemens.mp.game.MelodyComposer	
MelodyComposer()	Constructs a new MelodyComposer.
MelodyComposer(int[] notes, int bpm)	Constructs a new MelodyComposer with a list of notes and initial BPM.
void appendNote(int note, int length)	Appends a note to this object.
Melody getMelody()	Gets the Melody object ready for playback.
int length()	Returns the number of notes in the current melody.
static int maxLength()	Returns the maximum number of notes you can use.
void resetMelody()	Clears the current melody and starts again.
void setBPM(int bpm)	Sets the beats per minute.
com.siemens.mp.game.Melody	
void play()	Starts playing the melody.
static void stop()	Stops the current melody. (Notice that this method is static.)

Advanced Graphics and Gaming

The good news is that the SMTK includes an extensive set of classes to assist with advanced graphics and other gaming requirements. The classes available are all within the com.siemens.mp.game package:

- **Sprite.** This is an animated graphic with basic collision detection.
- **ExtendedImage.** This provides functionality to manipulate 1- or 2-bit images (black and white or black, white, and transparent).
- **GraphicObject.** This is an abstract base class representing a visible graphical object.

- **GraphicObjectManager.** This is a manager class for ordered drawing of a collection of GraphicObjects.
- **TiledBackground.** This is a limited tiling system.

The bad news is that of these classes, the only particularly useful one is ExtendedImage, which provides a limited form of pixel manipulation for 1- or 2-bit graphics. The Sprite and other game-oriented classes (GraphicObject, GraphicObjectManager, and TiledBackground) are relatively poor implementations of what you'll be doing in later chapters. If you're just starting out, you only want to develop on Siemens phones, and if you like painting naked camels, then you might benefit from these classes. Frankly, I wish Siemens had spent their programmer time (and class space) on developing better device functionality, such as color pixel manipulation or image reflection and rotation. Sprites and object managers are a great idea, but only if implemented well (and the Siemens Game API is far from that). Look toward MIDP 2 for a better implementation of some of these concepts (such as layers).

Motorola

Motorola, like Nokia, provides an excellent SDK for their MIDs. The Motorola J2ME SDK includes an excellent extensions API that is both highly functional and well put together. The SDK also includes emulators for all the major phone models.

The two major APIs included are the Lightweight Windowing Toolkit and the Game API. Of these, I'll only review the Game API. Don't get me wrong—the LWT is an excellent tool for applications requiring extra UI features, but these are less important for gamers so I'll just stick to the Game API.

The significant classes of the Game API provide functionality for:

- Graphics rendering using double buffering
- Sound effects and music
- Support for simultaneous key presses
- Sprites
- Direct pixel and palette manipulation
- Image scaling

In the following sections, you'll take a look at these in more detail. However, given that I've already covered two other APIs, I'll move a little faster. Ready?

Setup

To download the latest SDK and emulators, visit the Motocoder Web site at http://kb.motorola.metrowerks.com/motorola.

To compile you will need to add `cldc.zip`, `midp.zip` and `lwt.zip` to your CLASSPATH. They are located in the `Emulator7.5\lib` directory under the Motorola J2ME installation directory.

To test that everything is set up, I recommend loading the Launchpad (an application included with the SDK) and running some of the sample games. You can see the results in Figure 6.11.

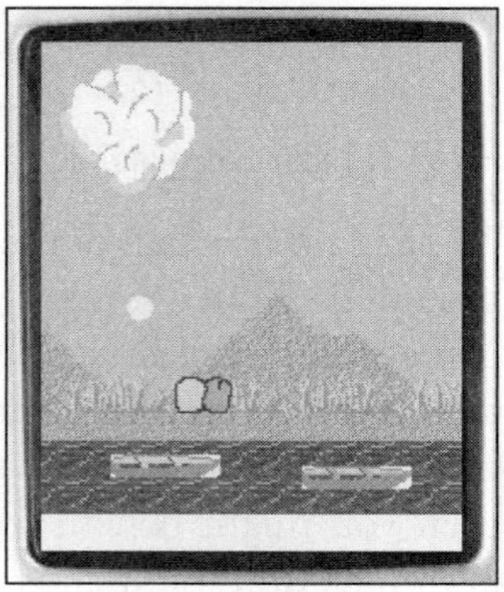

GameScreen

The `GameScreen` class provides functionality to cater to typical game requirements, such as buffered graphics and sound playback. It also provides an enhanced user input system that supports simultaneous key presses.

Figure 6.11 A Motorola game example running in the emulator.

Using `GameScreen` is relatively painless. (I'm hoping you don't like pain all that much.) However, it's a little different from the typical utility classes you've seen. `GameScreen` acts as a framework for graphics rendering, sound and music playback, and input handling, so you need to structure your game around a game loop with `GameScreen` at the core. During each pass through the game loop, you should check for input, process things, and then render the results onto `GameScreen`'s off-screen buffer before you finally flush the buffer onto the screen. Take a look at a sample of this process in action:

```
private void gameLoop(GameScreen gs)
{
    Graphics g = gs.getGraphics();

    // check key states
    int keys = gs.getKeyStates();
    if ((keyState & DOWN_KEY) != 0)  playerSprite.move( 0,  1);
    if ((keyState & UP_KEY) != 0)    playerSprite.move( 0, -1);
    if ((keyState & RIGHT_KEY) != 0) playerSprite.move( 1,  0);
    if ((keyState & LEFT_KEY) != 0)  playerSprite.move(-1,  0);

    // do other game processing here... such as AI
    ...

    // clear the background
    g.fillRect(getWidth(), getHeight());

    // draw player's sprite
```

```
playerSprite.draw(g);

// flush the buffer to the display
gs.flushGraphics();
```

Tip

For a full working example of this take a look at the `KeyTest` MIDlet in the Motorola demos directory (\Motorola\SDK v3.1 for J2ME\demo\com\mot\j2me\midlets)

The first thing to note here is how you grab a typical MIDP LCDUI `Graphics` object from
the `GameScreen` class (Table 6.12 lists the available methods). This lets you use all the normal graphics tools, with the rendering results going to `GameScreen`'s off-screen buffer.
Another thing to note is that (contrary to an obvious oversight in the API documentation)
`GameScreen` extends `javax.microedition.lcdui.Canvas`, so all the functionality of `Canvas` is
available as well.

After you get the `Graphics` context, the `getKeyStates` method call determines the current
state of key presses. This method returns an integer with bits set to indicate the combination of keys that are currently pressed. As you can see, you then just logically `AND` the results
to determine whether a particular key is pressed.

Tip

Given that key presses might happen very quickly—possibly at a time when you are not checking
the states of keys—you might miss that the user actually pressed the key. If your game is processing its main loop quickly, then generally you will want to respond to any key that was pressed since
you last checked—even if the key is down at that instant. To support this, `GameScreen` will indicate
that a key is down if it has been pressed since the last call to `getKeyStates`. You can disable this
latching behavior by just calling `getKeyStates` twice—once to clear it, and then again to check at
that instant. This will result in a true representation of whether the key is actually down at the time
you're calling.

After you check the key states, you can take action based on what the player is doing and
render the result to the off-screen buffer. Once everything is done, a call to `flushGraphics`
will take care of rendering the off-screen buffer onto the MID's display.

`GameScreen` also acts as the player for sound effects and music. There are two classes for producing sounds on Motorola MIDs: `SoundEffect`, which lets you play simple sounds, and
`BackgroundMusic` (Table 6.13 lists the API for both these classes), for playing MIDI
music. To determine whether the underlying device supports these functions, use the
`backgroundMusicSupported` and `soundEffectsSupported` methods.

Table 6.12 com.motorola.game.GameScreen Classes

Method	Description
GameScreen()	Constructs a new GameScreen.
void enableKeyEvents(boolean enabled)	Turns on or off key events.
int getKeyStates()	Gets the state map of the GameScreen keys.
void flushGraphics()	Draws any off-screen buffer content on the screen.
void flushGraphics(int x, int y, int width, int height)	Flushes only part of the buffer.
void paint(Graphics g)	Paints the GameScreen.
static int getDisplayColor(int color)	Asks the device to return the actual color as it would be rendered.
protected Graphics getGraphics()	Returns the LCDUI Graphics class associated with the GameScreen.
boolean backgroundMusicSupported()	Returns true if the MID can play music files.
void playBackgroundMusic(BackgroundMusic bgm, boolean loop)	Starts playback of a background music object.
void playSoundEffect(SoundEffect se, int volume, int priority)	Starts playback of a sound effect.
boolean soundEffectsSupported()	Returns true if the underlying device supports sound.
void getMaxSoundsSupported()	Returns the number of simultaneous sounds the device can play back.
void stopAllSoundEffects()	Kills all sound effects currently playing.

Table 6.13 Sound and BackgroundMusic Classes

Class	Description
com.motorola.game.SoundEffect	
static SoundEffect createSoundEffect(String resource)	Creates a sound effect based on a resource loaded from a URL.
com.motorola.game.BackgroundMusic	
static BackgroundMusic createBackgroundMusic(java.lang.String name)	Creates background music loaded from a URL.

You can use SoundEffect to load a local sound resource from a file and then make it available for playback. In essence, you set up a sound resource and then fire it whenever you need to play back the sound. A sound resource is typically in the form of a WAV file. Take a look at an example:

```
SoundEffect explosionSound = null;
try
{
    explosionSound = SoundEffect.createSoundEffect("/whabam.wav");
}
catch(FileFormatNotSupportedException fe)
{ }
```

From this code, you can get the general idea of how things work. Actually, it's simpler than you think. The SoundEffect class has a single static method called createSoundEffect, to which you pass the name of a resource. The resource name can also be a URL pointing to an HTTP resource, such as http://your-site.com/explode.wav.

The BackgroundMusic class is just as simple, except the resource you're loading is a type 0 or 1 MIDI music file (MID). For example:

```
BackgroundMusic karmaChameleon = null;
try
{
    karmaChameleon =
        BackgroundMusic.createBackgroundMusic("http://boy-george.com/kc.mid");
}
catch(FileFormatNotSupportedException fe)
{ }
```

When you have a sound or music resource ready to go, you can start playback by calling the GameScreen class's playBackgroundMusic and playSoundEffect methods.

Sprites and PlayField

Motorola also included good implementations of a general-purpose Sprite class and world manager in the form of the PlayField class. As with Siemens, I'm not going to go into the details about these classes because you'll be developing better implementations in later chapters. Feel free to browse the javadoc for details. Motorola has done a good job, but we're going to do a better one.

ImageUtil

Like Nokia, Motorola provides some excellent image tools, including direct pixel access and image scaling (no rotation or reflection, though). Silly, isn't it? You get rotation from Nokia and scaling from Motorola. Maybe if you get players to buy one of each and hold them really close together, you can combine the effects somehow. Not!

Motorola's direct pixel access methods are the best of the manufacturer bunch. You just grab 24-bit RGB values straight from an image. No worries about underlying implementations, you are removed from the gory details, thankfully. To grab the pixel data, use the getPixels method in the ImageUtil class (Table 6.14 lists the API). This will return an array of integers with color data in the form of 0x00RRGGBB. You can manipulate this data (as you did in the Nokia section) and then draw those pixels back onto an image.

The ImageUtil class also provides a method to scale an image to a different size. Like reflection and rotation in the Nokia API, scaling can be very useful (though not as useful as reflection and rotation) for creating different versions of the same sprites, such as creating bigger versions of the same enemy ship to represent stronger types.

To scale an image, call the getScaleImage method and pass in the source image and the new size. You can also choose from three types of scaling methods that vary considerably in performance: SCALE_AREA, SCALE_REPLICATE, and SCALE_SMOOTH. Feel free to experiment.

Table 6.14　com.motorola.game.ImageUtil

Method	Description
static void getPixels(Image src, int[] rgbData)	Gets the pixel data from an image.
static void getPixels(Image src, int x, int y, int width, int height, int[] rgbData)	Gets the pixel data from a region of an image.
static void setPixels(Image dest, int[] rgbData)	Sets pixel data on an image.
static void setPixels(Image dest, int x, int y, int width, int height, int[] rgbData)	Sets pixel data in a region on an image.
static Image getScaleImage(Image src, int width, int height, int method)	Returns a scaled version of the original image.

PaletteImage

The PaletteImage class (Table 6.15 lists the methods) allows you to manipulate an image's palette, rather than having to adjust pixels as well. This is a much simpler and faster way to change just the color components of the image, and you can use it to generate some interesting effects.

A good example of pixel color manipulation is the trick you did in the Nokia API, where you changed one color on an image to another. You can do the same thing by adjusting the palette for the image, rather than the pixels themselves. For example:

```
PaletteImage redStripe = new PaletteImage("redstripe.png");

// Get the palette entries
int[] palette = new int[redStripe.getPaletteSize()];
palette = redStripe.getPalette();

// Find our max red and change it to max green
for (int i=0; i < redStripe.getPaletteSize(); i++)
{
    if (palette[i] == 0xFF0000)
        redStripe.setPaletteEntry(i, 0x00FF00);
}
Image greenStripe = redStripe.getImage();
```

Tip

Although there is no support for alpha channels, you can use the setTransparentIndex to indicate one of the palette entries that will render transparently.

Table 6.15 com.motorola.game.PaletteImage

Method	Description
PaletteImage(byte[] data, int offset, int length)	Constructs a new PaletteImage.
PaletteImage(String name)	Constructs a new PaletteImage using data loaded from the named resource.
Image getImage()	Returns an image with the adjusted palette.
int[] getPalette()	Gets the current palette as an array on 24-bit RGB integers.
int getPaletteEntry(int index)	Gets a specific palette entry using an index.
int getPaletteSize()	Gets the size of the palette.
void setPalette(int[] newPalette)	Sets a new palette for the image.
void setPaletteEntry(int index, int color)	Sets the specified entry in the palette.
void setTransparentIndex(int index)	Changes the transparent index.
int getTransparentIndex()	Returns the index of the transparent color.

Other Extensions

So far you've reviewed the APIs from Nokia, Siemens, and Motorola. It doesn't end there, though—pretty much every major MID manufacturer worth their salt has support for J2ME in some phone models. Some of these manufacturers also provide assistance to developers in the form of emulators or device extension APIs such as the ones you've reviewed in this chapter. Table 6.16 provides a list of Web sites for some additional development resources available from other manufacturers.

Table 6.16 Other Manufacturer Extensions

Manufacturer	Web Site
Samsung	http://www.samsungmobile.com/gbr/index.jsp
Sony Ericsson	http://www.ericsson.com/mobilityworld/sub/open/technologies/java/index.html
BlackBerry	http://www.blackberry.net/developers/na/index.shtml
LG	http://java.ez-i.co.kr (watch out, it's in Korean!)

Conclusion

Getting sick of APIs? I know I am. The exercise, however, is a good one. As you've seen, some of the functionality (such as device control, imaging tools, and sounds) can dramatically enhance your game over the default MIDP 1.0 functionality. Nowadays I wouldn't consider developing a game that did not include at least some of these extensions.

Of course, the problem is how to do this without ending up with code that resembles a game addict's bedroom. Typical methods for abstracting and organizing this type of code might have worked in the big world, but they can carry too high of a price in terms of class resources to be useful for J2ME. In Chapter 14, "The Device Ports," you'll explore techniques that keep the bedroom sparkling without requiring a complex web of interfaces and classes.

But before you move on to the main event, there's one more warm-up act. You've looked into the history, talked about tons of APIs and tools, and seen more sample code than a hamster on acid (no, I don't know why they see sample code when they're on acid), but it's hard to see how this all comes together as an actual game. In the next chapter you'll do just that—it's game time!

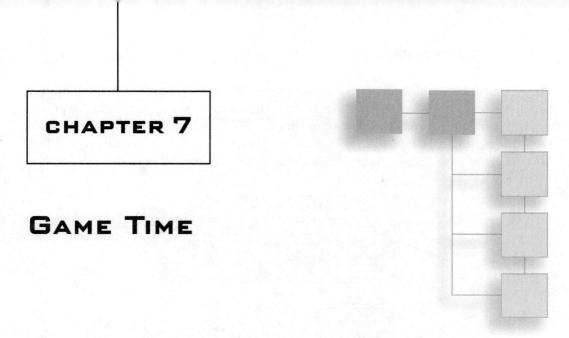

CHAPTER 7

GAME TIME

R eviewing the APIs has been a good exercise; you can see how much (and how little) power you have when developing a game for MIDs. But great APIs a game
does not make. (I sound like Yoda again.) In this chapter, you'll use those APIs to
create an actual game. Are you ready to dodge some trucks?

Game Time

You've covered a lot of ground in the past few chapters; now it's finally time to bring it all
together into something that you can play. It won't be a blockbuster, but it will have many
of the constructs that any game requires.

A word of warning, though: I'm going to do a lot of things in the game code that aren't
the best practice for MID programming (even though they might be good in the larger
programming environments). The point is not to worry too much about the details just
yet; you'll use this game as a basis for improvement in Part III, "Game On."

Game Design

So what sort of game shall we make? Do you remember *Frogger*? It was a cute little game
where you helped a little frog hop across a busy highway, dodging trucks, cars, and other
obstacles along the way. In this chapter, you're going to create a similar game. I decided on
this type of game because of its simplicity. At this stage I don't want to swamp you with
huge amounts of game code (although I'm sorely tempted to, even if just to show off what
you can really do). For now, you'll just explore the components of a basic game, concen-
trating on how to use what you've learned in the previous chapters in a real game context.

The game (dubbed *RoadRun*) presents the player with the challenge of helping a little wombat across a busy highway (see Figure 7.1). The player can jump to the next or previous lane using the up and down arrows, or along a lane using the left and right arrows. To keep things simple, I've decided to exclude the poisonous barbs the wombat could fire into the driver's eye (causing him to veer wildly and smash into other cars).

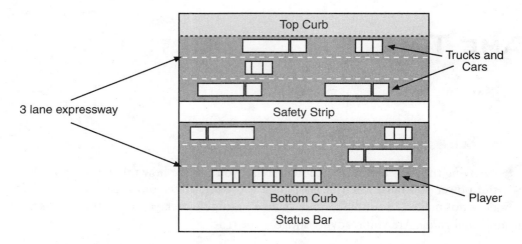

Figure 7.1 In *RoadRun*, the player tries to navigate across six lanes of high-speed traffic without getting squished.

The Application Class

Given the (albeit simple) game design, you can move on to the classes you'll need to get the job done. The first and most obvious is a MIDlet class to represent the application. I prefer the convention of using the application name without tacking MIDlet on the end for this class, so call your first class RoadRun.

The role of this class, like any good MIDlet, will be to act as your connection to the Application Manager (it will call the MIDlet startApp, pauseApp and destroyApp methods to let you know when the game is starting, pausing, or about to be destroyed). Here's the complete class:

```
import javax.microedition.midlet.*;
import javax.microedition.lcdui.*;


/**
 * The application class for the game RoadRun.
 * @author Martin J. Wells
 */
```

```java
public class RoadRun extends MIDlet
{
    private MainMenu menu;

    /**
     * MIDlet constructor instantiates the main menu.
     */
    public RoadRun()
    {
        menu = new MainMenu(this);
    }

    /**
     * Called by the game classes to indicate to the user that the current game
     * is over.
     */
    public void gameOver()
    {
        // Display an alert (the device will take care of implementing how to
        // show it to the user.
        Alert alert = new Alert("", "Splat! Game Over", null, AlertType.INFO);
        // Then set the menu to be current.
        Display.getDisplay(this).setCurrent(alert, menu);
    }

    /**
     * A utility method to shutdown the application.
     */
    public void close()
    {
        try
        {
            destroyApp(true);
            notifyDestroyed();
        }

        catch (MIDletStateChangeException e)
        { }
    }

    /**
     * Handles Application Manager notification the MIDlet is starting (or
```

```
 * resuming from a pause). In this case we set the menu as the current
 * display screen.
 * @throws MIDletStateChangeException
 */
public void startApp() throws MIDletStateChangeException
{
    Display.getDisplay(this).setCurrent(menu);
}


/**
 * Handles Application Manager notification the MIDlet is about to be paused.
 * We don't bother doing anything for this case.
 */
public void pauseApp()
{
}


/**
 * Handles Application Manager notification the MIDlet is about to be
 * destroyed. We don't bother doing anything for this case.
 */
public void destroyApp(boolean unconditional) throws MIDletStateChangeException
{
}


}
```

As you can see, this is the most basic of MIDlets. You just implement the required methods, instantiate your menu, and make it the current display. This code won't work as it is though; you need to implement the menu system (the MainMenu class).

The Menu

To start the game, present the player with a splash screen and menu. This is just a simple form with text introducing the title of the game and offering an option to either start playing or quit. This screen also serves as an anchor point to return to when play has ended. You'll see this in action later. For now, here's the menu class:

```
import javax.microedition.lcdui.CommandListener;
import javax.microedition.lcdui.Form;
import javax.microedition.lcdui.Command;
import javax.microedition.lcdui.Displayable;
```

```java
/**
 * A simple menu system for RoadRun using commmands.
 * @author Martin J. Wells
 */
public class MainMenu extends Form implements CommandListener
{
    private RoadRun theMidlet;
    private Command start;
    private Command exit;

    /**
     * Creates a new menu object (while retaining a reference to its parent
     * midlet).
     * @param midlet The MIDlet this menu belongs to (used to later call back
     * to activate the game screen as well as exit).
     */
    protected MainMenu(RoadRun midlet)
    {
        // the Form constructor
        super("");

        // a connection to the midlet
        theMidlet = midlet;

        // add the welcome text
        append("\nWelcome to\n");
        append("R-O-A-D R-U-N");

        // create and add the commands
        int priority = 1;
        start = new Command("Start", Command.SCREEN, priority++);
        exit = new Command("Exit", Command.EXIT, priority++);

        addCommand(start);
        addCommand(exit);

        setCommandListener(this);
    }

    /**
     * Handles the start (activate game screen) and exit commands. All the work
```

```
 * is done by the RoadRun class.
 * @param command the command that was triggered
 * @param displayable the displayable on which the event occurred
 */
public void commandAction(Command command, Displayable displayable)
{
    if (command == start)
        theMidlet.activateGameScreen();

    if (command == exit)
        theMidlet.close();
}
}
```

This class extends `javax.microedition.lcdui.Form` to provide a simple placeholder for the intro text (your splash screen). The constructor then adds this text along with the `start` and `exit` commands.

The `commandAction` method handles the two commands, both of which use the `theMidlet` field to make a callback to the application class. `exit` simply calls the `close` method on the MIDlet. `start`, however, calls a method you haven't implemented yet, `activateGameScreen`. Of course, before you can activate it, you need to know what exactly a `GameScreen` is.

The Game Screen

The `GameScreen` class represents the core of your game. This includes object movement, graphics rendering, and reading and reacting to input.

Because you have to start somewhere, begin with the graphics. To implement this for *RoadRun,* you need to derive a class from the MIDP LCDUI's low-level `Canvas` to represent your game's screen. Take a look at the starting code for the `GameScreen` class:

```
import javax.microedition.lcdui.Canvas;
import javax.microedition.lcdui.Graphics;

public class GameScreen extends Canvas
{
    private RoadRun theMidlet;

    public GameScreen(RoadRun midlet)
    {
        theMidlet = midlet;
    }
```

```
protected void paint(Graphics graphics)
{
}
```

```
}
```

Again, this is skeleton stuff. You need to do quite a bit more to make things happen. Before you can really add any action in here, you need something more fundamental. You need to pull out the defibrillators, yell "Clear!," and start your game's heart.

The Game Loop

At the heart of any action game is a processing loop used to carry out all the tasks that keep things moving. You need to move those trucks and cars, detect input from the player, check for collisions, and render everything to the screen—and you need to do it quickly enough to give the player the impression that it's something like reality.

To do this, you use what's commonly termed a *game loop*. Essentially, you have the application run around like a dog chasing its tail as fast as it can. You then carry out any necessary tasks as part of this looping process. The number of times per second the dog completes a circle (and this is one quick dog) is known as the application's CPS (*cycles per second*). Figure 7.2 illustrates this concept.

To implement a game loop, you need an execution process independent of the application so that you can maintain control over it (such as pausing). In Java, you do this by creating a separate thread using the rather appropriately named Thread class.

Adding this to the class is pretty easy. First change the GameScreen class so that it implements the Runnable interface. The Runnable interface is required for a class, in this case the GameScreen class, to become a target of execution for a new thread.

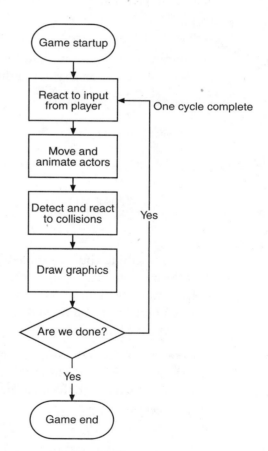

Figure 7.2 The components of a simple game loop

```
public class GameScreen extends Canvas implements
Runnable
```

Next add the thread initialization process to the GameScreen constructor.

```
public GameScreen()
{

    ...

    // create the game thread
    Thread t = new Thread(this);
    t.start();
}
```

This is simpler than it looks. First you construct the Thread object, assigning this instance of the GameScreen class as the Runnable target, and then you call the start method to get things going.

To comply with the Runnable interface, you also have to add a run method. This is the method called as soon as you call the start method.

```
private boolean running=true;

public void run()
{
    while(running)
    {
        // do... everything!
    }
}
```

There's something you can immediately gather from all of this: The fastest the game can go is the maximum CPS. Therefore, the application is now running at the fastest CPS possible. Any code you now add to the game loop will slow this down. Knowing the base CPS at this point in the game and then watching it decrease progressively is an excellent method of tracking the impact of your code. Now add a CPS meter to the application.

Calculating CPS is pretty simple; you just increment a counter every time you go through the game loop. To find out the cycles per second, you also check whether a second has passed, and then record the total. First, you need to add the following tracking fields to the GameScreen class:

```
private int cps=0;
private int cyclesThisSecond=0;
private long lastCPSTime=0;
```
You can then use these fields in the game loop. For example:
```
public void run()
```

```
{
    while(running)
    {
        repaint();

        if (System.currentTimeMillis() - lastCPSTime > 1000)
        {
            lastCPSTime = System.currentTimeMillis();
            cps = cyclesThisSecond;
            cyclesThisSecond = 0;
        } else
            cyclesThisSecond++;
    }
}
```

This code calculates the amount of time that has passed to determine whether a second has elapsed (1000 milliseconds). If it has, you set the lastCPSTime to now (the current time) and mark the CPS rate (since we now know how many cycles occurred up to 1000 milliseconds); otherwise, you increment the number of cycles so far.

I've added a repaint method call so you can display the CPS on the screen. When repaint is called the system will (at some point in the very near future) call the GameScreen paint method to draw everything.

Now you can revise the paint method to draw the number of CPS.

```
protected void paint(Graphics graphics)
{
    graphics.setColor(0x00000000);
    graphics.fillRect(0, 0, getWidth(), getHeight());
    graphics.setColor(0x00ffffff);
    graphics.drawString("cps=" + cps, 0, 0, Graphics.LEFT
| Graphics.TOP);
}
```

As you can see from the results in Figure 7.3, your CPS starts out very high! Unfortunately it's just an illusion. As you add features (and start to behave like a proper game), you'll see this number drop significantly.

Because you are now rendering a frame on each pass, you can say this is now also your number of FPS (*frames per second*).

Figure 7.3 Output from a simple GameScreen showing the starting CPS.

This works nicely, but it's also a bit silly. Do you really need to be cycling this fast? For a start, you'll find your game becomes very jerky when you start to move and animate things. This is because you're hogging the CPU. You need to give the underlying operating system time to do its work as well (such as rendering your graphics). Don't cycle unnecessarily.

To keep things looking smooth, you need to maintain a reasonable frame rate—say 50 per second. If you can achieve this, you should be nice to your operating environment and put your MIDlet to sleep using the Thread.sleep method while doing all your required processing.

For how long should you sleep? There's no need to go overboard and compromise your application's performance because you sent it off to sleep for too long. Therefore, how long you sleep should be relative to the spare time you have. (Sometimes this might be no time at all.) Modify the cycle loop to check whether you have any time left, and then sleep for only that time.

To calculate how much time you have left, you first need to know how much time you allotted to each cycle. If you're under that time at the end of the cycle, you should sleep for the difference. If you set your maximum number of cycles per second to 50, then each cycle has 20 milliseconds to finish. Take a look at the code to do this:

```java
private static final int MAX_CPS = 50;
private static final int MS_PER_FRAME = 1000 / MAX_CPS;
public void run()
{
    while(running)
    {
        // remember the starting time
        long cycleStartTime = System.currentTimeMillis();

        ... process the cycle (repaint etc)

        // sleep if we've finished our work early
        long timeSinceStart = (cycleStartTime - System.currentTimeMillis());
        if (timeSinceStart < MS_PER_FRAME)
        {
            try
            {
                Thread.sleep(MS_PER_FRAME - timeSinceStart);
            }
            catch(java.lang.InterruptedException e)
```

```
        { }
      }
    }
  }
}
```

I've made things a little clearer (and more flexible) by using two constants to figure the maximum cycle rate (50) and the subsequent number of milliseconds to which this translates (20). The modified cycle code remembers the cycleStartTime and then sleeps for any leftover time using Thread.sleep(MS_PER_FRAME - timeSinceStart).

Tip

In this example the CPS and FPS are effectively the same. In more advanced scenarios you can separate the timing of these, using one rate for redrawing (FPS) and one for other parts of the game (CPS), such as physics and collision detection. If necessary, you can take this even further by allocating processing budgets for different parts of the system depending on their priority, although this is getting a bit heavy-duty for your purposes.

If you run this code now, you'll notice the CPS drops to something near your desired maximum rate. As an exercise, try changing the sleep time to 1. The CPS won't return to your previous super-high levels because the sleep method is quite an expensive call to make.

Adding the Graphics

Now that you have a basic framework going, you can get on with the task of creating the graphics for the game. The first thing you'll cover is a rendering technique known as double buffering; after that, you'll move on to drawing the game world.

Double Buffering

As you saw in reviewing the MIDP APIs, rendering graphics generally just involves adding code to the paint method. You grab a graphics context and draw on the display. Unfortunately, if you're doing this through a high-speed game loop (as you did earlier), you'll run into some ugly display issues. The problem is something like holding a stage play with no curtain—you need time to get everything ready before you open the curtain and let everyone take a peek. It's the same with your MID—you need to prepare everything off-screen and, when you're ready, render it in one go.

To create this process you need to add another area, or buffer, where you can safely render off-screen. You then have two buffers—one on-screen, representing what you last rendered, and one off-screen, to which you can render anytime. That's why you call this *double-buffering*. You can see this process illustrated in Figure 7.4.

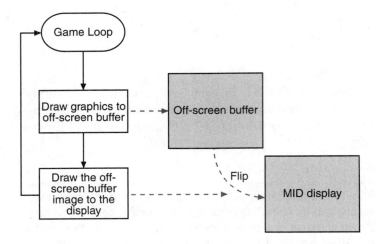

Figure 7.4 To eliminate drawing process artifacts, you render to an off-screen buffer and then draw the entire screen to the display in one quick step.

To add double buffering to *RoadRun*, you need to initialize an off-screen buffer. I do this using a resource setup method called from the constructor.

```
private Image offScreenBuffer;

public GameScreen()
{

   ...

   initResources();
}

private void initResources()
{
   offScreenBuffer = Image.createImage(getWidth(), getHeight());
}
```

You also need to modify the paint process to render your off-screen buffer. You'll notice that in the following code, I've also added another method called renderWorld. You'll get to that one in the next section.

```
protected void paint(Graphics graphics)
{
   renderWorld();
   graphics.drawImage(offScreenBuffer, 0, 0, Graphics.LEFT | Graphics.TOP);
}
```

Drawing the World

Drawing the world is a relatively painless process. You just use the built-in vector drawing tools to render a simple version of the freeway. Because you're using vector-based drawing to set up the world, you can be a little more flexible about how the world is drawn. This starts with the idea that the lane height (the vertical distance between each lane) is the primary unit for rendering the entire level. As you saw in Figure 7.1, you need three curbs (top, middle, and bottom), six lanes (three at the top and three at the bottom), and space for the status bar along the bottom.

To space things out well, you set the status bar to a static height of 10 pixels. (This is generally a good size for the small font.) laneHeight is then calculated inside the initResources method as the height of the display minus the status bar divided by 9 (three curbs and six lanes. Because you only need to calculate these numbers once, the code to carry this out belongs in the initResources method.

```
private static int statusLineHeight=10;
private int laneHeight=0;
private static final int topMargin = 3;

private void initResources()
{
    ...
    // set up our world variables
    int heightMinusStatus = getHeight() - statusLineHeight;
    laneHeight = ((heightMinusStatus) / 9);
}
```

Once you have things set up, you can add the renderWorld method to create your expressway.

```
private void renderWorld()
{
    // grab our off-screen graphics context
    Graphics osg = offScreenBuffer.getGraphics();
    int y=0;

    // draw the top roadside
    osg.setColor(0x00209020);
    y += (laneHeight)+topMargin;
    osg.fillRect(0, 0, getWidth(), y);

    // curb edge
    osg.setColor(0x00808080);
    osg.drawLine(0, y-2, getWidth(), y-2);
```

```
osg.setColor(0x00000000);
osg.drawLine(0, y-1, getWidth(), y-1);

// draw the first three lanes
osg.setColor(0x00000000);
osg.fillRect(0, y, getWidth(), laneHeight * 3);

// draw the line markings on the road
osg.setStrokeStyle(Graphics.DOTTED);
osg.setColor(0x00AAAAAA);
y += laneHeight; osg.drawLine(0, y, getWidth(), y);
y += laneHeight; osg.drawLine(0, y, getWidth(), y);
y += laneHeight; osg.drawLine(0, y, getWidth(), y);

// draw the middle safety strip
osg.setColor(0x00666666);
osg.fillRect(0, y-2, getWidth(), 2);
osg.setColor(0x00aaaaaa);
osg.fillRect(0, y, getWidth(), laneHeight); y+= laneHeight;
osg.setColor(0x00666666);
osg.fillRect(0, y - 2, getWidth(), 2);

// draw the next three lanes
osg.setColor(0x00000000);
osg.fillRect(0, y, getWidth(), laneHeight * 3);

// draw the line markings on the road
osg.setStrokeStyle(Graphics.DOTTED);
osg.setColor(0x00AAAAAA);
y += laneHeight; osg.drawLine(0, y, getWidth(), y);
y += laneHeight; osg.drawLine(0, y, getWidth(), y);
y += laneHeight; osg.drawLine(0, y, getWidth(), y);

// curb edge
osg.setStrokeStyle(Graphics.SOLID);
osg.setColor(0x00808080);
osg.drawLine(0, y, getWidth(), y);
y++;
osg.setColor(0x00000000);
osg.drawLine(0, y, getWidth(), y);

// draw the bottom roadside
osg.setColor(0x00209020);
```

```
osg.fillRect(0, y, getWidth(), y + (laneHeight * 2));
y += laneHeight * 2;

// draw the status bar along the bottom
osg.setColor(0, 0, 128);
osg.fillRect(0, getHeight() - statusLineHeight, getWidth(), getHeight());
osg.setFont(Font.getFont(Font.FACE_PROPORTIONAL, Font.STYLE_PLAIN, Font.SIZE_SMALL));
osg.setColor(0x00ffffff);
osg.setColor(0x00ffffff);
osg.drawString("" + cps + " cps", 5, getHeight() - statusLineHeight + 1,
               Graphics.LEFT | Graphics.TOP);
}
/**
 * @return The height of a lane.
 */
public int getLaneHeight()
{
    return laneHeight;
}
```

Figure 7.5 Not bad for a little bit of drawing code!

I know that's a lot of code, but it's nothing you haven't seen already. Take note, however, that you're doing all your drawing to the off-screen buffer's Graphics context, not to the screen. I've also moved the CPS rate-drawing code out of the paint method and onto the status bar rendered at the bottom of the screen. Figure 7.5 shows the results.

Linking to the Application

The next step for GameScreen is to integrate it into the application class. If you remember back when you created the menu form, there was a call to an "international method of mystery" named activateGameScreen. Now that you have the GameScreen ready, integrate it with RoadRun and implement the *activate* method.

```
public class RoadRun extends MIDlet
{
    ...

    private GameScreen gameScreen;

    ...

    public void activateGameScreen()
    {
        gameScreen = new GameScreen(this);
```

```
        Display.getDisplay(this).setCurrent(gameScreen);
    }
```

With GameScreen now integrated with the application, your stage is set. Let's go hire some actors!

The Actors

What your game needs now is some action. To get things moving, you need what I refer to (rather abstractly) as actors. According to my definition, an actor is an object that can move around. So for your game, the player's object (the wombat) and the cars and trucks that speed along the road are all actors. To be able to move, all of these objects must have a 2D position (x and y) in your world. Movement is just a change in this position over time.

Although having a position is common to all of these objects, there are still a few differences for your game. First, you draw each actor differently on the screen, so you need a way to track the type of actor and thus do the correct rendering. The cars and trucks also differ in that they move at varying speeds along the highway.

Many Roles

With all this in mind, take the object-oriented high road and create a hierarchy that appropriately represents what you need. As you can see in Figure 7.6, the Actor class is an abstract base class for your WombatActor and VehicleActor classes. WombatActor adds its unique rendering, and the VehicleActor class adds the concept of speed.

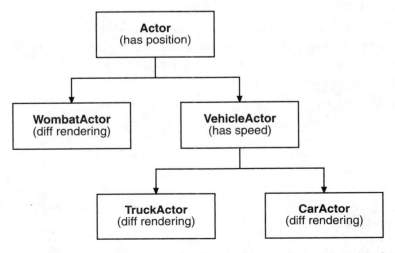

Figure 7.6 The action in *RoadRun* is implemented using a hierarchy of actors.

The Actor class represents an on-screen object in the game that will move around. To handle this it first needs to maintain a position (in the following source code you can see this represented using the x and y integers). In order to give it life you add a cycle method which you can call from the game loop and finally a render method so it can draw itself on the screen. Since the functionality is common to the vehicles, I've implemented code to handle getting and setting positions. The cycle and render methods however are left ready to be overridden to implement the WombatActor and VehicleActor specifics.

```java
import javax.microedition.lcdui.Graphics;

/**
 * An abstract base class for higher level Actors. This class handles basic
 * position as well as maintaining a link to the GameScreen. A class extending
 * this needs to implement the cycle and render methods.
 */
abstract public class Actor
{
    protected GameScreen gameScreen;
    private int x, y;

    /**
     * Constructs a new Actor.
     * @param gsArg The GameScreen this Actor belongs to.
     * @param xArg The starting x position.
     * @param yArg The starting y position.
     */
    public Actor(GameScreen gsArg, int xArg, int yArg)
    {
        gameScreen = gsArg;
        x = xArg;
        y = yArg;
    }

    /**
     * Called by the main game loop to let the Actor have a life. Typically an
     * implementation should use the deltaMS (the number of milliseconds that
     * have passed since the cycle method was last called) to carry out movement
     * or other actions relative to the amount of time that has passed. The
     * default implementation in the base class does nothing.
     * @param deltaMS The number of milliseconds that have passed since the last
     * call to cycle.
     */
    public void cycle(long deltaMS) { }
```

```
/**
 * Called by the main game loop to draw this Actor to the screen. It is
 * intended that a child class override this implementation in order to
 * draw a representation of the actor (in a way it sees fit).
 * @param g The Graphics context upon which to draw the actor.
 */
public void render(Graphics g) { }

/**
 * Returns the width of the Actor (can be overriden by a child class to
 * return a different size).
 * @return Width of the actor.
 */
public int getActorWidth()
{
    // square by default
    return getActorHeight();
}

/**
 * Returns the height of the Actor (can be overriden by a child class to
 * return a different size). The default implementation (the most common
 * case) is to use a value slightly smaller than the lane height.
 * @return Height of the actor.
 */
public int getActorHeight()
{
    return gameScreen.getLaneHeight() - 2;
}

/**
 * @return The current x position of the actor.
 */
public int getX() { return x; }

/**
 * Sets the current x position of the actor. We also check to see if the
 * actor has moved off the edge of the screen and wrap it around.
 */
public void setX(int newX)
{
    x = newX;
```

```
    // we wrap on the x-axis on a constant number to maintain an
    // equal distance between all vehicles
    if (x < -32)
        x = gameScreen.getWidth();

    if (x > gameScreen.getWidth())
        x = -getActorWidth();
}


/**
 * @return The current y position of the actor.
 */
public int getY() { return y; }

/**
 * Sets the current y position of the actor. We also check to see if the
 * actor has moved off the edge of the screen and wrap it around.
 */
public void setY(int newY)
{
    y = newY;

    // we don't wrap on the y-axis
    if (y < gameScreen.getLaneYPos(0))
        y = gameScreen.getLaneYPos(0);

    if (y > gameScreen.getLaneYPos(8))
        y = gameScreen.getLaneYPos(8);
}

}
```

As you can see, the Actor class nicely wraps up an x and y position in your game world. As a convenience for later use, you also have each actor object keep a reference to the GameScreen object that created it. The interesting part of the Actor class is in the two base methods—cycle and render. Your subclasses will override these methods to implement any cycling or rendering they need to do. (You'll see this in action a little later.)

I've included the methods for getting and setting the position of the actor. The set methods also test to make sure the object isn't off the edge of your world and reset the position if required. Take note that the x and y integer fields for position are declared private, not protected. This is intentional, to ensure that the only access to these fields is via the set and get methods.

The Wombat

The code for the next object, the `WombatActor`, follows. For this class you extend `Actor` and override the `render` method to draw your wombat (a green square).

```java
import javax.microedition.lcdui.Graphics;

/**
 * The main player actor, the Wombat.
 * @author Martin J. Wells
 */
public class WombatActor extends Actor
{
    /**
     * Constructs a new WombatActor object using the specified GameScreen and
     * position.
     * @param gsArg The GameScreen this Actor is associated with.
     * @param xArg The x starting position.
     * @param yArg The y starting position.
     */
    public WombatActor(GameScreen gsArg, int xArg, int yArg)
    {
        super(gsArg, xArg, yArg);
    }


    /**
     * Renders the actor to the screen by drawing a rectangle.
     * @param graphics The graphics context to draw to.
     */
    public void render(Graphics graphics)
    {
        graphics.setColor(0x0044FF44);
        graphics.fillRect(getX(), getY(), getActorWidth(), getActorHeight());
    }


    /**
     * An overridden version of the Actor setX method in order to stop the
     * wrapping it does. You want the wombat to stop on the edge of the screen.
     * @param newX The new x position.
     */
    public void setX(int newX)
    {
        super.setX(newX);
```

```
    // non-wrapping version for the wombat
    if (getX() < 0)
        setX(0);

    if (getX() > gameScreen.getWidth()-getActorWidth()-2)
        setX(gameScreen.getWidth() - getActorWidth()-2);
    }
}
```

The only significant change here is the setX method. Since you don't want your wombat to wrap to the other side when it moves beyond the edge of the screen, you override setX to put on the brakes.

Movement

The VehicleActor object is a little bit different. The purpose of the class is to implement movement for the cars and trucks that speed along the expressway. Here's the code:

```
/**
 * An Actor that serves as a base class for the vehicles (such as CarActor and
 * TruckActor). The common functionality is the movement in the cycle method.
 * @author Martin J. Wells
 */
abstract public class VehicleActor extends Actor
{
    protected int speed;          // speed (along x axis only)
    private long fluff = 0;

    /**
     * Constructs a new Vehicle setting the GameScreen, starting position (x, y)
     * and the speed at which it should move.
     * @param gsArg GameScreen Actor is associated with.
     * @param xArg The starting x position.
     * @param yArg The starting y position.
     * @param speedArg The speed of the vehicle.
     */
    public VehicleActor(GameScreen gsArg, int xArg, int yArg, int speedArg)
    {
        super(gsArg, xArg, yArg);
        speed = speedArg;
    }

    /**
```

```
 * A cycle method that moves the Actor a distance relative to its current
 * speed (the value of the speed int) and the amount of time that has passed
 * since the last call to cycle (deltaMS). This code uses a fluff value in
 * order to remember values too small to handle (below the tick level).
 * @param deltaMS The number of milliseconds that have passed since the last
 * call to cycle.
 */
public void cycle(long deltaMS)
{
    long ticks = (deltaMS + fluff) / 100;

    // remember the bit we missed
    fluff += (deltaMS - (ticks * 100));

    // move based on our speed in pixels per ticks
    if (ticks > 0)
        setX( getX() - (int) (speed * ticks) );
}


}
```

This is a good example of the purpose of a cycle method. In your VehicleActor's case, you move the actor along the x-axis. The question is how far do you move it? You'll notice that I have added a speed field to the class and initialized it using a revised constructor. The cycle method uses this field to move the actor at a rate of pixels per tenths of a second. When the GameScreen calls the cycle method for this actor, you also get the total time that has passed since the last cycle call. The amount you need to move is simply the time since the last cycle (in tenths of a second) multiplied by your movement speed.

It all sounds easy, doesn't it? There's a little problem, though. In your game, the GameScreen class will call the cycle method with a gap of about 20 milliseconds. However, because you want to move in tenths of a second, there will be no movement in any single call. Are you with me on this? It comes down to how you figure the number of tenths of a second. (In the code I refer to these as *ticks*.) If you take the number of milliseconds the GameScreen gives you each cycle (about 20) and divide it by 100 to get number of ticks, you'll naturally get a number that is less than zero (for example, 20 / 100 = 0.2). The problem is that you're throwing away the remainder of the calculation because you don't have any support for floating-point numbers. Therefore, the solution is to use a technique known as *remainder memory*, or more cutely as *fluffing*.

Doing this is easier than it sounds. Notice the fluff field I've added to the class. On each pass through the cycle, you use this to remember any leftovers from the calculation, and then add that on to your total the next time. After a few cycles, you'll accumulate enough fluff to have at least one full tick. The good news is that this method is safe no matter what timing you use in the game. If the frame rate is changed, you won't have to adjust your speed; it will always remain time-relative.

Cars and Trucks

Your final two classes, CarActor and TruckActor, are both derived from VehicleActor. In these you override the render method to carry out drawing specific to each type.

```java
import javax.microedition.lcdui.Graphics;

/**
 * A VehicleActor that represents a truck (the only customization is the
 * size and the drawing code).
 * @author Martin J. Wells
 */
public class TruckActor extends VehicleActor
{
    /**
     * Constructs a new truck setting the GameScreen, starting position (x, y)
     * and the speed at which it should move.
     * @param gsArg GameScreen Actor is associated with.
     * @param xArg The starting x position.
     * @param yArg The starting y position.
     * @param speedArg The speed of the vehicle.
     */
    public TruckActor(GameScreen gsArg, int xArg, int yArg, int speedArg)
    {
        super(gsArg, xArg, yArg, speedArg);
    }

    /**
     * Get the Actor width (overriden to set the width properly).
     * @return The width of the truck.
     */
    public int getActorWidth()
    {
        return 28;
    }

    /**
     * Draws a truck using rectangles.
     * @param graphics The graphics context on which to draw the car.
```

```
    */
    public void render(Graphics graphics)
    {
        int u = getActorHeight();

        // the front
        graphics.setColor(0x00aa9922);
        graphics.fillRect(getX(), getY(), 4, u);
        // the trailer
        graphics.setColor(0x00aa9922);
        graphics.fillRect(getX()+9, getY(), 18, u);
        // the cab
        graphics.setColor(0x00ffcc66);
        graphics.fillRect(getX() + 4, getY(), u-3, u);


    }
}
```

The CarActor is very similar.import javax.microedition.lcdui.Graphics;

```
/**
 * A VehicleActor that represents a little car (the only customization is the
 * size and the drawing code).
 * @author Martin J. Wells
 */
public class CarActor extends VehicleActor
{
    /**
     * Constructs a new car setting the GameScreen, starting position (x, y)
     * and the speed at which it should move.
     * @param gsArg GameScreen Actor is associated with.
     * @param xArg The starting x position.
     * @param yArg The starting y position.
     * @param speedArg The speed of the vehicle.
     */
    public CarActor(GameScreen gsArg, int xArg, int yArg, int speedArg)
    {
        super(gsArg, xArg, yArg, speedArg);
    }

    /**
     * Get the Actor width (overriden to set the width properly).
```

```
 * @return The width of the car.
 */
public int getActorWidth()
{
    return 12;
}


/**
 * Draws a car using rectangles.
 * @param graphics The graphics context on which to draw the car.
 */
public void render(Graphics graphics)
{
    int u = getActorHeight();

    graphics.setColor(0x00aa9922);
    graphics.fillRect(getX(), getY(), u, u);
    graphics.fillRect(getX() + (u / 2) + 5, getY(), u, u);
    graphics.setColor(0x00ffcc66);
    graphics.fillRect(getX() + u - 2, getY(), u, u);
}
}
```

Due to the power inherited in the base classes (VehicleActor and Actor), there's very little to do in these classes other than draw the car and truck graphics.

Bringing Them to Life

At this point you need to take a step back. Before you can use your actors, you need to set up the GameScreen class to support them. Start by adding a Vector collection to store all your actors, as well as a field for your main character, the hapless wombat.

```
/**
 * The main drawing and control class for the game RoadRun.
 * @author Martin J. Wells
 */
public class GameScreen extends Canvas implements Runnable
{
    private Vector actorList;
    private WombatActor wombat;
    ...
```

You then modify the initResources method to set up the actorList vector with the starting actors. I've added a convenience method to calculate the Y pixel position of a given lane.

```java
public int getLaneYPos(int lane)
{
    // convenience method to return the y position of a lane number
    return (lane * laneHeight)+1+topMargin;
}


/**
 * Initialize the resources for the game. Should be called to setup the game
 * for play.
 */
private void initResources()
{

    ...

    actorList = new Vector();

    // add the wombat
    wombat = new WombatActor(this, getWidth() / 2, getLaneYPos(8));
    actorList.addElement( wombat );

    // add the top vehicles
    for (int i=1; i < 4; i++)
    {
        actorList.addElement(new TruckActor(this, 1, getLaneYPos(i), (i * 2) + 1));
        actorList.addElement(new CarActor(this, getWidth()/2, getLaneYPos(i), (i*2)+1));
    }

    // add the bottom vehicles
    for (int i = 5; i < 8; i++)
    {
        actorList.addElement(new TruckActor(this, 0, getLaneYPos(i), i));
        actorList.addElement(new CarActor(this, getWidth() / 2, getLaneYPos(i), i));
    }
}
```

To breathe life into all of your actors, you need a master cycle method in the GameScreen class.

```java
private long lastCycleTime;
```

```java
/**
```

```
 * Handles the cycling of all the Actors in the world by calculating the
 * elapsed time and then call the cycle method on all Actors in the local
 * Vector. At the end this method also checks to see if any Actor struck
 * the Wombat.
 */
protected void cycle()
{
    if (lastCycleTime > 0)     // since cycling is time dependent we only do it
        // with a valid time
    {
        long msSinceLastCycle = System.currentTimeMillis() - lastCycleTime;

        // cycle all the actors
        for (int i = 0; i < actorList.size(); i++)
        {
            Actor a = (Actor) actorList.elementAt(i);
            a.cycle((int)msSinceLastCycle);
        }
    }
    lastCycleTime = System.currentTimeMillis();
}
```

Not a lot to this, really. The main processing is the looping through of all the actors within the vector and calling the cycle method (passing in the delta time since you last called). To make this work we then need to modify the run method to call cycle on every pass. Here's the complete revised run method.

```
/**
 * Called when thread is started. Controls the main game loop including the
 * framerate based on the timing set in MS_PER_FRAME. On every cycle it
 * calls the cycle and repaint methods.
 */
public void run()
{
    while(running)
    {
        // remember the starting time
        long cycleStartTime = System.currentTimeMillis();

        // run the cycle
        cycle();
        repaint();
```

```
    // update the CPS
    if (System.currentTimeMillis() - lastCPSTime > 1000)
    {
        lastCPSTime=System.currentTimeMillis();
        cps = cyclesThisSecond;
        cyclesThisSecond = 0;
    } else
        cyclesThisSecond++;

    // Here we calculate how much time has been used so far this cycle. If
    // it is less than the amount of time we should have spent then we
    // sleep a little to let the MIDlet get on with other work.
    long timeSinceStart = (cycleStartTime - System.currentTimeMillis());
    if (timeSinceStart < MS_PER_FRAME)
    {
        try
        {
            Thread.sleep(MS_PER_FRAME - timeSinceStart);
        }
        catch(java.lang.InterruptedException e)
        { }
    }
}

    // If we've reached this point then the running boolean has been set to
    // false by something (such as a quit command) and it's time to fall back
    // to the menu system. The gameOver method displays an alert telling the
    // user their time has come and then returns to the menu.
    theMidlet.gameOver();
}
```

Now there's one final thing to do before your world will come alive. You need to draw these actors on the screen. To do this, modify the renderWorld method to cycle through the current actor list and call each actor's render method.

```
/**
 * Draws the background graphics for the game using rudimentary drawing
 * tools. Note that we draw to the offscreenBuffer graphics (osg) not the
 * screen. The offscreenBuffer is an image the size of the screen we render
 * to and then later "flip" (draw) onto the display in one go (see the paint
 * method).
 */
```

```
private void renderWorld()
{
    ...

    // now draw all the actors
    for (int i=0; i < actorList.size(); i++)
    {
        Actor a = (Actor)actorList.elementAt(i);
        a.render(osg);
    }
}
```

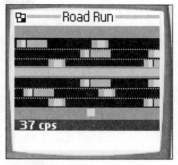

Things are moving along nicely now. As you can see in Figure 7.7, if you run this code you'll see lots of cars and trucks whizzing by. Pretty cool, huh?

Figure 7.7 The Actors in action.

Input Handling

Watching those cars and trucks cruising along is very entertaining, I know—I could just watch it for hours. The real action, however, is in accepting the challenge of navigating your little wombat across the road without turning it into a photo opportunity for road-kill.com. To do this, you need to get some input from the player and translate that into movement.

Guiding your wombat requires reading and reacting to input from the MID. You can do this by adding a keyPressed event handler to the GameScreen class.

```
/**
 * Called when a key is pressed. Based on which key they hit it moves the
 * WombatActor.
 * @param keyCode The key that was pressed.
 */
protected void keyPressed(int keyCode)
{
    switch (getGameAction(keyCode))
    {
        case UP:
            wombat.setY(wombat.getY() - laneHeight);
            break;
        case DOWN:
            wombat.setY(wombat.getY() + laneHeight);
            break;
```

```
        case RIGHT:
            wombat.setX(wombat.getX() + laneHeight);
            break;
        case LEFT:
            wombat.setX(wombat.getX() - laneHeight);
            break;
    }
}
```

Inside this method, you interpret the key that was struck and move the wombat the appropriate distance along either the x- or y-axis. The setX method in the wombat class will take care of limiting the movement to the screen boundaries.

Collision Detection

Since you have both the vehicles and the wombat moving, the potential exists for the two to collide (rather a bad idea from the wombat's perspective). To get this going, you need to add code to determine when a collision occurs, and then react accordingly.

Collision detection can be a complex business. Thankfully, your requirements are relatively simple for *RoadRun*. The only potential collision is between the wombat and one of the vehicles. Life is also easier because of the limited number of objects with which the wombat can potentially collide. You can therefore implement collision detection by checking that the wombat's bounding rectangle is not intersecting any of the vehicles' rectangles. To do this, add some code to the Actor class.

```
/**
 * Simple collision detection checks if a given point is in the Actor's
 * bounding rectangle.
 * @param px The x position of the point to check against.
 * @param py The y position of the point to check against.
 * @return true if the point px, py is within this Actor's bounding rectangle
 */
public boolean isCollidingWith(int px, int py)
{
    if (px >= getX() && px <= (getX() + getActorWidth()) &&
        py >= getY() && py <= (getY() + getActorHeight()) )
        return true;
    return false;
}


/**
 * Determines if another Actor has collided with this one. We do this by
 * checking if any of the four points in the passed in Actor's bounding
```

```
 * rectangle are within the bounds of this Actor's (using the isCollidingWith
 * point method above)
 * @param another The other Actor we're checking against.
 * @return true if the other Actor's bounding box collides with this one.
 */
public boolean isCollidingWith(Actor another)
{
    // check if any of our corners lie inside the other actors'
    // bounding rectangles
    if (isCollidingWith(another.getX(), another.getY()) ||
        isCollidingWith(another.getX() + another.getActorWidth(), another.getY()) ||
        isCollidingWith(another.getX(), another.getY() + another.getActorHeight()) ||
        isCollidingWith(another.getX() + another.getActorWidth(),
                        another.getY() + another.getActorHeight()))
        return true;
    else
        return false;
}
```

This code determines whether a collision occurs by checking whether any of one object's corners are within the bounding rectangle of another. You can see this concept illustrated in Figure 7.8. As a convenience I'm using two methods; one determines whether a collision occurs between the actor and another, and the other is a utility method to check whether the actor has collided with a single 2D point.

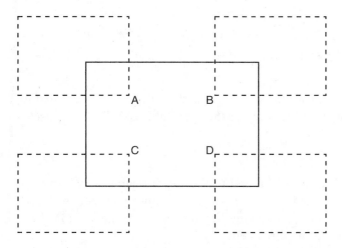

Figure 7.8 A simple method of collision detection involves determining whether any of the four corners (A, B, C, and D) of any object exist inside the bounding rectangle of another object.

Tip

Consider wrapping this type of geometry in a Point and Rectangle class. The actor's position would then be set using a Point (which would encapsulate x and y). A Rectangle class would then encapsulate a Point along with a width and height—as well as a host of 2D geometry tools, such as the intersection test used earlier for collision detection. The only issue with this approach is the potential cost of two additional classes in your final JAR.

Next you need to add the code that calls this collision detection method into the master cycle of the GameScreen. Here's the complete code for revised cycle method:

```
protected void cycle()
{
    if (lastCycleTime > 0)
    {
        long msSinceLastCycle = System.currentTimeMillis() - lastCycleTime;

        // cycle all the actors
        for (int i = 0; i < actorList.size(); i++)
        {
            Actor a = (Actor) actorList.elementAt(i);
            a.cycle((int)msSinceLastCycle);

            // check if any hit the wombat
            if (a.isCollidingWith(wombat) && a != wombat)
                running = false;
        }

    }
    lastCycleTime = System.currentTimeMillis();
}
```

To check for collisions, the cycle code calls the isCollidingWith method on the wombat for every actor. (Make sure you're not checking whether the wombat is colliding with itself.)

Game Over

If a collision is detected, you need to trigger an end to the current game. To do this, the collision-checking code changes the running Boolean to false. If you remember the thread code, you know that this will cause the main game thread to fall through its while loop. Now modify it to do something when the thread ends.

```
public void run()
{
    while(running)
    {
        ...
    }

    // fall back to the splash form at the end of our loop
    theMidlet.gameOver();
}
```

Finally you can add the gameOver method to the application class. This will display an alert message and then change the display back to the menu.

```
/**
 * Called by the game classes to indicate to the user that the current game
 * is over.
 */
public void gameOver()
{
    // Display an alert (the device will take care of implementing how to
    // show it to the user.
    Alert alert = new Alert("", "Splat! Game Over", null, AlertType.INFO);
    // Then set the menu to be current.
    Display.getDisplay(this).setCurrent(alert, menu);
}
```

And without further ado, your masterpiece is complete. Congratulations, you've now covered all the elements required to make a fully functioning game!

If you want to push on with the game yourself, I recommend adding some simple scoring. For example, you could keep track of the number of times the wombat crosses the road before a timer counts down, and then award points for each crossing. The more times you cross, the higher the points awarded. When the time is up, move the player to a new level, increasing the speed of the vehicles and the value of the points along the way. I also recommend making death a little less permanent—maybe just use the time penalty of having to restart.

Conclusion

It won't set the world on fire, but *RoadRun* has all the elements required to make a J2ME game. To be honest, it's better than some of the professional games available.

Go pick up a new BMW convertible as a personal reward for getting this far. If the dealer wants some money, just explain that you've learned how to make a J2ME game and you deserve it! Making J2ME games isn't easy. If you understood everything in this chapter (and trust me, I wasn't going slowly), then you're already a micro-game programmer.

However, you're not here to make average games. In Part III, you'll learn how to push the edge of J2ME gaming. From preprocessors to animation, build scripts to localization, obfuscation to physics, it's time to go pro.

PART III

GAME ON

CHAPTER 8

The Project 247

CHAPTER 9

The Graphics 269

CHAPTER 10

The Action 303

CHAPTER 11

The World 367

CHAPTER 12

The Game 433

CHAPTER 13

The Frontend 465

CHAPTER 14

The Device Ports 493

CHAPTER 15

The Optimizing 519

CHAPTER 16

The Localization 535

Now it's time to get serious about your game development. In Part 3, "Game On," you'll see how to design and then create a high-quality game using sprites, scrolling worlds, and physics.

To give things a professional feel, you'll also see how to add a splash screen and menu system before moving on to advanced subjects such as creating an automated build system, porting the game to multiple devices, optimizing performance, and finally, localizing your game for different languages.

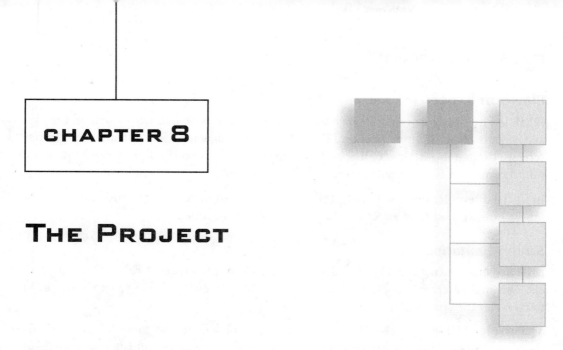

CHAPTER 8

THE PROJECT

In this chapter you'll learn how to design a J2ME game from scratch. Initially you'll review the limitations of J2ME devices and, most importantly, how that will impact your game design. Then you'll move on to creating your own game design. (Don't worry, you won't be writing any long, boring documents.)

The State of Play

So here you are; you've covered all the foundation areas of J2ME technology, and you've even made a little game. However, a professional J2ME game today needs to be a lot slicker than yet another *Frogger* clone. So in Part 3, you'll learn how to cover more ground than the wombat in *RoadRun*.

J2ME game development is an exciting area right now, and I don't see that changing anytime soon. Every week there seems to be yet another high-powered, full-color, big-screen, Java-enabled phone released by manufacturers. I'm not going to bore you with the stats—just visit your local mobile phone shop and browse through the selection. Anything mid-range and up is a J2ME-ready machine just waiting for your game to bring it to life. The size of the market for your games today is already large; the size of tomorrow's market is downright scary.

Thankfully, we're a little beyond the micro-caveman days of SMS, WAP, and monochrome J2ME games. Today, it's well designed, high-quality games with crisp color graphics and addictive game play. Modern J2ME games are just as much fun to make as they are to play.

Platform Issues

J2ME is a new platform with its own idiosyncrasies, so a game that works well on the bigger systems is often impractical on J2ME. You need to take into account smaller, dimmer screens, limited input, slow CPUs, and some pretty severe resource limitations to design a micro game that is practical, usable, and above all, fun.

In the next few sections you'll look at the practicalities of micro gaming and, more importantly, how these should affect the design of your J2ME game.

Screen Limitations

MID screens are small LCD-based displays typically in the range of 100–200 square pixels. This makes screen real estate a scarce commodity. When developing a game, you need to consider the size of graphics.

The average MID's LCD also lacks brightness and color depth, so those beautifully rendered graphics that look great on a PC can appear dim and washed out when you see them on an actual device screen. In addition, the reduction to the average 12-bit (or lower) color depth will have quite an impact on presentation quality. Keep in mind that PC emulators won't emulate this feature, so you should try your graphics out on a real phone in a bad lighting situation.

Low-end LCDs also have issues with the speed at which pixels can change color. This slowness can create a noticeable blurring or ghosting of images, especially if those images are moving quickly across the screen. In cases where graphics change quickly, such as action games, you might need to slow things down so the player can keep track of the graphics. Don't underestimate the effect blurring can have on game play. If you're planning an action game, you need to keep your implementation flexible enough to slow things down if necessary.

Control Freaks

If you've played games on your phone, I'm sure you'd agree the input isn't the greatest. It's easy to appreciate the placement, size, and tactile response of a typical PC keyboard far more after you poke away at a phone keypad for any length of time. The typical size and keypad placement makes it difficult to pull off what you would consider simple on a keyboard or game pad, and you need to keep this in mind when you design the input for your game.

The placement of keys isn't the only issue. Most MIDs don't support simultaneous key presses. You won't truly appreciate how restrictive this can be until you rely on this feature in an action game. Imagine a side-scrolling shooting game in which you can't move down and fire at the same time! Typical MIDs also have a high latency on key presses, so your game might frustrate a player if you rely too much on instant responses.

These control limitations can cause some major issues, so if you're planning to create an action game, you need to consider these restrictions carefully and do your best to work around them. One effective method is to automate some control aspects, such as an optional auto-fire or auto-thrust.

A good game also uses keypad-friendly controls or repeat functions so the player doesn't have to press another key. For example, if you have multiple pop-up windows in your game, such as an inventory, map, and character info screens, you should consider displaying them all sequentially using the same key, instead of assigning different keys to each option.

Processor Power

Due to size and power consumption constraints, MIDs typically have low-end CPUs. The slow performance is accentuated by the lack of floating-point hardware because you need to spend extra time doing that work as well. When you are programming the game, you must constantly keep in mind the CPU performance of the real device (not the emulator).

From a design perspective, there's nothing in particular you need to avoid. In fact, I encourage you to go ahead and develop anything you want. There are plenty of methods to reduce the CPU requirements for code. Just keep things flexible and leave yourself twice as much time to optimize as it took you to develop something in the first place.

Storage Limits

One day you'll be happily coding away, the game will be going great, half the features will be done and then boom . . . `java.lang.OutOfMemory`! It'll be quite a shock, and development will suddenly come to a grinding halt. At this point the memory constraints of MIDs will finally hit home. If you're only halfway through all the features of the game, how on earth can you add anything more if you can't create variables or instantiate classes?

Memory, or more accurately the size of the application heap, is usually the first MID limitation you'll encounter. (JAR file size and CPU limits don't usually show up on emulators.) Modern gaming MIDs can have quite a range of memory capabilities—anything between 100 KB and 500 KB is common. This might not sound too bad until you consider that all those pretty game graphics take up heap memory as well (in their much larger decompressed states). A game with reasonable-quality graphics can find itself with less than 100 KB to play with. Instantiate a few objects and a reasonably-sized level, and you're out of space.

There is another type of storage you should also keep in mind—the non-volatile RAM used by the RMS. Unlike PC hardware, you won't have virtually unlimited space in which to store saved games or other state information. Thankfully, though, you normally have enough space to meet the needs of a standard game; just don't plan to have a history of 50 saved games.

Game Types

In your quest to make a great J2ME game, your first consideration should be the type of game to make. More specifically, what type of game is suited to micro devices? Take a look at some of the classic gaming genres and consider how well they might suit MIDs.

Action Games

Action games are by far the most popular for any hardware platform, including J2ME. Since the caveman days, there has always been something instinctively fun about trying to spear a speeding mammoth. (It's a guy thing, okay?!)

The sky is really the limit on the type of action game you can develop. From simple vertical scrolling shooters to in-seat car racing, there's plenty of room to create a solid but still quite original game.

If you've played many J2ME games, you might have noticed a tendency to simplify game play. This is mostly to compensate for the limited input controls. Reducing the complexity of game control is an easy way to ensure that the game isn't too hard to handle on a typical MID. For example, most side-scrolling shooting games (well, the good ones anyway) provide an auto-fire option so the player doesn't have to hit the move and shoot keys simultaneously.

So should you make an action game? Well, the bad news is that action games are probably the most difficult to develop on J2ME because they combine so many resource-hungry elements. You need real-time physics (even if it's basic motion), collision detection, animation, multi-layer moving backgrounds, precision input, AI, sound, and some pretty graphics, too. All of these things combined will stress almost any MID.

The good news is that action games are both fun to develop and fun to play, so your chances of having a commercial success are higher given the popularity of the genre. Gamers understand action games almost instinctively, so assuming you stick to the standard styles of games (even if you mix in your own elements), you'll be using a reliable formula for success.

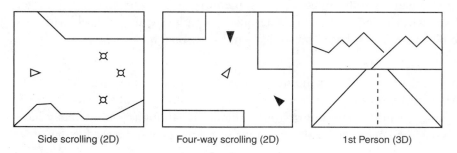

Side scrolling (2D)   Four-way scrolling (2D)   1st Person (3D)

Figure 8.1 Examples of 2D and 3D perspective games

Puzzle Games

Puzzle games are typically much simpler than action games, although they can be just as successful if they are done well. Jigsaws, word games, memory games, sliders, and many others are all tried-and-true material.

Puzzle games are a pretty interesting type of game to create for J2ME. Done well, they can be addictive and very popular. You can also mix puzzle-style games with other genres. Adventure games work very well with puzzle games, as do action games; the mighty *Tetris* is a great example of a mix of puzzle and action.

If you're considering creating a puzzle game, I recommend taking a basic puzzle scenario and applying it to a more interesting (and exciting) environment; the classics *Lode Runner* and *Penguin* are excellent examples of this. Both games involve figuring out a basic sliding puzzle, but the settings in ice and rock caves (as well as the risk of being squished as a result of an error) make things far more interesting than in traditional sliding puzzles.

Adventure Games

Classic adventure role-playing games (RPGs) can translate very well to J2ME. The slower game action results in less reliance on the limited input and device horsepower. On the flip side, though, adventure games rely quite heavily on exploration of new environments as a key motivator for players, and this typically translates into new graphics. Limited JAR space will be the dragon you'll have to slay to make a great adventure game.

There are three main types of adventure games—top-down perspective (including isometric-style games such as *Diablo*); first-person perspective, where the player "sees" as though he is in the game world; and storybook, where the player sees (and reads) the game as distinct pages. All of these game types are good choices for J2ME game development.

Strategy Games

Strategy games are typically either real-time (RTS), such as *Warcraft* and *Command & Conquer*, or turn-based, such as *Heroes of Might and Magic* and *Chess*. The settings and perspective can vary enormously, but generally strategy games simply involve the acquisition and tactical deployment of available resources for the greatest gain. Doing this against other players (even AI ones) is even more fun.

Simulation games also fall into this category. These types of games involve the management of a deeply complex system (usually as it's evolving), such as an ant colony, amusement park, or town. (*The Sims* is an excellent example of a simulation, even if it's somewhat original.) A simulation game is more about understanding and affecting the inherent nature of the simulated system than it is about employing a proactive strategy. This is great because not only do you get to play a strategy game, but you can also learn a great deal about the simulated entity along the way. Even if you won't say it out loud, you have to admit that finding out how ant farms really work is pretty cool! If you're considering developing a strategy game, think about teaching the player the nature of something along the way.

So can you make a strategy game using J2ME? You bet. In fact the platform is well suited to most turn-based strategy games, as long as they don't require fast input or high-speed action. RTS games are a little more difficult, though. They require a great deal of CPU power to handle the graphics, animation, unit movement, and AI (for path finding and enemy strategy). In addition, RTS games can involve the control of many units very quickly. Try selecting those 20 defense tanks using only the keypad while the enemy is rushing your base! To make an RTS, you need to carefully consider the input limitations and automate as much as possible. This might include simplifying the terrain and movement systems or removing requirements for fast-response, complex input from the game design.

Strategy games, like most micro games, will never be the same as they are on bigger systems, so don't try to make them that way. Adapt to the platform; you'll be surprised how easy it can be to rework things to suit the more restrictive format. Who knows, maybe you'll create a new game genre along the way.

Traditional Games

Traditional games, such as gambling, card, board, and dice games, are a much scoffed-at genre. However, keep in mind that a very large part of your potential market won't (or can't) play complex action or strategy games. Want to bet with me that the default solitaire game installed on most PCs is the most popular game in the world? Scary, I know.

Traditional games don't necessarily have to be boring. You can easily beef them up with good graphics and sound (strip poker, anyone?) or mix in other genres. Consider inventing your own dice game or adding a little strategy or action to a classic slot machine game.

Designing Your Game

I'm sure you're as eager as hell to start developing a game, but before you get into some code again, you need to work through how to design a great game.

Just because J2ME games are smaller than their big-system cousins, developing them isn't necessarily a walk in the park. Completing a commercial-grade J2ME game typically takes two to three months of hard work. No, really; let me say it again. If you're serious about making a great game, it's going to take months. You're not going to get anything good done in a few weeks.

Although this timeframe pales in comparison to the 2 to 3 years of development time for average PC games, you're still making a significant investment to develop your game. Therefore, it's important to be as sure as you can about the quality of your game before you run off and develop it.

Having said all that, one of the great aspects of J2ME projects is the short development timeframe—usually only a few months. Instead of working (or slaving) away for years on only a small facet of a game project, a J2ME programmer can work on all aspects of a project and have an end always in sight. Short projects are typically easier to manage and cost far less—and, to be honest, it's easier to stay interested in a project for a few months than it is for a few years.

Because projects are short and labor is the most significant part of development costs, you can go from idea to completed (hopefully revenue-generating) product in a few months using a small team (or even alone). This isn't an "indie" pipe dream; it's possible to develop something as good as (or better than) products from some of the best studios in the world. The best part is, you can do it by yourself, part-time, using only a broken pink crayon . . . okay, maybe you need a computer, too.

The low cost of development (and by cost I mean time as well as money) lets you be far more creative with your game design. With a reasonable toolset and basic game programming skills, the sky is the limit on the design of your game. The low cost means if the design isn't working, you're wasting a few weeks or months, not a few years.

The Platform

Most J2ME game designers start out as PC or console designers (even if they're amateurs). This leads to the most common mistake made by new J2ME developers—designing a game based on PC concepts rather than MID ones. If you're in that category, let me open the Almanac of J2ME Game Design and tell you a few things again—and this time I really want you to listen. The screens are tiny; the input is slow to respond; the keys are hard to handle; you can't use simultaneous key presses; the JAR and memory size will severely limit your graphics, sound, and level resources; the CPUs are slow; and above all, you can't rely on the emulator to tell you whether the game is running well!

If you're not listening now, you will be exactly 54 percent of the way into development when you get your first `java.lang.OutOfMemory` exception! These concepts are fundamental to designing a good game. Meet them head on and work around them; don't try to ignore them or hope that players will just use the PC emulator for your game. J2ME games are great fun to make and play, but only if you work within the true constraints of the device.

Minimum Requirements

Before you start designing you need to decide quite early on the basic MID required to play your game. For most types, this comes down to three minimum requirements—screen size, color support, and JAR size.

Deciding on screen size is a reasonably easy exercise. Most gaming-class MIDs are greater than 100 pixels square, so this is a reasonable starting point. In later sections you'll review how to develop games to dynamically adjust to the size of the device. Although this is a good idea, it is only effective to a certain degree. You need to establish a minimum size in order to set the basic dimensions of your graphics. Keep this a little loose at this stage; when it comes to the technical implementation you can adjust the size if there's a good reason to do so.

So suppose your minimum screen size is around 100×100 pixels. The next decision is whether to design the game for color. If you drop the monochrome graphics from your design, you're potentially limiting quite a portion of the market. Do you really care, though? The vast majority of new phones are color. Are people who still buy monochrome mobiles the sort of people who buy games? I recommend designing a game for color from the ground up. If the game is a commercial success in the color phone market, you'll likely be invited to port the game to lower-end devices anyway (assuming this is practical).

The minimum JAR file size a MID can handle is again something with which you can be a little flexible. However, setting a general indication is a good idea at this stage because it will focus the design on the largest limitation. My absolute minimum size is usually 64 KB. Anything after that is an optional extra the game has to be able to live without in the low-end versions. Now just to clarify, that means in order to run our game the MID must support a JAR size of at least 64K—anything less and the game won't run.

Reference Device

Next you need to choose a reference device. This won't be the only device you support—it's just the device chosen to serve as the primary target platform. The reference device you choose should not exceed (at least by much) your minimum requirements. Most importantly, choose a device on which you really like to develop. (Having access to the real phone is a bonus as well.)

Due to their extensive J2ME hardware support, excellent online resources, great phones (and emulators), consistent platform, and obvious commitment to gaming, the first annual Marty award for preferred reference device goes to . . . the Nokia Series 40 (crowd roars).

You'll notice I haven't picked a particular phone model. That's because the folks at Nokia are kind enough (and smart enough) to categorize all their devices into different series.

The Series 30 are small, monochrome screen devices with limited resources. The next step up, the Series 40, has a 128 × 128 pixel color display and a maximum 64-KB JAR file size (although many support larger sizes). You can see a typical Series 40 device in Figure 8.2. This is perfect for your needs at this stage. The next level up, the Nokia Series 60, is also an excellent platform, but the features are a little too far beyond your minimum requirements for it to be a practical reference device.

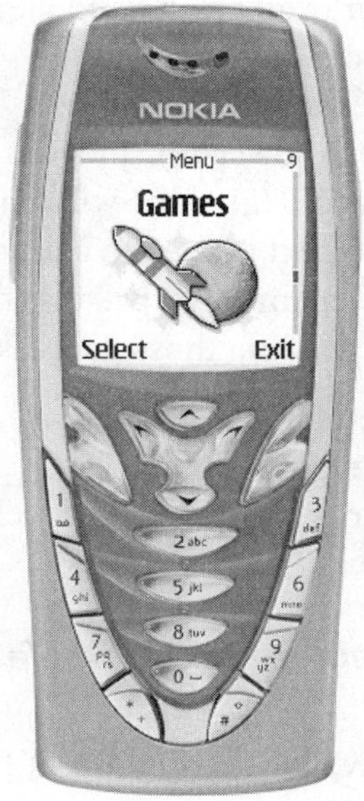

As you saw in Chapter 6, Nokia's LCDUI toolkit provides a host of great features, including access to the full screen area, transparency, and imaging tools such as rotation and reflection. These are important features for which you'll specifically code when you do your device porting. For now, though, you'll be sticking to only those features supported by the standard MIDP.

Platform Setup

That's basically it for deciding what type of platform you need to support. Requirements such as minimum screen capability and JAR size are not set in stone. The important thing is to have a solid starting point from which to base your design.

Figure 8.2 The Nokia 7210 emulator, our Series 40 reference device

Now that you have a basic platform, you should take a little time to set up your development environment by obtaining your reference device's emulator and work through any sample applications the emulator includes.

When you're ready, you can move on to figuring out what sort of game you want to make.

What Makes a Good Game?

And so we come to the ultimate question: What makes a game addictive? Why is one game just a bit more compelling than another? Understanding this is probably the key to whether your game will be a huge success, yet another shooter clone, or a sad reject nobody wants to dance with. There are five requirements to make a game great—it must be fun, addictive, compelling, cool, and above all, commercially successful.

Goals

The absolute number one thing a great game needs is goals. Present players with as many as you can simultaneously, and then progressively reward them as they achieve things. Even better, increase the challenge of goals as you go.

For example, a good game will present a power-up to a flying spaceship, and then reward the player for picking it up by enhancing his ship (and maybe including some groovy new weapon-fire graphics as well). This will give the player an immediate goal to acquire the next power-up, and you've established a goal just by presenting the power-up in the first place. This alone will make a good game. But a great game will take this further by making the next power-up a little harder to get—maybe you have to shoot down a certain number of enemies to get it. This way, you're not only giving the player goals, but you're also expanding those goals as he progresses. This always makes for highly addictive game play.

Some types of goals are inherent in many gaming genres. Action games, for example, set the goal of the player getting through to the next level. The goal is for the player to progress past the obstacles you place in his path, and his reward is seeing those cool new areas.

Balance and Completeness

A good game needs to balance the progression through challenges and rewards. Players have an expectation of how much time it will take to complete a game. (It's surprisingly short for most J2ME games—typically two to five play hours.) You need to present them with content at a steady pace. You should think of it a little like a tap—turn it on too fast and you'll give away too much of your game early on. I know the temptation will be to start your player with those rapid-fire Vulcan cannons, but there's no need. The player will prefer to earn them along the way anyway. Start off slowly and use your content (game play elements) as a reward in a progressive manner.

Game balance also means not making things too difficult too quickly. Players need a challenge, but it can't be so great that they get frustrated and give up. The opposite is even more the case; if a game is too easy, a player will give up even faster than if it's too much of a challenge. So how do you know when you've struck the right balance? Easy—just play the game from the start and measure whether things are too difficult or easy as you go. (Having friends play the game is also a great idea.) If this sounds like a lot of work, you're right—it is. Play testing and game balancing are difficult and very time-consuming processes, but they make the difference between fun and frustration.

Originality

I'm sorry to say it, but game players generally don't want new games—they want better versions of previously great experiences. A truly original game might be a groundbreaker, but the chances are against it being commercially successful even if it's fun. So does that mean your game should just be a clone of others? Hell no—you have to make your game a new experience for players, but try to take a workable formula and then just push out the edges a little. The more successful you become at development, the more you'll be able to push those edges, and the more original your game will be.

Technology

Games are a unique medium because they have such a strong mix of technology and entertainment. Technology, however, is not the entertainment; it's just the mechanism that delivers it to the player. Contrary to what might seem like popular opinion, people don't play games because they are technically superior. Players might see the latest 3D rendering trick as cool, but only because it means better content and therefore better entertainment value for them.

However, technology is one of those things you can't get wrong. A great game requires great technology. It needs to run smoothly, look good, and deliver the game's entertainment value without a hitch. In other words, it should be so slick that the player never has to think about it.

Don't get caught up in technology too much. If you want to push the boundaries a little, make sure you don't try it on your first game. And when you do, add a few slick things to a new game and keep everything else tried and true. Nothing will kill your motivation faster than endless crash bugs and nightmare math problems.

The Inspiration

Designing a J2ME game is a difficult exercise—ironically, I find that the more I do, the harder it seems to get—so be prepared to commit some serious mental energy over a reasonable period of time to come up with a solid design for your game. The good news is that this time is more than worth it. The beginnings of a hit game lie in coming up with a realistic, workable, and entertaining design. I guarantee the final game won't be the same as the original plan. This is a good thing, but it's important to get things off on the right foot with a design that reflects the foundation of what makes your game good.

The first step to any good design is a little thing called inspiration, and the best source of that is (you guessed it) other games. Go out and play all the J2ME emulator games you can find. Then go buy some commercial games for your phone and play them to the end. (No, really, I mean it—don't just play the demos!) This will give you design inspiration and provide a technical benchmark from which to work. As a bonus, you'll see the sort of quality a commercial game requires, the length of the game, and technical implementations. You'll also get the basic feel of players' expectations.

While playing some of these games, you might come across what seem to be strange limitations or other peculiarities. Don't dismiss these immediately! There are some great developers out there, so take note of how things are commonly done. Even if you think it's a bit weird (or you just think you could do far better), there's usually a good reason why things were done that way. Keep the platform limits in mind when you are reviewing games.

Visualize Things

Once you have a good dose of inspiration, you need to settle on the type of game you want to make. Above all, pick something that you're excited about—something you have no doubt will be great fun to play (and hopefully develop). If nothing leaps out, by all means start with something standard, like an action game.

After you have an idea for your game (even if it's pretty vague at this stage), move on to creating a mock-up of the core play screens. Try to keep things as close to the actual scale of the game as possible. This is worth quite a bit of time because you'll be mentally working through a great deal of how the game feels as you create the mock-up. Then you can move on to other screens that involve different game scenarios. When you do, try to imagine how the game would feel if you were really playing it. Don't worry if you find this hard at first; it's something you'll get better at with practice. While you go through this visualization process, note the top ten things that really kick in the design. (This list can change often.) What is really great about this game? If you struggle to come up with ten, then think twice about the design.

Keep the list of good game-design practices in mind as you work through your design. What goals can you set for the player? How does the game progress through stages? What motivates the player to keep going?

As you move along, don't worry too much about the technical implementation. You need to be aware of basically what's possible, but for now stick to designing the basic concept of your game, and then build up a list of game features you'd like to have. Keep these ideas modular so that when you get to the technical implementation, you can add or remove components easily.

If the game still works for you after this type of visualization (I usually find about one in five makes it past this level), then get someone else off whom you can bounce the idea. Another programmer or artist is an excellent choice for this. If the design still comes up good after they've shredded it a bit (hopefully they're now excited about the game as well), then you can move on to creating a design document.

The Design Document

Writing a design document is traditionally not a great deal of fun. For most PC games, they tend to be long-winded, jumbled messes that don't help anybody, including the author. But they're still a required tool in the game-design process for two reasons. First, the process of creating a design document forces you to consider many of the aspects of your game design that you likely skipped over in those excited 2:00 a.m. debates. It all sounded good at the time, but in the cold light of a structured design, you'll quickly find that some aspects just don't work as well as you thought they would. Second, a good design document serves as a background reference for your game. Anybody who works on the project can quickly come up to speed on your idea by reading the document. I include my Top Ten Things That Kick about This Game section as well. Periodically rereading the list can be motivating and help keep you focused on the things that make your game fun.

Design documents also bring some order to development. It's only natural to break the game into sub-modules as you progress through the design. This will help you organize the development later.

Tip

A design document is also an excellent base for your game's user guide, so none of it is really going to waste. In fact, if you're having trouble creating your document, consider writing something like a guide for potential players of the game. This will force you to think from the perspective of the player.

While working as a game producer, I used to receive design documents from budding game developers. It amazed me how long, overly complicated, and boring they tended to be. We're in the games business! A design doc should be fun, easy to read, and above all, make you wet your pants about the game. Leave the deep discussion on UI issues or sound system implementation notes to the technical specification (if you even decide to have one).

The easiest way to write a good design doc is to keep it short. For J2ME games, this is especially easy because the games just don't have the breadth of features to fill ten pages, let alone 200. Start with the idea of writing two to three pages; if the doc ends up slightly longer, that's okay. But it should be concise, fun, and above all, make you remember why you really want to make this game.

To get started, write down all your ideas, but don't let yourself become caught up in the format, structure, wording, or grammar. Just blast away as though you were explaining the game to another game addict. If something doesn't make sense, don't worry too much; just keep banging away with all those ideas. Leave the editing and structuring until after you have the bulk of the content. The most organizing I do at this point is putting a heading on each idea section.

After you've laid down everything, go back and organize the document into the following broad sections.

- **Introduction.** Write a two- to three-paragraph sales pitch on the game. Don't try to fit in everything in detail; just lay down a broad overview of what you're trying to achieve. At the end of this section, make a top-ten list of the things that really sell the game idea. Remember, keep it short.
- **Setting.** Describe the setting for your game. You might find this works better as part of the introduction. For J2ME games, settings are usually quite simple anyway.

- **Game Play.** Describe the basics of game play. Where does the player start? How do they progress through the game? This is where you need to organize things into the goals and rewards you're presenting to the player. I tend to list these in connected series, such as all the power-ups and how to get them. If your game has different levels or areas, list these and feel free to describe the setting, challenges, and any other interesting ideas along the way.

- **Interface.** Outline the user interface and game controls, such as the main menu items and their functions, along with all the in-game control keys. You might find that a simple storyboard showing the progression from splash, menu, and game screen helps as well.

- **Features.** List any features or ideas you have not covered in previous sections, such as online high scores or a random level generator.

- **Platform.** Detail the minimum requirements and reference device details. List any ideas on future features you'd like to take advantage of on different phone models.

- **Resources.** Create a summary list of all the sound, graphic, and level resources you think your game needs. Then estimate the size of each resource and total the amount at the end. If you're not sure about the size, go mock up some graphics and save them as PNGs. The total size needs to be quite a bit less than the total JAR size to leave room for the class files.

  Also consider making some of these resources optional. Maybe you can reuse graphics by overlaying decal sprites. I guarantee you'll run out of JAR space, so try to get an idea early on about what you absolutely can't live without.

- **Tech Notes.** List any technical implementation notes or ideas you have. Don't talk about the obvious; just describe anything special you want to do.

As you work through your design document you might find that some aspects become frustrating or confusing. Don't ignore these; the reason you're doing this in the first place is to force you to think through your idea properly. If there are issues now, you're far better off resolving them on paper than after you've started coding.

The Development Process

After you've completed the design document, you're ready to begin development (assuming you still want to create the game). Next I'll review a little about how you should tackle the development process.

Creating a Prototype

Rather than just leaping in to develop the entire game, at this point you should aim to create a working prototype. The point of a prototype is to prove the viability of the game's design. Your aim should be to mock up how things should work. Don't worry about splash screens, menus, saving the games, or even proper art—just throw something together with basic game play. The goal is to prove the game works before you commit serious resources.

If you're starting from scratch without an existing game code base to work from, then a prototype can take quite a bit of time—50 percent of your total project time is not unreasonable. There's no problem with this because most of your prototype code will be reusable in the final game, anyway.

After playing with your prototype, you'll typically have to go back and revisit the design. Some aspects of the game will work, and some won't. Be very conscious of what's fun, and cut or rework the things that don't come up well.

Developing the Game

When you're satisfied that your prototype game is on the right track, you can start to flesh out things like graphics, levels, bosses, and everything else that makes a kick-ass game. The order of development is up to you, although I prefer to concentrate everything on the core game play and then wrap up by doing the splash, menus, save/load, and other little touches at the end.

While you are developing, you need to keep a close watch on your JAR size. As you add graphics and classes (and even methods), the amount of space you have left will decrease. Being aware of the differences in size as you progress will help you track the effects new features will have, and will also trigger the space alarm bell.

When the JAR is about 80 percent of its maximum size—it's surprising how fast you can get to this limit—you need to seriously consider whether something is worth adding. If you're working on the core of the game play, you also need to reserve quite a bit of space for the menus and splash screen. (A good splash graphic could easily cost 7 KB to 10 KB of JAR space by itself.) Also keep in mind that some distributors or carriers will require a small amount of space for their own uses (such as copy protection).

Tip

When you figure your current resource size, you can assume a savings of 10 to 20 percent of your class file sizes by using an obfuscator. You'll learn more about exactly how to do this in later chapters. You'll get further savings from the JAR file compression process, although it will only impact data and class files, not image files. (The PNG format is already heavily compressed.)

One of the great things about J2ME development is that projects end! You will reach a point, usually before you've finished even half of the features you planned, where you just run out of CPU cycles, JAR space, memory, or all of these combined. If you haven't spent literally years on PC game development projects, you can't know how great it is to actually wrap up a game and move on to something else. With J2ME development, you have to! There's no space to add anything (even new methods) without removing something else. Wrap it up and send it off; then move on to the next project.

Tip

The secret to making a great game is in the time you spend polishing things. It is all the little extras you add, the endless hours spent perfectly balancing the game play, that extra boss monster or cool bonus level. . . . A game will go from average to good and from good to great based solely on the level of little extras you add. Be sure to leave at least as much time for tweaking and tuning your game as you did for developing it.

Finish What You . . .

A final word of development advice: If you've never done any professional game development, let me let you in on a little secret. You're going to fail. Trust me. No matter how great you are (and I'm not saying you're not great), the reality of actual game production is something you can only experience firsthand. The chances of creating a commercially successful game the first time around are very low. Your goal for your first production should be to learn as much as you can about the process. To accomplish this, I would strongly recommend taking things all the way through to completion. Even if the game is not good enough to really do that well, there's a huge difference between a half-completed, might-have-been-great game and a finished, average game. The secret to making great games is to make bad games first.

Being successful at writing games is very much about the reality of game production. How good a game can you really make? How long will development of all those features take? How does the game finally come together? It's all about understanding what's practically possible—and more important, what players want out of a great game. The way to gain that understanding is pretty easy—finish some games.

Games are very complex beasts (yes, even J2ME games), so as you near the end of production, you're going to end up with something. It's not going to be what you designed, but it will be a game. (Hopefully it will be something like your design, although you'd be surprised how much a game can change during production.) It's only as the game matures into reality that you can appreciate the one factor that decides whether you have succeeded or not—is it fun to play?

Taking a game to completion involves a great deal of work (usually about ten times what you originally thought it would take). Following through on a single production lets you see the full breadth of problems faced at each stage of production. If you give up partway through your next game, you'll likely succeed right up to the point where your previous game failed. At this point you'll run into an issue you didn't encounter before. Understanding the complexities of implementing a save game feature, adding sound, localizing for different languages, or just performing the endless tweaking you need to balance the game experience. . . . All these issues sound easy in isolation, but at the end of production (or what you think should be the end of production), these things can become frustrating nightmares. The moral of the story is, try to wrap up the game, whether it's a great game or not, before you move on to your next project. Next time around you'll get everything right because you'll know what to expect.

All right, I'll get off my soapbox now. Now let's go over what sort of game you're going to make.

Tip

As programmers, it's only natural for us to start working on a new platform by developing an engine, or at least a toolbox from which to establish our new games. The same applies to J2ME. You will need a good set of tools; however, given the space constraints, you really don't have room to waste on proper physics code, graphics effect routines, or any other great chunk of code unless your game really needs it. As you develop your code base, keep it modular enough that you can leave out large chunks when a game doesn't need it.

Your Idea

As you progress through Part 3, your goal is to develop a professional-quality J2ME game. To do so, you first need to put all this sage game design advice into action and consider what features you'll have in your game.

You've already determined the minimum requirements and the reference device, so now you can choose the game type.

Game Type

Because you're here to work on the more advanced aspects of J2ME game development, the best type of game to develop should also be the hardest—an action game. So what sort of action game will it be?

The most popular type of J2ME action game is the scrolling shooter. In this type of game, the player controls a ship (or other character) that remains reasonably static on screen while the terrain scrolls horizontally or vertically around it. The player is able to move around on the screen, dodging baddies (or blowing them away) as they scroll by. It's a classic formula game that players will instinctively understand.

To make things a little more interesting, though, you can make this a four-way scrolling space shooter. As you can see in Figure 8.3, this means the player will be able to fly in both horizontal and vertical directions at the same time. Think of it as something like *Asteroids*, but with a scrolling world below the player.

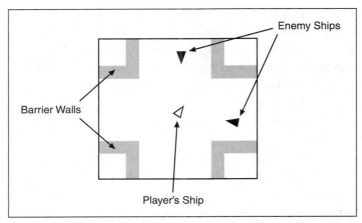

Figure 8.3 In a four-way scrolling space shooter, the player's ship is located in the center of the screen.

Game Name

Before you go any further, you should give your new project a name. Because it involves space, ships, and blowing things apart, call it *Star Assault*. I know that's not the best name, but it's all I could come up with at the time, okay? Send me an e-mail if you come up with something better . . . er, on second thought, don't.

Setting

Now you need a little background for the game. This is typically pretty easy for action or adventure games. (I'm not sure what the background plot to *Tetris* is—maybe you have to stop an invasion by an evil race of box shapes!)

Is a background story worth creating? It's really up to you. I add them because I feel they add strength to the game design. The plot doesn't have to be complicated, but setting the scene can really help motivate the team (especially the graphics guys), and it gives you a way to visualize the game more easily. Aside from that, backgrounds are usually fun to write.

To give you an idea what I mean, here's the background for *Star Assault*. (Get some tissues; it's a sad saga.)

> *The massive bulk of the Britanic, the United Space Command's flagship Star Carrier, slid across space, eclipsing the sun of an alien world like some long-lost titan of the heavens. In its belly lay the hope of mankind—an offer of peace. A peace that many dared to believe would end this war to end all wars.*

The death toll, now standing in the billions, came at a ten-fold cost to the Alien Horde. But the Terran onslaught that had begun with heroes had slowly turned to ruin. A victory of numbers hollowed only the more by the next being ever greater. Endless . . . infinite, it seemed. The Horde had kept coming.

Now the battle cry of the would-be conqueror had turned to a plea of mercy. The offer of peace, purported as already accepted by the Horde, need only be delivered to come into force. The Britanic, along with her crew of more than 200,000, was now deep within the alien home world's intricate web of defenses, on its way to complete a simple mission. . . .

A Hurricane class assault fighter swept in from routine patrol, its sensors staring back at the pilot with an impossible emptiness where the Star Carrier should have been. The scattered debris was the only evidence of what had become of the Britanic.

Now, lost deep inside an alien defense grid, the way home betrayed, a lone fighter had only the memories of comrades to cling to—memories that were soon ablaze in flames of rage. Vowing to avenge them all, one fighter, accompanied only by the ghosts of lost comrades, would brandish the greatest weapon mankind had ever known . . .

Revenge.

Game Play

A player begins a new game of *Star Assault* at the controls of a shiny new Hurricane class assault fighter. The aim of the game is to fly the ship through a maze of defenses to try to locate the jump-gate that leads to the next level.

As the player progresses, he has to work through ever more complicated, randomly generated levels, doing battle against enemy mines, defense turrets, and fighters.

Given that control of the ship is more difficult than in the typical scrolling shooter, you should be more forgiving of mistakes by having the ship bounce off walls, rather than explode on impact. This bouncing effect will also apply to weapons (which will create some interesting combat techniques as a bonus).

Features

Star Assault has a whole host of features that form the basis of the game. The following sections detail these features.

Configuration

In case the player is using a phone with a non-standard layout, you should let them reconfigure the default numeric keys. Certain game functions, such as vibration and auto-fire, should also be configurable.

Four-Way Scrolling

This game uses a four-way scrolling model that provides more free-flowing game play than the more restricted single-dimension scrolling games. Because of this, you need to deal with extra issues such as a more restricted viewing area (caused by centering the view on the ship) and extra graphics to accommodate the 360-degree turning. It's nothing you can't handle, though.

Enemy AI

The evil of the Horde will come in the form of three types of enemy units—mines (dumb floating bombs), turrets (fixed units that can sense the player's ship and then turn and fire), and fighters (smart ships that will target the player and chase after him, guns blazing).

Random Level Generator

To keep things interesting, *Star Assault* will generate a new level as the player enters. This will add to the game's replayability (how many times a player wants to come back and play again), as well as remove the need for you to store level data as a resource.

Level Graphics

Each level will be a connected series of rooms, so the primary level graphics are the tiles that form the walls of each room. For *Star Assault*, you should keep this simple and use a basic square tile for the walls.

To make things a little more interesting, you'll draw a background star field behind the level tiles. This will scroll at a different rate than the level to create a cool visual illusion that the stars are far off in the distance.

Save Game

Players won't be impressed if they have to restart the game every time they play, so you should implement a save game function that automatically persists the current level (keep in mind that it was randomly generated) and other game state information to non-volatile memory via the RMS, and then gives the player a resume option when he returns.

Interface

The game controls for *Star Assault* are pretty simple. The main control of the ship is by the left and right arrow keys. To keep things simpler for the player, the ship will auto-thrust forward (slowly).

Given that many modern MIDs have arrow pads, and you have the up direction free, you might as well make the up arrow the fire button. On most phones, this means players will be able to play with only their thumbs on the arrow pad.

Resources

Table 8.1 contains a list of all the resources I initially estimate this project will require. As you can see, it's a surprising amount for a relatively simple game project.

The total estimate for graphics is 19 KB, which should leave you plenty of room for your class files.

Table 8.1 Resource List

Graphic Name	Estimated Size	Purpose
Player Ship	2 KB	The player's ship facing 16 directions
Enemy Mine	2 KB	Animated spinning mine
Enemy Turret	2 KB	Enemy turret facing 16 directions
Enemy Fighter	2 KB	Enemy ship facing 16 directions
Level Tiles	1 KB	Tiles for the world
Star Field	1 KB	Star graphics for the backgrounds
Splash	5 KB	A title graphic for the splash
Weapons Fire	1 KB	Graphics for weapons fire (flying and exploding)
Explosion	2 KB	Big animated explosion representing the end of an enemy (or us)
Shields	1 KB	Animated shield for showing impact effects

Conclusion

As you can see, the process of designing a J2ME game isn't all that difficult. Even though you might consider it a pain, going through an organized design process is a necessary step along the road from idea to finished product.

No matter what you come up with, though, what you've designed is not a great game. A great game comes after you've developed your idea fully. It comes from all those little extras you add in—the homing missiles, the ten different enemy types, the extra-slick graphics, and all that endless tweaking to balance game play. I fully expect this polishing phase to take nearly as long as the original development time, so try to allocate tons of extra time in your schedule for tweaking your end product. It will make all the difference.

Now that you've done the design, let's bring *Star Assault* to life.

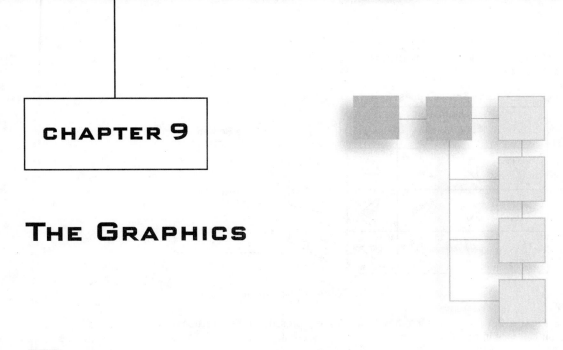

CHAPTER 9

THE GRAPHICS

B rilliant graphics are an integral part of most J2ME games, and *Star Assault* is no different. In this chapter, you'll move on to advanced topics such as multi-frame image loading and sprite animation. By the time you're finished, you'll have a set of robust imaging classes ready to support the action in your game.

Sprite Basics

As an action game, *Star Assault* depends heavily on graphics as the primary feedback mechanism for the player. You'll need to draw level tiles, the player's ship, enemy units, and those cool-looking explosions. To bring these to life requires more than just drawing simple images; what you need are sprites!

Sprites are collections of images (or frames) that represent all of the various states of a graphical entity. When the game is running, you quickly switch between these frames to give the illusion of animation.

The ship the player controls in *Star Assault* is a good example of a sprite. As you can see in Figure 9.1, you use 16 frames to represent the directions the ship can face. As the player turns the ship (using the arrow keys), you quickly change the onscreen image to represent the direction the ship object is facing, thus giving the illusion the ship is actually turning.

Another good example of a sprite is the explosion you'll display when an enemy or the player is defeated. To display the explosion, you use a sequence of 20 frames, each one representing one part of the total animation. When you play back these images in sequence, it gives the illusion of a blast and then a slowly dissipating smoke cloud. Figure 9.2 shows the actual frames for the full explosion animation.

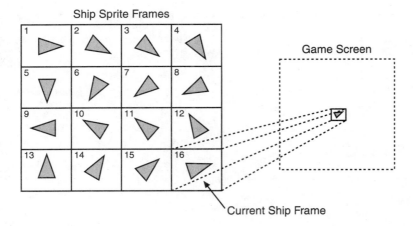

Figure 9.1 The ship sprite has 16 frames to represent all the directions it can face in the game.

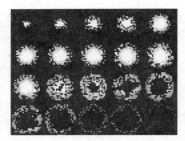

Figure 9.2 The 20 frames that make up your explosion animation

So how do you go about making your own sprites? First you need to obtain some source material in the form of image files.

Preparing Graphics

Regardless of whether someone else creates the graphics for your project or you do them yourself, you will have to format the source images into something you can conveniently load for your sprites. The next few sections will show you how to do this.

Layout

Firstly, MIDP uses the PNG image file format for all graphics, so you (or the artists, if you can convince them) will need to use a 2D graphics application to lay out and save your images using this format. I use Adobe Photoshop, although other applications such as

Jasc's Paint Shop Pro and GIMP on Linux are just as good. (They may be even better by now; I'm stuck on Photoshop out of habit.)

Using your graphics program, you should then create a single image file and lay out all the frames of your sprites in even rows and columns (to line things up use the grid and guide-line tools in your graphics application). Try to keep things in even rows so you don't end up with any blank areas in your image and waste image file space. As you saw in Figure 9.2, I arranged the explosion sprite frames into four rows of five frames each.

Tip

> Images are expensive in terms of both JAR space and heap (when they are decompressed into memory), so try to reduce the number and size of images as much as possible. Consider reusing all or part of some graphics for other elements in your game. (You'll be surprised how reusable some graphics can be.) You should also try to reduce the total number of frames used for animations; MIDs typically don't need very many anyway. The 20-frame explosion animation illustrated in Figure 9.2 looks perfectly fine with eight frames, and even quite passable with four frames.

Saving Header Space

There's an added bonus to merging all the frames of a sprite into a single image file. PNG files, like most graphical formats, require a minimum amount of space, known as a *header*, before you store any image data. With PNGs, this required space is around 200 bytes. That might not sound like much now, but as you can see in Figure 9.3, if you mul-tiply that by every frame, for every state of every sprite, it can quickly turn into a great deal of wasted JAR space.

Not Saving Header Space

Now that you're undoubtedly convinced you should merge every image into one giant PNG, I should tell you about the drawbacks of doing so. The most significant effect is something you're undoubtedly already very familiar with—paletificatalisation.

Had trouble with that one, didn't you? All right, I admit it—that's not really a word. I just made it up. (Wow, maybe it'll catch on . . . in Tibet.) Anyway, paletificatalisation is just my term for the effects of merging images. To understand this concept, you first need to know that the level of compression you can achieve using the PNG format is closely tied to the size of the palette your image has (in other words, the number of unique colors it uses). The wider the variety of colors, the more space every pixel takes. It follows, therefore, that you can keep the size of PNG files down by storing images of similar color. This is great for most sprite frames, which tend to use a very similar palette, but if you use a single image file with separate sections for many colors, you're likely to end up increasing the total image size due to the larger palette required to represent all your images.

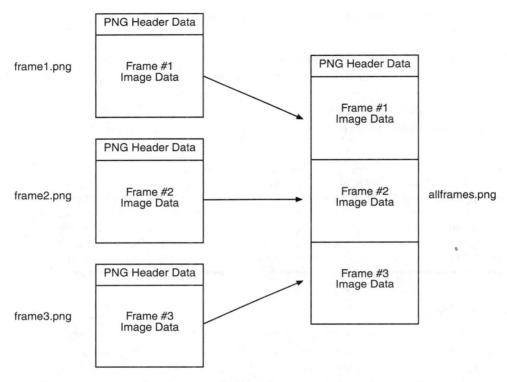

Figure 9.3 Individual images (left) each include a header which is not required when combined (right).

Tip

You can achieve very high compression rates using the PNG image format. Most graphics programs will provide options when you save the file. To reduce the file size, try using an 8-bit color format (PNG-8 instead of PNG-24), disabling dithering, and, if possible, reducing the palette size. (You'll be surprised how few colors you really need in an image.) You should also always turn off interlacing, which is pointless on MIDs, and disable transparency if you're targeting a device that doesn't support it.

To optimize properly, you often need to have different versions of PNG files for different MID builds. Unfortunately, this can become very confusing due to the large numbers of different image files you need to manage. To help you with this, you'll look at using an automated build system in Chapter 14, "The Device Ports."

Optimizing your PNG files can typically save you 50 to 80 percent in terms of file size when compared to the typical default save options, so it's worth spending some time tweaking the settings. However, keep in mind that this saves JAR space, not heap memory. When the image is later loaded into memory, it will decompress to the same size regardless of how much you optimized it. How much heap it will take depends on the phone.

Image Colors

MIDs typically use a much lower color depth (12-bit or less) than PCs (24-bit). If your artists jump at the horror of this, just tell them to load an image on a phone screen and try to spot the difference in a 12-bit image file. I'll bet you they can't do it.

Unfortunately, there's no 12-bit default palette you can load in your graphics program to simulate how the image will actually look on a MID. The only way to do this is to load the image on the actual device and find out for real. As you'll see, though, the translation of your image palette when it is displayed on a particular phone doesn't have much of an impact anyway. The screens are just too small to notice fine-grained color differences.

I recommend that you use very strong, very bright colors. MIDs will wash out what looks like a bright image on a PC, so pump up the contrast and brightness to make things really stand out.

Tip

If you're really after every inch of space in an image file, one technique is to reduce your palette by merging similar colors. Many advanced graphics applications have tools to assist with this process. You'd be surprised how many colors you can merge without a noticeable impact on the presentation of an image.

Loading the Images

Next I want to work through how to load up the frames of your sprite using the MIDP graphics tools. Figure 9.4 shows the image file containing the frames for the player ship, enemy fighter (the red one), and enemy turrets. This file also includes the four frames for the shielding animation.

The two ships and the turret each have 16 frames, arranged in a 4 × 4 layout. Each frame is 16 × 16 pixels. The shield frames, however, are 4 frames, each 20 × 20 pixels. (This is so they poke out of the edges when drawn underneath the ship sprites—it's a pretty good-looking effect, actually, but I'll get to that later.)

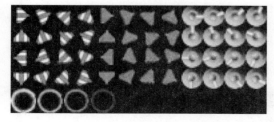

Figure 9.4 The frames for the player's ship as well as two enemy types laid out in a single image.

Extracting the Image

To use these images in your game, you need to extract only the portion of the image that contains the frames you want. First, you load the entire image from the file:

```
Image fileImage = null;
try
{
    fileImage = Image.createImage(filename);
}

catch (IOException ioe)
{
    System.out.println("can't load file: " + filename);
}
```

Your problem now is how to extract just the portion of the image you want. As you can see in Figure 9.5, if you want to create an image containing only the shield frames, you need to exclude everything else in the file. The area you want is below the 16 frames for the player's ship, so you need to start 64 pixels down and then grab a portion of the image 80 pixels across (4 × 20 pixels for each shield frame) and 20 pixels down.

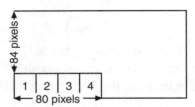

Figure 9.5 You need to extract only the part of the greater image that contains your frames.

Here's a good question: How can you extract only a part of a larger image (in your case, the 20 × 80 pixel shield frames)? MIDP does not support any method to draw only part of an image. To do this, you need to use a little drawing trickery. Here's the code:

```
/**
 * Extracts a portion of an image using clipping.
 * @param source The source image.
 * @param x The starting x position of the clipping rectangle.
```

```
 * @param y The starting y position of the clipping rectangle.
 * @param width The width of the clipping rectangle.
 * @param height The height of the clipping rectangle.
 * @return A new Image object containing only the portion of the image
 * withing the x, y, width, height rectangle.
 */
public final static Image getImageRegion(Image source, int x, int y, int width, int
height)
{
    // create a placeholder for our resulting image region
    Image result = Image.createImage(width, height);

    if (x + width > source.getWidth() || y + height > source.getHeight())
        System.out.println("Warning: attempting extract using (" +
                        x + "," + y + "," + width + "," + height + ") when image is " +
                        "(" + source.getWidth() + "," + source.getHeight() + ")");

    // draw the image, offset by the region starting position
    result.getGraphics().drawImage(source, -x, -y, Graphics.TOP|Graphics.LEFT);

    return result;
}
```

Did you spot the trick? Let me explain how this works. To extract the correct image portion, you first create a new image the same size as the area you want to extract. The method does this with the following line:

```
Image result = Image.createImage(width, height);
```

Next, all you need to do is draw the source image (the big one) onto this new target area, offset by the position of the area you want to extract. Figure 9.6 illustrates what I mean.

As you can see, all you're doing is drawing the source image starting at 0, −64. The image drawn onto the target at position 0, 0 is what was on the source image starting at 64. Here's the code the method uses to do this:

```
result.getGraphics().drawImage(source, -x, -y,Graphics.TOP|Graphics.LEFT);
```

A quick thanks goes out to the MIDP developers for allowing that one!

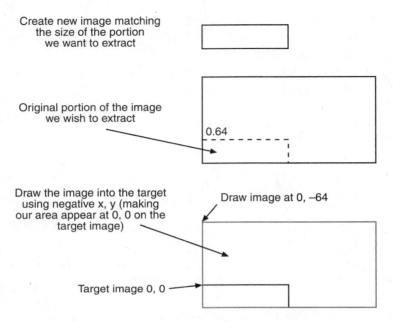

Create new image matching the size of the portion we want to extract

Original portion of the image we wish to extract

0.64

Draw the image into the target using negative x, y (making our area appear at 0, 0 on the target image)

Draw image at 0, –64

Target image 0, 0

Figure 9.6 Using clipping to extract a portion of an image

Separating the Frames

Now that you know how to grab only a portion of an image, you can use this code to extract the individual frames for an animation from the larger composite image. For the shields, this would be the four 20 × 20 pixel images located on the bottom right of your file. The following method uses the getImageRegion method to do this:

```
/**
 * Gets an array of images by breaking a larger image into smaller frames.
 * @param sourceImage The image to extract the frames from.
 * @param sourceX The starting x position in the source image to use.
 * @param sourceY The starting y position in the source image to use.
 * @param framesWide The number of frames across the source image to extract.
 * @param framesHigh The number of frames down the source image to extract.
 * @param frameWidth The width of each of those frames.
 * @param frameHeight The height of each of those frames.
 * @return An array containing an image for each frame.
 */
public final static Image[] extractFrames(Image sourceImage, int sourceX,
                                int sourceY,
                                int framesWide, int framesHigh,
                                int frameWidth, int frameHeight)
```

```
{
    // extract all the frames from the source image
    Image[] frames = new Image[framesWide * framesHigh];
    int frameCount = 0;

    for (int fy = 0; fy < framesHigh; fy++)
        for (int fx = 0; fx < framesWide; fx++)
            frames[frameCount++] =
                    getImageRegion(sourceImage, sourceX + (fx * frameWidth),
                                   sourceY + (fy * frameHeight),
                                   frameWidth, frameHeight);
    return frames;
}
```

This method is quite simple. First, you create an array of images to hold your results. Two for loops (one inside the other) then loop through every frame (fx) along each row (fy), using the getImageRegion method to extract the frame you want. The result is stored in the image array and then returned.

Using the method is also pretty easy. Here's how you'd pull out the shield frames from the ship.png image file:

```
Image[] shieldFrames = ImageSet.extractFrames(shipImage, 0, 64, 4, 1, 20, 20);
```

This line extracts four frames across and one frame down starting at position 0, 64 in the source image, with each frame being 20 × 20 pixels.

Once you have the array of frame images, you can draw them by accessing the array element that corresponds to the frame you want. For example, if you wanted to draw the last shield image, you could use

```
graphics.drawImage(shieldFrames[3], 0, 0, Tools.GRAPHICS_TOP_LEFT);
```

Getting Some Action

Now that you have the code to load up the frames of a sprite, it's time to see it in action. In the following example, you load the ship frames and then spin the red ship around by cycling through all the frames. I've excluded the standard MIDlet support methods as well as the image extraction methods I've already covered.

Tip

You'll find the source code and a working JAD/JAR for this example on the CD under the Chapter 9 source code directory using the name SpriteTest.

```java
import javax.microedition.midlet.*;
import javax.microedition.lcdui.*;
import java.io.IOException;

/**
 * An example that demonstrates the use of the ImageSet class to create a sprite.
 * Note that this is used as a precursor to creating a Sprite class, not as an
 * example of how to use the Sprite class.
 * @author Martin J. Wells
 */
public class SpriteTest extends MIDlet implements CommandListener, Runnable
{
    private static int SHIP_FRAME_WIDTH = 16;
    private static int SHIP_FRAME_HEIGHT = 16;

    private MyCanvas myCanvas;
    private Command quit;
    private Image[] shipFrames;
    private boolean running;
    private int currentFrame;

    /**
     * A custom canvas that will draw the current frame in the animation.
     */
    class MyCanvas extends Canvas
    {
        /**
         * The overidden Canvas class paint method takes care of drawing the
         * current frame.
         * @param graphics The graphics context on which you draw.
         */
        protected void paint(Graphics graphics)
        {
            graphics.setColor(0);
            graphics.fillRect(0, 0, getWidth(), getHeight());

            graphics.drawImage(shipFrames[currentFrame], getWidth() / 2, getHeight() / 2,
                            Graphics.HCENTER | Graphics.VCENTER);

        }
    }
```

```
/**
 * Constructor loads the ship.png file (make sure this image file is in the
 * JAR (and not in a subdirectory) for this code to work. After loading the
 * image we extract the frames, create an image set then setup the canvas.
 */
public SpriteTest()
{
    try
    {
        // Construct the image and extract the red ship frames
        Image shipImage = Image.createImage("/ship.png");
        shipFrames = ImageSet.extractFrames(shipImage, 4 * SHIP_FRAME_WIDTH,
                                            0, 4, 4, SHIP_FRAME_WIDTH,
                                            SHIP_FRAME_HEIGHT);
    }
    catch (IOException ioe)
    {
        System.out.println("unable to load image");
    }

    // Construct the canvas
    myCanvas = new MyCanvas();

    // And a way to quit
    quit = new Command("Quit", Command.EXIT, 2);
    myCanvas.addCommand(quit);

    myCanvas.setCommandListener(this);

    // create the thread that will carry out the animation.
    running = true;
    Thread t = new Thread(this);
    t.start();
}

public void run()
{
    while (running)
    {
        // Increment the current frame. Note that this is not a particularly
        // good way to do animation. See the Sprite class for how to handle it
        // properly (using timing).
```

```
        currentFrame++;
        if (currentFrame > 15)
            currentFrame = 0;

        // Request a canvas repaint.
        myCanvas.repaint();
        try
        {
            // Hang around a bit.
            Thread.sleep(100);
        }
        catch (InterruptedException e)
        {
        }

    }
}


/**
 * Handles Application Manager notification the MIDlet is starting (or
 * resuming from a pause). In this case we set the canvas as the current
 * display screen.
 * @throws MIDletStateChangeException
 */
protected void startApp() throws MIDletStateChangeException
{
    Display.getDisplay(this).setCurrent(myCanvas);
}


/**
 * Handles Application Manager notification the MIDlet is about to be paused.
 * We don't bother doing anything for this case.
 */
protected void pauseApp()
{
}


/**
 * Handles Application Manager notification the MIDlet is about to be
 * destroyed. We don't bother doing anything for this case.
 */
protected void destroyApp(boolean unconditional)
        throws MIDletStateChangeException
```

```
    {
    }


    /**
     * The CommandListener interface method called when the user executes
     * a Command, in this case it can only be the quit command we created in the
     * constructor and added to the Canvas.
     * @param command The command that was executed.
     * @param displayable The displayable that command was embedded within.
     */
    public void commandAction(Command command, Displayable displayable)
    {
        try
        {
            if (command == quit)
            {
                running = false;
                destroyApp(true);
                notifyDestroyed();
            }
        }

        catch (MIDletStateChangeException me)
        {
            System.out.println(me + " caught.");
        }
    }
}
```

Figure 9.7 The results of the SpriteTest MIDlet (it's far more exciting in real life).

Figure 9.7 shows the output from the full MIDlet. Not bad for a thread and some simple image tools.

Note

I find this type of little test MIDlet pretty useful. You can use it to check whether an animation looks good when running on an MID. Feel free to replace the ship graphics with any sprite you require for your game.

You've covered quite a bit to get things to this stage, including loading images, isolating regions, and extracting frames. There are still a few issues to deal with, though. For example, how do you handle animation at different speeds, and what if a sprite has more than one animation? So far, all you have are arrays of images; for *Star Assault*, you'll need a few more tricks.

Advanced Sprites

Sprites are one of the most important and time-consuming parts of MID game development. Organizing images, extracting frames, setting up animation timing, and then drawing the sprites on the screen are all routine tasks when you are putting together a game. *Star Assault* is no different. For a simple game, there is a surprising number of sprites.

In the next section you'll look at more advanced sprite techniques and tools, such as using image sets, handling multiple state sprites, and doing proper animation.

States Versus Frames

Using arrays of images for all your sprite frames works quite well, but imagine if your ship had many different animations, such as one for when the guns fire, a custom explosion animation, and maybe even an after-burner jet. These all require different sequences of frames, possibly of different sizes, each with their own animation speeds. Each of these animations represents a different state the ship sprite can have.

Another good example of a sprite having multiple states is the MR-313 high-impact radial plasma shells your ship fires. (Okay, we'll just call them bullets from now on. . . .) These bullets have two quite distinct states—flying, in which they cycle through a little sparkle animation, and exploding, which is a short animation played when the bullets hits something. You can see the frames for these two states in Figure 9.8.

Coding sprites with multiple states, each with distinct animations, quickly becomes a confusing mess if you're dealing with a large number of sprites (or even a small number sometimes). Therefore, you should encapsulate the many states of a sprite into a single image set. You can think of this as a set of sprite states.

Tip

The more sophisticated your sprites become, the more important states will get. If you were coding a game such as *Diablo*, for example, you could use a separate state for the walking, attacking, and blocking animation sequences used by the player character. Each of these states can have different image sequences, frame sizes, and animation speeds.

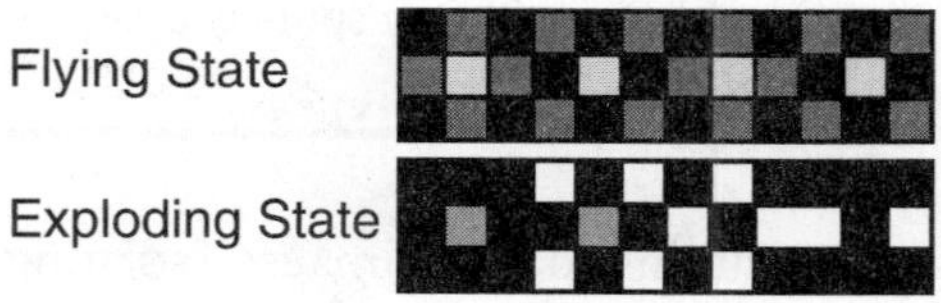

Flying State

Exploding State

Figure 9.8 The two sets of image frames we use for bullets corresponding to the flying and exploding states.

Creating Image Sets

To encapsulate the concept of image sets, you can use the rather appropriately named Image-Set class. The primary purpose of this class is to manage the array of frame images (including details on the frame width and height), as well as the speed at which the frames for that state should animate. There is, however, another important reason why you need this class. This might be something you've wondered already: Why have ImageSet classes at all; why not just have a Sprite class? What more is there to a sprite than states and animation?

There's a good reason why you separate image sets from sprites. Unfortunately, I can't remember what it was at the moment, so let's move on to something else and you can just trust me, okay?

Had you going for a second there! All right, to understand why you separate image sets from sprites, I'd like you to think about the underlying images. MIDs have such a limited amount of memory that you obviously can't afford to have a set of images for every copy of a sprite. Take a look at the bullets as an example. In *Star Assault*, the ships can all fire bullets. This can quickly result in many bullets flying around during big fights, which in turn requires many bullet objects. Although you need to have each bullet animate independently of all the other bullet objects, you don't want to require a copy of all the image frames as well. It would be a disastrous waste of memory!

The ImageSet class, therefore, acts as a container for the various arrays of images required for each state. A Sprite class, on the other hand, contains all the data for a particular instance of a sprite, such as the state it's in, the current frame, and how long before it should switch to the next frame in the animation. As you can see in Figure 9.9, the three bullet sprite instances share this same ImageSet. This allows you to have only a single copy of the images in memory, yet still have independent sprites utilizing these graphics.

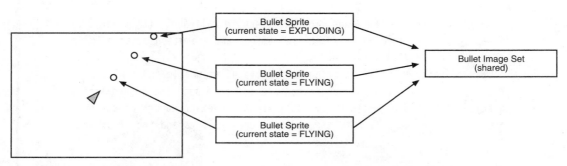

Figure 9.9 The separation of images from sprites lets you share graphics among sprites, even if they are of different types.

All right, take a look at the complete `ImageSet` class. Thankfully there's nothing too complicated in there.

```java
import javax.microedition.lcdui.Image;
import javax.microedition.lcdui.Graphics;
import java.io.IOException;

/**
 * A container for sets of image frames; typically sprites. A single set
 * is made up of one or more states. Each state represents an animation sequence
 * including Image objects for the frames, animation timing and frame
 * dimensions. An example use of this class would be to animate a little dude.
 * If he had two states of existence, standing (which has short breathing
 * animation) and walking (which has a much longer animation), this would be
 * implemented by creating an ImageSet object and then adding two states, each
 * with their own Image array for all the animation frames (use the static
 * methods at the end of this class to load a clipped file image and then
 * extract the image frame array from it). You can then use a Sprite class
 * associated with this ImageSet to draw the character to the screen as well as
 * keep track of animation frames.
 * @author Martin J. Wells
 */
public class ImageSet
{
    private int totalStates;              // incremented by addState method only
    private Image[][] stateFrames;
    private int[] stateAnimTime, stateFrameWidth, stateFrameHeight;

    /**
     * Constructor for a new image. You will need to call addState to add the
     * various states (and their associated images and animation data) before
     * the object is really usable.
     * @param numStates The initial number of states (since ImageSet uses an
     * array internally (for speed) it costs a lot to expand the internal size
     * beyond this number -- typically you'll know the exact number of states
     * beforehand anyway. If not, the addState code will expand the array when
     * required.
     */
    public ImageSet(int numStates)
    {
        stateAnimTime = new int[numStates];
        stateFrameWidth = new int[numStates];
        stateFrameHeight = new int[numStates];
```

```java
        stateFrames = new Image[numStates][];
    }


    /**
     * Adds a new state to the ImageSet including an array of images and the
     * number of milliseconds to animate the entire state (NOT each frame). If
     * this is not an animating set then just use 0 for the animtime. To animate
     * you will need to create a Sprite object linked to this ImageSet.
     * @param frames An array of javax.microedition.lcdui.Image objects.
     * @param animTime The number of milliseconds delay to animate ALL frames.
     */
    public final void addState(Image frames[], int animTime)
    {
        int state = totalStates++;

        if (state >= stateFrames.length)
        {
            // expand the number of states
            stateAnimTime = Tools.expandArray(stateAnimTime, 1);
            stateFrameWidth = Tools.expandArray(stateFrameWidth, 1);
            stateFrameHeight = Tools.expandArray(stateFrameHeight, 1);
            stateFrames = Tools.expandArray(stateFrames, 1);
        }

        stateAnimTime[state] = animTime;
        stateFrameWidth[state] = frames[0].getWidth();
        stateFrameHeight[state] = frames[0].getHeight();
        stateFrames[state] = frames;
    }


    /**
     * Gets the number of frames for a particular state in the ImageSet.
     * @param state The state you want to know about.
     * @return The number of frames in that state.
     */
    public final int getTotalFrames(int state)
    {
        return stateFrames[state].length;
    }


    /**
     * Gets the total amount time to animate all the frames of a given state.
```

```
     * Note this is not the delay per frame.
     * @param state The state you want to know about.
     * @return The animation delay (in milliseconds) corresponding to the given
     * state.
     */
    public final int getAnimTime(int state)
    {
        return stateAnimTime[state];
    }


    /**
     * Gets the amount of time to spend on each frame of a set to animate it.
     * This is just a convenience method that returns the animation time for
     * a state divided by the total number of frames.
     * @param state The state you want to know about.
     * @return The number of milliseconds delay for each frame of a given state.
     */
    public final int getAnimTimePerFrame(int state)
    {
        return stateAnimTime[state] / stateFrames[state].length;
    }


    /**
     * Draws a specific frame of this sprite onto a graphics context.
     * @param target The target graphics context to draw on.
     * @param state The state corresponding to the frame being drawn.
     * @param frame The number of the frame you want to draw.
     * @param targetX The x-position to draw the frame.
     * @param targetY The y-position to draw the frame.
     */
    public final void draw(Graphics target, int state, int frame, int targetX, int tar-
getY)
    {
        if (stateFrames[state][frame] != null)
            target.drawImage(stateFrames[state][frame],
                            targetX, targetY, Tools.GRAPHICS_TOP_LEFT);
    }


    /**
     * Extract an Image corresponding to a particular state and frame.
     * @param state The state you're after.
     * @param frame The frame you're after.
```

```
 * @return The image corresponding to the given frame in the given state.
 */
public final Image getFrame(int state, int frame)
{
    return stateFrames[state][frame];
}


//
// STATIC IMAGE TOOLS
//


/**
 * Static utility method to load up a portion of an image from a file. Note
 * that the file must be in your JAR (or otherwise accessible) by the MID in
 * order to be loaded.
 * @param filename The name of the resource file to load.
 * @param originX The starting x position of the file image you want to load.
 * @param originY The starting y position of the file image you want to load.
 * @param width The width of the image you want to clip to.
 * @param height The height of the image you want to clip to.
 * @return A new Image object containing only the rectangle of originX,
 * originY, width and depth.
 */
public final static Image loadClippedImage(String filename, int originX, int originY,
int width,
                                                      int height)
{
    try
    {
        // load full image from file and create a mutable version
        Image fileImage = Image.createImage(filename);
        // use the getImageRegion method to extract out only the bit we want.
        return getImageRegion(fileImage, originX, originY, width, height);
    }

    catch (IOException ioe)
    {
        System.out.println("can't load file: " + filename);
        return null;
    }
}
```

```
/**
 * Static utility method to load up a portion of an image from a file. Note
 * that the file must be in your JAR (or otherwise accessible) by the MID in
 * order to be loaded. The width and height of the portion is assumed to be
 * the size of the file image.
 * @param filename The name of the resource file to load.
 * @param originX The starting x position of the file image you want to load.
 * @param originY The starting y position of the file image you want to load.
 * @return A new Image object containing only the rectangle starting at
 * originX, originY.
 */
public final static Image loadClippedImage(String filename, int originX, int originY)
{
    try
    {
        // load full image from file and create a mutable version
        Image fileImage = Image.createImage(filename);

        // shortcut out of here so we can avoid creating another image if they
        // are just using this method to load an image normally (no clipping).
        if (originX == 0 && originY == 0) return fileImage;

        // use the getImageRegion method to extract out only the bit we want.
        return getImageRegion(fileImage, originX, originY, fileImage.getWidth(),
fileImage.getHeight());
    }

    catch (IOException ioe)
    {
        System.out.println("can't load file: " + filename);
        return null;
    }
}

/**
 * Extracts a portion of an image using clipping.
 * @param source The source image.
 * @param x The starting x position of the clipping rectangle.
 * @param y The starting y position of the clipping rectangle.
 * @param width The width of the clipping rectangle.
 * @param height The height of the clipping rectangle.
 * @return A new Image object containing only the portion of the image
```

```
    * within the x, y, width, height rectangle.
    */
   public final static Image getImageRegion(Image source, int x, int y, int width, int
height)
   {
       // create a placeholder for our resulting image region
       Image result = Image.createImage(width, height);

       if (x + width > source.getWidth() || y + height > source.getHeight())
           System.out.println("Warning: attempting extract using (" +
                             x + "," + y + "," + width + "," + height + ") when image
is " +
                             "(" + source.getWidth() + "," + source.getHeight() +
")");

       // draw the image, offset by the region starting position
       result.getGraphics().drawImage(source, -x, -y, Tools.GRAPHICS_TOP_LEFT);

       return result;
   }

   /**
    * Gets an array of images by breaking a larger image into smaller frames.
    * @param sourceImage The image to extract the frames from.
    * @param sourceX The starting x position in the source image to use.
    * @param sourceY The starting y position in the source image to use.
    * @param framesWide The number of frames across the source image to extract.
    * @param framesHigh The number of frames down the source image to extract.
    * @param frameWidth The width of each of those frames.
    * @param frameHeight The height of each of those frames.
    * @return An array containing an image for each frame.
    */
   public final static Image[] extractFrames(Image sourceImage, int sourceX,
                                           int sourceY,
                                           int framesWide, int framesHigh,
                                           int frameWidth, int frameHeight)
   {
       // extract all the frames from the source image
       Image[] frames = new Image[framesWide * framesHigh];
       int frameCount = 0;

       for (int fy = 0; fy < framesHigh; fy++)
```

```
        for (int fx = 0; fx < framesWide; fx++)
            frames[frameCount++] =
                        getImageRegion(sourceImage, sourceX + (fx * frameWidth),
                                    sourceY + (fy * frameHeight),
                                    frameWidth, frameHeight);
    return frames;
    }
}
```

As you can see, the ImageSet class manages a two-dimensional array of images, which includes all the frames for all the states, along with the animation delay time (in milliseconds) and the width and height of the frames in each state.

Tip

I recommend you also move the image extraction methods from earlier in this chapter into this class (as statics) because this is their logical home.

Using Image Sets

When you construct an ImageSet, you can specify the number of states it initially has. Then you just call addState for each new state you have, passing in the array of images for the frames and the animation speed. For example, here's the code to construct the bullet ImageSet:

```
bulletImageSet = new ImageSet(2);
Image sourceImage = ImageSet.loadClippedImage("/general.png", 0, 0)
Image[] flyingFrames = ImageSet.extractFrames(sourceImage, 0, 0, 1, 1, 3, 3);
Image[] explodingFrames = ImageSet.extractFrames(sourceImage, 0, 3, 4, 1, 3, 3);

int flyingState = bulletImageSet.addState(flyingFrames, 200);
int explodingState = bulletImageSet.addState(explodingFrames, 500);
```

The addState method returns an assigned integer for each of the new states you add. You can use this to later reference these different states. For example, when your bullet object hits something, you can then draw images from the exploding state (rather than flying state) using the ImageSet draw method.

```
bulletImageSet.draw(graphics, explodingState, 0, 100, 100);
```

This will draw the first frame of the bullet in the exploding state. To complete this properly, you'd need to add timing code to change the frame according to the animation speed. That's something I'll get to soon.

Okay, now you've seen how to use image sets to create different arrays of images to represent the various states of an object. This all works quite well; however, there's a fair amount of work you'll need to do to animate the frames and keep track of various states. Because all of your graphics-based objects are going to be doing this, you should take a look at bringing this all together in the Sprite class.

Before you get to that, though, you need to take care of a little housekeeping.

The Tools Class

You might have noticed that the previous class used a few utility methods from a mysterious Tools class. This is just a repository for any static utility methods used in your game classes. You'll continue to add little things you need as you go along, so here's the foundation of this class and the methods used by ImageSet:

```
import javax.microedition.lcdui.Image;
import javax.microedition.lcdui.Graphics;


/**
 * A bunch of static tools.
 * @author Martin J. Wells
 */
public final class Tools
{
    /**
     * Commonly used so we precalc it.
     */
    public static final int GRAPHICS_TOP_LEFT = Graphics.LEFT | Graphics.TOP;


    /**
     * Take an array of existing objects and expand its size by a given number
     * of elements.
     * @param oldArray The array to expand.
     * @param expandBy The number of elements to expand the array by.
     * @return A new array (which is a copy of the original with space for more
     * elements).
     */
    public final static int[] expandArray(int[] oldArray, int expandBy)
    {
        int[] newArray = new int[oldArray.length + expandBy];
        System.arraycopy(oldArray, 0, newArray, 0, oldArray.length);
        return newArray;
    }
```

```
/**
 * Take a 2D array of existing objects and expand its size by a given number
 * of elements.
 * @param oldArray The array to expand.
 * @param expandBy The number of elements to expand the array by.
 * @return A new array (which is a copy of the original with space for more
 * elements).
 */
public final static Image[][] expandArray(Image[][] oldArray, int expandBy)
{
    Image[][] newArray = new Image[oldArray.length + expandBy][];
    System.arraycopy(oldArray, 0, newArray, 0, oldArray.length);
    return newArray;
}


}
```

The two forms of `expandArray` are used by the `addState` method of the `ImageSet` class to increase the size of the array of states if the initial capacity is not large enough. It's not the most efficient of methods, but because you generally know the number of states you have in the first place, you won't be calling it often.

I've also included a `GRAPHICS_TOP_LEFT` static integer. This is just a pre-calculation of a very commonly used setting to save a little processing time.

The Sprite Class

Image sets give you the frames and animation timing data for a sprite; however, to make the sprite come alive, you need to implement the animation code and keep track of which state and frame you're currently viewing. It would be silly to put all this into each of the game objects (such as `Bullet` and `Ship`), and the code doesn't belong in the `ImageSet` class because it's shared by all instances of the sprite. The logical place for this is, of course, in a `Sprite` class.

Aside from handling images and states, you only have one major thing left to do (and that's really what the `Sprite` class is here to care of)—animation. Since you already have all your sprite states, frames, and timing data ready to go, it's much easier to tackle animation. All you need to do now is add timing.

You first saw game timing in Chapter 7; in that example, you learned that the basics for timing in *RoadRun* came from cycling through a loop once for each frame in your game. On each pass you only calculated the total time that had elapsed since the last cycle. All movement (actor cycling) was then factored by this amount of time, resulting in the proper motion of the cars and trucks. You simply moved an amount of space relative to the time that had passed.

Animation is exactly the same. You have a number of frames to cycle through, so all you need to do is step through each frame at a rate equal to the animation speed. For example, if the bullet explosion state had four frames and an animation speed of 500 ms per frame the animation would complete a full explosion cycle in 2000 milliseconds.

The Sprite class's job is to keep track of the current state and frame and then handle the animation based on the associated ImageSet animation timing. Take a look at the code:

```java
import javax.microedition.lcdui.Graphics;

/**
 * A state manager for a game sprite. Use in conjunction with an ImageSet in
 * order to draw animated, multi-state sprites. For each instance of an animated
 * graphic you should create one corresponding Sprite object. Graphics are
 * shared using a common ImageSet. To animate you must call this class's cycle
 * method.
 * @author Martin J. Wells
 */
public class Sprite
{
    private int currentFrame;
    private int currentState;
    private long currentStateBegan;              // time this currentState started
    private ImageSet imageSet;
    private long lastFrameChange;
    private int totalCycles;

    /**
     * Constructor for a Sprite object requiring the source image set and the
     * starting state and frame.
     * @param is The imageSet which is the source of graphics for this Sprite.
     * @param startingState The starting state (normally 0).
     * @param startingFrame The starting frame (normally 0).
     */
    public Sprite(ImageSet is, int startingState, int startingFrame)
    {
        imageSet = is;
        setState(startingState, true);
        currentFrame = startingFrame;
    }

    /**
     * Change to a specific frame.
     * @param f The frame to change to.
```

```java
 */
public final void setFrame(int f)
{
    currentFrame = f;
}


/**
 * Change to a different state.
 * @param s The state to change to.
 * @param force Normally we won't change if that is already the current
 * state. However this has the effect of not resetting the state began time
 * and totalCycles counter. Set this to true to force those to be reset.
 */
public final void setState(int s, boolean force)
{
    if (currentState != s || force)
    {
        currentState = s;
        currentFrame = 0;
        totalCycles = 0;
        currentStateBegan = System.currentTimeMillis();
    }
}


/**
 * Resets all state information such as the current animation frame, total
 * number of completed cycles and the time the state began.
 */
public final void reset()
{
    currentFrame = 0;
    totalCycles = 0;
    currentStateBegan = 0;
    lastFrameChange = 0;
}


/**
 * Get the time the last state change occurred.
 * @return Time last state was changed in milliseconds since epoch.
 */
public final long getWhenStateBegan()
{
    return currentStateBegan;
```

```
}

/**
 * @return The total time spent in the current state.
 */
public final long getTimeInCurrentState()
{
    return (System.currentTimeMillis() - currentStateBegan);
}

/**
 * @return The current state.
 */
public final int getCurrentState()
{
    return currentState;
}

/**
 * @return The current frame number.
 */
public final int getCurrentFrame()
{
    return currentFrame;
}

/**
 * Draws the current sprite frame onto a specified graphics context.
 * @param target The target to draw the image frame onto.
 * @param targetX The target x position.
 * @param targetY The target y position.
 */
public final void draw(Graphics target, int targetX, int targetY)
{
    imageSet.draw(target, currentState, currentFrame, targetX, targetY);
}

/**
 * Cycles the current sprite's animation and goes forward by the number of
 * frames corresponding to the amount of time that has elapsed.
 * @param deltaMS The amount of time that has passed in milliseconds.
 */
public final void cycle(long deltaMS)
```

```
    {
        // change frame if we are animating (and enough time has passed)
        if (imageSet.getTotalFrames(currentState) > 1 &&
                imageSet.getAnimTime(currentState) > 0)
        {
            long deltaTime = System.currentTimeMillis() - lastFrameChange;
            if (deltaTime > imageSet.getAnimTimePerFrame(currentState))
            {
                currentFrame++;
                lastFrameChange = System.currentTimeMillis();
                if (currentFrame >= imageSet.getTotalFrames(currentState))
                {
                    currentFrame = 0;
                    totalCycles++;
                }
            }
        }
    }


    /**
     * @return The total number of cycles this sprite has animated through.
     * Very useful for determining if a sprite has finished its animation.
     */
    public final int getTotalCycles()
    {
        return totalCycles;
    }
}
```

Using the Sprite class is pretty easy. Once you have an ImageSet ready, you can simply construct a Sprite by passing it in along with a starting state and frame. For example:

```
bulletSprite = new Sprite(bulletImageSet, flyingState, 0);
```

This creates a new Sprite using bulletImageSet for images and animation timing. It also sets the current state to be the flyingState reference you previously recorded.

The Sprite class also has convenience methods to change the current state or frame, although generally the cycle method will switch frames for you.

You'll notice that I've also made the Sprite object keep track of exactly when a state change occurs. Game classes can then use this data to find out how long a sprite has been in a given state. For example, the bullets in *Star Assault* have a limited lifetime (about three seconds). Instead of tracking the lifetime of the bullet in the Bullet class, you can check the time the bullet has been in the flying state using the getTimeInCurrentState method.

Using a simple test each cycle, you can determine whether a bullet is old enough to be removed from the game world.

The Sprite class also tracks the total number of times it has cycled through the current animation. This is very useful if you want to know when an animation has gone through a certain number of iterations. For example, using the getTotalCycles method, the Bullet class can determine when its explosion animation has completed. After it has gone through once, you remove the bullet from the screen. Again, this saves you from doing the same sort of thing inside higher-level game object classes.

More Action

Now that you have a fully operational Sprite class, you can put it to use. In the following example, I've created a few alien proximity mine sprites and let them spin through their animations. Notice how I'm using the same image set for three distinct sprites. I'm also starting the animation at slightly different frames to demonstrate the sprites' independence.

```
import javax.microedition.midlet.*;
import javax.microedition.lcdui.*;
import java.io.IOException;

/**
 * A demonstration of the ImageSet and Sprite classes.
 * @author Martin J. Wells
 */
public class AdvancedSpriteTest extends MIDlet implements CommandListener,
        Runnable
{
    private static int MINE_FRAME_WIDTH = 16;
    private static int MINE_FRAME_HEIGHT = 16;

    private MyCanvas myCanvas;
    private Command quit;
    private boolean running;
    private Sprite mineSprite1;
    private Sprite mineSprite2;
    private Sprite mineSprite3;

    /**
     * An inner class canvas used to draw the three animating mines.
     */
    class MyCanvas extends Canvas
    {
        /**
```

```
    * Paints the mine sprites onto a blank canvas.
    * @param graphics The graphics context to draw onto.
    */
   protected void paint(Graphics graphics)
   {
      // Set the color to black and draw a complete rectangle in order to
      // clear the screen.
      graphics.setColor(0);
      graphics.fillRect(0, 0, getWidth(), getHeight());

      // Draw each of the sprite objects at different positions on the
      // screen.

      // Draw the first sprite at position 25, 25.
      mineSprite1.draw(graphics, 25, 25);
      // Draw the first sprite at position 50, 50.
      mineSprite2.draw(graphics, 50, 50);
      // Draw the first sprite at position 75, 75.
      mineSprite3.draw(graphics, 75, 75);
   }
}


/**
 * Constructor for our demo that loads up the mine graphics and uses these
 * to create an image set and then three sprites. It then creates a canvas as
 * well as a quit command.
 */
public AdvancedSpriteTest()
{
   try
   {
      // Load up the mine.png image and then use extract frames to rip out
      // the frames of the image. In this code we start at position 0, 0 in
      // the mine.png (which means our mine frames are in the top left of
      // the file) and then load 3 frames across and 2 down -- a total of
      // 6 frames.
      Image[] frames = ImageSet.extractFrames(Image.createImage("/mine.png"),
                                        0, 0, 3, 2,
                                        MINE_FRAME_WIDTH,
                                        MINE_FRAME_HEIGHT);
      // Create an ImageSet for the mine frames.
      ImageSet set = new ImageSet(1);
```

```
        // Set the animation speed to be 500 (so we'll animate through all 6
        // frames in half a second (500 ms).
        set.addState(frames, 500);

        // Create the first Sprite with a starting state of 0 and starting
        // frame of 0.
        mineSprite1 = new Sprite(set, 0, 0);
        // Create another sprite (using the same mine graphics - ImageSet) but
        // this time set the starting frame to 3 in order to offset the
        // animation a little. Changing the starting frame like this stops
        // all the mines animating with exactly the same frames.
        mineSprite2 = new Sprite(set, 0, 3);
        // For the last one we start at frame 5.
        mineSprite3 = new Sprite(set, 0, 5);
    }
    catch (IOException ioe)
    {
        System.out.println("unable to load image");
    }


    // Construct the canvas.
    myCanvas = new MyCanvas();

    // And a way to quit.
    quit = new Command("Quit", Command.EXIT, 2);
    myCanvas.addCommand(quit);

    myCanvas.setCommandListener(this);

    // Create a thread to do the animation and then redraw the Canvas.
    running = true;
    Thread t = new Thread(this);
    t.start();
}

/**
 * Executed when we start the Thread for this class. Calls cycle on the three
 * Sprite objects as well as asking for a repaint on the Canvas.
 */
public void run()
{
    while (running)
```

```
        {
            myCanvas.repaint();

            // Call the cycle method in order to have it advance the animation. To
            // save on code here I've just used a simple value of 100 to represent
            // the amount of time that has passed. This isn't accurate but it will
            // do for a demo of sprites. You should replace this with proper code
            // to track and determine the time difference between each cycle call.
            mineSprite1.cycle(100);
            mineSprite2.cycle(100);
            mineSprite3.cycle(100);

            try
            {
                Thread.sleep(100);
            }
            catch (InterruptedException e)
            {
            }

        }
    }

    /**
     * Handles Application Manager notification the MIDlet is starting (or
     * resuming from a pause). In this case we set the canvas as the current
     * display screen.
     * @throws MIDletStateChangeException
     */
    protected void startApp() throws MIDletStateChangeException
    {
        Display.getDisplay(this).setCurrent(myCanvas);
    }

    /**
     * Handles Application Manager notification the MIDlet is about to be paused.
     * We don't bother doing anything for this case.
     */
    protected void pauseApp()
    {
    }

    /**
```

```
 * Handles Application Manager notification the MIDlet is about to be
 * destroyed. We don't bother doing anything for this case.
 */
protected void destroyApp(boolean unconditional)
        throws MIDletStateChangeException
{
}


/**
 * The CommandListener interface method called when the user executes
 * a Command, in this case it can only be the quit command we created in the
 * constructor and added to the Canvas.
 * @param command The command that was executed.
 * @param displayable The displayable that command was embedded within.
 */
public void commandAction(Command command, Displayable displayable)
{
    try
    {
        if (command == quit)
        {
            running = false;
            destroyApp(true);
            notifyDestroyed();
        }
    }

    catch (MIDletStateChangeException me)
    {
        System.out.println(me + " caught.");
    }
}

}
```

And Beyond

That's about all you need for your sprite system in *Star Assault*. While it's not overly complicated, it has everything you need for your game. Being a programmer, though, I'm sure you already have 50 ideas for expanding the functionality I've presented. The problem is, you've already used about 8 KB of JAR space just creating your three classes (ImageSet, Tools, and Sprite). Because you already have pretty much everything you need, you can't afford to waste precious JAR space on functionality not directly used by the current project.

Being forced to include only what you absolutely need makes engine development extremely difficult. You'll blow 64 KB faster than you can say, "Sorry sir, I confused you with a giant pretzel." Try to keep this in mind when you look to add more capabilities to your classes—it'll save you from removing code later.

Having said that, there are certainly plenty of development situations in which you will need extra functionality, so here are a few ideas for how to expand the capabilities of your sprite system. It's up to you when and where you use these ideas—just be ready to sacrifice something else in exchange for them.

- **Reverse animation.** Add the option to have animations play either forward or backward (or maybe even sideways!).

- **Transitioning.** Support the concept of states that can transition to other states. When adding a state, you could specify which state should follow, either automatically (after a set number of cycles) or manually, by calling a `nextState` method.

- **Triggers.** Commonly, you'll want to know when an animation or state transition occurs. To help with this, you could have the `Sprite` class call you back when these events occur. Any class wanting to listen to these events could implement a `SpriteEventListener` interface. Although this might sound expensive, consider how much code you waste polling to see whether these events have occurred anyway.

- **Image set manager.** As the name implies, you can add a manager for all of your game's image sets. You can use this to centralize image loading and unloading (or nulling), as well as to keep all graphics access code in one place. Centralizing management will also help you keep track of the graphics that are currently in memory at any point in time, which can prove very useful when you're running low on RAM.

- **Resource data.** Instead of putting your graphics meta-data (frame size and layout, animation speed, and state setup) in code, consider storing it in a separate resource data file. Artists can then modify the file without needing to bother the all-important programmer. You could even write some simple MIDlets for artists to load and test sprites independent of the game.

Conclusion

`ImageSet` and `Sprite` are useful classes. You'll find that most games will use these in some form or another. For *Star Assault*, you'll see how all the graphics for your sprites are loaded and handled as you put the game together in the next few chapters.

Now that you have most of the graphics requirements for the game out of the way, you can take a look at advanced techniques for driving the action of your game.

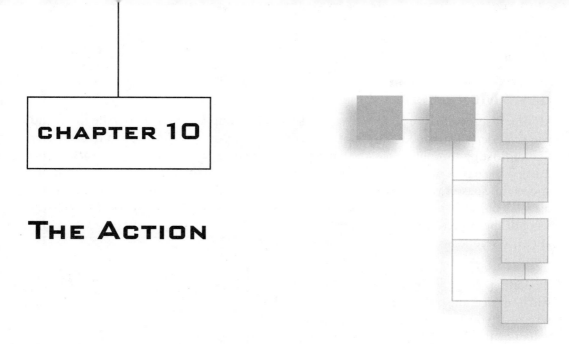

CHAPTER 10

THE ACTION

E instein once said, "Reality is merely an illusion, albeit a very persistent one." This couldn't be truer for game development—although maybe he should have changed it to "There is no spoon." Either way, his statement is especially meaningful with respect to your role in creating games—an art that involves the weaving of a careful illusion of reality, a reality you can then play with as you please. The beginnings of that illusion come from the images you use to portray your objects, but to bring them truly to life requires something more. What you need is the magic of motion.

In this chapter, you'll explore the fundamentals of moving your game objects around using basic physics, along with how to detect when those objects collide with each other. You'll wrap up with a look at how to add a little intelligence for your arch nemesis in *Star Assault*—the dreaded ships of the Horde.

Getting Some Action

In the last chapter I covered how to load all those beautiful images created by your artists (or yourself) and draw them on the screen. You even saw some basic animation. But although they're important, sprites are like international supermodels—they look great, but there's not a lot going on behind the scenes. (My apologies to all you supermodel readers.)

To bring your game objects to life, you need to simulate movement. To do this, you use physics—or, more specifically, dynamics (the area of physics relating to motion). Don't worry; I'll keep the math to a minimum.

Basic Movement

Motion is something we all intuitively understand. Get up and walk across the room and you've undertaken a good bit of motion. Whether it's an apple falling from a tree or a star fighter floating through space, the concepts of movement are the same. In *RoadRun* you learned the basics of how to move an object around on the screen. You give it a position, and as time passes you adjust that position based on a constant speed. For example, if you place an object at position 50, 50 on the screen, and then add 1 to the y component each second, the object will move to position 50, 75 after 25 seconds—a total distance of 25 pixels along the y-axis.

By adding to the y component of the position, you'll notice the object moved down on the screen. If you take away from the y position, it will of course move upwards. The same applies to adjusting the x component. By adding, you'll move to the right; subtracting will result in movement to the left.

This is the simplest form of movement—constant speed in a straight line (either horizontally or vertically in relation to the screen). Things get a little more complicated, however, if you want to move in an arbitrary direction (at an angle).

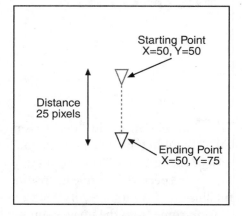

Figure 10.1 An example of basic movement by adding to the y position of an object over time.

Moving at an Angle

You saw that adding to or subtracting from the x- and y-axis components on an object's position will result in it moving along a straight line. If you increment x and y simultaneously you will move both horizontally and vertically (in other words, diagonally) across the screen. The way you move depends on whether you're adding or subtracting values on either the x or y-axes.

You can think of the movement in any of these directions in terms of degrees around a circle. Movement along the x-axis is 0 degrees (east), following counter-clockwise around the circle for all 360 degrees (see Figure 10.2).

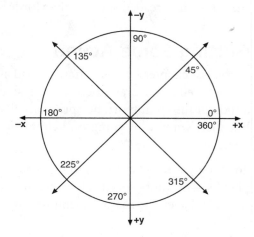

Figure 10.2 The 360 degrees of directions

Cartesian Space

Before we go any further, I need to clarify something regarding the difference between working in screen coordinates and Cartesian coordinates. In Figure 10.3 you can see the Cartesian and screen coordinate systems side by side. The difference is pretty simple, actually. In Cartesian space the y-axis proceeds upward, whereas it proceeds downward in the screen coordinate system. The x-axis is the same in both. As you can see in Figure 10.3, position 50, 50 in Cartesian space is located in the top-right quadrant of the square, whereas it's in the bottom-right quadrant with screen coordinates.

Screen coordinates reflect the way in which you view a computer screen. When you look at a computer monitor, the origin (0, 0) point is in the top-left corner. As you move down, the value of y increases. It's a common misconception to say that screen coordinates can't be negative. Although it's true that you can't draw anything on a screen at a negative position (that would be an interesting trick), you can certainly have an object at a negative screen coordinate—it just won't appear on the screen.

The main effect on your movement code is that whenever you use a calculation that's based on Cartesian coordinates (such as trigonometry), you need to invert any resulting y-value. You will see this in action a little later in the chapter.

Directional Movement

Movement along a straight line is simple; you just add or subtract from either the x- or y-axis. The way you go depends on which axis you change. If you adjust both axes simultaneously, you'll move diagonally.

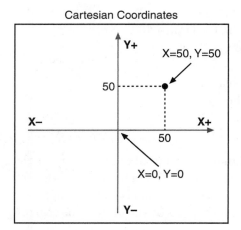
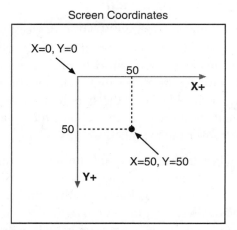

Figure 10.3 In Cartesian space the y-axis extends upward.

If you take that a little further, you can see that making different size adjustments to either axis will result in movement in a different direction. For example, suppose you add 2 to both the x and y-axes. If you then moved 20 times, you would end up at position 40, 40 (see Figure 10.4). If you refer back to Figure 10.2, you can see the movement was at an angle of 315 degrees (down and to the right). This works for all directions, you move simply by adjusting the amount of either the x or y value you change on every movement step.

This is all nice to know, but if you want your ship in *Star Assault* to move in any direction, how do you figure out how much to move on each axis? Your goal should be to face the ship at a particular angle and then just move it in that direction. In order to do that, you need to figure out the distance you want to move on each axis corresponding to that angle. For that you need to use a little trigonometry.

In Figure 10.5, I've modified the diagram in Figure 10.4 to show the right-angle triangle you'll use as the basis for calculating your values. As you can see, Side a, the adjacent, represents the x-axis distance; Side b, the opposite, represents the y-axis distance; and Side c is the hypotenuse of the triangle (in this case, the line from the starting point to the end).

If you say your ship's direction is 60 degrees, you first need to know how far to move along the x and y-axes based on this angle. You can determine the x component using the cosine of this angle (the ratio of the adjacent, or x-axis side, over the hypotenuse) and the y component from the sine (the ratio of the opposite, or y-axis side, over the hypotenuse).

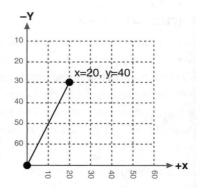

Figure 10.4 You can move an object diagonally by making simultaneous adjustments to both the x and y-axes.

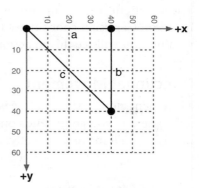

Figure 10.5 A right-angle triangle formed from the coordinates of the origin and target points.

However, because sine and cosine both work with radians, you'll need to convert the angle into radians before you do any calculations. Since there are 2π radians (approximately 6.28) in 360 degrees, you know that the number of degrees to a radian is equal to (approximately) 360 divided by 6.28, or 57.3. So if you divide 60 degrees by the number of degrees per radian (57.3), you'll end up with 1.047 radians.

With your radians in hand, you can now use the sine and cosine trigonometry functions to determine the results you need.

$$x = \cos(1.047) = 0.50$$

$$y = \sin(1.047) = 0.86$$

Notice something wrong with the result? The y-axis result is a positive number, but if you refer back to Figure 10.2, you'll see that 60 degrees faces upwards relative to the screen. If we were to add the y-axis result from the calculation above we would move down instead of up. This problem is caused by the mismatch of screen and Cartesian coordinates you saw in the previous section. To fix it you just invert the y-axis result. The calculation should therefore be:

$$x = \cos(1.047) = 0.50$$

$$y = -\sin(1.047) = -0.86 \qquad \text{// Inverted sin to map to screen coordinates.}$$

If you now start from the origin point and keep adding 0.50 to the x component and -0.86 to the y, you'd be moving at 60 degrees!

You might be thinking that this all works fine for easy angles (0 to 90 degrees), but what about as you move further around the circle? The values will have to be negative to move in the right direction. The good news is that you don't have to make any adjustments. As the angles move around the circle (through each quadrant), you'll get either negative or positive values. Figure 10.6 shows my previous diagram with angles in 45-degree increments. As you can see, the values go negative where appropriate. For example, the cosine of 180 degrees is −1 (the x component), and the sine is 0 (the y component). If you add this to an object's position, it will move backward along the x-axis, or 180 degrees.

This all works rather nicely; however, before you put all this into some real game code, you still have one more problem to solve. You've probably noticed that these calculations all rely on floating-point values to be correct. (Imagine radians without floating points.) Thus before you can get to some examples of all this in action, you first need to review how to handle floating-point values.

Simulating Floating-Point Math

Since J2ME (or more specifically, the CLDC) doesn't include any support for non-integer values, you're going to find it rather difficult to use trigonometry. To get around this limitation, you need to simulate floating point values using the built-in types you have.

Fixed-point mathematics is not all that hard to simulate. You can just split an integer into two distinct components—one for a value behind the decimal place and another for a value after the decimal place. Because an integer in Java is 32 bits, you have room for around 4 billion numbers, so even if you use half of all those decimal places for fractional values, you still have enough room for reasonably large numbers on the other side.

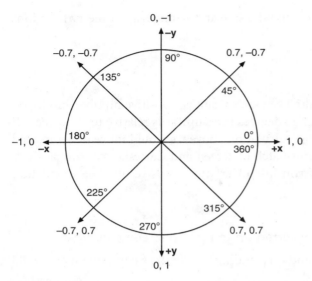

Figure 10.6 Examples of the x and y-axis adjustments for moving at different angles.

Although simulating fractions isn't all that difficult, what about all those math functions you take for granted, such as cosine, square root, and exponent? I don't know about you, but I'd rather be writing game code than trying to rewrite math functions.

MathFP

Thankfully there are a few libraries available that take care of all the work for you. They use built-in types to simulate pretty much all the functionality you'll need. For the purposes of *Star Assault*, you'll use the MathFP library written by Onno Hommes. MathFP has an excellent range of features, including variable precision and versions using both `long` and `int` base types. I've found it to be a robust, reliable, and extremely fast solution. You can download the library from `http://home.rochester.rr.com/ohommes/MathFP`.

Note

MathFP is subject to a license agreement, so be sure to read the conditions before you use the library in a publicly released product. It should only be used for non-commercial purposes.

I chose MathFP because it's a stable and simple system I felt best demonstrated the use of floating point within J2ME. Other floating point libraries are available which also do the job, such as:

JMFP (http://sourceforge.net/projects/jmfp)

FPLib (http://bearlib.sourceforge.net/)

ShiftFP (http://sourceforge.net/projects/shiftfp/)

MathFP has a number of different implementations you can use (all located in the classes directory). The two that will be useful to you are net.jscience.math.MathFP, which uses a long as its base type, and net.jscience.math.kvm.MathFP, which uses an int as the base type. Unless you're doing something with seriously high precision, you won't need to use a long (8 bytes) as the base type, so you can save space and use the net.jscience.math.kvm.MathFP class (using a 4-byte integer).

Note

Don't forget to add this entry to your class path. You'll also need to include this class in your game's JAR file, in the location /net/jscience/math/kvm/MathFP.class.

Using MathFP

Once you have things set up, using MathFP is very painless. Here's how you create an FP (fixed-point) value:

```
int xFP = MathFP.toFP("0.1");
```

The first thing you'll notice is that I didn't declare a type or object called MathFP; I just created an integer variable and then used the MathFP library to fill in the value. All MathFP methods are static, and the class is declared abstract as well.

Because there is no way to actually express a fractional value using J2ME (you'll get a language error), I've used the MathFP library's toFP(String) to convert a string representation of my value into an FP equivalent. If you were to print the variable xFP out to the screen, you'd actually see 1677721. How does this relate to 0.1, you ask? Never mind—that's MathFP's internal representation of the value of 0.1. If you want to print out the value, you first need to ask MathFP to decode it for you.

```
System.out.println( MathFP.toString(xFP) );
```

And you'll see your original value again—0.1.

As you can see, you must never make the mistake of thinking that an FP value is an integer in the normal sense. Although it uses the integer type to store data, that's where the similarity ends. If you want to work with FP values, you must use the corresponding MathFP methods. This is why I add the two letters at the end of the name of a variable. When I first used MathFP, I found that I often forgot a value was an FP and so I used it in conjunction with regular integers. This would result in weird, hard-to-find bugs. I'm not normally a fan of adding type identifiers to variable names (Hungarian notation); however, because you'll commonly need both integer and FP equivalent values (such as having a distinct variable x and xFP) and there's no built-in type protection available from the compiler, I think it's worth doing in this case.

Table 10.1 lists all the main methods in the MathFP API. As you can see, you have just about everything you'll need.

Table 10.1 net.jscience.math.kvm.MathFP

Method	Description
static int abs(int n)	Returns the absolute value of n.
static int acos(int r)	Returns the arc cosine of r (radians).
static int add(int n, int m)	Returns the sum of n and m.
static int asin(int r)	Returns the arc sine of r (radians).
static int atan(int r)	Returns the arc tangent of r (radians).
static int atan2(int y, int x)	Returns the principal of the arc tangent of y/x (radians).
static int convert(int a, int b)	Changes the precision of an FP value.
static int cos(int r)	Returns the cosine of r (radians).
static int cot(int r)	Returns the cotangent of r (radians).
static int div(int n, int m)	Divides n by m and returns the result.
static int exp(int x)	Returns the natural number raised to the power of x.
static int getPrecision()	Returns the current precision used.
static int log(int s)	Returns the logarithm of s.
static int max(int n, int m)	Returns the greater of n and m.
static int min(int n, int m)	Returns the lesser of n and m.
static int mul(int n, int m)	Multiplies n by m and returns the result.
static int pow(int b, int e)	Returns a value raised to another.
static int round(int x, int d)	Rounds a value to a certain precision.
static int setPrecision(int p)	Alters the level of precision used by the library.
static int sin(int r)	Returns the sine of r (radians).
static int sqrt(int s)	Returns the square root of s using 24 iterations.
static int sqrt(int s, int i)	Returns the square root of s using I iterations. Use a lower number of iterations to increase the speed of this operation. However the result will be less precise. Valid values are 6 to 24 with 24 being the most accurate (and slowest).
static int sub(int n, jnt m)	Subtracts m from n and returns the result.
static int tan(int r)	Returns the tangent of r (radians).
static int toFP(int i)	Converts a normal integer to an FP.
static int toFP(String s)	Converts a string to an FP.
static int toInt(int f)	Converts an FP back to an integer (discarding the fraction).
static String toString(int f)	Converts an FP into a string.
static String toString(int f, int d)	Converts an FP into a string (with rounding).

Using these methods is also very easy. Here's an example of multiplying and then dividing an FP value:

```
int xFP = MathFP.toFP("0.10");
int yFP = MathFP.toFP("0.2");
int zFP = MathFP.mul(xFP, yFP);
System.out.println( MathFP.toString( zFP ) );    // 0.20
zFP = MathFP.div(xFP, yFP);
System.out.println( MathFP.toString( zFP ) );    // 0.05
```

A Moving Example

All right, you've figured out how to move at an arbitrary angle, and with the MathFP library you have the functionality to do it. Now you can put everything together and make a little ship fly around the screen in any direction you want. Here's the code:

Tip

The complete code and a working JAD/JAR for basic movement are on the CD under the Chapter 10 source code directory "Direction Movement".

```
import net.jscience.math.kvm.MathFP;
import javax.microedition.midlet.*;
import javax.microedition.lcdui.*;
import java.io.IOException;

/**
 * A demonstration of moving an on-screen object in an arbitrary direction.
 * @author Martin J. Wells
 */
public class DirMoveTest extends MIDlet implements CommandListener, Runnable
{
    private static int SHIP_FRAME_WIDTH = 16;
    private static int SHIP_FRAME_HEIGHT = 16;
```

To save time you should always pre-calculate MathFP values if you can.

```
    public static final int FP_PI2 = MathFP.mul(MathFP.PI, MathFP.toFP(2));
    public static final int FP_DEGREES_PER_RAD = MathFP.div(MathFP.toFP(360), FP_PI2);
    public static final int FP_22P5 = MathFP.toFP("22.5");

    private GameScreen myCanvas;
    private Command quit;
```

```
private boolean running;
private Sprite shipSprite;

/**
 * A custom canvas class that handles drawing, cycling and input for a basic
 * movement example.
 */
class GameScreen extends Canvas
{
```

Note the addition below of properties to hold the position of the Ship and its current direction. Note that I'm using MathFP values for the ship's position, whereas the direction is just a plain old integer value (since we don't ever need to deal with fractional angles). The code that actually moves the ship is in the cycle method.

```
// ship properties
private int shipXFP;          // x position (as a MathFP)
private int shipYFP;          // y position (as a MathFP)
private int direction;        // current direction in degrees

/**
 * Constructor that sets up the position of the ship.
 */
public GameScreen()
{
    shipXFP = MathFP.toFP(50);
    shipYFP = MathFP.toFP(50);
}

/**
 * Canvas paint implementation which clears the screen and then draws
 * the ship at its current position.
 * @param graphics The graphics context on which to draw.
 */
protected void paint(Graphics graphics)
{
    // Clear the screen.
    graphics.setColor(0);
    graphics.fillRect(0, 0, getWidth(), getHeight());
```

Here you can see the alignment of the ship's direction to an appropriate frame by dividing the direction by 22.5. You then set the ship sprite frame to match this value, and it will take care of the rest. We use MathFP to properly handle the fractions.

```
int frame = MathFP.toInt(MathFP.div(MathFP.toFP(direction), FP_22P5));

// Set the ship sprite frame to be the one matching the direction.
shipSprite.setFrame(frame);

// Draw that frame on the screen.
shipSprite.draw(graphics, MathFP.toInt(shipXFP),
                MathFP.toInt(shipYFP));
}


/**
 * Moves the ship based on the angle it's facing.
 */
public void cycle()
{
```

This code is where we change the x and y position of the Ship based on the cosine and sine functions, respectively. Because these methods work in radians, not degrees, you convert the direction angle before you use it.

Note

Trigonometry functions are very slow. In Chapter 15, "The Optimizing," you'll look at methods to speed this up.

```
// Move the ship according to its current direction (in radians).
int dirRadians = MathFP.div(MathFP.toFP(direction),
    FP_DEGREES_PER_RAD);
// Add the x component of the movement (cos radians)
shipXFP = MathFP.add( shipXFP, MathFP.cos(dirRadians) );
// Add the y component of the movement (negative sin radians). We
// use negative sin to convert from Cartesian to screen coordinates.
shipYFP = MathFP.add( shipYFP, -MathFP.sin(dirRadians) );

// Check our position and wrap around to the other side of the canvas
// if we have to.
if (MathFP.toInt(shipXFP) < 0)
    shipXFP = MathFP.toFP(myCanvas.getWidth()-1);
if (MathFP.toInt(shipXFP) > myCanvas.getWidth())
    shipXFP = MathFP.toFP(0);
if (MathFP.toInt(shipYFP) < 0)
    shipYFP = MathFP.toFP(myCanvas.getHeight() - 1);
```

```
        if (MathFP.toInt(shipYFP) > myCanvas.getHeight())
            shipYFP = MathFP.toFP(0);
    }


    /**
     * React to keys pressed by the user.
     * @param keyCode The code of the key the players pressed.
     */
    protected void keyPressed(int keyCode)
    {
        int action = getGameAction(keyCode);
```

This example also adds support for turning the Ship when the user hits either the left or right arrow key. The following code reads the key and then adjusts the direction angle appropriately.

You might wonder why I've added 23 degrees. This is because your ship sprite has 16 frames, so if you divide 360 by 16, you know that each frame represents 22.5 degrees. (In this case it doesn't make any difference whether you move in 22.5- or 23-degree increments.) Each time you get a key press, you adjust the direction by 23. This means you'll always be flying in a direction that closely matches the way the picture of the ship is facing. If you didn't do this, you'd be flying one way but the ship would be facing another direction.

```
        // Based on the key they pressed we adjust the facing angle by an
        // increment equal to the facing directions of the ship (16 possible
        // translates to 22.5 which we round up to 23).
        if (action == RIGHT) direction -= 23;
        if (action == LEFT) direction += 23;

        // Wrap the direction around if it's now invalid.
        if (direction < 0) direction = 359-23;
        if (direction > 358) direction = 0;
    }
}


/**
 * MIDlet constructor loads up the ship graphics and then creates a
 * corresponding ImageSet and Sprite. It then constructs a canvas and quit
 * command.
 */
public DirMoveTest()
{
```

```java
    // Load up the standard ship graphics and make up a Sprite.
    try
    {
        Image[] frames = ImageSet.extractFrames(Image.createImage("/ship.png"),
                                        0, 0, 4, 4,
                                        SHIP_FRAME_WIDTH,
                                        SHIP_FRAME_HEIGHT);

        ImageSet set = new ImageSet(1);
        set.addState(frames, 0);
        shipSprite = new Sprite(set, 0, 0);
    }
    catch (IOException ioe)
    {
        System.out.println("unable to load image");
    }

    // Construct a canvas.
    myCanvas = new GameScreen();

    // And a way to quit.
    quit = new Command("Quit", Command.EXIT, 2);
    myCanvas.addCommand(quit);
    myCanvas.setCommandListener(this);

    running = true;
    Thread t = new Thread(this);
    t.start();
}

/**
 * Runnable interface run method that cycles the ship and requests a repaint
 * of the Canvas.
 */
public void run()
{
    while (running)
    {
        myCanvas.repaint();
        myCanvas.cycle();

        try
        {
```

```
                // Simple timing - sleep for 100 milliseconds.
                Thread.sleep(100);
            }
            catch (InterruptedException e)
            {
            }
        }
    }


    /**
     * Handles Application Manager notification the MIDlet is starting (or
     * resuming from a pause). In this case we set the canvas as the current
     * display screen.
     * @throws MIDletStateChangeException
     */
    protected void startApp() throws MIDletStateChangeException
    {
        Display.getDisplay(this).setCurrent(myCanvas);
    }


    /**
     * Handles Application Manager notification the MIDlet is about to be paused.
     * We don't bother doing anything for this case.
     */
    protected void pauseApp()
    {
    }


    /**
     * Handles Application Manager notification the MIDlet is about to be
     * destroyed. We don't bother doing anything for this case.
     */
    protected void destroyApp(boolean unconditional)
            throws MIDletStateChangeException
    {
    }


    /**
     * The CommandListener interface method called when the user executes
     * a Command, in this case it can only be the quit command we created in the
     * constructor and added to the Canvas.
```

```
   * @param command The command that was executed.
   * @param displayable The displayable that command was embedded within.
   */
  public void commandAction(Command command, Displayable displayable)
  {
      try
      {
          if (command == quit)
          {
              running = false;
              destroyApp(true);
              notifyDestroyed();
          }
      }

      catch (MIDletStateChangeException me)
      {
          System.out.println(me + " caught.");
      }
  }


}
```

To see how all this works you can just load and run the DirMoveTest.jad in the Direction Movement example directory under Chapter 10 source code on the CD.

That about wraps up basic movement; however, in *Star Assault* you're dealing with spaceships, so you can make things a little more interesting by applying a more realistic space flight model using directional velocity, thrust, and acceleration.

Advanced Motion

In the previous example, you had your ship flying around quite nicely. However, that example used a very simple flight model. The ship had a constant speed, and the direction it faced was the direction it moved. In *Star Assault*, you're going to make things a little more interesting by using a more complex flight model.

If you recall games such as *Asteroids* and *Subspace*, you'll remember that the flight mechanics were quite different than the previous example. The ship would move in a particular direction until it was pushed in another by some force (such as the ship's thrusters). To understand the mechanics of how this works, you need to look at a few physics concepts, namely velocity and acceleration.

Velocity

Velocity is simply the speed at which your ship is moving. In the previous example, the ship's velocity was the result of the calculations:

```
shipXFP = MathFP.add( shipXFP, MathFP.cos(dirRadians) );
shipYFP = MathFP.add( shipYFP, -MathFP.sin(dirRadians) );
```

The velocity was the value returned by the cosine and sine functions. As you changed direction, the velocity instantly adjusted to a new value relative to this new direction. The code then adjusted the ship's position according to this velocity.

Does this feel wrong to you? I know it did to me at first. Because velocity is really just the speed at which something is traveling (such as a speedboat cruising along at 80 mph), how can adjusting the velocity change the direction your ship (or speedboat) is going? If you change the velocity, shouldn't the vessel just speed up or slow down?

The difference is that you're dealing with velocity in two dimensions here. You can adjust the speed of movement in both the x and y directions, thus your speedboat can not only speed up and slow down going forward and backward, but it can also do the same going sideways! (I want one of these boats.)

Your ship floating through space is a much more reasonable example. You can easily imagine it flying along at a constant velocity. You can also see how the direction the ship is facing doesn't necessarily have anything to do with this velocity.

In the diagram in Figure 10.7, your ship is moving at a velocity of 0.7 on x and 0.7 on y, (equivalent to 315 degrees) even though it is facing toward 0 degrees. The only reason the ship changes direction (velocity) when you change the angle is because the code reacts to it instantly (hence the name *instant velocity*). The important point is that there's no difference between the direction the ship is floating and its velocity; they're the same thing.

However, for your space flight model, you don't want instant velocity; what you want is for the ship to float along until thrusters push it in a new direction. To simulate that, you'll need to adjust the ship's velocity using acceleration.

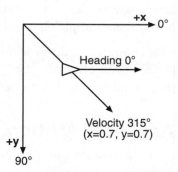

Figure 10.7 Movement of a ship in a direction different to the one it is facing

Acceleration

Acceleration is simply a measure of a change in velocity. If your ship is currently moving at a certain velocity, you can change that by applying acceleration to it. Like velocity, acceleration has both an x and a y component when you're dealing in two dimensions.

Therefore, by applying acceleration to your ship's velocity, you can vary the direction in which it's traveling.

As you can see in Figure 10.8, the ship is traveling at a velocity of (x, y) 0.7, 0.7 (315 degrees) while facing 0 degrees. Assuming the thrusters push the ship in the direction it's facing (by thrusting out the back); applying that thrust will adjust the velocity toward the direction it's pointing. This way, the ship's velocity and the direction it's floating are pushed by the thrusters.

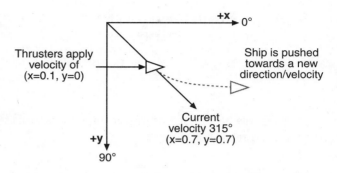

Figure 10.8 By applying acceleration to existing velocity an object moves "toward" a new direction.

Tip

You can simulate your floating ship slowing down (due to the effects of friction) simply by decreasing the overall magnitude of its velocity over time. Of course, this won't have much of an effect if the thrusters are on full blast all the time. (It will never have a chance to slow down.) You could get around this by making thrust only apply when a key (such as the up arrow) is pressed.

Free Flight

I know this is all rather theoretical, so let's put it all together into some code. The changes are all in the GameScreen inner class.

Tip

The complete code, including a working JAD/JAR for the advanced movement can be found on the CD under the Chapter 10 source code directory "Advanced Direction Movement".

```
/**
 * A Canvas used to draw and move a little ship sprite.
 */
class GameScreen extends Canvas
{
    // ship properties
    private int shipXFP;          // x position (as a MathFP)
    private int shipYFP;          // y position (as a MathFP)
    private int direction;        // current direction in degrees
```

```
private int xVelFP;             // x velocity (as a MathFP)
private int yVelFP;             // y velocity (as a MathFP)

private int maxVelFP = MathFP.toFP("2");
private int thrustFP = MathFP.toFP("0.2");

...

/**
 * Moves the ship based on the angle it's facing using directional
 * acceleration and velocity.
 */
public void cycle()
{
    // move the ship according to its current direction (in radians)
    int dirRadians = MathFP.div(MathFP.toFP(direction), FP_DEGREES_PER_RAD);
```

This code is where you can see the main difference between instant velocity and applying acceleration. Based on a thrust value the code calculates by how much we'll change the velocity (the acceleration).

```
    // Calculate the acceleration for this cycle by multiplying the direction
    // by the thrust on both x and y.
    int xAccFP = MathFP.mul(thrustFP, MathFP.cos(dirRadians));
    int yAccFP = MathFP.mul(thrustFP, -MathFP.sin(dirRadians));
```

You then just add this acceleration value to the current velocity.

```
    // Increase the velocity by the amount of acceleration in this cycle.
    xVelFP = MathFP.add(xVelFP, xAccFP);
    yVelFP = MathFP.add(yVelFP, yAccFP);
```

Because velocity is now increasing through acceleration you need to add some code to put a cap on it. Notice that I'm capping both positive and negative velocity. Without this, the ship would soon be moving at breakneck speed.

```
    // Cap our velocity to a controllable level.
    if (xVelFP > maxVelFP) xVelFP = maxVelFP;
    else if (xVelFP < -maxVelFP) xVelFP = -maxVelFP;
    if (yVelFP > maxVelFP) yVelFP = maxVelFP;
    else if (yVelFP < -maxVelFP) yVelFP = -maxVelFP;
```

Everything else is basically the same as the simple movement system

```
    // Move the ship according to its current velocity.
    shipXFP = MathFP.add(shipXFP, xVelFP);
```

```
    shipYFP = MathFP.add(shipYFP, yVelFP);

    // Check our position and wrap around if we have to.
    if (MathFP.toInt(shipXFP) < 0)
        shipXFP = MathFP.toFP(myCanvas.getWidth() - 1);
    if (MathFP.toInt(shipXFP) > myCanvas.getWidth())
        shipXFP = MathFP.toFP(0);
    if (MathFP.toInt(shipYFP) < 0)
        shipYFP = MathFP.toFP(myCanvas.getHeight() - 1);
    if (MathFP.toInt(shipYFP) > myCanvas.getHeight())
        shipYFP = MathFP.toFP(0);
    }


    ...

}
```

Thankfully, not too much has changed. The major addition is to the `cycle` method, where you'll notice you now calculate acceleration based on a constant thrust value (an arbitrary number representing how much force is coming out of the back of the ship) that is multiplied by the directional component of the x and y-axes.

Flying the ship around using this flight model is actually quite a lot of fun. You can zoom around and do slide-outs all over the screen. It's amazing how such a small amount of code produces a cool physics model like this. Check out the example on the CD and if you'd like, adjust the thrust and maximum velocity to see the effects. If you reduce thrust especially you'll see how the `Ship` slides a lot more (due to the reduced effects of lower acceleration).

Next I'll show you how to make things even more interesting and take a look at using your velocity in a different way by making the ship bounce off the side of the screen when it hits. Sound hard? Actually, it's easier than you might think.

Adding Bounce

In the current example code, you detect whether the ship has moved beyond the screen by checking if its position is beyond any of the edges.

If you detect this has happened, you then react by changing the position of the ship so it will appear on the other side of the screen (wrapping around the world). If you want the ship to bounce off the edge instead, you need to adjust its velocity. The question is, what type of adjustment do you make?

Bouncing, believe it or not, is actually very similar to jumping. For example, suppose you're walking along a footpath and you decide to jump. What happens? Well, before you jumped you only had horizontal velocity (think of it like the x-axis). When you leap into the air, you effectively accelerate the vertical component of your velocity. This means you move both vertically and horizontally; hence your jump covers a certain amount of distance. While you're in the air, another force comes into play—gravity. This force slowly pushes down the vertical velocity component. The combination of jumping acceleration and the pull of gravity creates the arc of movement when you jump (also known as a *parabola*). But we're getting ahead of ourselves. . . .

Think about how this works for bouncing as well. If I have a ball and I throw it straight down, it has a certain vertical velocity. Assuming it's not a squash ball, it will rebound against the floor and then fly back up. When it impacts the floor, the vertical velocity is inverted. Note that I said the vertical velocity is changed, *not* the horizontal. Figure 10.9 illustrates what I mean.

If you throw the ball forward and down at the same time, it has both horizontal and vertical velocity. Thus when it hits the floor, the angle of the surface causes a reaction only in the vertical component. This causes the ball to bounce (the vertical component will reverse), but the horizontal velocity is not affected so it will continue in that direction (see Figure 10.10).

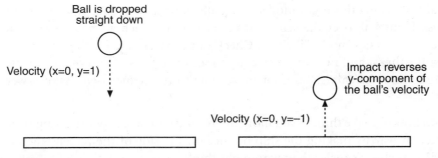

Figure 10.9 Bouncing an object is carried out by reversing its y-axis direction.

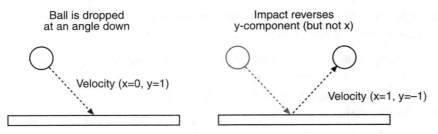

Figure 10.10 A bouncing ball with both horizontal and vertical motion

All right, so now you know that to bounce, all you need to do is figure out which component of your velocity to reverse. This is actually pretty easy because you're dealing with flat surfaces, so the component you reverse is the direction perpendicular to the plane you hit. Did I lose you? Actually, it's simpler than it sounds. In the diagram in Figure 10.11, you can see an example of perpendicular angles.

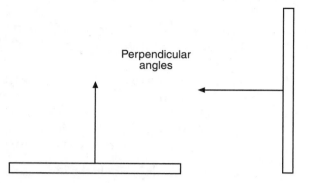

Perpendicular angles

Figure 10.11 An example of a perpendicular direction (angle)

I want you to think about what's actually happening to the ball when it hits the floor. If you throw it straight down and it hits a flat surface, why does this only affect the vertical velocity? The answer is in the force created by that horizontal surface. Because it's flat, it cancels out (or in this case, reverses) the entire vertical component because the surface blocks anything from moving further downward. There's nothing blocking the horizontal movement, though, so it remains unaffected.

All right, so you know that if the ball hits a horizontal floor you reverse the vertical velocity, and if it hits a vertical wall you invert the horizontal velocity. The same thing applies to your ship; when you detect that it hits either side, you reverse the x-axis velocity. If it hits the top or bottom, you reverse the y component. You can add code to the cycle method of the previous example to do this. Notice also that I'm remembering the position before we collided so that we can back out of the collision state. If this wasn't there you would find the object "sticks" forever in a collision state when it hits the edge (forever bouncing against the wall)—we'll see a more detailed example of this a little later in this chapter.

The first step is to remember the Ship's position before you move it. This is used later to back out of a collision if it occurs.

```
// Save the original position (so if it collided we can back out of
// this movement)
int origXFP = shipXFP;
int origYFP = shipYFP;
```

Next you can move the Ship using the same acceleration code from previous examples.

```
// Calculate the acceleration for this cycle by multiplying the direction
// by the thrust on both x and y.
int xAccFP = MathFP.mul(thrustFP, MathFP.cos(dirRadians));
int yAccFP = MathFP.mul(thrustFP, -MathFP.sin(dirRadians));
```

```
// Increase the velocity by the amount of acceleration in this cycle.
xVelFP = MathFP.add(xVelFP, xAccFP);
yVelFP = MathFP.add(yVelFP, yAccFP);

// Cap our velocity to a controllable level.
if (xVelFP > maxVelFP) xVelFP = maxVelFP;
else if (xVelFP < -maxVelFP) xVelFP = -maxVelFP;
if (yVelFP > maxVelFP) yVelFP = maxVelFP;
else if (yVelFP < -maxVelFP) yVelFP = -maxVelFP;
```

Everything else is basically the same as the simple movement system.

```
// Move the ship according to its current velocity.
shipXFP = MathFP.add(shipXFP, xVelFP);
shipYFP = MathFP.add(shipYFP, yVelFP);

// Check our position and if we're hitting an edge reverse a velocity
// component.
if (MathFP.toInt(shipXFP) < 1 ||
    MathFP.toInt(shipXFP)+SHIP_FRAME_WIDTH >= myCanvas.getWidth())
{
    // back out of the collision position
    shipXFP = origXFP;
    xVelFP = MathFP.mul(xVelFP, MathFP.toFP("-1.0"));
}
if (MathFP.toInt(shipYFP) < 1 ||
    MathFP.toInt(shipYFP)+SHIP_FRAME_HEIGHT >= myCanvas.getHeight())
{
    // back out of the collision position
    shipYFP = origYFP;
    yVelFP = MathFP.mul(yVelFP, MathFP.toFP("-1.0"));
}
```

All I'm doing in this code is detecting the impact and then reversing a velocity component by multiplying it by −1. It's simple, but if you play with the demo it's also lots of fun. Feel free to play around with values less than 1 to reduce the level of bounce or greater than 1 to see much bigger bounces. I use a value of around 0.8 to let the bounce slowly fade after a few impacts.

Because *Star Assault* only deals with perfect horizontal and vertical surfaces, this about covers your requirements for bouncing objects. However, if you're developing a game in which you have surfaces at other angles, you will need to adjust the velocity components based on the relative parts of the x and y-axes affected by the angle of the impact.

Collision Detection

Most action games have many objects flying around on the screen. Whether it's a spear heading toward a mammoth, a car flying along a track, or in the case of *Star Assault*, bullets hurtling toward doomed enemies, you need to determine when any of the objects collide.

Tip

> The complete code and a working JAD/JAR for the following collision detection code are on the CD under the Chapter 10 source code directory "CollisionTest".

Basic Intersection

In Chapter 7, the *RoadRun* game had a basic form of collision detection. Every cycle you would check whether the bounding rectangle of your main actor (the wombat) was intersecting with any of the vehicles. If this was the case, then splat—time for another wombat!

This type of collision detection works by checking whether any of the four corner points of one rectangle lie within another. You can see this illustrated in Figure 10.12.

The code for this is the same as our collision detection from the Actor class in Chapter 7, for example:

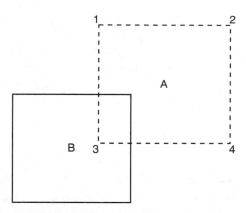

Figure 10.12 An intersection of two rectangles.

```
/**
 * Simple collision detection checks if a given point is in the Actor's
 * bounding rectangle.
 * @param px The x position of the point to check against.
 * @param py The y position of the point to check against.
 * @return true if the point px, py is within this Actor's bounding rectangle
 */
public boolean isCollidingWith(int px, int py)
{
    if (px >= getX() && px <= (getX() + getActorWidth()) &&
        py >= getY() && py <= (getY() + getActorHeight()) )
        return true;
    return false;
}
```

```
/**
 * Determines if another Actor has collided with this one. We do this by
 * checking if any of the four points in the passed in Actor's bounding
 * rectangle are within the bounds of this Actor's (using the isCollidingWith
 * point method above)
 * @param another The other Actor we're checking against.
 * @return true if the other Actor's bounding box collides with this one.
 */
public boolean isCollidingWith(Actor another)
{
  // check if any of our corners lie inside the other actor's
  // bounding rectangle
  if (isCollidingWith(another.getX(), another.getY()) ||
      isCollidingWith(another.getX() + another.getActorWidth(), another.getY()) ||
      isCollidingWith(another.getX(), another.getY() + another.getActorHeight()) ||
      isCollidingWith(another.getX() + another.getActorWidth(),
                              another.getY()+ another.getActorHeight()))
      return true;
  else
      return false;
}
```

Nothing too complicated there, right? Although this works quite well, it's also extremely slow. Since you'll be doing a great deal of collision detection in your game, it's pretty important to do it as quickly as possible, so take a look at an alternative rectangle intersection test known as *plane exclusion*.

Intersection through Exclusion

To understand how this works, you need to think the opposite of how you normally would to determine whether two things collide. Instead of trying to determine whether the rectangle intersects another, ask if it *doesn't*. For example, suppose the left edge of one rectangle is beyond the right edge of another. In that case there's no possible way the rectangles can intersect, right? One of them is beyond the opposite side of the other, so it just can't happen. You can see what I mean in Figure 10.13. None of the A rectangles could ever be in a collision state with B if the left side is beyond the right edge of B.

You can use this test to exclude one plane. If you are able to exclude all four planes (top, bottom, left, and right), then it's not possible that the rectangles intersect. If you can't exclude them all, then logically there has to be an intersection somewhere. As you can see, Figure 10.14 covers all the possible places one rectangle can be in relation to another.

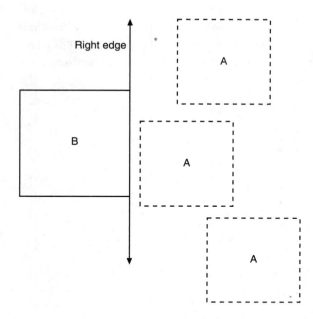

Figure 10.13 Because the left-hand side of all the A rectangles is beyond the right-hand side of B, it is not possible that the two rectangles are colliding.

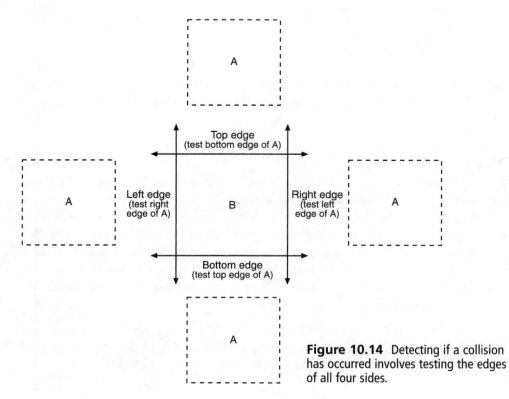

Figure 10.14 Detecting if a collision has occurred involves testing the edges of all four sides.

The following code does this by comparing two rectangles: a and b. The first rectangle is made up of the coordinates ax, ay, aw and ah, where ax and ay are the top-left point of a rectangle with a width of aw and a height of ah. The second rectangle is the same except you use the b set of variables. Here's the code:

```
/**
* Test for a collision between two rectangles using plane exclusion.
* @return True if the rectangle from the b coordinates intersects those
* of a.
*/
public static final boolean isIntersectingRect(int ax, int ay,
                                               int aw, int ah,
                                               int bx, int by,
                                               int bw, int bh)
{
    if (by + bh < ay || // is the bottom of b above the top of a?
        by > ay + ah || // is the top of b below bottom of a?
        bx + bw < ax || // is the right of b to the left of a?
        bx > ax + aw)   // is the left of b to the right of a?
        return false;

    return true;
}
```

Nice and simple, isn't it? You'll find this method is also extremely fast because of the low number of comparisons. Since it's used in many places, you should place it in a general Tools class.

Reacting to a Collision

Once you've determined that two objects have collided, you need to do something about it. The easiest thing to do would be to ignore it, but then what was the point of detecting the collision in the first place? The next easiest thing would be to remove one or both of the objects from your world. This is common in the case of a rocket hitting a ship. You have the ship show some type of "ouch" graphic (such as an explosion or shield impact), and then you remove the bullet from the game world. The more complicated case is to have both objects remain in the game world but react in some way to the collision. To do this, you need to manage things better.

Imagine you've just arrived at the scene of an accident where two cars (Porsches) have collided. Your job is to rectify the situation—fix the cars, deal with all the consequences of the crash, and then send everybody on their merry way—in about 10 milliseconds.

The first problem you have to deal with is that the cars are still in a collision state (their rectangles are intersecting), so you need to back them out of this position before you can do anything else. If you fail to do this, you would detect the collision state again the next time around (endlessly). The easiest method to reverse the state of a collision is to simply go back in time a little. You can do this by placing the objects where they were before they collided. For example you add the following code to the `cycle` method that moves your Actors:

```
// remember our position
int lastXFP = xFP;
int lastYFP = yFP;

// move
xFP = MathFP.add(xFP, xVelFP);
yFP = MathFP.add(yFP, yVelFP);

// test for collision
if (checkCollision(this))
{
    // if we hit something move back to where we were
    xFP = lastXFP;
    yFP = lastYFP;
}
```

Unfortunately, you still have a problem. When the game resumes, your Porsches, which are still heading in the same direction, will just smash into each other again! Backing the cars out of the collision state is an important step, but if you want both cars to continue you need to adjust their directions so they don't just slam into each other again. Say, here's an idea: Why don't you use that great bounce code you just figured out? When the Porsches impact, you could make them rebound off each other.

In the previous section, you saw that to bounce something off a surface, you need to invert either the horizontal or vertical velocity components based on the edge of the surface you hit. This was pretty easy in the previous example because you knew exactly which side of the screen the ship had hit. In this case, however, your collision code only determines whether or not they collided—*not* the edge upon which they collided. You need to determine this edge before you know which way to bounce.

You can determine the edge by comparing the position of the intersecting corner relative to the collision point. However, the code to do this is typically complex, quite slow, and not entirely accurate. The easier, more accurate method is to test for collisions separately on each component of your velocity as you move. Essentially, you move on the x-axis, and then test for a collision. If the collision occurs at that point, you know you've hit a vertical edge. Then you move on the y-axis and repeat the test, except this time a collision means you hit a horizontal edge. You can see this illustrated in Figure 10.15.

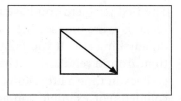

Figure 10.15 A cheap, fast way to determine on which edge a collision occurs is to change and test each axis separately.

If this all sounds familiar, that's because it is. The advanced movement example earlier in the chapter used this method to detect collisions on the edge of the screen and bounce off (without getting stuck). Here it is again so you don't have to flick back:

```
// Save the original position (so if it collided we can back out of
// this movement).
int origXFP = shipXFP;
int origYFP = shipYFP;

// Move the ship.
shipXFP = MathFP.add(shipXFP, xVelFP);
shipYFP = MathFP.add(shipYFP, yVelFP);

// Check our position and if we're hitting an edge reverse a velocity
// component.
if (MathFP.toInt(shipXFP) < 1 ||
    MathFP.toInt(shipXFP)+SHIP_FRAME_WIDTH >= myCanvas.getWidth())
{
    // back out of the collision position
    shipXFP = origXFP;
    xVelFP = MathFP.mul(xVelFP, MathFP.toFP("-1.0"));
}
if (MathFP.toInt(shipYFP) < 1 ||
    MathFP.toInt(shipYFP)+SHIP_FRAME_HEIGHT >= myCanvas.getHeight())
{
    // back out of the collision position
    shipYFP = origYFP;
    yVelFP = MathFP.mul(yVelFP, MathFP.toFP("-1.0"));
}
```

Advanced Collision Detection

The methods you've reviewed so far are very simple collision detection techniques. They certainly won't cover very complex collision cases. For example, if an object is moving fast enough, it's possible that a single step (cycle) could take the object completely beyond an object with which it should have collided. You can see this illustrated in Figure 10.16.

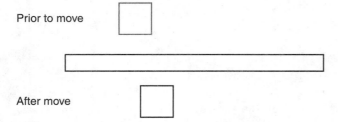

Figure 10.16 If an object is moving fast enough, it's possible it could "jump" completely over an obstruction.

For many J2ME games you won't have to worry (or care) about this case. If you do, however, you will need to detect collisions based on the path of the object, not just where it ends up. One technique for doing this is to do an intersection test for the line from the center of the object's starting position to the center of its end position, against all four sides of the other object. Figure 10.17 illustrates this.

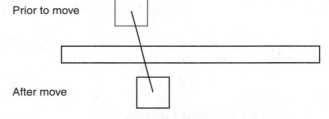

Figure 10.17 A quick method to determine collisions on fast moving objects is to test the intersection of a line representing its path against the lines of the other object's bounding rectangle.

Line intersection tests are complex processes, so doing this test four times for every object comparison is slow going. Doing this type of collision test for all the objects flying around in the game is rarely worth it.

Another method for detecting collisions between two objects is to test whether their bounding circles overlap. You can do this quickly by comparing the sum of the radii of both objects squared against the sum of the distance between the objects squared. If the radius result is greater than the distance, then the circles collide.

To figure out the radius you simply use half the value of the height or width, whichever is greater. Here's the original collision method modified to use a bounding circle test. If you're going to use this, I recommend pre-calculating and storing the radius values for speed.

```
/**
 * Returns true if b intersects a (uses bounding circle comparison)
 */
public static final boolean isIntersectingRect(int ax, int ay, int aw, int ah,
                                               int bx, int by, int bw, int bh)
{
```

```
int radius = (Math.max(aw, ah)/2) + 1;
int anotherRadius = (Math.max(bw, bh)/2)+1;

int radiusSquared = radius * radius;
int anotherRadiusSquared = anotherRadius * anotherRadius;

// if the distance squared < the square of the two radii then
// the circles overlap
int distanceX = ax - bx;
int distanceY = ay - by;

if (((distanceX * distanceX) + (distanceY * distanceY)) <
        (radiusSquared + anotherRadiusSquared))
    return true;
else
    return false;
}
```

A Collision Example

In the following example, you will bring together all the components of collision detection. You'll create five ships and have them fly around in random directions. When they collide, they'll bounce off each other before they continue. To accomplish this, I've separated the ship and game screen components into their own classes. To bring all this together I've also created a simple MIDlet class called CollisionTest and expanded out the Tools class with a few extras (like a random number generator). Also because it's getting a little sophisticated, I've split out all the code relating to the little ships into a new Ship class.

First up is the MIDlet class to handle everything, CollisionTest:

```
import javax.microedition.midlet.*;
import javax.microedition.lcdui.*;

/**
 * An example that creates some ships and flies them around bouncing off each
 * other.
 * @author Martin J. Wells
 */
public class CollisionTest extends MIDlet implements CommandListener, Runnable
{
    private GameScreen gameScreen;
    private Command quit;
    private boolean running;
```

```
/**
 * Constructor for the MIDlet creates the GameScreen object, adds a quit
 * command and then creates a thread to do our cycling and painting.
 */
public CollisionTest()
{
    // Construct a canvas
    gameScreen = new GameScreen();

    // And a way to quit
    quit = new Command("Quit", Command.EXIT, 2);
    gameScreen.addCommand(quit);
    gameScreen.setCommandListener(this);

    // Create the game thread.
    running = true;
    Thread t = new Thread(this);
    t.start();
}


/**
 * Runnable interface run method that cycles the ship and requests a repaint
 * of the Canvas.
 */
public void run()
{
    while (running)
    {
        gameScreen.repaint();
        gameScreen.cycle();

        try
        {
            // Simple timing - sleep for 100 milliseconds.
            Thread.sleep(100);
        }
        catch (InterruptedException e)
        {
        }

    }
}
```

```
/**
 * Handles Application Manager notification the MIDlet is starting (or
 * resuming from a pause). In this case we set the canvas as the current
 * display screen.
 * @throws MIDletStateChangeException
 */
protected void startApp() throws MIDletStateChangeException
{
    Display.getDisplay(this).setCurrent(gameScreen);
}

/**
 * Handles Application Manager notification the MIDlet is about to be paused.
 * We don't bother doing anything for this case.
 */
protected void pauseApp()
{
}

/**
 * Handles Application Manager notification the MIDlet is about to be
 * destroyed. We don't bother doing anything for this case.
 */
protected void destroyApp(boolean unconditional)
        throws MIDletStateChangeException
{
}

/**
 * The CommandListener interface method called when the user executes
 * a Command, in this case it can only be the quit command we created in the
 * constructor and added to the Canvas.
 * @param command The command that was executed.
 * @param displayable The displayable that command was embedded within.
 */
public void commandAction(Command command, Displayable displayable)
{
    try
    {
        if (command == quit)
        {
            running = false;
```

```
            destroyApp(true);
            notifyDestroyed();
        }
    }

    catch (MIDletStateChangeException me)
    {
        System.out.println(me + " caught.");
    }
}

}
```

Next is a modified version of the GameScreen class that creates five Ship objects (you'll see the Ship class in just a moment) and places them in a vertical row down the screen. It then gives each Ship a random direction and a velocity so they'll all fly off in different directions. When collision is detected, the Ships will bounce off each other before continuing.

```java
import javax.microedition.lcdui.Canvas;
import javax.microedition.lcdui.Graphics;

/**
 * A GameScreen (Canvas with game logic) that creates five Ships then flies them
 * off in random directions. If a collision occurs the Ship will bounce off
 * before continuing.
 * @author Martin J. Wells
 */
public class GameScreen extends Canvas
{
    private Ship[] ships;

    /**
     * Constructor for the GameScreen that creates the five Ships.
     */
    public GameScreen()
    {
```

This is where the five Ships are constructed and positioned in a vertical down the center of the screen. In this example we set them all off in different directions so they collide (the random directions are set in the Ship constructor).

```java
        // Create 5 ships positioning them in a vertical line down the center of
        // the screen.
        ships = new Ship[5];
```

```
    for (int i = 0; i < ships.length; i++)
        ships[i] = new Ship(getWidth()/2, 20*i, this);
}
```

In the render method the main addition is to loop through the array of Ships and call their render methods to draw them on the screen. It's the same thing with the cycle method, which again just loops through calling the cycle method for all the Ships.

```
/**
 * Canvas paint implementation which clears the screen and then draws
 * the ships at their current positions.
 * @param graphics The graphics context on which to draw.
 */
protected void paint(Graphics graphics)
{
    graphics.setColor(0);
    graphics.fillRect(0, 0, getWidth(), getHeight());

    // Cycles through the array of Ships and draws them all on the canvas.
    for (int i = 0; i < ships.length; i++)
        ships[i].render(graphics);
}


/**
 * Calls the cycle method on all the Ships in the array.
 */
public void cycle()
{
    for (int i = 0; i < ships.length; i++)
    {
        Ship s = ships[i];
        s.cycle();
    }
}
```

For the collision test we need to deal with detecting if a collision occurs between one Ship and the other four.

```
/**
 * Called by the Ship class to test whether a collision has occured between
 * one ship (the s paramater) and any other Ship in the array.
 * @param s The Ship to test against.
 * @return True if the Ship s is colliding with another.
 */
```

```
public boolean checkCollision(Ship s)
{
    // did this ship hit another?
    for (int j = 0; j < ships.length; j++)
    {
        Ship another = ships[j];
        // First we test that Ship s is not the element of the array being
        // tested.
        if (another != s &&
            Tools.isIntersectingRect(s.getX(), s.getY(), 16, 16,
                                     another.getX(), another.getY(), 16, 16))
            return true;
    }
    return false;
}

}
```

Since our little spaceships are getting a bit complicated I've placed all the logic in a new class called Ship. This class handles the movement and drawing of the Ships.

```
import net.jscience.math.kvm.MathFP;
import javax.microedition.lcdui.*;
import java.io.IOException;

/**
 * Class to handle the drawing and movement of a little spaceship. Image is
 * loaded in a Sprite from the ship.png file.
 * @author Martin J. Wells
 */
public class Ship
{
    private static int SHIP_FRAME_WIDTH = 16; // size of the ship in pixels
    private static int SHIP_FRAME_HEIGHT = 16;

    // Some pre-calculated values to speed things up.
    public static final int FP_PI2 = MathFP.mul(MathFP.PI, MathFP.toFP(2));
    public static final int FP_DEGREES_PER_RAD = MathFP.div(MathFP.toFP(360),
                                                            FP_PI2);
    public static final int FP_22P5 = MathFP.toFP("22.5");

    private static ImageSet shipImageSet;  // the one and only imageset
```

```java
private int xFP;                          // x position (as a MathFP)
private int yFP;                          // y position (as a MathFP)
private int direction;                    // current direction in degrees

private int xVelFP;                       // x velocity (as a MathFP)
private int yVelFP;                       // y velocity (as a MathFP)

private int maxVelFP = MathFP.toFP("2");
private int thrustFP = MathFP.toFP("0.2");

private Sprite shipSprite;
private int worldWidth;                   // size of the world (so we can wrap)
private int worldHeight;
private GameScreen gameScreen;

/**
 * Constructs a ship starting at a given location.
 * @param x The starting x position.
 * @param y The starting y position.
 * @param gs The GameScreen this Ship belongs to (used to call back for
 * collision detection)
 */
public Ship(int x, int y, GameScreen gs)
{
    gameScreen = gs;

    // Load up the images for the Ship. Note that shipImageSet is a static
    // so this code will only be run once (after that shipImageSet will not
    // be null).
    if (shipImageSet == null)
    {
        // Set the width and height of the world (we only do this once as
        // well).
        worldWidth = gs.getWidth();
        worldHeight = gs.getHeight();

        try
        {
            Image[] frames = ImageSet.extractFrames(Image.createImage("/ship.png"),
                                        0, 0, 4, 4,
                                        SHIP_FRAME_WIDTH,
                                        SHIP_FRAME_HEIGHT);
```

```
            shipImageSet = new ImageSet(1);
            shipImageSet.addState(frames, 0);
        }
        catch (IOException ioe)
        {
            System.out.println("unable to load image");
        }
    }

    // Create a Sprite for this instance of the Ship.
    shipSprite = new Sprite(shipImageSet, 0, 0);

    // Set the starting position.
    xFP = MathFP.toFP(x);
    yFP = MathFP.toFP(y);

    // Set a random direction.
    direction = Tools.getRand(0, 359) / 23 * 23;
}

/**
 * Calculates the correct frame based on the Ship's direction and then draws
 * that frame in on the screen at the Ship's current position.
 * @param graphics The graphics context upon which to draw.
 */
public void render(Graphics graphics)
{
    // Calculate the frame by dividing the direction by 22.5 degrees (360
    // degrees divided by 16 frames equals 22.5).
    int frame = MathFP.toInt(MathFP.div(MathFP.toFP(direction), FP_22P5));
    shipSprite.setFrame(frame);
    shipSprite.draw(graphics, MathFP.toInt(xFP), MathFP.toInt(yFP));
}

/**
 * Movement for the Ship. Collision detection is done by asking the
 * GameScreen class through the checkCollision method. This is done because
 * the GameScreen is the one with the array of Ships.
 */
public void cycle()
{
```

```
// move the ship according to its current direction (in radians)
int dirRadians = MathFP.div(MathFP.toFP(direction), FP_DEGREES_PER_RAD);

int xAccFP = MathFP.mul(thrustFP, MathFP.cos(dirRadians));
int yAccFP = MathFP.mul(thrustFP, MathFP.sin(dirRadians));

xVelFP = MathFP.add(xVelFP, xAccFP);
yVelFP = MathFP.add(yVelFP, yAccFP);

// Cap the velocity to a controllable level
if (xVelFP > maxVelFP)
    xVelFP = maxVelFP;
else if (xVelFP < -maxVelFP) xVelFP = -maxVelFP;
if (yVelFP > maxVelFP)
    yVelFP = maxVelFP;
else if (yVelFP < -maxVelFP) yVelFP = -maxVelFP;

int lastXFP = xFP;
xFP = MathFP.add(xFP, xVelFP);

// Test for collisions, after x movement.
if (gameScreen.checkCollision(this))
{
    xVelFP = MathFP.mul(xVelFP, MathFP.toFP("-1"));
    xFP = MathFP.add(lastXFP, xVelFP);
}

int lastYFP = yFP;
yFP = MathFP.add(yFP, yVelFP);

// Test for collisions, after y movement.
if (gameScreen.checkCollision(this))
{
    yVelFP = MathFP.mul(yVelFP, MathFP.toFP("-1"));
    yFP = MathFP.add(lastYFP, yVelFP);
}

// Check the position and wrap around if we have to.
if (MathFP.toInt(xFP) < 0) xFP = MathFP.toFP(worldWidth - 1);
if (MathFP.toInt(xFP) > worldWidth) xFP = MathFP.toFP(0);
if (MathFP.toInt(yFP) < 0) yFP = MathFP.toFP(worldHeight - 1);
if (MathFP.toInt(yFP) > worldHeight) yFP = MathFP.toFP(0);
```

```
    }

    /**
     * @return The x position of the Ship.
     */
    public int getX()
    {
        return MathFP.toInt(xFP);
    }

    /**
     * @return The y position of the Ship.
     */
    public int getY()
    {
        return MathFP.toInt(yFP);
    }

}
```

As I mentioned earlier you will also need to add a random number generator to the Tools class to set the random directions on the Ships.

```
public final class Tools
{
    private static final Random randomizer = new Random();

    /**
     * A method to obtain a random number between a miniumum and maximum
     * range.
     * @param min The minimum number of the range
     * @param max The maximum number of the range
     * @return
     */
    public static final int getRand(int min, int max)
    {
        int r = Math.abs(randomizer.nextInt());
        return (r % ((max - min + 1))) + min;
    }

    ...
```

Actors

Back when you developed *RoadRun*, one of the primary classes was `Actor`, a relatively simple object used to represent anything that could move around in the game. It contained the object's position (x, y), dimensions (width, height), and methods for drawing and cycling the object.

Tip

> The complete code and a working JAD/JAR for the following code are on the CD under the Chapter 10 source code directory "EnemyTest".

For a game such as *Star Assault*, you'll need to expand the original `Actor` object to handle your new physics, collision detection, and AI systems. This new `Actor` class will serve as the base class for the game's ships, enemy mines, turrets, fighters, and even the bullets these will fire.

The New Actor Class

The revised `Actor` class is simply an abstraction of much of the functionality in the `Ship` class; however, I've modified the movement code to use proper timing. Here are the changes needed to turn the `Ship` into a useful `Actor` base class for future development.

The first change is to the class name and type. I've renamed it to `Actor` (obviously) and declared it `abstract`—we'll see the `abstract` methods soon. I've also added in a fluff variable for use later in the movement code and a new constructor.

```
abstract public class Actor
{

    ...

    private long fluff = 0;

    /**
     * Constructs an Actor at position x, y facing direction d and setting
     * a maximum velocity and starting speed and thrust. (Note the
     * maxVelFPArg, speedFPArg and thrustFPArg must be MathFP values.)
     */
    public Actor(int x, int y, int d, int thrustFPArg, int speedFPArg,
                int maxVelFPArg)
    {
        worldWidth = GameScreen.getGameScreen().getWidth();
        worldHeight = GameScreen.getGameScreen().getHeight();
```

```
    xFP = MathFP.toFP(x);
    yFP = MathFP.toFP(y);
    direction = d;

    maxVelFP = maxVelFPArg;
    thrustFP = thrustFPArg;
    // Set the Actor's current speed.
    setVel(speedFPArg);
}
/**
 * Changes the current speed of the actor by setting the velocity based on
 * the current direction.
 * @param speedFPArg The speed to travel at (as a MathFP value).
 */
public final void setVel(int speedFPArg)
{
    xVelFP = MathFP.mul(speedFPArg,
                        MathFP.cos(getRadiansFromAngle(direction)));
    yVelFP = MathFP.mul(speedFPArg,
                        -MathFP.sin(getRadiansFromAngle(direction)));

    // Cap the velocity to a reasonable level.
    if (xVelFP > maxVelFP)
        xVelFP = maxVelFP;
    else if (xVelFP < -maxVelFP) xVelFP = -maxVelFP;
    if (yVelFP > maxVelFP)
        yVelFP = maxVelFP;
    else if (yVelFP < -maxVelFP) yVelFP = -maxVelFP;
}
```

Next we need to add in the abstract methods. You will need to implement these in any class that extends Actor.

```
/**
 * Abstract method to render the Actor. You must implement this method
 * in order to use this class.
 */
abstract public void render(Graphics graphics);
/**
 * Abstract method to return the width of the Actor.
 */
abstract public int getWidth();
```

```
/**
 * Abstract method to return the height of the Actor.
 */
abstract public int getHeight();
```

Next is the cycle method. For this Actor class we do the calculations for movement and then check collisions by calling back the GameScreen.

```
/**
 * A cycle method that moves the Actor a distance relative to its current
 * speed (the value of the speed int) and the amount of time that has passed
 * since the last call to cycle (deltaMS). This code uses a fluff value in
 * order to remember values too small to handle (below the tick level).
 * @param deltaMS The number of milliseconds that have passed since the last
 * call to cycle.
 */    public void cycle(long deltaMS)
{
    int ticks = (int) (deltaMS + fluff) / 100;

    // remember the bit we missed
    fluff += (deltaMS - (ticks * 100));

    if (ticks > 0)
    {
        int ticksFP = MathFP.toFP(ticks);

        // move the ship according to its current direction (in radians)
        int dirRadians = MathFP.div(MathFP.toFP(direction), FP_DEGREES_PER_RAD);

        int xAccFP = MathFP.mul(thrustFP, MathFP.cos(dirRadians));
        int yAccFP = MathFP.mul(thrustFP, -MathFP.sin(dirRadians));

        xVelFP = MathFP.add(xVelFP, xAccFP);
        yVelFP = MathFP.add(yVelFP, yAccFP);

        // cap our velocity to a controllable level
        if (xVelFP > maxVelFP) xVelFP = maxVelFP;
        else if (xVelFP < -maxVelFP) xVelFP = -maxVelFP;
        if (yVelFP > maxVelFP) yVelFP = maxVelFP;
        else if (yVelFP < -maxVelFP) yVelFP = -maxVelFP;

        int lastXFP = xFP;
        xFP = MathFP.add(xFP, MathFP.mul(xVelFP, ticksFP));
```

```
        // test for collisions, after x movement
        if (GameScreen.getGameScreen().checkCollision(this))
        {
            xVelFP = MathFP.mul(xVelFP, MathFP.toFP("-1"));
            xFP = MathFP.add(lastXFP, xVelFP);
        }

        int lastYFP = yFP;
        yFP = MathFP.add(yFP, MathFP.mul(yVelFP, ticksFP));

        // test for collisions, after y movement
        if (GameScreen.getGameScreen().checkCollision(this))
        {
            yVelFP = MathFP.mul(yVelFP, MathFP.toFP("-1"));
            yFP = MathFP.add(lastYFP, yVelFP);
        }

        // check our position and wrap around if we have to
        if (MathFP.toInt(xFP) < 0) xFP = MathFP.toFP(worldWidth-1);
        if (MathFP.toInt(xFP) > worldWidth) xFP = MathFP.toFP(0);
        if (MathFP.toInt(yFP) < 0) yFP = MathFP.toFP(worldHeight-1);
        if (MathFP.toInt(yFP) > worldHeight) yFP = MathFP.toFP(0);
    }
}
```

You may notice that this class doesn't require a reference to the GameScreen when it's constructed. In previous code, I've used this reference to carry out collision detection. If you look at the revised cycle code you'll see a call to:

```
GameScreen.getGameScreen().checkCollision(this))
```

Revised Ship Class

Using the new Actor class as a base, you can now revise the Ship class. As you can see in the following code, things are much simpler now (and more organized). The main code that has been removed is the cycle method.

```
import net.jscience.math.kvm.MathFP;
import javax.microedition.midlet.*;
import javax.microedition.lcdui.*;
import java.io.IOException;

public class Ship extends Actor
```

```
{
```

The first thing you can see about this new Ship class is that we no longer need any of the position and movement code. That's all now handled by the Actor base class.

```
private static int SHIP_FRAME_WIDTH = 16;
private static int SHIP_FRAME_HEIGHT = 16;

public static final int FP_22P5 = MathFP.toFP("22.5");

private static ImageSet shipImageSet;  // the one and only imageset

private Sprite shipSprite;

public Ship(int startX, int startY)
{
```

To properly construct the Ship you have to now call the Actor constructor first.

```
    super(startX, startY, 0, MathFP.toFP("0.2"), MathFP.toFP("0.0"),
        MathFP.toFP("2.0"));
    if (shipImageSet == null)
    {
        try
        {
            Image[] frames = ImageSet.extractFrames(Image.createImage("/ship.png"),
                                                0, 0, 4, 4,
                                                SHIP_FRAME_WIDTH,
                                                SHIP_FRAME_HEIGHT);

            shipImageSet = new ImageSet(1);
            shipImageSet.addState(frames, 0);
        }
        catch (IOException ioe)
        {
            System.out.println("unable to load image");
        }
    }

    shipSprite = new Sprite(shipImageSet, 0, 0);
}

public void render(Graphics graphics)
{
```

```
        int frame = MathFP.toInt(MathFP.div(MathFP.toFP(getDirection()), FP_22P5));
        shipSprite.setFrame(frame);
        shipSprite.draw(graphics, getX(), getY());
    }

    public int getHeight()
    {
        return SHIP_FRAME_HEIGHT;
    }

    public int getWidth()
    {
        return SHIP_FRAME_WIDTH;
    }
}
```

Revised Game Screen

In the previous version of the Ship class, I passed a reference to the GameScreen object to know the size of the world (in order to detect when you hit the edge of the screen) and to check whether the Ship had collided with anything. This was getting a little cumbersome, so you'll notice in the revised Actor and Ship classes that I've switched to using a simpler system. Because there is only ever one instance of the GameScreen object, I simply have the object store a static reference to itself, and then use a static method to gain access to it from anywhere.

GameScreen has also been updated to use a Vector to contain all the actors in the game. This will serve you later when you start dynamically adding and removing objects from the game.

Here's the revised version of the class:

```
import javax.microedition.lcdui.Canvas;
import javax.microedition.lcdui.Graphics;
import java.util.Vector;

public class GameScreen extends Canvas
{
```

Note this code uses a Vector, not an array to store Actors. This is so we can dynamically add and remove Actors later on.

```
    private Vector actors;
```

This is a static reference to the one and only instance of the GameScreen (known as a *singleton*). This is initialized in the constructor and then accessed using the getGameScreen method.

```
private static GameScreen theGameScreen;    // the one and only

public GameScreen()
{
    theGameScreen = this;

    // This code now uses a Vector instead of an array.
    actors = new Vector();

    // create 5 ships
    for (int i = 0; i < 5; i++)
        actors.addElement( new Ship() );
}
```

A new static method to return the one and only instance of the GameScreen object.

```
public final static GameScreen getGameScreen()
{
    return theGameScreen;
}
```

The main difference in the revised paint and cycle methods is to use the Actor vector, rather than an array.

```
protected void paint(Graphics graphics)
{
    graphics.setColor(0);
    graphics.fillRect(0, 0, getWidth(), getHeight());

    for (int i = 0; i < actors.size(); i++)
        ((Actor)actors.elementAt(i)).render(graphics);
}

public void cycle()
{
    for (int i = 0; i < actors.size(); i++)
        ((Actor) actors.elementAt(i)).cycle(100);
}

public boolean checkCollision(Actor s)
{
```

```
        // did this ship hit another?
        for (int j = 0; j < actors.size(); j++)
        {
            Actor another = (Actor)actors.elementAt(j);
            if (another != s &&
                Tools.isIntersectingRect(s.getX(), s.getY(), s.getWidth(), s.getHeight(),
                                        another.getX(), another.getY(),
another.getWidth(), another.getHeight()))
                return true;
        }
        return false;
    }

}
```

Adding Weapon Fire

Flying your ship around is fun, but to get things really moving, you can add some weapon fire! With your revised Actor class, this is now surprisingly easy. To start, you need to create a type of actor for the missiles fired by your ships—the Bullet class. When a ship fires, you'll construct a new Bullet object with a starting direction and speed to make it look like the bullet is flying out from the front of the ship.

Tip

Constructing objects under J2ME is extremely slow. In Chapter 11, "The World," you'll see how to use object pooling to avoid this delay.

The first thing you need to do is figure out where the Bullet object should start in the world. At first you might think this is just the position of the ship; however, it will look a bit strange if the bullet starts inside the body of the ship. You also need to start bullets at different positions if you want to implement something like dual forward firing weapons.

To figure out where your bullet should start, you need to be able to pick a starting point and then project it along a particular angle path for a certain distance. As you can see in Figure 10.18, if you want to fire your weapon you project from the center of the ship along its current direction so your bullet can start slightly in front.

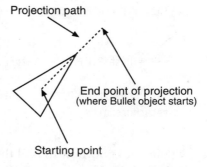

Figure 10.18 To find the point where a Bullet originates, you project outwards from the center of the ship in the direction it's facing.

The code to do this is basically exactly the same as your previous motion code. You just start at a certain position and then apply your movement code to the distance you need to project. Here's the new method for the Actor class (it can be static since it doesn't rely on any instance data in the Actor class):

```java
/**
 * Projects a point starting at x, y outwards at an angle for the specified
 * distance. The result is an array of two integer with the x and y point
 * of the projected point.
 * @param startX The starting x position.
 * @param startY The starting y position.
 * @param angleToProjectAt The angle to project along.
 * @param distanceToGo The distance to go.
 * @return An array of 2 integers with the x and y position of the projected
 * point.
 */
public final static int[] getProjectedPos(int startX, int startY,
                                          int angleToProjectAt,
                                          int distanceToGo)
{
    int angleInRadians = MathFP.div(MathFP.toFP(angleToProjectAt),
                                    FP_DEGREES_PER_RAD);

    int dx = MathFP.cos(angleInRadians);
    int dy = -MathFP.sin(angleInRadians);

    int xFP = MathFP.toFP(startX);
    int yFP = MathFP.toFP(startY);
    int distanceFP = MathFP.toFP(distanceToGo);

    xFP = MathFP.add(xFP, MathFP.mul(dx, distanceFP));
    yFP = MathFP.add(yFP, MathFP.mul(dy, distanceFP));

    int[] result = {MathFP.toInt(xFP), MathFP.toInt(yFP)};
    return result;
}
```

Now that you know how to find the origin point of a new bullet, you can create the bullet itself. This class is very similar to the Ship actor; I've just added specific drawing code, changed the size returned by the getWidth and getHeight methods, and added some code to limit each Bullet's lifetime.

```java
import net.jscience.math.kvm.MathFP;
import javax.microedition.midlet.*;
```

```
import javax.microedition.lcdui.*;
import java.io.IOException;

/**
 * A Bullet Actor is a simple flying object fired from a Ship. It has a limited
 * lifetime of 3 seconds using code in the cycle method after which the object
 * is removed from the GameScreen.
 * @author Martin J. Wells
 */
public class Bullet extends Actor
{
```

The `Bullet` class uses its own graphics through an `ImageSet` and `Sprite` class.

```
    private static ImageSet bulletImageSet;  // the one and only imageset
    private Sprite bulletSprite;
```

The constructor is basically the same as the `Ship` except it has different velocity and thrust values. This code then loads up the graphics from the general.png image file and breaks out the four frames each three pixels square.

```
    /**
     * Creates a new Bullet at the specified starting position and facing
     * direction. This is called by the Ship class when the player hits the fire
     * key.
     * @param startX The starting x position..
     * @param startY The starting y position.
     * @param direction The starting direction.
     */
    public Bullet(int x, int y, int direction)
    {
```

Note in the following call to the `Actor` constructor the `Bullet` does not have any thrust, only velocity. Because it has no thrust the direction value has no real effect (since there's no "push" behind that direction). When the bullet then strikes something, it will apply the bounce change to the velocity which will cause it to go the other way. If you were to set a thrust value, the bullet would hit the wall, bounce away, then fly right back at the wall again, and again, and again (the same as the ship does).

```
        super(x, y, direction, MathFP.toFP("0.0"), MathFP.toFP("2.0"),
            MathFP.toFP("2.0"));

        if (bulletImageSet == null)
        {
            try
            {
            {
```

```
            Image[] frames = ImageSet.extractFrames(Image.createImage("/general.png"),
                                                    0, 0, 4, 1, 3, 3);
            bulletImageSet = new ImageSet(1);
            bulletImageSet.addState(frames, 0);
        }
        catch (IOException ioe)
        {
            System.out.println("unable to load image");
        }
    }

    bulletSprite = new Sprite(bulletImageSet, 0, 0);
}
```

The render method is basically the same as the Ship except that the bullet graphic doesn't face a particular direction so you don't need to worry about setting that.

```
/**
 * The render method is basically the same as the Ship except that the bullet
 * graphic doesn't face a particular direction so you don't need to worry
 * about setting that.
 * @param graphics The graphics context upon which to draw the bullet.
 */
public void render(Graphics graphics)
{
    bulletSprite.draw(graphics, getX(), getY());
}
```

The cycle method calls the base class cycle (Actor) which handles the movement, then we cycle the Sprite object so it will animate (progress to the next frame) before checking the amount of time the object has been around and destroy it by calling the GameScreen.removeActor method (we'll see the removeActor method next).

```
/**
 * The cycle method calls the base class cycle (Actor) which handles the
 * movement, then we cycle the Sprite object so it will animate (progress to
 * the next frame) before checking the amount of time the object has been
 * around and destroy it by calling the GameScreen.removeActor method.
 * @param deltaMS The amount of time that has passed since the last call to
 * cycle (in milliseconds).
 */
public void cycle(long deltaMS)
{
    super.cycle(deltaMS);
```

```
    bulletSprite.cycle(deltaMS);

    //Tterminate this bullet if it's older than 3 seconds
    // See below for the GameScreen method this code calls.
    if (bulletSprite.getTimeInCurrentState() > 3000)
        GameScreen.getGameScreen().removeActor(this);
}
```

A `Bullet` is a tiny object in the game so we give it a size of one pixel square.

```
public int getHeight() { return 1; }
public int getWidth() { return 1; }
}
```

This is about as simple as an `Actor` class object can get. One interesting addition, though, is the use of the `Sprite getTimeInCurrentState` method to give your `Bullet` objects a lifetime. If this time passes three seconds (3000 milliseconds), you use the `GameScreen` method to remove the bullet from the world.

The next step to getting firing to work is to register the fire key press and then have the `Ship` object respond by firing a bullet. A simple way to do this would be to just construct a `Bullet` object each time the key is pressed, however this means players will be able to fire every time they hit a key (with no limits on their rate of fire). The same would apply to enemy ships which would just rapidly blast away at the player without limits.

To implement a fire rate limiter we first need to add some member to the `Ship` class to track whether the ship is firing (the `firing` boolean), when the last shot took place (`timeLastFired`), and how long this ship has to wait between shots (`firingDelay`).

```
public class Ship extends Actor
{
    // Weapons fire.
    private boolean firing;             // Is the ship currently firing?
    private int firingDelay=500;        // The delay between shots (in ms)
    private long timeLastFired;         // Used to track when I can fire again
```

The next step is to add code to the `cycle` method to detect when the firing flag is true, check the time to see if enough has elapsed before the next shot can be made, and then to construct the actual `Bullet` object.

```
public void cycle(long deltaMS)
{

    ...

    if (firing)
    {
```

```
            // Calculate the amount of time that has passed. If it's greater than
            // the firing delay then the Ship is clear to fire again.
            long timeSinceLastFire = (System.currentTimeMillis() - timeLastFired);
            if (timeSinceLastFire > firingDelay)
            {
                int[] nosePos = Actor.getProjectedPos(getX()+ (SHIP_FRAME_WIDTH/2),
                                                      getY()+ (SHIP_FRAME_HEIGHT/2),
                                                      getDirection(), 12);

                // Add the new bullet actor to our world.
                GameScreen.getGameScreen().addActor(
                    new Bullet(nosePos[0], nosePos[1], getDirection()) );

                // Update the time the last fire took place (now).
                timeLastFired = System.currentTimeMillis();
            }
        }
    }
```

Since you'll also need a way of triggering the firing process a method needs to be added to the Ship class.

```
    public final void setFiring(boolean b)
    {
        firing = b;
    }
```

The final step is to trigger firing when the player hits the up arrow by setting the firing boolean to true, and then turn off firing when the key is released. This means the ship will continue to fire while the key is down.

```
public class GameScreen extends Canvas
{
    ...

    protected void keyPressed(int keyCode)
    {
        ...

        if (action == UP)
            playerShip.setFiring(true);
    }

    protected void keyReleased(int keyCode)
    {
```

```
    ...
    if (action == UP)
        playerShip.setFiring(false);
}
```

The Enemy

One of the things that makes action games fun is battling enemies. Whether they are German U-boats, backpack-nuke-wielding terrorists, or Horde space fighters, there's a certain satisfaction in blowing them away.

However, you can't just throw some red fighters in *Star Assault*. The enemy has to be able to detect the presence of the player and then react in a semi-intelligent way. Take the case in which your intrepid player flies by an enemy turret. What should the turret do in reaction to the player? To begin with, it needs to detect the player's presence within a certain range. If the player is within that range, the turret should figure out which direction it should turn to best aim at the player, and then fire if the angle is close enough. The following sections will show you how to code all of this.

The end result will be a cool little demo where an enemy ship will follow the player's ship around the screen. You can check out the result in the Chapter 10 source code directory under "Enemy Test".

Computing Distance

The first thing your AI needs to be able to do is figure out how far away the player is. If the distance is beyond a certain limit, the turret doesn't need to do anything because there's nothing to react to. You need to figure the distance between the two points. You can do this by using the Pythagorean Theorem, which states that the square of the hypotenuse is the sum of the squares of the other two sides. That is:

$$c[2] = a[2] + b[2]$$

Now, if you recall that any two points (x1, y1) and (x2, y2) form a right triangle, you can then calculate the length of the *a* side (the x-axis side) as x2–x1 and the length of the *b* side (the y-axis side) as y2–y1. You can see this illustrated in Figure 10.19.

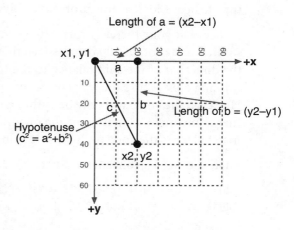

Figure 10.19 You can compute the distance between two points using the Pythagorean Theorem.

To calculate the length of *c*, you just take the square root of *a[2]* + *b[2]*. Here's the code to do that:

```
public final static int distance(int x1, int y1, int x2, int y2)
{
    int dx = (x2 - x1) * (x2 - x1);
    int dy = (y2 - y1) * (y2 - y1);
    if (dx == 0 || dy == 0) return 0;

    try
    {
        return MathFP.toInt(MathFP.sqrt( MathFP.toFP( dx + dy ) ));
    }

    catch(ArithmeticException ae)
    {
        return 0;
    }
}
```

You should add this method to the `Actor` class.

Targeting an Angle

Now that you know the distance between your turret and the player, you know when to wake up and take some notice. The next problem is getting your turret to turn and aim at the ship, so you need to figure out the direction of the location of the ship relative to the turret. Take a look at this problem in Figure 10.20.

Notice that your turret is currently facing about 60 degrees, whereas the ship lies to the southeast at around 300 degrees (relative to the turret's position). You need to figure out the direction of the ship relative to the turret based on their positions. You can calculate this angle by taking the tangent of the *b* side over the *a* side. This will return the angle. However, the angle will only be within a range of 0 to 90 degrees, so you need to do a further adjustment to figure out the quadrant the other object is in and adjust the angle to match. Here's the code to do this. (Again, this should go in your `Actor` class.)

First, you need a convenient way to go from degrees to radians.

```
public static final int FP_PI2 = MathFP.mul(MathFP.PI, MathFP.toFP(2));
public static final int FP_DEGREES_PER_RAD = MathFP.div(MathFP.toFP(360),
                                                        FP_PI2);
public final static int getAngleFromRadians(int radiansFP)
{
    return MathFP.toInt(MathFP.mul(radiansFP, FP_DEGREES_PER_RAD));
```

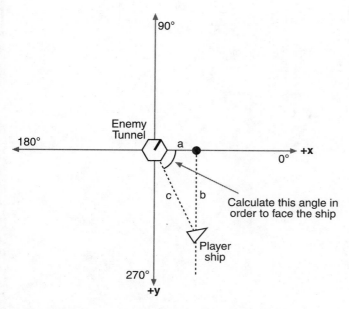

Figure 10.20 An enemy turret currently facing 60 degrees needs to turn towards the player's ship by changing direction to face at 300 degrees.

```
}

public final static int getRadiansFromAngle(int angle)
{
    return MathFP.div(MathFP.toFP(angle), FP_DEGREES_PER_RAD);
}
```

Next we calculate the facing angle.

```
public final static int getFacingAngle(int x1, int y1, int x2, int y2)
{
    // figure the two sides of our right angle triangle
    int a = MathFP.toFP(Math.abs(x2 - x1));
    int b = MathFP.toFP(Math.abs(y2 - y1));

    if (a == 0) a = FP_ONE;
    if (b == 0) b = FP_ONE;

    int bovera = MathFP.div(b, a);

    int angleInRadians = MathFP.atan(bovera);
```

```
    int angle = getAngleFromRadians(angleInRadians);

    // now adjust for which quadrant we're really in
    if (x2 < x1)
    {
        // left side
        if (y2 < y1)
            return angle + 180;
        return angle + 90;
    }
    else
    {
        // right side
        if (y2 < y1)
            return angle + 180;
        return angle;
    }
}
```

Using this code, you can calculate which way to face, but there's still something else you need to know about this angle. Which way should the turret turn in order to face your ship as quickly as possible? It's going to look a bit silly if the turret is facing five degrees away from the ship and it decides to turn completely around the other way. You need to know whether turning clockwise or counterclockwise is the fastest route to a particular direction. Here's a static method for the Actor class that figures this out for you:

```
public final static boolean isClockwise(int angleA, int angleB)
{
    if (angleA > angleB)
        return (Math.abs(angleA - angleB)) < (angleB + (360 - angleA));
    else
        return (angleA + (360 - angleB)) < (Math.abs(angleB - angleA));
}
```

Turning through Spin

Now that you know the direction your turret needs to face and which way to turn, you need to actually make the turret turn that way and then stop when it reaches the correct direction. To do this, you need to add controlled spin to the Actor class.

Spinning is simply turning at a constant rate expressed in degrees per tick (hundredths of a second). This rate represents how fast any actor can turn, and it can vary from actor to actor. For example, the player can turn his ship at a rate of 22.5 degrees per tick, thus completing a full 360-degree turn in approximately 1.6 seconds, whereas the turret turns at a slower rate of only 10 degrees per tick. This makes it easier for the player to outmaneuver the turret because the turret will have to slowly track the player. Higher-level turrets can then increase this rate to make them more accurate and thus more dangerous.

Spin is also used when the player holds down the left or right arrow key. All you do is set the player's ship to have a spin rate of either 22.5 or –22.5, depending on which direction the player hits. When the player releases the key, you just set the spin rate back to 0. For example you could just add the following code to the GameScreen class (we'll get to the setSpin method in just a second):

```
protected void keyPressed(int keyCode)
{
    int action = getGameAction(keyCode);
    if (action == RIGHT)
        playerShip.setSpin(MathFP.toFP("22.5"));
    if (action == LEFT)
        playerShip.setSpin(MathFP.toFP("-22.5"));
}


protected void keyReleased(int keyCode)
{
    int action = getGameAction(keyCode);
```

Notice below I don't use the MathFP.toFP. This is because zero is always zero, so there's no need to convert it.

```
    if (action == RIGHT)
        playerShip.setSpin(0);
    if (action == LEFT)
        playerShip.setSpin(0);
}
```

The code to actually spin the object is even easier. You need to add a member to track both the rate at which the object can spin (you'll use this for the enemy) and the current spin rate.

```
private int currentSpinFP;          // current spin rate (can be negative)
private int spinRateFP;             // spin ship capability (can be negative)
```

To support these you need to add some get and set methods for the spin value. I've also added a way to set the direction (safely).

```
    /**
     * Gets the spin rate for this Actor in degrees per second.
     * @return The current spin (turning).
     */
```

```
public int getSpin()
{
    return MathFP.toInt(spinFP);
}


/**
 * Set the spin rate for this Actor in degrees per second.
 * @param newSpin The spin rate (as a MathFP value).
 */
public void setSpin(int newSpinFP)
{
    spinFP = newSpinFP;
}
/**
 * Change the Actor's current direction.
 * @param newDirection The new direction to face (in degrees).
 */
public void setDirection(int newDirection)
{
    direction = newDirection;
    if (direction < 0) direction = (359 + (direction));    // add the neg value
    if (direction > 359) direction = (newDirection - 360);
}
```

To spin the ship, you simply modify the cycle method of the Actor to change the direction based on the current spin rate. As you can see, all you're doing is adding (or taking away, in the case of a negative value) the spin from the current direction.

```
// spin based on degrees per tick
if (currentSpinFP != 0)
    setDirection(direction + MathFP.toInt(MathFP.mul(ticksFP, currentSpinFP)));
```

All right, you can now turn the player's Ship based on a key hit by setting the spin value. But you need to do a little more to have your turrets turn toward the player automatically. Next you can add a target direction which the Actor cycle code will automatically turn towards (using the shortest route).

To support this we first add a targetDirection to the Actor class as well as a boolean to indicate whether this is active or not. The targetDirection is initialized with the value of negative one so that we know a target direction has not been set. You don't want to use zero for this because it's a valid angle.

```
private boolean autoSpinning;
private int targetAngle=-1;
```

```
public final void setTargetDirection(int angle)
{
    // set an angle this actor wants to face; the actor will start spinning
    // at its default spin rate towards the target angle - see cycle for
    // the actual spin code
    targetAngle = angle;
    autoSpinning = false;
}
```

Next you need to modify the cycle code to turn towards the target angle if it's enabled. This code checks whether the Actor has a value in the targetAngle field not equal to a negative one. If it does, the Actor automatically starts spinning in the correct direction. Once it's at the right angle, the Actor then stops spinning.

```
// move towards our target direction, if we have one
if (targetAngle != -1)
{
    if (!autoSpinning)
    {
        // start spin in the dir of the target angle
        setSpin(isClockwise(getDirection(), targetAngle) ? -maxSpinRate : maxSpinRate);
    }

    // and check if we've made it to the target direction
    if (targetAngle == direction)
    {
        // cancel turning
        setSpin(0);
        setTargetDirection(-1);
        autoSpinning = false;
    }
}
```

Aligning Directions

Introducing precise spin to the Actors shows you another problem very quickly—sprite alignment. In Figure 10.21, you can see all the frames for your enemy turret. Since we're no longer moving in nice even increments of 22.5 degrees the turret can face an angle that cannot be represented by these frames.

Figure 10.21 The 16 frames of the turret graphic

The problem is that you're now turning the ship to directions you can't render properly on the screen. This will produce weird results, such as the Ship flying in a slightly different direction than the way it's facing on the screen and the turret bullets coming out in slightly wrong directions.

One way to fix this is to only allow an actor to change to a direction it can accurately represent. But this is messy, and you lose the accuracy of actual direction changes. What you really need is two directions—one that represents the direction in which the actor is really facing (the real direction) and another that represents a direction aligned to a particular degree increment (the aligned direction). All your code to manipulate your direction will then continue to work perfectly based on the real direction member, and you can use the aligned direction for drawing, moving, and firing.

To do this, you need to make a few adjustments to your Actor class. First, add the different direction members (real and aligned) as well as the degrees to which you want to align.

```
private int realDir;               // actual direction in degrees
private int alignedDir;            // aligned direction
private int alignedDivDegreesFP;   // degrees per facing division
```

You need to initialize the member to an appropriate value in the Actor constructor. For example, in the following code, the alignedDivArg is what's passed into the constructor:

```
wantAlignment = false;
if (alignedDivArg > 0)
{
    alignedDivDegreesFP = MathFP.div(360, alignedDivArg);
    wantAlignment = true;
}
```

You then need to change the direction methods in the Actor class. The major change is to the setDirection method. This now does all the work of updating the aligned direction whenever the real direction changes.

```
/**
 * Change the Actor's current direction.
 * @param newDirection The new direction to face (in degrees).
 */
public void setDirection(int newDirection)
{
    realDir = newDirection;
    if (realDir < 0) realDir = (359 + (realDir));   // add the neg value
    if (realDir > 359) realDir = (newDirection - 360);

    // set the facing direction to be the closest alignment
```

```
        if (wantAlignment)
            alignedDir = getAlignedDirection(realDir);
        else
            alignedDir = realDir;
    }
/**
 * Gets the closest aligned direction to the passed in direction (in
 * degrees).
 * @param dir The direction to align (in degrees).
 * @return A direction which aligns to the number of divisions the Actor
 * supports.
 */
public final int getAlignedDirection(int dir)
{
    int divisions = MathFP.toInt(MathFP.div(MathFP.toFP(dir),
                                            alignedDivDegreesFP));
    int roundedDivisions = MathFP.toInt(MathFP.mul(MathFP.toFP(divisions),
                                            alignedDivDegreesFP));
    if (roundedDivisions < 0) roundedDivisions = 0;
    if (roundedDivisions > 359) roundedDivisions = 0;
    return roundedDivisions;
}


/**
 * @return The current aligned direction.
 */
public final int getDirection()
{
    return alignedDir;
}


/**
 * @return The current real direction (not aligned).
 */
public final int getRealDirection()
{
    return realDir;
}
```

You'll notice I've updated the getDirection method to now return the aligned direction, not the real one. Anything using getDirection will now use a value properly aligned to the capabilities of the actor.

Creating an Enemy

In the next example you'll see how to add some control logic to enemy ships so that they'll chase after you. Before you can do that though you need to add support in the Ship class for the enemy graphics and properties.

Firstly, you need a boolean to indicate whether this is an enemy or player Ship as well as support for the two distinct sets of images used to draw them.

```
public class Ship extends Actor
{
    private boolean isEnemy;
    private static ImageSet playerShipImageSet;
    private static ImageSet enemyShipImageSet;
```

In the Ship constructor you'll need to load up two sets of ship images: the yellow ones for the player and the red ones for the enemy. All these images are within the one image file.

```
public Ship(boolean isEnemyArg, int startX, int startY)
{
    super(startX, startY, 0, 16, MathFP.toFP("0.2"), MathFP.toFP("0.0"),
        MathFP.toFP("2.0"), MathFP.toFP("-1.0"), 23);

    if (playerShipImageSet == null)
    {
        try
        {
            Image shipGraphic = Image.createImage("/ship.png");
```

Here we extract two sets of images now instead of just one. The red fighter frames (the enemy) start four frames across in the file (4 * 16).

```
            // Extract out the image frames for the player ship.
            Image[] playerShipFrames = ImageSet.extractFrames(shipGraphic,
                0, 0, 4, 4, SHIP_FRAME_WIDTH, SHIP_FRAME_HEIGHT);
            playerShipImageSet = new ImageSet(1);
            playerShipImageSet.addState(playerShipFrames, 0);

            // Extract out the image frames for the enemy ship.
            Image[] enemyShipFrames = ImageSet.extractFrames(shipGraphic,
                4*16, 0, 4, 4, SHIP_FRAME_WIDTH, SHIP_FRAME_HEIGHT);
            enemyShipImageSet = new ImageSet(1);
            enemyShipImageSet.addState(enemyShipFrames, 0);
        }
        catch (IOException ioe)
        {
```

```
            System.out.println("unable to load image");
        }
    }
```

Based on the isEnemyArg value we set the isEnemy flag and then initialize the ship sprite with the appropriate images.

```
    // Set the ship sprite based on the type. If it's an enemy we use the
    // red ship frames.
    isEnemy = isEnemyArg;

    if (isEnemy)
        shipSprite = new Sprite(enemyShipImageSet, 0, 0);
    else
        shipSprite = new Sprite(playerShipImageSet, 0, 0);
}
```

That's it for creating an enemy type; next I'll show you how to give it a brain.

Creating a Brain

Finally, our AI is ready to come together. You have all the tools you need to have your enemies act and react within the game. To make all this come alive, you need to give your actors a brain. Don't worry—it's nothing like the HAL9000. All you need is control logic to check for conditions and then react appropriately. For your enemy ships and turrets, you check whether the player is within a sensible range and then turn toward him. For example here's a revised Ship cycle method that adds basic logic to the enemy:

```
/**
 * Cycling for the Ship calls Actor.cycle to handle movement. It then checks
 * to see if this is an enemy type ship and updates the direction based on
 * the relative angle of the player's ship from the enemy one.
 * @param deltaMS The amount of time that has passed since the last cycle
 * (in milliseconds).
 */
public void cycle(long deltaMS)
{
    super.cycle(deltaMS);

    if (isEnemy)
    {
        // If insufficient time has passed to do an AI update we just add the
        // deltaMS time to the counter. If enough time has passed it executes
        // the Enemy AI code (this is only done periodically since it's
        // typically expensive stuff you don't want to do every frame).
```

```
if (msSinceLastAIUpdate < msPerAIUpdate)
   msSinceLastAIUpdate += deltaMS;
else
{

   msSinceLastAIUpdate -= msPerAIUpdate; // take off one update's worth

   // Calculate the distance to the player so we ignore cases where
   // the player is too far away to bother with.
   Ship playerShip = GameScreen.getGameScreen().getPlayerShip();
   int distanceToPlayer = distanceTo(playerShip);
   if (distanceToPlayer < ENEMY_IGNORE_DISTANCE)
   {
      // Figure out the angle we need to face to fly directly towards
      // the player's ship.
      int facingAngle = getFacingAngle(getX(), getY(), playerShip.getX(),
                                       playerShip.getY());
      // Set this to be our target direction. The Actor.cycle method
      // will take care of turning this ship until it faces the target
      // angle we set here.
      setTargetDirection(facingAngle);
   }
}
```

You'll notice I've wrapped the code to check the distance and then adjust the turn within a time check. There's no need to do an AI update every cycle; in fact, it's a complete waste of time. Having an update rate of about one second is usually more than enough to make your enemies seem responsive. This also gives you more freedom to make this code more complex if you need to.

Conclusion

In this chapter, you've covered moving objects around in arbitrary directions, computing angles and distance, and adding basic AI to your enemies. To see how it all comes together take a look at the "EnemyTest" example in the Chapter 10 source code on the CD. It's a really cool look at an enemy ship chasing after the player's. I've even added code to fire a bullet when you hit the up key.

As you'll see from the demo doing all this in the area of a single screen is getting a little silly. In the next chapter, you'll look at how to create a larger world in which your actors can play.

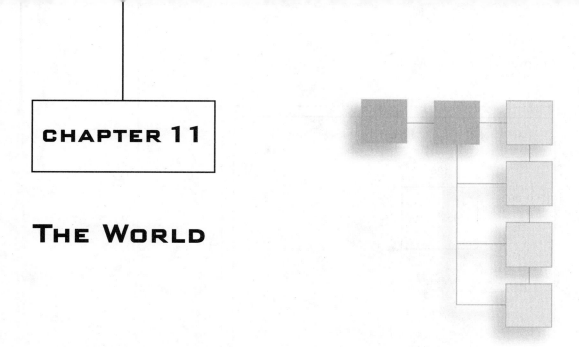

CHAPTER 11

THE WORLD

Most action and adventure games need levels (or worlds) in which the hero can roam. In this chapter, you'll walk through how to add a level system to the game, including support for multiple layers (backgrounds), and rendering, as well as how to generate level content using either code (such as a random level generator) or map editors. You'll also look at how to improve performance by better managing your objects.

A New World

You used the concept of a game world quite a bit in the previous examples. A world (also known as a level, stage, or map) is simply a container for all the objects in a game. To encapsulate this concept we'll create a new class in this chapter called (you guessed it) World. This new class will take over some of the functionality of the current GameScreen in that it now acts as the container and manager of the actors. GameScreen will instantiate the World instance for your game and then make calls to cycle and render all the actors onto its Canvas.

Nature of the Universe

Up until now, you've kept your game worlds simple by limiting them to the size of the screen and only dealing with basic actor objects. This isn't enough for *Star Assault* (or most other action- or adventure-style games) so I want to expand things a little.

In Figure 11.1, you can see the layout of a game world that is 1000 pixels square. This is obviously much larger than the size of the screen, so at any point in time what's on the screen only represents a small portion of the entire world. This area, known as the *view port*, stays relative to the position of the player object (such as the ship in *Star Assault*), thus creating the scrolling effect you see so often.

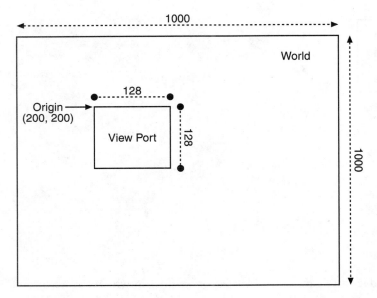

Figure 11.1 A game world can be much larger than the screen size. The section of the world visible on the screen at any point in time is known as the *view port*.

Managing game play within this larger environment requires quite a few changes to the way you've been coding your game. First, you'll need to expand your coordinate system beyond the screen.

World Coordinates

Having a larger world means you need to store the position of all the actors using coordinates relative to the world, not the screen. To then draw an actor on the screen, you have to translate its world position into a relative screen position. For example, take the case of an actor located at position 250, 250 in the world. If your screen is only 128 × 128, there's no way you'll ever see that actor without changing your view port because it lies beyond the edge of the screen.

In Figure 11.1, the top left of the view port is set to a point of 200, 200. Because the screen is 128 × 128 pixels, you should see all the actors with world positions between 200, 200 and 328, 328. Take a look at how you'd modify the actor-rendering code to handle this.

```
public class World
{
    ...
```

```
public void render()
{
    for (int i = 0; i < actors.size(); i++)
    {
        Actor a = (Actor) actors.elementAt(i);
        if (a.getX()-a.getWidth() > viewX && a.getX() < viewWidth &&
            a.getY()-a.getHeight() > viewY && a.getY() < viewHeight)
            a.render(g, viewX, viewY);
    }
}
}
```

In this code, you're testing whether an actor's bounding rectangle lies somewhere in the view port (including a case in which only part of the actor extends down onto the screen). Notice that I've added two parameters to the actor's render method call. This is used to draw the image at the correct location on the screen (relative to the current view port coordinates). This is simpler than it sounds. All you need to do is offset its world position by the view port origin. For example, here's the Ship actor's render method with an origin offset added:

```
public class Ship extends Actor
{
    public void render(Graphics graphics, int offsetX, int offsetY)
    {

        ...
        shipSprite.draw(graphics, getX()-offsetX, getY()-offsetY);
    }
}
```

Assuming your view position is at 200, 200, the rendering code will draw your actor with a world position of 250, 250, at position 250 minus 200, or at 50, 50 on the screen.

Scrolling the View Port

If you continue on with the previous example, imagine the ship at world position 250, 250 is moving. If you don't keep your view port at the same position, the ship will eventually fly off the area of the world covered by the screen. What you need to do next is control the position of the view port to stay focused on the action. Typically, this will be a position that keeps the player's actor (such as his ship in *Star Assault*) in the center of the screen (see Figure 11.2).

Doing this is a lot easier than it sounds. You adjust the view port position on each game cycle to the center position of the player's actor, minus half the screen width and height.

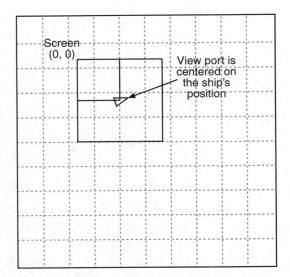

Figure 11.2 Scrolling is achieved by moving the view port over the world to follow the player's ship.

For example, the following code is a modified version of the `GameScreen` cycle method, which modifies the view position:

```
public void cycle()
{
    world.setView(playerShip.getX() + playerShip.getWidth()/2 - getWidth()/2,
                  playerShip.getY() + playerShip.getHeight()/2 - getHeight()/2);
    world.cycle();
}
```

As you can see, I'm referring to a `World` class. (You'll get to that one soon.) The `setView` method simply updates the `viewX` and `viewY` members later used in a world `render` method.

Once you have this in place, the player's ship actor will remain centered in the screen with the world scrolling around it. If you want to have the ship stay in a different part of the screen, such as on the far left in a side scroller or at the bottom in a vertical scrolling game, simply adjust the position of the view relative to where you want the actor to appear.

Panning the View Port

One reason horizontal (side) or vertical scrolling games are popular for small screens are they maximize the available screen space for seeing what's coming. However, since *Star Assault* is a four-way scrolling game, with the player in the center, you can only give the player half a screen's warning. Even with a typical platform game you'll find you'll need to adjust the view port in order to maximize the amount of available space. In this section you'll use a technique known as "panning" to move the view port around in order to make more screen space available to see the action.

Right now the view port is positioned so the player's ship is always kept in the center of the screen. If you want to let the player see more of the action then you logically need to update the view port to focus more on the areas of the screen where the action is. The question is what determines the best view? There are a few techniques for determining the correct view, ranging from complex to simple. One sophisticated method is to check the locations of enemy ships within a few screens' distance of the player and balance the position of the view (based on a system of weightings varying according to the distance of each enemy) to try and fit everybody on the screen. This is typically buggy though and has the added issue of effectively warning a player where the enemy is coming from.

Another far simpler system is to pan the view according to the direction the player is facing. Since the player will naturally turn to face the action anyway, this is usually a great method for just about any game type. In this section you'll implement a panning view for use in *Star Assault*.

It really is hard to describe exactly how a panning view works, so I'd highly recommend you playing around with the demonstration MIDlet on the CD under the Chapter 11 source code directory "SimpleWorldTest" in order to get a feel for it in a real game.

To make the process of adjusting the view to an optimal location, you could just set the view port position each cycle. Unfortunately this will create a very direct effect with the view spinning as the player changes direction. It's a disconcerting overreaction to what might be a very temporary direction adjustment by the player (and it'll also likely make the player motion sick). Instead, our view system will slowly move "toward" the optimal point. This is what gives that smooth "springy" panning camera effect that you're after. To do this you need to set a rate at which the view will move toward the optimal point in pixels per second. The higher this number, the faster the view move pans towards this point, and thus the faster it will react to the player's direction changes (feel free to try out different numbers). For this example I'm using a value of 22 pixels per second.

Okay, time to look at some code. To add a directional panning view to *Star Assault* you first need to add some new variables to the GameScreen class in order to track the current view position.

```
public class GameScreen extends Canvas
{
```

The view panning code you'll add later will update the currentViewPosX and currentViewPosY to be the top left-hand corner of the view port.

```
    private int currentViewPosX;
    private int currentViewPosY;
```

This is the actual number of pixels the view can move in one millisecond (0.022). A MathFP value is used since it's a fraction. You'll see this in action in the panning code later. The panPixelsToMoveFP keeps track of how many pixels to move, again as a MathFP value.

```
private int pixelsPerMSFP = MathFP.div(22, 1000);
private int panPixelsToMoveFP=0;
```

To get all this to work you need to know how much time has passed in the GameScreen cycle method. These two variables are used to track that.

```
private long msSinceLastCycle;
private long lastCycleTime;
```

Next, you need to add the panning code to the GameScreen cycle method.

```
public void cycle()
{
```

First, the code calculates the amount of elapsed time in milliseconds.

```
msSinceLastCycle = System.currentTimeMillis() - lastCycleTime;

if (msSinceLastCycle > 0)
{
```

To calculate how far to move the view, the code multiplies the number of elapsed milliseconds since the last execution of the cycle method by the number of pixels to move per millisecond. Since this value is commonly less than 1 pixel (since the cycle method is commonly called up to 80 times per second), the next line rounds up the number of whole pixels that the view can be repositioned by.

```
panPixelsToMoveFP += MathFP.mul(pixelsPerMSFP,
                        MathFP.toFP((int)msSinceLastCycle));
// Figure out how many whole pixels to move.
int wholePixels = MathFP.toInt(panPixelsToMoveFP);
```

Next, you calculate the optimal point the view should be at based on the direction the player's ship is facing. The target view position is calculated by projecting outwards from the front of the ship by around a third of the screen's width. This will leave a reasonable amount of room around the edge of the view, rather than panning all the way to the edge.

```
// Calculate the ideal position for the view based on the
// direction the player's ship is facing.
int[] targetViewPos = Actor.getProjectedPos(
        playerShip.getX(), playerShip.getY(),
        playerShip.getDirection(), getWidth() / 3);
```

Once the target point has been calculated, you next move toward that point by the number of whole pixels. The following code simply checks the relative coordinates of the target point and adjusts each axis.

```
// Adjust the current move slightly towards the ideal view
// point.
if (currentViewPosX < targetViewPos[0])
    currentViewPosX += wholePixels;
if (currentViewPosX > targetViewPos[0])
    currentViewPosX -= wholePixels;
if (currentViewPosY < targetViewPos[1])
    currentViewPosY += wholePixels;
if (currentViewPosY > targetViewPos[1])
    currentViewPosY -= wholePixels;
```

After successfully moving, the number of whole pixels is subtracted from the current pixel movement count.

```
// Take away the pixels that were moved.
panPixelsToMoveFP = MathFP.sub(panPixelsToMoveFP,
                               MathFP.toFP(wholePixels));
```

Next you set the World view port to correspond to the newly adjusted position. Half the screen's width and height are subtracted because you want the target point to end up in the center of the screen.

```
            world.setView(currentViewPosX-getWidth()/2,
                          currentViewPosY-getHeight()/2);
        }
    }
    world.cycle();
```

Finally, you record the time of this cycle in order to calculate the elapsed time the next time around.

```
    lastCycleTime = System.currentTimeMillis();
}
```

Creating a Tile Engine

Imagine for a moment that you're creating a game with a large world (1000 × 1000 pixels). The next thing you'd need to do is fill the world with objects that the player will collide with, fire at, or pick up. Assuming you use your current system, you would create an Actor object for all of these items and then add them dynamically to a Vector object. Given that your level is reasonably large (around 10 screens, or 1 million square pixels), you would probably have upwards of 500 items in a level. Unfortunately, your current system will never work for a world with that density.

First, constructing tens of objects in J2ME is a very slow process; constructing hundreds is simply not practical. (It would literally take minutes on some MIDs!) Constructing this many objects would also cause serious problems in terms of memory space.

Next, you'd need to call the `cycle` method on all these actors. Without any form of organization, you'd have to do this for every actor in the world, on every game cycle! This is not only impractical; it's a waste of time. If an actor is nowhere near the player, or if the actor doesn't move or change anyway, there's no need to bother calling the `cycle` method.

Rendering a world of this size has similar problems. Because drawing is extremely slow, you need to check whether an actor is actually within the view port before you bother to draw it on the screen. Checking whether an actor's rectangle falls within the boundary of the view port is a reasonably expensive test. With your current system, you would again need to do this on every cycle.

Last, and certainly not least (as if there aren't enough problems already), is the issue of collision detection. If you have 500 actors in the world, you would need to check whether any of these objects collides with any other object. That would require 500 tests against 500 objects—a total of (gulp) 250,000 collisions tests!

Now, some of these limits are because of J2ME (object construction speed and memory limits); however, even a modern PC will turn purple trying to do 250,000 collision tests 50 times a second.

There are many methods you can use to get around these problems. For 2D games, the most common solution is tiling. *Tiling* is a technique that takes advantage of the fact that much of the content in a game world is static. Take the walls of a room, for example; the player might collide with these, but they generally don't move, turn, or animate. For these static elements, there's no need to use a full `Actor` object. All you really need is a basic type to identify the element (such as a wall) and its position.

In order to do this, you first need to separate your game world into different layers—one for your dynamic actors (the actor layer) and one for the more static elements (the tile layer). Take a look at Figure 11.3 to see what I mean.

The Tile Map

Tiling takes its name from the way it divides a layer into equally-sized squares that are much like the tiles on that shower wall you stare at thinking of game ideas all the time. Suppose you have a game world of 800 pixels square. You can divide it into 16 pixel areas

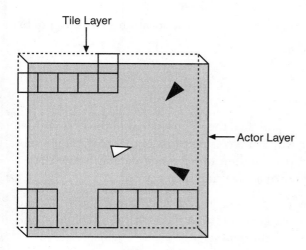

Figure 11.3 The view of a game world divided into two distinct layers: a static layer of tiles and an active layer of Actor.

(tiles), which would give you 50 tiles across and 50 tiles down, for a total of 2500 tiles. Because a tile is not a full class Actor (you don't need to store attributes such as position or direction), you can use a single byte for the type of tile at a given location. Your code can then represent the world using an array of these bytes. For example:

```
byte tileMap[50][50];
```

Tip

Since there is a large number of elements in a tile map, I use a byte (requiring only a single byte of memory) rather than a short (2 bytes) or int (4 bytes). This means you can only have 256 different tiles in your game, which is more than enough for most games.

Notice it's an array of 50 × 50 bytes, not 800 × 800. You're only storing a byte for the type of tile at each 16-pixel location, not every pixel.

To differentiate between different tiles and no tile at all, you can declare some simple byte constants.

```
public static final byte NO_TILE = 0;
public static final byte WALL_TILE = 1;
```

You can now alter the type of tile at any location simply by changing the value at the corresponding array point. To access any point relative to the world, you need to divide by the size of the tile. For example, you can set a wall tile at world location x=320, y=120 by using:

```
int tileX = 320;
int tileY = 120;
tileMap[ tileY / 16 ][ tileX / 16 ] = WALL_TILE;
```

As you can see, you're referencing first the y and then the x component of the array, rather than x and then y. You may be wondering why I'm accessing y first in the array, rather than x. This is really just to follow the general convention of accessing data as a row then a column. You can think of it like reading down a page, and then across.

You can access this array using any code. For example, this code creates a border around your tile map. Take note of my use of the variables tx, for a tile x position (column) and ty, for a tile y position (row). You'll be seeing these a lot.

```
// Set the array elements down the left and right sides of the world.
for (int tileY=0; tileY < 50; tileY++)
{
    tileMap[tileY][0] = WALL_TILE;
    tileMap[tileY][49] = WALL_TILE;
}
// Set the array elements across the top and bottom.
for (int tileX = 0; tileX < 50; tileX++)
{
    tileMap[0][tileX] = WALL_TILE;
    tileMap[49][tileX] = WALL_TILE;
}
```

Rendering the Tile Layer

Rendering your tile layer is also quite simple. All you need to do is draw an image corresponding to the byte type in each array position. First, however, you need some images to draw.

The images for your tiles should be the same size (16 × 16 pixels) in order to align correctly. If you load these images into an ImageSet using the same order for your byte values, you can reference each frame using that byte. This makes life much easier than trying to map your types to a particular image.

```
Image tileGraphics = ImageSet.loadClippedImage("/world.png", 0, 0, 16, 16);
tiles = new ImageSet(1);
tiles.addState(new Image[]{tileGraphics}, 0);
```

To render the tiles, you first need to figure out which part of the tile map lies within the current view port. Because tiles might appear only partly onscreen, you'll include one tile row above and below the screen size. In this code I'm assuming the current view port coordinates are in the viewX and viewY variables.

```
// Calculate which tiles to start at.
int startTileX = (viewX / 16) - 1;
int startTileY = (viewY / 16) - 1;

// Calculate which tile we should stop at (both across and down).
int endTileX = ((Math.abs(viewX) + viewWidth) / 16) + 1;
int endTileY = ((Math.abs(viewY) + viewHeight) / 16) + 1;

// check where within tile map range
if (endTileX > tilesWide) endTileX = tilesWide;
if (endTileY > tilesHigh) endTileY = tilesHigh;
if (startTileX < 0) startTileX = 0;
if (startTileY < 0) startTileY = 0;
```

Once you know the starting and ending tiles, you can loop through drawing the tiles on the screen.

First you need a byte to hold each tile map entry as it is read.

```
byte t = 0;
```

Next you start a loop for all the rows of the tile map that need to be drawn, then all the columns. This starts at startTileY and goes down until we get to the last viewable row at endTileY, then for each of these it goes across the map from startTileX to endTileX.

```
for (int drawTileYy = startTileY; ty < endTileY; drawTileY++)
{
    for (int drawTileX = startTileX; drawTileX < endTileX; drawTileX++)
    {
```

Inside the double loop you can access the entry corresponding to this location. Since most tile maps contain empty space, the code also does a quick check to see if it can just ignore this entry if the byte equals the default value 0 (NO_TILE).

```
        tileType = tileMap[drawTileY][drawTileY];
        if (tileType == NO_TILE) continue; // quick abort if it's nothing
```

Now comes the tricky bit. Based on the byte value, this code draws an image from the ImageSet loaded in the constructor. To keep this simpler I've mapped the frames in the graphics file to the same byte values in the map. That way the code doesn't need to translate the values when drawing them—if the tile map byte is the number two, the second frame from the loaded world images will be drawn (note that I take one away from the byte value to account for zero meaning no tile in the world).

Finally, to figure out where to draw the tile, the code multiples the tile x (tx) and tile y (ty) values by the tile size again, and takes away the view port offset.

```
        // draw the image using tile type - 1 (WALL_TYPE=frame 0)
        // we offset drawing by the view port origin
        tiles.draw(g, 0, tileType-1, (drawTileX * TILE_WIDTH) - viewX,
                                     (drawTileY * TILE_HEIGHT) - viewY);
    }
}
```

Tile Collision Detection

Now that you're using your tile layer for all the walls in your game, you need to add code to detect collisions between the tiles and actors. The good news is that because tiles are at a fixed location and there are relatively few of them, your collision tests are extremely fast.

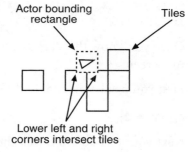

Figure 11.4 To check whether an actor is colliding with any tiles, you check the tile map entries that lie underneath the actor.

In order to determine whether an actor has collided with a tile, all you need to do is look at what tiles are "underneath" that actor. If you do this for all the possible tile positions that fall within the actor's bounding rectangle, you can determine whether it's in a collision state (see Figure 11.4) if any of those entries in the tile map are not equal to TILE_NONE (byte 0).

The code to do this is relatively simple. The following method checks the tiles under a given rectangle by stepping through all the tile-sized areas within an actor's rectangle.

```
for (int tileY=actorToCheck.getY(); tileY <= actorBottom;
     tileY += TILE_HEIGHT)
{
    for (int tileX=actorToCheck.getX(); tileX <= actorRightSide;
         tileX += TILE_WIDTH)
    {
        if (getTile(tileX, tileY) > NO_TILE)
            return true;
    }
}
```

The getTile method just grabs the tile at a given location (with some sanity checking).

```
public final byte getTile(int x, int y)
{
   int tileX = x / 16;
   int tileY = y / 16;
   if (tileX < 0 || tileX >= tilesWide || tileY < 0 || tileY >= tilesHigh) return -1;
   return tileMap[ tileY ][ tileX ];
}
```

Tip

If you're getting lost as to how all this comes together, you can take a look at a complete example in the CD Chapter 11 source directory, "SimpleWorldTest".

As you can see, collision detection against tiles is much faster than against dynamic actors. You only need to do four (very quick) array checks for each actor, instead of doing a full rectangle intersection for all actors.

Animated Tiles

So far your tiles have been simple static images. Sometimes, though, it's nice to animate tiles to bring those backgrounds to life. One method is to make the animating parts of your backgrounds actors, but then you're back to the performance issues.

Another method is to draw your tiles using sprite objects and just cycle the one copy of a sprite object for all the tiles of a particular type. To do this, you need to modify the tile rendering code to draw a sprite instead of an image frame. For example:

```
byte tileType = 0;
for (int tileY = startY; tileY < endTileY; tileY++)
{
   for (int tileX = startX; tileX < endTileX; tileX++)
   {
      tileType = tileMap[tileY][tileX];
      switch(tileType)
      {
         case NO_TILE: continue; // quick abort if it's nothing

         case WALL_TILE:
            tiles.draw(g, 0, tileType-1, (tileX * TILE_WIDTH) - viewX,
                                         (tileY * TILE_HEIGHT) - viewY);
            break;

         case GLOWING_WALL_TILE:
```

```
                torchSprite.draw(g, (tileX * TILE_WIDTH) - viewX,
                                    (tileY * TILE_HEIGHT) - viewY);
            break;
        }
    }
}
```

Inside the cycle code for your world, you need to call the `cycle` method for all your world sprites (such as the `torchSprite` used in the previous code). This will cause all the tiles associated with the sprites to animate.

The only issue you might have with this system is that all tiles will animate using the same frames at the exact same time. Under certain circumstances it's something you'll really notice, such as a line of animated torches along a wall all dancing perfectly in sync. A clever way I've used to get around this (without having to use separate sprite objects for every tile) is to offset the frame displayed by the position of the tile (a fixed number). For example:

```
case GLOWING_WALL_TILE:
    // offset the frame by a fixed number (relative to position)
    int offsetFrame = (tileX + tileY) % torchImageSet.getTotalFrames();

    // add the offset to the current frame number
    int f = (torchSprite.getCurrentFrame() + offsetFrame);

    // wrap around the frame count if you have to
    if (f > torchImageSet.getTotalFrames())
        f -= torchImageSet.getTotalFrames();

    torchImageSet.draw(g, 0, f, (tileX * TILE_WIDTH) - viewX,
                                (tileY * TILE_HEIGHT) - viewY);
    break;
```

This code uses the position of the tile (`tileX + tileY`) as a Modula offset to the current frame. Notice I'm using the image set to draw a specific frame, not the sprite (which would draw the current frame based on the sprite animation timing). The end result is that each tile draws a slightly different frame based on its position.

Activator Tiles

Adding a tile layer has significantly reduced the number of actors required in your world because you no longer need objects to represent static elements. However, there are still quite a few elements in the game that need to be proper objects. If you think about fighting your way from the start of a complex level to the end, it's not unreasonable to encounter upwards of 100 enemies. Although this isn't as high as your original 500, you're still talking about a significant number of actors contained within the world. (Does this bring back all those memories of collision detection, construction delays, and memory hogging?)

To solve this problem, you need to answer a simple (but classic) question. If a tree falls in your world, and the player isn't around to see it, did it really happen? In your case, the answer is no. If a player is nowhere near an enemy, then you certainly don't need that enemy to be a full object. It's only when the player moves into the object's area of effect that you want to bring the enemy to life. This same concept applies to many aspects in your game. You only want to activate things when the player moves into range.

To introduce this, you need a way to trigger code based on the player's location. As soon as you detect the player getting close, you execute that code and activate the component of the game. The player will be none the wiser. Because you already have a sophisticated tile system, you can also use it to trigger game events using special tile types known as *activator tiles*. For the purposes of *Star Assault*, your activator tiles are pretty simple. You use a specific type of tile to represent an enemy unit (a mine, fighter, or turret). For more sophisticated game types, you could make activators spawn enemies of different types over time or otherwise alter the game. Most of this, however, will come back to the same basic process—when it is within range, the activator tile executes code and removes itself from the world. The first code you need is for some new tile types for your activators. I've added some bounding constants as well (such as START_ACTIVATOR_TILE). You'll use these in the following code to test for certain types of tiles.

```
public static final byte NO_TILE = 0;

public static final byte WALL_TILE = 1;

// Since you'll likely have many different activator type
// tiles you use a range (starting from the first entry through
// to the last entry).
public static final byte START_ACTIVATOR_TILE = 2;
public static final byte FIGHTER_ACTIVATOR_TILE = 2;
public static final byte END_ACTIVATOR_TILE = 2;
```

A good place to detect an activator tile now is when you draw it. Here's the original tile rendering code with the activator added. Notice I'm using the bounding constants to check for a range of tile types.

```
for (int drawTileY = startTileY; drawTileY < endTileY; drawTileY++)
{
    for (int drawTileX = startTileX; drawTileX < endTileX; drawTileX++)
    {
```

```
        if (drawTileY >= 0 && drawTileX >= 0)
        {
            tileType = tileMap[drawTileY][drawTileX];
            if (tileType == NO_TILE) continue; // quick abort if it's nothing
```

This is where the code detects if the tile at this location is an activator by checking if the tile number is in the START_ACTIVATOR_TILE to END_ACTIVATOR_TILE range. If it is, the work is then done by an activateTile method, which you'll see below.

```
        if (tileType >= START_ACTIVATOR_TILE &&
            tileType <= END_ACTIVATOR_TILE)
            activateTile(drawTileX, drawTileY)
        else
        {
            xpos = (drawTileX * TILE_WIDTH) - viewX;
            ypos = (drawTileY * TILE_HEIGHT) - viewY;

            if (xpos > 0 - TILE_WIDTH && xpos < viewWidth &&
                ypos > 0 - TILE_HEIGHT && ypos < viewHeight)
            {
                tiles.draw(graphics, 0, 0, xpos, ypos);
            }
        }
    }
  }
}
```

Inside the World class activateTile method you can now do whatever you want based on the tile type. For *Star Assault*, you simply replace the tile with the type of enemy you want.

```
private final void activateTile(int tileX, int tileY)
{
  byte tileType = tileMap[tileY][tileX];
  int xpos = (tileX * TILE_WIDTH);
  int ypos = (tileY * TILE_HEIGHT);

  switch (tileType)
  {
    case FIGHTER_ACTIVATOR_TILE:
        Ship s = new Ship(this, true, xpos, ypos);
        addActor(s);
        break;
  }
```

```
    // clear the activator tile
    tileMap[tileY][tileX] = NO_TILE;
}
```

That last line is pretty important. If you don't remove the activator, it will trigger again on the next cycle. You'll end up creating about 80 actors per second until the MID explodes!

Non-Collidable Tiles

Often in worlds you'll want to have certain types of tiles which do not collide with the player (floor for example). Doing this with your tile engine is pretty simple. First you need to set up a mechanism to detect whether you want a tile to cause a collision with the player object or not. With a traditional tile engine, you'd add a flag indicating this to the tile map data, but with J2ME that's a waste of precious memory. Instead, you can use a type range like we did with the activators to indicate which tiles are "real". For example, here's the tile static list again with a real tile range added:

```
public static final byte NO_TILE = 0;

public static final byte START_REAL_TILE = 1;
public static final byte WALL_TILE = 1;
public static final byte END_REAL_TILE = 1;

// Activator tiles are not within the real tiles range.
public static final byte START_ACTIVATOR_TILE = 100;
public static final byte FIGHTER_ACTIVATOR_TILE = 100;
public static final byte END_ACTIVATOR_TILE = 100;
```

Next you simply modify the collision code to ignore anything other than this range. For example:

```
for (int tileY=actorToCheck.getY(); tileY <= actorBottom;
     tileY += TILE_HEIGHT)
{
    for (int tileX=actorToCheck.getX(); tileX <= actorRightSide;
         tileX += TILE_WIDTH)
    {
        byte tileType = getTile(tileX, tileY);
        if (tileType >= START_REAL_TILE &&
            tileType <= END_REAL_TILE)
            return true;
    }
}
```

Background Layers

So far you've seen how to create two distinct layers for your game—the tile layer and the actor layer. You don't have to stop there, though; you can add further layers if you want. Typically, though, any additional layer will tend to be for backgrounds, rather than for yet more tiles or actors—it's just not worth the added memory and processing.

Background layers (and you can certainly have more than one) are usually at a different scale than the other layers. This means they scroll at a different relative speed to the primary layers. This is the effect you'll often see used in side-scrolling or car-driving games in which the backgrounds move much slower than the player does. This difference in speed is what creates the illusion that the backgrounds are far away. To do this you can just create another tile layer using a scrolling speed different than the current view port.

For *Star Assault*, you'll create a similar effect using a background star field (rather than a new tile map). As you can see in Figure 11.5, you'll draw the star field below the other layers by drawing it first.

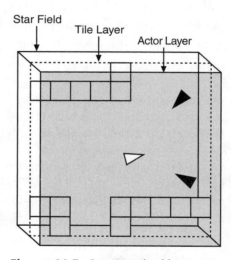

To give the illusion of great distance, the scroll speed of the star field will be very low relative to the front layers. This means you only need a small area for the entire field (256 × 256 pixels). In addition, you don't need any collision detection, activator tiles, or map editing, so there's no need to create a complex data array. You can just whip up some code to generate a random-looking blob of stars.

Figure 11.5 *Star Assault* adds an additional drawing layer for a scrolling background star field.

```
public final class Tools
{
    ...

    /**
     * Draws a background star field using little star images (ranging in size
     * from 1 to 3 pixel square; loaded from the general.png image file). The
     * field is drawn as a 256 by 256 pixel map of stars using a simple
     * placement method of incrementing a value to give an impression of
     * distribution of stars across the map.
     * @param graphics The graphics context upon which to draw.
     * @param offsetX The relative x offset of the current view port.
     * @param offsetY The relative y offset of the current view port.
     * @param viewWidth The width of the current view port.
```

```
 * @param viewHeight The height of the current view port.
 */
public final static void drawStarField(Graphics graphics,
                                       int offsetX, int offsetY,
                                       int viewWidth, int viewHeight)
{
    // Load the static star graphics inmageset.
    if (smallStarImages == null)
        smallStarImages = ImageSet.extractFrames(ImageSet.loadClippedImage(
                        "/general.png", 0, 0), 0, 6, 4, 2, 3, 3);

    // Draw the stars on the background by running through all the positions
    // in the 256 by 256 star map jumping in different increments to give
    // a scattered but consistent distribution of stars.
    int jumpBy = 160;
    for (int i = 0; i < (256 * 256); i += jumpBy)
    {
        int starX = i / 256 - (offsetX);
        int starY = i % 256 - (offsetY);

        // Check whether the star image will fit on the current view and then
        // draw a frame relative to the position in the map.
        if (starX > -MAX_STAR_WIDTH && starX < viewWidth &&
            starY > -MAX_STAR_HEIGHT && starY < viewHeight)
            graphics.drawImage(smallStarImages[i % smallStarImages.length],
                        starX, starY, Graphics.TOP | Graphics.LEFT);

        // Change the jump value increment to randomize the distribution
        // somewhat.
        jumpBy += 33;
    }
}
```

This code looks complex, but basically I'm just playing with numbers in order to generate a random-looking group of stars. The offset passed into the method call determines how much you scroll. When you draw the star field you should keep this offset value relative to the view port, but scaled up according to how fast you want it to move relative to the player. For example:

```
// Draw a star field scrolling 10 times slower than the view.
Tools.drawStarField(g, viewX / 10, viewY / 10, viewWidth, viewHeight);
```

You can see the final result in Figure 11.6, although it's a much cooler effect when you see it moving!

You can use images as part of your background by using a tile layer. Given the slow scrolling speed, the total size of a background tile map can be much smaller than your previous one. You can also use much larger tiles, say 64 × 64 pixels.

Figure 11.6 A screenshot of the scrolling star field background in action (it looks much cooler as you fly around).

Putting It All Together

You've covered a lot of different territory in the last few sections. To bring it all together as a working system, you'll need to create a new version of the GameScreen class that supports the World class. You'll then need to wrap up all the code presented so far into the World class itself.

Below is an outline of the revised GameScreen class (I've left out the unimportant bits). As you'll see, most of the work is passed off to a new World instance.

```
/**
 * GameScreen class now modified to support a World class. The main
 * difference is the world takes care of cycling, rendering and
 * handling actors (so there's no more Actor vector required).
 */

public class GameScreen extends Canvas
{
    private Ship playerShip;
    private World world;

    /**
     * Constructs a new GameScreen which in turn constructs a new world 10 by
     * 10 tiles in size with a view port the size of the screen. A player ship
     * is then constructed and added to this world.
     */
    public GameScreen()
    {
        ...

        // Construct a new world 10 by 10 tiles in size using a view port the
        // size of the screen.
        world = new World(10, 10, getWidth(), getHeight());

        // Create the player ship and add it to the world.
```

```
      playerShip = new Ship(world, false, 20, 20);
      world.addActor(playerShip);
}
/**
 * Canvas paint method used to render the world.
 * @param graphics The graphics context upon which to draw the Actors.
 */
protected void paint(Graphics graphics)
{
    graphics.setColor(0);
    graphics.fillRect(0, 0, getWidth(), getHeight());

    world.render(graphics);
}


/**
 * Called by the run method to set the view port to center on the player's
 * ship and then cycle the world.
 */
public void cycle()
{
    world.setView(playerShip.getCenterX() - getWidth()/2,
                  playerShip.getCenterY() - getHeight()/2);
    world.cycle();
}


/**
 * React to keys pressed by the user.
 * @param keyCode The code of the key the players pressed.
 */
protected void keyPressed(int keyCode)
{
    int action = getGameAction(keyCode);

    if (action == RIGHT)
        playerShip.setNegPeakSpin();
    if (action == LEFT)
        playerShip.setPeakSpin();
    if (action == UP)
        playerShip.setFiring(true);
}


/**
```

```
 * React to key being released. For this example the code stops the spin.
 * @param keyCode The code for the key that was released.
 */
protected void keyReleased(int keyCode)
{
    int action = getGameAction(keyCode);
    if (action == RIGHT)
        playerShip.setSpin(0);
    if (action == LEFT)
        playerShip.setSpin(0);
    if (action == UP)
        playerShip.setFiring(false);
}
}
```

Since we're now using a World instead a GameScreen the Actors need to be modified to use this as a reference, for example:

```
abstract public class Actor
{
    private World world;                    // the world this actor is within.
    ...

    public Actor(World worldArg, ...)
    {
        world = worldArg;
```

You'll then need to change the various Actor derived classes, such as Ship and Bullet, to set the new parameter in the constructor.

Next you need to create a World class as a new home for the tiles and actors. Since you've pretty much seen all the code for this already I'll save some trees and let you refer to the CD "SimpleWorldTest" project in the Chapter 11 source code directory for a complete example (note that an example of activator tiles appears in the GeneratedWorldTest example).

Building Worlds

Creating a tile engine is only the beginning of constructing a world. All you really have so far are the tools to create your game environments; what you need to do next is create that environment. First you should take a look at what makes up a game level.

Level Design

Up until now what you've been doing is creating an engine for your game. This isn't the game, though; it's just a bunch of tools. The first time you'll really start to see your game come to life is when you begin the level design process. Designing this environment for your game can be quite a challenge—level design is a serious profession in itself now.

To create the levels, I recommend that you first create a list of all the content elements in your game. This is basically just a list of new elements the player could encounter, such as terrain, enemies, and any new capabilities.

When you have the list, you should then consider at what point in your game you will introduce each component. Depending on the size and complexity of your content, you'll want to keep the player interested without overwhelming him with new features and using up all your content too quickly.

New content is also your primary reward for the player who meets your challenges. This doesn't always have to be defeating a massive boss monster; it could be just for progressing through the game. Consider this when you're designing your levels. Present a challenge, and then reward the player with something new. This is also important because you don't want to use up all your content too quickly. You'll find that J2ME games have a very limited scope on game features, so you need to time their introduction to keep the player feeling rewarded throughout the life of the game.

You should also be somewhat considerate of first-time players of your game. While you don't want to bore people with ridiculously simple (read slow and boring) introductions, you should start out slowly to give them a chance to work their way into the game play.

For *Star Assault* I'm keeping things simple by having only two significant content elements—level complexity and your three enemy types (drones, turrets, and fighters). If this were a commercial game project, I would also add a variety of boss enemies (for placement at the end of some levels), a series of power-ups that the player can pick up along the way to enhance his ship, and a few more tile sets to represent some different environments (star bases, asteroid fields, and so on).

Constructing levels is a time-consuming process, so investing some solid time into methods to make level design easy and fast is well worth the effort. The quality of your tools can significantly impact your overall development speed and thus the quality of your game (because you'll be able to use all that extra time on improvements). You'll also find level design to be an iterative process. As you continue to tweak all the parameters of the game and inevitably implement new content ideas, you'll constantly modify levels to maintain a good balance. If modifying your levels is a painstaking exercise, you'll find yourself cutting corners or excluding features just because it's "too hard to redo the map." The moral of the story is: Invest time in your tools. Invest time in your tools. Invest time in your tools. Invest time in your tools. Invest time in your tools. Invest time in your tools. Invest time in your tools. Invest time in your tools. Got it yet? It's one of the keys to developing a great game. Take the time to work with your tools to make the process of creating your game easier. It'll come back a hundredfold in the quality of your final game.

All right, so how do you go about creating those levels? Well, because you're using a tile engine you really need to be able to fill in that tile map array with bytes corresponding to the contents of the level. There are a number of methods you can use to construct a world; which one you use depends on the type of game you're making. Thankfully, there are also quite a few tools out there to help in the process. However, as with most things, you need to make some adjustments to suit the micro world. Take a closer look at the various methods and tools you can use to build your world.

Array Maps

The simplest method to create a level is to initialize the tile map array using Java code. For example, the following code creates a 10 × 10 tile map; the 0s represent empty tiles and the 1s represent wall tiles.

```
byte[][] level0 = {
    {0, 0, 0, 0, 0, 0, 0, 0, 0, 0},
    {0, 1, 1, 1, 1, 1, 0, 0, 0, 0},
    {0, 1, 0, 0, 0, 1, 0, 0, 0, 0},
    {0, 1, 0, 0, 0, 1, 1, 1, 1, 0},
    {0, 1, 0, 0, 0, 0, 0, 0, 1, 0},
    {0, 1, 0, 0, 0, 0, 0, 0, 1, 0},
    {0, 1, 0, 0, 0, 1, 1, 1, 1, 0},
    {0, 1, 1, 1, 1, 1, 0, 0, 0, 0},
    {0, 0, 0, 0, 0, 0, 0, 0, 0, 0},
    {0, 0, 0, 0, 0, 0, 0, 0, 0, 0}
};
```

This might seem like a pretty silly way to make levels, but keep in mind this is J2ME. More sophisticated map-editing systems will cost you in terms of code (and map data files); array initialization code will end up being extremely small in a compiled JAR file. If your requirements are very light and the levels aren't going to change too often, then creating a level directly using Java code might be a good idea.

Using code to generate levels doesn't stop here, though. You can use more sophisticated code to generate highly complex (and fun) level content. In the next section, you'll look at how to generate some sophisticated levels using a random level generator.

Random Level Generator

A great way to keep things fresh for players (and thus increase replayability) is to generate new levels for them using a random level generator. Many games (such as *Diablo*) use random level generators so effectively it's hard to tell the difference between hand-edited maps and generated ones.

There are many forms of map generator techniques, most of which are tailored to the type of map that is being generated. From fantasy dungeons such as those used in *Diablo* to complex terrain generators used in real-time strategy games, the generators are custom-built to suit the game requirements. As an example, you'll build a relatively simple corridor-room system for *Star Assault*. You can see an example of the levels you'll be generating below.

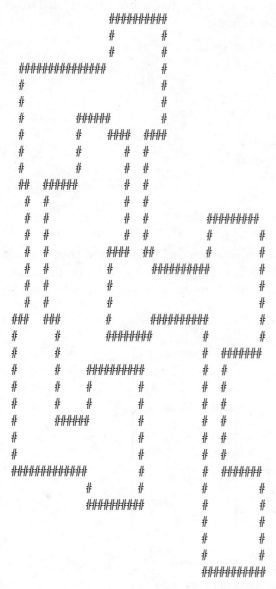

To keep things organized all the code will go into a new LevelGenerator class.

Creating Rooms

In Figure 11.7 you can see two rooms connected by a corridor. This is the basic building block of your generator. The system is quite simple. Based on a starting room, move a random distance in a random direction (directly left, right, up, or down) and create another room. Then build a corridor between these two to connect them.

The first step in generating the level is to construct a room. To do this you just need to set all the bytes of a rectangle in the tile map, for example:

```
// Set the array elements down the left and right sides of the room.
for (int tileY=topOfRoom; tileY < heightOfRoom; tileY++)
{
    tileMap[tileY][0] = WALL_TILE;          // Left side.
    tileMap[tileY][widthOfRoom-1] = WALL_TILE; // Right side.
}
// Set the array elements across the top and bottom.
for (int tileX = leftSideOfRoom; tileX < widthOfRoom; tileX++)
{
    tileMap[0][tileX] = WALL_TILE; // Top.
    tileMap[heightOfRoom-1][tileX] = WALL_TILE; // Bottom.
}
```

Once you have a room, the next step is to create another at a distance and then connect the two using a corridor. In the left-hand illustration in Figure 11.8 you can see the results of this and you can also see your next problem: there are no doors, so the player won't be able to move from room to room.

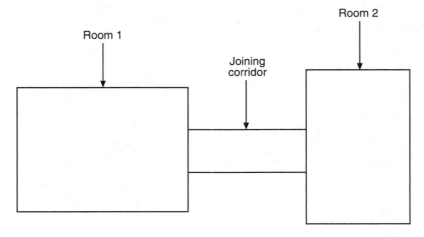

Figure 11.7 Your random level generator creates random rooms and then connects them using corridors.

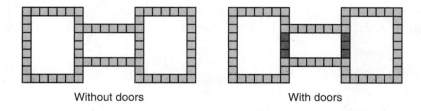

Without doors   With doors

Figure 11.8 Two rooms connected by a corridor (left) need the overlapping tiles (excluding corners in this case) to be inverted to create doorways (right).

In the illustration on the right, I've highlighted the parts of the walls that need to be opened up in order to let the player fly through. Notice something? The doors are where the walls for the rooms intersect (I've excluded the corners in this example). A simple method of opening doorways therefore is to just change any part of the wall that overlays another into an opening. In effect what you need to do is "invert" tiles as you create the walls for each room.

To do this you start with a method that takes care of inverting tiles.

```
public class LevelGenerator
{
    /**
     * Inverts an existing map tile between either empty or a wall tile.
     * @param tileX The x position of the tile to invert.
     * @param tileY The y position of the tile to invert.
     */
    private void invertTile(int tileX, int tileY)
    {
        // Turn an empty tile into a wall or vice versa.
        if (tileMap[tileY][tileX] == World.WALL_TILE)
            tileMap[tileY][tileX] = World.NO_TILE;
        else
            tileMap[tileY][tileX] = World.WALL_TILE;
    }
```

Next is a method to set the tiles corresponding to a room rectangle by inverting the tiles already on the map. (From Figure 11.8 you can also see the code should not invert the corner tiles. This is because for this type of tile map you always want them to be walls in order to avoid ugly gaps in the edges of the doorways. Setting corners separately is also useful later on if you decide to have special tile graphics for corners or junctions.)

```
    /**
     * Toggles tiles in the tilemap to either a wall or an empty space (based on
```

```
 * what is there already) in an outline rectangle using the supplied bounding
 * coordinates. Note that corners are NOT inverted, they are always set as
 * walls.
 * @param roomTileX The starting x position of the room to create.
 * @param roomTileY The starting y position of the room to create.
 * @param roomTilesWide The width of the room to create.
 * @param roomTilesHigh The height of the room to create.
 */
private void addWallsToMap(int roomTileX, int roomTileY,
                              int roomTilesWide, int roomTilesHigh)
{
    // Add the top and bottom line.
    for (int tileX = roomTileX; tileX < roomTileX + roomTilesWide; tileX++)
    {
        // Invert the tiles along the top.
        invertTile(tileX, roomTileY);
        // Invert the tiles along the bottom.
        invertTile(tileX, roomTileY + roomTilesHigh - 1);
    }

    // Left and right side lines.
    for (int tileY = roomTileY + 1; tileY < roomTileY + roomTilesHigh - 1;
        tileY++)
    {
        // Invert the tiles down the left side.
        invertTile(roomTileX, tileY);
        // Invert the tiles down the right side.
        invertTile(roomTileX + roomTilesWide - 1, tileY);
    }

    // Mark corners as walls (not inverted).
    tileMap[roomTileY][roomTileX] = World.WALL_TILE;
    tileMap[roomTileY][roomTileX + roomTilesWide - 1] = World.WALL_TILE;
    tileMap[roomTileY + roomTilesHigh - 1][roomTileX] = World.WALL_TILE;
    tileMap[roomTileY + roomTilesHigh - 1][roomTileX + roomTilesWide - 1] =
            World.WALL_TILE;
}
```

When you're trying to create each new room, you need to make sure that there is available space on the map and that the size and position of the room leave enough area to create a corridor between them.

To do this the generator needs to keep track of the locations of all previous rooms using a room array like this:

```
private int[] roomX;
private int[] roomY;
private int[] roomW;
private int[] roomH;
```

To now add a room you just combine the code to add the walls to the map and to add an entry to the room array. This following method, addRoom, also uses the supplied level number to fill the room with enemy.

```
/**
 * Adds a room to the level by setting all the bytes in the tilemap to be
 * walls. Note that existing wall tiles will be inverted by this process
 * (except for corners) in order to "carve out" doorways where the walls
 * between rooms and corridors overlap.
 * @param level The level number is a relative density level used to fill
 * the room with objects.
 * @param tileX The x position of the new room.
 * @param tileY The y position of the new room.
 * @param tileWidth The width of the new room.
 * @param tileHeight The height of the new room.
 */
private void addRoom(int level, int tileX, int tileY, int tileWidth,
                     int tileHeight)
{
    addWallsToMap(tileX, tileY, tileWidth, tileHeight);

    roomW[roomCount] = tileWidth;
    roomH[roomCount] = tileHeight;
    roomX[roomCount] = tileX;
    roomY[roomCount] = tileY;
    roomCount++;
```

The following code adds the enemy to the room by picking a random location inside the room and setting it to be a FIGHTER_ACTIVATOR_TILE.

```
// Add enemy to this room (we base the number on the level they're on)
int maxEnemy = level + 1;
if (maxEnemy > 10) maxEnemy = 10;
int numEnemy = Tools.getRand(0, maxEnemy);

int numAdded = 0;
```

Since the location picked for a new fighter might already be populated, the code keeps try-ing until the `tries` count is past the rather arbitrary value `maxEnemy * 2`.

```
int tries=0;

while (numAdded < numEnemy && tries++ < maxEnemy * 2)
{
    // Pick a random tile and try to add an activator there (may be filled
    // by another one)
    int randomTileX = Tools.getRand(tileX + 1, tileX + tileWidth - 2);
    int randomTileY = Tools.getRand(tileY + 1, tileY + tileHeight - 2);

    if (tileMap[randomTileY][randomTileX] == World.NO_TILE &&
            (randomTileX != playerStartX && randomTileY != playerStartY))
    {
        numAdded++;
        tileMap[randomTileY][randomTileX] = World.FIGHTER_ACTIVATOR_TILE;
    }
}
```

Now that you have the code to add a single room, you're almost ready to start generating the level. First though you need a few more helper methods to get the job done.

Utility Methods

The code for all this starts with a few utility methods. The first is used to return a random direction from a list of available ones.

When inside the main loop the code will try to create a room in a random direction (left, right, up or down), however it's better to try directions that haven't previously failed first since they have a better chance of not being blocked (by the map dimensions or another room). To track previously tried directions, the code uses an array of four boolean (representing the four directions) which are set to true if a direction has been tried. The following code returns a random choice from the array entries that are false (excluding the true ones).

```
/**
 * Based on an array of booleans this returns a random choice from a limited
 * list of ones that are currently false. The level generator uses this to
 * randomly choose a direction, but only from ones that have not previously
 * been tried (set to true in the array).
 */
private static final int getRandDir(boolean[] dirs)
```

```
{
    // we only do a random test on the number of available dirs, so let's
    // find out how many there are first
    int numDirs = 0;
    for (int i = 0; i < 4; i++)
        if (!dirs[i]) numDirs++;

    if (numDirs == 0) return 0;

    // now pick one at random
    int n = 0;
    if (numDirs > 1)
        n = Tools.getRand(0, numDirs - 1);

    // and return the dir corresponding to the nth result by figuring
    // the array index of the nth true value
    int c = -1;
    int i = 0;
    while (i < dirs.length)
    {
        if (!dirs[i++]) c++;
        if (c == n) return i - 1;
    }

    return 0;
}
```

The loop code also checks to see if all directions have been tried for the current room (if it has, the directions are reset so it can retry them all again). The following method tests whether an array of booleans are all true.

```
/**
 * @param b An array of booleans to test.
 * @return True if all the booleans in the array are true.
 */
private static final boolean areAllTrue(boolean[] b)
{
    for (int i = 0; i < b.length; i++)
        if (b[i] == false) return false;
    return true;
}
```

Another utility method used by the main loop tests whether a proposed new room is close to another room on the map. To keep the map uncluttered, the code ensures a distance of at least three tiles between each room.

```
/**
 * Checks to see if the supplied rectangle is within 3 tiles of any other
 * room (including corridors).
 * @param tileX The x position of the room to be checked.
 * @param tileY The y position of the room to be checked.
 * @param tilesWide The width of the room to be checked.
 * @param tilesHigh The height of the room to be checked.
 * @return True if the rectangle (room) is within 3 tiles of another.
 */
private final boolean isRectNearRoom(int tileX, int tileY, int tilesWide,
                                     int tilesHigh)
{
    for (int i = 0; i < roomCount; i++)
    {
        if (Tools.isIntersectingRect(tileX, tileY, tilesWide, tilesHigh,
                                     roomX[i] - 3, roomY[i] - 3,
                                     roomW[i] + 3, roomH[i] + 3))
        {
            return true;
        }
    }
    return false;
}
```

The Main Loop

All right, with background and all the utility methods out of the way, you're ready for the main loop. Since this is a pretty lengthy process, here's the basic pseudo-code for the entire process.

- Pick a level width and height and create a corresponding tile map array.
- Choose the number of rooms you'd like in the level.
- Create a starting room with a random size within one of the four corners of the map.
- Start looping until you've either reached the target room count, or you've tried so many times that you have to give up. (Do the following inside the loop.)
- Pick a random size for a new room.
- Pick a random size for a corridor to connect that room to the existing one.

- Starting from the current room, pick a random direction (left, right, up, or down) from directions not previously tried for this room.
- Mark the chosen direction as tried.
- Test if the new room and connecting corridor will fit on the map and that it does not collide with another room already on the map.
- If the room fits, set the added room to be the last one (not the corridor) and add it to the map. If the room did not fit then just go back to the top to try another direction.

Pretty dense I know, but there's no rocket science going on here; the process is basically to create rooms and connecting corridors in random directions, keeping track of what you're doing along the way. Here's the complete code for the generateLevel method. I'll explain things along the way.

```
public byte[][] generateLevel(int level)
{
```

The level integer is an arbitrary number used to alter the size and density of the level being generated. Level 1 for example is only a few rooms, with each room containing a small number of enemy; level 10 has significantly more rooms and a larger number of enemy in each of those rooms. There's no solid formula to how the level corresponds to difficulty; it's a game balancing thing that you just tweak as you flesh the game's playability out.

```
// Set the size of the level relative to the level number provided.
width = 30 + (level * 2);
height = 30 + (level * 2);
```

The size of a level needs to be capped to a reasonable map since it directly corresponds to the size of the tileMap byte array, and therefore the amount of memory being consumed.

```
// Cap the level to a reasonable maximum.
if (width > 100) width = 100;
if (height > 100) height = 100;

// Construct a new tile map based on this size and clear it.
tileMap = new byte[height][width];

// The minRooms is used later to determine when to stop generating new
// rooms. It's more of a target than an exact number though.
int totalRooms = 10 + (level * 2);

System.out.println("Generating level: " + level + " minRooms: " +
                   totalRooms + " width: " + width + " height: " + height);
```

To track all the rooms created in a level we use an array for each room's x, y tile position, the width and height as well as whether the room was a corridor joining two others. This is mostly used by the code to determine if there is enough space to place a new room.

```
roomX = new int[totalRooms];
roomY = new int[totalRooms];
roomW = new int[totalRooms];
roomH = new int[totalRooms];
```

When creating a room there is a reasonable minimum and maximum size set.

```
// The minimum size of each room.
int minRoomHeight = 6;
int minRoomWidth = 6;
int maxRoomHeight = 10;
int maxRoomWidth = 10;
```

The first step in the generation process is to create a room. In order to give the generation system the best chance of creating lots of rooms we always start in one of the corners, rather than near the center of the map.

```
int corner = Tools.getRand(0, 3);
int roomStartX = 3;
int roomStartY = 3;

switch (corner)
{
    // case 0 is top left (3,3) (which is already initialized)
    case 1: // top right
        roomStartX = width - maxRoomWidth;
        roomStartY = 3;
        break;
    case 2: // bottom right
        roomStartX = width - maxRoomWidth;
        roomStartY = height - maxRoomHeight;
        break;
    case 3: // bottom left
        roomStartX = 3;
        roomStartY = height - maxRoomHeight;
        break;
}
```

Once the position of the first room has been set, the following code adds it to the map with a random width and height within the previously specified range.

```
addRoom(level, roomStartX, roomStartY,
        Tools.getRand(minRoomWidth, maxRoomWidth),
        Tools.getRand(minRoomHeight, maxRoomHeight));
```

Next the player's start position for the level is set to be the center of the first room.

```
playerStartX = roomX[0] + (roomW[0] / 2);
playerStartY = roomY[0] + (roomH[0] / 2);
```

Since the addRoom method call above also fills the room with enemy fighters, you need to clear the tiles directly around the player in order to not give them a nasty surprise when entering a level. To do this, the code just sets all the tiles close to the player start point to World.NO_TILE.

```
for (int ty = 0; ty < 3; ty++)
    for (int tx = 0; tx < 3; tx++)
        tileMap[playerStartY - 1 + ty][playerStartX - 1 + tx] =
                World.NO_TILE;
```

Since the generator needs to connect rooms together it keeps track of the last room created using this value. You'll see it in action a little later. For now this value is set to be the array index of first room created.

```
int lastRoomIndex = 0;
```

If a new room is not valid (too big, for example) the generator will loop around for another go trying all the different directions. If all the directions are exhausted, they are reset and the generating will have another go, ad infinitum. To stop it from going forever, the tries counter is used to stop the loop after a reasonable number of attempts have been executed.

```
int tries = 0;
```

The following two variables are used inside the loop when creating new rooms.

```
int newRoomX = 0;
int newRoomY = 0;
```

The roomCount integer is incremented every time a new room is successfully added to the map.

```
roomCount = 1;
```

The code will randomly try to attach a corridor and room using one of the four directions (left, right, up, and down). If this step fails, such as when there's no space left on the map, or another room is in the road, the generator attempts another direction. To make this efficient, it tracks which directions it has already tried using an array of four `boolean`s (one for each direction).

```
boolean[] dirsTried = new boolean[4];
```

Next is the main `while` loop for creating the rooms. On each pass it will attempt to create a room along with a connecting corridor. The process ends when the generator has either created the required number of rooms, or the number of passes has reached a high level (100).

```
while (roomCount < totalRooms - 1 && tries < 100)
{
    tries++;
```

To add a room to the map, you need to place it relative to the previous room, and then connect back using a corridor. The first step is to grab the details of the previously created room. In the first pass, this is set to be the first room created outside the loop.

```
// Grab the info on the last room created.
int lastRoomX = roomX[lastRoomIndex];
int lastRoomY = roomY[lastRoomIndex];
int lastRoomW = roomW[lastRoomIndex];
int lastRoomH = roomH[lastRoomIndex];
```

Based on the minimum and maximum room sizes the generator randomly chooses a width and height for the new room.

```
// Pick a random size for the new room.
int newRoomW = Tools.getRand(minRoomWidth, maxRoomWidth);
int newRoomH = Tools.getRand(minRoomHeight, maxRoomHeight);
```

Here the code checks that all the directions away from the last room have already been tried. If they have then it's likely one or more failed because the random room and connecting corridor size were too large or misplaced. In this case the code resets the previously tried boolean array back to all false so the system can have another go around. If the room really is surrounded by blocks, then the tries counter will cut the process off after a certain number of attempts. (This could be optimized to detect a case where the generator just keeps failing on the same room.)

```
// If all the previous directions have been tried we reset them
// and start again.
if (areAllTrue(dirsTried))
{
```

```
        // reset the tried dirs to have another go
        for (int i = 0; i < 4; i++)
            dirsTried[i] = false;
    }
```

Now the generator picks a random direction for the next room to be placed and then records the attempt by setting the corresponding boolean in the array to true.

```
        // Pick a random dir from the ones that have not previously been tried.
        int dir = getRandDir(dirsTried);

        // Mark this direction as tried.
        dirsTried[dir] = true;
```

Next, a corridor is randomly sized and placed to link the last and new rooms together. By default, it assumes the chosen direction was either left or right and initializes the values according to that direction. If it turns out to be up or down it redoes the number for that. In each case the corridor size (either width or height) is fixed so that it does not exceed the size of the room it's connecting to.

```
        // Figure the corridor dimensions to connect up this new room.
        int corridorWidth = Tools.getRand(4, 10);
        int corridorHeight = Tools.getRand(4, minRoomHeight - 2);
        if (dir == UP_DIR || dir == DOWN_DIR)
        {
            corridorWidth = Tools.getRand(4, minRoomWidth - 2);
            corridorHeight = Tools.getRand(4, 10);
        }
```

With the corridor and room size chosen, the following code will attempt to randomly position the new room and corridor on the map. The tricky bit is figuring out how much space to leave for all the different directions.

```
        // If the room is to the left or right.
        if (dir == LEFT_DIR || dir == RIGHT_DIR)
        {
            // First choose a new x position (it's relatively fixed based on the
            // position of the previous room and the width of the corridor
            // (already chosen above).
            if (dir == LEFT_DIR)  // to the left
                newRoomX = lastRoomX - newRoomW - corridorWidth + 2;
            if (dir == RIGHT_DIR) // to the right
                newRoomX = lastRoomX + lastRoomW + corridorWidth - 2;

            // Next determine the vertical position of the new room. This code
```

```
        // ensures enough space is left available to fit in the corridor
        // (positioned on the left or right).
        int lowPoint = Math.max(1, lastRoomY + corridorHeight - newRoomH);
        int highPoint = lastRoomY + lastRoomH - corridorHeight;
        newRoomY = Tools.getRand(lowPoint, highPoint);
    }

    // If the room is above or below.
    if (dir == UP_DIR || dir == DOWN_DIR)
    {
        // First choose a new y position (it's relatively fixed based on the
        // position of the previous room and the height of the corridor
        // (already chosen above).
        if (dir == UP_DIR)
            newRoomY = lastRoomY - corridorHeight - newRoomH + 2;
        if (dir == DOWN_DIR)
            newRoomY = lastRoomY + lastRoomH + corridorHeight - 2;

        // Next determine the horizontal position of the new room. This code
        // ensures enough space is left availble to fit in the corridor
        // (positioned on the above or below).
        int lowPoint = Math.max(1, lastRoomX + corridorWidth - newRoomW);
        int highPoint = lastRoomX + lastRoomW - corridorWidth;
        newRoomX = Tools.getRand(lowPoint, highPoint);
    }
```

With the new room position and size figured out, you can now test to see if it actually fits on the map, and it isn't too close (or overlapping) another room.

```
        // Check to see if this new room is within the dimensions of the map.
        if (Tools.isRectWithinRect(0, 0, width - 1, height - 1,
                                   newRoomX, newRoomY, newRoomW, newRoomH))
        {
            // Check the room is not too close (or overlapping) another room.
            if (!isRectNearRoom(newRoomX, newRoomY, newRoomW, newRoomH))
            {
```

Now clear to add this room (and the corridor) to the map. The final step is to figure out the x and y position of the corridor and also place it on the map.

```
                addRoom(level, newRoomX, newRoomY, newRoomW, newRoomH);

                // Add the corridor connecting the new room to the last one.
                int corridorX = 0;
                int corridorY = 0;
```

```
// Connect a new room either to the left or right.
if (dir == LEFT_DIR || dir == RIGHT_DIR)
{
    if (dir == LEFT_DIR)
        corridorX = lastRoomX - corridorWidth + 1;
    if (dir == RIGHT_DIR)
        corridorX = lastRoomX + lastRoomW - 1;

    corridorY = Tools.getRand(Math.max(lastRoomY, newRoomY),
                              Math.min(lastRoomY + lastRoomH -
                                       corridorHeight,
                                       newRoomY + newRoomH -
                                       corridorHeight));
}

// Connect a new room either above or below.
if (dir == UP_DIR || dir == DOWN_DIR)
{
    if (dir == UP_DIR)
        corridorY = lastRoomY - corridorHeight + 1;
    if (dir == DOWN_DIR)
        corridorY = lastRoomY + lastRoomH - 1;

    corridorX = Tools.getRand(Math.max(lastRoomX, newRoomX),
                              Math.min(lastRoomX + lastRoomW -
                                       corridorWidth,
                                       newRoomX + newRoomW -
                                       corridorWidth));
}

// Draw the corridor on the tilemap.
addRoom(level, corridorX, corridorY, corridorWidth,
        corridorHeight);
```

Since a room was successfully added to the map, the generator now makes it the last room so that the next room will extend out from this one.

```
// Set the last room index to be the room we added (step back by
// an extra one to skip the corridor just added to connect the
// new room to the last one).
lastRoomIndex = roomCount-2;
            }
        }
    }
```

After completing the while loop the new map is returned.

```
    return tileMap;
}
```

To now use our level generator, you need to call it from the World class in order to fill in the tileMap before starting the game. For example, here's a method for the World class to generate a new level:

```
public void generateLevel(int levelNum)
{
    LevelGenerator lg = new LevelGenerator();
    tileMap = lg.generateLevel(levelNum);

    tilesWide = tileMap[0].length;
    tilesHigh = tileMap.length;
    int levelStartX = lg.getPlayerStartX();
    int levelStartY = lg.getPlayerStartY();

    playerShip.setX(levelStartX * TILE_WIDTH);
    playerShip.setY(levelStartY * TILE_HEIGHT);
}
```

And finally, call this method from an appropriate location to create a new level, such as the GameScreen constructor.

```
public GameScreen()
{
    // Set a reference to ourselves (singleton).
    theGameScreen = this;

    // Construct a new world 10 by 10 tiles in size using a view port the
    // size of the screen.
    world = new World(10, 10, getWidth(), getHeight());

    // Create the player ship and add it to the world.
    playerShip = new Ship(world, false, 20, 20);
    world.addActor(playerShip);
    world.setPlayerShip(playerShip);

    world.generateLevel(1);
}
```

Hopefully you didn't find any of that particularly difficult. It's a complicated process (and a bit of a brain bender sometimes) but in the end it's quite a basic system for creating a level. For a simple example, look at the CD Chapter 11 source code directory "Generated-WorldTest" as well as the finished *Star Assault* source code for a look at how it would integrate into a completed game.

Using Generators Effectively

I've used random level generators successfully in plenty of game development situations. You'll be surprised how often you can use them to enhance your game.

Once you have this system up and going, you can easily add special rooms and other level components to spice up what's happening. For *Star Assault*, you could add lines of turrets that stretch across the room, fighter bays (rooms with bunches of fighters in formation), or even special grids to make navigating more difficult. The possibilities are pretty much endless.

The best use of generators, however, is typically in combination with other map generation systems. For example, you can use a random generator for parts of your level, and then use hand-edited rooms at certain locations. In turn, you can assist the generator greatly by placing anchor points on your map that it can use as references to generating different content (such as a boss indicator).

In the next section, you'll look at another great way of creating level content—map editors.

Using a Map Editor

Probably the most flexible and powerful world creation method is to use a dedicated application known as a *map editor*. A map editor lets you visually edit the contents of your map using drawing tools. In other words, what you typically see on the screen is what you'll see in your level.

Map editors come in a variety of shapes and sizes, some obviously better than others. The two most suitable (and popular) for J2ME development are Mappy (http://www.tilemap.co.uk), shown in Figure 11.9, and Tile Studio (http://tilestudio.sourceforge.net), shown in Figure 11.10. Both of these tools are excellent for typical 2D game development requirements.

Of these two tools, I prefer Tile Studio due to the extra support for making edits to tile graphics (on the fly) and a programmable export system that lets you output data in almost any format you can imagine. This is, however, somewhat of a preference choice; I'm aware of other J2ME game developers successfully using Mappy as an editor.

Figure 11.9 The Mappy map editor

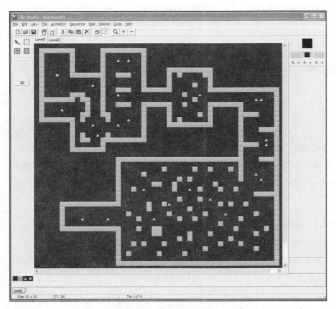

Figure 11.10 Tile Studio offers additional features such as tile graphic editing and customized export.

You can download Tile Studio (for Windows) from the Web site listed a moment ago. Once you have it installed, you will need to create a new project.

Tip

> For a working example, you can load up the two levels from the StarAssault.TSP project file (under the MapEditedWorld Chapter 11 source directory on the CD).

Editing the Map

To edit using the actual tiles from your game, you first need to import the graphics into the project using the Import Tiles option from the Tile Studio File menu. This feature supports PNG files, so you should have no trouble loading up the tile packs for your game. (Make sure when you load the tile image you set the Tile Width and Tile Height options to 16.)

Once you have the tiles loaded, they will appear along the bottom of the screen. The next thing to do is set up special tiles for the elements in the game which are not represented as graphical tiles. The activator tiles are a good example of this. You want to be able to add them onto the map, but there's no graphical tile in the world.png file that represents it, so there's no tile to place. To get around this you add custom tiles to represent special functions.

Tip

> Tile Studio is based around having one set of tiles for all the maps within a project. If you have different sets of tiles in your game, you'll have to merge them into a single image file in order to edit maps using Tile Studio. If that's not suitable, you can create a different project for levels using other tile sets. Generally I just throw everything into one image file designed for use only with Tile Studio. The final image files for the project are still separate.

The first is a blank tile representing an empty tile space in our game. This is a blank tile with an index of 0, rather than Tile Studio's default "null" tile which has an index of -1. You can create this new tile by selecting the original world tile and then hitting the insert key. To edit the tile, press Ctrl+Tab to switch to the tile editor mode and draw on it using the basic tools. For the blank tile I just filled it with black. To switch back to the map editor mode press Ctrl+Tab again. You're then free to draw anywhere on the map using this new tile.

Tip

> When creating a new map, always start by filling it with the zero index tiles so as not to confuse the map loader introduced later in the chapter.

The two tiles to the right of the original world tile are exactly the same type of special case. The first is the fighter activator and the second is an indicator as to where the player's ship should start in the map. To support this, the World class file needs some new tile indices defined.

```
public class World
{
    public static final byte NO_TILE = 0;
    public static final byte WALL_TILE = 1;
    public static final byte START_ACTIVATOR_TILE = 2;
    public static final byte FIGHTER_ACTIVATOR_TILE = 2;
    public static final byte END_ACTIVATOR_TILE = 2;
    public static final byte PLAYERSTART_TILE = 3;
```

The important thing to take note of here is the byte values I've assigned to each of these tiles are the same as the tile index in Tile Studio. It's vital that these two things remain in sync, so if you add, delete, or move a tile, you'll need to adjust the World class indices to match.

Tip

You can rearrange tiles (and their corresponding index value) anytime by selecting them and pressing Ctrl+Shift and the left or right arrow key.

The next thing to do is switch between the tile editor and map editor modes using Ctrl+TAB. You can then create a new map using the File menu's New Map command. Give it a name, such as "Level1" and a reasonable size (say 50 × 50 tiles).

Tip

Use the View menu's Background Color option to change the color from the default black to something like dark gray. This will help highlight areas of your map that have not been filled in with content.

To edit your map, just select the tile you want and then draw on the map window. To remove a tile, right-click in the top-right tile panel to select no tile, and then draw over the area you want to erase. There are plenty of other features in Tile Studio, so feel free to play around with it.

Tip

When editing a map, you'll find it annoying to have to select tiles from the bottom row all the time. An equivalent shortcut is to right-click on an existing tile on the map. This will select that tile as the current one. You'll find this a much faster method of editing.

Once you have a map created, the next step is to get the data into your game. To do that, you first need to export the map data out of Tile Studio.

Exporting Maps

One of the issues with using map editors is that they tend to use file formats designed for bigger systems. If you export all the data for a 50 × 50 map from Tile Studio, it can easily be 40 KB (or more). And that's for one map! If you make a game with 10 levels, you'll have serious JAR space issues. Thankfully, Tile Studio has an excellent customizable export system (Code Generator). You'll use this to export the data in a more suitable format.

To create a custom export, you need to create a TSD (*Tile Studio Definition*) file. A TSD is a text file containing instructions on the format of the file that you want to make. For details on exactly what you can control, I recommend taking a look at the Tile Studio tutorial. For the purposes of *Star Assault*, you'll export the map data as a series of tile numbers (separated by spaces). Here's the TSD to do this:

```
#file levels.dat
#tileset
#map
!<MapIdentifier>~<MapWidth:"%2d"><MapHeight:"%2d">
#mapdata
<TSMidTile:"%2d">
#end mapdata
#end map
#end tileset
#end file
```

Caution

Don't be tempted to indent your TSD files as you would with source code. This isn't valid, and it will cause the TSD compiler to report (rather obscure) errors.

To create a new TSD, just place a file containing this text into the directory where you installed Tile Studio. To select it as the current exporter, restart Tile Studio, hit Shift+F10, and select your TSD from the drop-down list. To export the current map, you can then just hit F10. The exporter will create a file named levels.dat (as specified in the TSD file) based on the contents of the map you're editing. Here's an excerpt from the generated file for the two Star Assault levels.:

```
!Level1~5050 0 0 0 0 0 0 0 0 0 0 0 0 0 0 0 0 0 0 0 0 0 0 0 0 0 0 0 0 0 0 0 0 0 ...
!Level2~3030 0 0 0 0 0 0 0 0 0 0 0 0 0 0 0 0 0 0 0 0 0 0 0 0 0 0 0 0 0 0 0 0 0 ...
```

As you can see, this file format is very simple. The exclamation mark is used to indicate the start of the level name string, and tilde (~) terminates it. Immediately following this is the number of tiles wide and high. All the rest of the numbers are the entries corresponding to all the tiles on the map.

The resulting file is around 8 KB, which is still too large for your purposes. Thankfully, though, the compression (ZIP) used by JAR files reduces this to a far more acceptable 400 bytes. Not bad for two levels.

Note

It is possible to reduce this size even more. One method is to apply a simple run-length encoding algorithm. To do this, you could save a tile number and run-length value for the repeating values. For example, if the file contained a series of 20 tile 0s in a row (which is quite common), you could save that as the tile number, 0, and then a 20. When you re-create the map, you interpret the values and place 20 of that tile type in the map.

This is quite a simple thing to implement; after doing so, you get results of around 600 bytes (down from 8000) for the original map file. After JAR compression, the size is around 250 bytes. It all sounds good, but frankly, I found it not worth the added complexity, code, and mess of converting files to save only 150 bytes on each map in the end.

Loading Maps

Loading the map from this file format is pretty easy. In the following code, you read through the file until you get to the correct level and then load all the byte data for the tiles that make up that level. The result is a tileMap array containing all of the entries for the map.

Here's the World class's level loader from *Star Assault*. You can see a complete example of this working in the MapEditedWorld directory under the Chapter 11 source code directory on the CD.

```
/**
 * Loads a level from the map data file using its name as the key.
 * @param levelName The name of the level to load.
 */
public void loadLevel(String levelName)
{
    try
    {
```

The levels.dat file contains the data for all the levels in the game. The first step is to load this file and create an input stream.

```
InputStream is = null;
is = this.getClass().getResourceAsStream("/levels.dat");
```

Since there are many levels in the one file, you need to read through the file checking the level name strings until you reach the named level (the parameter to the method call). The actual reading of a string is done by the readString method (shown next).

```
boolean foundLevel = false;

// Loop through until you get to the correct level.
int b = is.read();
while (b != -1 && !foundLevel)
{
    // Level name starts with a ! and terminates with a ~ character.
    // The readString method wraps up reading the string from the
    // stream.
    if (b == '!')
    {
        // Got a start of level name char, read the name string.
        String ln = readString(is, (byte) '~').toLowerCase();

        if (ln.equals(levelName.toLowerCase()))
            foundLevel = true;
    }

    // If the level hasn't been found yet you continue reading.
    if (!foundLevel)
        b = is.read();
}
// Test if the end of the file was reached, in which case the level
// load failed (possibly because of the wrong level name being used).
if (b == -1)
    throw new Exception("unknown level: " + levelName);
```

After reading through the level names, you're now positioned at the start of the level data for the map you want. The first step is to read the width and height variables and then construct a corresponding byte array (tileMap).

```
// Load the level. Start by reading the height and width from the file.

byte[] buffer = new byte[2];
is.read(buffer);
String tws = new String(buffer, 0, 2);
is.read(buffer);
String ths = new String(buffer, 0, 2);
tilesWide = Integer.parseInt(tws);
```

```
tilesHigh = Integer.parseInt(ths);

tileMap = new byte[tilesHigh][tilesWide];
```

Next you read all the tiles into the tile map. Each tile is represented by 2 bytes (tile numbers can go up to a maximum of 99). The data is read into a 2 byte buffer and then added to the tile map.

```
int bytesRead=0;

for (int ty=0; ty < tilesHigh; ty++)
{
    for (int tx = 0; tx < tilesWide; tx++)
    {
        bytesRead = is.read(buffer);
        if (bytesRead > 0)
        {
            tws = new String(buffer, 0, 2).trim();
            if (tws.indexOf("-") != -1)
                // If this starts throwing exceptions when loading the map
                // check that the tile indecies in your map file doesn't
                // have -1's in it. This is the default index for the
                // empty tile in TileStudio. Always fill your levels with
                // blank (NO_TILE) entries before editing it.
                System.out.println("Oops, read a - at " + tx + ", " + ty);

            byte c = Byte.parseByte(tws);
            if (c == PLAYERSTART_TILE)
            {
                playerShip.setX(tx * TILE_WIDTH);
                playerShip.setY(ty * TILE_HEIGHT);
            } else
            {
                // All other tiles are handled either as walls or
                // activators.
                tileMap[ty][tx] = c;
            }
        }
    }
}
```

```
    catch (Exception e)
    {
        System.out.println("Exception loading map file : " + e);
        e.printStackTrace();
    }
}
```

The readString method takes an input stream and keeps reading bytes until it hits the specified terminator character. It then returns the string of characters read up to that point as a String object. Again, this belongs in the World class.

```
private String readString(InputStream is, byte terminator)
{
    try
    {
        StringBuffer sb = new StringBuffer();
        int b = is.read();
        while (b != -1)
        {
            if (b == terminator)
            {
                return sb.toString();
            } else
                sb.append((char)b);

            b = is.read();
        }

        return null;
    }

    catch(IOException e)
    {
        System.out.println("IOException: " + e);
        e.printStackTrace();
        return null;
    }
}
```

And that's it! You're now ready to load a level by calling the loadLevel method, such as from a GameScreen startNewLevel method.

Other Editors

Those are the basics of editing and then loading a map into your game. As you can imagine, though, building mapping and other editing tools can go quite a bit further.

Map files are not the only level files you can have. If you want to externally manage other aspects of the game, such as special event triggers, story lines, or object properties, consider adding another resource file type for the job. You don't have to have an editor to support it; just use a text editor for simple files. As well as improving your code base (by keeping it abstracted from the specifics of your game data) you'll find other members of your team can participate more fully in the development process because they have the power to edit that much more of the game content without pestering the all-important programmer.

Finally, after you develop a few games (don't try this on your first one), consider devoting some time to writing your own editing tools. Nothing will be more powerful or flexible than an editor dedicated to your engine's capabilities.

Advanced Object Management

Now that you have your level editing worked out, you can start to populate the game with lots of content, which inevitably means lots of actors. Through the use of activator tiles, you've dramatically reduced the total number of actors because now you don't need to bother creating actors until the player is near them. However, there can still be quite a few actors flying around when the action gets heavy. In addition, the weapons you added in the previous chapter are going to mean there are a lot more bullet-type actors floating around. Having this many actors introduces a few more challenges for you to solve.

The first problem you'll encounter is when you try to construct all these objects. It's a hopelessly slow process under J2ME (on pretty much all MIDs), so it will slow down the game overall. In the case of weapons fire, this will introduce a noticeable lag between when the player hits a key and when he sees a bullet appear.

The second issue relates to cleaning up all those objects when you've finished with them. The garbage collector process will be working overtime to clear out all those dead enemy and bullet objects. Because there can be literally hundreds created in a short time span, the garbage collector can drag the performance of the game down with it.

Finally, one of the most common errors encountered with J2ME games is the dreaded OutOfMemory exception. The number one reason this happens is excessive object construction, which in turn creates fragmentation in the available heap memory. Even if you're carefully managing your objects and memory, excessive object construction will cause memory issues. It won't happen overnight, but it will happen.

Unfortunately, if your game is constructing many objects, these issues simply do not go away. The only solution is the most obvious—don't construct objects. Take a look at how to avoid object construction using another method of managing your actors, known as *object pooling*.

Object Pooling

If you think about your problem with constructing objects, you'll see that the normal way of doing things is pretty silly. Object construction is an expensive exercise, yet every time the ships fire you're constructing a `Bullet` actor. The bullet then flies around for a while before being cleared (at some point) by the garbage collector. Your game repeats this process again and again.

Consider something else about the nature of weapons fire in your game. How many bullets would you say would be flying around at the height of the action? Something like 20 is probably about right; after that, things would be too confusing on the screen to notice more—and you'd likely be running in the opposite direction anyway.

The basic concept of using object pooling is to create a set (or pool) of objects which are then handed out upon request. Instead of constructing an object, you grab an existing one from the pool and then initialize it as though it were a new one. For example, to fire a bullet, you would get a `Bullet` object from the pool and then reset its position, speed, animation state, and other parameters to starting values. For all intents and purposes, the object would look and feel like a newly constructed one. When you're finished (the bullet has expired or hit something), you set it to be invisible and uncollidable and then tell the pool that the object is available again. The end result is that you only need to construct the objects for your pool once, rather than every time they're used, and there's never any need to remove them from memory, so the garbage collector is no problem.

Object pooling isn't all good news, though, and it's not suitable for all cases. For example, at this point you might be asking yourself what happens if the number of objects you need exceeds the number in the pool. The choices are to expand the pool to meet the requirement, constructing a new object along the way; to deny access to a new object, which has to be properly handled by your code; or to forcibly reuse an object that's already been handed out.

Take the example of the bullets in your world. If you were to create a pool of 20 bullets (quite a practical number, actually), what would you do in a case where a ship tries to fire a twenty-first bullet? You can use any of the options I've mentioned quite effectively for enemy weapons fire; however, if it's the player trying to fire, then having nothing come out the other end isn't really an option. This leaves you with either reusing another bullet object or constructing a new one. Before you decide which method to use, consider another problem.

Using the activator tile system in your game, the player will slowly encounter more and more enemies. The general idea is that the player will fly onto the screen, thus triggering the activators and causing ships and turrets to be grabbed from the pool and initialized. The player then destroys them (releasing them back to the pool) before continuing. However, there are situations in which the player might not bother (or need to) destroy the enemy. In a large level, you can quickly see how you'll end up with quite a few actors lying about, basically doing nothing until the level ends. Although there are other potential solutions to this problem, such as timing enemy actors out automatically, you'll still end up having to construct new actors because the pool empties. The easier method is to simply reuse the oldest object in the pool. This way, you'll avoid constructing new objects and force your game to stay within an acceptable limit.

All right, enough background. Take a look at how to code an object pooling system for *Star Assault*.

Linked Lists

The primary thing your object pooling system has to handle is storing references to all the objects in the pool, and then handing them out on request. One method to do this would be to store the references in a Vector object kept inside the object pool, and then just mark the object as it is used. To release the object, you just find it in the vector and mark it as available again.

Can you spot the problem with this? To find an available object, you need to traverse the entire vector! Consider your drawing, cycling, and collision detection code as well. You need to cycle any actors currently in use; however, this number typically is very small compared to the total number in the pool. Looking through the entire vector on every cycle is a horrible waste of time. More to the point, there's just no need to cycle every actor if most of them aren't currently in use.

Vectors are also a pretty slow method of accessing objects anyway. They're slow to traverse and even slower to update.

To get around this, think about what you really need to do to manage a basic object pool. Get a free object, release it back, and traverse the list. The key here is that you don't need to directly access any particular object in the list. The best storage method therefore is to use a *linked list*.

A linked list is like a chain of objects. The first object stores a reference to the second; the second stores a reference to the third; and so on. If you start at the first object (known as the *head*), you can traverse the list by looking at each object's reference to the next one. You can see this illustrated in Figure 11.11.

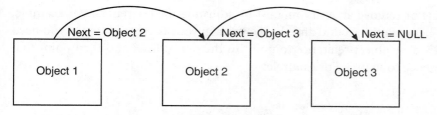

Figure 11.11 A linked list is a chain of linked-between objects.

To implement a simple linked list system for your Actor objects, you can simply add a next object reference to the class, along with methods to access and change it.

```
private Actor nextLinked;            // link to next actor if we're in a list

public final Actor getNextLinked()
{
    return nextLinked;
}
public final void setNextLinked(Actor nextLinked)
{
    this.nextLinked = nextLinked;
}
```

You can then add objects to the end of the list by setting the next-object values. For example:

```
Actor actor1 = new Actor();
Actor actor2 = new Actor();
Actor actor3 = new Actor();

actor1.setNextLinked( actor2 );
actor2.setNextLinked( actor3 );
actor3.setNextLinked( null );
```

end code

To then traverse the list, you simply follow the next reference trail, starting from the head of the list. For example:

begin code

```
Actor currentActor = actor1;
while(currentActor != null)
{
    System.out.print( currentActor.toString() + " " );
    currentActor = currentActor.getNextLinked();
}
```

Traversing a linked list is both very fast and simple.

You can also insert or remove an entry in a list by adjusting the references. For example, to insert an item between the second and third entries in your current example, you need to change item 2's next-object reference to point to the new object, and then point that object's next reference to item 3. For example:

```
Actor newActor = new Actor();
actor2.setNextLinked( newActor );
newActor.setNextLinked( actor3 );
```

To remove object newActor, you simply reverse the process by pointing actor2's next reference at actor3 (again) and setting newActor's next object reference to null. (See Figure 11.12.)

```
actor2.setNextLinked( actor3 );
newActor.setNextLinked( null );
```

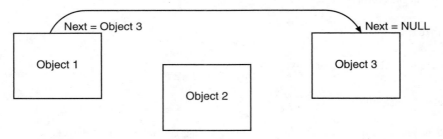

Figure 11.12 To remove an object from a linked list, you simply change the references to the object's prior and next links in the chain.

There's a slight problem, though. Removing b from the list is much easier because you know the structure of the list. In a typical game environment, though, you're not going to know that actor2 references newActor—all you'll have is newActor. To determine which item references newActor, you need to traverse the entire list!

The way around this is pretty easy: Have each object store not only a reference to the next object, but one to the previous object as well. You have two links to every object; hence, you call this a *doubly linked list*. To implement this, you just add a previous link to the Actor class.

```
private Actor prevLinked;                          // link to previous actor
public final Actor getPrevLinked()
{
    return prevLinked;
}
```

```
public final void setPrevLinked(Actor prevLinked)
{
    this.prevLinked = prevLinked;
}
```

Now when you adjust the list, you need to maintain both the next and previous references. For example:

```
Actor actor1 = new Actor();
Actor actor2 = new Actor();
Actor actor3 = new Actor();

actor1.setPrevLinked( null );
actor1.setNextLinked( actor2 );

actor2.setPrevLinked( actor1 );
actor2.setNextLinked( actor3 );

actor3.setPrevLinked( actor2 );
actor3.setNextLinked( null );
```

As a bonus, you can now traverse the list backward as well as forward.

```
Actor currentActor = actor3;
while(currentActor != null)
{
    System.out.print( currentActor.toString() + " " );
    currentActor = currentActor.getPrevLinked();
}
```

Mutually Exclusive Lists

All right, consider your object pooling system again. You now have a way of storing all the objects in the list. To create the object pool, you construct a bunch of objects you need and then hand them out upon request. This hand-out process also needs to keep track of which objects are currently in use. This is great, but in order to find a free object, you'll again have to traverse the entire list every time. If you have a reasonably large pool of objects, this is going to cost you in performance.

To get around this problem, you'll use two doubly linked lists as a mutually exclusive pair. Don't worry, it's simpler than it sounds. Basically, you'll have two linked lists—one for free objects and one for used objects. When you grab an object off the free list, all you have to do is adjust the references so that it appears on the used list, and vice versa. (See Figure 11.13.)

Free Objects

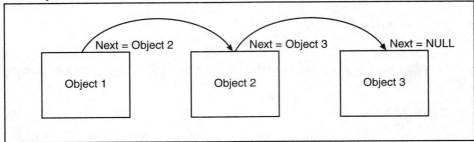

Used Objects

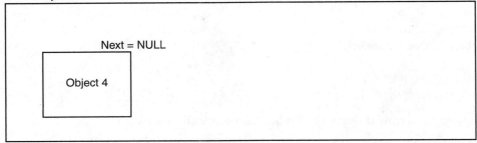

Figure 11.13 In a mutually exclusive linked list pair no object can exist in more than one list at any point in time.

Using this system, it's now blindingly fast to gain access to a free or used object. Before you look at the code for this, I need to cover one more thing.

Tracking Object Use

There's one final thing your object pooling system needs. As I mentioned in the introduction, you might run out of objects. In other words, the pool might reach a point at which it has already handed out all it has available, but then another request comes in. At this point, you might have decided the best method is to forcibly reuse the object that has been in use the longest—the one least likely to still be on the screen. One minor issue, though: How do you keep track of which object has been out the most time?

To do this, you don't need to do any fancy timing or other tricks. When you first hand out an object, you consider that one the oldest. In the release code, you check to see whether the object returning to the pool is what you considered the oldest. If it is, you set the current first item on the list to be the oldest, and so on.

Take a look at the complete code to implement your actor pooling system.

The Actor Pool Class

To make all this work, let's wrap up the two doubly linked lists and the tracking of the oldest object in use into a complete class for actor pooling. Here's the final code:

```
public class ActorPool
{
```

The firstFree and lastFree members are used to track the head and tail of the free list. Similarly, the firstUsed and lastUsed is for the Actor currently "checked out" by the game. oldestUsed is a special variable used to track which is the oldest actor handed out, and the first object to be discarded if too many objects are in use at any one point in time.

```
    private Actor firstFree;      // ref to the head of the free actor list
    private Actor lastFree;
    private Actor firstUsed;      // ref to the head of the used list (oldest)
    private Actor oldestUsed;
    private Actor lastUsed;
```

To construct an ActorPool you pass in an array of previously constructed objects (the pool won't construct them for you).

```
    public ActorPool(Actor[] initObjects)
    {
        if (initObjects == null || initObjects.length < 2)
            return;

        // initialize the linked list of free objects
```

If the caller passed in a list of objects, these are added to the list. The first object in the array is the firstFree item in the free list and the last item is the lastFree.

```
        firstFree = initObjects[0];
        lastFree = initObjects[initObjects.length - 1];
```

The constructor now loops through all the objects in the array and creates the doubly linked list chain.

```
        for (int i = 0; i < initObjects.length; i++)
        {
```

If this is not the last object in the list, you set this object's link to the next object to point to the next object in the array. Otherwise the next link is set to null making it the end of the list.

```
            if (i < initObjects.length - 1)
                initObjects[i].setNextLinked(initObjects[i + 1]);
            else
                initObjects[i].setNextLinked(null);
```

If this is not the first object, you set the link to the previous object to be the one prior to this one in the array. If it is first, the prior reference is set to null (start of the list).

```
        if (i > 0)
            initObjects[i].setPrevLinked(initObjects[i - 1]);
        else
            initObjects[i].setPrevLinked(null);
    }
}
```

This method returns the next free actor from the available object pool (the free list). It then marks that object as used by removing it (unlinking) from the free list and appending it onto the used list. If there are no available free actors, the oldest used actor is handed out instead.

```
public Actor getNextFree()
{
```

First you check if there are any actors in the free list. If firstFree is null that means there's none left.

```
    if (firstFree != null)
    {
```

Since you have a free actor available on the free list you need to now remove it from the free list and append it to the used list. To do this there are a series of cases you need to deal with to clean up the reference links.

If there is another actor after the first one on the free list (because the firstFree's reference to the next reference is not null) then you need to cancel the next actor's reference to the first one. In other words, the second actor on the free list has a reference back to the first actor. That reference needs to be set to null now since the first object is being removed from the list. (This might seem a little confusing at first, but try to keep up as this type of operation is repeated many times managing linked lists.)

```
        // if there's an actor linked next after firstFree you set the second
        // actor's reference back to the first to null.
        if (firstFree.getNextLinked() != null)
            firstFree.getNextLinked().setPrevLinked(null);
```

Next you grab a reference to the next object on the free list (after the first one). Later you'll set this as the firstFree object. If the next reference is null (there is no next) that's okay, you'll just be setting firstFree to null, which indicates there are no more free objects.

```
        Actor newFirstFree = firstFree.getNextLinked();
```

Now begins the process of adding the firstFree actor onto the used list. Since the firstFree actor is appending onto the end of the used list, the firstFree's next object reference is set to null.

```
// now link this actor onto the end of the used list
firstFree.setNextLinked(null);
if (lastUsed != null)
{
```

If there are any items on the used list already then lastUsed will not be null. In that case the firstFree actor is now the end of the list so you make adjustments by setting the lastUsed actor to have a next actor reference to the firstFree, and then set lastUsed to be the new end of the list (firstFree).

```
    firstFree.setPrevLinked(lastUsed);
    lastUsed.setNextLinked(firstFree);
}
lastUsed = firstFree;
```

Next the oldestUsed reference is updated to be firstFree if you didn't previously have a lastUsed reference (it was null). This only happens if there were no entries on the used list.

```
if (oldestUsed == null)
    oldestUsed = firstFree;
```

Likewise, if there is no first used actor (the head of the used list) then firstFree, the newly added used list object, is set to be the head of the used list.

```
if (firstUsed == null)
    firstUsed = firstFree;
```

Next you need to check for a case where you're handing out the last actor on the free list. If so the lastFree reference (the tail of the free list) is set to null.

```
// if we're giving out the last one then clear lastFree
if (lastFree == firstFree)
    lastFree = null;
```

Everything is now done for this case. The previously set newFirstFree, which is either the actor after firstFree (it's next) or null, in this case is the end of the free list. The firstFree actor, having now been properly placed into the used list is now returned to the caller.

```
    Actor r = firstFree;
    firstFree = newFirstFree;

    return r;
}
```

Next is the case where there are no free actors on the free list. In this case you need to return the actor that's been handed out the longest (oldestUsed).

```
Actor actorToReturn = oldestUsed;
if (oldestUsed == null)
{
```

If oldestUsed is null that means the entire used list has been traversed (by subsequent calls to this method). In that case you start again at the top of the used list.

```
oldestUsed = firstUsed;
actorToReturn = oldestUsed;
}
```

Now make the oldest reference the one after the current oldest (since you're about to hand the current oldest reference out as an object). Note that you don't need to worry about moving this from the free list to the used list (like you did above) because this object is already on the used list.

```
oldestUsed = oldestUsed.getNextLinked();
return actorToReturn;
}
```

When an actor is no longer required in the game, such as when a bullet's lifetime has expired, or the player destroys an enemy ship, you need to release it back from the used list into the available pool (the free list).

```
public void release(Actor actorToRelease)
{
```

If the actor you want to release has a link to a previous actor (not the first on the used list), then that reference is no longer valid. This reference is changed to point to the actorToRemove's next reference effectively removing the actorToRemove object from the link chain.

```
if (actorToRelease.getPrevLinked() != null)
    // join the break in the used list
    actorToRelease.getPrevLinked().setNextLinked(
            actorToRelease.getNextLinked());
```

The same thing is done to the actorToRemove's next linked actor. Its link back to actorToRemove is changed to reference the one before actorToRemove.

```
if (actorToRelease.getNextLinked() != null)
    actorToRelease.getNextLinked().setPrevLinked(
            actorToRelease.getPrevLinked());
```

Next you check to see if the actor being released back to the free pool was the current oldest one. If so, the oldest reference is changed to be the actorToRelease's next linked actor.

```
if (oldestUsed == actorToRelease)
    oldestUsed = actorToRelease.getNextLinked();
```

If the actorToRelease was the head or tail of the used list, then you need to change the reference to the next (or previous) actor appropriately.

```
if (firstUsed == actorToRelease)
    firstUsed = actorToRelease.getNextLinked();
if (lastUsed == actorToRelease)
    lastUsed = actorToRelease.getPrevLinked();
```

That takes care of removing the actor from the used list. Now you can add it onto the end of the free list. Since it's going to be placed on the end, the first step is to set the actorToRelease's next actor reference to be null.

```
actorToRelease.setNextLinked(null);
```

Next you have to handle the special case where the free list is currently empty in which case the actorToRelease becomes the one and only entry on the free list.

```
if (firstFree == null)
{
    firstFree = actorToRelease;
    actorToRelase.setPrevLinked(null);
}
```

Now you need to add the actorToRelease onto the end of the free list. If there is already an entry on the end of the list, you make actorToRelease equal to lastFree and set the existing lastFree's next reference to be the new end of the list (actorToRelease).

```
if (lastFree != null)
{
    actorToRelease.setPrevLinked(lastFree);
    lastFree.setNextLinked(actorToRelease);
}
else
    actorToRelease.setPrevLinked(null);

lastFree = actorToRelease;
}
```

That's the basics of our actor pooling system out of the way. To see the complete class check the ActorPool.java file in the Chapter 11 source code directory on the CD. (For a working example of actor pooling, look at the complete *Star Assault* project also on the CD.)

Adapting the World to Pooling

Now that you have an object pooling system available, you need to modify the world to use it. The first major change is to how you construct the bullets and ships. Instead of creating them on the fly, you'll construct a bunch of them when the world class constructs. Because you want to treat ships and bullets a little differently, later on you'll create a pool for each type.

Tip

Constructing the objects for your pool is a very slow process. To get around this delay, especially if you're dealing with more than 40 objects, you can have the pool construct objects on the fly as it needs them (up to a maximum). This also serves to keep the number of actors to exactly what's required, which in turn reduces overall memory use.

The only downside of this is the delay created when the pool constructs the objects, such as firing bullets. If you're dealing with a small number and you're reasonably sure of the maximum number of objects the player will encounter, then pre-create them.

If neither system is quite right for you, consider using a hybrid. Have the pool create a minimum starting number of objects, and then dynamically construct more as required (up to a maximum).

```
private ActorPool enemyShipPool;
private ActorPool bulletPool;
public World(int tilesWideArg, int tilesHighArg, int viewWidthArg,
                int viewHeightArg){

    ...

    // construct the object's pools for ships and bullets
    Ship ships[] = new Ship[20];
    for (int i = 0; i < ships.length; i++)
        ships[i] = new Ship(this);
    enemyShipPool = new ActorPool(ships);

    Bullet bullets[] = new Bullet[20];
    for (int i = 0; i < bullets.length; i++)
        bullets[i] = new Bullet(this);
    bulletPool = new ActorPool(bullets);
}
```

To gain access to the pool, add some convenience methods. For example:

```
public final Bullet getBulletFromPool()
{
    return (Bullet)bulletPool.getNextFree();
}

public final void releaseBullet(Bullet b)
{
    bulletPool.release(b);
}

public final Ship getEnemyShipFromPool()
{
    return (Ship) enemyShipPool.getNextFree();
}

public final void releaseShip(Ship s)
{
    enemyShipPool.release(s);
}
```

The next change to the world is how you handle actor construction. Instead of creating a new object each time, you acquire an old one and clean it up by reinitializing (because you can't be sure where it's been). To handle this, the actors need to move much of their setup code out of the constructor and into an init method. To fire a bullet, for example, you grab it from the pool and then call the init method. (See the *Star Assault* project source code on the CD for the Ship and Bullet class for a complete example of the init method.)

```
int[] nosePos = Actor.getProjectedPos(getCenterX(), getCenterY(),
                                      getDirection(), 12);
// get a bullet from the pool and init it to what we want
Bullet newBullet = getWorld().getBulletFromPool();
newBullet.init(nosePos[0], nosePos[1], getDirection());
```

Next take a look at the updated drawing code based on pooling. The main change here is to traverse the linked list, rather than using a vector. Note also that you're only traversing the used actors list, not the free one, so only actors used in the game will be drawn. (The same also applies to the cycle and collision detection code.)

```
Actor ship = enemyShipPool.getFirstUsed();
while (ship != null)
{
```

```
        if (Tools.isPointInRect(ship.getX(), ship.getY(), viewX - TILE_WIDTH,
                                viewY - TILE_HEIGHT, tw * TILE_WIDTH,
                                th * TILE_HEIGHT))
            ship.render(g, viewX, viewY);
        ship = ship.getNextLinked();
    }


Actor bullet = bulletPool.getFirstUsed();
while (bullet != null)
{
    if (Tools.isPointInRect(bullet.getX(), bullet.getY(), viewX - TILE_WIDTH,
                            viewY - TILE_HEIGHT, tw * TILE_WIDTH,
                            th * TILE_HEIGHT))
        bullet.render(g, viewX, viewY);
    bullet = bullet.getNextLinked();
}
```

Similarly, you need to modify collision detection and cycling to use the pools. Again, this all belongs in the World class.

```
protected final void cycle()
{
    if (lastCycleTime > 0)
    {
        long msSinceLastCycle = System.currentTimeMillis() - lastCycleTime;
```

The following code is the main change to the world's cycle method. Again, instead of looping through a vector, you traverse the linked list.

```
        Actor a = enemyShipPool.getFirstUsed();
        while (a != null)
        {
            a.cycle(msSinceLastCycle);
            a = a.getNextLinked();
        }
```

The same applies to the bullets list: traverse each link in the list until you get a null.

```
        // now cycle all the bullets (we only cycle used ones)
        Actor bullet = bulletPool.getFirstUsed();
        while (bullet != null)
        {
```

```
        bullet.cycle(msSinceLastCycle);
        bullet = bullet.getNextLinked();
      }
    }

    lastCycleTime = System.currentTimeMillis();
}
```

The collision detection code is again basically the same; you just add the linked list loop,

```
public final boolean checkCollision(Actor hitter, int x, int y, int w, int h)
{

    ...

    // if this is the playerShip then we check if we hit another
    // enemy ship (we don't care if enemy ships hit each other)
    if (hitter == playerShip)
    {
        Actor a = enemyShipPool.getFirstUsed();
        while (a != null)
        {
            if (a.isCollidable && a.isCollidingWith(playerShip))
            {
                a.onCollision(playerShip);
                playerShip.onCollision(a);
                return true;
            }
            a = a.getNextLinked();
        }
    }

    return false;
}
```

The code I've presented so far is only an example of what's required for a complete game. Take a look at the complete *Star Assault* project on the CD to see how this can all come together in a game.

Conclusion

As you've seen, the construction and management of your game's world is a significant development task. Through the use of a tile engine, you were able to dramatically increase the performance of the game world by replacing static actors with much simpler tiles.

In this chapter you also saw how to generate level content for your games using static arrays, random generators, and map editors. These techniques should serve you for creating a huge variety of games.

In the next chapter, you'll look at how you can bring all the tools you've created so far into the structure of a game.

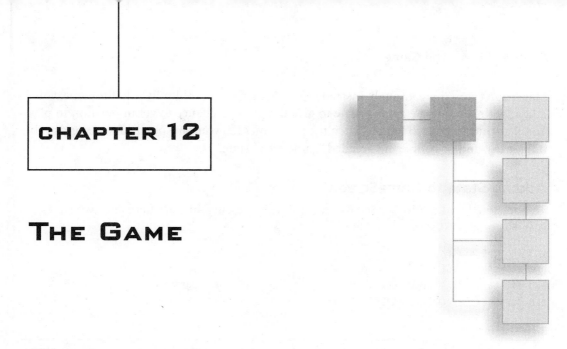

CHAPTER 12

THE GAME

I f you take the graphics, action, and world code you've developed so far, you have what seems to be most of the tools you need for your game. There's still something missing, though. For want of a better term, you can think of that something as the glue that turns a bunch of classes into the game.

In this chapter, you'll bring everything together by adding game state, persistence (save games), and the concept of the game's primary actor—the player's star fighter. By the time you're done, *Star Assault* will start looking like a real game.

The Game Screen

As you saw in past examples, the GameScreen class serves as the primary controller of your game play. In the following sections, you'll expand the functionality of this class to support different states, the player's ship (including damage and lives), and saving and loading the game.

To start with, take a look at how to better manage the state of the game.

Game State

To make *Star Assault* a professional-quality game, you need to add support for some additional game states. A *state* is just a mode in which you place the game to handle different game situations. A good example of two states is playing (normal game play) and paused (where the game just treads water while waiting to return to the play state).

States don't stop there, though. Instead of throwing the player blindly into the game, you'll add a "get ready for the action" state to give the player a chance to get in position to play. You'll also add a state to handle when the player dies (so you can spend a few seconds rubbing it in), and of course the dreaded "game over" state.

Adding State to GameScreen

To add state handling to GameScreen, start by adding a current state field and two states—PLAYING and PAUSED.

```
private int state;
private static int t=0;
public static final int PLAYING = t++;        // game in progress
public static final int PAUSED = t++;         // paused
```

Tip

Notice the use of the incrementing integer t for the state types. This is just an easy way to add and remove entries in the list without having to renumber them.

You'll also add a convenience method to change the state of the game.

```
public final void setState(int newState)
{
    state = newState;
}
```

To implement the various states, you need to next move the thread construction code and run method from the application class in the GameScreen class.

```
public class GameScreen extends Canvas implements Runnable, CommandListener
{
    ...

    private boolean running;
    private int state;

    public GameScreen(StarAssault midlet)
    {
        ...

        // create the game thread
```

```
        Thread t = new Thread(this);
        t.start();
    }
```

An example `run` method now able to handle a new "paused" state is coded below. This method replaces the existing `GameScreen` `cycle` method previously called by the application class's `cycle` method (which is also no longer necessary).

```
public void run()
{
    try
    {
        while(running)
        {
            // remember the starting time
            cycleStartTime = System.currentTimeMillis();

            if (state != PAUSED)
            {
                world.cycle();
                repaint();
                ...
                // sleep if we've finished our work early
                timeSinceStart = System.currentTimeMillis() - cycleStartTime;

                if (timeSinceStart < MS_PER_FRAME)
                {
                    synchronized (this)
                    {
                        wait(MS_PER_FRAME - timeSinceStart);
                    }
                }
                else
                    Thread.yield();

            } else          // PAUSED
            {
                // just hang around sleeping if we are paused
                try
                {
                    Thread.sleep(500);
                }
```

```
            catch (java.lang.InterruptedException e)
            {
            }
        }
    }

    ...
```

This modified version of the run method checks to see whether you're in the paused state before doing any rendering or cycling. If the game is paused, you just sleep for short amounts of time, waiting for the state to return to normal.

This is only the start of your state code. Next, add a state that gives the player a small amount of time before you start the game.

```
public static final int STARTING_UP = t++;
```

To implement this, you need to change the run method so that when the game is in this state the world and actors are rendered, but nothing is cycled. This way, the player will be able to see what's going on, but nothing will move. After a timeout (say three seconds), you'll switch into the PLAYING state, and off they'll go.

Before you look at the changes to the run method, add support for the timeout of this state. You'll find that knowing how long you've been in a state is a pretty common requirement, so you should add some generic support to the GameScreen class.

```
private long timeStateChanged;

public final void setState(int newState)
{
    state = newState;
    timeStateChanged = System.currentTimeMillis();
}
```

Now take a look at the revised run method to support the starting-up state. Notice I've separated the handling of the rendering (repaint) and cycling code. You only cycle if the game is underway, but you always render (unless the game is paused).

```
public void run()
{
    try
    {
        while (running)
        {
            ...
```

```
        // run the cycle (only if they're playing)
        if (state == PLAYING)
          world.cycle();

        if (state == STARTING_UP)
        {
            long timeSinceStateChange = System.currentTimeMillis() -
                                        timeStateChanged;
            if (timeSinceStateChange > 3000)
                setState(PLAYING);
        }
```

Note that we don't bother drawing when in the paused state because it takes too much processing power. The screen won't be blank though, the last rendered screen will stay on the screen (unless something else is drawn over the top, such as the menus).

```
        // always draw unless we're paused
        if (state != PAUSED)
        {
            repaint();


            ...
```

So how do you use the starting-up state? Well, first you set it to be the initial state when the player starts the game, but it's really more for when the player starts a new game or life and he needs a moment to gather his bearings. You'll see all of this in action a little later in the chapter—along with some additional states such as "game over" and "dying"—when you handle the death of the player's ship.

The Primary Actor

Star Assault involves the player piloting his ship around an alien maze of doom, wreaking as much havoc as possible. His ship, a Hurricane-class deep-space assault fighter, is just another type of actor. However, because it's the player, there's a clear relationship between the ship and the game screen (the controller of game play).

The first thing you need to do is create the player's ship and ensure that you keep a solid reference to it. You can do all this inside the GameScreen constructor.

```
private Ship playerShip;
public GameScreen()
{
    // create the world and playerShip
    world = new World(screenWidth, screenHeight);
```

Note here I'm using a new version of the `Ship` constructor that takes only the `World` argument. The `init` method now takes care of setting the type and position. You can see a complete example in the final *Star Assault* source code on the CD.

```
playerShip = new Ship(world);
playerShip.init(Ship.PLAYER_SHIP, 0, 0);

world.setPlayerShip(playerShip);

...
}
```

You need to add a `setPlayerShip` method (and corresponding field) to the `World` class for this to work.

```
/**
 * @param a The Actor object that represents the player in the game.
 */
public final void setPlayerShip(Ship a)
{
    playerShip = a;
}
```

The `World` class now differentiates between regular actors and the primary, so you need to modify the rendering, cycling, and collision detection to accommodate this. For example, you'll need to specifically render the player actor last in the `World` render method.

Notice the `PLAYER_SHIP` constant I'm using in the `init` method called from the revised `Game-Screen` constructor above? This is so you can differentiate between the different types of ships you want. Next you'll see how to create player (and enemy) ship types.

Ship Types

In *Star Assault* you have a number of different types of ship class actors flying around the game. The simplest is the drone; it's something like a floating mine. The challenge for the player is to simply avoid hitting it. This is a good type of enemy for introducing the player to the game because it doesn't fight back. The next enemy type, the turret, is a stationary gun that is able to turn 360 degrees and fire at the player. The turret can detect the player's presence and turn toward him. Finally, the fighter is just like a turret except it can fly around as well. The player's ship is basically the same as the fighter, but with slightly modified specs to make it a little bit faster and more maneuverable.

If you were developing this in a normal environment, you would use quite a few classes to represent all these capabilities. For example, I would create a `TargetingActor` class to represent the functionality of an actor being able to detect and target the player's ship. I would then extend this class to create `TurretActor` and `FighterActor` classes, and then I would add all the specific code for these ship types into overridden methods (drawing, special physics, custom AI). Finally, I'd create a `HurricaneActor` class to represent the player's ship. Wouldn't it be lovely? Unfortunately, I just wasted 5 to 10 KB of JAR space just on classes.

Classes are very expensive in terms of resources; you really have to think twice about creating one, which unfortunately means you have to ditch some of the tried and true practices of object-oriented development (such as extensive inheritance trees). For *Star Assault* you already have more classes than you'd think (`GameScreen`, `Actor`, `ActorPool`, `Sprite`, `ImageSet`, `Ship`, `Bullet`, `Tools` and the `World`), and you haven't yet added menus, splash screens, or resource handlers. Without even blinking, you can have 20 classes, minimum. Creating five classes just to represent different ship types isn't practical.

To get around this, you can go back to the tried and true method of using a type indicator to change the type of class being instantiated. This typically results in a bunch of nested `if` and `switch` blocks spread throughout the code, which, as you can imagine, can quickly turn into a mess. If things start to get too unruly, consider adding another class or two if you really think it's worth it.

Adding types to your actors is pretty easy. You simply put a type field and methods to access it in the `Actor` class.

```
abstract public class Actor
{

    ...
    public static final int SHIP_START = 0;
```

If you later want to move the ship indices for some reason (such as making room for other actor types), you can do so simply by adjusting this `SHIP_START` value.

```
    public static final int PLAYER_SHIP = SHIP_START + 1;
```

The following order of ship types is important. For example, to detect if a ship is an enemy, you test if its type value is between the `ENEMY_SHIP_START` and `ENEMY_SHIP_END` values.

```
    public static final int ENEMY_SHIP_START = SHIP_START + 2;
    public static final int ENEMY_AI_START = SHIP_START + 3;

    public static final int ENEMY_FIGHTER = SHIP_START + 4;
    public static final int SHIP_END = SHIP_START + 5;
```

Notice I've also added a new range type ENEMY_AI_START. This is used later in the cycle code to only carry out AI operations for enemy ships. If you later add different enemy types (such as those in the next section), you can change whether they use the AI code, or remain dumb.

```
public static final int BULLET_START = 1000;
public static final int PLASMA_CANNON = BULLET_START + 1;
public static final int BULLET_END = BULLET_START + 2;

private int type;     // type of actor (instead of subclassing)

public final int getType()
{
    return type;
}

public final void setType(int type)
{
    this.type = type;
}


    ...


}
```

Are you wondering why I'm doing this in the Actor class and not the Ship class? This is so you can differentiate between all Actor class types without having to use the unbelievable slow instanceof operator. There are plenty of cases in which you'll want to know the type of a particular actor (most importantly, whether it's a Bullet or Ship class). Using the instanceof operator for this is a waste of precious CPU power. By moving the type into the Actor class, you can differentiate any class of Actor, as well as its subtypes. Add some methods to the Actor class to help with this.

```
public final boolean isEnemyShip()
{
    return (type > ENEMY_SHIP_START && type < SHIP_END);
}

public final boolean isBullet()
{
    return (type > BULLET_START && type < BULLET_END);
}
```

You can now determine whether an Actor is a Bullet or Ship simply by calling these methods, rather than using instanceof. In the section "The Shield Effect" later in this chapter, you'll see how you use this method to detect the type of collision that occurs.

Now that you have your type set up, you need to adjust the Ship class to take this into account. The following init method adds support for the four distinct types of ships in the game.

```java
public class Ship extends Actor
{

    ...

    /**
     * Initialize an instance of a ship. May be called at any time to reuse this
     * instance of the object as another type.
     */
    public final void init(int typeArg, int x, int y)
    {
```

This method starts by setting up some default values used by all the ship types.

```java
        int firingDelay = 500;
        int alignedDiv = 16;
        int thrust = 0;
        int speed = 0;
        int maxVel = 0;
        int dir = 0;
        int bounceVel = Actor.FP_MINUS_05;
        int maxSpinRate = 23;
```

Next the actor type is set, then based on this type you make changes to the default values. The enemy fighter for example has a slower speed, maximum velocity, firing rate, and thrust than the player's ship.

```java
        setType(typeArg);

        switch (getType())
        {
            case PLAYER_SHIP:
                shipSprite = new Sprite(yellowShipImageSet, 0, 0);
                speed = 2;
                maxVel = 2;
                thrust = 2;
                break;
```

```
        case ENEMY_FIGHTER:
            shipSprite = new Sprite(redShipImageSet, 0, 0);
            speed = 1;
            maxVel = 1;
            thrust = 1;
            firing = true;
            firingDelay = 2000;
            break;
    }
    super.init(null, x, y, thrust, speed, maxVel, dir, alignedDiv,
            bounceVel, maxSpinRate);
}


    ...


}
```

Expanding the Enemy

Now that you have different ship types you can add some extra flavor to the game by introducing the Drone (a dumb floating mine) and the Turret (a sort-of fixed position fighter that will turn and shoot at the player). To support this you'll need to add extra types to the Actor class.

```
public static final int ENEMY_SHIP_START = SHIP_START + 2;
public static final int ENEMY_DRONE = SHIP_START + 3;
public static final int ENEMY_AI_START = SHIP_START + 4;
public static final int ENEMY_TURRET = SHIP_START + 5;
public static final int ENEMY_FIGHTER = SHIP_START + 6;
public static final int SHIP_END = SHIP_START + 7;
```

Notice that I've left the ENEMY_DRONE outside of the ENEMY_AI_START range. This will ensure the drones don't come chasing after you!

The next change you need is to load up graphics to represent the new enemy. For the mine, I've used a six-frame spinning globe animation and a 16-direction turret gun looking thing (that's the technical name) for the turret.

Since all the code to load up and prepare the images is getting a little large, it's best to move it out into a separate Ship class setup method.

```
public final static void setup()
{
    Image shipImage = ImageSet.loadClippedImage("/ship.png", 0, 0);
```

Here is the new code to load up the drone images from the separate file mine.png. The turret frames are already within the ship.png file.

```
Image droneImage = ImageSet.loadClippedImage("/mine.png", 0, 0);

yellowShipImageSet = new ImageSet(16);
redShipImageSet = new ImageSet(16);
turretImageSet = new ImageSet(16);
droneSet = new ImageSet(1);

Image[] yellowDirImages = null;
Image[] redDirImages = null;
Image[] turretImages = null;
```

The drones and turret images are then extracted from the file images. The turret uses 16 states to represent the 16 directions it can face. The mine, however, only faces one direction, but has six frames of animation. The following code extracts these six frames (arranged in two rows of three tiles) and then sets the ImageSet to animation a complete cycle over an 800 millisecond period.

```
Image[] droneImages = ImageSet.extractFrames(droneImage,
                          0, 0, 3, 2, 16, 16);
droneSet.addState(droneImages, 800);

yellowDirImages = ImageSet.extractFrames(shipImage, 0, 0, 4, 4, 16, 16);
redDirImages = ImageSet.extractFrames(shipImage, 4 * 16, 0, 4, 4, 16, 16);
turretImages = ImageSet.extractFrames(shipImage, 8 * 16, 0, 4, 4, 16, 16);

for (int i = 0; i < 16; i++)
{
    Image[] yellowFrame = {yellowDirImages[i]};
    yellowShipImageSet.addState(yellowFrame, 0);

    Image[] redFrame = {redDirImages[i]};
    redShipImageSet.addState(redFrame, 0);
```

This is where the turret images are initialized in the same way the ship images are.

```
    Image[] turretFrame = {turretImages[i]};
    turretImageSet.addState(turretFrame, 0);
}
}
```

Next you need to add initialization code to the Ship class's init method to support the two new ship types.

```
public final void init(int typeArg, int x, int y)
{
    ...

    switch (getType())
    {
        ...

        case ENEMY_DRONE:
            shipSprite = new Sprite(droneSet, 0, 0);
            alignedDiv = 0;
            dir = Tools.getRand(0, 359);
            speed = maxVel = 1;
            thrustFP = 0;
            bounceVelFP = Actor.FP_MINUS_1;
            break;
        case ENEMY_TURRET:
            rechargeRate = 0;
            speed = 0;
            maxSpinRate = 5;
            firingDelay = 2000;
            shipSprite = new Sprite(turretImageSet, 0, 0);
            firing = true;
            break;
    }

    ...

    super.init(null, x, y, thrustFP, MathFP.toFP(speed),
                MathFP.toFP(maxVel), dir, alignedDiv,
                bounceVelFP, maxSpinRate);
}
```

To draw the new enemy types, you'll also need to update the Ship class's render method to detect the type and use the correct graphics.

```
public final void render(Graphics g, int offsetX, int offsetY)
{
```

Here's where you handle the special case enemy drone image; in all other cases you use the current ship sprite and set the direction to correspond to the correct frame. For the enemy drone, the sprite animation code will take care of animating the image as long as you call the sprite's cycle method.

```
if (getType() != ENEMY_DRONE)
{
    int s = MathFP.toInt(MathFP.div(MathFP.toFP(getDirection()),
                                    Actor.FP_225));
    if (s != shipSprite.getCurrentState())
        shipSprite.setState(s, false);
}

shipSprite.draw(g, getX() - offsetX, getY() - offsetY);
}
```

The drone relies on you calling the sprite object's cycle method so you'll need to add that call to the Ship classes cycle method.

```
public final void cycle(long elapsedTime)
{
    super.cycle(elapsedTime);

    if (getType() == ENEMY_DRONE)
        shipSprite.cycle(elapsedTime);
    ...
}
```

For a complete example of the new enemy types check the *Star Assault* project on the CD.

Dealing with Damage

I've got a personal thing about games in which you die due to a hit by a lone stray bullet. It's just not fair, damn it! (Smacks the machine.)

In *Star Assault*, you'll give the ships an extra chance by adding shielding. When the ship takes damage from collisions with enemy ships or bullets, you reduce the shield level by varying amounts. It's only when the energy level of the shield falls below zero that things get fatal. To make it fair, you'll give shields to the enemy as well (although they won't be as strong, of course).

Adding Energy

The first step to adding shielding is to add a current energy level to the Ship class.

```
private int energy;                    // current reactor core energy level
private int energyMax;                 // max level
private int rechargeRate;              // recharge rate (energy per sec)
private int msPerRecharge;             // how many MS to equal one recharge
private long msSinceLastRecharge;      // multicycle counter for recharge
```

A little overly complicated just for an energy level, isn't it? That's because you're going to make things a little more interesting by recharging the shields slowly over time. This lets the player take damage and, if required, withdraw from the fight for a moment (letting the shields power back up) before returning for more action.

The energy field represents the current level of shield power. The maximum level you'll let this reach is the current energyMax. The rechargeRate represents how fast you'll re-energize the shields. You use the other two fields to manage the recharge process.

The first thing you need to do to make this work is initialize the shield level. If you look at the code in the previous section, you'll notice I snuck it in already. The init method sets up the energy and energyMax fields based on the type of ship. You also set the recharge rate, along with the msPerRecharge field.

To recharge the shields, you modify the cycle code for the Ship to increment the energy level based on the recharge rate over time.

```
public final void cycle(long deltaMS)
{
    ...

    if (rechargeRate > 0 && energy < energyMax)
    {
        if (msSinceLastRecharge < msPerRecharge)
            msSinceLastRecharge += deltaMS;
        else
        {
            energy++;
            msSinceLastRecharge -= msPerRecharge;
            if (energy > energyMax) energy = energyMax;
        }
    }
}
```

Note that this code will give a shield to all ship types, including turrets and drones. The strength of that shield is set in the Ship class's init method based on the type. For example:

```
public final void init(int typeArg, int x, int y)
{
    ...

    energyMax = 1000;
    energy = energyMax;
    rechargeRate = 50;

    switch (getType())
    {
        ...
```

The ships all use the default values, except the enemy turret, which has a shield but no recharge.

```
        case ENEMY_TURRET:
            ...
            rechargeRate = 0;
            energyMax = 200;
            break;
    }

    if (rechargeRate > 0)
        msPerRecharge = 1000 / rechargeRate;

    ...
}
```

For convenience later, you should also add some access methods for the maximum and current energy levels.

```
public final int getEnergy()
{
    return energy;
}

public final int getEnergyMax()
{
    return energyMax;
}
```

The Shield Effect

Because the ships no longer explode when they're hit by weapons fire (or other ships), you need to give the player some other indication of the impact. To do this, you flash a circular shield that slowly fades away around the ship. The image frames for the shield effect are within the ship PNG (shown in Figure 12.1).

To add the shield effect to the Ship class, you first need to load the images and create a sprite.

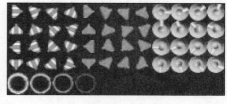

Figure 12.1 The ship.png also contains the four frames for the shield effect in the lower left-hand corner.

```
public class Ship extends Actor
{
    ...

    private static ImageSet shieldImageSet;
    private Sprite shieldSprite;

    ...

    public Ship(World worldArg)
    {
        super(worldArg);

        // load up the images (static) if we haven't done so already
        if (shieldImageSet == null)
            setup();
    }

    public final static void setup()
    {
        Image shipImage = ImageSet.loadClippedImage("/ship.png", 0, 0);
        Image[] shieldImages = null;
        shieldImages = ImageSet.extractFrames(shipImage, 0, 4 * 16, 4, 1, 20, 20);
        shieldImageSet.addState(shieldImages, 200);

        // init other images for ship
        ...
    }

    ...

}
```

Now you have the images ready, so it's time to get your shield effect going. The trigger you use is whenever the ship takes damage. You set a flag to indicate that you want to display the shields, and then use the sprite state to indicate when you should turn them off. For example, here's a new method for the Ship class:

```
public final void takeDamage(int damageLevel)
{
    energy -= damageLevel;
    showShields = true;
}
```

This method is also decrementing the energy level based on the damage done by an impact. Typically, you call this method from the collision notifier (recall that the collision notifier is called from the Actor class whenever a collision takes place—check the *Star Assault* Actor class cycle method for an example).

```
public final void onCollision(Actor actorItHit)
{
    if (actorItHit == null) return;
```

First you need to test that the owner (the actor that created this object) is not the same. This stops you from hitting your own bullets. The code then tests if the actor that this actor hit is a bullet and reacts (takes damage).

```
    if (actorItHit.getOwner() != this)
    {
        if (actorItHit.isBullet())
        {
            Bullet bulletItHit = (Bullet) actorItHit;
            takeDamage(bulletItHit.getDamage());
            actorItHit.setCollidable(false);
        }
    }
```

In a case where any of the ships collide, this ship takes a big damage hit. For most enemy types this will be fatal.

```
    // if we hit an enemy ship, take a big hit
    if (!a.isBullet())
        takeDamage(250);

}
```

Now you need to react to the state of the showShields Boolean set in the takeDamage method. The first thing to do is draw the shield sprite when you display the ship in the Ship class's render method.

```
public final void render(Graphics g, int offsetX, int offsetY)
{
    // draw the 20 x 20 shield sprite underneath the 16 x 16 ship
    // sprite (the edges will stick out)

    if (showShields)
        shieldSprite.draw(g, getX() - offsetX, getY() - offsetY);

    // draw the ship
    ...

}
```

Next you need to turn the shields off when they have gone through the cycle once (the flash and then fade sequence). To do this, you can use the Sprite class's getTotalCycles method. As soon as this reaches 1, you know you're finished. Again, this all belongs in the Ship class.

```
public final void cycle(long deltaMS)
{
    ...

    if (showShields)
    {
        shieldSprite.cycle(deltaMS);

        if (shieldSprite.getTotalCycles() > 0)
        {
            shieldSprite.reset();
            showShields = false;
        }
    }
}
```

Energy Bar

Players now have to manage the level of shield energy they have left. Letting it get below zero will result in destruction, so you should add an energy bar to give the player a visual indicator as to the current level of shielding. An example of this is illustrated in Figure 12.2. The small green bar in the bottom-left corner of the screen is the current shield level.

To add an energy bar, you modify GameScreen's rendering code to draw a few filled rectangles. Because drawing rectangles is not particularly fast, you need to use a small image to cache the results of the drawing. It's much faster to just draw the image (instead of the rectangles). If the bar value changes, you redraw the cached image. Here's the GameScreen code to do this (note that I've reorganized the GameScreen class by moving initialization code into a new initResources method):

Figure 12.2 An energy bar indicates the player ship's current shield level.

```
private void initResources()
{
    // create the cache image for the energy bar (width is kept relative
    // to the size of the screen)

    barWidth = screenWidth / 5;
    barHeight = 6;
    energyBarImage = Image.createImage(barWidth, barHeight);


    ...


}


/**
 * update the energy bar image
 */
private final void updateEnergyBar(int barFill, boolean showRed)
{
    Graphics g = energyBarImage.getGraphics();

    // clear the background
    g.setColor(0);
    g.fillRect(0, 0, energyBarImage.getWidth(), energyBarImage.getHeight());

    // draw a white(ish) border
    g.setColor(0xaaaaaa);
    g.drawRect(0, 0, barWidth, 6);
```

```
    if (showRed)
        g.setColor(0xcc2222);
    else
        g.setColor(0x22cc22);

    g.fillRect(1, 1, barFill, 5);
}
private final void renderWorld(Graphics graphics)
{
    ...
    // draw the playerShip energy bar
    int pixelsPerEnergyPoint = playerShip.getEnergyMax() / barWidth;
    int barFill = playerShip.getEnergy() / pixelsPerEnergyPoint;
```

If the bar hasn't changed value (in terms of the number of pixels to draw), then we don't need to redraw the image.

```
    if (lastDrawnBarValue != barFill)
    {
```

The updateEnergyBar has a parameter to draw the bar in red. This is set to true in the method call below if the player's shields are below 50 percent. I've used a cheap method to do this without fractions by dividing the max energy level by the current energy. If the result (rounded down) is greater than one then they have less than half of their energy left.

```
        updateEnergyBar(barFill, playerShip.getEnergy() > 0 &&
                            playerShip.getEnergyMax() /
                            playerShip.getEnergy() > 1);
        lastDrawnBarValue = barFill;
    }
    graphics.drawImage(energyBarImage, 6, screenHeight - 12,
                    Tools.GRAPHICS_TOP_LEFT);

    ...

}
```

Dealing with Death

There's a slight issue with the current game play in *Star Assault*. Although your shielding system now absorbs damage, there are no consequences for that energy level falling below zero. All the ships just keep flying. What you need to do is properly handle the death of both the player and enemy ships.

Like shielding, the first step in this process is to give some visual feedback that the ship is going down for the count. To do this, you draw an explosion sprite in place of the ship when it reaches this point. After the explosion has faded away, you can deal with the results.

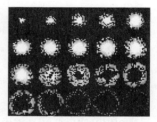

Figure 12.3 The frames of the explosion sprite.

Figure 12.3 shows the explosion sprite you'll use; it's a simple sequence of frames showing a fireball that fades away slowly.

To use the explosion sprite, you need to add an explosion image set and initialize the images in the Ship class's static setup method.

```
public class Ship extends Actor
{
    private static ImageSet explosionSet;

    public final static void setup()
    {
        Image explosionImage = ImageSet.loadClippedImage("/explode.png", 0, 0);
        Image[] explosionImages = ImageSet.extractFrames(explosionImage,
                                                  0, 0, 1, 4, 25, 25);
        explosionSet.addState(explosionImages, 500);
        ...
```

Just like you did with shields, add a Boolean to indicate when the ship is in the exploding state and set it in the Ship class's takeDamage method.

```
public final void takeDamage(int damageLevel)
{
    energy -= damageLevel;
    showShields = true;

    if (energy < 0)
    {
        exploding = true;
        showShields = false;
    }
}
```

Once you have the Boolean set, you can use it when rendering the ship as a special case in the Ship class's render method.

```
public final void render(Graphics g, int offsetX, int offsetY)
{
```

```
if (exploding)
    explodingSprite.draw(g, getX() - offsetX - 2, getY() - offsetY - 2);
else
{
    // normal ship drawing code
    ...
```

Hopefully this is all getting familiar now. Next you can use the `cycle` method to trigger the consequences of the ship's death. For the non-player ships, you just ask the world to remove the ship. You then notify the game screen that a ship has died, and it will handle the adjustment to the scoring or cases in which the player's ship has died. Here's an update `Ship cycle` method.

```
public final void cycle(long deltaMS)
{

    ...

    if (exploding)
    {
        explodingSprite.cycle(deltaMS);

        if (explodingSprite.getTotalCycles() > 0)
        {
            explodingSprite.reset();

            if (getType() != PLAYER_SHIP)
                // if this is not the player ship then just have the
                // world release the ship back into the pool
                world.releaseShip(this);

            else
            {
                // big vibration if player died
                Tools.vibrate(10, 800);

                // tell the game screen about it
                GameScreen.getGameScreen().notifyShipDied(this);
            }
        }
    }

    ...
}
```

Your ships will now explode with a rather gratifying animation. Next take a look at how the game screen should handle the death of these ships properly.

To make things a little more challenging for the player, you can implement a limited number of lives. When the player has gotten himself destroyed more than the allotted number of times, you'll transition to a "game over" state.

To implement this, you just add a lives counter field and the notifyShipDied handler to the GameScreen class.

```
private int lives=3;

public void notifyShipDied(Ship ship)
{
    if (ship == playerShip)
    {
        lives--;
        if (lives == 0)
        {
            setState(GAME_OVER);
        }
        else
        {
            world.restart();
            setState(DYING);
        }
    }
}
```

The World class method restart is required to reset the level back to a starting state. For example:

```
/**
 * Restart the level
 */
public void restart()
{
    // reset all the ships (used only of course)
    Ship s = (Ship) enemyShipPool.getFirstUsed();
    while (s != null)
    {
        Actor next = s.getNextLinked();

        // Final check used to remove any inactive or exploding actors.
```

```
                // This can happen sometimes if actors were not given enough time
                // to complete their death sequence before this restart method was
                // called. For example, if the player collides with an enemy ship
                // before dying it won't have time to finish its exploding state and
                // suicide before we get this call in here. Without this check we
                // could end up with floating, half-dead phantom objects.
                if (!s.isVisible() || s.isExploding())
                    releaseShip(s);
                else
                    s.reset();

                s = (Ship) next;
            }
            playerShip.reset();

            // release all the bullets
            Actor a = bulletPool.getFirstUsed();
            while (a != null)
            {
                Actor next = a.getNextLinked();
                releaseBullet((Bullet) a);
                a = next;
            }
        }
```

I've introduced two new game states here—DYING, which you use to delay restarting play a little, and GAME_OVER, as a result of the player running out of lives. Handling these two new states is relatively simple. First you draw the game over message on the screen, if required. Here's an example of the code you would add to the GameScreen's renderWorld method.

```
private final void renderWorld(Graphics graphics)
{
    ...

    if (state == GAME_OVER)
    {
        graphics.setColor(0x00ffcc66);
        graphics.setFont(defaultFont);
        graphics.drawString("GAME OVER", getWidth() / 2, getHeight() / 2,
                            Tools.GRAPHICS_TOP_LEFT);
    }
}
```

Next you add the revised `cycle` code for `GameScreen`. Here's where you really deal with these state changes. Notice that after you display GAME OVER for a little while, you call an `activateMenu` method; I'll cover this in the next chapter. (I think you can imagine what it does, though.)

```
public void run()
{
    try
    {
        while (running)
        {

            ...

            if (state == PLAYING)
                world.cycle();

            // if we're in the starting up state, wait a moment then
            // progress to playing
            if (state == STARTING_UP)
            {
                long timeSinceStateChange = System.currentTimeMillis() -
                                            timeStateChanged;
                if (timeSinceStateChange > 3000)
                    setState(PLAYING);
            }

            if (state == GAME_OVER)
            {
                long timeSinceStateChange = System.currentTimeMillis() -
                                            timeStateChanged;
                if (timeSinceStateChange > 3000)
                {
                    setState(GAME_DONE);
                    theMidlet.activateMenu();
                }
            }

            // if they died we wait 1 second before restarting play
            if (state == DYING)
            {
```

```
            long timeSinceStateChange = System.currentTimeMillis() -
                                        timeStateChanged;
            if (timeSinceStateChange > 1000)
                setState(STARTING_UP);
        }


        ...
```

That's about it. If you were to play through this game now, you'd find it feels much more like a typical action game. You now have the challenge of staying alive for as long as possible.

Saving and Loading

Star Assault is starting to look like a real game now. If you put together the fun of trying to stay alive, progressing to new levels, and encountering new types of enemies, you'll quickly find yourself getting engrossed in the game.

The next thing you need to do is provide a way for the player to save the game and resume progress at a later stage. To do this, you'll save the game state to a record store, and then load it back again.

As you saw in Chapter 5, record stores are simple to use. You just open or create a store, construct an array of bytes, and then write it out. To keep things simple, you'll save your game at the start of a new level, rather than midway through it. This means you only need to store the tile map (rather than the attributes of all the actors as well). To accomplish this, you add a saveLevel method to the World class.

```
public boolean saveLevel()
{
    RecordStore store = null;

    try
    {
        try
        {
            // Our save/load system only supports a single current saved level so
            // to make room you need to delete any current saved level first.
            RecordStore.deleteRecordStore("Level");
        }
        catch (RecordStoreNotFoundException rse)
        { }

        store = RecordStore.openRecordStore("Level", true);
```

```
ByteArrayOutputStream byteOutputStream = new ByteArrayOutputStream();
DataOutputStream dataOutputStream = new DataOutputStream(byteOutputStream);

// write out the number of tiles we have
dataOutputStream.writeInt(tilesWide);
dataOutputStream.writeInt(tilesHigh);

// write the tile map
for (int ty=0; ty < tilesHigh; ty++)
    for (int tx=0; tx < tilesWide; tx++)
        dataOutputStream.writeByte(tileMap[ty][tx]);

dataOutputStream.flush();

// delete the old one and add the new record
byte[] recordOut = byteOutputStream.toByteArray();
try
{
    // try to set the existing record (we'll get an invalid exception
    // if it doesn't exist)
    store.setRecord(1, recordOut, 0, recordOut.length);
}
catch (InvalidRecordIDException ir)
{
    // add the record
    store.addRecord(recordOut, 0, recordOut.length);
}

dataOutputStream.close();
byteOutputStream.close();

return true;
}

catch (IOException io)
{
    System.out.println("IOException: " + io);
    return false;
}
catch (RecordStoreException rse)
{
```

```
            System.out.println("RSException: " + rse);
            return false;
        }

        finally
        {
            try
            {
                if (store != null)
                    store.closeRecordStore();
            }

            catch (RecordStoreNotOpenException e)
            {
            }

            catch (RecordStoreException e)
            {
            }
        }

    }
```

In this method you create an output stream and then write the size and contents of the map. You then convert this DataOutputSteam into a byte array and use the record store methods to write it out.

Loading the data back up is even easier.

```
public void loadLevel()
{
    // load up the tilemap from RMS for the current level
    RecordStore store = null;
    try
    {
        store = RecordStore.openRecordStore("Level", true);

        ByteArrayInputStream byteInputStream = new
ByteArrayInputStream(store.getRecord(1));
        DataInputStream dataInputStream = new DataInputStream(byteInputStream);

        tilesWide = dataInputStream.readInt();
```

```
        tilesHigh = dataInputStream.readInt();

        tileMap = new byte[tilesHigh][tilesWide];
        for (int ty = 0; ty < tilesHigh; ty++)
            for (int tx = 0; tx < tilesWide; tx++)
                tileMap[ty][tx] = dataInputStream.readByte();

        // now restart the world for this level
        restart();

        dataInputStream.close();
        byteInputStream.close();
    }

    catch (IOException io)
    {
        System.out.println("IOException: " + io);
    }
    catch (RecordStoreException rse)
    {
        System.out.println("RSException: " + rse);
    }

    finally
    {
        try
        {
            if (store != null) store.closeRecordStore();
        }

        catch (RecordStoreNotOpenException e)
        {
        }

        catch (RecordStoreException e)
        {
        }
    }
}
```

As you can see, it's basically the reverse of the save method. I've tried to keep things simple for the moment; however, in the final version of *Star Assault* you will need to write out and then read back the player's starting position, current number of lives, the level number, and anything else you need.

There are a few other things you need for handling save games as well. First, I've designed *Star Assault* so that when the player loses all of his lives and the game ends, you delete the current save game automatically. (This might be a bit harsh for some other game types so feel free to let them play on—maybe adding some other type of penalty rather than having to restart the game.) You can just wrap up a call to delete the record store to do this.

```
public void removeSavedGame()
{
    try
    {
        RecordStore.deleteRecordStore("Level");
    }
    catch (RecordStoreNotFoundException rse)
    {
    }
    catch (RecordStoreException e)
    {
    }
}
```

Next you need to be able to determine whether a save game currently exists. (You'll be using this in the menu system to display a Resume Game menu item if a save game exists.) To do this, you need a method that checks whether it can get the save record. Since this method is called every time the menu is displayed, you don't want to reload the entire level using the loadLevel method; this is not only slow but it would overwrite their existing game!

The following getSavedLevel method checks for the existence of a saved level without actually loading it. If a level is found it returns true, otherwise false.

```
public static boolean getSavedLevel()
{
    RecordStore store = null;
    try
    {
        store = RecordStore.openRecordStore("Level", false);
```

```
        ByteArrayInputStream byteInputStream = new
ByteArrayInputStream(store.getRecord(1));
        byteInputStream.close();
        return true;
    }

    catch (IOException io)
    {
        System.out.println("IOException: " + io);
        return false;
    }
    catch (RecordStoreNotOpenException rse)
    {
        return false;
    }
    catch (RecordStoreException rse)
    {
        System.out.println("RSException: " + rse);
        return false;
    }

    finally
    {
        try
        {
            if (store != null) store.closeRecordStore();
        }

        catch (RecordStoreNotOpenException e)
        {
        }

        catch (RecordStoreException e)
        {
        }
    }
}
```

Conclusion

Hopefully you've found this chapter to be pretty fun. Although you didn't explore a great deal of new technology, you still covered some important areas. The use of game state, for instance, lets you handle the different game modes required to make your game act professionally. You also saw how to react properly to collisions by adding ship damage, shielding, explosions, and life counts.

This chapter is really the first time you've worked on the game (not the tools). Everything else was just preparation, and now you're programming the challenge for your players. You should really think of this as the start of the project, not the end. It's at this point that you should really spend the time to add all those cool little things that make a game.

I'd highly recommend you look over the completed *Star Assault* game and the accompanying source code on the CD to get a feel for how all this comes together as a game.

You're not quite done yet, though. In the next chapter, you'll add the menus to drive the application.

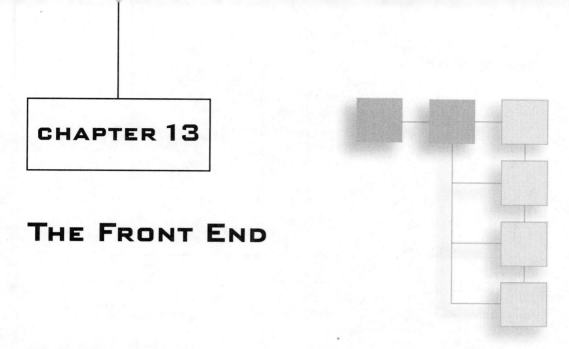

CHAPTER 13

THE FRONT END

When a player first starts up a J2ME game, you need to present him with a splash screen (to get him excited) and then a series of menus for the various options you've made available. For *Star Assault*, you'll let players configure the keys they want to use to control the fighter, as well as turn off (or on) features such as auto-fire, vibration, and drawing the background star field.

All these things combined are what you call the *front end* of the application. In this chapter you'll look at how the application class becomes the primary driver for these elements, along with how to develop a robust menu system without requiring loads of precious classes. By the time you're finished, *Star Assault* will look just like a real game.

Front End Overview

Every quality J2ME game needs a front end of some type, even if it's just a basic menu with New Game and Exit options. However, most games require quite a bit more. In Figure 13.1, you can see the front end you'll develop for *Star Assault*.

The front end begins when the MIDlet starts, at which point you display a splash screen. This serves to introduce the game, make a copyright and ownership statement, and get the player a little excited. Figure 13.2 shows the splash screen you'll create for *Star Assault*.

After the splash screen you present the main menu (see Figure 13.3) containing the various options to configure the game or get started playing. Like any good game, *Star Assault* has a variety of configuration options including enabling or disabling auto-fire, vibration, and the star field background (to increase rendering speed). The player can also reconfigure which keys correspond to different game actions (in case he is using an MID with a different keyboard layout than what you expect).

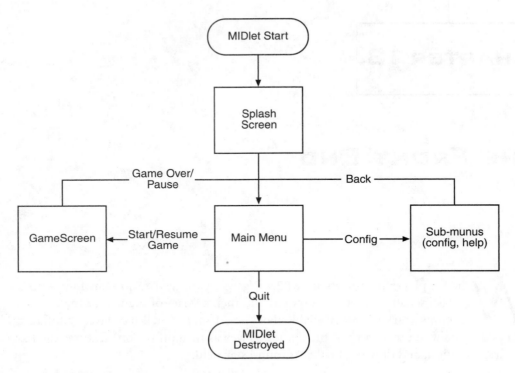

Figure 13.1 The flow of the application screens in *Star Assault*

Figure 13.2 A splash screen for *Star Assault*

Figure 13.3 The main menu provides options to manage the game and configuration options.

In the same way that GameScreen glues together all the game components, the MIDlet (or application class) drives the front end. You start developing the front end for *Star Assault* there.

The Application Class

As you saw when you developed *RoadRun*, your game starts and ends its life through the MIDlet class. In *Star Assault* you'll follow the same path; however, with the more complicated front end you need to make things a little more flexible.

First, to accommodate your new splash screen, menu system, and game screen, you have to be able to display a wide variety of different MIDP screens. Doing this is pretty easy; you just use the Display class' setCurrent method. However, at times you'll need to know which screen is currently active, so you need to keep track of what's currently displayed as well.

Take a look at your new application class (including support for GameScreen).

```
import javax.microedition.midlet.*;
import javax.microedition.lcdui.*;
import javax.microedition.rms.*;
import java.io.*;

/**
 * The application class for the game Star Assault.
 */

public class StarAssault extends MIDlet
{
    private static StarAssault theApp;
    private GameScreen gs;
    private boolean hasAGameRunning;
    private Displayable currentDisplay;
    public StarAssault()
    {
        theApp = this;
```

The code below refers to the Splash class; we'll get to this in the "Splash Screen" section later in the chapter.

```
        currentDisplay = new Splash(this);
```

The new application class retains a reference to the GameScreen class to notify it of changing in the application state.

```
        // init the game screen
        gs = new GameScreen(this);
    }
```

```
public static StarAssault getApp()
{
    return theApp;
}
```

When the application starts, you set the current display object (which will be the splash screen created in the constructor) to be the current displayable. If the game is being resumed (from a previously paused state), this code notifies the GameScreen it's time to get on with business.

```
public void startApp() throws MIDletStateChangeException
{
    activateDisplayable(currentDisplay);

    // if we are resuming the game then tell the game screen about it
    if (gs != null)
    {
        if (gs.getState() == GameScreen.PAUSED)
            gs.resume();
    }
}
```

Again, when the application is paused by the player for some reason (incoming phone call), this code lets the GameScreen know.

```
public void pauseApp()
{
    if (gs != null)
        gs.pause();
}

public void destroyApp(boolean unconditional) throws MIDletStateChangeException
{
}

public void close()
{
    try
    {
        destroyApp(true);
        notifyDestroyed();
    }
```

```
        catch (MIDletStateChangeException e)
        {
        }
    }

    public void createNewGame()
    {
        gs.startNewGame();
        activateGameScreen();
    }

    public void loadGame()
    {
        gs.loadGame();
        activateGameScreen();
    }
```

The activateGameScreen method takes care of placing the GameScreen in a state ready to play. If no game is currently underway it also sets up everything by calling the createNewGame method.

```
    public void activateGameScreen()
    {
        if (gs == null || gs.getState() == GameScreen.GAME_DONE)
            createNewGame();

        hasAGameRunning = true;
        gs.resume();
        currentDisplay = gs;
        activateDisplayable(gs);
    }
```

This method is called by the menu system to determine if a game is currently active, and thus the "Resume Game" menu item should be displayed.

```
    public boolean hasAGameRunning()
    {
        if (!hasAGameRunning) return false;

        if (gs.getState() != GameScreen.GAME_DONE)
            return true;
        else
            return false;
```

```
    }

    public static void activateDisplayable(Displayable s)
    {
        try
        {
            Display.getDisplay(getApp()).setCurrent(s);
        }
        catch (Exception e)
        {
            System.out.println("App exception: " + e);
            e.printStackTrace();
        }
    }

}
```

You'll notice added methods the menu system will use to load and save the current game as well as to handle pausing and resuming the game properly. You'll see those in action when you code up the menus.

Configuration Options

Like in any comprehensive game, you must let the player configure certain aspects of the application. Exactly what these options are depends on your game.

For *Star Assault* the first option is auto-fire. On some MIDs it's pretty difficult to hit a direction key and a fire key in an effective, coordinated way. This can be a result of input delays, key placement, or the lack of simultaneous key press support. When you turn on auto-fire, the ship will automatically fire its weapon as fast as possible.

Note

If you want to give players the option of auto-fire, consider the impact this might have on your game design. Having this option on should not adversely affect the state of play. For example, you might not be able to constrain weapons fire (such as a limited number of bullets or energy) or link special functionality to the fire key (such as holding it down to fire bigger blasts).

The second option you'll add is the ability to disable vibration. Vibration often sounds like a good idea at the time (and it is a good effect), but it can be difficult to tell the real impact of using it on actual handsets. Vibration can cause severe application delays (sometimes resulting in the game freezing) and it can drain batteries, especially if overused. It can also be just plain annoying sometimes.

Tip

Probably the best place to use vibration is when the player dies or the game is over. This isn't likely to be very often, and the player expects a delay (penalty) at this time anyway.

Another option (and this is more for demonstration purposes) is to let the player disable the background star field. Because this is an entirely optional component, players can elect to disable the field if it's causing confusion or slowing things down.

To store settings for these options, add the following fields to the StarAssault class:

```
private boolean optionAutoFire = false;
private boolean optionVibrate = true;
private boolean optionStarField = true;
```

The first three fields are boolean types representing whether an option is enabled or disabled. AutoFire defaults to off, while Vibrate and StarField default to on. Next, add access methods for the boolean fields.

```
public boolean isOptionAutoFire()
{
    return optionAutoFire;
}


public void setOptionAutoFire(boolean optionAutoFire)
{
    this.optionAutoFire = optionAutoFire;
}


public boolean isOptionStarField()
{
    return optionStarField;
}


public void setOptionStarField(boolean optionStarField)
{
    this.optionStarField = optionStarField;
}


public boolean isOptionVibrate()
{
    return optionVibrate;
}
```

```
public void setOptionVibrate(boolean optionVibrate)
{
    this.optionVibrate = optionVibrate;
}
```

To now use configuration options, add some code into the other game classes. For auto-fire you just change the Ship class init method to set firing to true if auto-fire is on.

```
public final void init(int typeArg, int x, int y)
{
    ...

    switch (getType())
    {
        case PLAYER_SHIP:

            ...

            firing = StarAssault.getApp().isOptionAutoFire();
            break;
```

To implement the optional star field you change the world render method to check before drawing.

```
public final void render(Graphics g)
{
    try
    {
        // draw the background stars
        if (StarAssault.getApp().isOptionStarField())
            Tools.drawStarField(g, viewX / 10, viewY / 10, viewWidth, viewHeight);
        ...
```

Configuring Keys

Another configuration option is the assignment of keys to actions in the game. You can let the player select which keypad numbers to use for left, right, and fire. Like the options you added previously, you start by adding fields to the StarAssault class.

```
private int leftKeyNum = 4;
private int rightKeyNum = 6;
private int fireKeyNum = 5;
```

To store the key settings you use an integer that corresponds to the actual keypad number you want to use for that function. Most MIDs use a phone-style keypad, hence the default numbers I used in this example.

Again, like for the other options, I've added access methods for the keys (you'll see the GameScreen class's setKeyBindings method later in this section).

```
public int getFireKeyNum()
{
    return fireKeyNum;
}

public void setFireKeyNum(int fireKeyNum)
{
    this.fireKeyNum = fireKeyNum;
    if (gs != null) gs.setKeyBindings();
}

public int getLeftKeyNum()
{
    return leftKeyNum;
}

public void setLeftKeyNum(int leftKeyNum)
{
    this.leftKeyNum = leftKeyNum;
    if (gs != null) gs.setKeyBindings();
}

public int getRightKeyNum()
{
    return rightKeyNum;
}

public void setRightKeyNum(int rightKeyNum)
{
    this.rightKeyNum = rightKeyNum;
    if (gs != null) gs.setKeyBindings();
}
```

Setting these values isn't much good if you don't actually use them. Because your input handling code uses Canvas key codes rather than integers, you need to add some support to map between these two types.

```
public static final int getKeyCodeFromNum(int n)
{
    switch (n)
```

```
    {
        case 0:
            return Canvas.KEY_NUM0;
        case 1:
            return Canvas.KEY_NUM1;
        case 2:
            return Canvas.KEY_NUM2;
        case 3:
            return Canvas.KEY_NUM3;
        case 4:
            return Canvas.KEY_NUM4;
        case 5:
            return Canvas.KEY_NUM5;
        case 6:
            return Canvas.KEY_NUM6;
        case 7:
            return Canvas.KEY_NUM7;
        case 8:
            return Canvas.KEY_NUM8;
        case 9:
            return Canvas.KEY_NUM9;
    }
    return Canvas.KEY_NUM0;
}
```

Now you're ready to add code to the GameScreen class to support configurable keys. For speed, cache the key codes.

```
public class GameScreen extends Canvas implements Runnable, CommandListener
{
    ...

    private int leftKeyCode;
    private int rightKeyCode;
    private int fireKeyCode;
    public GameScreen(StarAssault midlet)
    {
        ...

        setKeyBindings();
    }
```

```
public void setKeyBindings()
{
    leftKeyCode = StarAssault.getKeyCodeFromNum(theMidlet.getLeftKeyNum());
    rightKeyCode = StarAssault.getKeyCodeFromNum(theMidlet.getRightKeyNum());
    fireKeyCode = StarAssault.getKeyCodeFromNum(theMidlet.getFireKeyNum());
}
```

Because you're caching these values, you call the setKeyBindings method whenever the StarAssault class method changes the keys.

To make this all work, you simply adjust the input handling methods keyPressed and keyReleased to use these new values.

```
protected void keyPressed(int keyCode)
{
    ...
    // If the autofire is on you ignore the up key.
    if (!StarAssault.getApp().isOptionAutoFire())
    {
        if (action == GAME_A || keyCode == fireKeyCode || action == UP)
            playerShip.setFiring(true);
    }
}


protected void keyReleased(int keyCode)
{

    ...

    // If the autofire is on you ignore the up key.
    if (!StarAssault.getApp().isOptionAutoFire())
    {
        if (action == GAME_A || keyCode == fireKeyCode || action == UP)
            playerShip.setFiring(false);
    }
}
```

Saving and Loading Settings

Now that you've given the player the option to change the configuration of the game, you need to save his preferences.

The code to save the settings is a lot like the code to save the world. You simply create a record store named "Settings" and write out the data. The following is a method to save the settings in the application class. Note that this is an entirely separate operation to saving and loading the game (in the World class). Saving and loading settings is done whenever they are changed, not when playing the game.

```
public boolean saveSettings()
{
    RecordStore settings = null;
    try
    {
        try
        {
            // Remove any previous settings save record.
            RecordStore.deleteRecordStore("Settings");
        }
        catch (RecordStoreNotFoundException rse)
        {
            // No need to worry if it wasn't found as it could be the
            // first time they are saving the settings.
        }

        // Construct a new record store for the settings.
        settings = RecordStore.openRecordStore("Settings", true);

        // Output all the settings using a data stream.
        ByteArrayOutputStream byteOutputStream = new ByteArrayOutputStream();
        DataOutputStream dataOutputStream = new DataOutputStream(byteOutputStream);
        dataOutputStream.writeBoolean(optionAutoFire);
        dataOutputStream.writeBoolean(optionVibrate);
        dataOutputStream.writeBoolean(optionStarField);
        dataOutputStream.writeInt(leftKeyNum);
        dataOutputStream.writeInt(rightKeyNum);
        dataOutputStream.writeInt(fireKeyNum);

        dataOutputStream.flush();

        // delete the old one and add the new record
        byte[] recordOut = byteOutputStream.toByteArray();
        // Write the new record to the RMS.
        try
            {
```

```java
            settings.setRecord(1, recordOut, 0, recordOut.length);
        }
        catch (InvalidRecordIDException ir)
        {
            settings.addRecord(recordOut, 0, recordOut.length);
        }
        dataOutputStream.close();
        byteOutputStream.close();

        return true;
    }

    catch (IOException io)
    {
        System.out.println("IOException: " + io);
        return false;
    }
    catch (RecordStoreException rse)
    {
        System.out.println("RSException: " + rse);
        return false;
    }

    // In case there was any form of error you need to make sure the
    // record store is properly closed.
    finally
    {
        try
        {
            if (settings != null) settings.closeRecordStore();
        }

        catch (RecordStoreNotOpenException e)
        {
        }

        catch (RecordStoreException e)
        {
        }
    }
}
```

You'll see how and when to call the saveSettings method when you create the menus in the next section. Take a look at how to load these settings first.

```java
public boolean loadSettings()
{
    RecordStore settings = null;
    try
    {
        settings = RecordStore.openRecordStore("Settings", true);

        ByteArrayInputStream byteInputStream = new
ByteArrayInputStream(settings.getRecord(1));
            DataInputStream dataInputStream = new DataInputStream(byteInputStream);

        setOptionAutoFire(dataInputStream.readBoolean());
        setOptionVibrate(dataInputStream.readBoolean());
        setOptionStarField(dataInputStream.readBoolean());
        setLeftKeyNum(dataInputStream.readInt());
        setRightKeyNum(dataInputStream.readInt());
        setFireKeyNum(dataInputStream.readInt());

        dataInputStream.close();
        byteInputStream.close();

        settings.closeRecordStore();
        return true;
    }

    catch (IOException io)
    {
        System.out.println("IOException: " + io);
        return false;
    }
    catch (RecordStoreException rse)
    {
        System.out.println("RSException: " + rse);
        return false;
    }

    // In case there was any form of error you need to make sure the
    // record store is properly closed.
    finally
```

```
    {
        try
        {
            if (settings != null) settings.closeRecordStore();
        }

        catch (RecordStoreNotOpenException e)
        {
        }

        catch (RecordStoreException e)
        {
        }
    }
}
```

To load the settings, you simply call this method from the MIDlet constructor.

```
public class StarAssault extends MIDlet
{

    public StarAssault()
    {
        ...
        loadSettings();
    }
}
```

The Menus

Every game needs a menu system, even if it only contains options to start a new game and exit. For *Star Assault* you'll have quite a complex set of menus to let the player start or resume a game, configure available options, change the key setup, and view credits and information on how to play. Figure 13.4 shows all these options.

The easiest way to create a menu is to derive a class from the LCDUI List and add items for each menu option. Figure 13.5 shows an example of this.

When the user selects an option from the list, you simply undertake the action that corresponds to it. However, for each of the different menus you need to create another class derived from List. Seems like a bit of a waste, doesn't it? For *Star Assault* you'll have as many as five different menus, all of which are pretty much the same thing—just a list of options. Maybe there's a better way.

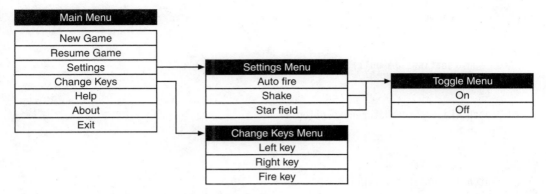

Figure 13.4 The menu structure for *Star Assault*

Figure 13.5 The resulting menu using a List object

To solve this problem you can use a special menu class that can dynamically change its items and responses to selections. You can display any number of menus and items, all using the same class.

To manage the menus, the DynaMenu class (what a cool name, you're thinking) starts by defining a constant for all the menus.

```
public class DynaMenu extends List implements CommandListener
{
    // Values have large increments so you can fit in more entries without
    // renumbering everything.
    private static final int MAIN_MENU = 100;
    private static final int SETTINGS_MENU = 110;
    private static final int AUTOFIRE_TOGGLE_MENU = 111;
    private static final int VIBRATE_TOGGLE_MENU = 112;
```

```
private static final int STARFIELD_TOGGLE_MENU = 113;
private static final int KEYSETUP_MENU = 120;
private static final int LEFTKEY_MENU = 121;
private static final int RIGHTKEY_MENU = 122;
private static final int FIREKEY_MENU = 123;
private static final int CONFIRM_NEW_GAME_MENU = 130;
private int currentMenu; // tracks which menu is current being displayed.
```

I've also added an integer field to keep track of which menu is currently being displayed.

To populate the list you use the List class' addElement method. Here's how to do this for the main menu:

```
public void goMainMenu()
{
    boolean savedLevel = World.getSavedLevel();

    Vector items = new Vector();
    items.addElement("New game");
    if (StarAssault.getApp().hasAGameRunning() || savedLevel)
        items.addElement("Resume game");
    items.addElement("Settings");
    items.addElement("Change keys");
    items.addElement("Help");
    items.addElement("About");

    String[] s = new String[items.size()];
    for (int i = 0; i < items.size(); i++)
        s[i] = (String) items.elementAt(i);
```

You'll see the setupMenu method later in this section.

```
    setupMenu("Main Menu", s, "Exit");

    currentMenu = MAIN_MENU;
}
```

You then need to call this from the constructor to switch to the main menu by default.

```
public DynaMenu()
{
    // Use an explicit list as it's the best type to reflect a menu (a simple
    // of items you can select from).
    super("", IMPLICIT);
    goMainMenu();
```

```
        setCommandListener(this);
    }
```

This code also checks to see whether a saved game currently exists or whether a game is in progress. If it is, then you add the Resume Game option as well. The setupMenu method does the hard work of populating the list.

First you clear any items currently displayed, and then you add an item on the list for every entry in the string array. If the backCommandName is anything other than null, you add a back command using that name. This way you can have Exit on the main menu and Back on the internal menus.

```
public void setupMenu(String title, String[] choices, String backCommandName)
{
    // Set the title of the menu.
    setTitle(title);

    // clear the current list & command
    int s = size();
    for (int i = 0; i < s; i++)
        delete(0);
    removeCommand(back);

    // add the new choices
    for (int i = 0; i < choices.length; i++)
        append(choices[i], null);

    // add the back command, if they wanted one
    if (backCommandName != null)
    {
        back = new Command(backCommandName, Command.BACK, 1);
        addCommand(back);
    }
}
```

Using this code you can now add setup methods for the other menus.

```
public void goSettingsMenu()
{
    setupMenu("Settings", new String[]{"Auto fire", "Shake", "Star field"},
            "Back");
    currentMenu = SETTINGS_MENU;
}
```

```
public void goKeySetupMenu()
{
    setupMenu("Key Setup", new String[]{"Left", "Right", "Fire"}, "Back");
    currentMenu = KEYSETUP_MENU;
}

public void goKeyNumMenu(String title, int menuId, int currentNum)
{
    setupMenu(title, new String[]{"Num-0", "Num-1", "Num-2", "Num-3", "Num-4",
                               "Num-5", "Num-6", "Num-7", "Num-8", "Num-9"}, null);
    // Set the selected item on the menu to match the currently configured key.
    setSelectedIndex(currentNum, true);

    currentMenu = menuId;
}
```

When you select an option related to a setting, you need to present two options (either yes and no or on and off). To handle all of these cases, you add a couple of generic menus.

```
public void goToggleMenu(String title, int menuId, boolean on)
{
    setupMenu(title, new String[]{"On", "Off"}, null);
    if (on)
        setSelectedIndex(0, true);
    else
        setSelectedIndex(1, true);

    currentMenu = menuId;
}

public void goYesNoMenu(String title, int menuId, boolean on)
{
    setupMenu(title, new String[]{"Yes", "No"}, null);
    if (on)
        setSelectedIndex(0, true);
    else
        setSelectedIndex(1, true);

    currentMenu = menuId;
}
```

All right, the real action in the DynaMenu class is where you respond to commands and switch to different menus. At first glance this might look a little complicated, but it's mostly just a big switch statement to handle selections. As a result of each selection, you either enact the results or switch to another menu.

```java
public void commandAction(Command command, Displayable displayable)
{
    // If they hit the back key you need to step back from the current
    // menu to a prior one in the hierarchy.
    if (command == back)
    {
        if (currentMenu == SETTINGS_MENU) goMainMenu();
        if (currentMenu == KEYSETUP_MENU) goSettingsMenu();
    }


    // Execute an item on one of the menus.
    if (command == List.SELECT_COMMAND)
    {
        String selected = getString(getSelectedIndex());
        switch (currentMenu)
        {
            // All the options for the main menu.
            case MAIN_MENU:
                if (selected.equals("New game"))
                {
                    // if they already have a game running then confirm that
                    // they want to create a new game
                    if (StarAssault.getApp().hasAGameRunning())
                    {
                        goYesNoMenu("Are you sure?", CONFIRM_NEW_GAME_MENU, false);
                    }
                    else
                        StarAssault.getApp().createNewGame();
                }

                if (selected.equals("Resume game"))
                {
                    // Check to see if they already have a game running, if they
                    // do then resume that game by reactivating the game screen.
                    // Otherwise you load the game from the RMS.
                    if (StarAssault.getApp().hasAGameRunning())
                        StarAssault.getApp().activateGameScreen();
```

```
            else
                StarAssault.getApp().loadGame();
        }
        if (selected.equals("Settings"))
            goSettingsMenu();
        if (selected.equals("Change keys"))
            goKeySetupMenu();
        if (selected.equals("Help"))
        {
            StarAssault.activateDisplayable(
                    new TextForm(this,
                            "Star Command Needs You! \nFight your way through " +
                            "the enemy defences to the warp tunnel exit on each
                            level." +
                            " Use 4 and 6 to turn and 5 to fire. "));
        }
        if (selected.equals("About"))
        {
            StarAssault.activateDisplayable(
                    new TextForm(this,
                            "StarAssault (C)opyright 2003, Martin J. Wells. All
                            rights reserved."));
        }
        break;

    case CONFIRM_NEW_GAME_MENU:
        if (getBool(selected))
            StarAssault.getApp().createNewGame();
        break;

        // SETTINGS...
    case SETTINGS_MENU:
        if (selected.equals("Auto fire"))
            goToggleMenu("Auto fire", AUTOFIRE_TOGGLE_MENU,
StarAssault.getApp().isOptionAutoFire());
        if (selected.equals("Shake"))
            goToggleMenu("Shake", VIBRATE_TOGGLE_MENU, StarAssault.getApp().
isOptionVibrate());
        if (selected.equals("Star field"))
            goToggleMenu("Star field", STARFIELD_TOGGLE_MENU,
StarAssault.getApp().isOptionStarField());
```

```
            break;

        case AUTOFIRE_TOGGLE_MENU:
            StarAssault.getApp().setOptionAutoFire(getBool(selected));
            StarAssault.getApp().saveSettings();
            goSettingsMenu();
            break;
        case STARFIELD_TOGGLE_MENU:
            StarAssault.getApp().setOptionStarField(getBool(selected));
            StarAssault.getApp().saveSettings();
            goSettingsMenu();
            break;
        case VIBRATE_TOGGLE_MENU:
            StarAssault.getApp().setOptionVibrate(getBool(selected));
            StarAssault.getApp().saveSettings();
            goSettingsMenu();
            break;

        // KEYS...
        case KEYSETUP_MENU:
            if (selected.equals("Left"))
                goKeyNumMenu("Left Key", LEFTKEY_MENU, StarAssault.getApp().getLeft
                KeyNum());
            if (selected.equals("Right"))
                goKeyNumMenu("Right Key", RIGHTKEY_MENU,
                StarAssault.getApp().getRightKeyNum());
            if (selected.equals("Fire"))
                goKeyNumMenu("Fire Key", FIREKEY_MENU, StarAssault.getApp().
                getFireKeyNum());
            break;

        case LEFTKEY_MENU:
            StarAssault.getApp().setLeftKeyNum(getKeyNum(selected));
            StarAssault.getApp().saveSettings();
            goKeySetupMenu();
            break;

        case RIGHTKEY_MENU:
            StarAssault.getApp().setRightKeyNum(getKeyNum(selected));
            StarAssault.getApp().saveSettings();
            goKeySetupMenu();
```

```
                break;

            case FIREKEY_MENU:
                StarAssault.getApp().setFireKeyNum(getKeyNum(selected));
                StarAssault.getApp().saveSettings();
                goKeySetupMenu();
                break;
        }
    }
}
```

The getBool method converts a string value like On/Off, Enable/Disable, and Yes/No to an equivalent boolean value. This is used in the menu items above when configuring options.

```
public static final boolean getBool(String s)
{
    if (s.equals("On")) return true;
    if (s.equals("Enable")) return true;
    if (s.equals("Yes")) return true;
    return false;
}
```

The getKeyNum method is another quick utility method used by the menu code to convert between a key number choice and an integer value.

```
public static final int getKeyNum(String s)
{
    String n = s.substring(4, 5);
    return Integer.parseInt(n);
}
```

In this example I'm also using a class called TextForm. This class lets you display a block of text on the screen and then return to the menu—perfect for your Help and About screens. Since this has to be an independent displayable, you need to use a Form object.

```
public class TextForm extends Form implements CommandListener
{
    private Command back;
    private Screen home;

    public TextForm(Screen homeArg, String displayText)
    {
        // call the Form constructor
        super("");
```

```
        home = homeArg;
        append(displayText);

        // add the exit
        back = new Command("Back", Command.BACK, 1);
        addCommand(back);
        setCommandListener(this);
    }

    public void commandAction(Command command, Displayable displayable)
    {
        if (command == back)
            StarAssault.activateDisplayable(home);
    }


}
```

The Splash Screen

To add that finishing touch to your game, you'll add what's called a *splash screen*. This screen really just serves to reinforce to the user what they've done (selected your game) and to get some hype going.

The splash screen is the first thing the player sees in your game, so make it pretty flashy. In fact, I recommend you spend quite a bit of time and resources on making the splash screen look downright sexy. Players have learned that good games start with really cool splash screens; it's just a sign of quality. If you put up a good front image, players will be willing to spend more time getting to know your game. The splash screen is also the strongest image you'll present of your game in any promotional activity (such as on a Web site).

For *Star Assault* you'll make an animated splash screen by drawing a title graphic and then scrolling your star field in the background. To do this, you need much of the functionality you've already seen in the GameScreen class. In fact, you can think of the splash screen as a mini-game in itself.

The Splash class needs to initialize the graphics and then, using a thread, render it and the star field until a key is pressed.

```
public class Splash extends Canvas implements Runnable
{
    private boolean running = true;
    private Image osb;    // Off screen buffer image
    private Graphics osg;    // graphics context for the off screen buffer
```

```
    private StarAssault theMidlet;
    private int starFieldViewY;
    private Image title;
    private int fontHeight;
    private Font font;

    public Splash(StarAssault midlet)
    {
        theMidlet = midlet;
        initResources();

        // create the timer thread
        Thread t = new Thread(this);
        t.start();
    }
```

The initResources method creates an off-screen buffer for rendering and then loads up the splash screen image.

```
    private void initResources()
    {
        // set up the screen
        osb = Image.createImage(getWidth(), getHeight());
        osg = osb.getGraphics();

        title = ImageSet.loadClippedImage("/splash.png", 0, 0);
        font = Font.getFont(Font.FACE_SYSTEM, Font.STYLE_PLAIN, Font.SIZE_SMALL);
        fontHeight = font.getHeight() + 2;

        osg.setFont(font);
    }

    private static final int MAX_CPS = 100;
    private static final int MS_PER_FRAME = 1000 / MAX_CPS;

    public void run()
    {
        try
        {
            while (running)
            {
                // remember the starting time
                long cycleStartTime = System.currentTimeMillis();
```

```
          // do our work
          repaint();

          // sleep if we've finished our work early
          long timeSinceStart = (cycleStartTime - System.currentTimeMillis());
          if (timeSinceStart < MS_PER_FRAME)
          {
             try
             {
                Thread.sleep(MS_PER_FRAME - timeSinceStart);
             }
             catch (java.lang.InterruptedException e)
             {
             }
          }
       }

       // fall back to the splash form at the end of our loop
       theMidlet.activateMenu();
    }
    catch (Exception e)
    {
       System.out.println("App exception: " + e);
       e.printStackTrace();
    }


}
```

This method renders the splash screen graphics to the screen. You can easily customize this to suit your own game requirements.

```
private void renderSplash()
{
    // clear the background
    osg.setColor(0);
    osg.fillRect(0, 0, getWidth(), getHeight());

    // draw a moving star field
    if (starFieldViewY++ > 128) starFieldViewY = 0;
    Tools.drawStarField(osg, 0, starFieldViewY, getWidth(), getHeight());

    osg.drawImage(title, getWidth() / 2, getHeight() / 2 - 10, Graphics.HCENTER |
Graphics.VCENTER);
```

```
        // draw text
        osg.setColor(0x00888888);
        osg.drawString("(C) 2003", getWidth() / 2, getHeight() - fontHeight * 3,
                        Graphics.HCENTER | Graphics.TOP);
        osg.drawString("Martin J. Wells", getWidth() / 2, getHeight() - fontHeight * 2,
                        Graphics.HCENTER | Graphics.TOP);
        // draw the copy line
        osg.setColor(0x00ffffff);
        osg.drawString("Press any key", getWidth() / 2, getHeight() - fontHeight * 1,
                        Graphics.HCENTER | Graphics.TOP);
    }

    protected void paint(Graphics graphics)
    {
        renderSplash();
        graphics.drawImage(osb, 0, 0, Graphics.LEFT | Graphics.TOP);
    }

    protected void keyPressed(int keyCode)
    {
        running = false;
    }
}
```

To use this class you need to change the MIDlet, so the first thing you do is construct the splash screen and set the currentDisplay field.

```
public StarAssault()
{
    ...

    currentDisplay = new Splash(this);
```

Keep in mind that it's the startApp method that gets the game going. You might recall this method; you use it to switch the display to whatever currentDisplay is pointing at. This will now be the splash screen.

```
public void startApp() throws MIDletStateChangeException
{
    activateDisplayable(currentDisplay);

    ...
}
```

You can easily add a timer as well as multiple screens without too much trouble. Often you can use the first screen to promote your company (or yourself) and then, after a few seconds, flip to the game graphics. I'll leave implementing that one up to you.

Conclusion

In this chapter you've seen how to construct the front end for your game, and *Star Assault* looks far more professional as a result. Creating a comprehensive, polished front end is a critical part of making a good game.

Using a dynamically constructed list, you were able to cover even complex menu systems using a single class. Although this doesn't take advantage of all the functionality available in the LCDUI (such as radio buttons for toggling options), it's still more than adequate for most game menu systems.

With the front end in place, you've now concluded the development of *Star Assault*. In the next chapter you'll look at how to take advantage of the capabilities of different devices, as well as how to automate many of those mundane development tasks using a build system.

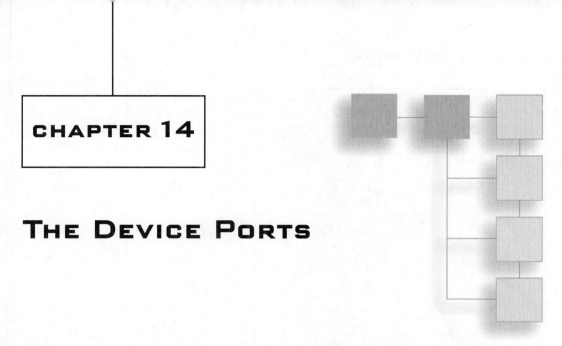

CHAPTER 14

THE DEVICE PORTS

S o far you've been developing *Star Assault* using only the standard features available in MIDP. In this chapter, you'll port the game over to use features made available to the reference device, the Nokia Series 40. You'll see how to use Nokia's FullCanvas to gain access to the extra screen space, how to use vibration, and how to take advantage of the image reflection and rotation capabilities to reduce the size of your graphics.

However, Nokia isn't the only port you'll need to use in order to produce a game. To help manage the process, you'll set up a build system to automate many of the mundane tasks involved. By the time you're finished, you'll be able to create multiple builds of your game with the press of a button.

Nokia Customization

The Nokia UI provides a host of cool features that can really enhance the quality of any J2ME game. For example, using the FullCanvas class you'll be able to utilize much more of the screen for your game. Likewise, you can use the imaging tools to reduce the size of graphics and add vibration support for a nice death effect.

In the next few sections, you'll modify *Star Assault* to take advantage of these new features. After you see what changes you need to make, I'll show you how to use build scripts and pre-processing to maintain a single code base for all the device ports you'll carry out in the future.

FullCanvas

Nokia's FullCanvas class is more or less the same as the MIDP Canvas class, just without the title bar and the mandatory LCDUI command line. As you can see in Figure 14.1, you gain quite a bit of screen real estate as a result. Adding support for FullCanvas is therefore quite worthwhile.

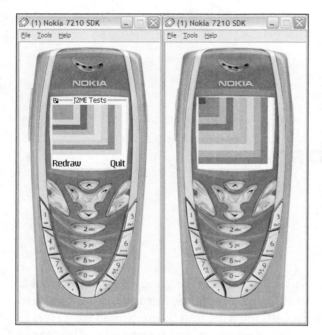

Figure 14.1 Taking advantage of the Nokia UI's full screen canvas means you gain extra space for games (left) than the normal LCDUI canvas (right).

Switching over to use FullCanvas is pretty easy. There are only two changes required. First, you need to derive the GameScreen class from FullCanvas, rather than Canvas. So instead of:

```
public class GameScreen extends Canvas implements Runnable, CommandListener
```

You'll use:

```
public class GameScreen extends FullCanvas implements Runnable
```

Notice I've also dropped the CommandListener interface. FullCanvas doesn't allow you to add commands (there's nowhere to draw them), so there's no point in having this interface.

Because you no longer have support for commands, you need to remove the code you use in the constructor to add the Menu command and set the listener. Here's the code you used to have in the constructor, now commented out:

```
public GameScreen(StarAssault midlet)
{
    ...
    // Command code
    // menu = new Command("Menu", Command.SCREEN, 1);
```

```
// addCommand(menu);
// setCommandListener(this);
```

You also need to remove the `commandAction` handler method.

Because you no longer have any commands, you might wonder how the player will exit to the menu. To support this, Nokia added two extra keys (`FullCanvas.SOFT_KEY1` and `FullCanvas.SOFT_KEY2`). These are the two keys you normally use to select commands on Nokia handsets; you can use them to bring up an in-game function or exit from a full-screen game. To support this, you simply check for these keys in the `keyPressed` method.

```
protected void keyPressed(int keyCode)
{
    ...
    if (keyCode == FullCanvas.KEY_SOFTKEY1 || keyCode == FullCanvas.KEY_SOFTKEY2)
    {
        pause();
        theMidlet.activateMenu();
    }
}
```

Because your game uses the `getWidth` and `getHeight` methods to dynamically set the size of the display, the game doesn't need any changes to adjust to the new screen size.

```
public GameScreen(StarAssault midlet)
{
    ...

    screenWidth = getWidth();
    screenHeight = getHeight();
```

That's it. *Star Assault* will now run in full-screen mode! Next you can look at adding Nokia vibration.

Vibration

Adding vibration to *Star Assault* is a good effect as well; however, you need to be careful not to overuse it. To implement this effect with the Nokia library, you simply call `DeviceControl.startVibra` with a limited time by adding a utility method to the `Tools` class.

```
public final static void vibrate(int strength, int time)
{
    if (StarAssault.getApp().isOptionVibrate())
    {
        DeviceControl.startVibra(strength, time);
    }
}
```

Using Reflection and Rotation

Probably the best of the Nokia UI features are in the imaging area, specifically the support for rotating and reflecting images. As you saw in Chapter 6, you can use the DirectGraphics class to draw an image reflected (either horizontally or vertically) or rotated by 90, 180, or 270 degrees.

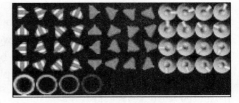

For *Star Assault*, many of the graphics (especially the fighters and turrets) are simply reflections or rotations of other images. Take another look at the ship graphics in Figure 14.2 and you can see what I mean.

Figure 14.2 The original ship graphics

If you look down the first column of yellow fighters, you can see that as you move down, each image is simply a 90-degree reflection of the previous one. This applies as you move across the columns too. If you take advantage of the Nokia tools, you can dispense with any image that is a 90-degree reflection of any other, so you can achieve the same result using the reduced set shown in Figure 14.3.

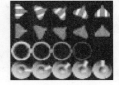

This version is less than half the number of bytes of the original, so it's well worth the trouble. You can add some code to generate the rest of the images on the fly.

Figure 14.3 Using reflection you need far fewer frames to represent all 16 directions.

Note

You'll notice something else different about the images you use for Nokia devices. That's right—transparency! Nokia supports this by default in PNG files.

Using reflection and rotation to simulate the different directions a sprite can move is a common trick, so I have some reasonably sophisticated methods to handle most situations.

First, you wrap up the reflection and rotation capabilities into a simpler method. The logical home for this is in the ImageSet class.

```
public final static Image getReflectedImage(Image source, boolean flipHorizontal,
boolean flipVertical)
{    // Create an image to draw onto and return.
    Image result = DirectUtils.createImage(source.getWidth(), source.getHeight(),
0x00000000);
    // Grab a reference to the Nokia UI DirectGraphics context for the result
    // image.
```

```
DirectGraphics rdg = DirectUtils.getDirectGraphics(result.getGraphics());
// Select the reflection required and execute it.
int flipType = 0;
if (flipHorizontal) flipType |= DirectGraphics.FLIP_HORIZONTAL;
if (flipVertical) flipType |= DirectGraphics.FLIP_VERTICAL;

rdg.drawImage(source, 0, 0, Tools.GRAPHICS_TOP_LEFT, flipType);

// Return the newly reflect image back to the requestor.
return result;
}
```

You can use this method to simplify reflection of an image horizontally or vertically (or both). For example, if you want to create another version of the enemy drone (the floating mine), using horizontally-reflected graphics you could just do:

```
Image droneImage = ImageSet.loadClippedImage("/mine.png", 0, 0);
droneSet = new ImageSet(1);
Image[] droneImages = ImageSet.extractFrames(droneImage, 0, 0, 3, 2, 16, 16);

// replace each image with a horizontally-reflected version
for (int i=0; i < droneImages.length; i++)
    droneImages[i] = ImageSet.getReflectedImage(droneImages[i], true, false);

droneSet.addState(droneImages, 800);
```

Nothing too difficult about that, but consider doing this for the ship (with its 16 directions). No really, I mean it—think about it for a second. As you can see in the revised graphics for your ships, you need to reflect all the angles in the first quadrant to the other three. Doing this using the previously mentioned method can quickly turn into a confusing mess. How about you write some code to handle all this?

Note

This method of reflection creates another copy of each image. While this is very fast, it also uses a lot of extra image memory. The built-in Nokia UI reflection code is actually so fast on most Nokia MIDs that it's possible to do this type of reflection in real-time, without having to create another copy of each reflection of the image. To do this I use an expanded version of the ImageSet class which adds an option for a particular state to be a reflection of another. You can see a complete example of this on the CD under the Chapter 14 source code directory.

Before you look at the code to do this, I'd better explain what I'm doing a little more. Depending on the game and the sprites you're working with, you need to do different forms of reflection. The number and type you do really come down to how many directions the sprite can face. A man walking in a 2D side-scrolling game only needs two directions, left and right. For this you only need one source image (and one reflection). For a monster in a top-down dungeon crawl, you would need as many as eight directions. For the more sophisticated hero graphics in a fantasy game (or in this case, the fighter in *Star Assault*), you use 16 directions. If you think back to your reflection tools, you can use copies of any image that is a 90-degree reflection of another. Figure 14.4 shows some of these typical cases; the colored fighters are the original source images.

As you can see in Figure 14.4, if you have a sprite with two directions you can simply mirror the first direction to get the other one. For four directions or more, you mirror all the source images both vertically and horizontally. In essence, you're reflecting each source image on its opposing axis. Take a look at a method to automate this process for any number of directions.

```
public final static Image[] getAxisReflections(Image[] source)
{
    int n = source.length;
    if (n == 0) return null;
```

First, the method takes an array of source images, and then, based on the number, it returns the axis reflections of these. To start, you need to figure out how many images are in the resulting array. For cases other than one or two, this is the number of source images minus one, multiplied by four (the maximum number of reflections any image can have). You can check this by looking at the diagram and counting the number of resulting images for the one with three source directions. The number of images in the result is

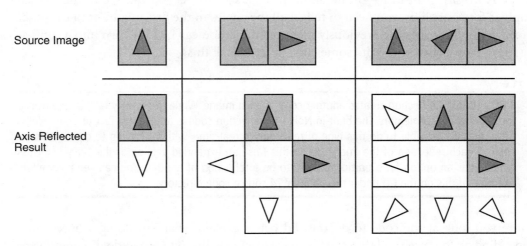

Figure 14.4 Common reflection cases for sprite graphics

equal to three minus one, which is two; multiply that by four, and you get a total of eight. If you did this for four source images, the result would be 12; for five images (the number in *Star Assault*), the result would be 16.

```
int total = (n - 1) * 4;
// special case for simple reflections
if (n < 3) total = n * 2;
```

Once you have the number of result images, you simply create an array and then copy in the source images.

```
Image[] result = new Image[total];

// copy the original images to the result
for (int i = 0; i < n; i++)
    result[i] = source[i];
```

Next you take care of the two easy cases, mirroring horizontally and vertically. Because there has to be at least one image, you always mirror source image zero vertically (feel free to default this to horizontal if you want) and place the resulting image halfway into the result. If the number of source images is greater than one, you also mirror the horizontal image into the result in a similar fashion.

```
// mirror the vertical (0 to 180)
result[total / 2] = getReflectedImage(source[0], true, false);

// mirror the horizontal (90 to 270)
if (n > 1)
{
    // you can think of total/4 as 90 degrees and total/2 as 180
    // keep in mind we're starting at 0 for array access
    result[total / 2 + (total / 4)] = getReflectedImage(source[n - 1],
                                        false, true);
}
```

The remaining code handles cases in which you have more than two source images. For each of these images, you reflect them into the other three quadrants of the circle. There's no rocket science to this; you just loop through those images and use vertical or horizontal reflection (or both) to mirror the images into the appropriate position in the result.

```
// mirror everything between 0 and 90 to the three other quadrants
if (n > 2)
{
    // now this gets a little messy; we need to mirror everything
    // in between 0 and 90 to the other quadrants. Since N > 2 we know we
```

```
        // have at least 1 image we need to reflect. First let's figure out how
        // many there are in the first quadrant, minus the two axes we already
        // took care of.
        int f = (n - 2);

        // now we mirror these to their opposing sides for the other 3
        // quadrants
        for (int i = 1; i <= f; i++)
        {
            result[total / 2 - i] = getReflectedImage(source[i], true, false);
            result[total / 2 + i] = getReflectedImage(source[i], true, true);
            result[total - i] = getReflectedImage(source[i], false, true);
        }
    }
    return result;
}
```

Now take a look at this code in a little more detail.

To use this code with your new fighter graphics, you adjust the image loading to suit the smaller PNG file, and then use the extractFrames method to create the rest.

```
yellowDirImages = ImageSet.extractFrames(shipImage, 0, 0, 5, 1, 16, 16);
yellowDirImages = ImageSet.getAxisReflections(yellowDirImages);
```

You can then use the image array in the same way you would if you loaded it directly from the image file. And you can use this code to reflect any number of source images.

That's where I'll stop with Nokia customization (although there are still plenty of things you could add).

All these code changes have created a problem, though. Your game no longer works with any MID other than a Nokia! At this point you could simply create different versions of the class files, but this quickly becomes hard to manage. What you'll look at next is how to use a build system to manage multiple versions of the same class.

Build Systems

Build systems are a traditional part of software development—they've been around almost as long as programming languages have. A build system lets you automate many of the typical development tasks such as compiling, packaging, and versioning. You can think of it as a big scripting system for your software projects.

One of the best reasons to use a build system is to automate rebuilding your projects to suit different device ports or languages. As you saw when you customized *Star Assault* to use the features available in the Nokia UI, you need to maintain different versions of your code in order to support different MID features.

As you start to add this support for more device formats, as well as for other languages, graphics, and resources, you'll quickly end up in a mess. A build system makes this process manageable (if not easy and fun).

Another great reason to use a build system is to access the extra tools available from third parties. You'll find a huge number of plug-ins for build systems that can automate all sorts of things for you. For J2ME development in particular, you can use the Antenna system (a plug-in for the Ant build system) to add features such as source code preprocessing and automated packaging and obfuscation (a class file optimization method that reduces file sizes).

For Java, the best build system is Ant, part of the open-source Apache Jakarta project. You can start by getting Ant set up and running.

Setting Up Ant

Ant is available free from its home page, `http://ant.apache.org`. You'll need to download the latest version (I've also included a copy on the CD) and unzip it to an appropriate directory on your machine. The system requirements for Ant are very light; basically, if you're using your machine for J2ME development, you should have no trouble using Ant.

Typically developers use Ant either from the command line or through integration in an IDE. Most modern IDEs directly support the use of Ant builds, so I recommend a little investigating as to what integration might be available.

To run Ant from the command line, you first need to set up the `ANT_HOME` environment to point to the directory where you unzipped the distribution (see Chapter 4 for a reminder on setting environment variables). For example:

```
set ANT_HOME= c:\java\ext\jakarta-ant-1.5.4
```

You should also add the `bin` directory to your path.

```
set PATH=%PATH%;%ANT_HOME%\bin
```

For Ant to function correctly, you also need to have the `JAVA_HOME` environment set to the location of your JDK. If you're not sure whether it's set correctly, then check. Having it set incorrectly can result in weird errors down the road. To make sure everything is set up correctly, enter the following at a command prompt:

```
ant -?
```

You can see the result in Figure 14.5.

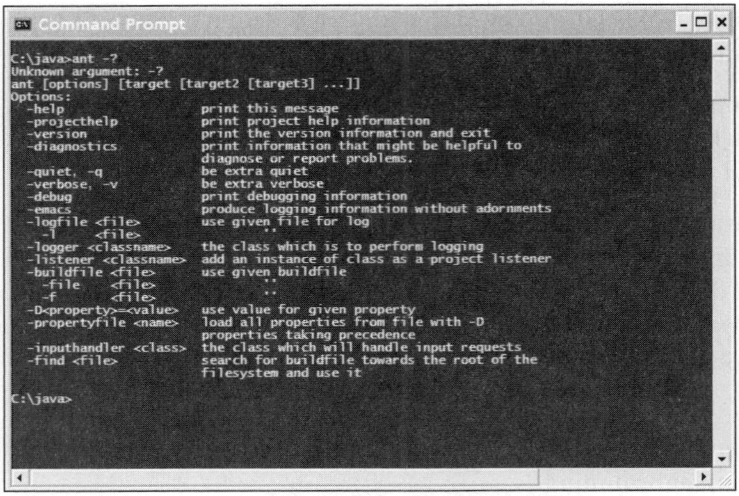

Figure 14.5 The output from executing the ant with the help option

Creating a Build File

To use Ant, you need to create an XML-formatted text file known as a *build* file. You can think of it a little like a scripting system, with the build files being your script and Ant being the interpreter.

The structure of an Ant build file follows the same thought process as traditional make files—that is, you define everything in terms of build *targets*. Take a look at a simple build file, and I'll show you what I mean.

Tip

You can see a complete example of a build.xml file in the *Star Assault* project directory on the CD.

```
<project name="My Project" default="compile">

    <target name="init">
        <property name="sourceDir" value="src" />
        <property name="outputDir" value="classes" />
    </target>

    <target name="clean" depends="init">
        <delete dir="${outputDir}" />
        <mkdir dir="${outputDir}" />
    </target>
```

```
  <target name="compile" depends="clean">
    <javac srcdir="${sourceDir}" destdir="${outputDir}" />
  </target>
</project>
```

In this example I'm defining three separate targets: init, clean, and compile. These are three tasks that I want to perform as part of the build process. init sets up the parameters (such as directory names), clean removes any files from a previous build process, and compile runs javac to build all the source files.

To run this build process with Ant, you would specify one of the targets. For example, run the following with the build.xml file in the current directory:

```
ant -f build.xml clean
```

This will execute all the tasks in the clean target. If you ran this build process, you'd see something like this:

```
$ ant -f build.xml clean
Buildfile: build.xml

init:

clean:
    [delete] Deleting directory C:\java\classes
    [mkdir] Created dir: C:\java\classes

BUILD SUCCESSFUL
Total time: 1 second
```

Notice how Ant processed the init target as well? That's because you defined the clean target to be dependent on the init target (depends="init"). Ant therefore executed the tasks in the init target first. If you look down at the compile target, you can see that it depends on the clean target. I reckon you can guess what happens if you build using that target. Here's the output:

```
$ ant -f build.xml compile
Buildfile: build.xml

init:

clean:
    [delete] Deleting directory C:\java\classes
    [mkdir] Created dir: C:\java\classes
```

```
compile:

BUILD FAILED
file:c:/java/build.xml:14: srcdir "C:\java\src" does not exist!

Total time: 1 second
```

As you can see, Ant executed the dependents (`init` and `clean`) prior to the `compile` task. Don't worry about the error.

Building up dependent targets is a little like programming, but in reverse. You get the hang of it pretty fast. Now take a closer look at the tasks that make up each of these targets—after all, they're doing all the work.

Tasks

Ant tasks are a little like statements in Java; each one carries out a specific task for you. Like everything in Ant build files, you write tasks using XML tags. A good example is the `delete` task used in the `clean` target.

```
<delete dir="${outputDir}" />
```

The great thing about Ant is the huge variety of tasks available, many of which are very natural to Java programmers. Table 14.1 is a short list of some of the more useful ones. I recommend reviewing the Ant manual for a complete list.

Table 14.1 Common Ant Tasks

Task	Description
copy	Copy a file or directory.
cvs	Access a CVS repository.
delete	Delete a file or directory.
echo	Output a message to the console.
exec	Execute another application.
get	Get a file using a URL.
jar	Jar a set of files.
java	Execute a java task. (Creates a new Virtual Machine)
javac	Compile some java source files.
mail	E-mail something to someone.
mkdir	Make a new directory.
mve	Move a file or directory.
sql	Execute an SQL statement.
zip	Create a zip archive.

One of the most powerful things about Ant is that it gives you the ability to create your own custom tasks. After you've become familiar with using it, I recommend you invest a little time learning how to make up new tasks. You'll be amazed what you can do.

Properties

In previous examples, you would have noticed the use of values such as ${blah}. A value such as this is an Ant property. It's just like any field (variable) you would use in a program. You can declare a property using the format:

```
<property name="outputDir" value="classes" />
```

This creates a new property you can access using ${outputDir}. Remember that you need to declare the properties in your build file before you use them.

As I did in the earlier example, it's common practice to declare properties for all your project-specific settings, such as specific directory or file names, inside an init target at the top of your project.

Using Antenna

Antenna is a library of tasks for Ant specifically to help with J2ME development. There's direct support for compiling, preverifying, packaging, obfuscating, and executing your MIDlets from your build script. There's also a very handy Java code preprocessor that you'll use to handle all those different build cases. Table 14.2 lists the important Antenna tasks.

Table 14.2 Antenna Tasks

Task	Description
wtkjad	Update or create JAD files (including all the properties).
wtkbuild	Similar to Ant's javac task, except it handles bootclasspath.
wtkpackage	Similar to Ant's jar task, but it adds better handling of JAD files and allows for other J2ME steps such as obfuscation and preverification.
wtkrun	Runs a MIDlet suite in the Wireless Toolkit's emulator.
wtkpreverify	Used for preverifying a set of classes. (Not normally required because the build and package tasks will do this for you.)
wtkobfuscate	Used for obfuscating a JAR file. (Not normally required because the packaging task will obfuscate as well.)
wtksmartlink	Detects and removes unnecessary classes from a JAR file.
wtkpreprocess	Java source preprocessor like you'd find in C.

Setting Up Antenna

You can obtain the latest copy of Antenna from `http://antenna.sourceforge.net`. To get it working with Ant, you need to copy the JAR file into Ant's `lib` directory. To make the tasks available in Ant, you need to declare them using Ant's `taskdef` task. To keep this nice and organized, I usually put my task declarations in a `setup` target and place it way down at the bottom of the build file (where I'll hopefully never have to look at it again). Here's the `setup` target, including the declarations for all the Antenna tasks:

```
<target name="setup">
   <!-- Antenna Setup -->
   <taskdef name="wtkjad" classname="de.pleumann.antenna.WtkJad"/>
   <taskdef name="wtkbuild" classname="de.pleumann.antenna.WtkBuild"/>
   <taskdef name="wtkpackage" classname="de.pleumann.antenna.WtkPackage"/>
   <taskdef name="wtkmakeprc" classname="de.pleumann.antenna.WtkMakePrc"/>
   <taskdef name="wtkrun" classname="de.pleumann.antenna.WtkRun"/>
   <taskdef name="wtkpreverify" classname="de.pleumann.antenna.WtkPreverify"/>
   <taskdef name="wtkobfuscate" classname="de.pleumann.antenna.WtkObfuscate"/>
   <taskdef name="wtksmartlink" classname="de.pleumann.antenna.WtkSmartLink"/>
   <taskdef name="wtkpreprocess" classname="de.pleumann.antenna.WtkPreprocess"/>
</target>
```

Keep in mind that for this to work, you need to execute the `setup` target before you use any of these tasks. The best method to do this is to make the `init` target depend on it. For example:

```
<target name="init" depends="setup">
```

Now that you have Antenna tasks ready to go, take a look at a basic build script for a J2ME project.

A Basic Build

For a J2ME project, the main components of a build file using Antenna carry out the following steps: initialize (and set up) the build, clean up any old files, compile the project, create the JAD file, create the JAR, and then run the emulator. Here's the entire thing, although I've excluded the `setup` target to keep it short:

```
<project name="StarAssault" default="run nokia" basedir=".">

   <!-- ......................... INIT ................................. -->
   <target name="init" depends="setup">
      <property name="wtk.home" value="c:\java\wtk104"/>
      <property name="midlet.name" value="StarAssault"/>
   </target>

   <target name="device build" depends="init">
```

```xml
    <property name="bd" value="build"/>

    <delete dir="${bd}/classes"/>
    <mkdir dir="${bd}/classes"/>

    <!-- compile -->
    <javac destdir="${bd}/classes" srcdir="${bd}/psrc"
        bootclasspath="${midplib}" debug="true" target="1.1"/>

    <!-- create JAD file -->
    <wtkjad jadfile="${bd}/${midlet.name}.jad"
        jarfile="${bd}/${midlet.name}.jar"
        name="${midlet.name}" vendor="Martin Wells" version="1.0.0"/>

    <!-- create JAR file -->
    <wtkpackage jarfile="${bd}/${midlet.name}.jar"
        jadfile="${bd}/${midlet.name}.jad"
        preverify="true"
        classpath="${midplib}"
        obfuscate="true">

        <fileset dir="${bd}/classes"/>
        <fileset dir="${bd}/res"/>
    </wtkpackage>
</target>

<target name="run nokia" depends="device build">
    <exec executable="C:\j2me\Nokia\Devices\Nokia_7210_MIDP_SDK_v1_0\bin\7210.exe">
        <arg line="build/${midlet.name}.jad"/>
    </exec>
</target>

... setup target

</project>
```

The first line of this example declares the project and sets the base directory to the current directory (.). For our purposes the current directory is wherever Ant is executed. All non-relative directories (ones that don't start with a /) you use in the project will be relative to this one. Using the directory from which you execute ant is typically fine. The project line also sets the default target to be run nokia. If you don't specify a target on the command line, the Ant interpreter will execute this one for you.

```xml
<project name="StarAssault" default="run nokia" basedir=".">
```

The next section is the typical property declaring an `init` target. You'll see these parameters in action in a bit.

```
<target name="init" depends="setup">
    <property name="wtk.home" value="c:\java\wtk104"/>
    <property name="midlet.name" value="StarAssault"/>
</target>
```

The next target, `device build`, is where all the action is. First you declare the target (depending on `init`) and then you set up a build directory property named "bd" (though you can name it something different if you like), in which all your build files will go later. After that you use `delete` and `mkdir` tasks to clean out the results of any previous builds. The `midplib` property is used to point to the correct MIDP libraries for the device you're building for.

```
<target name="device build" depends="init">
    <property name="bd" value="build"/>
    <property name="midplib" value="${wtk.home}/lib/midpapi.zip"/>
    <delete dir="${bd}/classes"/>
    <mkdir dir="${bd}/classes"/>
```

The next step in the build process is to compile the source. Here I'm just using the Ant javac task along with the appropriate `bootclasspath` and target version number. (Remember to use `target="1.2"` if you're using the Wireless Toolkit version 2.) You could use the Antenna task, but I don't think it really adds anything, so it's cleaner (and more flexible later) to just stick with `javac`.

```
<!-- compile -->
<javac destdir="${bd}/classes" srcdir="src"
        bootclasspath="${midplib}" debug="true" target="1.1"/>
```

After the classes have been compiled, you create the JAD file. You can add any additional attributes you want in here.

```
<!-- create JAD file -->
<wtkjad jadfile="${bd}/${midlet.name}.jad"
        jarfile="${bd}/${midlet.name}.jar"
        name="${midlet.name}" vendor="Martin Wells" version="1.0.0"/>
```

You can then package up your classes (and other files) into the JAR. To do so, you use the coolest of the Antenna tasks, `wtkpackage`. It preverifies and then JARs up everything all in one go. I'm including the content of the `classes` and `res` directories (where all your graphics and other resource files should go).

```
<!-- create JAR file using the specified JAD and other options -->
<wtkpackage jarfile="${bd}/${midlet.name}.jar"
            jadfile="${bd}/${midlet.name}.jad"
```

```
            preverify="true"
            classpath="${midplib}">

    <fileset dir="${bd}/classes"/>
    <fileset dir="${bd}/res"/>
</wtkpackage>
```

The final part of the build process is to run the game in an emulator. Again, I'm not using the Antenna task because I don't think it really adds anything. You can create any number of these types of tasks to run on different emulators.

```
<target name="run nokia" depends="device build">
    <exec executable="C:\j2me\Nokia\Devices\Nokia_7210_MIDP_SDK_v1_0\bin\7210.exe">
        <arg line="build/${midlet.name}.jad"/>
    </exec>
</target>
```

To get all this working, you need to place all your source files in the src directory and all the graphics and other resources in the res directory. If you then place the build.xml file in the root of your project's directory and execute ant (by itself), you'll have a fully auto-built project running in an emulator before you know it.

Obfuscation

The class files produced by the Java compiler (bytecode) retain much of the information you have inside your source—things like the full class, method, and field names (but not comments). Because humans never read bytecode, you might ask whether there is really a difference in calling a method a() rather than loadNewObjectFromHeapPoolInstanceNowPleaseOK(). If you used names like a(), your code would be hopelessly confusing, but to a bytecode interpreter it makes no difference. It does, however, make a big difference to the size of the resulting class file. All those long names equate to more actual bytes in the class, and thus the final JAR file.

An obfuscator (try saying that quickly while eating peanuts) simply "renames" all the string names in your class files with shorter names (such as a(), b(), and so on). The end result is typically a 20- to 50-percent reduction in the final size of your files.

To add support for this in your projects, you can use the ProGuard obfuscator by Mark Welch. You can download it from http://proguard.sourceforge.net.

To make the ProGuard obfuscator work with Antenna, you need to copy the ProGuard JAR file to the Ant lib directory. Now comes the really difficult and complicated part—enabling obfuscation using Antenna. Here's the wtkpackage task, this time with obfuscation enabled:

```
<wtkpackage jarfile="${bd}/${midlet.name}.jar"
            jadfile="${bd}/${midlet.name}.jad"
            preverify="true"
            obfuscate="true"
            classpath="${midplib}">

  <fileset dir="${bd}/classes"/>
  <fileset dir="${bd}/res"/>
</wtkpackage>
```

All you have to do is add the `obfuscate="true"` and, assuming you have the ProGuard JAR in the right place, Antenna takes care of the rest. Okay, so it wasn't that hard. . . .

Now you've got the basic build process out of the way. But Antenna still has one trick up its sleeve—the preprocessor. In the next section, you'll see how you can use the pre-processor to build multiple versions of the same project.

Preprocessing

Now you get to the really great thing about Antenna—the preprocessor. This nifty little fea-ture lets you generate different source code based on conditionals and includes that you can embed inside your source. Table 14.3 lists the preprocessor commands that are available.

For this to work, you need to add another step into the compile process. Before compil-ing the Java source files, you run them through the Antenna preprocessor task. The out-put from this is a new Java source file incorporating changes made by the preprocessor.

Table 14.3 Antenna Preprocessor Commands

Command	Description
#define	Defines an identifier for later use in an `ifdef`.
#undefine	Undefines an identifier so that an `ifdef` returns `false`.
#if	Tests an expression, such as `#if (DEBUG) || (TEST)`.
#elif	Tests an expression (as an alternative to an `if`).
#ifdef	Tests whether an identifier is defined, such as `#ifdef DEBUG`.
#ifndef	Tests whether an identifier is not defined.
#else	Used to include code as an alternative to an `#ifdef` or `#ifndef`.
#elifdef	Tests a new identifier as an alternative to a previous `#ifdef`.
#elifndef	Similar to `#elifdef`, but tests whether an identifier is not defined.
#endif	Used to close an i#fdef.
#include	Includes the contents of a file; must be closed with an `#endinclude`.

Obviously you can't overwrite your existing source code with the preprocessed ones (at least not more than once), so you need a new directory other than src to store the results of the preprocessor. For this I use build/psrc.

To use the preprocessor, you need to add a new task into the build file just prior to compilation (the javac task). Notice I've also changed the compile task to use the preprocessed source directory. Let me clarify this for you: You have to preprocess your files before they can be compiled.

```
<!-- preprocess -->
<property name="debug" value="debug"/>
<wtkpreprocess srcdir="src" destdir="${bd}/psrc" symbols="${debug}"
               verbose="true"/>


<!-- compile -->
<javac destdir="${bd}/classes" srcdir="${bd}/psrc"
       bootclasspath="${midplib}" debug="true" target="1.1"/>
```

Just before the wtkpreprocess task, I've declared a property called debug with the value debug. I then include this value in the symbols parameter when calling the preprocessor. You can use these symbols in any preprocessor expression (such as #ifdef).

All right, now you're ready to add some preprocessing instructions to your source code. Preprocessor commands are added directly into Java source code as comments, which means your IDE won't freak out. Here's an example of a conditional compile based on whether you declared the debug symbol:

```
//#ifdef debug
    System.out.println("I am in debug mode!");
//#else
    System.out.println("I am NOT in debug mode!");
//#endif
```

If you now run the preprocessor over this code (with the debug symbol set), you'll get a new file in the build/psrc directory with the code:

```
//#ifdef debug
    System.out.println("I am in debug mode!");
//#else
//#    System.out.println("I am NOT in debug mode!");
//#endif
```

Notice the preprocessed version of this code has the second print line commented out. This is all the preprocessor does; it simply comments out anything in the source that doesn't match the conditionals. Commenting is better than simply removing the source from the resulting file because it makes it easier to debug preprocessing results. (Sometimes preprocessing conditionals can get quite complicated so it's good to check the result.) This also means the line numbers won't change when you're debugging code.

Keep in mind that comments are only included in your source file if you've turned on debug output—and even if left in they will be removed by the obfuscator—so they take effectively no space in the resulting JAR file.

Note

Keep in mind that once you start using a preprocessor, you'll no longer be able to compile your code using an IDE; things just won't work as you intended. It might be worth exploring the capabilities of your system, though. Some IDEs let you run an Ant task prior to compiling.

The other useful preprocessor command is #include. This is great if you want to embed entirely different versions of files (such as resource tables) or alternative implementations of methods or classes. Typically, I try to avoid using #include because most IDEs don't deal well with fragments of Java code in different files.

Those are the basics of using the preprocessor, although actually it doesn't get much more complicated than that anyway. Next you'll see how to use the preprocessor to help you build different versions of the game for different conditions.

Multi-Device Builds

If you recall, at the start of the chapter you customized the *Star Assault* code to use special features available through the Nokia UI. Unfortunately, this means the current version of the game won't work on any devices that don't support these features—basically anything other than a Nokia. In this section, you'll see how to use Ant and Antenna to adapt your code to support multiple devices.

There are two main areas you need to cover to build different versions—resource management and device-specific code. Since I just covered the preprocessor, let's tackle the changes to the code first.

Device-Specific Code

The most convenient way to manage different source code versions is to use the preprocessor to embed conditionals based on the device you're building for directly inside the code. Although it would be cleaner (and more organized) to use device sub-classing (different versions of classes for different devices), you really can't afford the extra space these new classes would add to the JAR file.

A simple example of how to use the device preprocessor is the vibration code you saw earlier. You can use a preprocessor condition to wrap up the Nokia-specific code if you're building only a Nokia version. To do this, you first need to set a symbol in the call to the preprocessor that identifies the device for which you're building. In the following task, I'm using the dev property to indicate this.

```
<!-- preprocess -->
<property name="debug" value="debug"/>
<property name="dev" value="nokia"/>
<wtkpreprocess srcdir="src" destdir="${bd}/psrc" symbols="${debug}, ${dev}"
                verbose="true"/>
```

The value of dev is now available as a condition for the preprocessor. Here are the changes to the Tools class. Notice I've wrapped all the Nokia-specific code in if blocks.

```
//#ifdef nokia
import com.nokia.mid.ui.DeviceControl;
//#endif


...


public final static void vibrate(int strength, int time)
{
    if (StarAssault.getApp().isOptionVibrate())
    {
        //#ifdef nokia
            DeviceControl.startVibra(strength, time);
        //#endif
    }
}
```

You can see that it's easy to add different code versions based on different device values. Another good case is the use of plain old Canvas versus the enhanced Nokia FullCanvas class. For example:

```
//#ifdef nokia
public class GameScreen extends FullCanvas implements Runnable
//#else
public class GameScreen extends Canvas implements Runnable, CommandListener
//#endif
```

Unfortunately, mode IDEs aren't particularly happy with this type of code (but they get over it).

Those are the basics of multi-device code; you just keep wrapping the device-specific code inside preprocessor conditionals. Next you'll take a look at how to handle resources for different devices.

Managing Resources

As you saw at the start of this chapter, Nokia has some great features. Some of these, such as transparent PNGs and image reflection and rotation, require you to use different image files for different builds. Handling this manually (by copying files) might be okay for one or two devices, but when you're dealing with many devices or many types of different files it can become a real mess. Thankfully, you can use Ant to automate this process as well.

First you need to organize your resource files a little better. What you do is create a directory for all of the default resources—versions of the files (mostly images) that you'll use unless a particular device chooses to override them—as well as a directory for each device that has its own custom resources. The directory structure is listed in Figure 14.6; to help you understand, I've included the entire build structure as well:

Now here's the cool bit. When you build a version of the game, you use Ant to copy all the resources from the default directory (`res/default`) into the build resource directory for the device you're building (in this case, `build/nokia/res`). You then copy the device-specific resource over the top of this (`res/nokia` to `build/nokia/res`). Here's the Ant build to do this. (I've also included a revised version of the `wtkpackage` task using the new directory.)

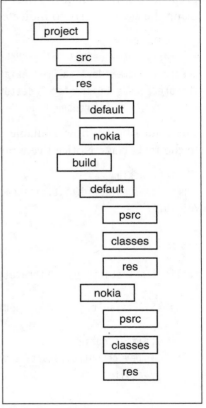

Figure 14.6 The directory structure

```
<!-- copy the default resources -->
<copy todir="${bd}/res">
    <fileset dir="res/default"/>
</copy>

<!-- copy over anything specific to this device -->
<copy overwrite="true" todir="${bd}/res">
    <fileset dir="res/${dev}"/>
</copy>

<wtkpackage jarfile="${bd}/${midlet.name}.jar"
            jadfile="${bd}/${midlet.name}.jad"
```

```
            preverify="true"
            classpath="${midplib}"
            obfuscate="true">
    <fileset dir="${bd}/classes"/>
    <fileset dir="${bd}/res"/>
</wtkpackage>
```

You can now move the Nokia-specific image files into the res/nokia directory and the original default version images into the res/default directory.

The Complete Build

All the components of your build process are ready to go now. However, there's still a little problem. In order to build different versions of the game, you would need to change the value of the dev property by editing the build file. This becomes annoying after a while, especially if you're constantly switching between versions for testing purposes (something I recommend you do quite a bit during development). Wouldn't it be nice if you could build a different version simply by using a different target?

To do this, you can set the device parameter and then "call" the device build target. For example:

```
<target name="build nokia" depends="init">
    <property name="dev" value="nokia"/>
    <property name="midplib"
        value="C:\j2me\Nokia\Devices\Nokia_7210_MIDP_SDK_v1_0\lib\classes.zip"/>
    <antcall target="device build"/>
</target>
```

Notice you set the midplib set prior to the call. This lets you use alternative libraries for compilation as well.

All right, now you have all the pieces, so let's take a look at the entire build file in one go. This version includes builds for Nokia, Vodafone, and the default device, as well as a convenient "build all" target.

```
<project name="StarAssault" default="compile" basedir=".">

    <!-- ......................... INIT ................................ -->
    <target name="init" depends="setup">
        <buildnumber file="ext/build.number"/>
        <property name="wtk.home" value="c:\java\wtk104"/>
        <property name="midlet.name" value="StarAssault"/>
        <property name="debug" value="debug"/>
    </target>
```

Build target specifically for a device using the Nokia UI. Note the use of a different `midplib` file.

```
<!-- ..................... DEVICE: NOKIA ....................... -->
<target name="build nokia" depends="init">
    <property name="dev" value="nokia"/>
    <property name="midplib"
value="C:\j2me\Nokia\Devices\Nokia_7210_MIDP_SDK_v1_0\lib\classes.zip"/>
    <antcall target="device build"/>
</target>
```

Executes the Nokia 7210 emulator.

```
<target name="run nokia" depends="build nokia">
    <exec executable="C:\j2me\Nokia\Devices\Nokia_7210_MIDP_SDK_v1_0\bin\7210.exe">
        <arg line="build/${dev}/${midlet.name}.jad"/>
    </exec>
</target>
```

Build target for the default MIDP 1 toolkit emulator.

```
<!-- ..................... DEVICE: DEFAULT ...................... -->
<target name="build default" depends="init">
    <property name="dev" value="default"/>
    <property name="midplib" value="${wtk.home}/lib/midpapi.zip"/>
    <antcall target="device build"/>
</target>

<target name="run default" depends="build default">
    <exec executable="C:\java\WTK104\bin\emulator.exe">
        <arg line="-Xdescriptor:build/${dev}/${midlet.name}.jad"/>
    </exec>
</target>
```

The following task is a method of building all of the targets in one go. This is something you might do when packaging up lots of different builds for a publisher.

```
<!-- ..................... BUILD ALL ...................... -->


<target name="build all" depends="init">

    <antcall target="build nokia"></antcall>

    <antcall target="build default"></antcall>

    <antcall target="build deftrans"></antcall>
```

```
      </target>



      <!-- .......................... TOOLS .............................-->
```

This is the bulk of the build process and is called by the different tasks to carry out a build on a specific device.

```
      <!-- ......................... DEVICE BUILD ....................... -->

   <target name="device build" depends="init">
      <property name="bd" value="build/${dev}"/> <!-- build dir -->
      <delete dir="${bd}/psrc"/>
      <delete dir="${bd}/classes"/>
      <mkdir dir="${bd}/psrc"/>
      <mkdir dir="${bd}/classes"/>
      <!-- preprocess-->
      <wtkpreprocess srcdir="src" destdir="${bd}/psrc" symbols="${dev},${debug}"
                     verbose="true"/>
      <!-- compile -->
      <javac destdir="${bd}/classes" srcdir="${bd}/psrc"
             bootclasspath="${midplib}" debug="true" target="1.1"/>
      <!-- create JAD file -->
      <wtkjad jadfile="${bd}/${midlet.name}.jad"
              jarfile="${bd}/${midlet.name}.jar"
              name="${midlet.name}" vendor="Martin Wells" version="1.0.0">
         <midlet name="${midlet.name}" class="${midlet.name}"/>
         <attribute name="MIDxlet-API" value="VSCL-1.0.1"/>
      </wtkjad>


      <!-- copy resources then package it up -->
      <copy todir="${bd}/res">
         <fileset dir="res/default"/>
      </copy>                  <!-- copy default resource -->
      <copy overwrite="true" todir="${bd}/res">
         <fileset dir="res/${dev}"/>
      </copy>                            <!-- copy overrides -->

      <wtkpackage jarfile="${bd}/${midlet.name}.jar" jadfile="${bd}/${midlet.name}.jad"
preverify="true"
              classpath="${midplib}"><!--obfuscate="true"-->
```

```
        <fileset dir="${bd}/classes"/>
        <fileset dir="${bd}/res"/>
    </wtkpackage>
  </target>

  <!-- ............................. SETUP ......................... -->
  <target name="setup">
    <!-- Antenna Setup -->
    <taskdef name="wtkjad" classname="de.pleumann.antenna.WtkJad"/>
    <taskdef name="wtkbuild" classname="de.pleumann.antenna.WtkBuild"/>
    <taskdef name="wtkpackage" classname="de.pleumann.antenna.WtkPackage"/>
    <taskdef name="wtkmakeprc" classname="de.pleumann.antenna.WtkMakePrc"/>
    <taskdef name="wtkrun" classname="de.pleumann.antenna.WtkRun"/>
    <taskdef name="wtkpreverify" classname="de.pleumann.antenna.WtkPreverify"/>
    <taskdef name="wtkobfuscate" classname="de.pleumann.antenna.WtkObfuscate"/>
    <taskdef name="wtksmartlink" classname="de.pleumann.antenna.WtkSmartLink"/>
    <taskdef name="wtkpreprocess" classname="de.pleumann.antenna.WtkPreprocess"/>
  </target>
</project>
```

Conclusion

Now that wasn't so hard, was it? A preprocessor really does allow you to take advantage of all those cool features made available by manufacturers.

Even though there are plenty of other methods, such as using implementation classes and interfaces, there's nothing quite as simple as just whacking in the customization exactly where you need it. No new classes or restructuring, and most importantly, no wasted precious JAR space—you must protect the precious.

Managing the resources for your builds is important as well. Using the simple process you set up in the build, you can split out different versions of your files based on each device type. I've also included a default resource directory for all those files that don't need customization. You certainly don't need to stop here. If you want, you can add different logical layers to this process, such as a split between default and default-transparent or a resource tree for one class of devices. You can easily adapt the copy process to take this into account.

With device ports out of the way, next you'll look at how to speed up your games using various optimization techniques.

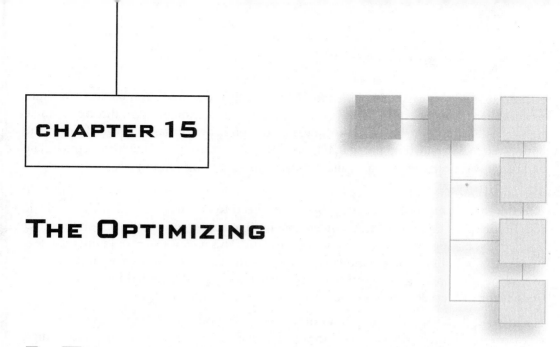

CHAPTER 15

THE OPTIMIZING

Now that you have a game basically working, it's time to work on optimizing performance. In this chapter, you'll start by looking at when and where it's best to optimize the code before you step through the use of the various tools at your disposal. You'll also work through a number of general techniques to improve the performance of your code in any game.

Speed, Glorious Speed

Sometimes I think half of game development is optimization. And with J2ME's typically limited CPU and RAM capabilities, it's even more important to squeeze as much as you can out of the devices. Depending on how you approach it—and whether a deadline is looming—optimizing code can be fun or frustrating. However, there is nothing quite like seeing your game's performance jump as you track down and eliminate the weak points in your code.

When to Optimize

I have a friend who is what you might call an "academic" programmer. He typically works on large-scale simulation systems (predicting little things like the motion of planets around a black hole). A few years ago he decided to try his hand at game programming. The work required the creation of a physics simulation of a dirt-racing bike. Being an expert in mathematical dynamics, he spent three months developing probably the best physics simulation I've ever seen. It was damn near perfect. Unfortunately—yep, you guessed it—that sports racing bike ran like a 30-year-old scooter. You couldn't measure performance in frames per second because it wasn't quick enough to get through a single frame! When fully integrated with the game, the poor performance dragged down the entire system. We ended up fixing it, but not without effectively starting from scratch. The end result was nowhere near as realistic, but it was a lot more fun to play.

The important point of this story is that optimization is an ongoing process, both in code direction and in the development process. You need to approach things with a realistic idea of the speed of your code. As you go, you need to keep a constant watch on the effect your code is having on the performance of the game. This means you should integrate features into the full game early and continually test the effects of your code on the game's overall performance—unlike my friend. If you're developing something you've never done before, it's even more important to keep a close eye on the effects of your code.

Having said that, I should also point out that optimization can be your enemy. Excessive or early optimization of your code can waste time and, believe it or not, introduce bugs. When you develop new code you have to be conscious of your game's overall performance, but you shouldn't go so far as to fine-tuning every bit of code. Concentrate on getting the functionality of your game going first, making sure your code runs well at a reasonable frame rate. Leave the intensive performance tweaking for later in the project.

Leaving extreme optimizing until later in the development cycle also means you don't waste time optimizing something that might not make it into your game. It's quite common to throw out parts as you come up against resource limitations (or just because an aspect doesn't work well), so you don't want to waste too much time optimizing it. This will happen more often than you think when you face the reality of J2ME JAR size limits.

Don't Optimize Blindly

This brings me to probably the most important aspect of optimization. Don't optimize code you *think* is slow; optimize what you *know* is slow. It amazes me how often I still make the mistake of thinking a part of my code is slow when in fact it's hardly affecting things at all.

In a similar vein, I've written plenty of code I thought was fast only to find out, after profiling, that it was a one-way ticket to Dogville. This is the trap of blind optimization. Get your code to work (and by all means make it work well), but before you go seriously out of your way to optimize things, spend some time figuring out where the real performance problems are.

So how do you go about doing this? Wouldn't it be great if you could get a report on the performance of your code? Imagine seeing (in percentage terms) how much time is spent in any given part of your game. The good news is, you can! Enter the method profiler. . . .

Method Profiling

Profiling involves tracking the memory and CPU usage of every part of your code while it's executing. You can then review exactly where things are slow (rather than where you think they're slow). Thankfully, Sun integrated profiling directly into the J2ME JVM, so you don't need to use a third-party profiling tool to get results. Sun's Wireless Toolkit includes an interface to the JVM's profiling output, which makes working with the profiling results a breeze.

To profile your game, use the Toolkit's Preferences tool to enable profiling, and then run the game with the Sun emulator (see Figure 15.1).

When you run your game you won't see anything regarding the profiler. It works away in the background, calculating the performance of your code. Once you exit your MIDlet, you'll see a performance report similar to Figure 15.2.

The profiling report contains two windows. On the left is the Call Graph pane, showing a hierarchy of all the method calls in your application. You can select the top node, <root>, to display all the method calls. The percentage number for each entry is the relative amount of time the application spent executing that method and all its children (methods called by that method). If you take a look at the example report, you can see that the game spent 81 percent of its time executing the EventLoop.run method. This is the primary game thread for the Sun emulator, so it's no surprise you spent the most time there. In Figure 15.2 you can see I've opened up this method to see what's going on in more detail.

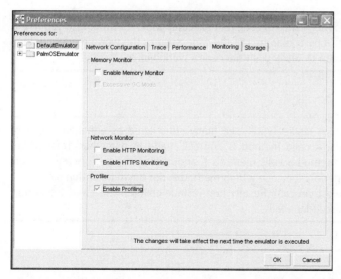

Figure 15.1 Enabling profiling using the default emulator

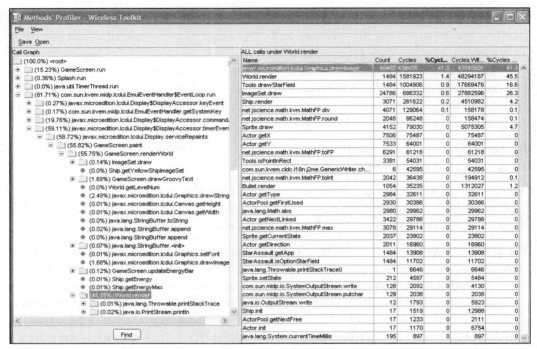

Figure 15.2 Sample results from a profiling session

Tip

Profiling works by measuring the performance of code that executes while it's running. If you're try-ing to improve the performance of a particular area of the code, such as the world rendering, then try to get lots of things on the screen to really push the code's workload.

Note

When you're reviewing performance results, you'll see many stats listed as either including or excluding children or descendants. A child method is any call made to a method from within another method. For example, if method a calls methods b and c, then the performance results excluding children would represent only the code within method a, not anything within b or c (nor any methods those methods would then call). Results that include children represent the perfor-mance all the way through the descendant calls.

On the right side is a detailed list of the methods called for the current Call Graph selection. I've selected the World.render method, so the right side is showing all of the calls made from this method. For each of these methods you can also see

- **Count.** The number of times this method was called.
- **Cycles.** The actual time spent executing this method (excluding children).
- **%Cycles.** The percentage of total execution time (excluding children).
- **Cycles with Children.** The execution time for this method (including children).
- **%Cycles with Children.** The percentage of total execution time for the selected method (including children).

Tip

You need to turn off obfuscation before running the profiler or all of your method names will be meaningless. You can do this by editing the build.xml file and commenting out the obfuscate="true" line in the wtkpackage task.

You can reorder the method list by clicking on the heading of the column. If you do this using the %Cycles with Children column, you can see that most of the time in this method is spent in calls to DrawImage. From here, you can look further into what and where you call this method to see whether it's possible to reduce the number of calls. For example, you could cut back on the total number of images drawn on the screen each cycle.

Feel free to browse around, looking at other performance results. Profiling is a little like a murder mystery; you need to analyze all the clues to find the real culprit. (Maybe it was the butler method in the DiningRoom class.)

Now that you've seen how to gather information on your code, take a look at the other side of the equation—memory management.

Memory Profiling

Most programmers don't rate memory profiling as a significant optimization technique. (It always takes a backseat to method profiling.) With Java, and especially J2ME, the amount of memory you use is more important than you think. Object creation is very slow, the heap is limited, and garbage collection can seriously degrade performance if it has to run too often (in order to clean up your objects). Thankfully, the Toolkit provides a great tool for profiling the memory habits of your game—the memory monitor.

You can enable the memory monitor similar to the way you used the profiler. Select it using the Toolkit Preferences, and then rerun your application (see Figure 15.3). I recommend you don't run both the profiler and the memory monitor at the same time because it will degrade the performance of your game too much.

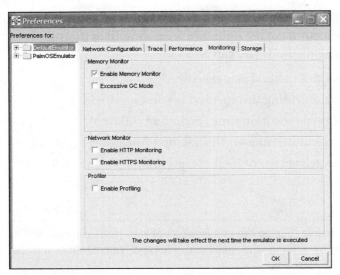

Figure 15.3 Enable the memory monitor using the default emulator preferences.

Unlike the profiler, the memory monitor displays a status screen as soon as you start the emulator. You can see an example of it in Figure 15.4. On this panel, you can track the type and number of objects as your code creates them. This is useful for tracking down when and where you're using memory excessively. Feel free to run other games using the monitor and see when and where they create similar objects.

Name	Live	Total	Total Size	Average Size
VM Internals	35	2973	5400	154
short	22	22	4752	216
char[ ]	175	480	4840	27
int[ ]	43	60	4508	104
short	64	64	2816	44
byte	20	20	3120	156
javax.microedition.lcdui.MutableImage	102	140	2448	24
javax.microedition.lcdui.Image[ ]	75	115	1592	21
java.lang.String	22	104	528	24
java.lang.Object[ ]	9	19	348	38
javax.microedition.lcdui.Image[ ][ ]	13	16	508	39
int	13	16	416	32
char[ ][ ]	4	4	256	64
GameScreen	2	2	352	176
javax.microedition.lcdui.ImmutableImage	9	17	216	24
java.util.HashtableEntry	8	8	224	28
byte[ ]	3	44	156	52
com.sun.kvem.midp.lcdui.KeyPadInputMeth...	1	1	132	132

Objects: 721   Used: 36240 bytes   Free: 463760 bytes   Total: 500000 bytes

Figure 15.4 Sample output from the memory monitor

Tip

The memory profiler (as with most heap profiling) is very slow under J2ME. Be prepared to wait quite a while for applications to start.

The memory monitor also shows you a cool little graph of the state of the heap (see Figure 15.5). Use this to keep track visually of how your game is using memory as it progresses. Watch especially for any time where memory exceeds the currently allocated heap (the dotted red line).

Garbage Monitoring

Java relieves you of the burden of having to manually clean up your objects when they are no longer in use. It does this by maintaining a *reference count* of all the objects you create. The garbage collection (GC) process runs periodically in the background, checking to see when this reference count falls to zero. When it does, the GC clears the object.

The process of cleaning up objects is normally very fast (hardly noticeable on a well-tuned application); however, if the object creation count begins to climb, the garbage collector will have to do more work to clear out old objects. This can quickly lead to serious drag on application performance. Unfortunately, the profiler won't tell you about the performance hit from the collector because it's not part of your direct application's performance.

You can trace the operations of the garbage collector using the Trace Garbage Collection option in the default emulator preferences (see Figure 15.6).

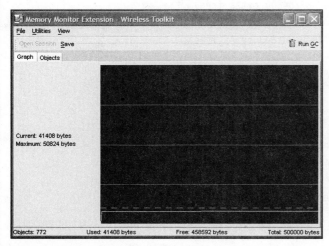

Figure 15.5 The memory monitor graph shows memory usage in real time (with pretty colors too!).

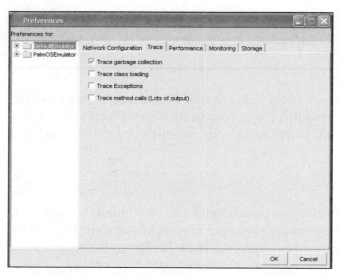

Figure 15.6 Enabling the garbage collection tracer using the default emulator preferences

Once you've selected this option, run the game again, and you'll see output similar to the following lines:

```
Collected 1036 bytes of garbage (109096/204800 bytes free)
Garbage collecting...
Collected 616 bytes of garbage (109048/204800 bytes free)
Garbage collecting...
Collected 1048 bytes of garbage (108940/204800 bytes free)
Garbage collecting...
Collected 616 bytes of garbage (108892/204800 bytes free)
Execution completed successfully
26266550 bytecodes executed
3537 thread switches
339 classes in the system (including system classes)
4418 dynamic objects allocated (334808 bytes)
96 garbage collections (291608 bytes collected)
Total heap size 204800 bytes (currently 98080 bytes free)
```

If you watch this output as your game runs, you'll get a good idea of how often the garbage collector is running.

Optimization

The best optimization is of course the one you never have to do in the first place. This is where experience and using your head really come into game development. There are plenty of ways to improve your code using a combination of tricks and brute force, but you should make sure you keep your eye on the ball. What's the ball, you ask? It's whether the game is fun. Don't spend all your time optimizing the hell out of something that isn't really adding to the fun anyway.

The easiest way to optimize is to simply not call the code in the first place. This doesn't necessarily mean you have to remove it; maybe you can call it in a different way (or just less). The main game loop is the most heavily pushed area of your game; always consider carefully whether something belongs in this area or whether you can call it less (say, every 100 frames).

With this in mind, techniques for optimizing your code tend to fall into two main areas—high-level optimizations, in which you look at the overall algorithm and structure of what you're doing, and low-level optimizations, in which you concentrate on isolated snippets of code, usually inside methods. Take a look at examples of both of these types in the following sections.

High-Level Optimizations

MIDs are fast. No, really—they are. Related to PCs they are, of course, dogs, but in general terms your average MID is still capable of executing millions of instructions per second. What makes them slow is your code—specifically, you trying to do too much too fast.

The reason I'm telling you this is to make sure you don't start a game project with the impression that things are already slow. It's not true; you need to write slow code to create a slow game. It won't happen right away, but you should keep in mind that at some point you'll end up writing the code that kills your application's performance. All the optimization tools I talked about earlier simply help you find out where your own code is slowing you down.

With this in mind, consider some of the high-level aspects of MID game programming that can affect performance.

Perception Is Reality

If you've ever had the opportunity to visit a movie set, you've seen how much of an illusion the moviemakers create. Through the eye of the camera everything looks perfect, but step behind the set and things are all wood, foam, and Gaffer Tape. For movies, perception really is reality.

Games are the same way—you only need to go as far as what's required for the game. This can apply to all aspects of your game development. Concentrate on what's fun and what plays well. Always keep in mind what you really need to do to carry this out, and dump the rest.

A good example of this is the collision detection in *Star Assault*—one of the most resource-intensive areas in the game. I took a few shortcuts in the interest of performance. None of these, however, really make much of a difference to game play. For example, for enemy ships and bullets you don't bother to check whether any hit each other—only whether they hit the player. This yields a dramatic savings because checking to see whether 20 ships and another 20 bullets hit any of the others (more than 1,000 collision checks) is quite slow. Does it really make a difference in the game if enemy ships don't collide with each other? It's only the player who is really important for the game.

Don't Create Objects

As I mentioned previously, creating objects is about as fast as unraveling barbed wire with a pair of tweezers. In Chapter 11 you saw how to use object pools to reduce the total number and frequency of object constructions. The end result was a dramatic increase in the performance of your game. The important lesson here is that you can optimize simply by not creating an object.

One problem with object construction is that profilers won't give you the whole picture. Although actually doing the construction process might not appear to create significant performance load, the aftereffects of increased garbage collection and reduced memory can have dramatic performance consequences.

I recommend you do a global search in your project for the `new` and `clone` keywords, and then carefully consider the implications of each object construction.

You should also be careful of inadvertently creating `String` objects. For example:

```
graphics.drawString(0,0, "Score: " + score);
```

This code will construct a new `String` object on every call, which in this case is every frame. It might be better to construct this string only when the score changes.

Drawing to the Screen

Usually by the time you're finished doing a whole heap of optimization on your game, you're rewarded with your game spending most of its time drawing the images on the screen. This is because the most time-consuming thing a game does is actually rendering the image (or any other drawing primitive call). Therefore, it's always an optimization if you can avoid doing that draw in the first place. If this requires even extensive checking (such as complex state checks or clipping setups) it's still almost always worth it to avoid or minimize how much screen rendering you do.

Methods of reducing screen drawing usually revolve around detecting whether something on the screen has changed, and if it hasn't, not updating that part of the screen. Another method is to increase the size of images being rendered in order to reduce the total number of individual render calls.

The Algorithm

The biggest and best high-level optimization you can make is always in the algorithm or method you're using. You're not breaking any new ground with J2ME game programming. Most of what you do is basic 2D game programming, so almost everything has been done (and optimized to death) already. Regularly spending time on sites such as Gamasutra (http://www.gamasutra.com), GameDev.net (http://www.gamedev.net) and flipCode (http://www.flipcode.com) will provide you with an abundance of game development material.

Low-Level Optimizations

Now that you've covered the general high-level optimizations, take a look at some lower-level stuff, mostly relating to code techniques.

Pre-Render Complex Graphics

As you already know, drawing anything using the LCDUI is slow going, so it's best to avoid it whenever possible. One method for doing this is to reduce complex rendering to a single pre-built image.

A good example of this is the code to draw the energy bar in Chapter 12 "The Game". Because the `fillRect` and `drawRect` methods are relatively slow, the energy bar was updated only if the values changed.

A further optimization along these lines would be to merge all your game status information into a single panel (score, lives, energy, and so on) and then update and render it all in one go.

Balance Classes Versus Memory

Creating new classes can be costly in terms of JAR space, so try to avoid it whenever possible. Instead of creating a new class to handle the specific logic of a sub-type, you can use conditional code such as `switch` statements. This is fine, but conditional sub-typing has one big issue—you can't use it for fields as well. If a particular type of object needs a field, then every object represented by your class is going to have a copy of that field as well. For example, suppose you have two types of cars—an automatic and a manual—both represented using the same `Vehicle` class. The manual car has an extra `boolean` field to represent whether the clutch is pressed. The class would look something like this:

```
public class Vehicle
{
    int speed;
    int gear;
    boolean isAutomatic;
    boolean isClutchEngaged;

    ...
}
```

Now suppose you create 1,000 automatic cars and one manual car. Do you see the problem yet? The 1,000 automatic car objects have an unnecessary field representing the clutch state. The automatic car type never uses this field so it's a waste of memory. Typically this isn't a problem at first (especially if you're only talking about a single `boolean` field), but as you add features to the game, you'll find yourself adding more and more type-specific fields to the same class, so the size of all instances of that class will continue to grow.

The solution is to just bite the bullet, create a new class specifically for that type (or branch), and move the fields into the new class. Although this costs in terms of an extra class, it can be worth it to save the extra memory. Try to consider beforehand whether a type is going to need a lot of specific fields, and create a sub-class if you think it's worth it. Unraveling complex type code can be a real pain if you let it go too far before you realize this.

However, there is a special case that you should keep in mind. If there can only be a single instance of a particular type, then make the fields for that type `static`. Because those fields will no longer be created for every instance, you don't need to sub-class to solve the memory issue. A good example of this is the player's ship in *Star Assault*. If you wanted to add a secondary weapon, you would need extra fields to track the firing rate and damage level. However, since there is only ever one of these objects in existence, you can just make the extra fields static.

Pre-Compute Complex Values

A great way to save on performance is to pre-calculate values so you don't need to call expensive methods. A good example of this is figuring out all the results for sine and cosine for all 360 degrees. To do this, you can simply initialize a static array for all the results. For example:

```
// lookup table for cos and sin value (0 to 359)
static int[] lookupCosFP = new int[360];
```

```
static int[] lookupSinFP = new int[360];

// static init
{
    for (int i = 0; i < 360; i++)
        lookupCosFP[i] = MathFP.cos(getRadiansFromAngle(i));
    for (int i = 0; i < 360; i++)
        lookupSinFP[i] = MathFP.sin(getRadiansFromAngle(i));
}
```

Now you can just look up the corresponding array value relating to the degrees you want. For example, this is how you use it in *Star Assault*:

```
xAccFP = MathFP.mul(thrustFP, lookupCosFP[alignedDir]);
yAccFP = MathFP.mul(thrustFP, lookupSinFP[alignedDir]);
```

In a similar vein, you can cache the results of other commonly called methods. The height and width of the main canvas are good candidates for this. For example, instead of always calling the getHeight and getWidth methods on a canvas, you can call them once and cache the results.

```
public class GameScreen extends Canvas implements Runnable, CommandListener
{
    ...

    private int screenWidth;
    private int screenHeight;

    public GameScreen(StarAssault midlet)
    {
        ...

        screenWidth = getWidth();
        screenHeight = getHeight();
```

Use Arrays

Whenever possible you should use an array instead of something like a vector. Arrays are significantly faster. The only issue you'll typically encounter is expanding the size of the array if the original allocation wasn't large enough. You can do that, but it requires reconstructing the entire array. For example here's a method from the Tools class:

```
public final static int[] expandArray(int[] oldArray, int expandBy)
{
    int[] newArray = new int[oldArray.length + expandBy];
```

```
    System.arraycopy(oldArray, 0, newArray, 0, oldArray.length);
    return newArray;
}
```

You should also try to use one-dimensional arrays whenever possible. Accessing elements in a two-dimensional array is twice as slow. Typically, you can still access the objects; you just need to do a little calculation yourself. For example, instead of doing this:

```
world[y][x] = 0;
```

It's much faster to do this:

```
world[y * tilesWide + x] = 0;
```

This code accesses the same location by multiplying the row count by the number of tiles wide in order to convert it to a one dimensional number.

Don't Use Arrays

Even though arrays are faster than vectors they're still slower than just accessing direct variables, so if possible remove array access altogether or look for opportunities to short-cut array access for common cases.

A good example of this is the revised ImageSet in the Chapter 14 source code directory. You'll find that most of the time states are reflected by a single image, rather than an array of images. In the revised version I've added code to use a single image frame, without accessing an array. Since this is a very commonly called method (to draw the ship frames), it can result in a nice time saving.

Use Quick Methods

Not all method calls in Java are equal in performance. The way you declare the method can have a dramatic effect on performance. The fastest type of method you can use is a static one, so try to move as much as you can into static method calls. You'll find this much easier with single-instance objects because there is only one copy of the object's data anyway, so you can easily make those static fields (and hence, static methods that manipulate those fields).

The second fastest are methods declared final. If you do this, you're telling the compiler there's no chance of the method being overridden by any sub-class. This means the call won't need to involve a dynamic reference; therefore, it's much faster. Declaring methods as final costs you very little. If you later find you need to sub-class the method, you can just remove the final declaration.

The two slowest methods to call are those in interfaces and anything declared with the `synchronized` keyword. You should try to avoid these method types as much as possible. For complete details on the different method types, refer to Appendix A "Java 2 Primer".

Tip

Contrary to what you might have been told, you don't need to use the `final` keyword to encourage inlining. HotSpot VMs (including J2ME VMs) are capable of detecting an inlining opportunity automatically, regardless of whether you declared the method `final`.

Turn Off Debug

Including debug symbols in your compiled application slows down performance and has a dramatic effect on JAR size. To disable it, you can simply modify the `javac` build task.

```
<javac destdir="${bd}/classes" srcdir="${bd}/psrc"
        bootclasspath="${midplib}" debug="false" target="1.1"/>
```

Other Tips

If you're looking for every ounce of speed, you should also consider all of the following general tips.

- Exceptions are horribly slow; don't use them for any normal part of the game's logic. Use them only for reporting real error states.
- Be careful using the `synchronize` keyword; it makes code extremely slow.
- The number of parameters in a method call affects the calling speed. You can gain a little by reducing the size and number of parameters.
- `switch` statements are much faster than `if` blocks.
- Avoid operations on `String` objects as much as you can; use a `StringBuffer`.
- Inner classes are slow; try to avoid them.
- Set references to `null` as soon as you're finished with them. Don't wait for finalization of an object to do this for your object's fields; if you're finished with something, set it (and all its fields) to `null` immediately.
- Don't waste time initializing an object to `null` or zero; the JVM will do this for you.
- Eat your greens; they make your brain work faster.
- Use statics wherever you can; they're extremely fast. This applies to both methods and fields; the rule is if it can be static, make it static.
- Avoid type casting.

Conclusion

Having done it so many times, I no longer regard optimization as a chore. In fact, I quite look forward to sitting down with something I've developed and exploring the performance bottlenecks.

One great motivator is to record your progress as you go. Write down how many frames per second you're getting at the start, and make notes as you go of the impact of your optimizations. It's fun to see just how much progress you can make. You can also make a little high-score list to see which optimizations have the most real impact.

Above all, keep your eye on the ball. You'll find that most of the time the greatest speed increase will come from rethinking the method you're using, rather than endlessly nitpicking code. Remember, the fastest line of code you can write is the one that never gets called! (Don't think about that for too long; your head will hurt.)

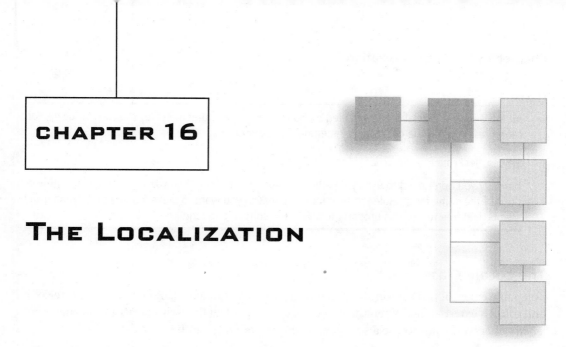

CHAPTER 16

THE LOCALIZATION

MIDs, and especially mobile phones, have spread throughout much of the world. That means much of the market for your game doesn't read English; to accommodate this you need to localize your game to suit different environments.

In this chapter, you'll create a simple language resource system and then adapt *Star Assault* to support localization.

Localizing

Different countries use distinct formatting for currency, date, time, and of course language. In the United States, for example, dates are formatted as MM/DD/YY, rather than the more common DD/MM/YY used in much of the world. Currency is another good example—there are plenty of different symbols in use.

Probably the most important localization, however, is the language used to display the game content, such as the menus and the story. Most J2ME distributors will require support for translation of your game into different languages. While most don't need you to actually translate the text, you need to provide a mechanism that lets the distributor do it for you without recompiling the game.

Take a look at how to add support for this localization to *Star Assault*.

Note

All MIDs have a special property called `microedition.locale` that indicates the current locale. You can access it using the `getProperty` method. For example:

```
System.getProperty("microedition.locale");
```

Typically you don't need to use this method because most of the time you build and distribute versions of the game for a single locale. If for some reason you want to make a game that dynamically adapts, feel free to use this property to select the correct language.

The Locale Class

To enable external translation, you need to move the language strings out of the game code and into an external file. When the game starts, you load all the strings into an internal map. Then, when you want to use a string, you simply grab it from the map using a key.

Tip

When you're designing your game, keep in mind that translated text might be considerably longer than the English equivalent. Leave plenty of space.

To get started, create a text file map of all the strings you need for the game. Here's an excerpt from the `locale.txt` for the English version of *Star Assault*.

Note

The following file is just an example of a specific language. Later in the section "The Build Step" you'll see how to use multiple files for different languages.

```
Application.Copyright=(C) 2003
Application.Author=Martin J. Wells
Application.Press key=Press a key

Main Menu.Title=Main Menu
Main Menu.New Game=New Game
Main Menu.Resume Game=Resume Game
Main Menu.Settings=Settings
Main Menu.Change Keys=Change Keys
Main Menu.Help=Help
Main Menu.About=About

...
```

The full file is quite a bit longer because it has to cater to every string you use in the game.

Okay, now you have your file ready, so let's take a look at your new `Locale` class. The first thing you need to do is load the contents of the text file. Take a look at the code:

```java
import java.io.InputStream;
import java.io.IOException;
import java.util.Hashtable;

public class Locale
{
    private final static Locale instance = new Locale();
    private static Hashtable map;

    public Locale()
    {
        //#ifdef debug
        System.out.println("Loading resources from locale.txt");
        //#endif

        map = new Hashtable();

        // load up the resource strings
        InputStream is = null;

        try
        {
            is = this.getClass().getResourceAsStream("locale.txt");

            boolean done = false;
            byte buffer[] = new byte[1];

            StringBuffer line = new StringBuffer();

            // read a line and add the entries
            while (!done)
            {
                int bytesRead = is.read(buffer);
                if (bytesRead != -1)
                {
                    if (buffer[0] == '\n')
                    {
                        String s = line.toString().trim();
```

```
                    // we ignore lines starting with #,  or if they don't have a
                    // = in them, or if the length is smaller than the min of
                    // 3 chars (ie. 'a=b')

                    if (!s.startsWith("#") && s.length() > 2 &&
                        s.indexOf('=') != -1)
                    {
                        String key = s.substring(0,
                            s.indexOf('=')).trim().toLowerCase();
                        String value = s.substring(s.indexOf('=')+1).trim();

                        map.put(key, value);

                        //#ifdef debug
                        System.out.println("Loading setting: " + key + "='" +
                                                value + "'");
                        //#endif
                    }
                    line.setLength(0);
                }
                else
                    line.append((char)buffer[0]);
            } else
                done = true;

        }

    }
    catch(IOException io)
    {
        System.out.println("Error loading resources: " + io);
    }

    finally
    {
        try
        {
            is.close();
        }

        catch(IOException io) { }
    }
```

```
    }

}
```

This code uses the (limited) I/O classes in MIDP to load the text file and store the values in a hash table. Next you add a method to the `Locale` class to gain access to these values.

```
public static String getString(String key)
{
    String s = (String)map.get(key.toLowerCase());
    if (s != null) return s;
    //#ifdef debug
    System.out.println("Attempt to get an unknown resource string: " + key);
    //#endif
    return key;
}
```

Adapting Star Assault

Now that you have the locale system ready, you need to modify the code in *Star Assault* to use it. For example, instead of displaying the New Game option in your menu using the code:

```
items.addElement("New Game");
```

you grab the string corresponding to your locale using:

```
items.addElement(Locale.getString("Main Menu.New Game"));
```

The details displayed in the splash screen are another good example. Here's the revised version:

```
osg.drawString(Locale.getString("Application.Copyright"), getWidth() / 2,
            getHeight() - fontHeight * 3,
            Graphics.HCENTER | Graphics.TOP);
osg.drawString(Locale.getString("Application.Author"), getWidth() / 2,
            getHeight() - fontHeight * 2,
            Graphics.HCENTER | Graphics.TOP);
```

Adapting the rest of the game is basically just the same process. Wherever there is a string, you move it to the locale file and then add a call to `getString` using the key.

The Build Step

The next step you need to accomplish is the ability to support the building of different versions based on locale using your Ant script. The first thing you need to do is make a home for the different versions of locale.txt for each language.

To do this, you add an extra directory called locale under the res directory for the project. You then place a locale text file with a name corresponding to the language. For example, I named the English version en.txt.

Once the files are in place, you need to modify build.xml to set the locale for which you want to build in the init target. For example:

```
<target name="init" depends="setup">
    ...
    <property name="locale" value="en"/>
</target>
```
You then copy the text file corresponding to the language for which you are building.
```
<target name="device build" depends="init">
    <property name="bd" value="build/${dev}-${locale}"/>       <!-- build dir -->
    ...

    <copy tofile="${bd}/res/locale.txt">
        <fileset file="res/locale/${locale}.txt"/>
    </copy>          <!-- copy locale files -->

    <wtkpackage jarfile="${bd}/${midlet.name}.jar"
                jadfile="${bd}/${midlet.name}.jad"
                preverify="true"
                classpath="${midplib}" obfuscate="true">
        <fileset dir="${bd}/classes"/>
        <fileset dir="${bd}/res"/>
    </wtkpackage>
</target>
```

Notice that at the top I've changed the build destination directory to now include the locale code (in addition to the device name). This is so I can build different versions for language and device, such as nokia-en (English) and nokia-fr (French).

Conclusion

Localizing is more prevalent with J2ME games than with other platforms. In fact, most distributors or publishers require easy translation. However, as you've seen in this chapter, localizing your game isn't very difficult, especially if you do it early.

With this completed, *Star Assault* is now a finished product. In Part Four of this book you'll look at how to take your product to market.

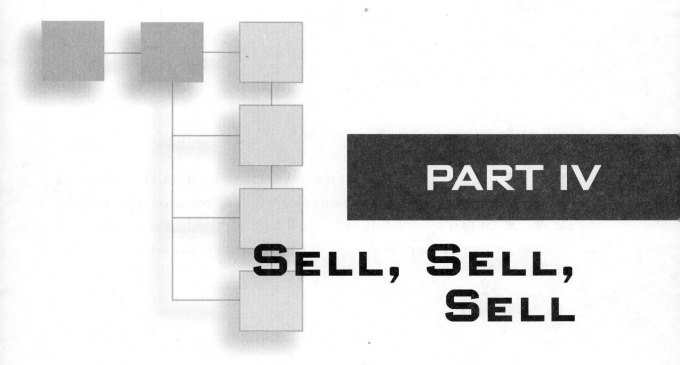

PART IV

SELL, SELL, SELL

CHAPTER 17

Marketing Material 543

CHAPTER 18

Sales Channels 553

Making games is fun, but if you want it to be anything more than a hobby, you're going to need to know how to "monetize your product," In Part 4, "Sell, Sell, Sell", you'll look at the different ways you can capitalize on your development and then how to go about marketing and selling your games.

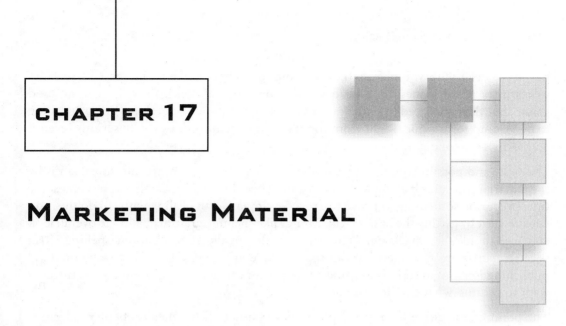

CHAPTER 17

MARKETING MATERIAL

To approach a publisher, you're going to need a little more than just the JAD and JAR files. The next step in preparing for publishing is creating the marketing material that will support your game. In this chapter, you'll look at exactly what you need to present a game professionally, including a game guide, screenshots, and even a video of the action.

Game Guide

The first thing you need to prepare to promote your game is a game guide. This is a three- to five-page document that gives the publisher an introduction to your game. To begin with, you should consider the goal of the document.

Without a doubt, the best way to approach a publisher is to demo your game in person. Nothing beats standing in front of the guy and showing him how cool the game is. Unfortunately, it's not always practical to do this, and even if you could, it's likely the publisher will want to then show the game off to others (without you being there all the time). I'm telling you this to give you the right frame of mind with which to approach the creation of a game guide. The guide exists to sell the game on your behalf. You need to emulate the impact a real demo would provide. Just like an in-person demo, your game guide needs to be well presented, professional, succinct, and above all, exciting!

Before you get into the actual document, I want to talk about the image you're presenting. One thing publishers have to battle is the vast number of budding game developers who have little or no professional experience (all of whom believe their game is the hottest thing ever made). It would amaze you just how much flak these guys have to deal with. To combat this, publishers naturally build barriers to weed out the amateurs. If a publisher has never dealt with you before, they're going to assume you're a lone-gun 12-year-old who thinks J2ME games are a groovy idea (for about a week). Publishers want good games, but they also need to build long-term relationships with developers who are going to be around for a while. Right from the start, you need to prove you're serious (even if you really are a lone-gun 12-year-old).

The first (and possibly only) chance a publisher has to judge your professionalism is by the material you submit along with your game. Therefore, it's critical that you spend some time preparing something to prove you're a developer worth dealing with. To do this, you need to start by getting the basics right. Things like spelling, grammar, and the overall look and feel should be smack on. (That's right—they really *do* care about spelling.) Just because games are fun doesn't mean these people aren't serious; in fact, you could say publishing is about as serious as game development can get. All right, enough lecturing; I want to get into what goes in this guide.

The point of the guide is to give a potential publisher all the details about your game. Don't worry; you don't need to write a novel. Basically you need three sections—why people would love to play this game, how the publisher can experience this amazing entertainment for himself, and a bunch of reference stuff the publisher will need if he gets into the details. Read on to take a look at each of these sections in a little more detail.

Tip

You can see a complete example of a Game Guide in the Chapter 17 directory on the CD.

Section 1: Introduction

The sole purpose of the introduction is to get a publisher excited enough about the game that he will bother to spend some time on it. Don't get me wrong; most publishers will take the time to have a thorough look at most games they receive. However, having an intro that gets the publisher excited helps him look at the game in the right frame of mind. If he starts out enthusiastic, you have a much better chance of success.

You should keep the introduction short and to the point; typically, about half a page is good. To write the introduction, you should start by playing the game for a bit to get things fresh in your mind. As you go, create a short list of features you think are really cool about the game. For *Star Assault*, that might be something like this:

- Fast-paced action
- New style of four-way scrolling shooter
- Great-looking color graphics and animation
- Random level generator that provides for a new experience every game

- Advanced physics (such as great flight mechanics and bouncing weapons fire)
- Smart enemy AI to keep you on your toes

You'll notice that what I call a feature is something relative to the J2ME world. For example, a four-way scrolling shooter is nothing new on other platforms. However, it hasn't been tried much in J2ME, so I'm considering it a feature.

Once you have this feature list, it's time to write the introduction. To do this, imagine you've gone to a trade show, booked some time with a potential publisher, and you now have his undivided attention. "Okay," he says. "What have you got for us?" Write an intro based on what you think you would say at that point. I always start by setting the scene for the game and then rolling through a demo. After you've written it try reading it back like a sales pitch; it'll help you add more punch to what you write.

Later in the chapter, you'll learn how to take screenshots of your game. You should include a few of these as you go along to illustrate what you're saying.

I typically include about half of my features in the text of the introduction (usually the best ones) and then add a list of additional features at the end. I just find that it balances the text well and leaves publishers with a "wow, there's even more" feeling.

Section 2: Playing the Game

After reading the intro, the publisher should be excited enough to want to give the game a go for himself. Section 2 needs to give him a step-by-step walkthrough of the action. This should be no longer than a page.

Starting with how to begin a new game, introduce the basic controls, the player's goals, and then the mechanics of game play. Along the way, remember to point out the strengths of your game. If you think something is cool, then tell them so! Contrary to what you might think, a publisher will only play the first few levels, so the walkthrough needs to communicate the entire experience in that time.

If you've added any cheat codes, you should point these out so the publisher can better see all the features. Features such as unlimited lives and the ability to jump to different levels or activate all the weapons and options are good things to include in the walkthrough.

Section 3: Reference

The final component you need is a reference section. This is where you put all the fine details about the game and yourself. Typically, I include the following:

- Details about the exact MIDs on which you've tested the game, as well as any comments about the portability of the game (such as support for different screen sizes, minimum JAR size, and support for localization)

- An interface summary that lists all the available game actions (the keys)
- A list of all menu commands and their functions
- A complete list of any cheat codes
- Details on any technical features of the game, if they are exceptionally good
- Company background and contact information

Tip

To give things a slightly more professional look, I always send documents as PDF files. This gives you a little more flexibility in your document creation capabilities, and you can be sure things will look exactly as you intended. One thing to watch out for, though: Acrobat (the software used to create PDF files) will try to recompress your images. This can result in your screenshots looking horrible. Be sure to tweak the PDF creation settings so the program doesn't recompress your images.

Taking Screenshots

A great promotional tool for your game is screenshots of the action, and they're surprisingly easy to create.

The simplest method is to use the Windows screen capture key, `Print Screen` (`PrtSc` on some keyboards). If you hold down the `Alt` and Print Screen keys, Windows will take a snapshot of the current application window and place it on the Clipboard.

To create the screenshot, run the game using the emulator. When the action reaches the point you want to snap, just hit `Alt+Print Screen`. To use the image, switch to a graphics application (such as Photoshop, Paint Shop Pro, or even Windows Paint) and paste the image into a new document. You then need to crop the image to show only the desired area of the screen (Figure 17.1). Finally, save it to an appropriate graphics file. (Use PNG or GIF files rather than JPEG files. They are smaller and provide a higher quality image.)

You should use this method to create a series of shots of the game. Usually three to eight is a good number. Try to show off as many different aspects as you can.

Tip

In the next section, you'll see how to use a screen capture application to take movies of your game in action. You can also use this software to capture screenshots. This has the added benefit of limiting the capture area to exactly what you want. In addition, you can immediately preview the results without having to switch away from the game.

Figure 17.1 Cropping a screenshot down to size using Adobe Photoshop

Making Movies

The next best thing to actually playing the game is seeing a little movie of the action. Given the small size of MID screens, it's quite practical to create a demo movie that is still small enough to distribute easily (especially via e-mail). Another good reason to create a movie is that some publishers will insist on seeing it before they do a full review of the game—a pretty sensible idea, really.

Carriers and distributors will also use game movies to market your game. The most common use is to embed an animated GIF inside a Web portal. In this section, you'll also look at how to create a cut-down version of your game movie as an animated GIF.

The Camera

To make a movie, the first thing you need is the equivalent of a camera to capture the images. You'll use video capture software capable of progressively grabbing the graphics from the screen as you play the game. You can then save the frames as an AVI file. There's plenty of software out there to do this; most of it is either free or very cheap. Personally I use SnagIt from TechSmith (see Figure 17.2). It's friendly and powerful, and if you decide to purchase it, it's extremely cheap. You can download a fully-functional 30-day evaluation version from http://www.techsmith.com.

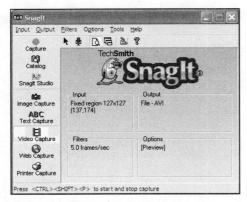

Figure 17.2 The SnagIt capture
application

Once you have downloaded and installed SnagIt, start up the application and select the
Video Capture option.

Next you need to set the capture area to the 128×128-pixel area used by the Nokia emulator. To begin, start the game in the emulator and position it alongside the SnagIt window; then, using SnagIt, select the Properties item from the Input menu. You'll see the
dialog box shown in Figure 17.3.

You can use the Select option to visually select the region you want to capture. When
you're satisfied, click on OK, and you'll see the capture region parameters updated to
match your selection.

Next you need to configure the type of video you want to output. Select the Properties
option from the Output menu, and then select the Video File tab (see Figure 17.4).

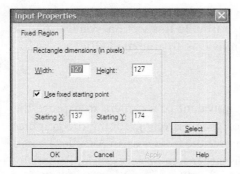

Figure 17.3 Setting the properties
ready to start capturing

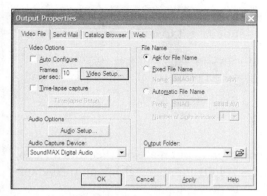

Figure 17.4 The video configuration options dialog box

Here you should adjust the number of frames to something like 10. Feel free to adjust the number, but keep in mind the higher the number, the larger the resulting video file. Use the Video Config button to adjust the quality to maximum; this will result in a much higher capture quality. (You'll introduce compression when you edit the video later; for now you want the highest-quality source material you can get.)

Okay, now you're ready to start shooting.

Shooting

The point of your movie is to give viewers a good impression of the best features of your game. To do this, you need to capture a variety of footage of the game as you play through different areas. At this stage you really shouldn't worry about exact timing or the length of what you're capturing; just go ahead and capture tons of stuff. You'll edit it all into something good later.

Tip

Using SnagIt you can also capture audio from a microphone as you go. If you think it's worth it, you can add a voiceover explaining features of the game. Most of the time, however, I find there just isn't enough time to say anything sensible without the file getting too big to handle (larger than 10 MB).

To start capturing you need both SnagIt and the game running at the same time. All you need to do is start playing the game. When you reach a section you want to start capturing, hit Ctrl+Shift+P (the default SnagIt hot key to begin capturing). SnagIt will paint a flashing rectangle around what you're currently capturing so you know everything is working.

When you've finished capturing, hit Ctrl+Shift+P again, and the recording will stop. You can then preview the result and choose to discard it or save it to a file (see Figure 17.5).

You should repeat this process to capture as many aspects of the game as you can, including the front end and menus. When you've got a good set of material, you can move on to editing.

The Editing

Now that you have a bunch of source material, you need to put it all together into a video. To do this, you can use a professional suite such as Adobe Premiere, although the default Windows XP Movie Maker application will certainly do the job.

When editing, try to run through a sort of high-speed tour of the game play. Start with the title and intro to the first level, and then jump through a series of action sequences. Use the editing tools to trim off anything not directly related to the action. The total sequence should go for about 30 seconds and result in a file no bigger than about 5 MB (depending on compression).

Making an Animated GIF

There are two popular types of animated GIFs used to promote J2ME games—movies and screen packs. The difference really comes down to the sizes of the resulting GIF files. A movie is simply a version of your AVI saved as an animated GIF, usually with a lower frame rate in order to reduce the file size. Typically, this GIF will be about one-tenth of the original video, but will still give the same general impression.

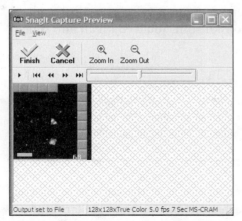

Figure 17.5 The SnagIt preview window lets you review a captured video and save it if required.

The absolute best tool I've seen to create animated GIFs is Ulead GIF Animator (see Figure 17.6). You can download a trial version from http://www.ulead.com.

Using GIF Animator, you can import the final AVI file and then manipulate the frame speed or sequence pretty much any way you want. You can also put together a sequence of frames by hand to create an extremely small file.

Another type of animated GIF to create for your game is a screen pack. This is just a selection of screen shots grouped together into an animated GIF and displayed with a slight delay. You can also use GIF Animator to create these.

Company Presence

As I've said before, J2ME game publishers are interested in establishing long-term relationships with developers. This is a good thing because if you get one game signed, you'll find it much easier to get subsequent games out the door. The side effect, however, is that the publisher wants to see you as a committed developer of more than just a single game.

Along with this, you also have the issue of professionalism. If you look like you're serious and committed, a publisher is going to commit more time to developing a relationship with you. If the game isn't something they want, they'll be more inclined to tell you what's wrong and then take another look when you fix it. Or if it's just not something they're interested in, maybe they'll be more inclined to listen when you release another title.

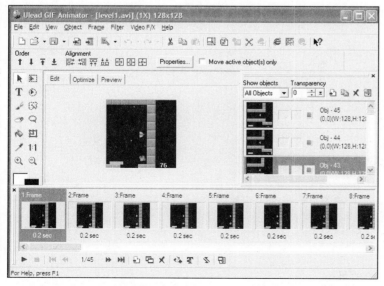

Figure 17.6 Using Ulead GIF Animator to create an animated GIF

The key to getting a publisher to believe you're serious is to be serious about yourself as a developer. If you're not an existing company, then become one. Establish a brand, create a logo, get a domain name, create a Web site, and always talk in terms of "we", not "I". If you're committed to being a leading J2ME game development house, they'll see it.

Conclusion

In this chapter, you saw how to create the marketing material to support your game. Although every publisher won't require all these elements, including them will show them that you're serious about your game.

In the next chapter, you'll see how to actually knock on the publisher's door.

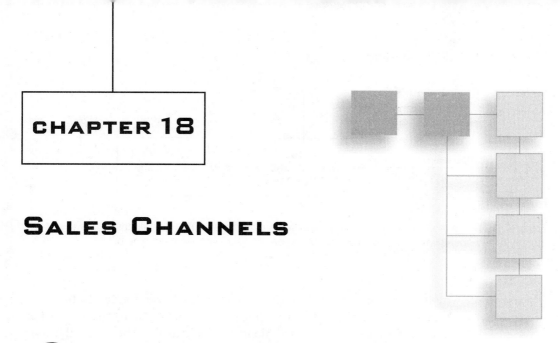

CHAPTER 18

SALES CHANNELS

One of the great things about developing J2ME games is the realistic chance you have to take a game to market and earn real revenue. Getting paid to write games—you gotta love that. To do it, though, you need to climb down from the ivory tower and journey into the murky swamp of—sharp intake of breath—business.

In this chapter you'll explore the methods available to obtain revenue from your newfound J2ME skills as well as how you can go about engaging the appropriate sales channels.

J2ME Business Model

To really understand how you can make money from your game, it's best to start by looking at exactly how the game can generate revenue. For the most part you'll deal with mobile (cell phone) games because these represent the vast majority of the J2ME game business.

Carrier Downloads

The most common way to obtain revenue from a game is for a mobile carrier to offer it as an optional "paid for" download. The reason this is popular really comes down to convenience. A mobile phone user can browse a list of game titles (on his phone), select one, and then purchase it instantly. The game then downloads over-the-air (OTA) and is ready to play immediately (see Figure 18.1). The charge for the game, typically only a few dollars, appears on the user's phone bill at the end of the month.

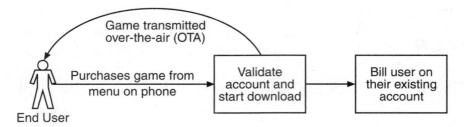

Figure 18.1 The most popular form of game sales is over-the-air (OTA) downloads directly to the phone with a charge then appearing on the user's mobile telephone bill.

It's easy to see why this type of sales mechanism is so popular. Users don't need to access the Internet and wade through myriad game options—they trust their carrier to offer a vetted selection of quality games. The download is direct to the phone, so the user doesn't need to fiddle around with transferring it from his PC. Payment is also easier because of the existing relationship (and trust on both sides), resulting in lower cost and a lower risk of charge-backs and fraud. All in all, it's a great system.

Carrier Revenue Shares

Because J2ME has networking facilities built in by default, you see new games that utilize the communications medium (especially on mobile phones) for multiplayer gaming as well as to download new content, such as new levels or episodes. To do this, the player has to transfer data across the carriage network, which results in charges for the airtime or data packets.

In some cases carriers may share a portion of this revenue with the content provider. This way the carrier can make a game available at a reduced rate or even for free and then rely on the network usage for payback.

Internet Downloads

Downloading a game directly onto your phone from the carrier's network is convenient; however, it's inherently limited to what the carrier elects to provide for you and what you can reasonably download over the mobile network—typically a few hundred kilobytes. It is possible to browse to external sites and download games, but this tends to be rare for most mobile phones (navigating to Internet sites might be possible, but it's certainly not popular).

On some devices, especially in the "smart" phone class, it's common to have the phone connected to the user's PC (via docking station, USB, or even Bluetooth). The user can then browse the Internet using his PC and then download the game onto his phone at high speed. Downloading and installing a multi-megabyte game is easy using this method.

Because no carrier is involved in this process, the user needs to establish a separate billing arrangement with the content provider. Once this arrangement is set up, it's usually an easy process to purchase and install games.

There's nothing really new about purchasing and downloading software from a Web site, so plenty of sites have already added J2ME sections to their portfolios. Handango (http://www.handango.com) is an excellent example of this (see Figure 18.2).

Designing for Revenue

How your game generates revenue can have quite an impact on the type of product you want to produce. Games sold directly through the phone, for example, such as in a carrier's portal, are an impulse purchase. Thus cheap pricing and focus on simple access are all about getting a player to make a snap decision to purchase the game. Games that succeed in this space need to be instantly attractive to the player. That means a catchy name, great-looking promo graphics, and possibly a style of game they readily understand. Tying the game to an existing franchise brand is also a popular method to gain immediate trust from the player.

On the other hand, if you're developing a game that earns revenue from the air time or data transfer, then you have the added goal of keeping the player online as long as possible. The game needs to be able to not only attract the player, but also keep him coming

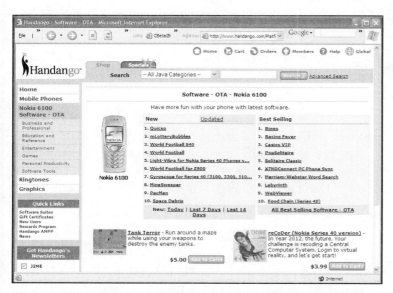

Figure 18.2 A Handango Web page (showing only software products for the Nokia 6100)

back for more—no simple feat. A continuous stream of updates or episodes is one method you can use to do this; multiplayer games that require constant interaction with other players are also a common option. The key is that you need to develop an experience that retains the player's attention over a longer period because this directly translates to the revenue your game generates.

Alongside this are games sold directly through Internet portals. These are a little different. Portal sites have more space in which to provide information, so potential players can view screenshots, movies, and even background stories before they choose to buy a game. They can also see reviews, recommendations, and sometimes even comments made by other players. The bad news is that if your game isn't that great, reviewers and users will slam it. The opposite is also true, though; if the game is great, the portal will help it succeed.

Ways to Market

Now that you've reviewed how players pay for your game, you can look at exactly how this translates into cash for you as the developer. To get your game out the door you can do one of two things—deal direct with a distributor (or carrier) or go via a publisher.

Distributors

Distributors are the direct channels to market. Basically, anyone who deals directly with an end customer is a distributor, although this definition can become blurry sometimes. This includes carriers (or carriage-related companies) as well as Internet portals or other direct sales systems. Some of the more popular distribution channels are Cingular Wireless, T-Mobile, Vodafone, Motorola iDEN/Nextel, and Handango.

The good thing about using a distributor is you're dealing directly with the channel. This translates to more contact with end customers, fewer delays, and usually a higher percentage of the revenue in your pocket.

To deal with a distributor, you need to establish a direct relationship. Most provide facilities to do this through a developer Web portal. To make your application available, some distributors require you to have your application certified. Nextel is a good example of this; if you choose to deal with them directly, you need to get the game certified. (This costs in excess of $1,000 per game.) Don't worry, though—not all distributors require this.

Keeping all this in mind, take a look at the more popular distributors out there.

T-Mobile

T-Mobile is a massive mobile network provider covering many countries in Europe and the United States. Being a subsidiary of Deutsche Telekom, they have a German heritage but have managed to extend well into many other countries. Given their size and reach, T-Mobile can be an excellent distribution method.

You can access the T-Mobile US developer portal at http://developer.t-mobile.com. From here it's free to register and then access a host of information on the J2ME partnership programs available.

Motorola iDEN/Nextel

Nextel is another massive mobile phone service provider based in the United States. Together with Motorola, they pioneered Java-based gaming in the United States in 2001, so they're old hands at it now. Since then, they've continued to provide excellent support for J2ME-based gaming across their product range.

Nextel lets anyone have a game appear on the network. To get started, you should visit their developer portal at http://idenphones.motorola.com/iden/developer/developer_home.jsp.

From here, you can register and gain access to materials that describe what's offered. The basic process is that you first need to check whether the game meets the technical criteria. To do this, you should download the Motorola iDEN SDK and check the game against their emulators. When you've finished any required tweaking, you're ready to submit the game for distribution.

There are two ways you can deal with Nextel—directly or via a publisher. If you choose to go direct, the next step is to get your game certified. This is done through a company associated with Motorola (called Quality Partners), and it costs approximately $1,000 per game. Once you have their stamp of approval, you can submit the game to Nextel. And here's the catch: Nextel has to approve your game before they will make it available. If they like the game enough, you can proceed to reviewing and signing a Software Distribution Agreement. Once you've done all that, the game will be ready to go live.

The other method is to go via a publisher. Instead of dealing with Motorola/Nextel directly, you can leave all that work to a publisher. Although you'll have to give up a portion of your revenue, this method is typically far easier in the long run. You should check the Motorola Web site for a list of current publishers.

AT&T Wireless

AT&T Wireless lets J2ME developers create applications for distribution through their mMode brand. You can check out mMode at http://www.attwireless.com/personal/features/mmode/index.jhtml.

To assist developers, AT&T has a dedicated site called devCentral. You can register and join the program free of charge at http://www.attwireless.com/developer.

The first step to getting a game on mMode is to work through AT&T's J2ME style recommendations. Complying isn't very hard, though; everything is pretty reasonable. When you're ready, you can submit the application for review. AT&T will then evaluate your game's potential to fit within the current mMode selection. For example, if they already have a host of side-scrolling action shooters, it's unlikely they'll want yet another one. An application has to add to their selection.

If the game is selected, you'll enter into an agreement with AT&T and then carry out work to integrate the game for distribution in the mMode portal.

Cellmania

Cellmania is a little bit different than other distributors. They provide a system, known as mFinder, that lets carriers manage the delivery of mobile products. The system is in use by many of the largest operators in the world, including:

- AT&T Wireless
- Telstra
- Cingular
- AirTel
- M1
- Orange

You can find out more information about Cellmania's developer opportunities at http://corp.cellmania.com/developers.

Submitting a game to Cellmania is extremely easy; you just complete an online form. However, note that you cannot upload a JAR or JAD; you need to supply a URL from which Cellmania can download the JAD and JAR files.

Following review, Cellmania will list your game in the directory within a few weeks. For the majority of sales then made, you'll get around 70 percent of the revenue.

Handango

Like Cellmania, Handango is not a carrier; they're a portal for applications. Once you register your game, it will be available for sale at http://www.handango.com. This is a pretty heavily trafficked site with more than 6 million visitors a month.

Handango also operates the application storefronts for many other companies, such as Nokia, Palm, Sony Ericsson, Dell, Hewlett-Packard, Casio, Handspring, and Psion. These companies basically re-brand Handango in order to sell applications for their products.

Like with Cellmania, you can expect around 70 percent of the revenue generated by your game. You can find out details about making your application available via Handango at the Web site. This is an extremely easy exercise because Handango does not do any quality assurance on the application.

The main problem with Handango is getting lost in the crowd. Because it's so easy to make an application available, there tends to be a great many in any category. Even a very successful title sold through Handango will only result in a few thousand sales; average games only sell a few hundred. If you're thinking of going with Handango, you should apply to be included in their further distribution to carriers and other portals (such as Nokia).

Using a Distributor

Using distributors to sell your game can be very effective. However, to make it work you'll have to devote some serious resources to establishing and maintaining relationships with multiple carriers. You need to work through the idiosyncrasies of each different channel and then spend time figuring out the best way to maximize its potential. If you just throw the application up, I can almost guarantee it will be quickly lost in the crowd, resulting in very little revenue for you. You have to work a channel to make it effective, and unfortunately this is rarely possible on your first title. With some experience and a better relationship with the distributor, you can work toward a position where your games start to sell well. To do this properly, you need to have a distributor who goes out of his way to help you succeed. Establishing that type of relationship requires building mutual trust and respect, and that takes time and effort. This is the only way you'll get those special deals such as premium placement and the opportunity to participate in promotions.

A slight step forward is to use one of the "aggregators" such as Cellmania or Handango. They'll take care of many of the details of working with the different carriers and other channels to get your game out the door quickly. Unfortunately, these guys deal with so many developers on so many different channels that it's hard to stand out from the crowd.

If you're a small development house, your best chance of success is to have someone who understands the business take care of all this for you. This role is filled by the publisher.

Publishers

Publishers are rather new to the J2ME marketplace. Up until recently, there just wasn't the diversity or revenue for the marketplace to be dominated by a publishing channel. Oh how things are changing!

Nowadays having a good publisher with the right influence and knowledge of the market can easily make the difference between success and failure of your games and your company. As the J2ME games industry continues to expand, you'll see the industry getting much more complex to manage. The number of distribution channels will increase dramatically, as will the forms of revenue you'll receive. Managing this without a publisher will become increasingly difficult.

Like in traditional PC game development, the role of the publisher is to bring a game product to market. This begins with the vetting of developers and their games to sort out the good (saleable) from the bad. The publisher then endeavors to build a strong relationship with you (even becoming part of the development process), providing a constant flow of ideas (including criticisms) to keep you on the right track. After the game is ready, they'll take care of getting it to market, as well as details such as translation into other languages. Because publishers only make money when people pay for your game, it's in their best interest to get the game selling as well as possible.

Typically it won't cost anything to form a relationship with a publisher or to have them take your game to market. Be suspicious if they start asking you for fees. The publisher will take care of getting the game out to the different channels and then collecting all the revenue. You will receive a portion of the revenue (a royalty) usually between 40 and 70 percent of the net proceeds (revenue minus direct costs).

Royalties aren't the only method of gaining revenue from a publisher. Once you have an established relationship, the publisher might offer you contract work to develop a new title on their behalf, clean or expand the functionality of an existing game, or port a game to other platforms. Revenue from this type of development tends to a fixed amount based on milestones, with the potential for (typically small) royalties.

Now that you have an idea of what publishers can do for you, take a look at the players in the market. One thing you might immediately notice is the absence (so far) of any publisher from the traditional games industry. Don't let that turn you off; there are some very professional, mature organizations out there doing great things for the industry.

- Unplugged—http://www.unplugged-inc.com
- Fifth Axis—http://www.fifthaxis.com
- Digital Bridges—http://www.digitalbridges.com
- Mforma—http://www.mforma.com
- Tira Wireless—http://www.tirawireless.com
- JAMDAT—http://www.jamdat.com

There are plenty of others out there, so don't read too much into the exclusion of any of them from this list. However, you shouldn't go wrong dealing with any of these companies; they're all pure publishers with solid backgrounds and good connections in the right parts of the industry.

Now that you have an idea of who the publishers are in the market, the challenge is how to get them to take you on as a developer. Read on to see what turns a publisher on.

Turning Publishers On

There's no doubt that writing video games is fun. Unfortunately, that also means every nerd and his robot dog also want to be video game programmers. You can't blame them; it really is a great thing to do for a living.

Unfortunately, this makes for a very crowded and very competitive marketplace. Not only that, the industry is filled with people trying to break in professionally. Because of the sheer volume, it's difficult for publishers to sort out the pros from the amateurs. The next few sections will examine the things a publisher will look for in evaluating your game—and you as a potential partner.

Game Concept

The first thing a publisher will look at is the overall concept of the game. Is it something that will get a potential player excited enough to part with some hard-earned cash? Does the game look catchy and interesting? Is it something players will understand?

They also look for originality of the game type. Writing a direct clone of another game is a surefire way of getting your game rejected.

If you're working with an existing licensee or brand, publishers will also evaluate its effect on the game's potential in the market.

Technical Capability

Next a publisher will evaluate you technically. But contrary to what many new developers think, most publishers really don't care much about how good you are technically; they care about whether the features you've implemented work well. The important thing is to concentrate on making a great game, not on showing off your technical skills.

Quality

Talking about technology leads us on to quality. Publishers put a great deal of stock into the quality of product. This means no bugs, ever. It might be acceptable to show off beta-quality stuff in the PC industry, but it isn't with J2ME. Most publishers expect a fully completed game with every i dotted and t crossed.

Make sure all your menu items work properly and that you haven't got any silly mistakes such as incorrect spelling or grammar. Most of all, play-test your game to death. There's no room for bugs.

If you think this is just publishers being picky, then consider their position. If a developer can't produce a quality product for the first game he submits, what will things be like down the road? The last thing a publisher wants is to have to constantly check your work and deal with angry distributors (and end-user returns) because of poor quality. This can jeopardize their relationships for all future dealings.

Presentation

A publisher will look at a game's overall presentation, starting with the quality of the graphics (and sound). Try to make everything as polished as you can; if it looks amateurish, then dump it.

They'll also look at how you present the game to the player, including any story elements. The game should immerse the player immediately and then keep him there. The interface should be simple to use and add to the game play, rather than detract from it.

Game Play

The next area is the hardest to get right—the quality of the game play. Publishers will evaluate the overall playability of the game. This really comes down to whether it's fun and addictive.

They will also look at how intuitive the game is. A new player should be able to get going without having to read any instructions. The game's controls also need to take into consideration the limitations of the device.

Finally the game needs to show a certain depth in order to keep players interested for a reasonable amount of time. This will translate directly to whether a player feels he got value for his money.

The Company

Given the short development cycle of J2ME games, publishers want to establish a relationship with a developer for hopefully many titles down the road. Part of their evaluation will include looking at you as an organization. Having a professional-looking Web site will help you with this.

Publishers will also look at any other games you've developed in the past, as well as any plans you have about future development ideas.

Overall Professionalism

Finally, publishers put a lot into how you deal with them. Yes, this is the games industry and it's all pretty casual, but that doesn't mean you shouldn't act professionally in any dealings with publishers.

Try to respond quickly to their queries and always follow through on something you said you would do (or tell them why you couldn't). Take their criticism as advice and don't react badly. Above all, never insult anybody—ever!

Okay, now that you have the lowdown on publishers, let's look at how you go about actually approaching them.

Approaching the Publisher

Armed with your knowledge of the market and all the marketing materials for the game, it's time to go knocking on some doors. There are quite a few methods for approaching a publisher. Which one you choose comes down to factors such as time, cost, and even personality.

In Person

The first method for contacting publishers is the most direct—go and see them. If you think you can become a successful developer without leaving that chair, then welcome to planet reality. At some point you need to get out there and show them what you've got.

Most publishers will take the time to see you if you're willing to turn up in person. In these days of electronic anonymity, showing up in the flesh is a powerful method of building a relationship. Just the fact that you're there shows a certain degree of professionalism and commitment to your work. It automatically buys you a relationship. In the future, actually having met the guy will go a long way toward your level of interaction and trust—and you can even make some good friends along the way.

Another great result of meeting a publisher in person is that you'll usually get direct feedback. Even if the publisher says they'll review your game in detail with the team later, they will usually tell you the good and bad about the game right then; in turn, you get to clarify what they mean. Sometimes publishers will even go so far as to actually show you an example of what they want. This feedback loop can save you months of time wasted trying to get to a shared vision.

Tip

You don't have to only see publishers; visit media organizations, carriers, and Web portals as well. Anybody who is in some way related to J2ME gaming is usually worth seeing in person. Even if they can't help you directly, there's a good chance these people will help point you in the right direction.

The downsides to showing up in person are time and money. It really isn't practical to fly to a country to visit one publisher and then fly back again. This is where the traditional business road show comes in. You just pack your bag and hit the road, visiting as many publishers (usually in one area) as you can in a few weeks. Feel free to fill in any gaps with visits to related organizations along the way. If you've never done a road show, I highly recommend it. There's nothing quite like living a month on the road, talking up your game to anybody who'll listen. Even if you don't succeed the first time, you'll find yourself gaining confidence for presenting your wares and gaining a lot of inside knowledge of the industry.

Trade Shows

Seeing people in person is very effective. However, it can get time consuming and expensive to visit too many companies, especially if they're far away. An alternative is to go to industry trade shows.

Although this isn't as good as going to a publisher's home turf, it can still be very effective—if only because you get to see so many publishers in such a short time. At a typical trade show you could easily see 20 or more companies in a single weekend.

At the moment, the main trade shows for J2ME are E3, JavaOne, GDC Mobile, and Milia. Of these, JavaOne and GDC (*Game Developers Conference*) are conferences for Java and game development, respectively. Both are well worth a visit regardless of the potential sales value. E3 and Milia are both pure trade shows; E3 in particular is all about publishers, distributors, and developers getting together. It's a spectacular, buzzing, super-hyped world of chaos like nothing you've ever seen. Definitely worth a visit, but be ready for a wild ride.

Tip

If you've ever heard the term *networking* and thought it had something to do with multiplayer gaming, you need to look again. Networking is about building and maintaining relationships with people (generally for business reasons). It's all about who you know in the gaming industry.

Networks of contacts are all about trust. Most people in business, especially gaming, waste a lot of time dealing with people who don't know what they're doing. Getting an introduction through a friend of a friend is an immediate way to gain that initial trust. This isn't something you might encounter occasionally; it's the driving force behind the majority of the industry.

Building a network is pretty easy; you'll encounter a lot of contacts by visiting trade shows and companies. Make sure you stay in touch and help them out if and when you can.

Over the Internet

Probably the easiest and most popular method for submitting a game to a publisher is over the Internet. All publishers invite developers to submit games to them online, usually by asking you to send an introductory e-mail containing a summary of the game.

Tip

If you want to catch a publisher's eye, send them a well-formatted HTML e-mail that includes an animated GIF showing off the game.

Have a look at the publishers' Web sites for the exact details on how to make a submission.

The Response

The best and worst thing about using a publisher is that the publisher gets to decide whether your game is good enough to take to market. If you approach a number of publishers and get turned down (or ignored) by all of them then—here's the bit every developer doesn't want to hear—your game is likely crap. If you're lucky, your game will be good enough that a publisher will take the time to tell you what's wrong. Most of the time you'll just a get a rejection or—gulp—silence. You need to take this the right way. The game industry is about selling games. If you can't get a publisher, then assume it's because the publisher doesn't think the game is going to make money. It doesn't matter whether the game is cool or even great fun to play; all that matters is whether a publisher thinks he can make money out of it. That's the reality; skill, effort, and fairness don't always play a part.

Tip

Integrity plays a big part in any dealings you have with a potential publisher. Always follow through on what you say, and don't leave things half-baked. Above all, remember that the games industry is like a big club. Fate will ensure that the guy you treat badly at one company will turn up at exactly the wrong time somewhere else.

It might well be that your first game is not good enough to picked up by a publisher. If that's the case, you've had a lesson in what not to do. Get back up, dust yourself off, and develop something that will sell.

Okay, you've finally developed something that a publisher likes. What's next?

Doing the Deal

If you've reached this point, congratulations are in order. A publisher thinks your game is good enough to take to market, and that's a huge endorsement from the people whose opinion counts when it comes to making money from games. Now it's time to do the deal.

I'll be honest with you here: Publishers in the PC game industry are not renowned for their commitment to help new developers break into the industry, nor are they particularly fair about it. However, given the short development timeframe for J2ME games, mobile game publishers need developers to produce multiple titles to be successful, and to do that they need to build a strong relationship with you over the long term. This means they'll be more likely to give you a good deal, treat you with respect, and not try to screw you over legally.

The next step is to get a lawyer. Unless you're pretty experienced legally and you can properly digest (and understand the implications of) a contract, I recommend you invest in some professional help. If you're not sure whether you can do it yourself, then you definitely need a lawyer. When searching for a lawyer look for someone experienced in game development—not just the local guy or someone your dad used once.

Once you're ready legally, there are some basic things you need to consider before signing the deal.

Tip

If a publisher claims an agreement is non-negotiable, walk away immediately. There's no such thing. There are plenty of other publishers willing to work a deal with you.

A lawyer will give you the details you need to handle the contract. However, there are a few things particular to game contracts worth mentioning.

- **Multiple games.** Never let a contract extend over more than one game. Ever! Always retain the option to renegotiate for any new games. There's no problem giving away a first right of refusal, which means the publisher gets a chance to bid for anything new you make, but there should never be an automatic agreement for any future games. Even if you've done a bad deal, J2ME games are small enough that you get a second chance on your next game.

- **Naming rights.** Make sure your name is included in any reference to the game, including any promotion. Basically, whenever the publisher refers to your game, they have to say your company's name as well. This will maintain your independence and help you build brand.

- **Other rights.** Be careful about giving up any rights other than the J2ME game. Any other use of the property, such as game ports or other content development, should be subject to a new agreement. Always retain the copyright to your material.

- **Exclusivity.** Some publishers will request that you give them exclusivity (with lots of creative reasons as to why they absolutely must have it). There are two key dangers with doing this. First, if for some reason the publisher behaves poorly or even just loses interest, you have no recourse; your game is basically dead in the water. Second, publishers perform far better under pressure of competition. Even if you don't use other publishers, the threat of you being able to do so should serve to keep them working for you. If you want to give exclusivity (and sometimes it can work to your advantage to have a publisher committed to your product), then limit the time of this option to six months at most.

- **Termination option.** A related option to exclusivity is an out clause for you as the developer. Try to get an option to be able to back out of the deal if the publisher doesn't reach set performance levels.

The main thing to remember when doing a deal is not to rush things. If you're not sure about something, get in contact with some other developers and ask their advice. It's exciting to be offered a deal, but don't let your enthusiasm guide you into a bad deal.

Conclusion

It takes time and effort to get a publishing deal—and even more time and effort to maximize its potential. There's every chance that you won't succeed on your first try, but I strongly advise you not to give up. Use that failure to force you into focusing on making a publishable game, even if it means not getting to develop exactly what you want. Sometimes failure is the only messenger that really gets through.

If you're new to the business of games, here's some news for you: Selling a game isn't easy. At times you'll feel disillusioned and depressed. You'll be abused, insulted, ignored, and endlessly lied to. You'll wonder whether it's all worth it. Thankfully, it is; there's nothing like writing games for a living. You just have to want to do it more than all the other amateurs out there.

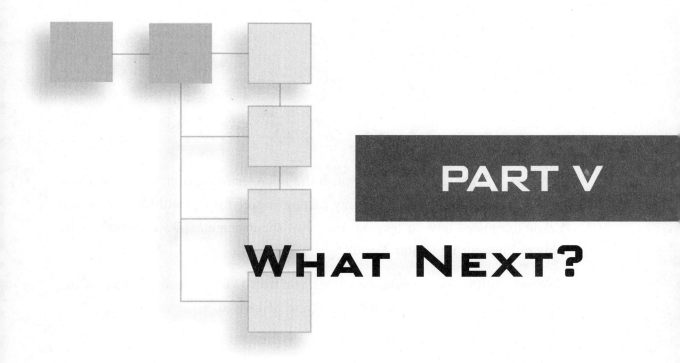

PART V

WHAT NEXT?

CHAPTER 19

CLDC 1.1 and MIDP 2.0 571

CHAPTER 20

The Isometric Engine 621

CHAPTER 21

Ray Casting 639

CHAPTER 22

Making the Connection 669

In Part 5, "What's Next?" you'll push the micro-gaming frontiers by developing both an isometric and 3D ray casting engine for use within your games. You'll also see how to take advantage of the average MID's connectivity by adding online scoring to Star Assault.

To keep up with what's around the corner, you'll also take an in-depth tour of the features in the next-generation CLDC 1.1 and MIDP 2.0.

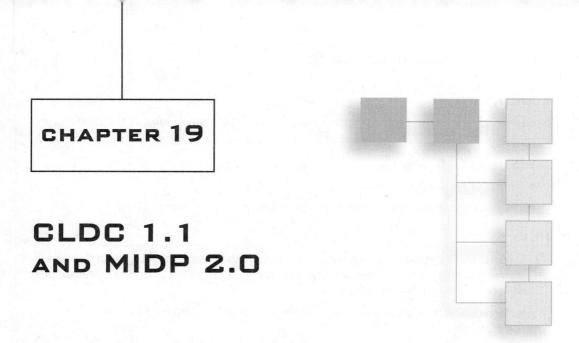

CHAPTER 19

CLDC 1.1
AND MIDP 2.0

Mobile technology is moving fast. When the original CLDC and MIDP specifications were created, the average mobile device lacked sound and color graphics and had a relatively slow CPU. Now there's a range of newer devices that offer a great deal more capability.

To accommodate the additional capabilities of this new breed, the original CLDC and MIDP standard were expanded to create CLDC 1.1 and MIDP 2.0. In this chapter, you'll explore the features now available in the second generation, as well as how to integrate MIDP 2 into your development process.

The Next Generation

In response to the growing capabilities of mobile devices, Sun released an expanded version 2 of the MIDP in November, 2002. The new version raises the bar on the capabilities and includes a host of new features.

Along with MIDP 2, the CLDC was expanded to version 1.1, also incorporating many new features. Note though that while you can employ CLDC 1.1 and MIDP 2.0 together, MIDP 2 does not require CLDC 1.1, so a device featuring MIDP 2 support does not necessarily implement CLDC 1.1. In fact, support for CLDC 1.1 is far behind MIDP 2. Therefore, most of the time you should target MIDP 2 and CLDC 1.0.4 for development.

CLDC 1.1

Even though it's not widely supported, you should take a quick look at the new features available in CLDC 1.1. The interesting additions are

- Support for floating point
- Support for weak references
- An increase in the minimum memory a device requires from 160 KB to 192 KB

Note

CLDC 1.1 also incorporates some more minor things you should take note of. None of these are life changers, but they're nice to have anyway (such as the `String.equalsIgnoreCase` method). These additions include the following features:

- Threads now have names—`Thread.getName()`—and you can interrupt them—`Thread.interrupt()`.
- The `NoClassDefFoundError` was added. This will be thrown if an unknown class is used.
- `Boolean.TRUE` and `Boolean.FALSE` were added.
- String now has `intern() to gain access to an internal string representation` and `equalsIgnoreCase()` methods which compares two strings regardless of case.
- Random now supports the `nextInt(int n)`.

The addition of floating point by default means you can now avoid the mess of using something like the MathFP library (which in turn saves you a little JAR space). In order to fully support floating point, the `Double` and `Float` classes have also been added.

MIDP 2

MIDP 2 is where all the really fun changes are. The new standard offers a great deal more for all types of MID developers, but especially for game programmers.

Handsets supporting MIDP 2 are starting to appear. Any Nokia Series 60 phone, for example, is usually MIDP 2 (though not CLDC 1.1) and other manufacturers are starting to release new handset versions also supporting the platform. Existing handsets, however, are generally not software upgradeable from MIDP 1 to MIDP 2. (Note though that most existing MIDP 1 capable devices are still being released with MIDP 1, not MIDP 2.)

The changes in MIDP 2 come in three main categories—things that you can count on in every implementation, things that are likely to be supported, and things that might be supported. Let's start with the things you know you can count on. These are

- An enhanced LCDUI with custom controls, spacers, and revised layout
- New imaging powers providing draw region, reflection and rotation, and RGB images

- A game library providing support for sprites and distinct drawing layers
- Support for sound (tones)
- PNG image transparency
- Onscreen feedback of any network usage
- The ability to share RMS data among MIDlets
- Secure HTTP (HTTPS)

Note

The MIDP 2 specification recommends that devices not let the user copy a MIDlet unless some type of copy protection system is in place.

The next set of functions is most likely supported, so for the most part you can count on these functions being available. A manufacturer will only exclude these if there's a good reason (such as a device limitation). For this reason most MIDP 2 implementations include these features, so it's quite reasonable to develop with these in mind. However, you will have to check whether they are supported on all devices (and networks) on which you intend to have your game run. The significant features in this category are

- WAV sounds (minimum 8 KHz mono)
- Datagram connections (UDP)
- Direct socket streaming connections (including secure ones)

In addition, optional components may be made available. Since it's completely optional for a manufacturer (or a network provider) to include these, you'll need to check on their availability on your target devices.

- Push protocols (where the MIDlet will "wake up" when traffic is received or at a certain time)
- Server sockets (allowing incoming connections to the device)
- Access to a device's serial ports

Note

MIDP 2 specifications require backward compatibility with all MIDP 1 functions. This means any MIDP 1 game will run on an MIDP 2 device.

Now that you've seen what's offered, take a look at how to set up for MIDP 2 development.

Is MIDP 1 an Upgrade to MIDP 2?

One thing you need to keep in mind about MIDP 2 is that it's a little like the different *Star Trek* series. The original version is still out there and well supported. The next generation is a lot more capable, has a much bigger budget, and looks a lot better, but it's certainly not an enhanced version of the original. They are separate entities designed to coexist. MIDP 2 is not intended to replace MIDP 1, no matter how old MIDP 1 looks compared to more modern versions.

This is illustrated by the common mistake of trying to use the version 2 Wireless Toolkit from Sun to develop MIDP 1 games. It's easy to understand the mistake; version 2 should be an upgrade of version 1, right? Well in this case, that's not quite correct. MIDP 2 is a new standard designed for a new range of more capable phones. In other words, most MIDP 1 devices won't be able to run MIDP 2. You need to use Toolkit 1 for MIDP 1 development and Toolkit 2 for MIDP 2 development.

Personally, I think Sun should have called MIDP 2 something like MIDP Generation 2 to try and reinforce the fact that it's not really an upgrade. After all, it's only natural for developers to assume something labeled 2.0 is a *replacement* for version 1.0.

The important thing is that the release of MIDP 2 does not signify the demise of MIDP 1. A device manufactured with the primary purpose of being a phone doesn't really need the capabilities mandated as part of the MIDP 2 specifications. Down at the budget phone end of the market, the manufacturers are under enormous pressure to keep handset prices down. Monochrome screens, limited memory, and slow CPUs aren't going anywhere anytime soon.

Developing with MIDP 2

To get started developing with MIDP 2, you'll need to download Wireless Toolkit version 2 (Toolkit 2) from Sun. You can download this from http://java.sun.com/products/j2mewtoolkit.

You'll find the Toolkit 2 (shown in Figure 19.1) to be familiar territory; pretty much everything remains the same. Once you have it installed you're ready to modify the build system to support an MIDP 2 target device.

Tip

Remember to copy your obfuscator JAR file (`retroguard.jar`) to the Toolkit 2 `bin` directory.

MIDP 2 Build System

To get started building MIDP 2 applications, you need to make some changes to your build system. Given that MIDP 2 is not a replacement, you need to make sure you can

Figure 19.1 The Wireless Toolkit 2.0's new features are almost exclusively related to MIDP 2 development.

continue to build for MIDP 1 as well. Thankfully, this isn't too difficult. Take a look at how to modify the build system for *Star Assault* to accommodate development on both platforms.

The first thing you need is a new build target for an MIDP 2 device. To handle this properly, you really want to build against the Toolkit 2 installation, not Toolkit 1. The build process gets the location of the Toolkit from the wtk.home parameter set inside the init target.

```
<project name="StarAssault" default="compile" basedir=".">
   <target name="init" depends="setup">
      <property name="wtk.home" value="c:\java\wtk104"/>
      ...
```

You then use this parameter inside a device's build target. For example:

```
<target name="build default" depends="init">
   <property name="dev" value="default"/>
   <property name="midplib" value="${wtk.home}/lib/midpapi.zip"/>
   <antcall target="device build"/>
</target>
```

To build for MIDP 2, obviously all you need to do is change the value of the wtk.home property to wherever you installed the Toolkit 2. For example:

```
<project name="StarAssault" default="compile" basedir=".">
   <target name="init" depends="setup">
      <property name="wtk.home" value="c:\java\wtk20"/>
      ...
```

Although this will work for building both MIDP 1 and 2 targets, it's not recommended practice by Sun—and it can be misleading if MIDP 2 features are accidentally compiled into an MIDP 1 device build. To solve this, one method might be to leave the wtk.home property set in the `init` target to be Toolkit 1, and then override the value for MIDP 2 builds. For example:

```
<project name="StarAssault" default="compile" basedir=".">
    <target name="init" depends="setup">
        <property name="wtk.home" value="c:\java\wtk104"/>
        ...
    </target>

    <target name="build default" depends="init">
        <!--OVERRIDE - WARNING THIS DOESN'T WORK WITH ANT -->
        <property name="wtk.home" value="c:\java\wtk20"/>
        <property name="dev" value="default"/>
        <property name="midplib" value="${wtk.home}/lib/midpapi.zip"/>
        <antcall target="device build"/>
    </target>
```

Ant, however, won't let you do this because you can't change property values after they've been set to an initial value. At this point, you could get rather complicated by inverting the build process to accommodate this; however, in practice I've found you just end up with an overly complex build system. The easier method is to specify the `wtk.home` directory in each of the build targets. For example:

```
<project name="StarAssault" default="compile" basedir=".">
    <target name="init" depends="setup">
        <!-- NO WTK.HOME SET -->
        ...
    </target>

    <target name="build default" depends="init">
        <property name="wtk.home" value="c:\java\wtk20"/>
        ...
    </target>
```

To run the game now, you need to add a target to execute the Toolkit 2 emulator. One problem you'll encounter when doing this is the current `MIDP_HOME` environment variable. Because it points to the Toolkit 1 directory, the Toolkit 2 emulator won't run. To handle this you need to override the environment variable with a different value when you execute the Toolkit 2 target. For example:

```
<target name="run defmidp2" depends="build default">
    <exec executable="C:\java\WTK20\bin\emulator.exe" >
        <env key="MIDP_HOME" value="c:\java\WTK20"></env>
```

```
    <arg line="-Xdescriptor:build/${dev}/${midlet.name}.jad"/>
  </exec>
</target>
```

Notice the addition of the `env` tag. This lets you set an environment variable when you are executing an application. In the preceding example, I'm pointing the environment variable to the Toolkit 2 installation directory.

Tip

If you get an untrusted domain error when you run the MIDP 2 emulator, then your `MIDP_HOME` environment variable is pointing to the wrong version of the Toolkit. Make sure it's set to the home directory where you installed the Toolkit 2 when you attempt to run an MIDP 2 application.

Along with the modifications to the build script, you'll likely need to set up your IDE to utilize the newer `midpapi.zip` class files included with the Toolkit 2. Because these are backwards-compatible, you can usually do this without disturbing the MIDP 1 build process.

When you have all this running, you'll be able to get *Star Assault* working on the MIDP 2 default emulator, as shown in Figure 19.2.

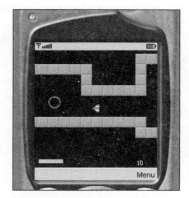

One thing to look out for is that the Toolkit 2 includes class files for CLDC 1.0, not CLDC 1.1, so you won't see any reference to new CLDC features. To develop for CLDC 1.1, you'll need the CLDC 1.1 RI (Reference Implementation), which is available at http://java.sun.com/products/cldc.

Okay, that's all you need to be set up for MIDP 2 development. Now you can take a more detailed look at what you can do with these new features.

Figure 19.2 *Star Assault* running in the MIDP 2 default emulator

Sound

One of the great additions to MIDP is the inclusion of sound. Whereas with MIDP 1 you were limited to a simple beep (through the `Alert` class) without using a device SDK, MIDP 2 lets you play tones and (on some implementations) even sampled audio (WAV files).

Note

The sound components of MIDP 2 are actually just a subset of the MMAPI (*Mobile Media API*)—JSR 135. You can check out the full API on the Java Web site.

The sound functions are available under the javax.microedition.media class hierarchy. The simplest sound you can make is to generate a tone using the Manager class method playTone. This call takes a frequency value representing the tone you want to play, duration in milliseconds, and a volume ranging between 0 and 100. Here's an example that plays a low tone for 500 milliseconds at half volume:

```
try
{
    Manager.playTone(20, 500, 50);
}
catch (MediaException e) { }
```

Every MIDP 2 device must support at least tone generation; however, they will most likely also support WAV file playback, which gives you far greater potential to add some great sound to games.

To play a WAV sound you need to add a resource file to the JAR and then load it as an input stream. You can then play it back using a Player object. For example:

```
try
{
    InputStream in = getClass().getResourceAsStream("/fire1.wav");
    Player p = Manager.createPlayer(in, "audio/x-wav");
    p.start();
}
catch (MediaException me) { }
catch (IOException ioe) { }
```

You also can check the state of a sound (such as whether it's already playing) using the getState() method.

Enhanced LCDUI

MIDP 2 adds quite a bit of functionality to the LCDUI, including support for custom items, better form layout, spacer items, changes to ChoiceGroup and List controls, commands on items, and tons of cool new things with graphics. In this section you'll explore in detail how all of these new features work.

CustomItem

MIDP 2 features a new CustomItem class, which lets you code your own LCDUI items and insert them into forms just like regular items—a bit like a Windows custom control. What the item does, including how it's drawn and reacts to input, is up to you. This is great for games in which you want to spruce up the UI a little, but you don't want to go as far as writing a complete interface.

To create your own item, derive a new class from `CustomItem` and fill in the abstract methods. Following is a simple example that creates a red item with severe emotional problems—it changes from happy to sad at the press of a key.

```
import javax.microedition.lcdui.*;
```

The first thing to notice is this class extends the new MIDP 2 `CustomItem`. Most of the work is done in the `paint` method.

```
public class SmileyItem extends CustomItem
{
    // the state of the item; true for happy, false for sad
    private boolean isHappy;

    public SmileyItem(String title)
    {
        super(title);
        isHappy = true;
    }

    public void change()
    {
        isHappy = !isHappy;
        repaint();
    }


    // overide abstract methods to fill in size details for the item
    public int getMinContentWidth()            { return 50; }
    public int getMinContentHeight()           { return 20; }
    public int getPrefContentWidth(int width)  { return getMinContentWidth(); }
    public int getPrefContentHeight(int height) { return getMinContentHeight(); }
```

The `paint` method is where we implement the custom rendering for this new item. You can do just about anything you want in here to make your own UI items.

```
    // We're responsible for drawing the item onto a supplied graphics canvas
    // for our custom smiley we just draw a red box and some text.
    public void paint(Graphics g, int w, int h)
    {
        // set color to red
        g.setColor(0xff0000);

        // fill the item area
        g.fillRect(0, 0, w - 1, h - 1);
```

```
    // change to white
    g.setColor(0xffffff);

    // set the font
    g.setFont(Font.getDefaultFont());

    // draw the smiley using text
    g.drawString(":" + (isHappy ? ")" : "("), getMinContentWidth()/2, 1,
                 Graphics.TOP | Graphics.HCENTER);
}
```

With a custom item we have to handle all the input ourselves, in this case we just change the state of the smiley no matter what they hit.

```
    protected void keyPressed(int keyCode)
    {
        change();
    }
}
import javax.microedition.lcdui.*;
import javax.microedition.midlet.*;
```

This class is a simple MIDlet to load up the custom item setup in the previous class.

```
public class CustomItemExample extends MIDlet implements CommandListener
{
    private Form form;

    public CustomItemExample()
    {
        form = new Form("A Custom Item");
```

This is where you add the new SmileyItem just like a regular Item object. In this way all the details of handling in the interface are taken care of for you.

```
        form.append(new SmileyItem("Smile"));
        form.addCommand(new Command("Exit", Command.EXIT, 0));
        form.setCommandListener(this);
    }

    public void startApp()
    {
        Display.getDisplay(this).setCurrent(form);
    }

    public void pauseApp()
```

```
    {
    }

    public void destroyApp(boolean unconditional)
    {
    }

    public void commandAction(Command c, Displayable s)
    {
        if (c.getCommandType() == Command.EXIT)
            notifyDestroyed();
    }

}
```

Tip

If you attempt to compile this class against MIDP 1 class files, you will get errors relating unimplemented abstract methods such as `getHeight` and `isFocusable`. If this happens, double-check that you are compiling against the MIDP 2 `midpapi.zip` JAR. You might need to carefully check the class path set in your IDE.

Figure 19.3 shows how this looks when running in the MIDP 2 default emulator.

Custom items can be really cool if you spend some time on them. Adding a steering wheel control to change values in a racing game, a rolling menu system with animation, or even just flashy text-entry boxes can all enhance the look and feel of your game. You can develop a control to do almost anything you want, and then have the convenience of simply adding it into a Form as you would any other Item.

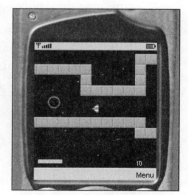

Figure 19.3 An example of a custom item that draws a white smiley face on a red rectangle

Form Control

Forms in MIDP 2 have some extra features as well. First, you can now choose a layout policy for items within a form. The device implementation uses these layout directives to alter the size and position of items for the best effect.

You can apply any of the layout directories listed in Table 19.1 to an item and see the effects. The exact layout and position, however, are up to the device, so you can't rely on an item appearing with the same position or size on all devices.

Table 19.1 Item Layout Options

Layout Directive	Description
LAYOUT_DEFAULT	Default layout (leave it up to the implementation)
LAYOUT_LEFT	Align the item to the left
LAYOUT_RIGHT	Align the item to the right
LAYOUT_CENTER	Center the item
LAYOUT_TOP	Align to the top
LAYOUT_BOTTOM	Align to the bottom
LAYOUT_VCENTER	Vertically center the item
LAYOUT_NEWLINE_BEFORE	This item will start on a new line
LAYOUT_NEWLINE_AFTER	This item will be the last one on a line (with a new line starting immediately after this item)
LAYOUT_SHRINK	Allow this item to shrink to the minimum width if required
LAYOUT_VSHRINK	Allow this item to shrink to the minimum height if required
LAYOUT_EXPAND	Expand the item as wide as possible
LAYOUT_VEXPAND	Expand the item as high as possible
LAYOUT_2	Indicate that MIDP 2 layout is in effect for this item

Figure 19.4 shows an example MIDlet with two custom smiley items added to a form. In this case the device lays out the two items with equal space.

If you now set the LAYOUT_EXPAND directive on the first item, you can see in Figure 19.5 how the implementation increases the width of the item up to the maximum available space (leaving the minimum room for the second item).

Figure 19.4 Two items added to a form with no layout options set

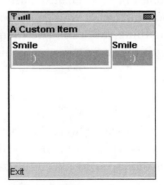

Figure 19.5 The first smiley item has the LAYOUT_EXPAND set, causing it to assume the majority of screen space (see FormLayoutExample).

```
import javax.microedition.lcdui.*;
import javax.microedition.midlet.*;

public class FormLayoutExample extends MIDlet implements CommandListener
{
    private Form form;

    public FormLayoutExample()
    {
        form = new Form("Layout Example");

        SmileyItem s1 = new SmileyItem("Smile");
```

This is the primary difference between this and the previous example. Here a new custom item is given a layout directive to expand across the screen. A second item added below does have this directive. From Figure 19.5 you can see how the first one expands to fill the remaining space on the layout line.

```
        // set the layout to expand this item as much as possible,
        // also indicate we are using MIDP 2 layout styles
        s1.setLayout(Item.LAYOUT_EXPAND | Item.LAYOUT_2);

        form.append(s1);

        SmileyItem s2 = new SmileyItem("Smile");
        form.append(s2);

        form.addCommand(new Command("Exit", Command.EXIT, 0));
        form.setCommandListener(this);
    }

    public void startApp()
    {
        Display.getDisplay(this).setCurrent(form);
    }

    public void pauseApp()
    {
    }

    public void destroyApp(boolean unconditional)
    {
    }
```

```
    public void commandAction(Command c, Displayable s)
    {
        if (c.getCommandType() == Command.EXIT)
            notifyDestroyed();
    }
}
```

Spacer Item

Now that you have more control over the layout of objects, you'll quickly find cases where you want to add space between items to organize the layout. MIDP 2 provides the Spacer class to let you do this.

Using a spacer is dead easy; simply construct it with the minimum horizontal and vertical space you need and then add it to the form as you would any other item. You can then use layout commands on the spacer to further control placement.

In the following example I've expanded the smiley arrangement to have two rows containing two smileys separated by a spacer. You can see the results in Figure 19.6.

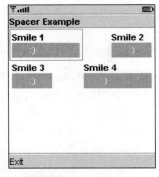

Figure 19.6 Smileys separated using spacer items

```
import javax.microedition.lcdui.*;
import javax.microedition.midlet.*;

public class SpacerExample extends MIDlet implements CommandListener
{
    private Form form;

    public SpacerExample()
    {
        form = new Form("Spacer Example");

        // ROW 1 ----------
        SmileyItem s1 = new SmileyItem("Smile 1");
        s1.setLayout(Item.LAYOUT_EXPAND | Item.LAYOUT_2);
        form.append(s1);

        // add a spacer in between the two smileys on the first row
        form.append(new Spacer(30, 30));
```

```
    // add the second smiley
    form.append(new SmileyItem("Smile 2"));

    // ROW 2 ---------
    form.append(new SmileyItem("Smile 3"));

    // add a spacer in between the two smileys on the second row
    form.append(new Spacer(30, 30));

    SmileyItem s4 = new SmileyItem("Smile 4");

    // expand the second smiley (expanding)
    s4.setLayout(Item.LAYOUT_EXPAND | Item.LAYOUT_2);
    form.append(s4);

    form.addCommand(new Command("Exit", Command.EXIT, 0));
    form.setCommandListener(this);
}

public void startApp()
{
    Display.getDisplay(this).setCurrent(form);
}

public void pauseApp()
{
}

public void destroyApp(boolean unconditional)
{
}

public void commandAction(Command c, Displayable s)
{
    if (c.getCommandType() == Command.EXIT)
        notifyDestroyed();
}
}
```

Due to their nature, spacer items cannot have commands, and you cannot navigate to them.

ChoiceGroup and List

The ChoiceGroup and List items also gain some new features in MIDP 2. First, you can now set a font for them to use. This adds some flexibility to how you want ChoiceGroups and Lists to appear; however, this is only a recommendation, and it doesn't work practically for all choice types (notably POPUPs).

The ChoiceGroup has a new POPUP type, which is something like a Windows drop-down menu. The GUI will display a single item picked from a list that drops down when you select the item. It's up to the implementation to draw how this control works, but most of the time you'll see a field with a down arrow indicating that more options are available.

Now you can also set a fit policy to indicate whether or not you want items in a list to wrap.

Note

ChoiceGroup and List now also have a deleteAll method to remove all the elements of a list in one go.

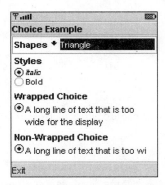

Figure 19.7 A demonstration MIDlet showing a drop-down style ChoiceGroup—a list containing items using different fonts, as well as two choices using different fit policies

You can see all these features in action in Figure 19.7 and in the following code.

```
import javax.microedition.lcdui.*;
import javax.microedition.midlet.*;

public class ChoiceExample extends MIDlet implements CommandListener
{
    private Form form;

    public ChoiceExample()
    {
        form = new Form("Choice Example");

        // a simple example of a popup list containing the
names of shapes
        ChoiceGroup c = new ChoiceGroup("Shapes", Choice.POPUP);
        c.append("Triangle", null);
        c.append("Square", null);
        c.append("Circle", null);
        form.append(c);

        // create an exclusive style choice with items representing different
```

```
    // fonts, then we set that style.
    ChoiceGroup c2 = new ChoiceGroup("Styles", Choice.EXCLUSIVE);
    c2.append("Italic", null);
    c2.append("Bold", null);
    c2.setFont(0, Font.getFont(Font.FACE_PROPORTIONAL, Font.STYLE_ITALIC,
                        Font.SIZE_SMALL));
    c2.setFont(1, Font.getFont(Font.FACE_PROPORTIONAL, Font.STYLE_BOLD,
                        Font.SIZE_SMALL));
    form.append(c2);

    // a wide list with wrapping on
    ChoiceGroup c3 = new ChoiceGroup("Wrapped Choice", Choice.EXCLUSIVE);
    c3.append("A long line of text that is too wide for the display", null);
    c3.setFitPolicy(Choice.TEXT_WRAP_ON);
    form.append(c3);

    // a wide list with wrapping off
    ChoiceGroup c4 = new ChoiceGroup("Non-Wrapped Choice", Choice.EXCLUSIVE);
    c4.append("A long line of text that is too wide for the display", null);
    c4.setFitPolicy(Choice.TEXT_WRAP_OFF);
    form.append(c4);

    form.addCommand(new Command("Exit", Command.EXIT, 0));
    form.setCommandListener(this);
}

public void startApp()
{
    Display.getDisplay(this).setCurrent(form);
}

public void pauseApp()
{
}

public void destroyApp(boolean unconditional)
{
}

public void commandAction(Command c, Displayable s)
{
```

```
        if (c.getCommandType() == Command.EXIT)
            notifyDestroyed();
    }


}
```

Item Commands

Now you can associate a Command with an Item. (In MIDP 1, Commands could only be added to a Form.) The MID will present commands associated with a particular item whenever it has focus (selected by the user).

To create an Item command, you simply construct a Command as normal and then use the new Item.addCommand method to associate it. To carry out actions when the Command is entered, use the Item.setItemCommandListener method.

In the following example, you can see a change Command added to your friend the SmileyItem. See Figure 19.8 for the results.

Figure 19.8 An example of an item command; note that the "change" command is only displayed when the smiley item is focused.

```
import javax.microedition.lcdui.*;
import javax.microedition.midlet.*;

public class ItemCommandExample extends MIDlet implements
        CommandListener, ItemCommandListener
{
    private Form form;
    private SmileyItem smiley;
    private Command changeEmotion;

    public ItemCommandExample()
    {
        form = new Form("Item Commands");

        // create a smiley item
        smiley = new SmileyItem("Smile");

        // create a command to change the type and add it as a command
        // onto the smiley item.
        changeEmotion = new Command("Change", Command.ITEM, 1);
        smiley.addCommand(changeEmotion);

        // set this class to be the listener for the command
```

```
        smiley.setItemCommandListener(this);

        form.append(smiley);
        form.addCommand(new Command("Exit", Command.EXIT, 0));
        form.setCommandListener(this);
    }

    public void startApp()
    {
        Display.getDisplay(this).setCurrent(form);
    }

    public void pauseApp()
    {
    }

    public void destroyApp(boolean unconditional)
    {
    }

    // form command listener
    public void commandAction(Command c, Displayable s)
    {
        if (c.getCommandType() == Command.EXIT)
            notifyDestroyed();
    }

    // item command listener
    public void commandAction(Command command, Item item)
    {
        if (command == changeEmotion)
        {
            smiley.change();
        }
    }
}
```

Graphics

One of the best areas of improvement for game development is in the revisions to the Graphics class. Now you can copy parts of the display using copyArea, draw triangles using fillTriangle, draw parts of an image using drawRegion, and figure out the actual color a device uses based on a particular RGB value using getDisplayColor.

If that's not enough, what's really cool is that you now have standard image rotation and reflection along with the power to directly manipulate images using RGB values. Read on to check these out in a little more detail.

Reflection and Rotation

Now you can draw a portion of an image on the screen using the new `Image.drawRegion` method. This is great, but the really cool thing is that this method also does reflection and rotation (similar to the Nokia UI).

Table 19.2 lists all the image manipulation options. Using these options, you can rotate or reflect an image in any 90-degree increment. Following is an example that rotates an image using every type. You can see the results in Figure 19.9.

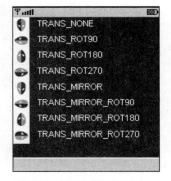

Figure 19.9 MIDP 2's new image manipulation lets you flip an image around.

Table 19.2 Image Manipulation (from javax.microedition.lcdui.game.Sprite)

Manipulation Option	Description
Sprite.TRANS_NONE	Copy with no alteration (default)
Sprite.TRANS_ROT90	Rotate the image region clockwise by 90 degrees
Sprite.TRANS_ROT180	Rotate the image region clockwise by 180 degrees
Sprite.TRANS_ROT270	Rotate the image region clockwise by 270 degrees
Sprite.TRANS_MIRROR	Reflect the image region vertically
Sprite.TRANS_MIRROR_ROT90	Reflect vertically and then rotate clockwise by 90 degrees
Sprite.TRANS_MIRROR_ROT180	Reflect vertically and then rotate clockwise by 180 degrees
Sprite.TRANS_MIRROR_ROT270	Reflect vertically and then rotate clockwise by 270 degrees

```java
import javax.microedition.lcdui.*;
import javax.microedition.lcdui.game.Sprite;
import javax.microedition.midlet.*;
import java.io.IOException;

public class GraphicsExample extends MIDlet
{
    private MyCanvas myCanvas;

    class MyCanvas extends Canvas
    {
        private Image alienHeadImage = null;
```

```
public MyCanvas()
{
    try
    {
        alienHeadImage = Image.createImage("/alienhead.png");
    }
    catch (IOException ioe)
    {
        System.out.println("unable to load image");
    }
}

protected void paint(Graphics g)
{
    g.setColor(0, 0, 0);
    g.fillRect(0, 0, getWidth(), getHeight());
    g.setColor(0xffffff);
    int y=0;

    // TRANS NONE
    g.drawRegion(alienHeadImage, 0, 0,
                 alienHeadImage.getWidth(), alienHeadImage.getHeight(),
                 Sprite.TRANS_NONE, 0, y, Graphics.TOP | Graphics.LEFT);
    g.drawString("TRANS_NONE", alienHeadImage.getWidth() + 10, y,
                 Graphics.TOP | Graphics.LEFT);
    y += alienHeadImage.getHeight();

    // TRANS ROT 90
    g.drawRegion(alienHeadImage, 0, 0,
                 alienHeadImage.getWidth(), alienHeadImage.getHeight(),
                 Sprite.TRANS_ROT90, 0, y, Graphics.TOP | Graphics.LEFT);
    g.drawString("TRANS_ROT90", alienHeadImage.getWidth() + 10, y,
                 Graphics.TOP | Graphics.LEFT);
    y += alienHeadImage.getHeight();

    // TRANS ROT 180
    g.drawRegion(alienHeadImage, 0, 0,
                 alienHeadImage.getWidth(), alienHeadImage.getHeight(),
                 Sprite.TRANS_ROT180, 0, y, Graphics.TOP | Graphics.LEFT);
    g.drawString("TRANS_ROT180", alienHeadImage.getWidth() + 10, y,
                 Graphics.TOP | Graphics.LEFT);
    y += alienHeadImage.getHeight();
```

```
            // TRANS ROT 270
            g.drawRegion(alienHeadImage, 0, 0,
                        alienHeadImage.getWidth(), alienHeadImage.getHeight(),
                        Sprite.TRANS_ROT270, 0, y, Graphics.TOP | Graphics.LEFT);
            g.drawString("TRANS_ROT270", alienHeadImage.getWidth() + 10, y,
                        Graphics.TOP | Graphics.LEFT);
            y += alienHeadImage.getHeight();

            // TRANS MIRROR
            g.drawRegion(alienHeadImage, 0, 0,
                        alienHeadImage.getWidth(), alienHeadImage.getHeight(),
                        Sprite.TRANS_MIRROR, 0, y, Graphics.TOP | Graphics.LEFT);
            g.drawString("TRANS_MIRROR", alienHeadImage.getWidth() + 10, y,
                        Graphics.TOP | Graphics.LEFT);
            y += alienHeadImage.getHeight();

            // TRANS MIRROR_ROT90
            g.drawRegion(alienHeadImage, 0, 0,
                        alienHeadImage.getWidth(), alienHeadImage.getHeight(),
                        Sprite.TRANS_MIRROR_ROT90, 0, y, Graphics.TOP | Graphics.LEFT);
            g.drawString("TRANS_MIRROR_ROT90", alienHeadImage.getWidth() + 10, y,
                        Graphics.TOP | Graphics.LEFT);
            y += alienHeadImage.getHeight();

            // TRANS MIRROR_ROT180
            g.drawRegion(alienHeadImage, 0, 0,
                        alienHeadImage.getWidth(), alienHeadImage.getHeight(),
                        Sprite.TRANS_MIRROR_ROT180, 0, y, Graphics.TOP | Graphics.LEFT);
            g.drawString("TRANS_MIRROR_ROT180", alienHeadImage.getWidth() + 10, y,
                        Graphics.TOP | Graphics.LEFT);
            y += alienHeadImage.getHeight();

            // TRANS MIRROR_ROT270
            g.drawRegion(alienHeadImage, 0, 0,
                        alienHeadImage.getWidth(), alienHeadImage.getHeight(),
                        Sprite.TRANS_MIRROR_ROT270, 0, y, Graphics.TOP | Graphics.LEFT);
            g.drawString("TRANS_MIRROR_ROT270", alienHeadImage.getWidth() + 10, y,
                        Graphics.TOP | Graphics.LEFT);
        }

    }

public GraphicsExample()
```

```
    {
        myCanvas = new MyCanvas();
    }

    protected void startApp() throws MIDletStateChangeException
    {
        Display.getDisplay(this).setCurrent(myCanvas);
    }

    protected void pauseApp()
    {
    }

    protected void destroyApp(boolean unconditional) throws MIDletStateChangeException
    {
    }
}
```

Image Arrays

One of the great new features in MIDP 2 is that you're able to represent images as arrays of integers. This gives you the power to manipulate the values and thus carry out image processing on the fly. You can use this feature for all sorts of cool things, such as increasing or decreasing image brightness, changing image size, creating shadows effects, or simply shifting colors.

MIDP 2 represents an image as an array of 32-bit integers, where each element corresponds to a single pixel in the image. The 32 bits correspond to 8 bits for each of the red, green, and blue elements and 8 bits for the alpha channel (also known as ARGB).

To create an RGB image you first need to construct an array of integers large enough to represent all its pixels. For example, the following code creates an image array and then sets all the pixels to be semi-transparent green.

```
// create a 10 by 10 image array
int numPixels = 10 * 10;
int[] rgbImage = new int[numPixels];

// fill pixel array with semi-transparent green
for (int i=0; i < numPixels; i++)
    rgbImage[i] = 0x5500FF00;
```

To render this on the display, you use the Graphics class's new drawRGB method. This takes the image array data, array offset (where in the array the image starts; usually this is the first byte, or zero), scan length (the number of array elements per row, typically the image width), the position at which you want the image to appear, the width and height, and finally whether you want the alpha channel processed. (If you're not using the alpha channel in your image array, you can use `false` in order to speed up rendering.) Here's an example that draws the image array you created a moment ago onto the display:

```
g.drawRGB(rgbImage, 0, 10, 75, 50, 10, 10, true);
```

Creating images like this is useful, but the real fun begins when you start manipulating existing images to create different effects. To do this, you first need to load an image to use. For example:

```
Image img = Image.createImage("/image.png");
```

You then need to construct an array large enough to hold an integer for every pixel in the image. You can get this simply by multiplying the image width by the height.

```
int[] rgbData = new int[(img.getWidth() * img.getHeight())];
```

You can now use the `Image` class's new `getRGB` method to populate the array.

```
// Extract the integers that make up the image into the rggData array.
img.getRGB(rgbData, 0, img.getWidth(), 0, 0, img.getWidth(),
            img.getHeight());
```

Now that you have all the image data in an array you can play around with it. A good way to utilize your new power is to recolor images to create different versions. In *Star Assault*, for example, you could create a set of enemy ships as a base and then dynamically color different versions to represent stronger enemy types. Using this method you can add much more variety to a game without adding to JAR space. Take a look at exactly how this is done using RGB images.

Tip
___
If you want to create a translucent shadow effect, you can do it easily by using an RGB image. Simply create a copy of the original image and then flip all pixels (that are not already transparent) to a transparent color, such as 0x5533333 (a transparent gray). To render the shadow, draw it before you draw the main image and offset its position to give it perspective.
___

Now that you can access the integers that represent pixels in the image, you can now start to manipulate that image by altering the colors represented in each pixel. In the next section you'll develop code to extract the color components, and then put them back into the image.

To manipulate pixels you first need to be able to split out the individual color components represented in the 32-bit integer. Each integer in the array is made up of four components, each using 8 bits (ARGB). In Figure 19.10, you can see how the four bytes represent each color.

Therefore, to represent any color, you can use the hex value corresponding to each of the color components you want. For example, 0x005500FF turns on half the bits for the red component and all the bits for blue, giving you a rather attractive shade of purple. You can see this illustrated in Figure 19.11.

Now imagine that you want to switch all those red pixels to green ones, keeping the exact same relative shade. To do this, you first need to isolate the different color components out of the integer value using a bit-wise AND mask. The mask should turn on (set to a value of 1) the bits representing the values you're after and turn off (set to a value of 0) the elements you don't want. When you use an AND operation on the original value combined with the mask, the result contains only values where the original bit was 1 and the mask was 1. Therefore, any bit turned on in the original color will come through, but only for the segment in which you're interested. Figure 19.12 shows an example of this.

Notice how only the bits that are 1 in both the value and the mask make it through to the result. This is how you isolate only the red portion of the color.

Byte 1	Byte 2	Byte 3	Byte 4
AAAAAAAA	RRRRRRRR	GGGGGGGG	BBBBBBBB

Figure 19.10 The bits that make up the four bytes for each pixel in an RGB image

00	55	00	FF
00000000	00001111	00000000	11111111

Figure 19.11 The bits that make up the RGB color 0x005500FF

	00	55	00	FF
Value	00000000	00001111	00000000	11111111

	00	FF	00	00
Mask	00000000	11111111	00000000	00000000

	00	55	00	00
Result	00000000	00001111	00000000	00000000

Figure 19.12 You can isolate certain components of an integer using a logical AND.

To do this in code, you use the hex equivalents of the bit value and the & (logical AND) operator. Here's a simple example to start with (you'll soon see how this can be used to manipulate complex color components):

```
int color = 0x005500FF;
int redMaskResult = (color & 0x00FF0000);        // result = 0x00550000
```

The redMaskResult integer now contains the value 0x00550000. This is great, but you're still not quite there. The problem is the red values are still sitting high in the integer value, so you need to shift them into the correct position for them to represent an integer containing only the red value. In effect, what you need is the value 0x00000055, not 0x00550000.

To shift the red bits over, you use the >> (bitwise shift) operator to move the value over the correct number of bits. Because the red component exists in the third byte, you need to shift it across by 2 bytes or 16 bits. You can see this in Figure 19.13.

To do a shift in code use the >> operator and the number of bits by which you want to shift. For example:

```
int redColor = redMaskResult >> 16;         // result = 0x00000055
```

If you take this a little further, you can see that to get the alpha component you would need to shift by 24 bits (3 bytes); likewise, the green would require 8 bits (1 byte). The green component sits at the end so it's already a normalized integer, and you don't need to shift anything. Here's the code to mask and shift out all the components. You'll notice I'm now combining the two steps into one line of code.

```
int p = rgbDate[i]; // Grab a pixel from the rgb array.
int alpha = ((p & 0xff000000) >> 24);
int red   = ((p & 0x00ff0000) >> 16);
int green = ((p & 0x0000ff00) >> 8);
int blue  = ((p & 0x000000ff) >> 0);
```

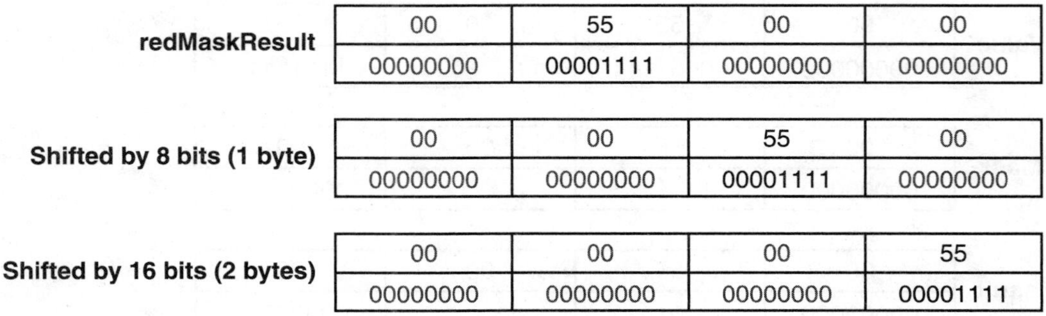

redMaskResult	00	55	00	00
	00000000	00001111	00000000	00000000

Shifted by 8 bits (1 byte)	00	00	55	00
	00000000	00000000	00001111	00000000

Shifted by 16 bits (2 bytes)	00	00	00	55
	00000000	00000000	00000000	00001111

Figure 19.13 To extract the red component of an RGB value you need to shift it into the first position in the integer.

You can now adjust these values as normal integers. If you want to increase the intensity of red in a pixel, you can simply increment the red integer value. To increase the general brightness, you can increase all the values. For example:

```
// increase brightness of image
red += 25;
green += 25;
blue += 25;
```

Now comes the last piece of the puzzle: How do you put the colors back into the ARGB format? Thankfully, this is much easier than extracting the values. You simply shift each component back into the correct position and then add them all together. For example:

```
int newColor = (alpha << 24) + (red << 16) + (green << 8) + blue;
```

And that's it. You can now extract the alpha and color components from any pixel, play around with the values, and then put them back. To give you an idea of how easy it can be to play around with images, take a look at a more comprehensive example.

In the following code, I load an image of an alien head that is black on one side and red on the other. Using the MIDP 2 RGB image tools, I recolor it to blue and then green. You'll notice in Figure 19.14 that the various shades of each color are maintained throughout the process.

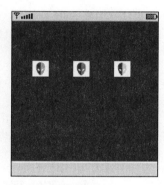

Figure 19.14 You can use RGB image tools to change images. In this example, the red elements of an image are flipped to blue and green.

```
import javax.microedition.lcdui.*;
import javax.microedition.lcdui.game.Sprite;
import javax.microedition.midlet.*;
import java.io.IOException;

public class RGBImageExample extends MIDlet
{
    private MyCanvas myCanvas;

    class MyCanvas extends Canvas
    {
        private Image redImage = null;
        private int[] blueRGBImage;
        private int[] greenRGBImage;

        public MyCanvas()
        {
            try
```

```
                {
                    // load up the original red alien head from a resource file
                    redImage = Image.createImage("/alienhead.png");

                    // create new versions by flipping color bytes around
                    blueRGBImage = flipImageColor(redImage, SHIFT_RED_TO_BLUE);
                    greenRGBImage = flipImageColor(redImage, SHIFT_RED_TO_GREEN);

                }
            catch (IOException ioe)
                {
                    System.out.println("unable to load image");
                }
        }

        protected void paint(Graphics g)
        {
            g.setColor(0, 0, 0);
            g.fillRect(0, 0, getWidth(), getHeight());

            // draw the original
            g.drawImage(redImage, 25, 50, Graphics.TOP | Graphics.LEFT);

            // draw the color-shifted images
            g.drawRGB(blueRGBImage, 0, redImage.getWidth(), 75, 50,
                        redImage.getWidth(), redImage.getHeight(), true);
            g.drawRGB(greenRGBImage, 0, redImage.getWidth(), 125, 50,
                        redImage.getWidth(), redImage.getHeight(), true);
        }

        private static final int SHIFT_RED_TO_GREEN = 0;
        private static final int SHIFT_RED_TO_BLUE = 1;
        private static final int SHIFT_GREEN_TO_BLUE = 2;
        private static final int SHIFT_GREEN_TO_RED = 3;
        private static final int SHIFT_BLUE_TO_RED = 4;
        private static final int SHIFT_BLUE_TO_GREEN = 5;

        public int[] flipImageColor(Image source, int shiftType)
        {
            // we start by getting the image data into an int array - the number
            // of 32-bit ints is equal to the width multiplied by the height
```

```
        int[] rgbData = new int[(source.getWidth() * source.getHeight())];
        source.getRGB(rgbData, 0, source.getWidth(), 0, 0, source.getWidth(),
                    source.getHeight());

        // now go through every pixel and adjust its color
        for (int i=0; i < rgbData.length; i++)
        {
            int p = rgbData[i];

            // split out the different byte components of the pixel by applying
            // a mask so we only get what we need, then shift it to make it
            // a normal number we can play around with
            int a = ((p & 0xff000000) >> 24);
            int r = ((p & 0x00ff0000) >> 16);
            int g = ((p & 0x0000ff00) >> 8);
            int b = ((p & 0x000000ff) >> 0);

            int ba=a, br=r, bb=b, bg=g; // backup copies

            // flip the colors around according to the operation required
            switch(shiftType)
            {
                case SHIFT_RED_TO_GREEN:    g = r; r = bg; break;
                case SHIFT_RED_TO_BLUE:     b = r; r = bb; break;
                case SHIFT_GREEN_TO_BLUE:   g = b; b = bg; break;
                case SHIFT_GREEN_TO_RED:    g = r; r = bg; break;
                case SHIFT_BLUE_TO_RED:     b = r; r = bb; break;
                case SHIFT_BLUE_TO_GREEN:   b = g; g = bb; break;
            }

            // shift all our values back in
            rgbData[i] = (a << 24) + (r << 16) + (g << 8) + b;
        }

        return rgbData;
    }

}

public RGBImageExample()
{
```

```
        myCanvas = new MyCanvas();
    }

    protected void startApp() throws MIDletStateChangeException
    {
        Display.getDisplay(this).setCurrent(myCanvas);
    }

    protected void pauseApp()
    {
    }

    protected void destroyApp(boolean unconditional) throws MIDletStateChangeException
    {
    }
}
```

Other Extras

So far I've only touched on the major new additions to the LCDUI. However, there are a host of other great extras that you'll also find useful. Briefly, these include

- Gauge can now use additional styles to indicate progress in different ways, such as the "I'm-doing-something-but-I-can't-tell-how-long-it-will-take-so-just-BACK-OFF-OK" style.

- StringItem can use different fonts via a setFont method.

- TextField and TextBox have the new input constraint types listed in Table 19.3.

- Form has the new methods getHeight, getWidth, and deleteAll. I'll let you guess what they do.

- Alerts can now contain Gauges as well as be interrupted using a special dismiss command. You can also set a listener for this event to catch when a user cancels something.

- StringItem and ImageItem can now set an appearance mode to PLAIN, HYPERLINK, or BUTTON to change how they look.

- For devices that support it, you can now control lights and vibration.

- Commands can now have an optional "long" text label, which will be used if space permits.

- You can now set up a notifier for you to be called back if the size of the screen changes for any reason (such as changing modes).

- You can now set an item to be current as well as a Displayable.

Table 19.3 New Text Input Constraints

Input Constraint Type	Description
SENSITIVE	Implementation cannot store the value internally.
UNEDITABLE	User cannot change contents.
NON_PREDICTIVE	Predictive input disabled.
INITIAL_CAPS_WORDS	Capitalize the first letter of every word.
INITIAL_CAPS_SENTENCE	Capitalize the first letter of every sentence.
DECIMAL	Restrict values to numbers plus a decimal point.

Game API

The MIDP 2 game library is probably the best set of features for game developers. It has two major areas—the GameCanvas, which improves the basic structure of a game application, and layers, which provide a standard mechanism for managing and drawing multiple graphics layers, including sprites.

To use the new Game API classes you need to import javax.microedition.lcdui.game.*. You'll tackle the GameCanvas first because it affects the fundamental structure of a gaming MIDlet.

GameCanvas

The GameCanvas class provides a version of the Canvas class with some extra capabilities for handling input and rendering.

For handling input, you no longer use the keyPressed method. GameCanvas takes care of interpreting events and setting a state for you, so all you need to do is check the state of keys using the getKeyStates() method. GameCanvas now also has the constants listed in Table 19.4 for all the standard game keys.

For example, in the following code you grab the key states and then check whether the left game key is down.

Table 19.4 Game Canvas Key States

```
LEFT_PRESSED
RIGHT_PRESSED
UP_PRESSED
DOWN_PRESSED
FIRE_PRESSED
GAME_A_PRESSED
GAME_B_PRESSED
GAME_C_PRESSED
GAME_D_PRESSED
```

```
int keyStates = getKeyStates();
if ((keyStates & LEFT_PRESSED) != 0)
    // do something incredibly exciting
```

This method of handling input, known as *polling*, has the side effect that you need to constantly check the state of keys in order to trigger effects based on any change of state (which is a general waste of time). Using the Canvas class, you used to be able to respond to direct events when they happened (through callback methods), so you knew, for example, when a key was released because the keyReleased method was called. With GameCanvas you need to continually check to see whether the state changed to achieve the same result. For example, in the following code you grab the key state and compare it to a saved one. If it has changed, you know the event has occurred.

```
previousState = currentKeyStates;
currentKeyStates = getKeyStates();
if ((currentkeyStates & LEFT_PRESSED) == 0 &&    // key is NOT pressed now
    (previouskeyStates & LEFT_PRESSED) != 0)     // but it WAS before
   // react to a key being released
```

GameCanvas also relieves you from much of the burden of managing the drawing state. When using Canvas you have to call repaint to trigger a call to your overridden paint method. You then use the graphics context passed into this method to do your drawing. GameCanvas simplifies this by making a graphics context available all the time. When you want to render the screen you *flush* it to the display using the flushGraphics method. This also means you don't have any issues with having your rendering code execute in a different thread than the rest of the game. GameCanvas also takes care of any double buffering (if it's required by the MID).

Using GameCanvas's new input and graphics means your run method is much simpler. You can check for input, cycle the game, and then do your rendering in a linear order—without needing to worry about who is calling what when.

```
public void run()
{
   while (true)
   {
      // set the state of the keys
      int keyState = getKeyStates();

      // code to handle input

      // code to paint to the GameCanvas graphics
      // use getGraphics() to grab the current graphics context

      // flip graphics
      flushGraphics();
```

```
        // pause if we need to
    }
}
```

Okay, now it's time to put all this into action. In the following example you can see the basics of a MIDlet that uses GameCanvas at its core.

Tip

The following code, along with all the example classes shown in this chapter can be found in the Chapter 19 source code directory on the CD.

```java
import javax.microedition.lcdui.*;
import javax.microedition.lcdui.game.*;
import javax.microedition.midlet.MIDlet;
import javax.microedition.midlet.MIDletStateChangeException;
import java.io.IOException;
```

This MIDlet class is basically the same as a MIDP 1 version. The real changes are in the custom canvas below.

```java
public class GameCanvasExample extends MIDlet
{
    private MyGameCanvas myCanvas;

    public GameCanvasExample()
    {
        myCanvas = new MyGameCanvas();
    }

    protected void startApp() throws MIDletStateChangeException
    {
        Display.getDisplay(this).setCurrent(myCanvas);
        myCanvas.start();
    }

    protected void pauseApp()
    {
    }

    protected void destroyApp(boolean unconditional) throws MIDletStateChangeException
    {
    }
}
```

This class extends the MIDP 2 GameCanvas rather than the MIDP 1 Canvas class.

```java
class MyGameCanvas extends GameCanvas implements Runnable
{
    private boolean running;
    private int x, y;
    private Image alienHeadImage = null;

    public MyGameCanvas()
    {
        super(true);

        x = getWidth() / 2;
        y = getHeight() / 2;

        try
        {
            alienHeadImage = Image.createImage("/alienhead.png");
        }

        catch (IOException ioe)
        {
            System.out.println("unable to load image");
        }
    }

    public void start()
    {
        running = true;
        Thread t = new Thread(this);
        t.start();
    }

    public void run()
    {
        Graphics g = getGraphics();

        while (running)
        {
```

The following code to handle the key states is quite different to how it's done in MIDP 1. You'll notice though that the end effect is the same as what is done in *Star Assault*; read keys and set a state value. In this example it checks if an arrow key is down and changes the position of the image accordingly.

```
// handle the state of keys
int keyStates = getKeyStates();

if ((keyStates & LEFT_PRESSED) != 0)    x--;
if ((keyStates & RIGHT_PRESSED) != 0)   x++;
if ((keyStates & UP_PRESSED) != 0)      y--;
if ((keyStates & DOWN_PRESSED) != 0)    y++;

if (x < 0) x = getWidth();
if (x > getWidth()) x = 0;
if (y < 0) y = getHeight();
if (y > getHeight()) y = 0;

// draw the world
g.setColor(0x000000);
g.fillRect(0, 0, getWidth(), getHeight());
g.drawImage(alienHeadImage, x, y, Graphics.VCENTER|Graphics.HCENTER);
```

This is the other major change from MIDP 1. You don't need to worry about setting up an off-screen buffer; you just call flushGraphics when ready to paint to the screen.

```
// flush the graphics buffer (GameCanvas will take care of painting)
flushGraphics();

// sleep a little
try
{
    Thread.sleep(10);
}
catch (InterruptedException ie)
{
}
        }
    }

}
```

Layer upon Layer upon . . .

The second major part of the Game API is direct support for layers. This includes a whole host of functionality revolving around managing distinct screens in a game, as well as support for basic game sprites.

When you developed *Star Assault* you used layers extensively. Basically, they're a way of separating the rendering of the different parts of your game. The star-field background, world tiles, and sprites are all examples of the different layers in a game. You can think of it a little like an onion, where each layer is drawn outward toward the viewer. When you combine them all, you get the final image of the game. Using layers, you can logically separate the distinct components in your game as well as manage the order in which they are drawn.

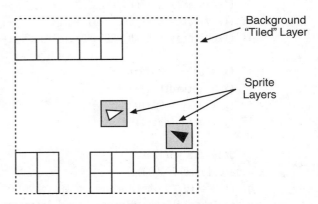

The two types of layers supported by MIDP 2 are tiled layers, using the TiledLayer class, and sprites, using the Sprite class. In Figure 19.15, you can see the different types of layers used in a typical game. You can have as many of these layers as you want.

Figure 19.15 The MIDP 2 game API provides for two distinct types of layers—tiles and sprites.

Note

The Layer class is an abstract base class for the TiledLayer and Sprite classes. I have no idea why, but Sun decided not to include a public constructor in the Layer class (only a private one), so you cannot derive a class directly from Layer.

Tiled Layer

Tiles are sets of equally sized graphics that you can arrange in a grid, or tile layer. By arranging (and repeating) these tiles, you can present proportionally large areas with small source images. In Figure 19.16, for example, you can see three tiles (each 16 × 16 pixels) representing horizontal, vertical, and cross pieces. Next to this is an example of these tiles arranged in a grid to form a series of interlocking lines.

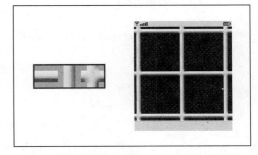

Figure 19.16 Using three very simple tiles, you can create a much larger "tiled" image.

Note

The performance of a `TiledLayer` is directly relevant to the size of each tile. The smaller each tile is, the slower it will render. Therefore, anything below 16 × 16 usually will cause issues.

To create your own tiled layer, you can construct a `TiledLayer` class, passing in the size of the grid, the source image, and the size of each tile frame. In the following example, you load the `pipes.png` image and use it to construct a `TiledLayer` with a grid size of 20 × 20. Each tile is 16 × 16 pixels.

```
try
{
    backgroundTilesImage = Image.createImage("/pipes.png");
}
catch (IOException ioe) { }


TiledLayer tileLayer = new TiledLayer(20, 20, backgroundTilesImage, 16, 16);
```

You can set which tiles appear in each cell using the `setCell` and `fillCells` methods. Each tile is referenced by the sequence number in which it appears in the tile image set. For example, the horizontal pipe is 1; the vertical is 2; and so on. So to create the lines in Figure 19.16, you can use

```
// draw horizontal lines
for (int y=0; y < 20; y+=5)
    tileLayer.fillCells(0, y, 19, 1, 1);    // set horizontal pipe

// draw vertical lines
for (int x=0; x < 20; x+=5)
    tileLayer.fillCells(x, 0, 1, 19, 2);    // set vertical pipe

// fill in the cross pieces
for (int y=0; y < 20; y+=5)
    for (int x=0; x < 20; x+=5)
        tileLayer.setCell(x, y, 3);                    // set the cross piece
```

Tip

One restriction with a `TiledLayer` is you can only associate it with one image. So what do you do if you have multiple sets of tiles or you want to do processing on images before they become tiles (such as changing colors)? To handle this, use the image tools to assemble a tile set image before you construct the `TiledLayer`, and then pass in the modified one. If you need to change a tile set after the `TiledLayer` has been created, use the `setStaticTileSet` method.

Keep in mind that the tile index starts at 1, not 0. Index 0 represents a blank (empty) tile, which is not drawn.

To make tile layers a little more interesting, you can add animation. The simplest way to do this is to periodically change the index of certain tiles. For example, you can add a set of animated tile frames at a certain position in the tile set—say, tile indices 10 to 20. When you populate the cells, start the animated tiles at index 10 and then periodically update any cell with an index between 10 and 20 by 1 (going back to position 10 if you pass 20). This will create an animated effect by changing the tile index to the next one in sequence.

This method is pretty simple. However, there's a major problem—it's about as quick as the International Convention on Slow Things' Really Slow Thing of the Year. In order to do the animation, you would have to check every cell in the grid to see whether its tile index falls into the animation range. For a tile map of 50 × 50, that's 2500 tests for every animation step. Not good.

A good general-purpose method to avoid this sort of thing is to use a secondary reference. To do this, you make a certain index range (say, anything negative or above a certain value) in the map have a special meaning. When the rendering goes to draw that tile index, it detects the special case and looks up a secondary reference to determine the actual tile type. Because there are very few entries in the secondary reference map (one for each animating tile type, rather than one for every instance of that tile), it's very fast to sweep through and update.

The TiledLayer supports this exact system for animation. A negative number indicates all animated tiles. You create a new special tile group using the createAnimatedTile method, which returns an index you can then use to reference the tile group. These start at –1 and go upward (or is that downward?), so the next one is –2, then –3, and so on.

Using the setCell and fillCells method, you can then populate the map with these negative values. To update the animation, you need to manage your own timer and then call the setAnimationTile method. When the MID sees a negative value, it will use whatever tile index has been set with the setAnimationTile method corresponding to that negative value. You can see this illustrated in Figure 19.17.

Tip

The animation tiles in TiledLayer are not limited to only doing animation. If you have any reason to use a secondary reference to group tiles together and then change them in one go, you can use the animation tile functionality. You could, for example, open all the doors on a level, turn off laser barriers, or even change scripted events. Feel free to use this functionality for more than just animation.

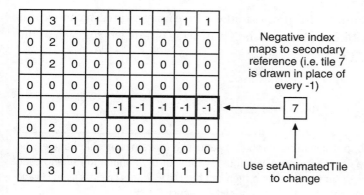

Figure 19.17 Using negative indices to reference animation tiles (which you can change separately to grid cells)

To render a `TiledLayer`, you can call its `paint` method from within your main game loop. For example:

```
tileLayer.paint(g);
```

That's all there is to tiled layers. Next you'll look at how sprites are handled. After you have that sorted out, you'll look at a complete `Game` API example using both tiles and sprites.

Sprites

The `Sprite` class provides basic functionality to create game sprites. In the `Game` API, these are implemented as distinct layers, so you can handle each sprite as a distinct layer when positioning and drawing. Sprites also support animation and image transforms.

To construct a sprite, you need to load up the image containing all the frames and then construct it using the frame size. For example, if your frames are 16 × 16 pixels, you can simply do:

```
Sprite mySprite = new Sprite(imageFrames, 16, 16);
```

Notice that you didn't specify how many frames there are in the image. The `Sprite` class assumes the entire image is for the sprite, so it simply divides the dimensions of the image by the tile size to figure out how many tiles there are.

To animate a sprite you need to set up your own timing process and then call `nextFrame` or `prevFrame` to progress through the frame sequence.

```
mySprite.nextFrame();
```

The animation sequence defaults to all the frames in the source image. You can change this sequence using the setFrameSequence method, passing in an array of integers for each of the frames. For example:

```
int[] seq = { 1, 2, 2, 2, 3, 3, 3, 4 };
mySprite.setFrameSequence(seq);
```

Tip

The Sprite class does not support animating through a sequence of frames. It only handles the order they are in. To animate a Sprite instance, you must write your own animation timing code (similar to that in the *Star Assault* Sprite class) and then call the MIDP 2 Sprite class's nextFrame to progress the animation to the next frame in the defined sequence.

The sequence doesn't have to reflect the number of frames you have in the original image, nor does it have to have any particular order. As you can see in the preceding sample code, you can even repeat frames.

Tip

Both Sprite and TiledLayer are derived from the abstract Layer base class. You can use the methods in this class to set a layer's position (move and setPosition), change visibility (isVisible and setVisible), and render (paint).

Sprites also support basic transformations. Using the setTransform method, you can mirror or rotate the image in the same way you did using the Graphics.drawRegion method. Transforms are done around a reference point in each image. The reference point is basically what the frame will spin around when it's transformed. If, for example, you set a reference point near the top of an image and flip it vertically, you'll find the reference point now toward the bottom of the image. If you want a demo of this, get a piece of paper with a drawing on it. Hold it flat on a table and put your finger on one point. Now turn the paper, and you'll see it rotate around the point where your finger is. That's the reference point for a transform.

The default reference point for a transform is 0, 0. Much of the time you want to rotate around the center of an image; you can do so using the following code:

```
// rotate around the center
mySprite.setRefPixelPosition(mySprite.getWidth()/2, mySprite.getHeight()/2);
mySprite.setTransform(Sprite.TRANS_ROT90);
```

Using different transforms for individual frames is not supported, so you'll need to manually change the transform each time you change the frame if you want to do this.

Sprites also provide some basic collision detection using the collidesWith methods. There are three methods available for checking against collisions with a TiledLayer, another Sprite, or an Image. You can specify whether you want rectangular or pixel-level collisions. A pixel-level collision will take into account any transparent pixels in the sprite when determining whether a collision has occurred. However, this is much slower than bounding-box collision, so I recommend you do that test before you test at the pixel level.

When checking against a TiledLayer, any cell with an index greater than zero will register a collision.

```
// test if the sprite collided with any tiles
if (mySprite.collidesWith( tiledLayer, false ))
{
    // If it did then do a more accurate test at the pixel level (slow).
    // Use true here to do a rectangular collision and false for a pixel
    // level collision.
    if (mySprite.collidesWith( tiledLayer, true ))
    {
        // explode!
    }
}
```

Note

When you transform a sprite using setTransform, the bounding box of the sprite (and thus the collision rectangle) is updated automatically.

Layer Manager

The LayerManager class handles the management and rendering of layers, including support for a single view port through which all layers are presented. Layers are drawn in what's termed the *z-order*. (You call it z because it reflects the third dimensional depth going down *into* the screen.) You can see this illustrated in Figure 19.18.

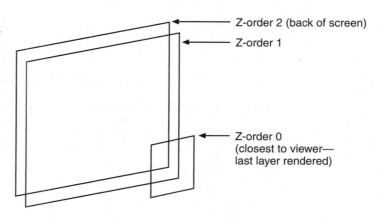

Z-order 2 (back of screen)

Z-order 1

Z-order 0
(closest to viewer—
last layer rendered)

Figure 19.18 The layer manager draws layers based on z-order, with 0 being the closest to the viewer (and the last one drawn).

To use the layer manager, you simply construct one and then add layers to it in the reverse order in which you want them to appear.

```
LayerManager layerManager = new LayerManager();

// add the sprite
mySprite = new Sprite(imageFrames, 16, 16);
layerManager.append(mySprite);

// add the background tile layer
TiledLayer tileLayer = new TiledLayer(20, 20, backgroundTilesImage, 16, 16);
layerManager.append(tileLayer);
```

Notice how I added the sprite first. This means it will appear on top of the background tile layer. You can also use the insert and remove methods to change the layer setup as well as change the order of layers.

To draw the layers, you use the LayerManager paint method. By default, this will render using the entire screen, starting at position 0, 0. If you want to change this you can use the viewPort method to set the x, y, width, and depth of the view.

Bringing It All Together

Now that you've seen all of the classes in the Game API, take a look at a more complete example. In this sample, you can see the use of a tiled background layer and a floating mine sprite that spins around. The position of the sprite is changed based on the state of the arrow keys.

```
import javax.microedition.lcdui.*;
import javax.microedition.lcdui.game.*;
import javax.microedition.midlet.MIDlet;
import javax.microedition.midlet.MIDletStateChangeException;
import java.io.IOException;
```

This is a simple MIDlet to show off a MIDP 2 custom canvas, this time using layers.

```
public class LayerExample extends MIDlet
{
    private AnotherGameCanvas myCanvas;

    public LayerExample()
    {
        myCanvas = new AnotherGameCanvas();
    }

    protected void startApp() throws MIDletStateChangeException
```

```java
    {
        Display.getDisplay(this).setCurrent(myCanvas);
        myCanvas.start();
    }

    protected void pauseApp()
    {
    }

    protected void destroyApp(boolean unconditional) throws MIDletStateChangeException
    {
    }
}

/**
 * A class which extends the new MIDP 2 Game Canvas.
 */

class AnotherGameCanvas extends GameCanvas implements Runnable
{
    private boolean running;
    private int x, y;
    private Image orbImage = null;
    private Image backgroundTilesImage = null;

    private Sprite orbSprite;
    private BackgroundLayer backgroundLayer = null;
    private LayerManager layerManager = null;

    public AnotherGameCanvas()
    {
        super(true);

        x = getWidth() / 2;
        y = getHeight() / 2;

        try
        {
            orbImage = Image.createImage("/orb.png");
            backgroundTilesImage = Image.createImage("/pipes.png");
        }

        catch (IOException ioe)
```

```
    {
        System.out.println("unable to load image");
    }
```

Note the construction of a layer manager, sprite, and background layer. The sprites and background layer are then added to the layer manager.

```
    layerManager = new LayerManager();

    // create the orb sprite and add it to the layer manager
    orbSprite = new Sprite(orbImage, 16, 16);
    layerManager.append(orbSprite);

    // add the background layer as well
    backgroundLayer = new BackgroundLayer(backgroundTilesImage);
    layerManager.append(backgroundLayer);
}

public void start()
{
    running = true;
    Thread t = new Thread(this);
    t.start();
}

public void run()
{
    Graphics g = getGraphics();

    while (running)
    {
        // handle the state of keys
        int keyStates = getKeyStates();

        if ((keyStates & LEFT_PRESSED) != 0)   x--;
        if ((keyStates & RIGHT_PRESSED) != 0)  x++;
        if ((keyStates & UP_PRESSED) != 0)     y--;
        if ((keyStates & DOWN_PRESSED) != 0)   y++;

        if (x < 0) x = getWidth();
        if (x > getWidth()) x = 0;
        if (y < 0) y = getHeight();
        if (y > getHeight()) y = 0;
```

Here's where the position of the sprite is updated and the animation takes place. This code advances one frame on each cycle.

```
// update the sprite position and animation frame
orbSprite.setPosition(x, y);
orbSprite.nextFrame();

// clear the display
g.setColor(0x000000);
g.fillRect(0, 0, getWidth(), getHeight());
```

This is the main difference with using a layer manager. Notice there's no code to draw the sprite or background layer. This is all taken care of by their inclusion in the layer manager. When you call paint on the layer manager, all the included layer will also be painted.

```
// draw the layers
layerManager.paint(g, 0, 0);

// flush the graphics buffer (GameCanvas will take care of painting)
flushGraphics();

// sleep a little
try
{
    Thread.sleep(5);
}
catch (InterruptedException ie)
{
}
        }
    }
}
```

An example of a background tiled layer that fills cells around the edges as well as cross pieces in the center.

```
class BackgroundLayer extends TiledLayer
{
    private static final int HORIZONTAL = 1;
    private static final int VERTICAL = 2;
    private static final int CROSS = 3;

    public BackgroundLayer(Image tiles)
    {
        super(20, 20, tiles, 16, 16);
```

```
        // draw horizontal lines
        for (int y=0; y < 20; y+=5)
            fillCells(0, y, 19, 1, HORIZONTAL);

        // draw vertical lines
        for (int x=0; x < 20; x+=5)
            fillCells(x, 0, 1, 19, VERTICAL);

        // fill in the cross pieces
        for (int y=0; y < 20; y+=5)
            for (int x=0; x < 20; x+=5)
                setCell(x, y, CROSS);
    }

}
```

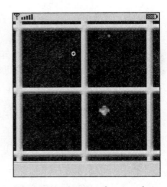

Figure 19.19 The results of a simple example of the Game API in action

You can see the final result in Figure 19.19.

Communications

MIDP 2 provides revised support for communications under the GCF (*Generic Connection Framework*). This includes support for server sockets, secure connections, and low-level connections using TCP or UDP. Read on to take a brief look at each of these.

Server Sockets

In MIDP 1 you could only create an outbound (client) connection. This meant communications had to originate from the MID and go outward to a server. In order to receive inbound connections, MIDP 2 added support for a server socket. You can instantiate one using the GCF's open method passed in with the type socket, but without the destination host portion specified. For example:

```
// create a server socket by excluding the host portion
ServerSocketConnection server = (ServerSocketConnection)
Connector.open("socket://:8888");
```

This will return a new ServerSocketConnection object linked to port 8888.

You then need to put the server socket into a wait mode so that it will accept incoming connections. This will *block* (sit there waiting until something happens) when you call it, so you would normally do this in another thread to your main application. To wait for a connection, use the acceptAndOpen method. When a new connection comes, this method will return a new SocketConnection object that represents the connection between your server and the new remote client.

```
// wait for a connection
SocketConnection client = (SocketConnection) server.acceptAndOpen();
```

You can then use the client SocketConnection just like you would any other type of connection. To read the data transmitted to you, use a DataInputStream; to send data, use a DataOutputStream.

```
// open streams linked to this client socket
DataInputStream dis = client.openDataInputStream();
DataOutputStream dos = client.openDataOutputStream();

// read client data
String result = is.readUTF();
// process request and send response
os.writeUTF(...);
```

When you're finished, remember to close any socket or stream instances you have.

```
// close streams and connections
is.close();
os.close();
client.close();
server.close();
```

Tip

Typically the best way to handle server socket processing is to create a central thread that handles incoming connections and another thread for each new client connection as it comes in. When the connection is then closed, you can remove the thread.

This method will let you communicate with clients, as well as accept other connections, without blocking on any one part of the process.

Secure Connections

MIDP 2 adds mandatory support for secure connections in the form of HTTPS (HTTP using the secure sockets layer). This provides for the encryption of information transmitted over the network.

You can get access to an HTTPS connection using the HttpsConnection object. For example:

```
HttpsConnection c = (HttpsConnection)Connector.open("https://www.secure.com/");
```

All communications over this socket will be encrypted automatically.

Low-Level Communications

MIDP 1 provided very minimal communications based on HTTP. With MIDP 2, you have access to lower-level IP socket types using either the TCP (streaming) or UDP (datagram) protocols.

Like with server sockets, the `Connector.open` method acts as a factory for new connections. To create a new stream socket use the form:

```
SocketConnection c = (SocketConnection)Connector.open("socket://host:port");
```

And for a datagram connection use:

UDPDatagramConnection c = (UDPDatagramConnection)Connector.open("datagram://host:port");Then you can use these connections as typical TCP and UDP sockets.

Push Registry

The MIDP 2 push registry is a cool new addition for game developers. Basically, it lets you wake up a MIDlet when a timer event goes off or when incoming traffic has arrived. This is really useful if you have a game that periodically updates data, or if you need to react when another party has done something (such as making a move in a chess game). All you need to do is register your MIDlet with the Application Management System (AMS), and it'll call you back when something happens.

To have the AMS listen for events, you need to register your MIDlet with it. You can do this statically, via JAD attributes, or dynamically, using the `javax.microedition.io.PushRegistry` API.

To register statically, add an attribute to the JAD file for your MIDlet in the following form:

```
MIDlet-Push-<n>: <ConnectionURL>, <MIDletClassName>, <AllowedSender>
```

Specify the connection as the URL of the incoming connection (basically the same as the connection URL you would use in your application). The MIDlet class name is the name of the class you want woken up when there's traffic, and the filter is a protocol-specific filter for the events to which you want to listen. Here's an example:

```
MIDlet-Push-1: socket://:79, com.your.SocketMidlet, 192.168.0.*
MIDlet-Push-2: sms://:500, com.your.SMSMidlet, *
```

You also register a connection from within your MIDlet using the API method `registerConnection`.

```
PushRegistry.registerConnection("socket://:79", this.getClass().getName(),
"192.168.0.*");
PushRegistry.registerConnection("sms://:500", this.getClass().getName(), "*");
```

Using the API, you also register for a wakeup call using the `registerAlarm` method. The AMS will trigger your MIDlet at the set time.

```
PushRegistry.registerAlarm(this.getClass().getName(), (new java.util.Date().getTime()) +
(60 * 10 * 1000));
```

Tip

> When you attempt to register an application with the push registry, the MID might ask permission from the user. If the user denies this option, your application will throw a `SecurityException`. Your MIDlet should expect this and deal with it appropriately.

If you later want to remove any of these registrations, you can use the `unregisterConnection` method. Static registrations are automatically removed when the MIDlet is uninstalled.

When a push registry event occurs, your application's `startApp` method is called. If you're wondering what method is called when your MIDlet is already running, the answer is none. The assumption is that if your MIDlet is running, you'll deal with any events in your own code. The push registry is only there for waking up MIDlets that are not already running.

To figure out why you were woken up, you can query the push registry's list of the connections ready for your application by using the `listConnections` method, which will return an array of strings using the connection URL format. Using this string, you can open a socket and read in the waiting data.

Conclusion

Because you now know that MIDP 2 is not really an upgrade, you have to ask the question of when it's right to develop for it. Right now devices supporting MIDP 2 tend to be toward the high end of the market, thus they represent a very small portion of the installed player base. Although this will change over time, at the moment the bulk of the market is still very much in MIDP 1 land. For this reason, I make MIDP 1 (usually with manufacturer extensions) my primary target for games and then port to MIDP 2 once completed (if it's worthwhile).

The main reason you'll want to develop for MIDP 2 is to take advantage of the new features that are not available (even with manufacturer extensions). Some of these features are downright cool, such as having your game wake up when network traffic arrives for it. Another reason is the lack of support for many of MIDP 2's features with manufacturer APIs, such as PNG transparency and sound. If your game relies on these features, then go for it.

Finally, due to MIDP 2 implementations covering things like layers and sprites—which manufacturers can choose to implement using native calls—you can expect games to run faster than MIDP 1 equivalents. Note that I said *expect*; you can just as easily encounter poor implementations (especially with tiled layers and image processing).

There's no doubt that MIDP 2 is significantly better than MIDP 1; keep your fingers crossed that it becomes the dominant platform sooner rather than later.

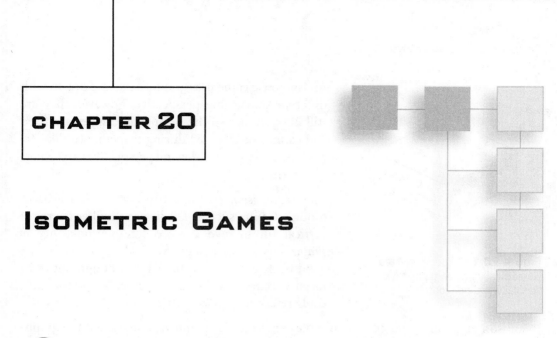

CHAPTER 20

ISOMETRIC GAMES

Sometime during the early '80s I remember peddling my bike (yeah, we rode bikes in those days) up to the local shop and rushing in, pocket jingling with change, only to find my favorite game machine had been replaced by something new. What I saw made me do a double take—instead of the typical 2D chomping semicircle or fruity sprites, I was confronted with the mind-blowing new perspective of a game called *Zaxxon*.

After I recovered from the initial shock (I was only a little kid, okay? This was a traumatic experience!), I found something oddly compelling about the 3D perspective of the game. The little ship was flying over and under walls! I left about six minutes later with empty pockets, vowing to return and master this new dimension.

Even though the ship was flying in three dimensions, this wasn't really a 3D environment; it was a clever use of 2D graphics drawn in a 3D perspective. The effect, commonly referred to as an *isometric perspective*, is still in use even today in games such as *Age of Empires*, *Diablo*, *Fallout*, and *StarCraft*.

Because isometric projection doesn't rely on heavy 3D hardware, it's perfectly suitable for J2ME game development as well. In this chapter, you'll see how to give your 2D games that 3D illusion.

What Is Isometric Projection?

The term *isometric projection* technically refers to viewing something with equal perspective on all angles. In Figure 20.1, you can see a block viewed isometrically. Notice how the box is tilted both vertically (forward) and horizontally (turned) to give it a 3D look. The box is isometrically projected.

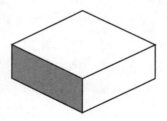

Figure 20.1 A cube projected isometrically has an equal tilt vertically and horizontally.

An isometric game uses graphics that are drawn with this type of viewing perspective; however, they are still 2D graphics so the perspective angles are fixed and cannot be changed during the game (unlike 3D engines, in which the viewing perspective can change in real time).

The term *isometric* has been a little overused, though. Games such as *Diablo* use a higher degree of vertical tilt to give a more side-on look. *Age of Empires* uses only a slight vertical tilt to give you a good birds-eye view of the field. Although not technically accurate, all of these games are still collectively referred to as isometric (or just "iso") games.

In an isometric game you can still use tiles like you did in *Star Assault*, except the graphics all have to be rendered at the correct perspective. You will, however, need to do quite a bit of work to figure out all those angles and drawing orders.

Vertical-Only Perspective

Another common style of iso game simplifies things by having a vertical tilt but no horizontal tilt. You can see what this looks like in the incredibly exciting Figure 20.2.

This type of projection provides a similar effect, but at the same time dramatically simplifies the rendering, math, and object management because you only need to deal with the single extra dimension.

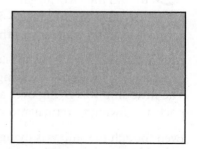

Figure 20.2 A cube projected with only a vertical tilt

Tip

Any projected perspective game that tilts horizontally always requires PNG transparency support to draw the overlapping tiles (since tiles must be the shape of a diamond, you'll always have to use transparency on the corners of the image). If you choose to make this type of game, keep in mind you're excluding most low-end MIDs (except Nokia). A vertical-only tilt perspective is possible without transparency; however, you'll be severely limited in your graphical options—the tree shown in Figure 20.3, for example, is not possible without transparent PNGs.

To demonstrate how all this works, you'll make a little demo with a tank driving around a forest. The cool thing is the tank will appear to drive behind the trees (and over the ground). You can see the final result in Figure 20.3.

To develop this demo you'll take the tile engine you developed for *Star Assault* and modify it to add perspective. The good news is, it's easier to do than you think.

The Graphics

The first thing you need to make an iso game is graphics that match the perspective you're portraying. Figure 20.4 shows the three images used for the demo.

Figure 20.3 An iso-perspective demo with a tank driving around a forest

The tank is very similar to sprites you have seen before. The only major difference is that it appears at a vertical tilt, like the tree. The freshly cut grass doesn't have any height to it so it's just rendered flat.

You might notice I'm using the PNG alpha channel for the shadows. The sprites use a highly transparent black, which creates the cool effect of casting a shadow that blends with the terrain over which the object is drawn. The tree's shadow, for example, is built

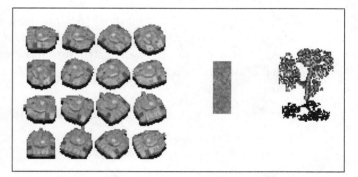

Figure 20.4 A tank, grass, and tree tiles rendered with an iso perspective.

into the image already and will darken the grass over which it's placed. (I guess it's just me, but I really do have a thing for alpha blending.) Try to resist the temptation to overuse alpha blending effects though; it takes extra time to render every one of those alpha pixels. If you don't want to use the alpha channel for shadows, you can simply use black pixels. Either way, you'll find that shadows really help to portray the feeling of depth in your graphics.

Tip

You can see a complete working example of an isometric engine in the Chapter 20 source code directory on the CD.

To get these graphics into the game you can use the ImageSet and Sprite classes developed for *Star Assault* (in Chapter 9, "The Graphics"). For example, to load the tank with its 16 states you need code very similar to how the original Ship class worked:

```
Image tankImage = ImageSet.loadClippedImage("/tank.png", 0, 0);
tankImageSet = new ImageSet(16);
Image[] tankImages = ImageSet.extractFrames(tankImage, 0, 0, 4, 4, 32, 32);

for (int i=0; i < 16; i++)
{
    Image[] s = { tankImages[i] };
    tankImageSet.addState(s, 0);
}
```

The Basic World

You might have noticed a bit more to the demo game than just an altered perspective. I've also added multiple layers so the tree can appear on top of the ground. To do this, you need to expand the basic world structure to handle these multiple layers. For this demo you'll only need two layers (the ground and the trees), but feel free to expand on this if you need more.

The first step is to expand the byte array you use to represent the tile. For example:

```
private int tilesDeep = 2;
private int tilesWide = 50;
private int tilesHigh = 50;
private byte[][][] tileMap;
```

You'll also need to add some tile types for this game:

```
public static final byte NO_TILE = 0;
public static final byte GRASS1_TILE = 1;
public static final byte GRASS2_TILE = 2;
public static final byte GRASS3_TILE = 3;
public static final byte TREE_TILE = 4;
```

To initialize these distinct layers you need to reference the depth as well. For example, to set a ground tile to be a certain type of grass, you would use the following line:

```
tileMap[0][8][8] = GRASS1_TILE;
```

To set a tree you need to use the higher layer. For example:

```
tileMap[1][8][8] = TREE_TILE;
```

Both of these tiles will now coexist happily on the same location.

Drawing with Perspective

Next you need to redo the rendering process so both layers are displayed. By itself this is pretty easy—simply render one layer and then the other. For example:

```
for (int td=0; td < tilesDeep; td++)       // go through all the layers
{
    for (int ty=startY; ty < th; ty++)
    {
        for (int tx=startX; tx < tw; tx++)
        {
            t = tileMap[td][ty][tx];
            if (td == 0 && t == NO_TILE) continue;

            xpos = (tx * TILE_WIDTH)- viewX;
            ypos = (ty * TILE_HEIGHT) - viewY;

            if (t > 0)
                tiles.draw(g, t-1, 0, xpos, ypos);
        }
    }
}
```

Keep in mind that to make it work properly in the iso perspective, you need to render the tiles so that foreground objects obscure background ones. You can see this illustrated in Figure 20.5.

The good news is, this is already how you're doing things: You progress upward through the y-axis, thus things are drawn effectively "toward" the screen. This is known as the *z-order* of drawing because it reflects the distance an object is from the viewer.

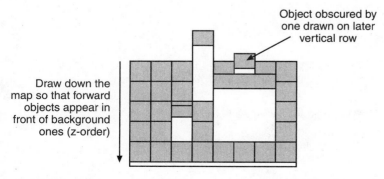

Figure 20.5 You need to render objects in order, toward the player, so they obscure those in the back (behind the player's view).

There's something else you need to handle, though. The tree tile is quite special because it has height that extends outside of its tile dimensions. Notice how the graphic is 48 × 48 pixels, even though the tiles in your engine are only 16 × 16 pixels. That's because the tree has perspective height; you need to accommodate this when you are drawing the tree. You can see this demonstrated in Figure 20.6.

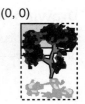

Image drawn at tile position (tree appears in the wrong place)

Notice that in the first picture the top of the tree image is aligned to the tile position. This is obviously incorrect and will prove very confusing if you try to drive around on this map—none of the trees will appear to be in the right spots.

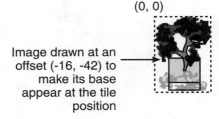

Image drawn at an offset (-16, -42) to make its base appear at the tile position

The trick to solving this is to offset the rendering of the tile image by an amount that moves the base of the object into the correct position. As you can see in the second image, once this is done the tree appears correctly relative to the tile.

Figure 20.6 You might need to offset the position of some tiles so the base of the object appears in the tile position (rather than on top of the object).

The easiest way to do this in the code is to detect the tile type as it's being rendered and then offset it. For example:

```
for (int td=0; td < tilesDeep; td++)       // go through all the layers
{
    for (int ty=startY; ty < th; ty++)
    {
        for (int tx=startX; tx < tw; tx++)
        {
            ...

            if (t > 0)
            {
                if (t == TREE_TILE)
                    tiles.draw(g, t-1, 0, xpos-16, ypos-42);
                else
                    tiles.draw(g, t-1, 0, xpos, ypos);
            }
        }
    }
}
```

This method can get a little cumbersome, though, so you might want to place the offsets for each tile type in a separate resource (text) file and load them when you load the images. This is also more convenient for artists because they can switch graphics without having to change the source and rebuild the game.

That's it for rendering the static tiles. Next you'll look at how to deal with actors (objects that move).

Handling Actors

Drawing the actors in your world presents a little more of a problem. If you recall, in *Star Assault* you drew all the tiles and then you drew the actors (ships, mines, and bullets) afterward as a separate process. Unfortunately, you can't do that with an iso perspective. What if the tank is driving behind a tree? As you can see in Figure 20.7, if you draw the tank after the tree it will look completely wrong—or you'll think tanks grow on trees.

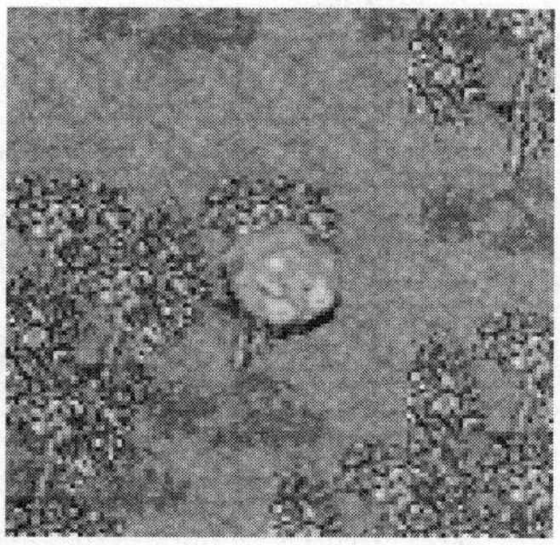

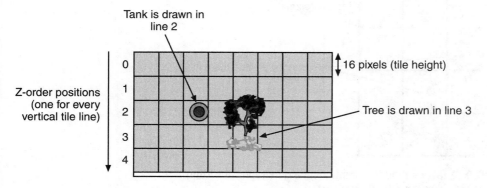

Figure 20.7 If you draw the actors after tiles (as you did in *Star Assault*), they will appear in front of tiles that are closer to the player (according to the new perspective).

Instead of drawing the actors in a separate operation after all the tiles, you need to draw them in the same pass. This is the same principal you saw when drawing the tiles; you simply need to draw the actors at the same time.

The key to understanding how all this works is the term "z-order". Because you're simulating a perspective in which the player looks straight down the field (with no side-on component), you only need to make sure objects are drawn at the correct depth level relative to that perspective (the z-order).

In Figure 20.8, you can see a screen divided into the typical 16×16-pixel tile grid. Each of the vertical rows is numbered progressively toward the screen according to its z-order

Tank is drawn in line 2

Z-order positions (one for every vertical tile line)

0
1
2
3
4

16 pixels (tile height)

Tree is drawn in line 3

Figure 20.8 You must draw actors at the correct vertical row (z-order) so they appear as though they are behind tiles.

position. As you can see, the tree is in row 3, while the tank is in row 2. If you draw things according to this order, the tank will appear correctly behind the tree.

To find out an actor's z-order, simply divide its y-position by the tile height. For example:

```
int currentZorder = playerTank.getY() / TILE_HEIGHT;
```

All sounds pretty easy so far, right? When you finish drawing a row of tiles you can simply find all the actors with a z-order matching the current row and draw them. The problem, however, is how you go about determining which actors are in that particular row. If you were to check every actor's position for every row you draw, it would take way too much time on a map with many actors. What you really need is a fast mechanism for tracking the z-order of all your actors. Enter sectors.

Using Sectoring

To speed up locating objects within a given space you can use a technique known as *sectoring*. This involves dividing the world into distinct subsections, and then storing references to all the actors currently within each sector. As actors move around, they are switched from one sector container to another.

Because sectors relate to a particular area on the map, what you're doing is effectively sorting objects into easily referenced geographical groups (see Figure 20.9).

Sectoring makes things faster because you can deal with all the objects in a world in small sections, rather than all in one shot. For example, if you want to determine which objects should be drawn in a current vertical row, you only need to check the sectors that are relative to the screen; you don't need to check any sectors outside of that range.

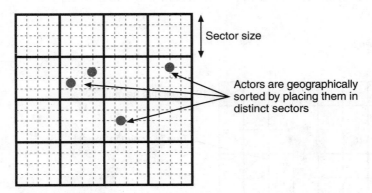

Sector size

Actors are geographically sorted by placing them in distinct sectors

Figure 20.9 A fast method for maintaining a geographical sorting of objects is to assign them to distinct sectors.

How large or small you make a sector comes down to the type of game you're making and how actors move around in it. If you make sectors too small, for example, you'll spend too much time moving actors between them. If they're too large, the processing you do on each sector will take too long (due to the high number of actors within each one). It's a bit of a balancing act that's dependent on your game type.

For your little tank demo, the most convenient system is to make a sector equal to the tile height so you can use it to reflect which actor is in each tile row. So one sector contains any object in one complete tile row extending all the way across the world. After you draw each tile row (z-order), you then draw all the actors in that sector (row).

Okay, take a look at a real example of this sectoring thing. The main thing you need is a container for the actor references in each sector. This needs to be very fast in order to move entries in and out, and it cannot use much storage. Most important, you don't want to bother storing much information for areas of the map that don't contain any actors. The best storage mechanism for this is (you guessed it) a simple linked list.

For the tank demo you'll make a sector for every vertical line, so you need an array pointing to the first actor object in each sector in the World class. For example:

```
Actor[] actorZMap = new Actor[tilesHigh];
```

To store objects in a doubly-linked list you need to maintain a link to both the next object and the previous one. The easiest (and most efficient) way to do this is to simply add two references to the Actor class, as well as methods to manage them.

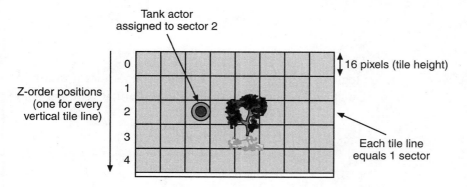

Figure 20.10 For your little tank game, you can make a sector equal to one tile row.

```
private Actor nextInZMap;          // used by zmap to ref next actor
private Actor prevInZMap;          // used by zmap to ref prev actor

public void setNextInZMap(Actor a) { nextInZMap = a; }
public Actor getNextInZMap() { return nextInZMap; }
public void setPrevInZMap(Actor a) { prevInZMap = a; }
public Actor getPrevInZMap() { return prevInZMap; }
```

Next you need to add (or move) actors to the appropriate linked list whenever they move. To catch these events you'll have the Actor class call a method in the World class whenever a position changes.

```
public void cycle(long deltaMS)
{

    ...

    if (ticks > 0)
    {
        // movement code...

        // tell the world we moved
        world.notifyActorMoved(this, lastX, lastY, x, y);
    }
}
```

In the World class you put the logic to manage the linked list in each z-order position in the notifyActorMoved method. Don't let the amount of code freak you out; it's simpler than it looks.

```
public void notifyActorMoved(Actor a, int oldX, int oldY, int x, int y)
{
    // figure out the z-order positions (Y tile position)
    int oldYTilePos = getTileY(oldY);
    int yTilePos = getTileY(y);

    // if they have indeed moved to another sector (vertical row) then
    // we need to move them from one linked list to another
    if (oldYTilePos != yTilePos)
```

```
{
    // go through all the actors in this sector's list until you find
    // this one - try the very fast case first (one item in list)
    if (actorZMap[oldYTilePos] == a && a.getNextInZMap() == null)
        actorZMap[oldYTilePos]=null;
    else
    {
        if (actorZMap[oldYTilePos] != null)
        {
            // we assume in this case that there must be at least two entries
            // in this linked list (since the above test failed)
            Actor actorToRemove = actorZMap[oldYTilePos];
            while (actorToRemove != a && actorToRemove != null)
                actorToRemove = actorToRemove.getNextInZMap();

            // if there was an entry matching the actor
            if (actorToRemove != null)
            {
                // set my next's prev to my prev (thus replacing me)
                if (actorToRemove.getNextInZMap() != null)
                    actorToRemove.getNextInZMap().setPrevInZMap(actorToRemove.
                    getPrevInZMap());
                // set my prev's next to my next
                if (actorToRemove.getPrevInZMap() != null)
                    actorToRemove.getPrevInZMap().setNextInZMap(actorToRemove.
                    getNextInZMap());

                // replace the head of the list if it was removed
                if (actorZMap[oldYTilePos] == actorToRemove)
                    actorZMap[oldYTilePos] = actorToRemove.getNextInZMap();

                // **NOTE: we don't bother updating a's next and prev because it will
                // be fixed up when we add it into another list (this is a move
                // function, not a remove)
            }
        }
    }

    // add the actor into the new spot. do the empty list case first
    // (the most common case).
    if (actorZMap[yTilePos] == null)
    {
```

```
            a.setNextInZMap(null);
            a.setPrevInZMap(null);
            actorZMap[yTilePos] = a;
        } else
        {
            // one or more, find the tail of the list and append this ref
            Actor tail = actorZMap[yTilePos];
            while (tail.getNextInZMap() != null)
                tail = tail.getNextInZMap();
            tail.setNextInZMap(a);

            a.setPrevInZMap(tail);
            a.setNextInZMap(null);
        }
    }
}


public final int getTileY(int y) { return y / TILE_HEIGHT; }
```

The result of this code is a maintained linked list for each sector. You can move actors around, and this code will now take care of making sure each of the sectors contains a list of only the actors in that specific area.

Now that you have all the actors sorted into the sectors, you can revisit the World class rendering code. Following is the revised code; this time you can see that you draw the first layer (the grass) and then, as you draw the upper layer (the trees), you also draw any actors that are in that tile row (sector).

```
public final void render(Graphics g)
{
    try
    {
        int startX = (viewX / TILE_WIDTH) - 5;
        int startY = (viewY / TILE_HEIGHT) - 5;
        int tw = ((Math.abs(viewX) + viewWidth) / TILE_WIDTH) + 5;
        int th = ((Math.abs(viewY) + viewHeight) / TILE_HEIGHT) + 5;

        if (tw > tilesWide) tw = tilesWide;
        if (th > tilesHigh) th = tilesHigh;

        int t=0;
        int xpos=0;
        int ypos=0;
```

```
for (int td=0; td < tilesDeep; td++)
{
    for (int ty=startY; ty < th; ty++)
    {
        for (int tx=startX; tx < tw; tx++)
        {
            if (ty >= 0 && tx >= 0)
            {
                t = tileMap[td][ty][tx];

                // quick abort if it's nothing and we're only doing the
                // ground layer (no actors to worry about)
                if (td == 0 && t == NO_TILE) continue;

                xpos = (tx * TILE_WIDTH)- viewX;
                ypos = (ty * TILE_HEIGHT) - viewY;

                if (t > 0)
                {
                    if (t == TREE_TILE)
                        tiles.draw(g, t-1, 0, xpos-16, ypos-42);
                    else
                        tiles.draw(g, t-1, 0, xpos, ypos);
                }

                // if this is the second pass then we draw the actors
                // at this z-order
                if (td==1)
                {
                    Actor a = actorZMap[ty];
                    while (a != null)
                    {
                        a.render(g, viewX, viewY);
                        a = a.getNextInZMap();
                    }
                }
            }
        }
    }
}

}
```

```
catch (Exception e)
{
    System.out.println("App exception: " + e);
    e.printStackTrace();
}
}
```

The end result of this is a lightning-fast sectoring system that does a great job rendering objects properly for your perspective view.

Collision Detection

Now that you've seen how to handle the drawing of objects with some perspective, take a look at how all this affects collision detection.

There are two main collision areas you need to cover—actors hitting tiles and actors hitting other actors. You'll deal with these separately in a moment.

Basic Tile Collisions

The good news is that not much changes, and what does only gets better. The basic tile collision system you use in *Star Assault* doesn't really change in an isometric view. The main thing is you no longer want to check for collisions at depth 0 (the ground layer). Other than that, things look pretty much the same. For example, here's the World class basic tile collision code for the tank demo.

```
public final boolean checkCollision(Actor hitter, int x, int y, int w, int h)
{
    // test if this actor object has hit a tile on layer 1 (we ignore layer 0)
    // we look at all the tiles under the actor (we do a <= comparison so we
    // include the bounding edge of the actor's rectangle)
    for (int iy=y; iy <= y+h; iy += TILE_HEIGHT)
    {
        for (int ix=x; ix <= x+w; ix += TILE_WIDTH)
        {
            if (getTile(1, ix, iy) > 0)
            {
                hitter.onCollision(null);
                return true;
            }
        }
    }
}
```

This will handle the basic detection of collisions between the actors (tanks) and any tiles in depth level 1 (trees). Next take a look at collisions between actors and other actors.

Actor Collisions Using Sectors

The good news is that sectoring can really enhance the performance of collision detection as well. In *Star Assault* you detected collisions among actors simply by checking against all the other actors in the world. Now that you have sectors you can localize your code to check only for collisions with nearby actors, which requires far less work in a map with many actors.

The simplest check you can make is to look up all the actors in the same sector and check whether they are in a collision state. For example here's revised code for the World class's collision system:

```
int sector = getTileY(hitter.getY());
Actor a = actorZMap[sector];
while (a != null)
{
    // remember to check we're not hitting ourselves!
    if (a.isCollidingWith(hitter) && a != hitter)
        // HIT!!!
    a = a.getNextInZMap();
}
```

There's a subtle bug in this code, though; an actor is contained within a sector based on its y-position. The problem is this is where the top of the actor is, so what about the bottom? As you can see in Figure 20.11, an actor can easily extend over its sector boundary—in fact, all actors with a height over one pixel will do this as they move downward—and thus collide with another actor that is not within the same sector.

To solve this you need to extend the checking to cover not only the actor's current sector, but also ones above and below it. The number of sectors you check comes down to the size of the biggest actor in your game. You need to check enough sectors to cover all cases.

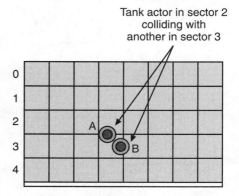

Figure 20.11 Actors can effectively exist in multiple sectors if they're large enough to overlap the sector boundary. In this case, an actor from one sector is colliding with one from a different sector.

For the tank demo you know the largest object is 32 pixels high (the tank). Therefore, the maximum number of (16-pixel-high) sectors that one object can exist in at any point in time is two. Therefore, if you check the sector the actor is in, plus the ones directly above and below, you'll be covering all possible collision cases.

Here's the revised collision code; I've factored out the collision logic to a separate method now.

```
public final boolean checkCollision(Actor hitter, int x, int y, int w, int h)
{
    // tile collision tests...

    // now test if this actor hit another actor in this or an adjacent
    // sector
    int sector = getTileY(y);
    Actor weHit = checkSectorCollision(hitter, sector, x, y, w, h);
    if (sector + 1 < actorZMap.length && weHit == null)
        weHit = checkSectorCollision(hitter, sector+1, x, y, w, h);
    if (sector - 1 >= 0 && weHit == null)
        weHit = checkSectorCollision(hitter, sector-1, x, y, w, h);

    if (weHit != null)
    {
        hitter.onCollision(weHit);
        return true;
    }

    return false;
}

private Actor checkSectorCollision(Actor hitter, int sector, int x, int y, int w, int
h)
{
    // check to see if we hit another actor in this sector (we ignore ourselves)
    Actor a = actorZMap[sector];
    while (a != null)
    {
        if (a.isCollidingWith(x, y, w, h) && a != hitter)
            return a;
        a = a.getNextInZMap();
    }
    return null;
}
```

Adding Windows

Another common technique used in isometric games is to have different collision states relative to the perceived height of an object. It might seem obvious, but a good example is the grass. Anything existing at depth 0 is not checked for collisions. You can extend this a bit further and have certain tile types that do not cause collisions with projectiles, but do collide with other actors. For your tank game, for example, you could have tiles such as pits, barbed wire, rivers, or bushes. In all these cases you'll obstruct the tank from moving but let weapons fire go through.

I find the easiest way to do this is to assign a certain range of tiles typed as windows. In the collision code you can compare the type of actor (whether it is a bullet or a projectile) with the tile range. If a projectile-type actor collides with a window range tile, you ignore it. For example, I define tiles such as:

```
public static final byte START_WINDOW_TILE = 12;
public static final byte BARBED_WIRE_TILE = 12;
public static final byte BUSH_TILE = 13;
public static final byte PIT_TILE = 14;
public static final byte RIVER_TILE = 15;
public static final byte END_WINDOW_TILE = 15;
```

Then the collision code needs to be adapted to check for the extra case. For example:

```
public final boolean checkCollision(Actor hitter, int x, int y, int w, int h)
{
    for (int iy=y; iy <= y+h; iy += TILE_HEIGHT)
    {
        for (int ix=x; ix <= x+w; ix += TILE_WIDTH)
        {
            // if we hit a tile in the above-ground layer
            byte t = getTile(1, ix, iy);
            if (t > 0)
            {
                // check and ignore if it's a projectile hitting a window
                // tile (isBullet is something borrowed from StarAssault)
                if (!hitter.isBullet() || t < START_WINDOW_TILE ||
                    t > END_WINDOW_TILE)
                {
                    hitter.onCollision(null);
                    return true;
                }
            }
        }
    }
}
```

Tip

Special tile types don't have to stop at windows. When you detect a collision between an actor and a special tile you can also do things such as changing the actor's physics (to make the tank slip in mud) or even the actor graphics (mud sprays).

Conclusion

Come on, tell me you don't think that little tank weaving in and out of trees is dead sexy. Hopefully you've found creating such a cool effect easy. I know you've cheated a little by creating a not-quite-really-an-iso engine, but for J2ME games right now, a vertical tilt engine is the best way to get the eye-candy value of a 3D perspective without the nightmare of managing too complex a system.

The isometric work you've done so far covers most games, but you can see that many things might need tweaking based on the exact type of game you are making. Fast-moving actors in big worlds, for example, might require modification to the sectoring system. Different projection angles might require more support for tile placement. Hopefully what you've seen in this chapter will give you enough background to adapt to most solutions. If not . . . well hey, you have to do some work sometime, you know.

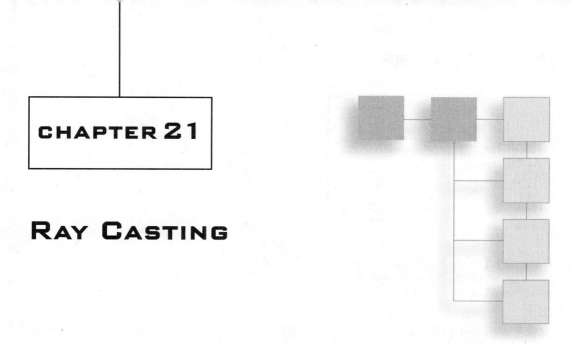

CHAPTER 21

RAY CASTING

I t might sound a little ambitious, but in this chapter you'll look at how to build a 3D engine for your average MID. It won't be anything like the modern PC 3D games, but it will certainly create a great 3D world effect you can use in many different game types.

To do this you'll use a simple technique known as *ray casting*, which thankfully doesn't require particularly complex algorithms or math. In fact, I think you'll be pretty surprised by how easy 3D can be.

What Is Ray Casting?

Thousands of years ago the ancient Greeks speculated on the mechanism of the wonder that is the human eye. One theory as to how it worked was that the eye itself fired rays outward, and the brain picked up the results once the rays bounced back. This is somewhat on the right track; they just got things a little backward. You perceive objects because light rays (well, photons actually) bounce off objects into your eyes.

The Greeks might not have discovered how the eye works, but they did provide us with the inspiration for a common method of generating a 3D visual scene, known as *ray tracing*. This technique involves starting at the observer's point of view and firing rays into a 3D world (see Figure 21.1). Based on whether the ray hit something and how far it went to do that, you draw a corresponding pixel. If you do this for every pixel on the screen, you'll generate a complete 3D view.

Tracing each of these rays is a relatively time-consuming process, though. Starting at the origin point, you move one unit forward and check whether you hit anything. If you did, you register the hit. (Effectively, you're bouncing the ray back to the viewer.) You can then

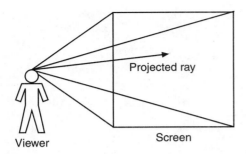

Figure 21.1 A ray-traced image is generated
by tracing rays into a 3D world and seeing
what they hit.

draw a different pixel based on the type of hit, such as the color of the object off which
the ray bounced. If you didn't hit anything, you move forward a little farther and check
again. You stop when you've reached the edge of your simulated vision (the horizon).

If you think that might take a while, consider the fact that you have to do this for every
pixel on the screen. For an MID with a 128 × 128-pixel screen, that's 16,384 times per
frame. Tracing that many rays even on a reasonably well endowed MID would give you a
frame rate of something like –2,000. In other words, you can forget it. The technique is
still a good one; you just need to tweak things a little.

The basic method of ray tracing works quite well for generating a presentable 3D image.
The reason it's slow is the sheer number of rays being traced to create each frame. Therefore, it follows that the best way to speed up the process is to reduce this number as much
as possible. If you think back to how you developed the tile engine, you might have
noticed how you reduced complexity by reducing the granularity of the world with which
you were dealing. Collision detection was a good example of this. Because you knew that
tiles only existed at certain points in the world (every 16 pixels), you only needed to check
those positions. The end result was that the number of checks you needed to perform was
reduced by 16 times.

Have you caught on to what you're going to do yet? It's basically pretty simply. To increase
the speed of ray tracing, you'll reduce the number of rays being traced. To do that, you'll
use a simplified form of ray tracing known as *ray casting*.

Essentially, ray casting is exactly the same as ray tracing except that you *cast* rays into the
world instead of tracing them. You can think of this as something like using a fishing rod
to cast to different points in the world. Instead of slowly tracing a line, you just dip in at
the points that count. In terms of your tile engine, this means you can jump along in 16-
pixel increments instead of one-pixel increments. In Figure 21.2 you can see an example

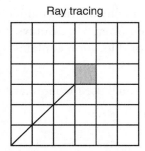 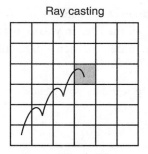

Figure 21.2 Ray casting involves tracing rays only at points where an object can exist.

of a ray being traced into a map to determine if and when it will collide with a tile. In the first case, ray tracing is used to check in one world-unit increments, whereas in the second case you jump in larger (tile-sized) increments. The resulting difference in speed is obvious: To strike the wall (the black tile) in this map with tracing could require hundreds of checks, whereas ray casting would require only three tests.

Like with a 2D tile engine, the use of ray casting limits you to placing objects in the world at set cell boundaries (tiles). It is possible to add objects (actors) that can move around freely; however, as with a tile engine, these are handled as a separate layer using fixed-perspective sprites (rather than 3D-rendered ones). Don't worry; you'll get to all that stuff after you finish your basic rendering engine.

Using ray casting (and a few other tricks you'll look at along the way), it's possible to create a very high-performance, cool 3D world effect—even with the limited power of an average MID. Figure 21.3 shows the end product.

All right, enough theory; you want to know exactly how to make this thing work. Ready to take a ride?

The Fundamentals

To build your ray-casting engine, you need to cover a few basic things first. Once you have all this in place you'll find the actual engine code to be much simpler.

The Map

Ray casting involves projecting rays into a representation of your world and determining if and where something was hit. The question

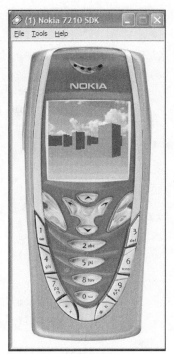

Figure 21.3 The J2ME ray-casting engine developed in this chapter

is, what exactly are you hitting? The answer is basically the same as in any 2D tile engine game: You need an array representing all the tiles in your world. Then when you cast rays, you'll check against this array to determine whether a particular world location contains a wall.

The code to create the map array is the same as you've seen before. You'll use the familiar World class to encapsulate all this.

N o t e

For a complete example of a raycasting engine, refer to the Chapter 21 source code directory on the CD.

```
public class World
{
    public static final int TILE_WIDTH=32;
    public static final int TILE_HEIGHT=32;

    private int tilesWide = 20;
    private int tilesHigh = 20;
    private byte[][] tileMap;

    ...
```

To give you somewhere to play around, you can simply add border walls and a grid of pillars. I've added this into the World class constructor.

```
// set up the map
tileMap = new byte[20][20];

// side walls
for (int tx=0; tx < 20; tx++)
{
    tileMap[0][tx] = 1;
    tileMap[19][tx] = 1;
}

// top and bottom walls
for (int ty=0; ty < 20; ty++)
{
    tileMap[ty][0] = 1;
    tileMap[ty][19] = 1;
}
```

```
// pillars every four tiles
for (int ty=0; ty < 20; ty+=4)
    for (int tx=0; tx < 20; tx+=4)
        tileMap[ty][tx] = 1;
```

Figure 21.4 shows the resulting tile map.

Field-of-View

Your ray-casting engine will present a view as though the player was looking into the world directly through the screen (known as a *first-person perspective*). Two-dimensional games in which you see the player's object (such as a ship) use a third-person perspective. Figure 21.5 illustrates the first-person perspective (ignore the man in the front, that's just to illustrate where the view is coming from).

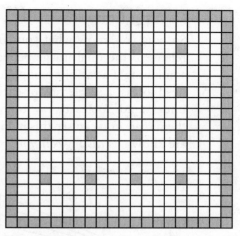

Figure 21.4 A grid of tiles used to represent the world

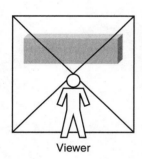

Viewer

Figure 21.5 Ray casting presents an image of the world in a first-person perspective.

The next thing you need to determine is exactly which rays to project and at what angles. If you picture yourself standing in the world you described earlier (the grid) and looking out across the tile map, you'll only be able to see a limited area based on the direction you're facing (unless you have eyes in the back of your head). The range of vision is known as your *field-of-view* (FOV). Your eyes have a natural FOV of around 100 degrees; however, due to the limits of the screen, an angle of about 60 degrees works best. Feel free to play around with different values to see the effects. (Setting the FOV to 360 is quite an experience.)

As you can see in Figure 21.6, if you project from the viewer's current point out into the tile map, you can determine what is within view based on the FOV.

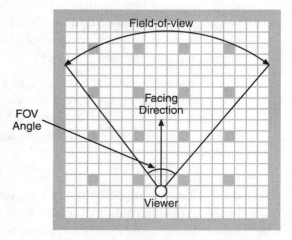

Figure 21.6 The field-of-view (FOV) represents the range of your virtual player's vision.

Casting Columns

So now you know what your field-of-view is, and you're probably wondering how this relates to the final image being displayed. For your simplified engine, you'll only draw something if a ray hits a populated tile. Because you're dealing with a 2D world, you only need to cast a single ray for each vertical screen column. This is an important concept to understand: You cast a ray for every vertical pixel line across the screen, not every pixel on the screen. You can see this in Figure 21.7; for every pixel wide you would cast a ray. These are known as *casting columns*.

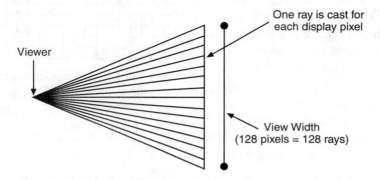

Figure 21.7 For each pixel across the screen you cast a corresponding ray into your world.

As each of these rays is cast, you check to see whether it hits anything. If it does, you can draw a vertical line representing the wall you struck. The position and size of the wall is based on distance the ray traveled. You can see the results in Figure 21.8. (I've added gaps to separate the rays visually.)

You've just seen essentially the core of a ray-casting engine. For every column, cast a ray, determine whether you hit something, and then draw a vertical bar based on the distance you went. Think about this for a second; it's the key to understanding how all this works.

Figure 21.8 You cast a ray for each vertical column. If a wall is struck, you draw a line based on the distance the ray went.

One other thing you need to do is determine the number of degrees per casting column. On your reference MID you would have 128 casting columns (one for each pixel across), so you can simply take the angle and divide it by the number of columns, right? Well there's a slight catch. Because you have a set number of pixels across, you need to round things out to make sure you go completely across the screen. For example:

```
columnsPerDegree = viewWidth / fov;   // 128 / 60 = 2.13 (rounded down to 2)
fovColumns = viewWidth / columnsPerDegree;   // 128 / 2 = 64 columns
halfFovColumns = fovColumns / 2;
```

The final variable, fovColumns, is the total number of casting columns you'll use. Notice you'll actually be drawing 64 degrees of view, rather than 60. halfFovColumns is something you'll need often later, so you pre-calculate it here to save time.

Focal Distance

Next you need to calculate the *focal distance* (also known as the *focal length*), which determines the distance between the viewer and the point of focus. For your purposes this is a somewhat arbitrary figure used to scale the size of objects.

To calculate the focal distance you use the FOV and the width of the final view image. Note that you're not using the height because you're dealing only with a 2D world map. (I'll get to more on this in a little while.)

Using the basic Nokia Series 40 MID, you would have a screen width of 128 pixels. You've already decided to use an FOV of 60 degrees. Now, based on these two values, figure out the distance between the projection plane and the viewer.

If you look carefully at Figure 21.9, you can see it's actually two right triangles. If you split it in half you can use basic trig to calculate your value. Because you only know the opposite side, which is the view width divided by 2 (64), and the angle, you need to use TAN to determine the adjacent (the distance). Let me explain this a little more—I just know you're dying to do some trig.

In Figure 21.10 you can see the triangle from Figure 21.9 separated out. I've also added trig labels to make this clearer.

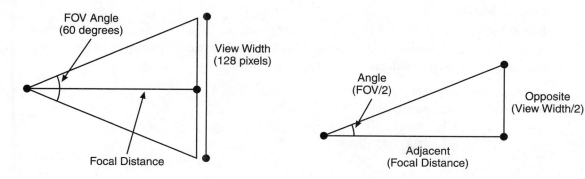

Figure 21.9 You determine the focal distance (used for scaling) using the viewing width and FOV.

Figure 21.10 The focal distance triangle. (Note that the width and FOV must be divided by 2.)

If you recall math class, you know that:

```
TAN(angle) = opposite / adjacent
```

Therefore, it follows that:

```
adjacent = opposite / TAN(angle)
```

It's pretty easy from this point; you simply fill in the values. The resulting code to determine your focal distance is

```
int focalDistance = (viewWidth/2) / TAN(FOV /2);
```

Just for your interest, the focal distance for your example MID, using an FOV of 64 degrees and a view width of 128 pixels, would be 64 / TAN(32), or around 110.

Here's the actual code for the World class you'll use; basically, it's the same except for the use of MathFP to handle the floating-point values.

```
int distFP = MathFP.div( MathFP.toFP(viewWidth/2),
                         MathFP.tan(Actor.getRadiansFPFromAngle(32)) );
focalDistance = MathFP.toInt(distFP);
```

In case you're wondering, the getRadiansFPFromAngle is a static Actor class method to convert degrees to radians.

```
public static final int FP_PI2 = MathFP.mul(MathFP.PI, MathFP.toFP(2));
public static final int FP_DEGREES_PER_RAD = MathFP.div(MathFP.toFP(360), FP_PI2);
public final static int getRadiansFPFromAngle(int angle)
{
    return MathFP.div(MathFP.toFP(angle), FP_DEGREES_PER_RAD);
}
```

Faster Math

Before you get into the actual engine, you need to add some general code to speed up these trigonometry calculations. Here's the World class code to create an array of lookup values corresponding to all 360 degrees:

```
// lookup table for trig values (0 to 359)
public static int[] lookupCosFP = new int[360];
public static int[] lookupSinFP = new int[360];
public static int[] lookupTanFP = new int[360];

// static init
{
    for (int i = 0; i < 360; i++)
```

```
{
    // build an array of pre-calculated trig values (much faster to just
    // look them up here). note we add 0.01 to avoid all divide by zero
    // cases.
    lookupCosFP[i] = MathFP.cos(MathFP.add(MathFP.toFP("0.01"),
                                Actor.getRadiansFPFromAngle(i)));
    lookupSinFP[i] = MathFP.sin(MathFP.add(MathFP.toFP("0 01"),
                                Actor.getRadiansFPFromAngle(i)));
    lookupTanFP[i] = MathFP.tan(MathFP.add(MathFP.toFP("0.01"),
                                Actor.getRadiansFPFromAngle(i)));
}
}
```

Notice I'm adding a small degree to each value; this is just a cheap way to avoid divide-by-zero problems later. The increment doesn't really affect the results, and you don't need to worry about catching all divide-by-zero cases (of which there are plenty).

The Engine

That's enough background; now you can get on with how to actually set up the rendering engine. In this section you'll look at how to use the fundamentals you just learned to cast rays into your world and then, based on the results, render the 3D scene.

Get ready; this is where things start to get a little more intense.

Horizontal and Vertical Rays

As I mentioned in the introduction to this chapter, ray tracing is about as fast as your mother's typing. Casting is faster because you sort of hop along in increments equal to the size of each tile in the map. This dramatically reduces the total number of castings you need to do. Because you're dealing with a 2D map, you actually need to cast two sets of rays to cover all the cases. If you take a look at Figure 21.11, you can see a very simple map containing a single wall and a ray being cast through it. In this example I'm taking an origin point and then

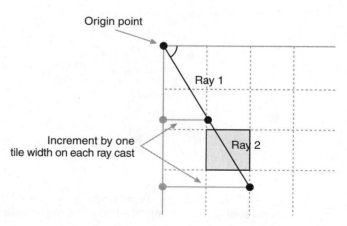

Figure 21.11 The first set of rays attempts to hit vertical walls. Each ray cast increments by one tile width. (The gray lines are the tile grid lines.)

moving in horizontal tile increments (by incrementing by one tile width on each ray cast) across the map until I hit something.

The black circles on the figure are the points to which each of the rays cast. At each of these points, you check whether a wall exists in the tile. Notice that because you're moving in tile-width increments, you're only hitting the vertical lines. In essence, you're casting along the vertical tile lines of the world. You might notice something else: You didn't actually hit the wall! The step between ray 1 and ray 2 meant you jumped right over the wall. To properly cover everything, you need to do the same process using the horizontal lines.

As you can see in Figure 21.12, moving in vertical tile steps gives you a quite different result. Due to the angle you had room to cast 3 rays, not 2, and of course you also hit our wall.

Figures 21.11 and 21.12 illustrate the basic *twin-casting* algorithm of a ray-casting engine. Starting at the origin point, you need to cast a ray across both vertical and horizontal lines until you get to the edge of the world or you hit something. Using this method you'll never miss a wall; as a bonus, you inherently know whether you struck a vertical or horizontal wall.

The next step in building your engine is figuring out how to actually cast those rays into the world.

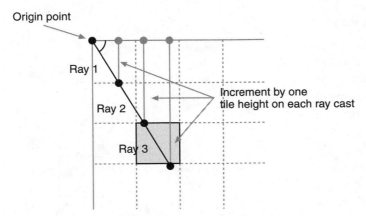

Figure 21.12 To cover the entire map, you also need to cast rays in tile-height increments (the horizontal tile boundaries).

Projecting a Ray

Each of the ray castings you do involves incrementing either the x- or y-axis, and then projecting out at a particular angle to determine the other component. Each of these tests requires you to project a ray given only one side of a triangle. Figure 21.13 shows an example of both a vertical and a horizontal increment.

Your goal here is to figure out the x and y coordinates of that target point. Notice how I've started at the origin point and then added the size of the tile to either the x- or y-component. You can then use TAN to discover the other size (either opposite or adjacent). For the adjacent component of the horizontal line, you can use

```
adjacent = opposite / TAN(angle)
```

However, for the opposite component of the vertical line calculation you need to be a little trickier and offset the angle by 90 degrees to invert the y-axis. For example, here's all the code to calculate the destination point on a vertical line:

```
// increment the origin point y by our tile size
int destinationY = originY + TILE_HEIGHT;

// figure out the x delta (distance we need to go to at current angle)
// note: I'm not properly checking the angle-90 for below zero cases
int distanceX = TILE_HEIGHT / TAN( angle - 90 );
int destinationX = originX + distanceX;
```

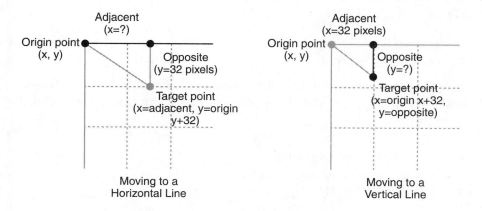

Figure 21.13 Casting a ray to the first horizontal and vertical line

For the horizontal line it's basically the same thing; you're just working with the opposing components.

```
// increment the origin point x by our tile size
int destinationX = originX + TILE_WIDTH;

// figure out the y delta (distance we need to go to at current angle)
int distanceY = TILE_WIDTH / TAN( angle );
int destinationY = originY + distanceY;
```

This all works fine; however, there's one more thing you need to deal with. Notice how I added the x and y values to the origin point; doing this will result in the destination point always being to the right and below the origin point, even if the angle was facing the opposite direction. Check out Figure 21.14 to see what I mean.

In this example the angle is around 40 degrees so the destination point is in the top-right quadrant relative to the origin point. To get to this point you need to take away the y-component, rather than adding to it. This is pretty easy to accommodate in code; you simply test the angle for each case and adjust the values accordingly. For example, here's the vertical test again, this time with the check added:

```
int destinationY = 0;
if (rayAngle > 180)   // if ray going down
    // increment the origin point y by our tile size
    destinationY = originY + TILE_HEIGHT;
else                  // going up
    // decrement the origin point y by our tile size
    destinationY = originY - TILE_HEIGHT;

int distanceX = TILE_HEIGHT / TAN( angle - 90 );
int destinationX = originX + distanceX;
```

The same thing applies to calculating out the horizontal step. This time, however, you're testing whether the ray went left or right. Again, remember that this is just pseudocode; you'll use MathFP in the final code.

```
int destinationX = 0;
if (angle < 90 || angle > 270)  // going right
    // increment the origin point x by our tile size
    destinationX = originX + TILE_WIDTH;
else                            // going left
    // decrement the origin point x by our tile size
    destinationX = originX - TILE_WIDTH;

// figure out the y delta (distance we need to go to at current angle)
int distanceY = TILE_WIDTH / TAN( angle );
int destinationY = originY + distanceY;
```

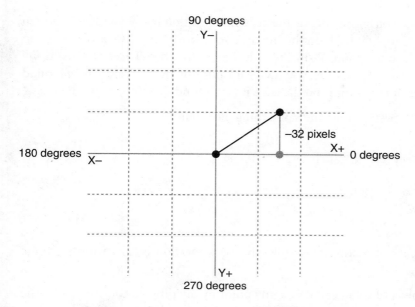

Figure 21.14 Based on the quadrant an angle is in, you might need to take away values rather than add them.

The First Step

In all the examples I've presented so far, the origin point has always been on a tile boundary. This is convenient for showing you how things work, but it's not practical for your engine. The origin point is going to be where the player is currently standing, so it's not going to stay on the tile boundaries. To accommodate this, you need to make the first cast a shorter one to align up to the tile boundary. You can see this in Figure 21.15.

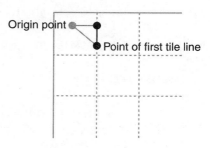

Figure 21.15 To align to the tile boundary you need to take a smaller initial step.

Doing this in code is quite simple; you just get the current tile position (based on the origin point) and then move one tile away. (The direction you move again depends on the angle.) For the horizontal tiles this is something like:

```
if (angle < 90 || angle > 270)    // if ray going right
    originX = ((startingX / TILE_WIDTH) +1) * TILE_WIDTH) + 1;
else                              // if ray going left
    originX = ((startingX / TILE_WIDTH) * TILE_WIDTH) - 1;
```

To get the tile coordinate you simply divide the current x position by the tile size. You then offset by one tile and multiply it back out by the tile size again. Notice I've also added 1 to the final number. This is so the point sits inside a tile, not on the edge. This ensures you will always hit the tile you want because when you divide the position by the tile size it will round down to the correct tile. If the point is on the edge it may round down to the wrong tile.

For the y-coordinate it's pretty much the same thing. For example:

```
if (angle > 180)
    originY = (((startingY / TILE_HEIGHT) +1) * TILE_HEIGHT) + 1;
else
    originY = (((startingY / TILE_HEIGHT) * TILE_HEIGHT) - 1;
```

Getting a Hit

You've covered the basics of casting rays now. The next question is how you determine whether you hit a wall.

Because a wall is simply a tile, you can check any point by dividing its coordinates by the tile sizes and checking the map array. For convenience, I wrap this into a World class function aptly named isWall (and some friends to help figure out tile positions—you might recognize some of these from *Star Assault*).

```
public final int getTileX(int x) { return x / TILE_WIDTH; }
public final int getTileY(int y) { return y / TILE_HEIGHT; }

public final byte getTile(int x, int y)
{
    int tx = getTileX(x);
    int ty = getTileY(y);
    if (tx < 0 || tx >= tilesWide || ty < 0 || ty >= tilesHigh) return -1;
        return tileMap[ ty ][ tx ];
}

private boolean isWall(int px, int py)
{
    if ( getTile( px, py ) == 1)
        return true;
    return false;
}
```

Calculating the Distance

Once you cast a ray and discover you got a hit, you need to be able to calculate exactly how far the ray went. This is important because you use the distance to scale the size of the wall (how far it is from the viewer). Figure 21.8 showed a good example of this. (Sorry to make you turn back a few pages.) In this figure, you can see that the rays cast against the side of the tile are further away from the viewer. Based on this distance the lines are drawn smaller, resulting in the effect of distance. It's simple, but it works really well.

Because you know the opposite and adjacent sides of your triangle, one method of getting the distance is to use the Pythagorean Theorem, which states that the square of the hypotenuse is equal to the square of the other two sides added together. This works, but it's a very expensive calculation to make, so you'll use something a little simpler.

A computationally faster method is to use sine and cosine based on the distance of each coordinate of the ray cast. Using an x-axis value, you can determine the hypotenuse by dividing it by the cosine of the angle. For a y-axis value, you need to use the sine. I wrap all this into a World class convenience function that takes both values and uses the larger of the two to determine the final result.

```
private int getDistanceFP(int dxFP, int dyFP, int angle)
{
    int distanceFP = 0;
    if ( MathFP.abs(dxFP) > MathFP.abs(dyFP) )
        distanceFP = MathFP.div(MathFP.abs(dxFP), lookupCosFP[angle]);
    else
        distanceFP = MathFP.div(MathFP.abs(dyFP), lookupSinFP[angle]);
    return MathFP.abs(distanceFP);
}
```

Adding Some Limits

To determine whether you hit something, the main ray-casting loop will fire a ray at a certain angle until it hits something. But what if there's nothing to hit? Or the thing is so far away in your world that it takes large number of casts to see it? To handle this you need to add some code to check for reasonable bounds when casting.

The first and simplest test is to make sure that a ray can possibly hit a tile line. There are a few cases in which it's simply impossible for a ray to get a hit, so you can detect these and not bother casting at all. In Figure 21.16, you can see the two angles each for horizontal and vertical casting.

The second test you need to make is to limit the distance a ray can go. Even with a small tile map you can have a ray being cast a relatively long way, with the resulting walls appearing very small. The problem is that to draw that wall, you've had to make a large number of cast steps to get there. This total number of ray casts will kill the performance of your ray-casting engine. You can think of it as something like the poly count in a 3D game—the higher the number of casts, the slower things will go. Those long-distance casts are the ones that really affect performance because it takes so many jumps to get there.

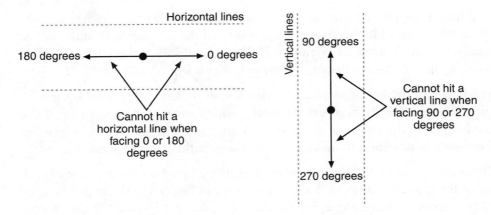

Figure 21.16 For vertical castings you don't need to bother testing angles of 90 or 270 degrees. Likewise, with horizontal castings it's impossible to hit any tile line with 0 or 180 degree angles.

The first distance test is to make sure you are even casting inside the tile map. You can do this by bounds checking each ray and aborting the casting if you've moved beyond the map dimensions. Here's a simple method to determine whether you're on a valid tile location:

```
private boolean isOnMap(int pointx, int pointy)
{
    if (pointx < 0 || pointy < 0) return false;
    if (pointx > TILE_WIDTH * tilesWide) return false;
    if (pointy > TILE_HEIGHT * tilesHigh) return false;
    return true;
}
```

Once you cast a ray, you can check whether it is on the map bounds and then abort the casting if you've gone beyond the map boundaries. You'll see this in action in the main casting loop a little later.

Even with the map boundary testing on, you still have cases in which with a large map you'll be drawing walls that are a very long distance away, costing a lot in terms of performance. To speed things up you can add a check to abort a ray cast past a certain distance.

```
static int HORIZON_DISTANCE_FP = MathFP.toFP(TILE_WIDTH * 20);
```

Then you can compare each ray's distance and abort the casting once it passes the horizon. Again, you'll see this in action in the main casting loop.

Through trial and error I've found that a distance of 20 tiles works quite well, although you can vary it based on the sort of performance you're getting with your world type.

The Main Loop

Okay, let's start to put all this together. The basic ray-casting loop is to start at your origin point and then, for all the angles in the FOV, cast rays into the world to determine whether you hit anything.

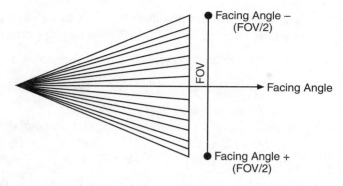

The first step is to determine the angles you need to cast. Assuming you know the facing angle of the player (this is just a variable that you'll change when the player turns), you can figure out the angles using the number of columns you'll be rendering. Because the player is facing the center of the view, you simply take off half the number of columns. You can see this illustrated in Figure 21.17.

Figure 21.17 In the main loop you cast a ray starting at the viewer's facing angle—half the field-of-view—all the way through to the facing angle plus half the field-of-view.

The code for your basic loop follows. I've also added in some variables you'll need in the casting code. For speed reasons I have both MathFP and normal integer versions of the player's origin point.

```
int startingXFP = MathFP.toFP(player.getX());
int startingYFP = MathFP.toFP(player.getY());
int startingX = player.getX();
int startingY = player.getY();

int rayAngle=angleChange(player.getDirection(), halfFovColumns);
int pixelColumn = 0;
int destinationXFP=0,destinationYFP=0;
int originXFP=0,originYFP=0;

for (int castColumn=0; castColumn < fovColumns; castColumn++)
{
    rayAngle = angleChange(rayAngle, -1);

    ... cast horizontal ray
    ... cast vertical ray
    ... if we got a hit then draw a wall segment

    // move across to the next column position
    pixelColumn += columnsPerDegree;
```

```
}
```

If you're wondering about the calls to `angleChange`, that's just a simple method to safely adjust an angle by any value (even negative ones). Here's the code:

```
private int angleChange(int a, int change)
{
    int angle = a + change;
    if (angle > 359) angle -= 360;
    if (angle < 0) angle = 360 - Math.abs(angle);
    return angle;
}
```

Now that you have the basic loop, you need to fill in the code to cast the horizontal and vertical rays. You have all the tools to do this now; all you have to do is put it all together. Here's the code to do the complete horizontal cast. Note that I'm now switching over to using `MathFP` for all the floating-point operations.

```
// --------- HORIZONTAL RAY ---------
// try casting a horizontal line until we get a hit

boolean gotHorizHit = false;
int horizDistanceFP = 0;

// if the ray can possibly hit a horizontal line
if (rayAngle != 0 && rayAngle != 180)
{
    // cast the first ray to the intersection point
    // figure out the coord of the vert tile line we're after
    // (based on whether we're looking left or right). Note we offset
    // by one pixel so we know we're *inside* a tile cell
    if (rayAngle > 180)
        originYFP = MathFP.toFP( (((startingY / TILE_HEIGHT) +1) * TILE_HEIGHT) + 1 );
    else
        originYFP = MathFP.toFP(((startingY / TILE_HEIGHT) * TILE_HEIGHT) - 1);

    destinationYFP = MathFP.sub(startingYFP, originYFP);
    destinationXFP = MathFP.div(destinationYFP, lookupTanFP[rayAngle]);
    originXFP = MathFP.add(startingXFP, destinationXFP);

    // get the distance to the first grid cell
    horizDistanceFP = getDistanceFP(destinationXFP, destinationYFP, rayAngle);

    while (!gotHorizHit)
```

```
    {
        // abort if we're past the horizon
        if (horizDistanceFP > HORIZON_DISTANCE_FP)
            break;

        // did we hit a wall?
        if (isWall(MathFP.toInt(originXFP), MathFP.toInt(originYFP)))
        {
            gotHorizHit = true;
            break;
        }

        // are we still on the map?
        if (!isOnMap(MathFP.toInt(originXFP), MathFP.toInt(originYFP)))
            break;

        int lastXFP = originXFP;
        int lastYFP = originYFP;

        // project to the next point along
        if (rayAngle > 180)   // if ray going down
            originYFP = MathFP.add(lastYFP, TILE_HEIGHT_FP);
        else                  // if ray going up
            originYFP = MathFP.sub(lastYFP, TILE_HEIGHT_FP);

        destinationYFP = MathFP.sub(lastYFP, originYFP);
        destinationXFP = MathFP.div(destinationYFP, lookupTanFP[rayAngle]);

        // move out to the next tile position
        originXFP = MathFP.add(lastXFP, destinationXFP);

        // add the distance to our running total
        horizDistanceFP = MathFP.add(horizDistanceFP,
                        getDistanceFP(destinationXFP, destinationYFP, rayAngle));
    }
}

if (!gotHorizHit)
    // make sure we don't think this is the closest (otherwise it would
    // still be 0). we use this later to determine which ray was closest
    horizDistanceFP = MathFP.toFP(99999);
```

Hopefully nothing in there is too scary. It's basically everything you've covered brought together in a complete loop. The end result of this code is two variables—gotHorizHit, which is set to true if the horizontal ray cast actually struck a wall, and horizDistanceFP, which will contain the distance the wall was if a hit occurred. If you didn't get a hit, the distance value is set to a large number (99999). I use a number this big so that it's impossible for it to really occur in the actual engine.

Next take a look at the vertical ray cast. This is the same thing except you're dealing with the vertical case. The basic structure is the same.

```
// --------- VERTICAL RAY ---------
boolean gotVertHit = false;
int vertDistanceFP = 0;

// if the ray can possibly hit a vertical line
if (rayAngle != 90 && rayAngle != 270)
{
    // cast the first ray to the intersection point

    // figure out the coord of the vert tile line we're after
    // (based on whether we're looking left or right). Note we offset
    // by one pixel so we know we're *inside* a tile cell.

    if (rayAngle < 90 || rayAngle > 270)   // if ray going right
        originXFP = MathFP.toFP(((((startingX / TILE_WIDTH) +1) *
                                TILE_WIDTH) + 1);
    else                               // if ray going left
        originXFP = MathFP.toFP(((startingX / TILE_WIDTH) *
                                TILE_WIDTH) - 1);

    destinationXFP = MathFP.sub(originXFP, startingXFP);
    destinationYFP = MathFP.div(destinationXFP,
                                lookupTanFP[angleChange(rayAngle,-90)]);
    originYFP = MathFP.add(startingYFP, destinationYFP);

    // get the distance to the first grid cell
    vertDistanceFP = getDistanceFP(destinationXFP, destinationYFP,
                                   rayAngle);

    while (!gotVertHit)
    {
        if (vertDistanceFP > HORIZON_DISTANCE_FP) break;

        // did we hit a wall?
```

```
    if (isWall(MathFP.toInt(originXFP), MathFP.toInt(originYFP)))
    {
        gotVertHit = true;
        break;
    }

    if (!isOnMap(MathFP.toInt(originXFP), MathFP.toInt(originYFP)))
        break;

    int lastXFP = originXFP;
    int lastYFP = originYFP;

    // project to the next point along
    if (rayAngle < 90 || rayAngle > 270)     // if ray going right
        originXFP = MathFP.add(lastXFP, TILE_WIDTH_FP);
    else
        originXFP = MathFP.sub(lastXFP, TILE_WIDTH_FP);

    destinationXFP = MathFP.sub(originXFP, lastXFP);
    destinationYFP = MathFP.div(destinationXFP,
                                    lookupTanFP[angleChange(rayAngle,-90)]);
    originYFP = MathFP.add(lastYFP, destinationYFP);

    // extend out the distance (so we know when we're casting
    // beyond the world edge)
    vertDistanceFP = MathFP.add(vertDistanceFP, getDistanceFP(
            destinationXFP, destinationYFP, rayAngle));
    }
}

if (!gotVertHit)
    // make sure we don't think this is the closest (otherwise it would
    // still be 0). we use this later to determine which ray was closest.
    vertDistanceFP = MathFP.toFP(99999);
```

Now that you've cast both rays, you've established whether one (and possibly both) of the rays struck a wall and exactly how far away that wall was from the viewer. With this information, you're now ready to draw the wall.

Drawing the Wall

Once you detect that a ray hit a tile, you can draw a segment of the wall using a vertical line. Based on the distance of the ray you adjust the size of this line. This is where that focal distance you worked out before comes into play. To get the size of the wall you first need to set a value corresponding to a full-size wall. In this case, I find that making walls twice as high as the tile size works well. Then you need to multiply this value by the focal distance to get the projected wall height.

```
static int PROJ_WALL_HEIGHT = TILE_WIDTH*2;
private int projWallHeight;

public World(int viewWidthArg, int viewHeightArg, Actor p)
{
    projWallHeight = MathFP.toFP(WALL_HEIGHT * focalDistance);
    ...
```

To get the size of the wall, you simply divide the distance (use the smaller of the two if both rays hit) into the projected wall height.

```
// remember we set the distance to 99999 if a ray didn't hit so it won't be
// used as the minimum in the code below
int distanceFP = MathFP.min(horizDistanceFP, vertDistanceFP);
int wallHeight = MathFP.toInt(MathFP.div(projWallHeight, distanceFP));
```

Once you have the height of the wall, the rest of the work is pretty easy. You simply need to determine where to start drawing the wall vertically and where to stop. To figure this out, you center the wall on the *projection plane*, which is just a fancy term for the height of the area on which you're drawing (typically the same as the screen height).

```
int bottomOfWall = (PROJ_PLANE_HEIGHT / 2) + (wallHeight/2);
int topOfWall = PROJ_PLANE_HEIGHT - bottomOfWall;

if (bottomOfWall >= PROJ_PLANE_HEIGHT)
    bottomOfWall = PROJ_PLANE_HEIGHT-1;
```

Finally you're ready to actually draw the wall. This is the easy part.

```
// draw the wall (pixel column)
g.setColor(0x777777);
g.fillRect(pixelColumn, topOfWall, columnsPerDegree, wallHeight);
```

Distortion

If you run the preceding code, you'll quickly find another problem . . . sorry, I mean challenge. Because you are basing the size of the wall on the distance the ray went, walls that are further away will appear smaller than those that are closer. This is what you intended, but as you can see in Figure 21.18, this has the effect of warping walls that should be straight.

Figure 21.19 demonstrates the problem a little better. See how the two rays to either side are more distant than the middle ray? This is what causes the distortion effect.

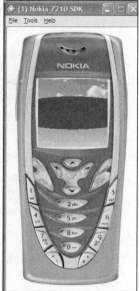

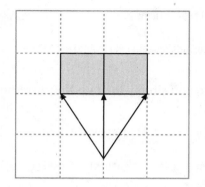

Figure 21.19 The distance of the outer rays causes the walls to be drawn smaller.

Figure 21.18 Because you used the distance to size walls, you have to compensate for the distortion this creates.

Believe it or not, this is how your eyes work. The eye presents a slightly curved image to your brain; you just don't notice because you're brain is compensating (and the curvature is outside your focal point). You can see what I mean by looking straight along a flat wall. If you focus on the center you'll see that the outer sides actually curve away slightly. Just like your brain, you need to compensate for this effect in your game.

The easiest method I've found to do this is to scale the wall height based on the ray being cast. The scale values correspond pretty much exactly to a circle surrounding the player—the further out you go, the bigger the compensation. Based on this, you can simply use the values of cosine from the facing angle outward. It's cute, I know, but it works like a charm.

Here's the code to pre-calculate the distortion values for all the FOV columns:

```
static int[] lookupDistortionFP;

public World(int viewWidthArg, int viewHeightArg, Actor p)
{
    // pre-calculate the distortion values
    lookupDistortionFP = new int[fovColumns+1];
    for (int i = -halfFovColumns; i <= halfFovColumns; i++)
```

```
lookupDistortionFP[i+halfFovColumns] =
        MathFP.div(MathFP.toFP(1),
        MathFP.cos(Actor.getRadiansFPFromAngle(i)));
...
```

When figuring the wall height, you simply look up the corresponding value to the angle and divide by it. For example:

```
if (lookupDistortionFP[castColumn] > 0 && distanceFP > 0)
    // adjust for distortion
    distanceFP = MathFP.div(distanceFP, lookupDistortionFP[castColumn]);
```

In Figure 21.20 you can see the results. This is much more like what you'd expect to see.

Wall Shading

So far your walls have all been drawn in one color. Another nice effect is to use a lighter color for all of one set of walls (say all the vertically aligned ones). The result is a simple lighting effect that gives some extra perspective to the view.

Figure 21.21 shows an example of this effect. The lines that make up the two walls shown on the left all use the same color, whereas on the right I've used a lighter shade for the horizontal rays. As you can see, the right-hand image looks much better.

Figure 21.20 After compensation for distortion, everything lines up nicely.

Figure 21.21 Shading walls makes for a much better 3D effect.

To create this effect you need to set the color of the line being drawn for each wall segment. You can determine this color by checking which ray hit the object (either vertical or horizontal). There's one issue you need to resolve first, though—tile edges.

At the edge of a tile you can get many cases in which the distance of both rays is equal (or close enough that it doesn't matter). You can see a simple case of this in Figure 21.22. The two rays being cast (horizontal and vertical) both hit around the corner of a tile. In some cases the vertical hit will return a (very slightly) smaller distance than the corresponding horizontal ray.

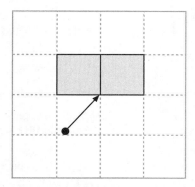

Figure 21.22 When casting rays near corners, you sometimes hit "hidden" walls.

The result of this on the screen is a change in color for wall segments that aren't actually corners. If you look down the left-hand wall in Figure 21.23, you can see the ugly results.

There are a few ways around this. The real problem is the rays are striking something that isn't really a wall in the first place; it's what you might term a *hidden edge*. To get around this, you could modify your map system to let you detect an edge that should be exposed to the world. This is nice, but unless you have another reason it's a bit of a waste of precious map space.

The second method (and the one I prefer for this case) is to add a little *edge detection*. What you do is assume that a wall runs along until there is a significant change in the distance of one ray type to another. That way, only a true corner will be picked up. Here's a modified version of the wall drawing code that adds edge detection. For completeness, I've included everything from the previous sections.

```
public class World
{
    // place this in the class's static list
    static int EDGE_IGNORE_FP = MathFP.toFP(5);


    ...

}
```

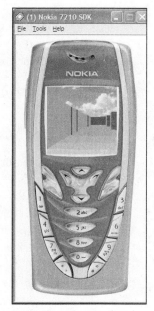

Figure 21.23 The left-hand wall shows the results of not detecting edges properly.

And here's the code to draw the wall slice, utilizing edge detection.
```
// --------- DRAW WALL SLICE ---------

// since it's possible (especially with nearby walls) to get a ray
// hit on both vertical and horizontal lines we have to figure out
// which one to use (the closest)
if (gotVertHit || gotHorizHit)
```

```
{
    int distanceFP = MathFP.min(horizDistanceFP, vertDistanceFP);
    int diffFP = MathFP.abs(MathFP.sub(horizDistanceFP, vertDistanceFP));

    boolean wasVerticalHit = true;

    if (horizDistanceFP > vertDistanceFP)
        wasVerticalHit = false;

    if (diffFP <= EDGE_IGNORE_FP)
        // if distance is the same then we hit a corner. we assume the
        // previous dir hit so as to give us a smooth line along walls
        wasVerticalHit = lastHitWasVert;

    if (wasVerticalHit)
    {
        // VERTICAL EDGE
        if (diffFP > EDGE_IGNORE_FP) lastHitWasVert = true;
        g.setColor(0x777777);
    }
    else
    {
        // HORIZONTAL EDGE
        if (diffFP > EDGE_IGNORE_FP) lastHitWasVert = false;
        g.setColor(0x333333);
    }

    if (lookupDistortionFP[castColumn] > 0 && distanceFP > 0)
        // adjust for distortion
        distanceFP = MathFP.div(distanceFP, lookupDistortionFP[castColumn]);

    if (distanceFP > 0)
    {
        int wallHeight = MathFP.toInt(MathFP.div(projWallHeight, distanceFP));

        int bottomOfWall = PROJ_PLANE_HEIGHT_CENTER + (wallHeight/2);
        int topOfWall = PROJ_PLANE_HEIGHT - bottomOfWall;

        if (bottomOfWall >= PROJ_PLANE_HEIGHT)
            bottomOfWall = PROJ_PLANE_HEIGHT-1;

        // draw the wall (pixel column)
```

```
        g.fillRect(pixelColumn, topOfWall, columnsPerDegree, wallHeight);
    }


    // and move across to the next column position
    pixelColumn += columnsPerDegree;
}
```

The end result of this is a smooth edge along all the walls.

Adding a Background Image

Your engine is really starting to come together now. To make it look
even better, you can add a background image to set the scene a little better.

To make a background image look good you need to create something with a horizon around the center of the screen. To give it an
outdoor look I've used a grass and blue sky combination for the
demo.

Adding the image into the ray-casting engine simply involves loading it up the normal way. For example:

Figure 21.24 A sample
background image

```
public World(int viewWidthArg, int viewHeightArg, Actor p)
{
    background = ImageSet.loadClippedImage("/background.png", 0, 0);
    ...
```

To use the background when rendering the ray-casting view, all you need to do is draw the
background image before you do anything else.

```
public final void render(Graphics g)
{
    // draw the background
    g.drawImage(background, 0, 0, Graphics.TOP|Graphics.LEFT);
```

Wrapping Up

Those are the basics of your ray-casting engine—see, I told you it wasn't that hard. Hopefully you've learned a little about the techniques you can use to create some interesting
types of games using 3D trickery.

However, turning this engine into a game requires a little more work. What you do next
really comes down to the type of game you want to make. In the next section I'll cover a
few areas you might need.

Advanced Features

Now that you've covered the basics of a ray-casting engine, you can move on to a few more advanced features you might add to support an actual game. These include collision detection, texture mapping, and sprites.

In the following sections I'll briefly cover ideas for extensions to the engine. I'll leave the development up to you.

Sprites and Actors

The current ray-casting engine is very similar to your basic tile engine before you added any concept of actors. To use ray casting in a game, you need to add these in and move them around the world.

The problem you have to solve is how to draw these actors on the screen. You can't use a normal sprite because the image will always appear the same size. Because you're dealing with a 3D view, you need to scale the sprite images to give the impression that they are far away. The first requirement for this is the ability to scale an image to any size. Because J2ME doesn't support that by default, you have to use a little extra code to do arbitrary scaling. I recommend checking out the `ScaleImage` class developed as part of the kobject project. You can go to http://sourceforge.net/projects/kobjects for more information. (Browse the source director and look for the class `/kobjects/utils4me/src/org/kobjects/lcdui/ScaleImage.java`.)

Once you have a scale image method ready, you need to create different versions of the actor images to display based on their distance from the viewer. The biggest problem with this is you can't scale images on the fly; it's just too slow. That means you need to pre-scale the images and store them for later use. Unfortunately, that chews memory for every copy of the same image. You need to keep your images small and make incremental jumps in the image sizes (say every 8 pixels instead of every 1) to get it all to work within the constraints of most MIDs. Even doing that, you can forget about having many different sprites.

You calculate the image size to use in more or less the same way as you figured the wall size; you just need to play around with the number to get a good balance. You might also find you need more precision up close, but you can increase the size gap as objects move away.

Collision Detection

Collision detection is basically exactly the same as it is in 2D tile games. The player is just another `Actor` object that moves around the world. You can grab the movement check code from the original Actor class and add it into the ray-casting engine. Of course, to add actors you'll need to add some sprites (see the previous section) to draw them in the game.

Once you detect a collision against a tile, you can react the same way you did in previous games. Try adding a projectile that fires from the player and bounces around the world. It's really cool.

Textures

The walls you currently render in the ray-casting demo use a simple draw line method. This is very fast and easy, but it's also pretty boring. By using textures you can map an image onto the wall to give it a much better look. To do texture mapping with your rendering process, you first need different-sized versions of the wall texture to map onto different-sized walls (based on their distances). You can use the scale image method again to create these.

To render the texture onto the wall, you need to draw a column of the image that matches the point the ray hit along the edge of the wall. To figure that out you can use the offset of the position after you hit it with a ray. For example:

```
if (gotHorizHit)
{
    // got a hit, let's work out what position along the cell wall the
    // ray struck
    cellPos = MathFP.toInt(destinationXFP) % TILE_HEIGHT;
}
```

To draw the texture part you need to set clipping so only the part of the image corresponding to that column is drawn. A combination of setClip and drawImage will get you there with a bit of tweaking.

Texture mapping is great, but again the major problem is storing the pre-scaled texture images. Because you need to create so many copies of the image, you'll quickly find that it uses very large amounts of precious memory. If you're using sprites, in most cases you won't have enough memory for textures as well. I'll give you a fair warning (which I know you'll ignore): Do the math on the total memory used by your scaled images before you bother coding. Trust me.

You might also want to consider another cheaper method of adding some texture to your walls: Use different colors when drawing the lines. For example, to draw a vertical edging across the bottom of every wall you can call the drawLine method twice—once to draw a small border segment, then you change the color, and call it again to draw the rest of the wall. Adding diagonal, checkered, and other patterns is relatively easy using this process. If you really get your stuff together, you can even draw brickwork and doorways.

Conclusion

As you saw, the basic concept of ray casting is pretty simple. You simply project rays into the world along the vertical and horizontal tile boundaries and, when you hit something, draw a wall relative to the distance the ray traveled. Do that for all the angles in the field-of-view, and you've got a reasonable 3D image.

The code you saw in this chapter does a good job of creating a ray-cast view; however, there's plenty of room to improve the performance and add cool features. Turning this basic engine into a game will be the fun part.

Ray casting won't produce results like *Quake III*, but it's an effective method for producing a great-looking 3D view you can use in all sorts of game types. Be creative with what you've got, and you'll be surprised how good the results can be.

CHAPTER 22

MAKING THE CONNECTION

One of the nice things mandated by the MIDP 1 specifications is that the device must be able to communicate via (at a minimum) HTTP. As a game developer, this means you can generally rely on being able to connect to the Internet from any MID.

In this chapter you'll explore the communications capabilities of your average MID and how you can practically utilize those capabilities in your games.

Mobile Communications

An MID is by definition a mobile device. That means in almost all cases they communicate without any type of fixed wires; in other words, they're wireless. There are three methods of communication you can practically use right now: SMS/MMS, Bluetooth, and HTTP. You should start by taking a look at these three in a little more detail.

SMS/MMS

SMS (*Short Message Service*) is available on almost all mobile devices (certainly all phones). Using the service you can send a short message (less than 160 characters) from one device to another using the target device's phone number. A target device need not be on the same carrier network.

SMS messages are not transmitted directly to the destination device; rather, an SMSC (*Short Message Service Center*) acts as a gateway to relay messages to their destinations.

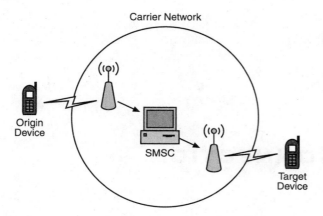

Figure 22.1 Short Message Service (SMS) messages are transmitted via an SMSC acting as a gateway to relay messages.

SMS is optionally supported as part of the Wireless Messaging API (WMA) version 1 (JSR 120). MMS is supported by the second edition of the WMA covered by JSR 205. Although support for WMA 1 or 2 isn't mandatory, it is becoming quite common for modern devices. Check the manufacturer specifications for each device to see whether it's supported.

Bluetooth

Bluetooth is a short-range radio (2.4 GHz Industrial Scientific Medical band) signaling system that provides communications between mobile devices within a range of about 10 meters (30 feet).

Figure 22.2 Bluetooth devices communicate directly with each other over short-range radio transmissions (at 2.4 GHz).

Bluetooth has gained very broad industry support, with more than 2,000 companies actively involved in its development and deployment. Due to its low range, Bluetooth transmitters are both compact (small and lightweight) and low cost, which allows manufacturers to include it within a device economically. Bluetooth is a popular feature of newer MIDs.

Unlike infrared, communicating via Bluetooth does not require line of sight. You simply need to get near another compatible device and bing . . . you're talking. Also unlike infrared, Bluetooth is not limited to one-to-one communication; multiple devices can have a little party together, which is great for multiplayer gaming.

Note

Do not confuse Bluetooth with IEEE 802.11b wireless LAN technology (and friends). Bluetooth is designed to provide inexpensive short-range (30 feet) communications at up to 1 Mbps. 802.11 is built for much larger devices, such as PCs, and communications at 11 Mbps at a range up to 300 feet.

Bluetooth is not part of the MIDP 1 specifications, but it is supported through the JSR 82 API. As with SMS, check the manufacturer specifications on your target devices to determine whether you have access to Bluetooth from Java.

HTTP

The only communications mechanism mandated as part of the MIDP 1 specifications is HTTP (*Hypertext Transfer Protocol*). Although this isn't a protocol you'd typically use as the basis for multiplayer games (a custom protocol based on UDP or TCP is more appropriate), it's still powerful enough to get a fair bit done.

An interesting thing to note about MIDP HTTP is that it may not necessarily be implemented over TCP. Most of the time MIDs use WAP (*Wireless Application Protocol*) instead. That's right—WAP lives!

To use HTTP you need to set up an HTTP server along with server-side code (servlets) to respond to your MID's requests. Access to the HTTP client is available by default with the MIDP 1 API.

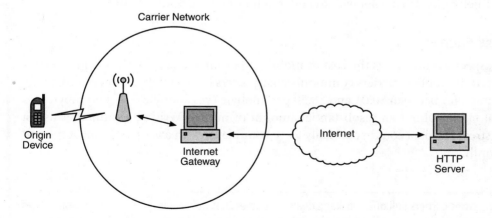

Figure 22.3 HTTP connections go via a carrier's Internet gateway.

Network Gaming

Now that you've seen what's basically available, I'd like to spend a minute going over the types of features you can develop with the communications you have available. More important, I want to give you a clear idea of what is and isn't possible.

Latency and Dropouts

I hate to throw cold water on anything, but don't get your hopes up too high with plans for multiplayer games, especially if you're dealing with anything in real time. Due to their nature, MIDs are not like broadband-connected PCs. In the real world you can expect low bandwidth (less than 20 Kbps even on so-called high-speed networks), very high latency (one to five seconds), and more dropouts than a physics course. These limitations don't mean you can't implement some great features based on wireless communications; you simply have to work within the limits.

Probably the most common mistake is to make a game that attempts to reflect a shared experience in real time. A good example of this is a multiplayer tank game. If two players face each other at nearly the same time and press the fire button, it's quite likely the messages relating to each command will arrive at a server up to five seconds late. Likewise, updates to the movement path of the tanks would be very erratic. These types of transmission delays (along with dropouts) would make the game pretty much unplayable.

Unfortunately, things don't really get any better on newer 3G networks. Although the overall throughput (the volume of data flowing to the phone) increases, the latency (the time it takes for data to get from the server to the phone and back) is more or less the same as current networks. Maybe 4G will do better, but don't hold your breath.

The Cost Factor

Another aspect to consider is the cost of mobile data transmissions. Unlike typical Internet connections, mobile carriers commonly charge users by the kilobyte for all traffic. The rates for this vary between $0.01 and $0.50 per kilobyte (yes kilobyte — *not* megabyte), so you're not talking about an insubstantial amount of money. Writing a game that uses a constant stream of data could potentially leave your player with a very large bill at the end of the month.

Tip

In some cases carriers will offer package deals for games that utilize a lot of bandwidth. Sometimes they even charge players a fixed monthly rate for the game and bandwidth. If you're contemplating something like this, it's usually a good idea to run it by your publisher (or carrier) first.

Practical Uses

That's all the bad news out of the way. The good news is you've got HTTP by default on all your MIDs. It might not be fast, but it's still enough to add some excellent features to your games. Take a look at some practical uses.

Meta-Games

A common method of utilizing the network for a J2ME game is to add any one of a number of extensions that broadly fall into the category of meta-games. A meta-game is essentially a part of your game play that exists above and beyond the actual game on the device. A classic example of this is an online high-scoring system. You can play the normal game standalone; however, you can choose to upload your score and see your ranking against all other players. The rank competition is a game in itself!

Tip

> Another great function that falls into the meta-game category is inter-player messaging. Based on your game type you might want to offer players the ability to send messages to each other.

Another common meta-game is to join groups of players into competing factions or clans. This might be as simple as unified scoring or as complex as having maps containing territories over which they fight.

All these types of meta-games are optional, so players who either cannot or don't want to incur the expense of network communications are not excluded from playing your game—they just don't participate in the greater meta-game.

By their nature, meta-games typically require very little bandwidth, with most communications occurring to update the state of play at any point in time. Because this is an optional component it's most commonly implemented as a separate feature the user needs to select, such as a Check My Online Ranking menu item.

New Content

Another excellent use of the network is to dynamically download new content for your game. This can include new graphics, levels, or any other data your game might use. Once you have downloaded the content, you can store the extra content in the MID's RMS, and you're not using precious JAR space.

The actual mechanics of how and where you make downloadable content available are again something you would want to discuss with your publisher or distributor.

Non-Real-Time Games

Non-real-time games (maybe you should term them unreal-time games) are simply games that don't pretend to operate in real time. A common example of this is any turn-based game, such as chess. Non-real-time games work well with mobile networking because they do not rely on low-latency and they generally don't require large amounts of bandwidth.

You're not limited to only turn-based games, though. As long as your game design allows a fair amount of time between transmissions and you don't constantly download data, you'll probably be okay. A strategy game, for example, could give players a certain number of moves per day (rather than enforcing turns). At the end of a game day, the server would then move everything simultaneously and return the results back to the players.

A Simple Networked MIDlet

HTTP communications from a MIDlet are carried out using the generic connection framework. This system uses a single "superconnector" factory for any type of supported connection. To make a connection to an HTTP server you simply open the URL and then read the response. In the following MIDlet example you'll create a connection to the java.sun.com Web site, download the homepage, and display the first few hundred bytes. You can build and run this example as a standalone MIDlet.

```java
import java.util.*;
import java.io.*;
import javax.microedition.midlet.*;
import javax.microedition.lcdui.*;
import javax.microedition.io.*;

public class NetworkingTest extends javax.microedition.midlet.MIDlet
{
    private Form form;

    public NetworkingTest() throws IOException
    {
        // Set up the UI
        form = new Form("Http Dump");
    }

    protected void pauseApp()
    {
    }
```

```
protected void startApp() throws MIDletStateChangeException
{
    // display our UI
    Display.getDisplay(this).setCurrent(form);
    communicate();
}

protected void destroyApp(boolean unconditional) throws MIDletStateChangeException
{
}

private void communicate()
{
    try
    {
        // Create an HTTP connection to the java.sun.com site
        InputStream inStream = Connector.openInputStream("http://java.sun.com/");

        // Open the result and stream the first chunk into a byte buffer
        byte[] buffer = new byte[255];
        int bytesRead = inStream.read(buffer);
        if (bytesRead > 0)
        {
            inStream.close();

            // Turn the result into a string and display it
            String webString = new String(buffer, 0, bytesRead);
            System.out.println(webString);
            form.append(webString);
        }
    }
    catch(IOException io)
    { }
}
```

This code shows the basic structure of communications between a MIDlet (the HTTP client) and an HTTP server. Create a connection, request a URL, and read back the response from the server. It's a simple transaction-style communications mechanism.

However, to use this in a game you need to do things a little differently. The first issue is the time it can take for communications to occur. Because of this delay you can't have the

MIDlet remain unresponsive to the user. At the very least, you need to provide a command to cancel out; even better, you could provide them with some feedback that stuff is happening. To do this you need to do your communications within a new thread. For example:

```
// create a new thread for the networking (inline class)
Thread t = new Thread()
{
    // declare a run method - not called until the thread is started
    // (see t.start below)
    public void run()
    {
        communicate();
    }
};

// start the thread (execute the contents of the run method above)
t.start();
```

Tip

Watch out for some of the Nokia emulators when you are doing network programming. Many of the older versions (including the 7210 v1.0 emulator) have a bug that shows up when you do multi-threaded HTTP requests while updating the display. The bug will crash your MID and output a Conflicting Stack Sizes error. If you encounter this, consider using a newer emulator in the same series. The 3300, for example, does not exhibit this behavior.

Now that you have some basic client communications working, take a look at the other side of the equation—the server.

The Server Side

To add communications to your games, you also need to set up an HTTP server that will listen for (and respond to) requests you make.

Because you're dealing with standard HTTP as the transport, you don't have to use a Java-specific solution for your server system. PHP, CGI, and Perl are all common solutions for server-side development. However, there is the obvious advantage to utilizing Java in dealing with a single code base (as well as working with only one language). You'll also find J2EE to be a powerhouse of functionality when you start getting more serious.

The best HTTP server solution for your purposes is Tomcat, part of the Apache software project.

Setting Up Tomcat

You can obtain Tomcat from the Apache binaries page at http://jakarta.apache.org/site/binindex.cgi. (The home page is http://jakarta.apache.org/tomcat/index.html.) Download the server archive in a format appropriate for your system and unzip it into a directory.

To get things working, navigate to the Tomcat /bin directory and execute the startup.bat (startup.sh for UNIX) file. After the server starts up, you can make sure that everything is working properly by opening up a Web browser and going to the URL http://localhost:8080/. If everything is set up correctly, you'll see an introduction page in your browser window.

Creating a Servlet

To handle incoming requests in Tomcat, you need to create a mini program that resides inside the server. These mini programs are known as *servlets*, and they are built according to Sun's J2EE specifications.

To create a servlet you need to create a class that extends the abstract javax.servlet.http.HttpServlet, and then implement either the doGet or doPost method to handle incoming requests.

Note

Note that to use javax you will need to have the servlets API to your class path. If you don't already have this you can find a version in the servlet-api.jar file under the common/lib subdirectory where you installed Tomcat.

Note

For your purposes you can use either an HTTP GET or POST request; however, GET uses the query string part of a URL for parameters—for example, http://localhost:8080/test.jsp?query=10. POST, on the other hand, transmits request parameters as a payload embedded into the request. The only real drawback to using GET (which is a little simpler) is you need to parse and unparse requests from the query string, and those query strings are limited in length. For these reasons, I recommend using POST.

Here's an example of a servlet that accepts POST requests and returns a hello in response.

```
import java.io.*;
import javax.servlet.*;
import javax.servlet.http.*;
```

```java
public class SimpleServlet extends HttpServlet
{
    public void doPost(HttpServletRequest req, HttpServletResponse res)
            throws ServletException, IOException
    {
        // open up the input stream and convert it into a string
        InputStream in = req.getInputStream();
        int requestLength = req.getContentLength();
        if (requestLength > 0)
        {
            StringBuffer sb = new StringBuffer(requestLength);
            for (int i=0; i < requestLength; i++)
            {
                int c = in.read();
                if (c == -1)
                    break;
                else
                    sb.append((char)c);
            }
            in.close();
            String rs = sb.toString();
            System.out.println("Got request: " + rs);
        }

        // process things
        // do something with the request

        // send back a response
        res.setContentType("text/plain");
        PrintWriter out = res.getWriter();
        out.write( " HELLO ");
        out.close();
    }

    public void doGet(HttpServletRequest req, HttpServletResponse res)
            throws ServletException, IOException
    {
        doPost(req, res);
    }

}
```

Once you have a servlet compiled into a class file, it's ready for deployment to the server.

Deploying a Servlet

To get a servlet functioning, you need to deploy it into the server. For Tomcat, you do this by first creating a new project directory for your application in the /webapps subdirectory of the Tomcat installation directory.

The project directory needs to contain another subdirectory named WEB-INF, and below that another directory named classes. The final structure should look like this:

```
/Tomcat-base-directory
    /webapps
        /test
            /WEB-INF
                web.xml (see below)
                /classes
                    SimpleServlet.class
```

Next you need to create a Web project file called web.xml in the WEB-INF directory. The contents of this file are used to set up the project. Here's an example:

```
<?xml version="1.0" encoding="ISO-8859-1"?>

<!DOCTYPE web-app
    PUBLIC "-//Sun Microsystems, Inc.//DTD Web Application 2.3//EN"
    "http://java.sun.com/dtd/web-app_2_3.dtd">

<web-app>
```

The first part of the web-app section is to set the concise (display) name and the long text description.

```
<display-name>Test</display-name>
<description>Simple Test Application</description>
```

Next you need to create a reference to the servlet class. This doesn't have to be a class in the WEB-INF/classes directory. In can be anything in the Tomcat class path. The servlet-name specified here is how this servlet is identified.

```
<servlet>
    <servlet-name>Test</servlet-name>
    <servlet-class>SimpleServlet</servlet-class>
</servlet>
```

Now the servlet has been defined you can use it by "mapping" it to a URL. In this case if the server sees an incoming URL of /hello (appended to the end of the application URL) the request will be passed to the referenced servlet (Test).

```
<servlet-mapping>
    <servlet-name>Test</servlet-name>
    <url-pattern>/hello</url-pattern>
</servlet-mapping>
</web-app>
```

The main function of this example web.xml file is to set up the servlet for access. This is done first by using the <servlet> to declare the mapping between a servlet nametag and a servlet class. You then use the tag to map to a specific URL (/hello).

To make the servlet work, you first need to copy the SimpleServlet.class file into the WEB-INF/classes directory.

To access your new project, you need to restart Tomcat and then navigate to the URL corresponding to the project. In your case this is just the directory name you used under webapps (test) plus the URL you specified pointing to the servlet in the web.xml file (/hello). Therefore, the full URL is http://localhost:8080/test/hello. If everything is working correctly, the server will respond with a "Hello".

Those are the basics of setting up your server and installing a servlet. In the next section you'll bring it all together in a working example.

Online Scoring for Star Assault

Now that you've covered all the basics of MIDlet networking, you can put it all to some practical use and add online scoring to *Star Assault*. The plan is pretty simple—you'll add some simple scoring (based on how many ships the player kills) and then after each game, you'll give the player the opportunity to submit his score online. Your servlet will then update a global rankings table and return a ranking order to the player.

Basic Scoring

The first thing you need to do is add scoring to the basic *Star Assault* game. To do this, you first need to track the score using an integer in the GameScreen class. For example:

Tip

You can see the complete online scoring system in the final *Star Assault* project in the source code directory in the CD.

```
public class GameScreen extends Canvas implements Runnable, CommandListener
{
    private int score;
    public void incScore(int i)
    {
        score += i;
    }
}
```

To register a score you modify the `onCollision` method of the `Ship` class to call the `incScore` method whenever an enemy ship dies a horrible death.

```
public class Ship extends Actor
{
    public final void onCollision(Actor a)
    {
        ...

        if (this.getType() != PLAYER_SHIP)
        {
            ...

            // add to the score
            GameScreen.getGameScreen().incScore(100);
        }
    }
    ...
```

You could get a lot fancier with scoring here (such as giving different points for the various types of enemies), but this works for this example.

Next you need to update the `GameScreen` class again to render the score to the player. You can do that by modifying the `renderWorld` method to draw the score in the top corner of the screen.

```
private final void renderWorld(Graphics graphics)
{
    ...

    graphics.setColor(0x00ffffff);
    graphics.setFont(defaultFont);
    graphics.drawString(""+score, getWidth()-2, 2, Graphics.TOP|Graphics.RIGHT);
```

That's all you need to add basic scoring to *Star Assault*. Next you'll add the online part of your scoring system.

The Online Scoring Class

To implement your online scoring system, you need to add a class that presents the user with a screen to submit and then check his online ranking. As we saw in Chapter 5, "The J2ME API," you can create a new display class by extending the LCDUI Form. The OnlineScoring class shown in the following code presents the user's score to him with the option to either cancel or transmit. If the player hits the send command, you then create a thread for communications, and it in turn calls the transmitScore method. Once a rank string is returned, you present it to the user using the same form.

```java
import javax.microedition.lcdui.*;
import javax.microedition.io.HttpConnection;
import javax.microedition.io.Connector;
import java.io.IOException;
import java.io.InputStream;
import java.io.OutputStream;

public class OnlineScoring extends Form implements CommandListener
{
    private int score;
    private Command cancel;
    private Command send;
    private Command ok;

    private HttpConnection httpConnection;
```

The constructor sets up a basic Form to transmit and display the score. All the action starts in response to the "Send" command.

```java
    public OnlineScoring(int scoreArg)
    {
        super("Online Score");
        score = scoreArg;

        append("Transmit score of " + score + "?");

        send = new Command("Send", Command.OK, 1);
        addCommand(send);
        cancel = new Command("Cancel", Command.CANCEL, 2);
        addCommand(cancel);

        setCommandListener(this);
    }

    public void showResult(String s)
```

```
{
    append(s);
}
```

When the "Send" command is executed this handler takes care of creating a thread and transmitting the score.

```
public void commandAction(Command c, Displayable s)
{
    if (c == send)
    {
        // get rid of the send command from the form
        removeCommand(send);

        // create a new thread for the networking
```

This is a neat trick if you haven't seen it before. The Thread class is declared inline in one statement. This saves having to create another specific class for the run method.

```
Thread t = new Thread()
{
    // declare a run method (not called until the thread is started
    // (see t.start below)
    public void run()
    {
        // send score to the server and retrieve the resulting rank
        // WARNING: this method will STALL until we get a response
        // or it times out
        String result = transmitScore();
```

Once you have a result, the current display text is removed and the result is shown.

```
        // delete the current text item
        delete(0);

        // present the result to the player
        showResult(result);

        // get rid of the cancel command and add an OK
        removeCommand(cancel);
        ok = new Command("OK", Command.OK, 1);
        addCommand(ok);
    }
};

    // start the thread (execute the contents of the run method above)
```

```
        t.start();
    }

    if (c == ok || c == cancel)
        StarAssault.getApp().activateMenu();
}
```

This is the method that takes care of all the communications to transmit the score to the server. Once a result has been received it returns it as a String.

```
public String transmitScore()
{
    InputStream in = null;
    OutputStream out = null;

    try
    {
        // submit score to server and read ranking response
        httpConnection = (HttpConnection) Connector.open("http://localhost:8080/
        StarAssault/updateScore");

        // close the connection after req/response (don't bother keeping it alive)
        httpConnection.setRequestProperty("Connection", "close");

        // set up for a post
        httpConnection.setRequestMethod(httpConnection.POST);
        String req = "" + score;
        httpConnection.setRequestProperty("Content-Length",
        Integer.toString(req.length()));

        // output the request
        out = httpConnection.openOutputStream();
        for (int i = 0; i < req.length(); i++)
            out.write(req.charAt(i));

        // read the result
        in = httpConnection.openInputStream();

        if (httpConnection.getResponseCode() == httpConnection.HTTP_OK)
        {
            int contentLength = (int) httpConnection.getLength();
            if (contentLength == -1) contentLength = 255;
            StringBuffer response = new StringBuffer(contentLength);
```

```
        for (int i = 0; i < contentLength; i++)
            response.append((char) in.read());

        String rankString = response.toString();
        return "You are currently ranked " + rankString + ".";
    }
    else
        throw new IOException();
}

catch (IOException e)
{
    return "Error transmitting score.";
}

finally
{
    if (httpConnection != null)
    {
        try
        {
            httpConnection.close();
        }

        catch (IOException ioe)
        {
        }
    }

    if (in != null)
    {
        try
        {
            in.close();
        }

        catch (IOException ioe)
        {
        }
    }

    if (out != null)
    {
```

```
        try
        {
            // clean up
            out.close();
        }

        catch (IOException ioe)
        {
        }
    }
  }
 }
}
```

The transmitScore method in this code calls the URL http://localhost:8080/StarAssault/ updateScore to submit the score to the server. You'll look at the corresponding servlet for this in the next section.

The Scoring Servlet

The scoring servlet implements the server-side component of your little system. Upon receiving a request (via a POST) you read the score, update a vector of all the scores, and then send back the player's ranking.

```java
import java.io.*;
import java.util.Vector;
import java.util.Collections;
import javax.servlet.*;
import javax.servlet.http.*;

public class ScoreServlet extends HttpServlet
{
    private static Vector topScores = new Vector();

    public void doPost(HttpServletRequest req, HttpServletResponse res)
            throws ServletException, IOException
    {
        // open up the input stream and convert it into a string
        InputStream in = req.getInputStream();
        int requestLength = req.getContentLength();
        if (requestLength < 1) throw new IOException("invalid request length");
        StringBuffer sb = new StringBuffer(requestLength);
        for (int i = 0; i < requestLength; i++)
        {
```

```
        int c = in.read();
        if (c == -1)
            break;
        else
            sb.append((char) c);
    }
    in.close();
    String rs = sb.toString();

    // process things
    System.out.println("New score uploaded: " + rs);

    int newScore = Integer.parseInt(rs);
    Integer newEntry = new Integer(newScore);
    topScores.add(newEntry);
    Collections.sort(topScores);
    int rank = topScores.indexOf(newEntry) + 1;
    String rankString = rankedInt(rank);
    System.out.println("Rank: " + rankString);

    // send back a response
    res.setContentType("text/plain");
    PrintWriter out = res.getWriter();
    out.write(rankString);
    out.close();
}

static public String rankedInt(int i)
{
    String result = "";

    String n = "" + i;
    int lastNum = Integer.parseInt("" + n.charAt(n.length() - 1));
    int lastTwoNums = 0;
    if (n.length() > 1)
        lastTwoNums = Integer.parseInt("" + n.charAt(n.length() - 2) +
n.charAt(n.length() - 1));

    if (lastNum >= 1 && lastNum <= 3)
    {
        if (lastTwoNums < 10 || lastTwoNums > 13)
        {
```

```
                        if (lastNum == 1) result = "st";
                        if (lastNum == 2) result = "nd";
                        if (lastNum == 3) result = "rd";
                }
            }
            else
                result = "th";

            return "" + i + result;
        }
    }
```

To now trigger the online process, you need to add code to the GameScreen class when it hits the game over state. For example:

```
    public void run()
    {
        try
        {
            while (running)
            {
                ...

                if (state == GAME_OVER)
                {
                    long timeSinceStateChange = System.currentTimeMillis() -
                            timeStateChanged;
                    if (timeSinceStateChange > 3000)
                    {
                        setState(GAME_DONE);
                        StarAssault.getApp().activateDisplayable(
                                new OnlineScoring(score));
                    }
                }
            }

            ...
```

That's it for your simple online scoring system. To make it work for a production game I'd do a few more things, such as saving the score to RMS and asking for the player's name. I'd also provide a screen the player could use to look up his current ranking at any time. The server side would also need to save the current rankings list to persistent storage, such as a database, since the current version will lose all the scores whenever you restart Tomcat (see the section "Server-Side Persistence" later in the chapter for more information).

Advanced Networking

What you've done in this chapter so far is probably the most basic of MIDlet networking. If you're planning to develop a multiplayer game, there are a few other things I'd like to cover to give you a heads-up on what you'll need to know.

Using Sessions

HTTP uses a stateless connection model, which means that each request is sent independent of any other request. By default there is no method to determine whether multiple requests have come from the same client.

The problem with this system occurs when the server side starts doing heavy processing. For example, suppose you wanted to save the score to a database. To validate the player you would first need to load up his account details using a validated user name and password. The way it works at the moment, you would need to do this for every single request for every user. For a multiplayer game involving many requests, this would quickly generate excessive load on your server, and it's pointless.

To get around this problem, J2ME adds the concept of a session. A single session represents any stream of connections from an individual client. Each session is then tracked by assigning a *session ID* to all the connections; this session ID is then passed back and forth by the client and server to track it (independently of the IP address). This is done either by embedding the session ID into the URL or by setting a cookie.

Note

A common misconception is that you can use the IP address of the client to represent a unique connection. Due to the use of NAT (*Network Address Translation*) and other relay technologies (such as proxies), you can quite commonly see connections coming from many different clients, all originating from a single IP.

You can obtain a session from within a servlet using a call to getSession on the request object. (The server will take care of associating a session with a request based on the session ID.)

```
HttpSession session = request.getSession();
```

You can tell whether this is a new session by calling the isNew method on the HttpSession object. Based on this you can carry out work to initialize the session for use, such as loading up details for a user.

```
if (session.isNew())
{
    // do init work for a new session
}
```

After you have made the call to getSession, the server will create a new session that is ready to use. You can now place data in the session, ready for later retrieval. For example, you could store a User object after the user has logged in successfully.

```
if (request.getParameter("username") != null)
{
    // load up the user from the database
    User u = new User(username);
    // set it in the session
    session.setAttribute("User-Object", user);
} else
{
    // retrieve the user object from the session
    User u = (User)session.getAttribute("User-Object");
    if (u == null)
        throw new Exception("oops, no user object set in session");
}
```

You now have a User object associated with the session on the server. Next you need to make sure your client properly identifies itself on each subsequent request. Normally an HTTP server will talk to a Web browser (an HTTP client), which will take care of handling the session ID for you. With a MIDlet, however, you need to take care of this manually. For example, if your server handles session IDs using cookies, you need to read the cookie (using the getHeaderField method), store the session ID it contains, and then set the session ID as a parameter in any future request you make using setRequestProperty.

Server-Side Persistence

There's a major problem with your little online scoring system: If you stop the server, the scores are lost. To resolve this you need to add code to *persist* the data by writing it to a file or database.

The most powerful (and flexible) solution is to use an SQL-compatible database. I recommend using the open-source MySQL database available from http://www.mysql.com. To access the database from Java you can use the JDBC (*Java Database Connectivity*) API. To talk to MySQL via JDBC, you also need to download and install the Connector/J JDBC driver (also available from the MySQL Web site).

Using JDBC is a good solution for very simple persistence; however, if you're getting serious you'll quickly find that manually handling SQL statements will become tiresome, buggy, and difficult to maintain. A better solution is to use an object/relational persistence system to automate the synchronization of Java objects with the database. That way you'll be able to deal purely with Java objects instead of having to map your SQL data to object instances and back again. You can find out more information on a popular (and free) persistence layer known as Hibernate at http://www.hibernate.org. Learning to use a persistence layer such as Hibernate is not easy, but I've found it substantially improves the development speed and overall quality of projects. Spend some time on it; it'll fundamentally change the way you work with SQL.

Multi-Server

There might be a point in the future when your game becomes so popular your server starts to have kittens handling the load. At this point you can buy a bigger server, but even that will only get you so far before you need to upgrade yet again. You also have the problem of your game being completely reliant on a single machine. If anything goes wrong, the whole game goes down until it's fixed. To resolve these issues you can design your server code and hardware setup to *distribute* the load among multiple servers.

Because you're dealing with HTTP as your protocol, you can take advantage of a host of technology already available to do this. Tomcat 5, for example, now includes a load-balancing system by default. Figure 22.4 shows a diagram of the basic structure of a distributed system.

For all intents and purposes, the load balancer in Figure 22.4 appears to the client device (MID) as an HTTP server. The load balancer will take a request and then have it handled by any of its available backend servers. The load balancer has the opportunity to make a decision about which server handles the request based on all types of factors (such as backend server load).

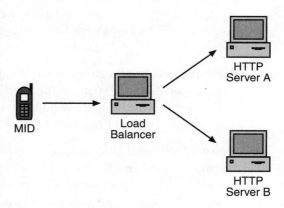

Figure 22.4 A load balancer acts as a request router to backend server resources.

You might be wondering what happens to your sessions in this case. If you create a session on one server, then what happens if on the next request the load balancer decides to route the request to a different server? You'd create another session. If you were to store data in that session, you'd start getting weird results as requests went to different servers. To accommodate this problem, load balancers are *session-aware*; they'll check whether a session ID has been set and then make sure all subsequent requests containing the same session ID are routed to the same server.

Session-aware load balancing solves the problem of session state; however, your current online scoring system would have another issue—server state. Each server will have its own instance of the online scores Vector. If you have 10 backend servers handling the score rankings, you'll have 10 completely different sets of scores and rankings. To resolve this you need to move the scores list into a memory state that can be shared among all servers.

The most common system for doing this is to use a database server accessible from all the machines. On each request you'll need to query the database, store the score, and then read back the updated ranking.

Using a database to share a game state among many servers works very well; however, the database itself can quickly become a critical point of load and failure if your system starts to get too big. At that point you might want to consider using a centralized application server such as JBoss (http://www.jboss.org) or moving to clustered DB caching based on the Clustered JDBC project (http://c-jdbc.objectweb.org).

Other Considerations

In this chapter you looked at the basics of adding network features to your game. As you can see, it's not particularly difficult to add elements that really improve game play. However, there are some serious pitfalls with multiplayer gaming that you should not ignore—and these are lessons I wish I'd been told about, instead of having to learn the (very) hard way.

First, because you'll commonly be dealing with multiple threads on both the client and server, you'll want to spend some time learning how to deal with the concurrency issues. (See the use of the synchronized keyword in Java.) If you ignore this, you'll find out why concurrency-related bugs are considered the most difficult to track down.

Second, you need to assume your client will be hacked by players. The online scoring example I used in this chapter would be figured out quickly by malicious players, who would then upload whatever scores they liked. Encrypting messages, moving much of the state to the server, and using tokens to validate messages are all techniques you should explore before embarking on a large multiplayer project. Above all, always consider how players can abuse an aspect you add to a game.

Conclusion

So far you've covered the basics of networking with MIDP, as well as some of the more advanced topics you'll need to handle when developing more sophisticated multiplayer games. As you can see, there's quite a bit more to multiplayer gaming. (Let's not get into massively-multiplayer or persistent-world issues—I could probably write a book on one of those subjects alone.) However, multiplayer games are one of the most exciting areas of mobile game development. I have no doubt that the most successful J2ME games of the future will utilize both the mobile and connected natures of the devices.

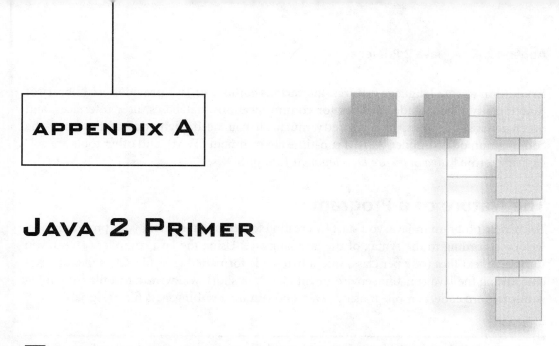

APPENDIX A

JAVA 2 PRIMER

I f you're new to Java programming or you just feel like a bit of a refresher, this section provides a rather fast introduction to the Java 2 programming language.

Java 2

Java is cool—no really; I mean it. It has pretty much everything you need in a programming language. It's modern, flexible, powerful, and most of all, easy to use. Java's performance in these areas isn't by luck; it was designed that way.

James Gosling, an employee of Sun Microsystems, created Java in the early 1990s as a robust, cross-platform programming environment based on C++. However, James (and friends) took the opportunity to simplify things a little. They removed elements such as direct memory management and access (which was inherently unportable), templates, preprocessing, auto-casting, operator overloading, and multiple inheritance. The end result is a much simpler language to use than C++ but which still has a majority of the functionality you need for your software projects.

Tip

Because Java is a Sun technology, I recommend regular visits to the official Java Web site at http://java.sun.com.

In addition to core language features, the various editions of Java provide a vast library of functionality that includes utilities for communications, databases, user interfaces, and other general purposes. Java is pretty much all you need, right out of the box. The combination of a compiler, APIs, a run-time environment (JVM), and other tools are collectively termed *Java Software Development Kits*, or SDKs.

The Nature of a Program

To create a program in Java, you start by creating text files that contain your program code, written according to the syntax of the Java language. Using the Java compiler (javac), you turn these text files (one per class) into a byte-code formatted class file. Class files are executed using the Java run-time environment (java). In short, you write a text file containing your program code, compile it using javac, and run the resulting class file using java.

Tip

Byte-code is the compiled form of Java code consisting of a concise instruction set designed to be executed with a Java Virtual Machine. It's machine language for a Java computer.

Most of the time, however, this process is simplified through the use of an IDE (*Integrated Development Environment*). Popular IDEs, such as JBuilder, Sun ONE Studio, IDEA, and Eclipse, take care of most of the work of compiling and packaging your class files. They also offer a host of other features to make your programming life easier.

Objects Everywhere

Java is a purely object-oriented programming language, so nothing can exist in Java that isn't part of an object. With that in mind, I think the best way to start understanding Java is to understand the nature of an object.

Fully appreciating exactly what an object is can be quite a leap, but it's nevertheless fundamental to understanding object-oriented development and, in turn, Java programming. Don't rush through this. You really need to fully grasp the nature of an object before you move on—it's fundamental to doing anything in Java.

So What Is an Object Anyway?

An object, like any program, is an abstract representation of something. When I talk about what an object is, all I'm really saying is what an object can represent abstractly. The great thing about objects is that unlike normal program code, object representations can be of both action and state—an object encapsulates both in one self-contained little package. In programming terms, an action is your code and state is your data (or variables). So why is this cool? Consider a game-programming example, as depicted in Figure A.1.

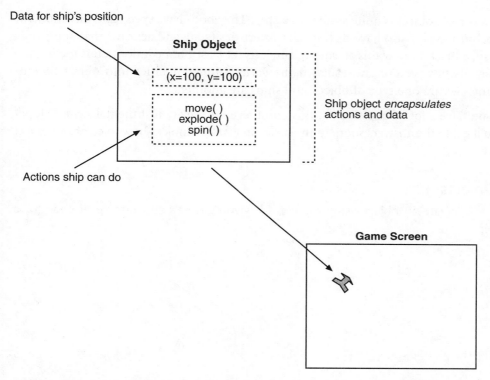

Figure A.1 An object encapsulates both state and actions. In this case, a ship is represented abstractly by the data of its position and the various actions available as program code.

In a typical space shooter, you use objects to represent everything—the player's space cruiser, the enemy ships, the meteorites . . . everything. Each of these objects encapsulates all of the states and actions they need. For example, the ship object has state data to represent its position, direction, and velocity, along with actions to keep it moving in the right direction (in other words, code to adjust its position over time) or to make it explode if it is hit by weapons fire. The important point is that the ship object contains all of these in one unit.

This is one of the great things about object-oriented coding. When you code objects, you code in terms of the things you're trying to represent. Your code and data are inherently divided into the sections that best represent what you're trying to achieve. This makes object-oriented programming a natural process. You can think and code in terms of the abstracts that make up your game.

I want to take this a little further. If you want the ship object to fire, all you need to do is adjust your object to include a fire action, right? Here's a good question, though: What does it fire? It isn't a ship object; that's just silly (or pretty cool, depending on your point of view). What you need is another object to represent a missile.

Your new missile object is quite similar to a ship. They both have speed and direction, for instance, but missiles also have distinct characteristics (state and actions) that apply only to a missile object. I know this all sounds obvious (at least I hope it does), but the important lesson is how you've encapsulated the various functionalities into object boundaries—missiles are one type of object, and ships are another.

I hope you have a lot of questions at this point, even if they're just mental itches. Hopefully you'll get to the answers soon. In the meantime, take a look at how to create an object using Java.

Java Objects

In Java, you create an object using the class keyword. Here's an example of code for a basic ship:

```
class Ship
{
    int x;
    int y;
    int color;

    void move(int newX, int newY)
    {
        x = newX;
        y = newY;
    }

    void setColor(int newColor)
    {
        color = newColor;
    }
}
```

This class represents your ship data (in Java these are called the *fields* of a class) in the form of three integers. The class also represents the actions in the form of the two *methods* move and setColor.

Instantiation

In Java, each new class becomes a new type in the language. So you can use the Ship class as the type of a new variable you create. Think of this as something like being able to rewrite the language as you go. Here's how you create a new instance of the Ship class in memory:

```
Ship myShip = new Ship();
```

What you've done is *instantiate* an object. You can then call `Ship` class methods (actions) on the `myShip` instance. For example:

```
myShip.move(100, 100);
```

Notice how I'm using the `Ship` class as a template for creating new objects of that type. This is an important distinction: `Ship` is the abstract class of an object, and `myShip` is one of those objects in existence. You can create as many of these instances of the `Ship` class as you want, but there can only ever be one type known as `Ship`. Here's an example in which you create three different `Ships`:

```
Ship myShip = new Ship();
Ship mySecondShip = new Ship();
Ship myThirdShip = new Ship();
```

You can now call the `move` method on any of these three ships, and they will move independently. You have three quite distinct `Ship` class objects.

Methods

As you just learned, fields (data) and methods (actions) make up a class. Now take a look at how to add a method to a class.

To create a method (known in other languages as a *procedure* or *function*), you first need to define a method header. This definition must contain the return type, method name, and an optional list of parameters. For example, the following header declares a method named `move` that takes two integers, `newX` and `newY`, and returns a `boolean` (true or false).

```
boolean move(int newX, int newY)
```

You can now add the code for the method directly below the header in what's called the method *body*. Inside the body, you can access the parameters using the names supplied in the header and return a value using the `return` keyword. You must write all the code for the method body within enclosing braces. For example:

```
boolean move(int newX, int newY)
{
    // method body
    System.out.println("move called with " + newX + " and " + newY);
    return true;
}
```

You can optionally set the return type in the method header to type `void`. In that case, a return statement is not required in your method, although you can use a return statement without a value if you just want to exit the method. For example:

```
void stop()
{
```

```
    if (speed == 0)
        return;

    // this code is never executed if speed is equal to 0
    speed=0;
}
```

Fields

A *field* is a variable defined at the class level. It's just like any other variable in Java, but what makes it special is that it lives in the scope of the class. Therefore, every instance of a class has its own set of these fields, which remain independent of any other instance of that class.

To add a field to a class, you simply declare a variable outside of any method. The following example declares three fields for your Ship class.

```
class Ship
{
    int x;
    int y;
    int color;
}
```

I'll get into the details of declaring variables a little later; for now, I want to stay on the object track.

Constructors

A constructor is a special method you use when you want to create an object. It lets you initialize the object in different ways depending on your needs. Take another look at your Ship class, for example. Suppose you wanted to set a different position for each Ship object you create. Here's an example of using a constructor to do that:

```
class Ship
{
    int x;
    int y;
    int color;

    public Ship(int startingX, int startingY)
    {
        x = startingX;
        y = startingY;
    }
}
```

As you can see, a constructor is just a method with no return type. (The built-in return value is actually the newly instantiated object itself.) You can do anything you would in a normal method; in this case, I just set the position to match the parameter values. To use your shiny new constructor, you need to adjust the call used to instantiate the object.

```
Ship myShip = new Ship();
Ship mySecondShip = new Ship(100, 200);
Ship myThirdShip = new Ship(300, 400);
```

As you can see, both of your constructors are in use here—one to create a normal ship and the other to initialize ships at a certain position.

Wait a minute! Did I just say both constructors? I hope you're confused, because if you look back at your class, it's obvious there is only one constructor declared. Where did the other one come from? And come to think of it, how come you were able to construct an object in the previous examples without any constructor at all?

The answer is the default constructor. The compiler automatically generates this special method if you leave it out. It's exactly the same as a constructor with no arguments—it will initialize all fields to their default values. Therefore, you can go ahead and create your own default constructor if you want to. Here's an example where I override the default constructor with my own:

```
class Ship
{
    int x;
    int y;
    int color;

    // the default constructor
    public Ship()
    {
        x = 100;
        y = 200;

        // color is not initialized so it will default
        // to zero
    }

    // the position constructor
    public Ship(int startingX, int startingY)
    {
        x = startingX;
        y = startingY;
    }
}
```

You should also note that the compiler will cease to generate a default constructor as soon as you supply any constructor of your own. So, in fact, the code to construct a ship using the default constructor would not have compiled after you added the position constructor, at least until you added the default constructor back in yourself.

One final point before I move on. When you're using multiple constructors you might encounter a case in which you want to call a constructor from another. You can use the this method call to reuse the functionality. For example:

```
class text
{
    int i;
    int a;

    public text()
    {
        i = 1;
    }

    public text(int b)
    {
        this();            // sets up i for us
        a = b;
    }
}
```

Objects and Memory

When you instantiate an object, it lives on the Java memory heap. This is a big pool of memory that you don't really need to worry about (although running out of it is not a good thing). The point is that memory management in Java is far simpler than it is many other languages that I won't name here. (Witness a coughing sound unmistakably similar to "C.") You just create objects, and . . . well, that's about it. You just create them, and the JVM will take care of the rest. Specifically, there's no way to free up memory you've already used.

At this point, you might be wondering why you won't eventually run out of memory. If there is no way to free the memory you've previously used, how does the memory get cleared? The answer is JVM's garbage collector. This nifty little bugger periodically sweeps the heap looking for objects that are no longer referenced by anything, and then discards them (thus freeing the memory).

Sounds simple, doesn't it? Well it is, but there are still a few things worth explaining about how this process works. The most important thing I want to mention is the concept of references.

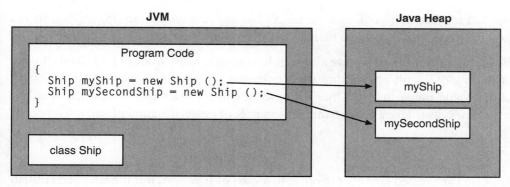

Figure A.2 Java classes are instantiated onto the Java heap.

A *reference* is a pointer (eeek!) to a Java object. Whenever you refer to a particular instance in your code, you're inherently maintaining a link to that object. As soon as you let go of that link, the object becomes unreferenced and is therefore a candidate for recycling by the big green garbage muncher. Take a look at an example because I know how confusing this can seem.

```
Ship myShip = new Ship();
myShip = null;
```

The first line creates a new Ship class object, allocated onto the heap. At this point the object has one reference to it—the variable myShip. Notice how the Ship class and myShip reference are different things. A reference is not the object; it's just a link to it. On the second line, I changed that reference to point to something else—in this case, nothing. At this point the reference count on the ship object is down to 0. The JVM keeps track of all these references so the next time the garbage collector periodically runs its process, it will know there are no longer any references to the Ship object and that it can go ahead and clear the memory.

Take a look at a slightly more complicated example:

```
Ship myShip = new Ship();
Ship yourShip = myShip;
myShip = null;
```

Any idea what's going to happen in this case? The important concept illustrated is the use of another reference to the same object—in this case, the yourShip object. I didn't construct anything; I just made yourShip refer to the same object. At this point the reference count on the object is 2. Even though I then set the original variable to null (thus reducing the reference count by 1), there is still a reference on the object so the garbage collector will pass it. If and when you set the final reference to null, the garbage collector will recycle it. Let's face it, if your code no longer has any reference to an object, then there's no point in keeping it around, is there?

While looking at references, you've also seen how objects really work in Java. To start with, you can only deal with objects through a reference, so there is no way to pass an object around by value, unlike in C++. Once you have the concept of a reference down, a lot of Java code becomes clear. Take a look at another example of object assignment and references.

```
Ship myShip;
myShip.move(100, 200);    // ERROR! Object not constructed.
```

In this case I've created a `myShip` reference to a class of type `Ship`, but it hasn't been initialized to anything. Thus the `move` method call will result in the computer exploding, likely taking most of the block with it in the process. Don't forget to take a hanky with you; my mum always told me you need a good hanky when you blow up the neighborhood. All right, so your computer won't explode (but imagining that it will certainly keeps the error rate down).

Tip

Another thing you might have noticed in the previous examples is that you assigned objects by reference. This means there is no way to copy an object. For example:

```
Ship yourShip = myShip;
```

This code does not create a clone of the original `Ship` object; it just creates another reference to the same object. If you want to create a copy of the original object, you need to use the `Clonable` interface.

Basic Syntax

You've taken a good look at objects and their importance in the Java landscape, but you're actually getting ahead of yourself. When it comes down to it, you need to follow the rules of the language (or the *syntax*) to code in Java. In the next few sections, you'll take a quick tour of the basic syntax that makes up the language.

Comments

Java has two methods for adding comments to your code. The simplest method uses the `//` token to tell the compiler to ignore the rest of the line. Here's an example you've seen before:

```
Ship myShip;
myShip.move(100, 200);    // ERROR! Object not constructed.
```

Alternatively, you can use a block comment, using the /* and */ tokens. This comment type can span multiple lines. For example:

```
/*
Ship myShip;
myShip.move(100, 200);  // ERROR! Object not constructed.
*/
```

Note that you cannot nest block comments; therefore, the following code is illegal:

```
/*
Ship myShip;
myShip.move(100, 200);   /* error!!! */
*/
```

Primitive Types

As shown in Table A.1, Java gives you a nice selection of primitive types from which to choose. Unlike many other languages, Java guarantees these primitive types to be the same size across any operating system. Therefore, you can safely assume an integer type will always use two bytes, no matter where it runs.

Table A.1   Primitive Types

Type	Description	Size	Range	Min/Max Values
boolean	Boolean value (true or false)	N/A	N/A	True or false
byte	Single-byte integer	8-bit (1 byte)	$-(2^7)$ to 2^7-1	−127 to 128
char	Unicode character	16-bit (2 bytes)	0 to $2^{16}-1$	0 to 65535
short	Short integer	16-bit (2 bytes)	0 to $2^{16}-1$	−32768 to 32767
int	Regular integer	32-bit (4 bytes)	$-(2^{31})$ to $2^{31}-1$	−2,147,483,648 to 2,147,483,467
long	Long integer	64-bit (8 bytes)	$-(2^{63})$ to $2^{63}-1$	−9,223,372,036,854,775,808 to 9,223,372,036,854,775,807
float	Single-precision floating point	32-bit (4 bytes)	$-(2^{63})$ to $2^{63}-1$	−
double	Double-precision floating point	64-bit (8 bytes)	$-(2^{63})$ to $2^{63}-1$	−

As you might have noticed in Table A.1, there are no unsigned types—they just don't exist in Java.

Literals

In Java there are six types of literals available—integers, longs, floats, characters, strings, and booleans. You can use a literal, also known as a *constant*, to create a value directly inside your code. I'll start with the simplest literal—integer.

An integer literal represents an integer value in decimal, hexadecimal (base 16), or octal (base 8). You can use a decimal constant simply by placing the integer value in your code. For an octal value, place a 0 before the number; for a hexadecimal number, use 0x or 0X. Here's all three in action; note that all of these statements are equivalent:

```
int a = 100;        // decimal
int a = 0144;       // octal
int a = 0x64;       // hexidecimal
```

To use a long literal, place an L after the number. For example, the following are all valid long numerical constants:

```
long a = 100L;
long a = 1234L;
long a = 0xBA12L;
```

You can use a floating-point literal in a similar fashion by placing an F after the number instead of an L. You can also use the constant E for an exponent and D for a double-precision number. Here are some examples:

```
float a = 100F;
float a = 1.23F;
float a = 1234.5678e+22F;
```

Note

CLDC 1.0 (the most common J2ME profile) does not support floating point values.

Character literals let you enter a character value directly into your code by placing it between single quotes. For example:

```
char c = 'a';
```

Table A.2 lists some special character literals available in Java. To use a special character, you must precede it with a backslash (\).

Table A.2 Special Characters

Character	Use
\n	Newline
\t	Tab
\b	Backspace
\r	Return
\f	Form feed
\ddd	Octal value
\'	Single quote
\"	Double quote
\\	Backslash

A string literal is very similar to a character literal, except you can place multiple characters between double quotes. For example:

```
String hi = "Hello there";
```

You can place any of the Java special characters inside a string.

```
String hi = "\tHello\n\"there\"";
System.out.println(hi);
```

That code would produce the following output:

```
    Hello
"There"
```

Finally, `boolean` literals are available in the form of `true` and `false`. You can use these directly in your code to assign a value. For example:

```
boolean a = true;
```

Declaring Primitive Types

Now that you know what primitive types are available, take a look at how to use them. To declare a variable using one of these types, use the keyword corresponding to that type, followed by an identifier for your new variable. You can use any combination of letters or numbers (as well as the underscore character) as an identifier; however, you can't start it with a number. Obviously, you also can't use reserved words or visible method names as identifiers.

Tip

Use identifiers (variable names) to provide a clear indication to the intent of the variable, even if it makes the name a little long. For example, use `speed` for the speed of a vehicle, rather than just `s`. You'll find that in the long run, your code is more organized and easier to understand (especially after you haven't looked at it for six months). The same tip applies to method and class names.

There's no real performance or size penalty for using full-length names. Although they do occupy more space in a class file, the process of obfuscating replaces long names with optimized ones. So leave obfuscation to the obfuscator.

Here are some examples of some different types of declarations:

```
int a;
long a;
float a;
boolean a;
```

The compiler will automatically assign a default value based on the variable's primitive type. For numerical values this will be 0; the boolean type defaults to false.

If you're not satisfied with the default values (damn, you're picky), you can provide an initial value using the assignment operator and a constant matching the type. (I'll talk more about assignment a little later.) For example:

```
int a = 100;
long a = 100l;
float a = 100f;
boolean a = true;
```

Also keep in mind that identifiers are case-sensitive, so a and A can refer to different variables.

Basic Operators

There are four types of basic operators available in Java—assignment, arithmetic, unary, and conditional. In the next few sections, you'll take a closer look at each of these operator types.

Assignment Operators

You've seen the most basic assignment operator, equals, used in quite a few examples already. For primitive types, equals does a by-value assignment of one variable to another. For example:

```
int a = 1;
int b = a;
a = b;
```

This code results in both a and b being equal to 1. For object types, the operator will assign the reference to the object, rather than to a copy of the object.

You can also chain equals assignment calls. For example, the following code assigns the value of 1 to all four variables:

```
a = b = c = d = 1;
```

Java also has a series of convenience assignment operators (+=, -=, *=, and /=) that do an assignment and a mathematical operation simultaneously. For example:

```
int a = 2;
int b = 4;
a += 2;    // a now 4
b *= 2;    // b now 8
```

Arithmetic and Unary Operators

The Java arithmetic and unary operators (+, -, *, /, and %) let you carry out basic mathematical operations on your variables. You can also chain these operators. For example:

```
int a = 1 + 2 + 3;    // a total of 6
```

The typical order of precedence also applies; therefore addition (+) and subtraction (-) have a lower precedence than multiplication (*), division (/), and mod (%). Thus 2 + 3 * 5 equates to 17, not 25. You can modify this order of precedence using brackets. For example, (2 + 3) * 5 equates to 25.

A unary operator lets you carry out an operation on a single element. The simplest of these operators are plus (+) and minus (-), which invert a number. For example:

```
int a = -2;
int b = -a;        // b equals 2
```

The other unary operators let you easily increment (++) and decrement (- -) a number. When you are using these operators within a larger statement, you can use the placement of the operator to specify whether to carry out the increment or decrement before or after the next statement. For example:

```
int a = 0;
if (a++ > 0)
   System.out.println("a=" + a);
```

In this case, there will be no output because the increment occurs after the statement evaluation. However, the following code will produce output:

```
int a = 0;
if (++a > 0)
   System.out.println("a=" + a);
```

Before I move on, there's one other operator you should take note of—the type caster. Sometimes you need to use this operator to give the compiler a little slap in the head. Take a look at an example, and then I'll explain what's happening in it.

```
int a = 10;
int b = 4;
float c = a / b;
System.out.println("c=" + c);
```

Now, you know that 10 divided by 4 is 2.5. Unfortunately, if you run this code the output will be 2.0. Confused? Here's what's happening. The divide-by statement involves two integers, so the result has to be another integer. Therefore, before you end up with the float result (c), a temporary variable is created and assigned to the integer value. This value is later implicitly cast into the final float value for the result. With me so far? The problem is that implicit conversion to an integer results in the loss of the floating-point portion of the result. For clarity, you can imagine that the statement actually reads:

```
float c = (int) a / b;
```

To get around the problem, you use the type cast operator to force the result type of the operation (the operator is the "(float)" in brackets). For example:

```
float c = (float) a / b;
```

Bit-Manipulation Operators

Java provides the operators you need to practice the black art of bit manipulation—AND (&), inclusive OR (|), exclusive OR (^), shift left (<<), shift right (>>), zero shift right (>>>), and complement (~). You can only carry out bitwise operations on byte, char, int, long, or short types.

The bitwise AND operator generates an integer result by comparing each of the bits of two integers to each other. If both compared bits are 1, the result for that bit position will be 1; otherwise, the result will be a 0 in that position. Bitwise inclusive OR is similar except that the result is 0 only if both bits in the original values are 0; otherwise, the result is 1. Similarly, an exclusive OR requires that the bits be different (one equal to 0 and one equal to 1).

The three bitwise shift operators let you move (or *shift*) the bits left or right by a certain number of spaces. For example, the following code shifts the bits representing the value binary 1 (00000001) four positions to the left, placing zeros in the new positions. The result is binary 16 (00010000).

```
int i = 1 << 4;
```

The bitwise complement operator simply toggles the bits in any number from 0 to 1 and vice versa.

Expression Operators

The final set of operators is a little different; you use them as part of an expression, usually relating to a condition in an if, for, while or other statement. The first operators, known as *equality operators*, are == and !=. These operators let you compare two expressions as equal or not equal. The result is a boolean (true or false). For example:

```
boolean b1 = 10 == 10;    // true
boolean b2 = 10 != 10;    // false
```

The result from this example will be that b1 is equal to true and b2 is equal to false.

You can also use relational expression operators (>, <, >=, and <=) in a similar way to compare two values. For example:

```
boolean b1 = 10 > 10;      // false
boolean b2 = 10 >= 10;     // true
boolean b3 = 5 < 10;       // true
boolean b4 = 5 <= 4;       // false
```

The final set of expression operators lets you carry out the Boolean operations AND (&&), OR (||), and NOT (!). These nifty little buggers (also known as logical operators) let you join two expressions, resulting in the combination of the two and carrying out a Boolean evaluation in the process. For example:

```
boolean b1 = 15 > 10 && 5 == 5;    // true
boolean b2 = 10 > 10 || 5 == 5;    // true
```

In the first case, the use of an AND operator means that both expressions must evaluate to true for the result to be true. The second statement uses OR, so only one of the statements needs to be true for the result to be true.

Take a look at another example, but this time something weird is going to happen.

```
int i=0;
boolean b2 = i == 1 || i++ > 0;
```

The problem here is that in Java, an expression evaluation will short-circuit as soon as the result is certain. So in this example, you'll never see the i++ executed because the i == 1 will always fail. (Since the statement was an OR, the failure of the first condition means the entire expression will also fail, so there's no point executing the other conditions.) Avoid relying on the execution of code within potentially short-circuited evaluations.

Before you move on, there's one other logical operator . . . NOT. (No, that's not a joke; there really is a NOT operator.) This one is a little special; it basically inverts the Boolean result of any singular expression. Here's an example:

```
boolean b1 = !(15 > 10)         // false (true inverted)
```

Statements and Blocks

Before you look at some of the other syntax, I'd like to clear up what I mean by the term *statement*. Like in C, a statement can contain multiple code elements separated by a semicolon (;). Here's an example of four valid statements:

```
int a = 0;
a = a + 1;;
int b = a;
```

Notice I said four statements, even though there are only three lines. That's because the second line actually contains two statements. (Notice the extra semicolon; this is considered to be an *empty statement*, and it is quite valid.)

You can group statements into a block simply by enclosing the code in braces ({ and }). For example:

```
{
    int a = 0;
    a = a + 1;
    int b = a;
}
```

A block can appear inside another block, thus creating a nested block.

```
{
    {
        int a = 0;
        a = a + 1;
        b = a;
    }

    int b = 0;
    b++;
}
```

Nesting blocks have another effect of which you should be aware. Any declarations (classes, methods, or variables) made within a block are not visible to any outer blocks. Because of this, you might sometimes need to adjust where you declare a variable to ensure that it's within the correct scope. Here's an example of an incorrect placement:

```
{
    while( true )
    {
        int i;          // oops, declared in the loop block
        i++;
        if (i > 10) break;
    }
}
```

Unfortunately, this while loop will spin forever because the variable i is re-declared on every pass. The correct code has the variable declaration outside of the while loop block.

```
{
    int i;          // that's more like it!

    while( true )
    {
        i++;
```

```
        if (i > 10) break;
    }
}
```

Conditionals

Conditional statements in Java let you control the flow of execution of your code. These statements include if, while, do, for, switch, and the ternary operator. I will start with the simplest—if.

The if Statement

The if conditional statement tests whether the result of an evaluation is true. This is where those expression operators really kick in. Here's an example:

```
if (10 > 15)
    System.out.println("True!");
System.out.println("Hello");
```

Because if only controls the following statement or block, the output of the preceding code is "Hello," not "True!" (because 10 is never greater than 15). I've indented the code to show which statements are subject to this condition. Keep in mind that this indenting has nothing to do with what's actually going on; it's just used to make the code clearer.

You can use any expression inside the brackets, including a joined one; the result can then be any value statement or block. For example:

```
if (10 > 15 && 10 > 9)
{
    System.out.println("One good statement...");
    System.out.println("deserves another.");
}
```

Caution

A common mistake for new coders is to place a semicolon at the end of a conditional statement. For example:

```
    if (10 > 15);          // oops
        System.out.println("True!");
```

If you were to execute this code, the string "True!" will always be output, which is not the intention of the code. The culprit is the extra semicolon at the end of the if line. The compiler treats this as an empty statement by the compiler; therefore, the result of the if is to execute an empty statement (which is the same as doing nothing). Execution then carries on to the next statement (println) as normal.

Optionally, you can use an else following the if statement to execute code if the expression result was false. Here's another example:

```
if (10 > 15)
    System.out.println("True!");
else
    System.out.println("False!");
```

The do and while Statements

The while statement is much cooler than the if statement. It lets you execute the same statement or block multiple times by a process known as *conditional looping*. Think of it like an if statement that keeps executing until the expression result is false. For example:

```
while (2 > 1)
    System.out.println("True!");
```

Of course, this code is not a good idea because the condition never evaluates to false. You'll just keep seeing an endless stream of "True!" (which is not my idea of fun). Here's a better, far more typical example:

```
int i = 0;
while (i < 10)
{
    System.out.println("i=" + i);
    i++;
}
```

This condition will output a limited number of strings before falling through to the next statement.

The do conditional is very similar to while; it just moves the condition to the end of the statement. For example:

```
int i = 0;
do
{
    System.out.println("i=" + i);
    i++;
} while (i < 10)
```

You primarily use the do statement when you want to execute a conditioned statement at least once. It is rarely used, however, because the for conditional is a more robust solution.

The for Statement

Java provides a more advanced conditional—the for statement. The nice thing about using for is that it can initialize, iterate, and test for an ending condition all in a single line. I've rewritten the while loop from the previous example using the more succinct for loop.

```java
for (int i=0; i < 10; i++)
    System.out.println("i=" + i);
```

Nice, huh? As you can see, for lets you provide three simple statements. (No, you can't put blocks in there.) The *initializer* is executed before the loop begins; the *conditional* is executed before each iteration through the loop to test whether the loop is complete; and an *update* statement is executed after each loop through but before the next condition test.

The switch Statement

The switch condition is for when you have many integer comparison cases. Using switch can dramatically reduce the required code for this type of operation. For example, here's the code to compare four integer values using if statements:

```java
if (i == 1)
    System.out.println("i=1");
if (i == 2)
    System.out.println("i=2");
if (i == 3)
    System.out.println("i=3");
if (i == 4)
    System.out.println("i=4");
```

Here's the equivalent code using a switch statement:

```java
switch(i)
{
    case 1:
        System.out.println("i=1");
        break;
    case 2:
        System.out.println("i=2");
        break;
    case 3:
        System.out.println("i=3");
        break;
```

```
    case 4:
        System.out.println("i=4");
        break;
}
```

Notice that at the end of each case line, I've included the keyword break. This is one of the nice things about a switch statement; if you leave the break out of the code, the next case is also executed. For example:

```
switch(i)
{
    case 1:
        System.out.println("Got one");
        break;
    case 2:
    case 3:
    case 4:
        System.out.println("i is 2, 3 or 4");
        break;
    default:
        System.out.println("i is something else");
}
```

You can also use the default keyword in a switch statement. That code is executed if no case matches.

The Ternary Operator

The ternary operator (?:) is a shortcut for evaluating a Boolean expression. Depending on the outcome, it will return one of two different results. For example:

```
int i=5;
String result = "Your number is " +
                ( (i <= 5) ? "less than or equal to" : "greater than") +
                " 5";
```

This is effectively the same as doing:

```
int i=5;
String result = "Your number is ";

if (i <= 5)
    result += "less than or equal to";
else
    result += "greater than";

result += " 5";
```

As you can see, the ternary operator lets you wrap up a conditional inside another statement.

The break keyword

As you briefly saw with the switch statement, the break keyword lets you exit a current block. Here's an example of a break used to exit an endless while loop:

```
int i = 0;
while(true)
{
   if (i > 10)
      break; // jump to exit point
   i++;
} // break exit point
```

You can also use break in conjunction with label much like a traditional goto statement. You can place a label almost anywhere, and then directly jump to it using the break statement. For example:

```
start_again:

int i = 0;
while(true)
{
   if (i > 10)
      break start_again;
   i++;
}
```

Unfortunately, your code is back to endlessly looping. As soon as the case to break is executed, you jump back up outside of the while statement and then execution starts all over again. I'll leave you to fix that.

Strings

In Java, you handle strings using the String object. String looks and feels exactly like any other Java-referenced object except for two minor changes: You can use the + and += operators to concatenate (join) strings, and strings cannot be altered. Once they are constructed, they are immutable. Here are some examples of String in action:

```
int i = 10;
String a = "abc";
a += "def";
String final = a + " - " + i;      // result is "abcdef - 10"
```

Being a full class object, String has a nice set of methods, such as substring, indexOf, and charAt, you can call to provide more advanced functionality.

Another note about strings (this applies in principle to all objects): When you want to determine whether two String objects are equal by comparing them, keep in mind that there are two quite distinct comparisons you can make. (And I guarantee you'll use the wrong one at some point in a Java program.) Have a look at the following example, and see whether you can spot what's wrong:

```
String a = "Hello";
String b = "Hello";
if (a == b)
    System.out.println("They are equal");
```

The problem is with the comparison inside the if statement. This looks like a comparison of the two strings "Hello" and "Hello," which should be equal—right? Wrong. If you think back to the details about objects and references, the if statement is comparing whether a is the same object reference as b, not whether they *contain* the same value. (The fact that they do contain the same value is irrelevant.) What you need to do is compare the contents of each object, not the object itself. For example, the following code is correct:

```
if (a.equals(b))
    System.out.println("They are equal");
```

The equals method, available for most objects, will logically compare the values of objects, rather than the references. (You can implement your own equals method for your classes. It's your decision as to what the equality of your objects really means.)

Quite often you will need to convert primitive type into a string. Thankfully, this is a relatively painless process using the String class's valueOf methods. These methods are static so you can call them on the String class, rather than a String object. For example:

```
String b = String.valueOf(700);
```

There's a slightly easier way to do this, but it's a little slower. You can use the concatenation operator. For example:

```
String b = "" + 700;
```

I had to add a string quote before the number literal to avoid a compile-time error. (String b = 700 is illegal because the compiler interprets this as you trying to assign a primitive type to an object reference.)

Tip

This is a simple look at the String class's capabilities. I recommend spending some time reviewing all the capabilities offered in this class.

Arrays

An array variable can store multiple variables in a single element. It can contain any type of variable, including objects, but this type must be the same for all elements.

To declare an array type, use the general variable declaration with the array operator either before or after the identifier name. For example, both of these declarations are for an array of integers:

```
int a[];
int[] a;
```

Before you can use an array variable, you have to initialize it using a list of expressions enclosed in braces. For example:

```
int[] a = { 10, 20, 30, 40 };
```

This code creates an integer array of four elements with the integer values 10 through 40. To access one of these elements, you use the array index operator:

```
int b = a[3];  // b is equal to 40
```

You should keep in mind that array access starts at zero, so the first entry in the array is at [0] and the last is at the array's length minus one.

To determine the size of an array, you can use a special property available with any array variable—length. Here's an example. (Note that this is not a method call.)

```
System.out.println(a.length);  // output is "4"
```

Arrays can also have more than one dimension. Here's the same example code expanded to an extra dimension:

```
int[][] a = { { 10, 20, 30, 40 }, { 50, 60, 70, 80 } };
int b = a[0][0];    // b is equal to 10
int b = a[1][3];  // b is equal to 80
```

Advanced Object-Oriented Programming

Earlier in this appendix you learned the basics of object-oriented programming, including how an abstract concept is encapsulated as a class through the use of Java fields and methods. As you can imagine (or you might already know), there's much more to object-oriented programming than encapsulation. In the next section, you'll look at the power of object relationships with inheritance, object scope, and visibility, and you'll learn a few other tricks along the way.

Basic Inheritance

Suppose you're working on a racing game involving many different types of cars and trucks, all tearing around a racetrack. To program this game using encapsulation, you would likely create a class to represent a Car type object and another for the Truck type object. As you wrote the code for these classes, you'd quickly find that a great deal of the functionality is similar, if not exactly the same. Both objects move around the track; even though they move at different speeds with different physics, these are only minor (parametized) differences. There are plenty of other similarities as well. Couldn't you (or shouldn't you) make these the same class? The problem is that they aren't the same type. Although much of the code is similar, there are still significant differences for each of these types.

The solution is to abstract out the shared components among these types into a shared class. Java then lets you have your final Car and Truck objects inherit this shared base of functionality. The name and type of this new base class is completely arbitrary; it's up to you what functionality you move into this class. For your Car and Truck class, you can say that these classes share their movement code but not their drawing code, so you'll create another Vehicle class to contain this.

Now I want you to stop for a second and think about this. I've found that a common misconception with inheritance is thinking there is a relationship between classes beyond what you define. Keep in mind that this is a completely abstract process. Given that you've only put the shared movement code into the Vehicle class, you don't necessarily have to call it a Vehicle. A better name is possibly the more abstract Mover class, which more adequately describes the limited functionality (see Figure A.3).

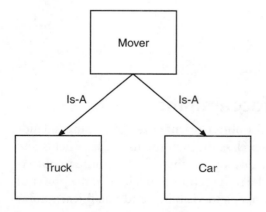

Figure A.3 The common components (movement) of your Car and Truck classes are abstracted into a Mover class.

Take a look at the code for this:

```
class Mover
{
    protected int x, y;

    public Mover()
    {
        x = 100;
        y = 100;
    }

    public void move(int newX, int newY)
    {
        x = newX;
        y = newY;
    }
}

class Car extends Mover
{
    public Car()
    {
    }

    public void draw()
    {
        // draw code
    }
}
```

The new addition here is the extends statement in the declaration of the Car class. This causes the class object to inherit all the functionality of the Mover class, which means you can now use the Mover class methods as though they were in the Car class. For example:

```
Car c = new Car();
c.move(10, 10);
System.out.println("Car position is " + c.x + ", " + c.y);
```

There's actually a subtle bug in the code for the previous example. The problem is that the Car object now encapsulates two classes. So when you instantiate the object, which constructor gets called—Car's or Mover's? The answer is Car's, which means the Mover constructor code to initialize the x and y positions is never called. To get around this, you use the super keyword to implicitly call the base class constructor.

```java
class Mover
{
    protected int x, y;

    public Mover()
    {
        x = 100;
        y = 100;
    }

    public void move(int newX, int newY)
    {
        x = newX;
        y = newY;
    }
}

class Car extends Mover
{
    public Car()
    {
        super();
    }

    public void draw()
    {
        // draw code
    }
}
```

The Car class constructor now calls the Mover constructor using the super method.

Now I want to tell you about one of the great powers of inheritance. Imagine you have a collection of all these Mover class objects (Car and Truck). You can now call the Mover class methods on any of the instantiated subclass objects. Still with me? Take a look at this in action:

```java
Vector allMovers;

public void startGame()
{
```

```
    // create our collection of movers
    allMovers = new Vector();

    // construct and add a car and truck to the collection
    allMovers.addElement( new Car() );
    allMovers.addElement( new Truck() );
}

public void moveAll(int x, int y)
{
    // loop through all our movers and call their move methods
    for (int i=0; i < allMovers.length(); i++)
    {
        Mover m = (Mover) allMovers.elementAt(i);
        m.move(x, y);
    }
}
```

As you can see, I've added a moveAll method that calls the Mover class's move method for all the Mover-derived objects, even though some of those are Car and Truck objects.

This example also begs the question, how do you know what type an object really is? To determine an object type at run time, use the instanceof operator. For example, this modified version of the moveAll method will only move Car class objects:

```
public void moveAll(int x, int y)
{
    // loop through all our movers and call their move methods
    for (int i=0; i < allMovers.length(); i++)
    {
        Mover m = (Mover) allMovers.elementAt(i);
        if (m instanceof Car)
            m.move(x, y);
    }
}
```

Object Base

It might also surprise you to find that you're using a form of inheritance with every object you create. All Java classes are automatically derived from the java.lang.Object class, which means they also inherit all the functionality of this class.

One nice available method is getClass, which returns a Class object representing the class of a particular object. For example, rewrite the moveAll method from the previous example, but instead of using the instanceof operator, get the Class object and compare its name to the one you want.

```
public void moveAll(int x, int y)
{
    // loop through all our movers and call their move methods
    for (int i=0; i < allMovers.length(); i++)
    {
        Mover m = (Mover) allMovers.elementAt(i);
        if (m.getClass().getName().equals("Car"))
            m.move(x, y);
    }
}
```

Method Overriding

Suppose you have a method in a base class that in some circumstances isn't quite appropriate. For example, imagine your Truck class has a slightly different version of movement, such as a speed limitation. In this case you can override the method in the base class with a more specific one.

```
class Truck extends Mover
{
    public Truck()
    {
        super();
    }

    public void move(int x, int y)
    {
        super.move(x, y);

        if (x > 10)
            x = 10;
    }
}
```

Notice the use of super again. What you've done here is create a new Truck class that extends the Mover object, just like Car, except you also implement a method exactly matching the base class's move method signature. This overridden version then calls the base class's version before it finally carries out a simple x position test and adjustment. From now on any call to the Truck object's move method will use this more specialized version.

Abstract

Consider for a minute the nature of the Mover class you've used in previous examples. It's not really anything concrete or usable, is it? In fact, you designed it to be a base class with no intention of ever instantiating it as an object. However, the way you've coded it now, any user of your racing game class library would be able to create a Mover object, even though this wasn't your intention. You can use the abstract keyword in the declaration of a class to make this impossible. Here's how you can enforce your design intention:

```
abstract class Mover
{
   ...
}
```

```
Mover m = new Mover();    // ERROR! Abstract class
```

The Mover object can no longer be constructed directly.

You can also use the abstract keyword on a method, but it has a slightly different meaning. Suppose later on you decide to enforce that every Mover-derived class must include a draw method. You can do this by adding an abstract method to the base class. This also saves you from having to implement anything for that method in the base class. For example:

```
class Mover
{
   ...

   abstract public void draw();     // abstract method; no body required
}

class Car extends Mover
{
   public void draw()
   {
      // draw code
   }
}

class Truck extends Mover
{
   ...

   // Error! Class must include a draw method
}
```

Interfaces

Up until now you've only seen examples of single inheritance, but imagine if you had a case in which you wanted to extend from more than one base class. For instance, you could create a Tank class by extending both the Mover and a new base class Firer. Deriving from more than one base class is known as *multiple inheritance*.

Java does not support a direct form of multiple inheritance, so you can't do something like this:

```
class Tank extends Mover, Firer     // Error!
```

In Java, you can't ever have a case where an object has a split class type; there can only ever be one parent type for any class. You can, however, make a class "look" like another one by using interfaces.

You can think of an interface as a completely abstract class. It has no fields (except static ones, but I'll get to that a little later), and all the methods are inherently abstract, with no code bodies. (Why didn't the abstract method go to the ball? Because it didn't have anybody to dance with! Sad, aren't I?)

Interfaces are really compiler tools that enforce that a class implements a known set of methods (or interfaces). You can create an interface in much the same way as you create a completely abstract base class. I want to revisit the Tank class again, this time using an interface:

```
class Mover
{
    ...
    abstract public void draw();
}


interface Firer
{
    ...
    abstract public void fire();
}


class Tank extends Mover, implement Firer
{
    ...

    public void move(int x, int y)
    {
        ...
```

```
    }

    public void fire()  // we now "comply" with the Firer interface
    {
        ...
    }
}
```

Now you can use the Tank class as both a Mover and a Firer. For example, here's a revised moveAll method from previous examples, except this time you have any Tank objects open fire as well:

```
public void moveAll(int x, int y)
{
    // loop through all our movers and call their move methods
    for (int i=0; i < allMovers.length(); i++)
    {
        Mover m = (Mover) allMovers.elementAt(i);
        if (m instanceof Mover)
            m.move(x, y);

        if (m instanceof Firer)
            m.fire();
    }
}
```

Notice that I'm checking whether the object m is an instance of the Firer interface. This is an important distinction; the object can *look* like many different types, but it is still actually only one type.

Visibility

By default, when you declare a field or method in a class, it is only visible (and thus accessible) to the code within members of that class; thus, it is private to that class. If you want to gain access to the declaration in a derived class, you can do so by declaring the field or method to be protected. If you want to allow any class access to the method or field, you can declare it as public. For example:

```
class Mover
{
    protected int x, y;  // x and y are now available to derived classes

    public Mover()
    {
```

```
        x = 100;
        y = 100;
    }

    public void move(int newX, int newY)
    {
        x = newX;
        y = newY;
    }
}

class Car extends Mover
{
    public Car()
    {
        super();
    }

    private void setup()
    {
        x = 50;         // this is now legal
        y = 50;
    }
}
```

In this example, the visibility of the two base class integers x and y is protected, so the direct access to these fields in the derived Car class setup method is now valid.

Tip

It is generally a good idea to limit the visibility of a method to private if it's intended for use only within a class (and is never called from outside the class). The same applies to protected scope; use it for methods that are used within a hierarchy, but which are not intended for use by outside (public) classes.

Inner Classes

In Java, you can declare classes within classes by creating *inner classes*. Typically, you create an inner class in a situation where you need a class but it exists only as a helper to another class. This is especially true if you do not intend to use the inner class by itself.

An inner class has access to all the fields and methods of its parent class (yes, even private ones). However, the parent class cannot access any private parts of the inner class.

As you can see in the following example, an inner class often serves to encapsulate components of the greater class.

```
class Car
{
    Color myColor;

    public Car(Color color)
    {
        myColor = color;
    }

    private void setup()
    {
        x = 50;             // this is now legal
        y = 50;
    }

    // inner class encapsulates color
    class Color
    {
        int r;
        int g;
        int b;

        public Color(int ar, int ag, int ab)
        {
            r = ar;
            g = ag;
            b = ab;
        }

        ...

    }
}


// application code...
{
    Car.Color red = new Car.Color(255, 0, 0);
    Car c = new Car( red );
}
```

Finalize

Earlier in this appendix, I reviewed the role of the garbage collector in cleaning up objects that are no longer referenced by your application. However, before the garbage collector destroys the object, you have an opportunity to do a little processing by implementing a finalize method.

Tip

After the call to finalize, the garbage collector will recheck the reference count for the object. If the reference is no longer zero, the garbage collector aborts the destruction of the object. Knowing this, it's possible to abort the destruction of an object simply by retaining a reference to it in your finalize method. (At least it's possible in theory.)

In practice, I don't recommend doing this. Although it's perfectly legal, you really shouldn't be at a point in your code where you have to rely on a trick like this. Just keep a reference on objects you don't want dumped, and they'll stay around as long as you want.

The finalize method is easy to add. Just override the method (which is declared in the Object base class) and add any code you want, such as code to free up resources. Here's an example:

```
class Car extends Mover
{
    public Car()
    {
        super();
    }

    protected void finalize() throws Throwable
    {
        // cleanup code
    }

    ...
}
```

Tip

If you're thinking you can move all that resource cleanup code into finalize methods, then I'm sorry—you're out of luck. The CLDC does not support finalize. Even if it did, under normal circumstances you should not rely on it as a means of cleaning up after yourself. Free up resources when you drop the reference to the object; there's no reason to rely on finalize.

This

The this reference is a special variable. It is accessible from within any class, and it represents the instance of the object itself. You can use this to check whether an object is accessing itself. For example:

```
public boolean isCollidingWith(Object another)
{
    if (this == another)      // can't collide with yourself
        return false;

    return myRect.intersects( another.getRectangle() );
}
```

You can also use this to access a class member, especially fields. This might be useful if you need to override visibility. For example:

```
class Test
{
    int i;

    public void setI(int i)   // argument has same name as field
    {
        this.i = i;  // using this to override default scope
    }
}
```

Statics

There are two types of statics in Java—fields and class initializers. Static fields differ from normal fields in that they share among all instances (objects) of that class, no matter how many objects the class contains. For instance, suppose you wanted to keep track of the number of Car objects you construct. Having a field in the Car class itself isn't going to be much help. For example:

```
public class Car
{
    private int totalCars;

    public Car()
    {
        totalCars++;
    }

    public int getTotalCars()
```

```
   {
      return totalCars;
   }
}

... // application code
{
   Car c1 = new Car();
   Car c2 = new Car();

   System.out.println(" total cars = " + c1.getTotalCars());
}
```

The intention of this code is to keep track of the total number of Car objects you have constructed. However, since the totalCars field is an instance field, the JVM will create a new copy every time you construct a new object; totalCars will never be higher than one. An alternative would be to move the totalCars variable to an outer scope. For example:

```
public class Car
{
   public Car()
   {
   }
}

... // application code
{
   int totalCars=0;

   Car c1 = new Car();
   totalCars++;

   Car c2 = new Car();
   totalCars++;

   System.out.println(" total cars = " + totalCars);
}
```

This solution now works, but it's not quite what you wanted. For a start, you've (arguably) broken the encapsulation of your Car class, and you now need to add code to increment (and later decrement) the car counter wherever you construct one. What you need is something in between, such as a variable that exists for all instances of a particle class. In

Java, you can do this by declaring a field to be static. Here's the static version of your car counter:

```java
public class Car
{
    private static int totalCars;          // now a static "class" field

    public Car()
    {
        totalCars++;
    }

    public int getTotalCars()
    {
        return totalCars;
    }
}

... // application code
{
    Car c1 = new Car();
    Car c2 = new Car();

    System.out.println(" total cars = " + c1.getTotalCars());
}
```

As you can see, I've changed the totalCars field declaration to include the static keyword, thus making it a class field. The totalCars++ increment code is now the same across all Car classes.

There's still one other problem, though. What if you want to access the number of cars from a different section of your game? Or what if you want to determine how many cars there are without having to actually construct any cars at all? Because you need to obtain a Car object before you can call the method, you will always need to have at least one Car object to call the getTotalCars method. This also seems a little silly. Why do you need an object to get access to a static field, since the totalCars value is not specific to an object? The answer is that you don't—what you need is to create a static method for the Car class.

```java
public class Car
{
    private static int totalCars;               // now a class field

    ...
```

```
public static int getTotalCars()      // static method
{
    return totalCars;    // access to a static member is ok
}
}
```

```
... // application code to get total cars
{
    System.out.println(" total cars = " + Car.getTotalCars());
}
```

The getTotalCars method is now static, so the application code can call using the Car class (Car.getTotalCars) rather than the object. In fact, a Car object is never constructed in the preceding code, so the result (correctly) is total cars = 0.

One final thing to keep in mind when using static methods is that the code cannot reference any object field directly. (Which one would it access, anyway?) Therefore, the following code is not legal:

```
public class Car
{
    private static int totalCars;           // static field
    private int color;                      // non-static field
    ...

    public static int getTotalCars()        // static method
    {
        if (totalCars > 10)
            color = 0xFF0000;               // Error, non-static field!

        return totalCars;
    }
}
```

Tip

Static methods are cleaner, faster, and easier to access than object methods. When you're adding a new method to a class, always ask yourself whether it can be a static method. You might be surprised by how many methods work just as well as statics.

Final

The final keyword tells the compiler that a particular element is immutable (in other words, it can't be changed). This is useful for both efficiency (the compiler can dramatically optimize methods or fields declared final) or because you want to make sure no extending class is able to override something. Here's an example:

```
public class Car
{
    private static final int DEFAULT_SPEED = 10;

    private int speed;

    public Car()
    {
        speed = DEFAULT_SPEED;
    }
}
```

Here I've used a final integer to improve the readability of the class. (Note that it's a common practice to use all uppercase in final fields.) You also have the option of initializing a final at a later stage, but the compiler will enforce that this initialization occurs before any use. For example:

```
public class Car
{
    private static final int DEFAULT_SPEED;       // blank final

    private int speed;

    public Car(int startingSpeed)
    {
        if (DEFAULT_SPEED == 0)
            DEFAULT_SPEED = startingSpeed;
        speed = DEFAULT_SPEED;
    }
}
```

The final keyword is available for methods as well. This has two effects. First, declaring a method final means that no subclass can override it, which might be a part of your class design. Second, the compiler might optionally inline a final method. (If you're familiar with C++, you likely know what I'm talking about already.) *Inlining* means the compiler can place a method directly into the calling area, instead of making a slower call to the method's code. This can have dramatic performance results.

Exceptions

Exceptions are objects that contain information about an event occurring outside of normal conditions—usually an error of some type. Typically you write code to throw an exception when this type of situation occurs. The exception then propagates back through the call stack (the previous methods) until it is caught in your code. You can think of an exception as something like an object containing an error report.

An exception can be a full class object, so it can have any elements you need to deal with the exceptional case when it occurs, such as any reason for the error. To create your own exception, you must extend the Exception class. To catch an exception, you must first wrap the code that might generate the exception in a try block. You can then use the catch keyword, followed by the exception class you want to catch. Here's an example of an exception being thrown and subsequently caught:

```java
public void setColor(int r, int g, int b)
{
    try
    {
        if (r > 255 || g > 255 || b > 255)
            throw new Exception("Invalid color");

        setColor(r, g, b);
    }

    catch(Exception e)
    {
        setColor(0, 0, 0);
    }
}
```

Sometimes you will encounter cases in which an exception might circumvent code you absolutely have to execute, such as code to release resources or carry out critical cleanup operations. The finally clause, which can follow any try block, is the place for this code. For example:

```java
public void setColor(int ar, int ag, int ab)
{
    int r = ar;
    int g = ag;
    int b = ab;

    try
```

```
    {
        if (r > 255 || g > 255 || b > 255)
            throw new Exception("Invalid color");
    }

    catch(Exception e)
    {
        System.out.println("fixing up bad color values");
        r = g = b = 0;
    }

    finally
    {
        setColor(r, g, b);
    }
}
```

If you don't want to handle an exception, you can declare your method so it throws the exception on the call stack (to the caller of the method and so on until it is handled). For example:

```
public void setColor(int ar, int ag, int ab) throws Exception
{
    int r = ar;
    int g = ag;
    int b = ab;

    try
    {
        if (r > 255 || g > 255 || b > 255)
            throw new Exception("Invalid color");
    }

    finally
    {
        setColor(r, g, b);
    }
}
```

In this case, the finally code is still executed, but the exception is passed back up to be handled by the method's caller as it sees fit.

Packages, Import, and CLASSPATH

Packages let you organize related classes into hierarchical collections. You can think of packages in terms of modules or libraries. Most of the functionality available in the Java API, such as java.lang and java.util, comes in the form of a package. You can create your own packages to better organize and segment functionality into modules.

To use a class from within a package, you actually don't need to do anything. As long as the class is visible to your application (via the CLASSPATH), you can reference it within your code. To do so, just add the package name to the class name. For example:

```
java.lang.String s = new java.lang.String();
```

Of course, having to add the full package name all over your code can get a little cumbersome. Wouldn't it be nice if the compiler could just assume which package you meant? I mean, how many String classes are there? Then you could just write:

```
String s = new String();
```

The compiler has a problem, though. The potential number of packages it has to scan can quite easily run into the thousands. (Just the Java API is hundreds of classes.) This would seriously slow down compiling, and it would have to happen on every compile. To solve this problem, you use the import keyword to limit the scope of the classes you intend to use. The same problem still holds true: The more you import, the longer the compiler will take to scan the import list. However, with a limited import scope, the length of time is usually negligible. Just don't go too ballistic on your import statements. Here's the example, rewritten with an import statement:

```
import java.lang.String;

class x
{
    String s = new String();
}
```

This works great, but you can imagine that with a big class, you might use hundreds of different classes (well, tens anyway). The import list would take up three screens! To avoid this, you can import using a wildcard. For example:

```
import java.lang.*;

class x
{
    String s = new String();
}
```

You can now use any class in the `java.lang` package without naming it specifically.

Tip

Try to avoid using wildcard imports when you can. Some packages are very large, and this can quickly slow down your compiles if you're not careful. Use a specific class import by default, and if the number of classes you're importing for a single package exceeds five, switch to the wildcard import. Some IDEs, such as IDEA, will automatically do this for you.

Packages are a great way to organize your work into modules. You can create your own packages using the `package` keyword. For example:

```
package my.utils;
import java.lang.*;

class x
{
    String s = new String();
}
```

However, for this to work you need to move the source for this class into a directory that matches the package name—in this case, a subdirectory called `my` under another directory called `utils`. So the final class name must appear as `my/utils/x.class`. This directory must be visible to your compile and run-time `CLASSPATH`.

`CLASSPATH` is very similar to any other type of system path—it declares the root paths to search for classes. You usually set the `CLASSPATH` using your IDE or from the command line. For example:

```
set CLASSPATH = c:\java\lib;.;
```

Tip

In Windows, `CLASSPATH` elements use a semicolon (;). In UNIX, they use a colon (:).

To make your classes available, you need to ensure that the class files are visible to the `CLASSPATH`.

INDEX

Symbols and Numerics

2D drawing tools, 159–160
*7 device (Sun), 3–4
+ (addition) operator, 707
& (AND) operator, 708
\ (backslash), 704
\b (backspace character), 704
{ } (braces), 710
- - (decrement) operator, 707
/ (division) operator, 707
" (double quote character), 704
\f (form feed character), 704
++ (increment) operator, 707
* (multiplication) operator, 707
\n (newline character), 704
| (OR) operator, 708
\r (return character), 704
' (single quote character), 704
- (subtraction) operator, 707
\t (tab character), 704
~ (tilde), 412

A

A380 Motorola phone, 45
abstract method, 342, 723
Abstract Windowing Toolkit (AWT), 123
acceleration, 318–319
acceptAndOpen method, 616–617
access methods, boolean types, 471–472
action
    collision detection
        advanced, 330–332
        code example, 332–342
        intersection, basic, 325–326
        intersection, through exclusion, 326–328
        reacting to, 328–330
        tiling, 378–379
    direction, alignment, 361–363
    enemy units
        angles, targeting, 356–358
        creating, 364–365
        distance, computing, 355–356
        isEnemyArg value, 365
        logic, creating, 365–366
        turning, through spin, 358–361
    movement
        acceleration, 318–319
        angles, 304
        basic movement, 304
        bouncing, 321–324
        Cartesian space, 305
        code, 311–317
        directional, 305–307
        discussed, 303
        fixed-point mathematics, 307
        floating-point math, simulating, 307–311
        free flight, 319–321
        MathFP, 308–311
        velocity, 318
    weapon fire, 349–354
action games, 250
action keys, 168
activate method, 225–226
activateGameScreen method, 216, 225–226, 469
activateMenu method, 457
activateTile method, 382
activator tiles, 380–383

Actor class
  abstract method, 342
  code, 342–345
  cycle method, 352, 360
  getRadiansFPFromAngle method, 646
  removeActor method, 352–353
  targetDirection method, 360
actors
  cycle method, 329
  isometric perspective, 627–628
  movement, 231–233
  primary
    discussed, 437
    enemy units, 442–445
    specifying, 438–442
  ray casting, 666
  render method, 238–239
  roles, defining, 226–231
addCommand method, 134, 184
addElement method, 481
addition (+) operator, 707
addState method, 290, 292
Adobe Photoshop, 240
advanced sprites, 297–301
adventure games, 251
alarms, registerAlarm method, 619
Alert class, 134
alignedDivArg method, 362
alignment, direction, 361–363
alpha color channel, DirectGraphics class, 188
AM (Application Manager), 79
AMS (Application Management System), 618
anchor-point types, fonts, 165
AND (&) operator, 708
angleChange method, 656
angles
  arcAngle method, 160
  movement, 304
  startAngle method, 160
  targeting, enemy units, 356–358
animation
  delay time, 290
  GIF files, 550–551
  reverse, 302
  tiles, 379–380
ANT tool, 76
Ant utility
  build files, 502–504
  properties, 505

  setting up, 501
  tasks, list of, 504–505
Antenna utility
  build file, 506–509
  obfuscation, 509–510
  preprocessing, 510–512
  setting up, 506
  tasks, list of, 505
Apache (Tomcat), 677
API (Application Programming Interface)
  discussed, 8
  Display class, 118
  MIDP API overview, 77
  MMAPI (Mobile Media API), 180
append method
  Form class, 135
  StringItem class, 141
application classes
  discussed, 36
  front end applications, 467–470
application management, J2ME, 21–22
Application Management System (AMS), 618
Application Manager (AM), 79
Application Programming Interface (API)
  discussed, 8
  Display class, 118
  MIDP API overview, 77
  MMAPI (Mobile Media API), 180
applications
  compilation, 58
  destroy method, 80, 84
  destroyApp method, 202
  front end
    application class, 467–470
    configuration options, 470–472
    key configurations, 472–475
    menus, 479–488
    overview, 465–466
    preferences, saving, 475–479
    splash screens, 488–492
  getAppProperty command, 70
  MIDP
    application descriptors (JADs), 33–34
    MIDlet JAR manifest attributes, 32
    run-time environment, 31
    suite packaging, 31
  pauseApp method, 79, 84, 202
  security, 20–21
  startApp method, 79–80, 84, 202, 491

arcAngle method, 160
architecture, J2ME, 14–15
archives, JAR file, 61–62
arcs, drawArc method, 160
arithmetic operators, 707–708
arrays
    array maps, world objects, 390
    DataOutputStream, 460–461
    declaring, 717
    images as, 593–600
    one-dimensional, 532
    optimization techniques, 531–532
    size determination, 717
    two-dimensional, 532
assignment operators, 706
AT&T Wireless, marketing distributors, 557–558
attributes, MIDlet JAR manifest, 32
audio, MIDP features, 37
auto-fire, *Star Assault* example, 470
AWT (Abstract Windowing Toolkit), 123

B

BACK command type, 119
backCommandName method, 482
background images, ray casting, 665
background layers, 384–386
background stories, game development, 264–265
backgroundMusicSupported function, 205
backlighting, device control, 177–178, 200
backslash (\), 704
backspace character (\b), 704
balance and completeness, good game design, 256
balance classes *versus* memory, 529–530
bit-manipulation operators, 708
bitwise shift, 593
BlackBerry Web site, 210
blinking effects, 197
blocks
    nested, 710
    statements and, 708
Bluetooth devices, mobile communications,
        670–671
board games, 252
bold characters, 163
boolean types
    access methods, 471–472
    discussed, 703
    getBool method, 487

bouncing, movement example, 321–324
braces ({ }), 710
break statement, 715
brightness, screen limitations, 248
browsers
    HotJava, 5–6
    Navigator, 6
buffers
    double-buffering, 221–222
    off-screen, 221--222
build systems
    Ant utility
        build files, 502–504
        properties, 505
        setting up, 501
        tasks, list of, 504–505
    Antenna
        build file, 506–509
        obfuscation, 509–510
        preprocessing, 510–512
        setting up, 506
        tasks, list of, 505
    MIDP 2, 574–577
    multi-device builds
        build file, 515–518
        device-specific code, 512–513
        resource management, 514–515
    reasons for, 500
    targets, 502–503
bulletImageSet method, 296
bullets, weapon fire, 349–354
byte type, 703
ByteArrayInputStream, 98
ByteArrayOutputStream, 98, 102
bytecode, 6–7

C

C++ language *versus* Java, 8
calendar classes, 26, 148
Call class, 199
cameras, movie making, 547–549
CANCEL command type, 119
cancel method, 90
Canvas class
    code, 152–156
    event response methods, 152
    general methods, 152
    Graphics objects, 151

canvas tools, MIDP features, 37
card games, 252
carrier downloads, sales channels, 553–554
case-sensitivity
    identifiers, 706
    INITIAL_CAPS_SENSITIVE input constraint
        type, 601
casting columns, 644–645
catch block, 86, 734
CDC (Connected Device Configuration), 15, 17
Cellmania, marketing distributors, 558
char type, 703
character literals, 704
checkered patterns, 667
choice types, List class, 125
ChoiceGroup class, 147–148, 586–588
class files, reverification, 58–59
class loaders, user-defined, 24
classes. *See also* objects
    Actor
        abstract, 342
        code, 342–345
        cycle method, 352, 360
        removeActor method, 352–353
        targetDirection method, 360
    adding fields to, 698
    adding methods to, 697–698
    Alert, 134
    application, 36, 467–470
    calendar, 26, 148
    Call, 199
    Canvas
        code, 152–156
        event response methods, 152
        general methods, 152
        Graphics objects, 151
    ChoiceGroup, 147–148, 586–588
    CLDC-specific, 25
    collection, 26
    CommandListener, 83, 120–122
    connection framework hierarchy, 27
    Connector, 90–91
    core, 21
    createSoundEffect, 207
    CustomItem, 578–581
    DateField, 148–149
    declaration, 83
    DirectGraphics
        clipping methods, 187

    color methods, 187
    image transparency, 192–193
    methods, list of, 189
    pixel data access, 193–197
    reflection, 191–192
    rotation, 191–192
    translation methods, 187
Display
    LCDUI, 114–118
    setCurrent method, 467
error, 27
exception, 27
ExtendedImage, 202
Font, 161–162
Form, 135–136
FullCanvas, 183–187, 493–495
GameCanvas, 601–605
GameScreen, 204–207, 216–217
    activateGameScreen method, 469
    applications, linking, 225–226
    cycle method, 232, 372, 435
    initResources method, 451
    keyPressed event, 239
    run method, 434
    setKeyBindings method, 473
Gauge, 150
GraphicObject, 202
GraphicObjectManager, 203
Graphics
    2D drawing tools, 159–160
    coordinates, 158–159
    drawing text, 161–164
    drawRGB method, 593
    images and clipping, 165–167
    methods, list of, 157–158
HttpConnection
    example code, 93–95
    methods, list of, 92
IllegalStateException, 184
ImageSet
    addState method, 290, 292
    code, 284–290
    discussed, 283
    draw method, 290
    expandArray method, 292
    getTimeInCurrentState method, 296
    isometric projection, 624
    reflection and rotation capabilities, 496–497

classes *(continued)*
    ImageUtil, 208
    inner classes, object-oriented programming,
       726–727
    input/output, 26
    Items, 137–139
    LayerManager, 611–612
    List
       addElement method, 481
       choice types, 125
       code, 126–129
       commandAction method, 129
       discussed, 124
       methods, 125
    Locale, 536–539
    MelodyComposer, 201–202
    MIDlet, 78
    Mover, 719–720
    networking, 36
    Nokia UI, 176
    PaletteImage, 208–209
    pclasses, 20
    Phonebook, 199
    PlayField, 207
    record management, 36
    RecordComparator, 104–106
    RecordEnumerator, 103–104
    RecordFilter, 106–108
    RecordListener, 108–110
    RecordStore, RMS, 96–97
    RMS (Record Management System), 96
    screen, 112
    SMS, 199
    SoundEffect, 207
    SoundListener, 180–183
    Sprite, 202, 207
       bulletImageSet method, 296
       code, 293–301
       cycle method, 296
       flyingState class, 296
       getTotalCycles method, 297
       isometric projection, 624
       overview, 292
    StringItem, 140–141
    system, 25–26
    TextForm, 487–488
    Thread, 217, 683
    TiledBackground, 203

    time, 26
    Tools, 291–292, 495–496
    type, 26
    user interface, 35–36
    utility, 27, 35, 112
CLASSPATH environment variable
    checking value of, using set command, 54
    discussed, 199, 737
    updating, for software installation, 54
CLDC (Connected, Limited Device Configuration)
    classes, 25
    CLDC 1.1 version, 572
    discussed, 15, 17
    security model, 19–21
    target platform characteristics, 18–19
clean target, build systems, 503
clipboard tools, 114
clipping
    clipRect method, 167, 187
    images, extracting, 276
    methods, DirectGraphics class, 187
    setClip method, 167, 667
clipRect method, 167, 187
clone keyword, 528
close method, 216
code
    abstract keyword, 723
    activate method, 225–226
    Ant utility, 501
    Antenna utility, 506–509
    arrays, 717
    break statement, 715
    build systems
       MIDP 2, 575–577
       multi-device systems, 515–518
    Canvas class, 152–156
    collision detection, 325–326, 332–342
    commandAction method, 85
    CommandListener class, 120–122
    comments, 702–703
    compilation stage, 7
    Connector class, 90
    constructors, 698–700
    CustomItem class, 579–581
    damage, recovering from
       energy levels, 446–447
       impact, protection, 448–450

destroy method, 84
Display class, 115–117
do statement, 712
event handling, 169–172
exceptions, 734
fields, adding to classes, 698
finalize method, 728
form control, MIDP 2, 583–584
front end applications
    application class, 467–470
    saveSettings method, 478–479
    saving and loading settings, 476–479
FullCanvas class, 184–187
GameCanvas class, 603–605
GameScreen class, 204–205, 216–217
getImageRegion method, 276–277
hello.java, 55–58
HttpConnection class, 93–95
HttpsConnection, 617–618
ImageItem class, 143–146
images
    as arrays, 594
extracting, 274–275, 277–281
ImageSet class, 284–290
inheritance, 719–721
initResources method, 223
inner classes, 727
interfaces, object-oriented programming, 724
interpretation stage, 7
isometric games
    basic world example, 624
    graphics, 624
    sectoring, 630–634
Item command, 588–589
Items class, 137–139
key configurations, 472–475
keyPressed event, 239–240
layers, 612–616
List class, 126–129
literals, 704–705
Locale class, 536–539
MelodyComposer class, 201–202
menu class, 214–216
menus
    backCommandName method, 482
    constants, 480
    displayed, tracking, 481
    getBool method, 487

setupMenu method, 481–482
    switching between, 484–487
methods
    adding to classes, 697
    overriding, 722
MIDlet application events, 80–82
movement, 311–317
    car and truck examples, 231–232
    free flight, 319–321
object management, 423–431
    linked lists, 419
    object pooling, 428–431
objects
    example code, 696
    instantiation, 687, 696
operators
    arithmetic, 707–708
    assignment, 706
    expression, 708–709
    ternary, 714–715
    unary, 707–708
pixel data access, DirectGraphics class, 195–196
pop-ups, 586–588
POST method, 677–678
pre-verification, 20
primitive types, declarations, 705–706
ray casting
    aborting, adding checks for, 654
    background images, 665
    casting columns, 645
    distortion, 661–662
    focal distance, 646
    main loop example, 655–659
    projecting a ray, 649–650
    shading effects, 663–665
readString method, 413, 415
RecordComparator class, 105–106
RecordFilter class, 107–108
RecordListener class, 108
records, writing data to, 99–101
rectangles, drawing, 190–191
reflection, 496–497
render method, 238–239
renderWorld method, 223–225
rotation, 496–497
run method, 237–238
saveLevel method, 458–460

code *(continued)*
  scoring
      basic structure, 680–681
      online scoring class, 682–686
      player ranking, 686–688
      rank strings, 682
  servlets, deploying, 679–680
  SocketConnection object, 616–617
  spacer items, 584–585
  splash screens, 214–216, 488–492
  Sprite class, 293–301
  sprites, animated, 609–611
  star fields, 384–386
  for statement, 713
  static fields, 729–732
  switch statement, 713–714
  TextBox class, 131–132
  TextForm class, 487–488
  tiling
      activator tiles, 381–382
      animated tiles, 379–380
      getTile method, 379
      non-collidable tiles, 383
  Timer object, 87–89
  Toolkit application code, 67–69
  Tools class, 291–292
  triangles, drawing, 190–191
  visibility, object-oriented programming, 725–726
  while statement, 712
  World class, 642–643
  world objects, 386–388, 396–398
collection classes, 26
collision detection
  actor collisions, using sectors, 635
  advanced, 330–332
  code example, 332–342
  intersection
      basic, 325–326
      tests, 242
      through exclusion, 326–328
  overview, 240–242
  ray casting, 666–667
  ray tracing, 640
  reacting to, 328–330
  tiling, 378–379, 634–635
color
  alpha color channel, DirectGraphics class, 188

color depth, screen limitations, 248
color shifting, pixel manipulation, 197
getDisplayColor method, 589
images, bright color, 273
methods, DirectGraphics class, 187
setColor method, 160
support, minimum system requirements, 254
command lines, 52
commandAction method, 85, 122
  catch block, 86
  List class, 129
CommandListener class, 83, 120–122
commands
  Ant utility tasks, 504
  Antenna utility, 505, 510–512
  exit, 216
  getAppProperty, 70
  go, 133
  Item, 588–589
  JAR, 61
  preverify, 53, 58–59
  Quit, 82, 133
  Send, 682–683
  set, 54
  start, 216
  taskdef, 506
commenting, 511–512
comments, 702–703
communication support, MIDP 2. *See also* mobile communications, 616–618
Compact Virtual Machine (CVM), 17
compilation
  applications, 58
  code stage, 7
  compile target, build systems, 503
completeness and balance, good game design, 256
complex values, pre-computing, optimization techniques, 530–531
concatenation, strings, 715
conditional looping, 712
conditional statements, 713
conferences, marketing tools, 564
configurations
  CDC (Connected Device Configuration), 15, 17
  CLDC (Connected, Limited Device Configuration), 15, 17–19
  front end applications, 470–472
  J2ME (Java 2 Micro Edition), 15–17

key configurations, front end applications, 472–475
  Star Assault example, 265
Connected, Limited Device Configuration (CLDC)
  classes, 25
  CLDC 1.1 version, 572
  discussed, 15, 17
  security model, 19–21
  target platform characteristics, 18–19
Connected Device Configuration (CDC), 15, 17
connections
  direct socket, 90
  framework hierarchy, 27
Connector class
  methods, list of, 91
  open method, 90
Connector.open method, 618
constructors, 698–700
contracts, publishers as marketing tool, 565–567
conversions, degrees to radians, 356–357
coordinates
  setX method, 231
  world objects, 368–369
copy command, Ant utility, 504
copyArea method, 589
copyrights, contracts, 566
core classes, 21
cost factor, network gaming, 672
CPS (cycles per second), 217–218, 220–221
createAnimatedTile method, 608
createSoundEffect class, 207
currentDisplay field, splash screens, 491
currentViewPosX method, 371
currentViewPosY method, 371
CustomItem class, 578–581
customization, Nokia
  FullCanvas class, 493–495
  reflection, 496–500
  rotation, 496–500
  vibration, 495
CVM (Compact Virtual Machine), 17
cvs command, Ant utility, 504
cycle method
  Actor class, 329, 352, 360
  discussed, 227
  GameScreen class, 232, 372, 435
  movement, 232
  Sprite class, 296

cycles per second (CPS), 217–218, 220–221
cycleStartTime method, 221

D

damage recovery
  discussed, 445
  dying actors, 452–458
  energy bars, 450–452
  energy levels, 446–447
  impact, protection, 448–450
  takeDamage method, 450, 453
data types, pixels, 194
DataInputStream array, 98
DataOutputStream array, 98, 102, 460–461
DateField class, 148–149
daylight effects, 197
ddd (octal value), 704
debug property, 511
debug symbols, optimization, 533
DECIMAL input constraint type, 601
declarations
  arrays, 717
  classes, 83
  methods, optimization techniques, 532–533
  primitive types, 705–706
decrement (--) operator, 707
#define command, 510
degrees, converting to radians, 356–357
delay time, 290
delete command, Ant utility, 504
delete method, Form class, 135
design of games
  balance and completeness, 256
  challenges, 211–212
  documentation, 258–260
  goal setting, 255–256
  inspiration, 257
  minimum system requirements, 254
  originality, 256
  overview, 252
  platform considerations, 253–255
  platform setup, 255
  reference device, 254–255
  technology, 257
  visualization, 258
destroy method, 80, 84
destroyApp method, 202

development process, gaming
    background stories, 264–265
    completion, finish what you started, 262–263
    game types, selecting, 262–263
    ideas, creating games from, 265–267
    JAR size considerations, 261–262
    prototypes, creating, 260–261
developmental tools
    downloading, 49–50
    JDK (Java Development Kit), 50
    micro devices, 10
device control
    Nokia, 177–178
    Siemens, 200–201
device-specific code, multi-device build systems,
    512–513
device-specific libraries, 173–174
diagonal patterns, 667
dice games, 252
Digital Bridges publisher, 560
direct graphics, Nokia, 180, 187–189
direct socket connections, 90
DirectGraphics class
    clipping methods, 187
    color methods, 187
    image transparency, 192–193
    methods, list of, 189
    pixel data access, 193–197
    reflection, 191–192
    rotation, 191–192
    stroke methods, 187
    translation methods, 187
direction
    alignment, 361–363
    directional movement, 305–307
    getDirection method, 363
    setDirection method, 362–363
directories
    creating, 50
    MIDP (Mobile Information Device Profile), 52
    res, 508
    src, 509
    utils, 737
display, MIDP device characteristics, 29
Display class
    LCDUI, 114–118
    setCurrent method, 467

distance, computing
    enemy units, 355–356
    ray casting, 652–653
distortion, ray casting, 660–662
distributors, marketing tools and
    AT&T Wireless, 558
    Cellmania, 558
    considerations for using, 559
    Handango, 558–559
    Motorola iDen/Nextel, 557
    T-Mobile, 556–557
division
    division (/) operator, 707
    in FP value, 311
do statement, 712
documentation, good game design, 258–260
doGet method, 677
doPost method, 677
double buffering, 221–222, 602
double-byte values, 142
double quote character ("), 704
double type, 703
doubly linked lists, 420
downloads, sales channels, 554–555
draw method, 290
drawArc method, 160
drawChar method, 161
drawChars method, 161
drawImage method, 667
drawImages method, 165
drawing
    rectangles, 190–191
    triangles, 190–191
    vector-based, 223
drawLine method, 159–160, 667
drawRect method, 160, 529
drawRGB method, 593
drawRoundRect method, 160
drawString method, 161–162
drawSubstring method, 161
dropouts and latency, mobile communication, 672
dying actors, damage recovery, 452–458
dynamic memory, 30

E

echo command, Ant utility, 504
Eclipse tool, 75–76

edge detection, 663
editing, movie making, 550
editors
    map, 407–409
    TextPlus, 76
    VIM, 76
elapsed time, 219–220
#elif command, 510
#elifdef command, 510
#elifndef command, 510
#else command, 510
empty statements, 708
emulators, SL55, 199
encryption, 617–618, 692
end of games, triggering, 242–243
#endif command, 510
endTileX method, 377
endTileY method, 377
enemy units
    angles, targeting, 356–358
    creating, 364–365
    distance, computing, 355–356
    isEnemyArg value, 365
    logic, 365–366
    primary actors, 442–445
    Star Assault example, 266
    turning, through spin, 358–361
energy bars, damage, recovering from, 450–452
energyMax method, 446
enumeration
    filtering, 106–108
    RecordEnumerator class, 103–104
environment variables
    CLASSPATH, 199, 737
        checking value of, using set command, 54
        updating, for software installation, 54
    MIDP_HOME, 53
    PATH
        adjusting in JDK binary directories, 51
        preverify command, 53
equality operators, 708–709
equals method, 716
error classes, 27
error handling, 22
event handling
    action keys, 168
    notification methods, 168

event methods
    Canvas class, 152
    RecordStore class, 97
examples. See code
exception classes, 27
exceptions
    object-oriented programming, 734–735
    RMS (Record Management System), 110
exec command, Ant utility, 504
exit command, 216
EXIT command type, 119
expandArray method, 292
explosions
    as sprite example, 269
    states, 282
exporting maps, 411–412
expression operators, 708–709
ExtendedImage class, 202
extracting images, 274–281, 290

F
features, design documentation, 260
field-of-view (FOV), 643
fields, adding to classes, 698
Fifth Axis publisher, 560
file formats, PNG, 143
files, manifest, 31–33
fillCells method, 607–608
fillRect method, 160, 529
fillRoundedRect method, 160
fillTriangle method, 589
filtering, RecordFilter class, 106–108
final keyword, object-oriented programming, 733
finalization callback, 22
finalize method, 728
finally clause, 734
first-person perspective, ray casting, 643
firstFree method, 423
fixed-point mathematics, 307
flags, unconditional, 85
Flash movies, in HTML pages, 21
flashLights method, 177
flight code, 319–321
float type, 703
floating-point math, 22, 307–311
fluffing, 232–233
flushGraphics method, 205, 602

flying states, 282
flyingState method, 296
focal distance, ray casting, 645–646
focal length, ray casting, 645–646
fog effects, 197
Font.getWidth method, 164
fonts
    anchor-point types, 165
    Font class, 161–162
    getFont method, 161
    types of, 163
for statement, 713
Form class, 135–136
form control, MIDP 2, 581–584
form feed character (\f), 704
forms, text messages, 140
Forum Nokia, 41
four-way scrolling, *Star Assault* example, 265
FOV (field-of-view), 643
fovColumns variable, 645
FPLib floating point library, 308
FPS (frames per second), 219
frames
    nextFrame method, 609
    prevFrame method, 609
    setFrameSequence method, 610
    states *versus*, 282
frames per second (FPS), 219
free flight, 319–321
front end applications
    application class, 467–470
    configuration options, 470–472
    key configurations, 472–475
    menus, 479–488
    overview, 465–466
    preferences, saving, 475–479
    splash screens, 488–492
full-screen drawing, Nokia, 183–187
FullCanvas class, 183–187, 493–495
functions. *See* methods

G

Gage, John, 5
gambling games, 252
Game API, Motorola, 203
game controls, *Star Assault* example, 266
Game Developers Conference (GDC), 564

game guide, marketing
    discussed, 543
    game playing, step-by-step walk through, 545
    introductions, 544–545
    reference section, 545
game loop, 217–221
game play, design documentation, 260
game state, 433–437
GameCanvas class, 601–605
gameOver method, 243
games
    action, 250
    adventure, 251
    design of
        balance and completeness, 256
        challenges, 211–212
        documentation, 258–260
        goal setting, 255–256
        inspiration, 257
        minimum system requirements, 254
        originality, 256
        overview, 252
        platform considerations, 253–255
        platform setup, 255
        reference device, 254–255
        technology, 257
        visualization, 258
    development process
        background stories, 264–265
        completion, finish what you started, 262–263
        game types, selecting, 262–263
        ideas, creating games from, 265–267
        JAR size considerations, 261–262
        prototypes, creating, 260–261
    Diablo, 282
    end of, triggering, 242–243
    isometric
        actors, drawing, 627–628
        basic world example, 624
        collision detection, 624, 635–636
        Diablo, 622
        drawing with perspective, 625–627
        graphics, 623–624
        isometric projection, 621–622
        sectoring, 628–634
        vertical-only perspective, 622–623
        windows, adding, 637

meta-games, 673
MIDP features, 37
naming, 264
non-real-time, 674
platform issues, 248–249
puzzle, 251
real-time, 251–252
RPGs (role-playing games), 251
simulation, 251–252
Star Assault
    auto-fire, 470
    enemy units, 266
    features, 265–266
    four-way scrolling, 265
    game controls, 266
    isometric perspective, 627–628
    random level generation, 266
    resources, 266–267
    splash screen, 465–466
    sprite example, 269
    vibration, 470–471
startup, 217
strategy, 251–252, 674
traditional, 252
Zaxxon, 621
GameScreen class, 204–207, 216–217
    activateGameScreen method, 469
    applications, linking, 225–226
    cycle method, 232, 372, 435
    initResources method, 451
    keyPressed event, 239
    run method, 434
    setKeyBindings method, 473
garbage collection (GC) process, optimization,
    525–526
Gauge class, 150
GC (garbage collection) process, optimization,
    525–526
GCF (Generic Connection Framework), 616
GDC (Game Developers Conference), 564, 616
generateLevel method, 399
Generic Connection Framework (GCF), 564, 616
geographical sorting, 628
get command, Ant utility, 504
GET method, 677
getAppProperty command, 70
getBool method, 487

getClass method, 722
getConcurrentSoundCount method, 179
getDirection method, 363
getDisplay method, 114–115
getDisplayColor method, 589
getFont method, 161
getGameAction method, 169
getHeaderField method, 690
getHeight method, 350, 495
getImageRegion method, 276–277
getKeyCode method, 169
getKeyName method, 169
getKeyNum method, 487
getKeyStates method, 205, 601
getRadiansFPFromAngle method, 646
getSavedLevel method, 462
getSession method, 689–690
getSupportedFormats method, 178
getTile method, 379
getTimeInCurrentState method, 296
getTotalCycles method, 297, 450
getWidth method, 350, 495
GIF files, animated, 550–551
Global System for Mobile Communications
    (GSM), 199
go command, 133
goal setting, good game design, 255–256
Gosling, James, 4–5, 693
gotHorizHit method, 658
GraphicObject class, 202
GraphicObjectManager class, 203
graphics
    enhancements, MIDP 2, 589–590
    flushGraphics method, 205, 602
    isometric games, 623–624
    MIDP device characteristics, 30
    Siemens, 202–203
Graphics class
    2D drawing tools, 159–160
    coordinates, 158–159
    drawing text, 161–164
    drawRGB method, 593
    images and clipping, 165–167
    methods, list of, 157–158
Graphics objects, Canvas class, 151
GSM (Global System for Mobile
    Communications), 199

H

halfFovColumns variable, 645
Handango, marketing distributors, 558–559
hardware platforms, differences between, 14
header space, 271–272
headers, methods, 697
heap memory, 30
height
    getHeight method, 350, 495
    laneHeight method, 223
hello.java code, 55–58
HELP command type, 119
Hibernate Web site, 691
hidden edges, 663
hierarchy, LCDUI, 113
high-level optimization, 527–529
high-level UI components, 123
horizDistanceFP method, 658
horizontal movement, 304, 322–323
horizontal rays, ray casting, 647–648
HotJava browser, 5–6
HTML (Hypertext Markup Language), 11
HTTP (Hypertext Transfer Protocol)
    mobile communication, 671
    servers, setting up, 676
HttpConnection class
    example code, 93–95
    methods, list of, 92
HTTPS (Secure HTTP), 573
HttpsConnection object, 617–618
HttpSession method, 689
Hypertext Markup Language (HTML)
    defined, 11
    servers, setting up, 676
Hypertext Transfer Protocol (HTTP)
    mobile communication, 671
    servers, setting up, 676

I

i-mode protocol, 11
lib directory, 52
IDE (Integrated Development Environment), 64,
    694
IDEA tool, 75–76
ideas, creating games from, 265–267
iDen 185s phone, 46

identifiers (variable names), 705–706
#if command, 510
if statement, 711–712
#ifdef command, 510
#ifndef command, 510
IllegalStateException class, 184
images
    as arrays, 593–600
    clipping, 167
    color, bright colors, 273
    drawImages method, 165
    extracting, 274–281, 290
    getImageRegion method, 276–277
    header space, 271–272
    image sets, creating, 283–290
    immutable, 143
    loading, 273
    mutable, 143
    PNG image file format, 143
    reflection, 191–192, 496–500, 590–592
    rotation, 191–192, 496–500, 590–592
    scaling
        getScaleImage method, 208
        pixel manipulation, 197
    transparency, 192–193, 209
ImageSet class
    addState method, 290, 292
    code, 284–290
    discussed, 283
    draw method, 290
    expandArray method, 292
    getTimeInCurrentState method, 296
    isometric projection, 624
    reflection and rotation capabilities, 496–497
ImageUtil class, 208
immutable images, 143
impact, protection from damage, 448–450
import statements, object-oriented programming,
    736–737
#include command, 510
increment (++) operator, 707
inheritance, 718–721, 724
init method, 429, 438
init target, build systems, 503
INITIAL_CAPS_SENSITIVE input constraint
    type, 601
INITIAL_CAPS_WORDS input constraint type,
    601

initialization process, threads, 218

initializer statements, 713

initResources method, 223, 236, 451, 489

inlining, 733

inner classes, object-oriented programming, 726–727

input
   input handling, 239–240
   input/output classes, 26
   input types, MIDP device characteristics, 29
   MIDP device characteristics, 30

insert method, 135

inspiration, good game design, 257

installations
   Nokia tools, 174–175
   SMTK (Siemens Mobility Toolkit), 198
   software
      CLASSPATH environment variable, updating, 54
      directories, creating, 50
      JDK, setting up, 51
      MIDP setup, 51–52
      MIDP_HOME variable, 53
      PATH environment variable changes, 52–53
      testing, 54
   Sun ONE Studio, 74
   Toolkit (J2ME Wireless), 64–65

instanceOf operator, 721

instantiation, 687, 696

int type, 703

Integrated Development Environment (IDE), 64, 694

inter-player messaging, 673

interfaces
   design documentation, 260
   LCDUI (Liquid Crystal Display User Interface), 112
   object-oriented programming, 724–725
   RMS (Record Management System), 96
   Runnable, 217–218
   SpriteEventListener, 302

Internet downloads, sales channels, 554–555

interpretation code stage, 7

intersection
   basic, 325–326
   tests, collision detection, 242
   through exclusion, 326–328

introduction
   design documentation, 259
   game guide, marketing, 544–545

InvalidRecordException, 110

isEnemyArg value, 365

isNew method, 689

isometric games
   actors, drawing, 627–628
   basic world example, 624
   collision detection, 624, 635–636
   Diablo, 622
   drawing with perspective, 625–627
   graphics, 623–624
   isometric projection, 621–622
   sectoring, 628–634
   vertical-only perspective, 622–623
   windows, adding, 637

italicized characters, 163

ITEM command type, 119

Item commands, 588–589

items, screen objects, 123

Items class, 137–139

J

J2EE (Java 2 Enterprise Edition), 9

J2ME (Java 2 Micro Edition)
   application management, 21–22
   architecture, 14–15
   CDC (Connected Device Configuration), 17
   CLDC (Connected, Limited Device Configuration), 17–19
   components of, 16
   configurations and profiles, 15–17
   defined, 9
   hardware platforms, differences between, 14

J2ME Wireless Toolkit. *See* Toolkit (J2ME Wireless)

J2SE (Java 2 Standard Edition), 9

JADs (application descriptors), 33–34

JAM (Java Application Manager), 63

JAMDAT publisher, 560

jar command, Ant utility, 504

JAR (Java Archive) file
   commands, 61–62
   game development process, 261–262
   minimum system requirements, 254

Jasc, Paint Shop Pro, 271

Java
C++ language *versus*, 8
defined, 6–9
history of, 3–6
language differences, 22–28
platform components, 7
sandbox, 20
Java 2 Enterprise Edition (J2EE), 9
Java 2 Micro Edition (J2ME)
application management, 21–22
architecture, 14–15
components of, 16
configurations and profiles, 15–17
defined, 9
hardware platforms, differences between, 14
Java 2 Standard Edition (J2SE), 9
Java API (Application Programming Interface), 8
Java Application Manager (JAM), 63
Java Archive (JAR) file
commands, 61–62
game development process, 261–262
minimum system requirements, 254
java command, Ant utility, 504
Java Database Connectivity (JDBC), 690
Java Development Kit (JDK), 50–51
Java Native Interface (JNI), 23
Java Virtual Machine Debugging Interface (JVMDI), 24
Java Virtual Machine (JVM)
defined, 6–7
discussed, 8, 694
language differences, 23–25
roles of, 9
javac command, Ant utility, 504
JBoss Web site, 692
JBuilder tool, 71–73
JDBC (Java Database Connectivity), 690
JDK (Java Development Kit), 50–51
JMFP floating point library, 308
JNI (Java Native Interface), 23
joining strings, 715–716
Joy, Bill, 5
JVM (Java Virtual Machine), 8, 694
defined, 6–7
language differences, 23–25
roles of, 9
JVMDI (Java Virtual Machine Debugging Interface), 24

K
kernel, MIDP device characteristics, 30
key configurations, front end applications, 472–475
key presses, simultaneous, platform issues, 248
keyPressed method, 168, 172, 239, 475
keyReleased method, 168, 475
keyRepeated method, 168
keywords
clone, 528
final, object-oriented programming, 733
new, 528
return, 697
synchronize, 533
KToolbar application (J2ME Wireless Toolkit), 65–70

L
laneHeight method, 223
languages, localization, 535–540
lastCPSTime method, 219
lastFree method, 423
latency and dropouts, mobile communication, 672
LayerManager class, 611–612
layers
background, 384–386
code, 612–616
LayerManager class, 611–612
sprites and, 609–611
tile layers, rendering, 376–378
tiled, 606–609
layout
form control options, MIDP 2, 582
modifiers, ImageItem class, 142
LCDUI (Liquid Crystal Display User Interface)
class hierarchy, 113
class summary, 112
CommandListener class, 120–122
commands, 118–120
DateField class, 148–149
discussed, 16, 77
Display class, 114–118
event handling, 168–172
Form class, 135–136
Gauge class, 150

Graphics class
  2D drawing tools, 159–160
  coordinates, 158–159
  drawing text, 161–164
  images and clipping, 165–167
  methods, 157–158
ImageItem class, 141–146
Items class, 137–139
List class, 124–130
overview, 111
screen objects, 123–124
screens, 113
StringItem class, 140–141
LEDs, device control, 177
level design, world objects, 388–390
levels
  generateLevel method, 399
  loadLevel method, 415
  startNewLevel method, 415
LG Web site, 210
libraries
  class libraries, 24
  device-specific, 173–174
  MIDP, 35–38
licensing, MathFP, 308
lighting
  backlighting, 177–178, 200
  flashLights method, 177
  light blasts, pixel manipulation, 197
  setLights method, 177
lines, drawLine method, 159–160, 667
linked lists, object management, 418–422
Liquid Crystal Display User Interface (LCDUI)
  class hierarchy, 113
  class summary, 112
  CommandListener class, 120–122
  commands, 118–120
  DateField class, 148–149
  discussed, 16, 77
  Display class, 114–118
  event handling, 168–172
  Form class, 135–136
  Gauge class, 150
  Graphics class
    2D drawing tools, 159–160
    coordinates, 158–159
    drawing text, 161–164
    images and clipping, 165–167

  methods, 157–158
  ImageItem class, 141–146
  Items class, 137–139
  List class, 124–130
  overview, 111
  screen objects, 123–124
  screens, 113
  StringItem class, 140–141
List class
  addElement method, 481
  choice types, 125
  code, 126–129
  commandAction method, 129
  discussed, 124
  methods, 125
listConnections method, 619
listeners
  CommandListener interface, 120–122
  RecordListener class, 108–110
  SoundListener class, 180–183
listening in, sound control, Nokia, 180–183
literals, 704–705
load balancing, 691
loading
  images, 273
  maps, 412–415
loadLevel method, 415, 462
Locale class, 536–539
localization, 535–540
locking records, 103
logic, creating, 365–366
logos, as marketing tool, 552
long type, 703
loops
  conditional looping, 712
  while, 242–243
low-level optimization, 529–533
low-level UI, 150–151
lower-level communication support, 618
lowest-common-denominator platform, 28

M

mail command, Ant utility, 504
manifest files, 31–33
maps
  exporting, 411–412
  loading, 412–415
  map editors, 407–409

marketing tools. *See also* **sales channels**
company presence, 551
distributors
AT&T Wireless, 557–558
Cellmania, 558
considerations for using, 559
Handango, 558–559
Motorola iDen/Nextel, 557
T-Mobile, 556–557
game guide
discussed, 543
game playing, step-by-step walk through, 545
introductions, 544–545
reference section, 545
GDC (Game Developers Conference), 564
logos as, 552
movie making, 547–551
networking, 564
professionalism, 551
publishers as, 567
discussed, 559–561
expectations of, 561–563
legal contracts, closing, 564
selection considerations, 563–566
screenshots, as promotion tool, 546
tradeshows, 564
Web sites as, 552
Master Control Program (TRON), 79
MathFP, 308–311, 646
MelodyComposer class, 201–202
memory
balance classes *versus,* 529–530
dynamic, 30
heap, 30
MIDP device characteristics, 29
non-volatile, 29–30, 96
objects and, 700–702
profiling, optimization, 523–525
RAM (random access memory), 30
remainder, 232
storage limits, platform issues, 249
volatile, 30
menu class, 214–216
menus
constants, 480
discussed, 479
displayed, tracking, 481

setupMenu method, 481–482
switching between, 484–487
messaging, inter-player, 673
meta-games, 673
method profiling, optimization, 521–523
methods
abstract, 723
acceptAndOpen, 616–617
activate, 225–226
activateGameScreen, 216, 225–226, 469
activateMenu, 457
activateTile, 382
addCommand, 134, 184
addElement, 481
adding to classes, 697–698
addState, 290, 292
alignedDivArg, 362
angleChange, 656
append
Form class, 135
StringItem class, 141
arcAngle, 160
backCommandName, 482
backgroundMusicSupported, 205
bulletImageSet class, 296
cancel, 90
Canvas class, 152
ChoiceGroup class, 148
clipRect, 167, 187
close, 216
commandAction
catch block, 86
discussed, 85, 122
List class, 129
CommandListener class, 123
Connector class, 91
Connector.open, 618
copyArea, 589
createAnimatedTile, 608
currentViewPosX, 371
currentViewPosY, 371
cycle
Actor class, 329, 352, 360
discussed, 227
GameScreen class, 232, 372, 435
movement, 232
Sprite class, 296
cycleStartTime, 221

DateField class, 149
declaring, optimization techniques, 532–533
delete, 135
destroy, 80, 84
destroyApp, 202
DirectGraphics, 189
Display class, 115
doGet, 677
doPost, 677
drawArc, 160
drawChar, 161
drawChars, 161
drawImage, 667
drawImages, 165
drawing, 290
drawLine, 159–160, 667
drawRect, 160, 529
drawRGB, 593
drawRoundRect, 160
drawString, 161–162
drawSubstring, 161
endTileX, 377
endTileY, 377
energyMax, 446
equals, 716
events, RecordStore class, 97
expandArray, 292
fillCells, 607–608
fillRect, 160, 529
fillRoundedRect, 160
fillTriangle, 589
finalize, 728
firstFree, 423
flashLights, 177
flushGraphics, 205, 602
flyingState, 296
Font class, 162
Font.getWidth, 164
Form class, 136
gameOver, 243
GameScreen class, 206
Gauge class, 150
generateLevel, 399
GET, 677
getBool, 487
getClass, 722
getConcurrentSoundCount, 179
getDirection, 363

getDisplay, 114–115
getDisplayColor, 589
getFont, 161
getGameAction, 169
getHeaderField, 690
getHeight, 350, 495
getImageRegion, 276–277
getKeyCode, 169
getKeyName, 169
getKeyNum, 487
getKeyStates, 205, 601
getRadiansFPFromAngle, 646
getSavedLevel, 462
getSession, 689–690
getSupportedFormats, 178
getTile, 379
getTimeInCurrentState, 296
getTotalCycles, 297, 450
getWidth, 350, 495
gotHorizHit, 658
Graphics class, 157–158
headers, 697
horizDistanceFP, 658
HttpConnection class, 92
HttpSession, 689
ImageItem class, 141
ImageUtil class, 208
init, 429, 438
initResources, 223, 236, 451, 489
insert, 135
isNew, 689
keyPressed, 168, 172, 239, 475
keyReleased, 168, 475
keyRepeated, 168
laneHeight, 223
lastCPSTime, 219
lastFree, 423
List class, 125
list Connections, 619
loadLevel, 415, 462
MathFP, 310
method body, 697
MIDlet class, 78
move, 721–722
moveAll, 721–722
msPerRecharge method, 446
nextFrame, 609
nextState, 302
Nokia device control, 177–178

methods *(continued)*
  Nokia sound control, 179
  notifyActorMoved, 630
  notifyDestroyed, 80
  notifyPaused, 80
  oldestUsed, 423
  onCollision, 681
  open, 90
  overriding, 722
  paint
    Canvas class, 152
    CustomItem class, 579
  PaletteImage class, 209
  panPixelsToMoveFP, 372
  pauseApp, 79, 84, 90, 202
  playBackgroundMusic, 207
  playSoundEffect, 207
  playTone, 201
  POST, 677–678
  prevFrame, 609
  previousRecord, 104
  PrintTask, 89
  readString, 413, 415
  rechargeRate, 446
  record access, RecordStore class, 97
  RecordComparator class, 105
  RecordListener class, 108
  RecordStore class, 97
  registerAlarm method, 619
  removeActor, 352–353
  removeCommand, 134
  render, 227, 238–239
  renderSplash, 490–491
  renderWorld, 222–225
  repaint, 219
  restart, World class, 455–456
  run, 218, 237–238, 434, 436, 683
  save, 462
  saveLevel, 458–460
  saveSettings, 478–479
  set, 135
  setAnimationTile, 608
  setARGBColor, 187–188
  setCell, 607–608
  setClip, 167, 187, 667
  setColor, 160, 187
  setCommandListener, 134, 184
  setCurrent, 115, 467
  setDirection, 362–363

  setFrameSequence, 610
  setGrayScale, 187
  setKeyBindings, 473
  setLights, 177
  setRequestProperty, 690
  setStaticTileSet, 607
  setTransform, 610
  setTransparentIndex, 209
  setup, 442, 726
  setupMenu,481–482
  setView, 370
  setX, 231
  sleep, threads, 220
  SoundEffectsSupported, 205
  soundStateChanged, 180
  startAngle, 160
  startApp, 79–80, 84, 202, 491
  startNewLevel, 415
  startTileX, 377
  startTileY, 377
  startVibra, 178
  startVibrator, 200
  static, 532
  stop, 179
  stopVibra, 178
  stopVibrator, 200
  store access, RecordStore class, 97
  StringItem class, 141
  takeDamage, 450, 453
  targetDirection, 360
  TextBox class, 131
  TextField class, 147
  tileMap, 399
  Timer object, 86–87
  TimerTask, 89
  translate, 187
  transmitScore, 682, 686
  triggerVibrator, 200
  unregisterConnection, 619
  updateScore, 686
  valueOf, 716
  viewX, 370, 377
  viewY, 370, 377
Mforma publisher, 560
micro devices
  application management, 21–22
  categories, 10
  developmental tools, 10
  revolution of, 9–10

MIDlets
application events, 80–82
creating, 55–57, 60
applications, compiling, 58
class file, preverification, 58–59
JAR (Java Archive) file, creating, 61–62
viewing, 59
methods, list of, 78
MIDlet JAR manifest attributes, 32
MIDP (Mobile Information Device Profile)
1.0 libraries, 35–36
2.0 library, 37–38
API overview, 77
applications
application descriptors (JADs), 33–34
MIDlet JAR manifest attributes, 32
run-time environment, 31
suite packaging, 31–33
directories, 52
discussed, 18–19
MIDP 2
build system, 574–577
ChoiceGroup class, 586–588
communication support, 616–618
CustomItem class, 578–581
form control, 581–584
GameCanvas class, 601–605
graphics enhancements, 589–590
images, as arrays, 593–600
item commands, 588–589
List class, 586–588
new features, 572–573
pop-ups, 586–588
push registry, 618–619
reflection and rotation enhancements, 590–592
sound functions, 577–578
spacer items, 584–585
specification, 573
minimum device characteristics, 29
target devices, 28–29
target software environment, 29–30
MIDP_HOME environment variable, 53
midplib property, 508
MIDs (Mobile Information Devices)
discussed, 16
Motorola, 45–46
Nokia, 40–44

non-volatile memory, 96
overview, 39
profile development, 30
Sony Ericsson, 44
minimum system requirements, game design, 254
mkdir command, Ant utility, 504
MMAPI (Mobile Media API), 180, 577
mobile communications
Bluetooth devices, 670–671
HTTP (Hypertext Transfer Protocol), 671, 676
load balancing, 691
network gaming
cost factor, 672
latency and dropouts, 672
practical uses, 672–673
scoring
basic structure, 680–681
online scoring class, 682–686
player ranking, 686–688
rank strings, 682
server-side persistence, 690–691
servlets, deploying, 679–680
sessions, use of, 689–690
SMS (Short Message Service), 669–670
SMSC (Short Message Service Center), 669
WAP (Wireless Application Protocol), 671
WMA (Wireless Messaging API), 670
Mobile Information Device Profile (MIDP)
1.0 libraries, 35–36
2.0 library, 37–38
API overview, 77
applications
application descriptors (JADs), 33–34
MIDlet JAR manifest attributes, 32
run-time environment, 31
suite packaging, 31
directories, 52
discussed, 18–19
MIDP 2
build system, 574–577
ChoiceGroup class, 586–588
communication support, 616–618
CustomItem class, 578–581
form control, 581–584
GameCanvas class, 601–605
graphics enhancements, 589–590
images, as arrays, 593–600
item commands, 588–589

Mobile Information Device Profile *(continued)*
   List class, 586–588
   new features, 572–573
   pop-ups, 586–588
   push registry, 618–619
   reflection and rotation enhancements,
      590–592
   sound functions, 577–578
   spacer items, 584–585
   specification, 573
   minimum device characteristics, 29
   Motorola, 45–46
   target devices, 28–29
   target software environment, 29–30
Mobile Information Devices (MIDs)
   discussed, 16
   MIDlets, 31
   Nokia, 40–44
   non-volatile memory, 96
   overview, 39
   profile development, 30
   Sony Ericsson, 44
Mobile Media API (MMAPI), 180, 577
mobile phones, UI (User Interface) for, 16
MobileSet tool, 71–72
monospace fonts, 163
Motocoder Web site, 203
Motorola
   A380 phone, 45
   Game API, 203
   GameScreen class, 204–207
   iDen 185s phone, 46
   ImageUtil class, 208
   marketing distributors, 557
   PaletteImage class, 208–209
   PlayField class, 207
   setup, 203–204
   Sprite class, 207
move method, 721–722
moveAll method, 721–722
movement
   acceleration, 318–319
   angles, 304
   basic movement, 304
   bouncing, 321–324
   car and truck examples, 231–232
   Cartesian space, 305
   code, 311–317
   cycle method, 232

   directional, 305–307
   discussed, 303
   fixed-point mathematics, 307
   floating-point math, simulating, 307–311
   free flight, 319–321
   MathFP, 308–311
   speed field, 232
   velocity, 318
Mover class, 719–720
movie making, marketing tools, 547–551
msPerRecharge method, 446
multi-device build systems
   build file, 515–518
   device-specific code, 512–513
   resource management, 514–515
multiple inheritance, 724
multiplication
   in FP value, 311
   multiplication (*) operator, 707
music. *See* **sound control**
mutable images, 143
mve command, Ant utility, 504

N

N-Gage (Nokia), 43
naming games, 264
naming rights, contracts, 566
NAT (Network Address Translation), 689
Naughton, Patrick, 5
Navigator browser, 6
NDS (Nokia Developer's Suite), 174
nested blocks, 710
Network Address Translation (NAT), 689
network gaming, mobile communications
   cost factor, 672
   latency and dropouts, 672
   practical uses, 672–673
networking
   classes, 36
   Connector class
      direct socket connections, 90
      methods, list of, 91
   Generic Connection Framework, 90–91
   HttpConnection class, 92–95
   as marketing tool, 564
   MIDP device characteristics, 29–30
   MIDP features, 37
new keyword, 528

newline character (\n), 704
Nextel, marketing distributors, 557
nextFrame method, 609
nextState method, 302
nighttime effects, 197
Nokia
    customization
        FullCanvas class, 493–495
        reflection, 496–500
        rotation, 496–500
        vibration, 495
    device control, 177–178
    direct graphics, 180, 187–189
    Forum, 41
    full-screen drawing, 183–187
    N-Gage, 43
    NDS (Nokia Developer's Suite), 174
    Nokia 3300, 42
    Nokia 3410, 41
    Nokia 3510i, 41
    Nokia 3650, 42
    Nokia 6820, 42
    Nokia 7700, 43
    Nokia 9290, 43
    Series 30, 40
    Series 40, 41
    Series 60, 42
    Series 80, 42
    Series 90, 42–43
    sound control
        full-screen drawing, 183–187
        listening in, 180–183
        playing tones, 178–180
        RTPL (Ring Tone Programming Language),
            180
        SMS (Smart Messaging Specification), 180
    tools, installing, 174–175
    triangles and polygons, 190
    UI classes, 176
    Web site, 174
non-collidable tiles, 383
non-real-time games, 674
non-volatile memory, 29–30, 96
NON_PREDICTIVE input constraint type, 601
notes, design documentation, 260
notifyActorMoved method, 630
notifyDestroyed method, 80
notifyPaused method, 80

O
Oak language, 4
obfuscation, 509–510
object-oriented programming
    abstract keyword, 723
    discussed, 717
    exceptions, 734–735
    final keyword, 733
    finalize method, 728
    import statements, 736–737
    inheritance, 718–721
    inner classes, 726–727
    interfaces, 724–725
    method overriding, 722
    object base, 721–722
    packages, 736–737
    static fields, 729–732
    this reference, 729
    visibility, 725–726
objects. *See also* classes
    constructors, 698–700
    defined, 694–695
    example code, 696
    graphics, Canvas class, 151
    instantiation, 687, 696
    memory and, 700–702
    object management
        code, 423–431
        discussed, 416
        linked lists, 418–421
        mutually exclusive linked lists, 421–422
        object pooling, 417–418, 428–431
        object use, tracking, 422
    reference counts, 525
    references, 701
    SocketConnection, 616–617
    TextBox
        code, 131–132
        Display class, 115
        LCDUI, 130–133
        methods, list of, 131
        TextField object *versus*, 114
    TextField, 114, 145–146
    Timer
        cancel method, 90
        methods, list of, 86–87
        pauseApp method, 90
        PrintTask method, 89

objects *(continued)*
    regular intervals, 87–89
    TimerTask method, 89
octal value (ddd), 704
off-screen buffers, 221–222
OK command type, 119
oldestUsed method, 423
onCollision method, 681
one-dimensional arrays, 532
open method, 90
operators
    arithmetic, 707–708
    assignment, 706
    bit-manipulation, 708
    equality, 708–709
    expression, 708–709
    instanceOf, 721
    relational expression, 708
    ternary operators, 714–715
    unary, 707–708
optimization. *See also* performance
    array usage, 531–532
    complex values, pre-computing, 530–531
    debug symbols, 533
    GC (garbage collection) process, 525–526
    high-level, 527–529
    low-level, 529–533
    methods, declaring, 532
    speed
        memory profiling, 523–525
        method profiling, 521–523
        optimization considerations, 520
        tips, 533
        when to optimize, 519–520
OR (|) operator, 708
origin points, ray casting, 651
originality, good game design, 256
OTA (over-the-air), carrier downloads, 553–554
output, input/output classes, 26
over-the-air (OTA), carrier downloads, 553–554
overriding methods, 722

P

P800 (Sony Ericsson), 44
P900 (Sony Ericsson), 44
packages, object-oriented programming, 736–737
paint methods
    Canvas class, 152

CustomItem class, 579
    repaint method, 219
Paint Shop Pro, Jasc, 271
paletificatalisation, 271
PaletteImage class, 208–209
panning view port, 370–373
panPixelsToMoveFP method, 372
PATH environment variable, 53
pauseApp method, 79, 84, 90, 202
PAUSED state, 434
pausing, 217
perception, high-level optimization, 527–528
performance, platform issues. *See also*
    optimization, 249
permission-based security, 37
Phonebook class, 199
phones
    Motorola series, 45–46
    Nokia series, 40–43
    Sony Ericsson series, 44
pixel data access, DirectGraphics class, 193–197
pixels
    data types, 194
    screen limitations, 248
placement control, MIDP features, 37
platforms
    components, 7
    design documentation, 260
    game design issues, 253–255
    hardware platforms, differences between, 14
playBackgroundMusic method, 207
PlayField class, 207
PLAYING state, 434, 436
playSoundEffect method, 207
playTone method, 201
PNG image file format, 143
PNG image transparency, MIDP features, 37
polling, defined, 602
polyphonic tones, MIDP features, 37
pop-ups, 586–588
portal sites, sales channels, 556
POST method, 677–678
pre-verification, 20
preferences, front end applications, 475–479
preprocessing, Antenna utility, 510–512
preverify command
    class files, 58–59
    PATH variable, 53

prevFrame method, 609
previousRecord method, 104
primary actors
    discussed, 437
    enemy units, 442–445
    specifying, 438–442
primitive types, 703, 705–706
procedures. *See* methods
processor power constraints, platform issues, 249
professionalism, marketing tools, 551
profiles, J2ME (Java 2 Micro Edition), 15–17
profiling, optimization
    memory profiling, 523–525
    method profiling, 521–523
ProGuard obfuscator (Mark Welch), 509
projection, ray casting, 649–650
projection plane, 660
projects, creating new, KToolbar application, 65
promotion tools. *See* marketing tools; sales
        channels
properties
    Ant utility, 505
    debug, 511
    midplib, 508
proportional fonts, 163
prototypes, game development process, 260–261
psclasses, 20
publishers, as marketing tool
    discussed, 559–561
    expectations of, 561–563
    legal contracts, 564
    selection considerations, 563–567
pulsing, pixel manipulation, 197
push protocols, MIDP 2, 573
push registry, MIDP 2, 618–619
Pythagorean Theorem, 653

Q

quit command, 82, 133

R

radians, converting degrees from, 356–357
RAM (random access memory), 30
random level generation
    map generation systems, 407
    Star Assault example, 266
    world objects, 390–391

rank strings, scoring, 682
ray casting
    aborting, adding checks for, 654
    background images, adding, 665
    casting columns, 644–645
    collision detection, 640, 666–667
    defined, 639–640
    distance, calculating, 652–653
    distortion, 660–662
    first-person perspective, 643
    focal distance, 645–646
    focal length, 645–646
    FOV (field-of-view), 643
    horizontal and vertical rays, 647–648
    main loop example, 655–659
    origin points, 651
    projecting a ray, 649–650
    ray tracing, 639
    shading effects, 662–665
    sprites and actors, 666
    textures, 667
    tile map example, 641–643
    twin-casting, 648
    vertical rays, 647–648
reactions, collision detection, 328–330
readString method, 413, 415
real-time games, 251–252
rechargeRate method, 446
record management classes, 36
Record Management System (RMS)
    classes, 96
    discussed, 95
    exceptions, 110
    interfaces, 96
    previousRecord method, 104
    RecordComparator class, 104–106
    RecordEnumerator class, 103–104
    RecordFilter class, 106–108
    RecordListener class, 108–110
    records
        locking, 103
        writing data to, 98–101
    RecordStore class, 96–97
RecordComparator class, 104–106
RecordEnumerator class, 103–104
RecordFilter class, 106–108
RecordListener class, 108–110

records
  locking, 103
  writing data to, 98–101
RecordStore class, RMS, 96–97
RecordStoreException, 110
RecordStoreFullException, 110
RecordStoreNotFoundException, 110
RecordStoreNotOpenException, 110
rectangles
  drawing, 190–191
  methods, 160
redMaskResult integer, 593
reference counts, objects, 525
reference device, game design, 254–255
Reference Implementation (RI), 49
reference section, game guide, marketing, 545
references, objects, 701
reflection
  DirectGraphics class, 191–192
  MIDP 2 enhancements, 590–592
  Nokia customization, 496–500
reflection, JVM language differences, 24
registerAlarm method, 619
relational expression operators, 708
remainder memory, 232
remote access methods, RecordStore class, 97
Remote Method Invocation (RMI), 24
removeActor method, 352–353
removeCommand method, 134
render method, 227, 238–239
rendering tile layers, 376–378
renderSplash method, 490–491
renderWorld method, 222–225
repaint method, 219
res directory, 508
resources
  design documentation, 260
  initResources method, 223, 236
  managing, multi-device build systems, 514–515
  Star Assault example, 266–267
restart method, World class, 455–456
return character (\r), 704
return keyword, 697
revenue, designing for, sales channels, 555–556
revenue shares, sales channels, 554
reverse animation, 302
RGB values
  drawRGB method, 593

getDisplayColor method, 589
RI (Reference Implementation), 49
ring-tone format, sound control (Nokia), 178
Ring Tone Programming Language (RTPL), 180
RMI (Remote Method Invocation), 24
RMS (Record Management System)
  classes, 96
  discussed, 95
  exceptions, 110
  interfaces, 96
  previousRecord method, 104
  RecordComparator class, 104–106
  RecordEnumerator class, 103–104
  RecordFilter class, 106–108
  RecordListener class, 108–110
  records
    locking, 103
    writing data to, 98–101
  RecordStore class, 96–97
role-playing games (RPGs), 251
rooms, creating, 392–396
Rosing, Wayne, 5
rotation
  DirectGraphics class, 191–192
  MIDP 2 enhancements, 590–592
  Nokia customization, 496–500
RPGs (role-playing games), 251
RTPL (Ring Tone Programming Language), 180
run method, 218, 237–238, 434, 436, 683
run-time environment, MIDP applications, 31
Runnable interface, 217–218

S

sales channels. *See also* **marketing tools**
  carrier downloads, 553–554
  carrier revenue shares, 554
  Internet downloads, 554–555
  OTA (over-the-air), 553–554
  portal sites, 556
  revenue, designing for, 555–556
Samsung Web site, 210
sandbox security, 20–21
save method, 462
saveLevel method, 458–460
saveSettings method, 478–479
scaling images
  getScaleImage method, 208
  pixel manipulation, 197

Schmidt, Eric, 5
scoring
    basic structure, 680–681
    online scoring class, 682–686
    player ranking, 686–688
    rank strings, 682
SCREEN command type, 119
screens
    LCDUI, 113
    limitations, 248
    screen objects, LCDUI, 123–124
    size, minimum system requirements, 254
screenshots, as promotion tool, 546
scrolling view port, 369–370
SDKs (Software Development Kits), 11, 173, 694
sectoring, isometric perspective, 628–634
secure connections, communication support,
        617–618
Secure HTTP (HTTPS), 573
security
    application, 20–21
    CLDC (Connected, Limited Device Configura-
        tion), 19–21
    MIDP features, 37
    permission-based, 37
    sandbox, 20–21
    virtual machine, 19–20
Send command, 682–683
SENSITIVE input constraint type, 601
Series 30 (Nokia), 40
Series 40 (Nokia), 41
Series 60 (Nokia), 42
Series 80 (Nokia), 42
Series 90 (Nokia), 42–43
server-side persistence, mobile communications,
        690–691
server sockets, communication support, 616–617
servers, HTTP, 676
servlets, 677, 679–680
session IDs, 689
sessions, mobile communications, 689–690
set command
    CLASSPATH variable, checking value of, 54
    Form class, 135
setAnimationTile method, 608
setARGBColor method, 187–188
setCell method, 607–608
setClip method, 167, 187, 667

setColor method, 160, 187
setCommandListener method, 134, 184
setCurrent method, 115, 467
setDirection method, 362–363
setFrameSequence method, 610
setGrayScale method, 187
setKeyBindings method, 473
setLights method, 177
setRequestProperty method, 690
setStaticTileSet method, 607
setTransform method, 610
setTransparentIndex method, 209
setup method, 442, 726
setupMenu method, 481–482
setView method, 370
setX method, 231
shading effects, 662–665
shadows, 197, 594
shell, defined, 52
ShiftFP floating point library, 308
shooting, movie making, 549–550
Short Message Service Center (SMSC), 669
Short Message Service (SMS), 669–670
short type, 703
Siemens
    device control, 200–201
    features, 198
    graphics and gaming, 202–203
    GSM (Global System for Mobile
        Communications), 199
    installation options, 198
    setup development, 199
    SL55 emulator, 199
    SMTK (Siemens Mobility Toolkit), 198
    sounds and tunes, 201–202
SIMULA language, 4
simulation games, 251–252
single quote character ('), 704
sites. See Web sites
SL55 emulator, 199
sleep method, threads, 220
slow performance, platform issues, 249
Smart Messaging Specification (SMS), 180
smileys, 580
SMS class, 199
SMS (Short Message Service), 669–670
SMS (Smart Messaging Specification), 180
SMSC (Short Message Service Center), 669

SMTK (Siemens Mobility Toolkit), 198
SnagIt (TechSmith), 547–549
SocketConnection object, 616–617
software
    installing
        CLASSPATH environment variable, updating, 54
        directories, creating, 50
        JDK, setting up, 51
        MIDP setup, 51–52
        MIDP_HOME variable, 53
        PATH environment variable changes, 52–53
        testing, 54
    playBackgroundMusic method, 207
Software Development Kits (SDKs), 11, 173, 694
software environment, MIDP, 29–30
Sony Ericsson, 44, 210
sorting, geographical, 628
sound control
    backgroundMusicSupported method, 205
    createSoundEffect class, 207
    getConcurrentSoundCount method, 179
    MIDP 2, 577–578
    Nokia
        listening in, 180–183
        playing tones, 178–180
        RTPL (Ring Tone Programming Language), 180
        SMS (Smart Messaging Specification), 180
    playSoundEffect method, 207
    Siemens, 201–202
    SoundEffect class, 207
    soundEffectsSupported method, 205
SoundEffect class, 207
soundEffectsSupported method, 205
SoundListener class, 180–183
soundStateChanged method, 180
spacer items, 584–585
special character literals, 704
specification, MIDP 2, 573
speed, optimization
    optimization considerations, 520
    profiling
        memory profiling, 523–525
        method profiling, 521–523
    tips, 533
    when to optimize, 519–520
speed field, movement, 232
spinning objects, 358–361

splash screens, 214–216
    current displayable, 468
    currentDisplay field, 491
    front end applications, 488–492
    renderSplash method, 490–491
    Star Assault example, 465–466
Sprite class, 202, 207
    bulletImageSet method, 296
    code, 293–301
    cycle method, 296
    flyingState method, 296
    getTotalCycles method, 297
    isometric projection, 624
    overview, 292
SpriteEventListener interface, 302
sprites
    advanced, 297–301
    defined, 269
    explosion example of, 269
    layers and, 609–611
    ray casting, 666
    Star Assault example, 269
    states versus frames, 282
sql command, Ant utility, 504
SQL-compatible database, server-side persistence, 690
src directory, 509
Star Assault game example
    auto-fire, 470
    configuration, 265
    enemy units, 266
    four-way scrolling, 265
    game controls, 266
    isometric perspective, 627–628
    random level generation, 266
    resources, 266–267
    splash screen, 465–466
    sprite example, 269
    vibration, 470–471
star fields, 384–386
start command, 216
startAngle method, 160
startApp method, 79–80, 84, 212, 491
startNewLevel method, 415
startTileX method, 377
startTileY method, 377
startup, games, 217
startVibra method, 178

startVibrator method, 200
statements
 break, 715
 conditional, 713
 do, 712
 empty, 708
 for, 713
 if, 711–712
 initializer, 713
 switch, 484–487, 713–714
 update, 713
 while, 712
states
 explosions, 282
 flying, 282
 frames *versus,* 282
 game state, 433–437
 PAUSED, 434
 PLAYING, 434, 436
static fields, object-oriented programming,
  729–732
static methods, 532
STOP command type, 119
stop method, 179
stopVibra method, 178
stopVibrator method, 200
storage limits, platform issues, 249
store access methods, RecordStore class, 97
strategy games, 251–252, 674
string literals, 705
StringItem class, 140–141
strings
 concatenation, 715
 joining, 715–716
stroke methods, DirectGraphics class, 187
subtraction (-) operator, 707
suite packaging, MIDP applications, 31
Sun One Studio tool, 73–75
Sun Web site, 64
Swing layout tools, 76
switch statement, 484–487, 713–714
synchronization, 690
synchronize keyword, 533
syntax
 arithmetic operators, 707–708
 arrays, 717
 assignment operators, 706
 bit-manipulation operators, 707–708

 comments, 702–703
 do statement, 712
 literals, 704–705
 primitive types, 703
 for statement, 713
 statements and blocks, 709–711
 strings, 715–716
 switch statement, 713–714
 ternary operators, 714–715
 unary operators, 707–708
 while statement, 712
system classes, 25–26
system fonts, 163
system requirements, game design, 254

T

T-Mobile provider, 556–557
T6xx (Sony Ericsson), 44
tab character (\t), 704
takeDamage method, 450, 453
target devices, MIDP, 28–29
target software environment, MIDP, 29–30
targetDirection method, 360
targets, build systems, 502–503
taskdef command, 506
technical implementation, design documentation,
  260
technology, good game design, 257
TechSmith, SnagIt, 547–549
termination options, legal contracts, 567
ternary operators, 714–715
testing, software installation, 54
text messages, adding to forms, 140
TextBox object
 code, 131–132
 Display class, 115
 LCDUI, 130–133
 methods, list of, 131
 TextField *versus,* 114
TextField object, 114, 145–146
TextForm class, 487–488
TextPlus editor, 76
textures, ray casting, 667
this reference, object-oriented programming, 729
Thread class, 217, 683
threads
 initialization process, 218
 sleep method, 220

ticks, defined, 232
tilde (~), 412
Tile Studio Definition (TSD), 411
tiled layers, 606–609
TiledBackground class, 203
tileMap method, 399
tiling
    activateTile method, 382
    activator tiles, 380–383
    animated tiles, 379–380
    background layers, 384–386
    collision detection, 378–379, 634–635
    getTile method, 379
    inverting, 393
    layers, rendering, 376–378
    non-collidable, 383
    overview, 373–374
    ray casting, 641–643
    tile map, 374–376
time
    elapsed, 219–220
    time classes, 26, 148
Timer object
    cancel method, 90
    methods, list of, 86–87
    pauseApp method, 90
    PrintTask method, 89
    regular intervals, 87–89
    TimerTask method, 89
Tira Wireless publisher, 560
Tomcat (Apache), 677
tones, sound control
    MIDP 2, 577–578
    Nokia, 178–180
Toolkit (J2ME Wireless)
    code example, 67–69
    features, 64
    installing, 64–65
    KToolbar application, 65–70
tools
    ANT, 76
    clipboard, 114
    downloading, 49–50
    Eclipse, 75–76
    IDEA, 75–76
    JBuilder, 71–73
    JDK (Java Development Kit), 50
    micro devices, 10

MobileSet, 71–72
    Nokia, installing, 174–175
    SMTL (Siemens Mobility Toolkit), 198
    Sun ONE Studio, 73–75
    Swing layout, 76
Tools class, 291–292, 495–496
tradeshows, as marketing tool, 564
traditional games, 252
transitioning, 302
translate method, 187
translation, localization, 535–540
translucent shadows, pixel manipulation, 197
transmitScore method, 682, 686
transparent images, 192–193, 209
triangles, drawing, 190–191
triggerVibrator method, 200
TRON (Master Control Program), 79
try block, 85, 734
TSD (Tile Studio Definition), 411
tunes. *See* sound control
twin-casting, ray casting, 648
two-dimensional arrays, 532
type caster, 707
type classes, 26

U
UDPDatagramConnection, 618
UI (User Interface)
    LCDUI, 16, 77
        Alert class, 134–135
        Canvas class, 151–156
        ChoiceGroup class, 147–148
        class hierarchy, 113
        class summary, 112
        CommandListener class, 120–122
        commands, 118–120
        DateField class, 148–149
        Display class, 114–118
        event handling, 168–172
        Form class, 135–136
        Gauge class, 150
        Graphics class, 156–167
        high-level UI components, 123
        ImageItem class, 141–146
        Items class, 137–139
        List class, 124–130
        low-level UI, 150–151

overview, 111
screen objects, 123–124
screens, 113
StringItem class, 140–141
TextBox class, 130–133
TextField class, 145–146
MIDP features, 37
mobile phones, 16
Nokia classes, 176
unary operators, 707–708
unconditional flag, 85
#undefine command, 510
underlined characters, 163
UNEDITABLE input constraint type, 601
Unplugged publisher, 560
unregisterConnection method, 619
update statements, 713
updateScore method, 686
user-defined class loaders, language differences, 24
user interface classes, 35–36
User Interface (UI)
LCDUI, 16, 77
Alert class, 134–135
Canvas class, 151–156
ChoiceGroup class, 147–148
class hierarchy, 113
class summary, 112
CommandListener class, 120–122
commands, 118–120
DateField class, 148–149
Display class, 114–118
event handling, 168–172
Form class, 135–136
Gauge class, 150
Graphics class, 156–167
high-level UI components, 123
ImageItem class, 141–146
Items class, 137–139
List class, 124–130
low-level UI, 150–151
overview, 111
screen objects, 123–124
screens, 113
StringItem class, 140–141
TextBox class, 130–133
TextField class, 145–146
MIDP features, 37

mobile phones, 16
Nokia classes, 176
utility classes, 27, 35, 112
utility methods, world objects, 396–398
utils directory, 737

V
valueOf method, 716
variable names (identifiers), 705–706
variables
CLASSPATH, 199, 737
checking value of, using set command, 54
updating, for software installation, 54
MIDP_HOME, 53
PATH
adjusting in JDK binary directories, 51
preverify method, 53
vector-based drawing, 223
velocity, 318
verification, pre-verification, 20
vertical movement, 304, 322–323
vertical-only perspective, isometric projection, 622–623
vertical rays, ray casting, 647–648
vibration, 178, 200
Nokia customization, 495
Star Assault example, 470–471
Video Capture option (SnagIt), 548
view port, 368
defined, 367
panning, 370–373
scrolling, 369–370
viewX method, 370, 377
viewY method, 370, 377
VIM editor, 76
virtual machine security, 19–20
visibility, object-oriented programming, 725–726
visualization, good game design, 258
volatile memory, 30

W
WAP (Wireless Application Protocol)
defined, 11
mobile communication, 671
WAV files, MIDP features, 37
weapon fire, 349–354
weather effects, pixel manipulation, 197

Web sites
AT&T Wireless, 557
Blackberry, 210
Eclipse, 75
Hibernate, 691
IDEA, 75
JBoss, 692
LG, 210
as marketing tool, 552
Motocoder, 203
Nokia, 174
as sales channels, 554–555
Samsung, 210
Sony Ericsson, 210
Sun, 64
T-Mobile, 557
TechSmith, 547
Welch, Mark (ProGuard obfuscator), 509
while loop, 242–243
while statement, 712
width, getWidth method, 350, 495
windows, isometric perspective, 637
Wireless Application Protocol (WAP)
defined, 11
mobile communication, 671
Wireless Markup Language (WML), 11
Wireless Messaging API (WMA), 670
Wireless Toolkit. *See* **Toolkit (J2ME Wireless)**
WMA (Wireless Messaging API), 670
WML (Wireless Markup Language), 11
world objects
array maps, 390
code, 386–388
coordinates, 368–369
level design, 388–390
maps
exporting, 411–412
loading, 412–415
map editors, 407–409
object management
discussed, 416
linked lists, 418–421
mutually exclusive linked lists, 421–422
object pooling, 417–418
object use, tracking, 422

random level generation, 390–391
restart method, 455–456
rooms, creating, 392–396
saveLevel method, 458–460
tiling
activateTile method, 382
activator tiles, 380–383
animated tiles, 379–380
background layers, 384–386
collision detection, 378–379
getTile method, 379
inverting, 393
layers, rendering, 376–378
non-collidable, 383
overview, 373–374
tile map, 374–376
utility methods, 396–398
view port, 368
defined, 367
panning, 370–373
scrolling, 369–370
writing data, to records, 98–101

X

x-coordinates
Graphics class, 158–159
movement, 304–307
Mover class, 720

Y

y-coordinates
Graphics class, 158–159
movement, 304
bouncing example, 322
directional, 305–307
Mover class, 720

Z

Z600 (Sony Ericsson), 44
Zaxxon, 621
zip command, Ant utility, 504
zip compression, 412

Gamedev.net

The most comprehensive game development resource

- The latest news in game development
- The most active forums and chatrooms anywhere, with insights and tips from experienced game developers
- Links to thousands of additional game development resources
- Thorough book and product reviews
- Over 1000 game development articles!
  Game design
  Graphics
  DirectX
  OpenGL
  AI
  Art
  Music
  Physics
  Source Code
  Sound
  Assembly
  And More!

Gamedev.net

TAKE YOUR GAME TO THE
XTREME!

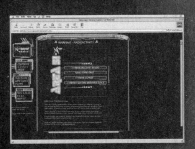

Xtreme Games LLC was founded to help small game developers around the world create and publish their games on the commercial market. Xtreme Games helps younger developers break into the field of game programming by insulating them from complex legal and business issues. Xtreme Games has hundreds of developers around the world. If you're interested in becoming one of them, then visit us at **www.xgames3d.com**.

www.xgames3d.com

License Agreement/Notice of Limited Warranty

By opening the sealed disc container in this book, you agree to the following terms and conditions. If, upon reading the following license agreement and notice of limited warranty, you cannot agree to the terms and conditions set forth, return the unused book with unopened disc to the place where you purchased it for a refund.

License:
The enclosed software is copyrighted by the copyright holder(s) indicated on the software disc. You are licensed to copy the software onto a single computer for use by a single user and to a backup disc. You may not reproduce, make copies, or distribute copies or rent or lease the software in whole or in part, except with written permission of the copyright holder(s). You may transfer the enclosed disc only together with this license, and only if you destroy all other copies of the software and the transferee agrees to the terms of the license. You may not decompile, reverse assemble, or reverse engineer the software.

Notice of Limited Warranty:
The enclosed disc is warranted by Course PTR to be free of physical defects in materials and workmanship for a period of sixty (60) days from end user's purchase of the book/disc combination. During the sixty-day term of the limited warranty, Course PTR will provide a replacement disc upon the return of a defective disc.

Limited Liability:
THE SOLE REMEDY FOR BREACH OF THIS LIMITED WARRANTY SHALL CONSIST ENTIRELY OF REPLACEMENT OF THE DEFECTIVE DISC. IN NO EVENT SHALL COURSE PTR OR THE AUTHOR BE LIABLE FOR ANY OTHER DAMAGES, INCLUDING LOSS OR CORRUPTION OF DATA, CHANGES IN THE FUNCTIONAL CHARACTERISTICS OF THE HARDWARE OR OPERATING SYSTEM, DELETERIOUS INTERACTION WITH OTHER SOFTWARE, OR ANY OTHER SPECIAL, INCIDENTAL, OR CONSEQUENTIAL DAMAGES THAT MAY ARISE, EVEN IF COURSE PTR AND/OR THE AUTHOR HAS PREVIOUSLY BEEN NOTIFIED THAT THE POSSIBILITY OF SUCH DAMAGES EXISTS.

Disclaimer of Warranties:
COURSE PTR AND THE AUTHOR SPECIFICALLY DISCLAIM ANY AND ALL OTHER WARRANTIES, EITHER EXPRESS OR IMPLIED, INCLUDING WARRANTIES OF MERCHANTABILITY, SUITABILITY TO A PARTICULAR TASK OR PURPOSE, OR FREEDOM FROM ERRORS. SOME STATES DO NOT ALLOW FOR EXCLUSION OF IMPLIED WARRANTIES OR LIMITATION OF INCIDENTAL OR CONSEQUENTIAL DAMAGES, SO THESE LIMITATIONS MIGHT NOT APPLY TO YOU.

Other:
This Agreement is governed by the laws of the State of Massachusetts without regard to choice of law principles. The United Convention of Contracts for the International Sale of Goods is specifically disclaimed. This Agreement constitutes the entire agreement between you and Course PTR regarding use of the software.